Little Buddhas

AAR

AMERICAN ACADEMY OF RELIGION

RELIGION, CULTURE, AND HISTORY

Series Editor
Jacob N. Kinnard, Iliff School of Theology

A Publication Series of
The American Academy of Religion
and
Oxford University Press

Anti-Judaism in Feminist Religious Writings
Katharina von Kellenbach

Cross-Cultural Conversation *(Initiation)*
Edited by Anindita Niyogi Balslev

On Deconstructing Life-Worlds
Buddhism, Christianity, Culture
Robert Magliola

The Great White Flood
Racism in Australia
Anne Pattel-Gray

Imag(in)ing Otherness
Filmic Visions of Living Together
Edited by S. Brent Plate and David Jasper

Cultural Otherness
Correspondence with Richard Rorty, Second Edition
Anindita Niyogi Balslev

Feminist Poetics of The Sacred
Creative Suspicions
Edited by Frances Devlin-Glass and Lyn McCredden

Parables for Our Time
Rereading New Testament Scholarship after the Holocaust
Tania Oldenhage

Moses in America
The Cultural Uses of Biblical Narrative
Melanie Jane Wright

Intersecting Pathways
Modern Jewish Theologians in Conversation with Christianity
Marc A. Krell

Asceticism and Its Critics
Historical Accounts and Comparative Perspectives
Edited by Oliver Freiberger

Virtuous Bodies
The Physical Dimensions of Morality in Buddhist Ethics
Susanne Mrozik

Imagining The Fetus
The Unborn in Myth, Religion, and Culture
Edited by Vanessa R. Sasson and Jane Marie Law

Victorian Reformation
The Fight over Idolatry in the Church of England, 1840–1860
Dominic Janes

Schleiermacher on Religion and The Natural Order
Andrew C. Dole

Muslims and Others in Sacred Space
Edited by Margaret Cormack

Little Buddhas
Children and Childhoods in Buddhist Texts and Traditions
Edited by Vanessa R. Sasson

Little Buddhas

Children and Childhoods in Buddhist Texts and Traditions

Edited by Vanessa R. Sasson

OXFORD
UNIVERSITY PRESS

OXFORD
UNIVERSITY PRESS

Oxford University Press is a department of the University of Oxford.
It furthers the University's objective of excellence in research, scholarship,
and education by publishing worldwide.

Oxford New York
Auckland Cape Town Dar es Salaam Hong Kong Karachi
Kuala Lumpur Madrid Melbourne Mexico City Nairobi
New Delhi Shanghai Taipei Toronto

With offices in
Argentina Austria Brazil Chile Czech Republic France Greece
Guatemala Hungary Italy Japan Poland Portugal Singapore
South Korea Switzerland Thailand Turkey Ukraine Vietnam

Published in the United States of America by
Oxford University Press
198 Madison Avenue, New York, NY 10016

Library of Congress Cataloging-in-Publication Data
Little Buddhas : children and childhoods in Buddhist texts
and traditions / edited by Vanessa R. Sasson.
pages cm
Includes bibliographical references and index.
ISBN 978-0-19-986026-5 (alk. paper) – ISBN 978-0-19-994561-0 (pbk.: alk. paper)
1. Children—Religious aspects—Buddhism. I. Sasson, Vanessa R., editor of compilation.
BQ4570.C47L58 2012
294.3083—dc23
2012006211

ISBN 978-0-19-986026-5
ISBN 978-0-19-994561-0

1 3 5 7 9 8 6 4 2
Printed in the United States of America
on acid-free paper

For Darshan

CONTENTS

PART TWO: Children and Childhoods in Buddhist Traditions

ACKNOWLEDGMENTS

As a graduate student many years ago, I had the privilege of watching Victor Hori demonstrate *paṭicca-samuppāda* to a class by providing an elaborate history of the button on his shirt. He took the students around the world, from the oil fields of Saudi Arabia to a production line in China, to the land that grew the crops to feed the infinite number of beings involved in the process, and to the sun, the rain, the stars, and even the Big Bang. It took the better part of an hour and he barely skimmed the surface of this interconnected web of reality. I think he would appreciate my comparing an edited volume to the button on his shirt.

If I am permitted to acknowledge everyone and everything from the Big Bang to the very remote past in one sweeping gesture, I nevertheless find myself with quite a few people to thank. First and foremost, I would like to extend my profound gratitude to the nineteen contributors to this volume. While scholars always stand on the shoulders of those before them, the research produced for this volume is quite new, with relatively few secondary sources to lean on. Many months (and even years) of thinking, rethinking, undoing, and rewriting were required. A number of the contributors volunteered their time and expertise to read each other's material and provide feedback, creating a kind of cyber-conference that many attended at various points during this process. I am most grateful to all the contributors for the work and time they dedicated to this volume, but in particular Amy Langenberg who was a champion at every stage from beginning to end.

I am also grateful to those contributors who participated in a panel at the 2009 annual meeting of the American Academy of Religion, which likewise helped us contextualize and think through the issues emerging from this study.

I am especially grateful to my editors, Jacob Kinnard and Cynthia Read, who have been most generous with their time and encouraging about this project. Working with them and with the team at Oxford University Press has been a great pleasure, two times over.

I thank also my friends and colleagues at Marianopolis College who are consistently supportive of my research, as well as my friends and colleagues at McGill University's Faculty of Religious Studies. Both environments have nourished me in their own ways. I thank, moreover, the International Institute for

Studies in Race, Reconciliation, and Social Justice at the University of the Free State for its continued support in the shape of an ongoing Research Fellowship.

Most of all, though, I thank my teachers (especially and always Barry Levy and Victor Hori) and my family, for I would not be the little that I am without them. I am forever grateful to my parents and sisters for their ongoing support, love of stories, adventure, and soft couches to recline on, and my beautiful husband, Sébastien, who is forever my guide and gentle friend. I make him crazy at times—of this I am certain! But, hopefully, the laughter I see in his face makes it all worth it. His loving patience and his nudging humor are my lifelines.

As for Darshan, our precious son—this book is for you. You are my deepest inspiration.

CONTRIBUTORS

Elijah Ary is both a Western Tulku and an academic. Recognized at age eight by the Dalai Lama as the reincarnation of a renowned Tibetan scholar, he spent six years from 1986 to 1992 studying Buddhist philosophy at Sera Monastery in South India. He currently holds a Ph.D. in the Study of Religion from Harvard University and teaches Tibetan religious history at the École Pratique des Hautes Études in Paris, France.

Thomas Borchert is an Associate Professor of Religion at the University of Vermont. His research is focused on monastic education and religion and politics in China and Thailand. His articles have appeared in the *Journal of Asian Studies*, *Journal of the American Academy of Religion*, and the *Journal of Church and State*, among others. He received his Ph.D. from the University of Chicago in 2006 and is currently revising a manuscript on monastic education among the Dai-lue.

Wei-Yi Cheng is an Assistant Professor at the Department of Religious Studies, Hsuan Chuang University (Taiwan). She is the author of *Buddhist Nuns in Taiwan and Sri Lanka: A Critique of the Feminist Perspective* (London: Routledge, 2007). Her research interests include women in Buddhism, contemporary Buddhist culture (especially Taiwan and Sri Lanka), and similar topics.

Kate Crosby is the Director of the Centre for Buddhist Studies at the School of Oriental and African Studies, University of London (SOAS). As the Seiyu Kiriyama Reader in Buddhist Studies at SOAS, she teaches Buddhist studies, especially Theravada Buddhist literature and practice as well as Pali and Sanskrit language and literature. Her current areas of research are continuity and diversity in Theravada Buddhism and technologies of directed transformation in the Buddhist cultural milieu, using text-historical and social anthropological approaches. Recent research projects have included an examination of the *lik long* literature and poetic training of the Shan of Burma and northern Thailand, monastic disrobing practices throughout the Theravada world, and the literature and sponsorship of *boran yogavacara* meditation, the so-called “tantric Theravada” of Sri Lanka and mainland Southeast Asian Buddhism. She is co-editor of the Routledge journal *Contemporary Buddhism*.

Melissa Anne-Marie Curley is Assistant Professor of Japanese religions at the University of Iowa. Her research focuses on modern Japanese Buddhism, particularly Pure Land. She has recently contributed to Ugo Dessì's *The Social Dimension of Shin Buddhism*, and the forthcoming *Blackwell Companion to Buddhism*, edited by Mario Poceski and Michael Zimmerman. With Victor Sōgen Hori, she edited *The Kyoto School: Neglected Themes and Hidden Variations*, the second in Nanzan's Frontiers of Japanese Philosophy series.

Karen Derris is an Associate Professor and Chair of the Religious Studies Department at the University of Redlands. Her research and publications consider primarily the intersections of literature, ethics, and history in Theravada Buddhism. Her recent publications include "When the Buddha Was a Woman: Reimagining Tradition in the Theravada" (*Journal of Feminist Studies in Religion*, 2008) and a co-edited reader, *Defining Buddhism(s)* (Sheffield: Equinox Press, 2007).

Christoph Emmrich (Ph.D. in Classical Indology, Heidelberg University, 2004) is currently working on and with Newar girls in the Kathmandu Valley (Nepal) and their involvement in Buddhist practices related to marriage, image consecration, temporary ordination, and female education. In his forthcoming monograph titled *Buddhist Rituals for Newar Girls: Mimesis and Memory in the Kathmandu Valley* he confronts the personal and ethnographic remembrance of singular ritual events with the history of their local and academic exegesis on the basis of ritual manuals reaching back to the early seventeenth century. Christoph Emmrich works in the fields of Newar Buddhism, Pali and Burmese literature and Tamil Jainism and has covered themes such as the historiography of ritual failure, the relationship of soteriology, temporality and language, and the shifting religious affiliation of literary texts. After past appointments at the University of Heidelberg, the Università degli Studi di Firenze and the University of Michigan, Ann Arbor, he currently teaches South and Southeast Asian Buddhism at the University of Toronto. Recent studies include "On the Road to Mawlamyine. Transit and Translation through a Burmese Buddhist Novel, forthcoming; The Ins and Outs of Jains in Tamil Literary Histories. *Journal of Indian Philosophy*, in press; Emending Perfection. Prescript, Postscript and Practice in Newar Buddhist Manuscript Culture, in *Buddhist Manuscript Cultures: Knowledge, Ritual and Art*, S. Berkwitz, J. Schober, and C. Brown, eds. (London: Routledge, 2008), 140–55; All the King's Horses and All the King's Men. The 2004 Red Matsyendranātha Incident in Lalitpur, *Indologica Taurinensia* 32 (2006), 31–65.

Monica Lindberg Falk received her Ph.D. in social anthropology from Gothenburg University, Sweden. She is the vice director and senior lecturer at the Centre for East and South-East Asian Studies at Lund University, Sweden. Her research interests include gender, Buddhism, anthropology of disaster, religious movement and social change in South-East Asia. Her scholarship includes extensive fieldwork in Thailand. She has published a monograph and several articles on themes related to gender and Buddhism, socially engaged Buddhism, and Buddhism and crises. One of her current research projects is gender and Buddhism's role in the recovery process after the 2004 tsunami catastrophe in Thailand. Another of her research projects is about gender and student mobility within Asia.

Frances Garrett is Associate Professor of Tibetan and Buddhist Studies in the Department for the Study of Religion at the University of Toronto. She received her Ph.D. from the University of Virginia in 2004. Her current research considers the intersections between tantric practice, ritual and occult knowledge, and medical theory, and what these tell us about the processes of institutional and ideological change in Tibet.

Winston Kyan is Assistant Professor of Art History at the University of Utah. He received his B.A. in comparative literature from Brown University and his M.A. and Ph.D. in art history from the University of Chicago (2006). His current manuscript project focuses on the intersection of image, text, and bodily practices in medieval Chinese Buddhist art (third to tenth centuries) within the context of religious exchange and material trade along the Silk Road. Dr. Kyan's interest in the relationship between visual culture, human migration, and cultural interaction also extends to the modern and contemporary periods, and he has written essays and interviews on Chinatowns as sites of transnational visual culture and on contemporary art of the Asian diaspora. His most recent article, "Family Space: Buddhist Materiality and Ancestral Fashioning in Mogao Cave 231," appeared in *The Art Bulletin* (March/June 2010).

Amy Paris Langenberg is Instructor of Religion at Auburn University, where she also teaches in the Women's Studies Program. She holds a 2008 Ph.D. in Religious Studies from Columbia University and has taught at Brown University, Brandeis University, and Dartmouth College. Her research interests include Buddhist law, the intersection of aesthetics and religion, Buddhism and medicine, and the gender history of Indian Buddhism. Her most recent article, "Pregnant Words: South Asian Buddhist Tales about Pregnancy and Child Protection," is forthcoming in *History of Religions*. She is currently working on a project concerning Indian Buddhist understandings of, ritualization of, and critique of human fertility.

Miriam Levering is Professor of Religious Studies and Asian Studies Emerita at the University of Tennessee. She is also the International Advisor for Rissho Kosei-kai, a Buddhist lay organization that originated in Japan. Prof. Levering has written or edited *Rethinking Scripture: Essays from a Comparative Perspective* and *Zen Inspirations*. She specializes in the History of Chinese Chan Buddhism and in Women and Gender in Chan and Zen Buddhism. She is now working on a translation into English of the Chinese Chan text "The Letters of DahuiZonggao," an important text in Chinese Chan, Japanese Zen, and especially Korean Son Buddhism.

Todd Lewis is the father of two children, Nathan and Melissa, both of whom have lived with him during research sojourns in Asia. He is also Professor of World Religions at the College of the Holy Cross in Worcester, Massachusetts. He has studied Buddhism in the Kathmandu Valley since 1979. Co-author of the textbook *World Religions Today*, his scholarship on Newar Buddhism include several dozen articles as well as two books, *Popular Buddhist Texts from Nepal: Narratives and Rituals of Newar Buddhism* (New York: SUNY, 2000) and, most recently, *Sugata Saurabha: A Poem on the Life of the Buddha by Chittadhar Hridaya of Nepal* (New York: Oxford, 2010).

Justin McDaniel received his Ph.D. in 2003 from Harvard University's Department of Sanskrit and Indian Studies. Presently he teaches Buddhism and Southeast Asian Studies at the University of Pennsylvania. His research foci include Lao, Thai, Pali, and Sanskrit literature, Southeast Asian Buddhism, Japanese Buddhism, ritual studies, manuscript studies, and Southeast Asian history. His first book is on the history of Buddhist monastic education in Laos and Thailand, *Gathering Leaves and Lifting Words* (Seattle: University of Washington Press, 2008). It won the Harry Benda Prize from the Association of Asian Studies for the best first book in Southeast Asian Studies (2008–2009). His second book is a study on material culture and ritual in Thai Buddhism: *The Lovelorn Ghost and the Magic Monk: Practicing Buddhism in Thailand* (New York: Columbia University Press, 2011). His recent publications appear in the *Bulletin del"École Françaised" Extrême-Orient (Étudesthématiques), Journal of the International Association of Buddhist Studies, Aséanie, Journal of Religion and Film, Material Religion, Manusya*, and the *Journal of the Siam Society*, as well as contributions to collected articles on Buddhism and Modernity, Pali literature, Palm-leaf Manuscript research, and liturgical studies. In 2012 he was named a Guggenheim Fellow.

Hillary Rodrigues (Ph.D. McMaster) is professor of Religious Studies at the University of Lethbridge. His publications include *Krishnamurti's Insight* (Nepal: Pilgrims, 2001), *Ritual Worship of the Great Goddess* (SUNY, 2003), and *Introduction to the Study of Religion* (London: Routledge, 2009). He has edited *Studying Hinduism in Practice* (London: Routledge, 2011), a volume in the *Studying Religions in Practice* series. He has been honored with the University of Lethbridge's Distinguished Teaching Medal and the Board of Governors Chair in Teaching.

Jeffrey Samuels is Associate Professor in the Department of Philosophy of Religion and Coordinator of Asian Studies at Western Kentucky University. His research interests center on the intersection of religion and culture in

South and Southeast Asia. He has published articles on Buddhist monastic culture, pedagogical practices, and research methods in the *Journal of the American Academy of Religion, Modern Asian Studies, Religion, Journal of the International Association of Buddhist Studies, Contemporary Buddhism, American Behavioral Scientist, South Asian Diaspora*, and others. Along with co-editing *Approaching the Dhamma: Buddhist Texts and Practices in South and Southeast Asia* with Anne Blackburn in 2003, he has published *Attracting the Heart: Social Relations and the Aesthetics of Emotion in Sri Lankan Monastic Culture* (Honolulu: University of Hawaii Press, 2010). He is currently writing a social history of Theravada Buddhism in Malaysia.

Vanessa R. Sasson is a professor of Religious Studies in the Liberal Arts Department of Marianopolis College where she has been teaching since 1999. She is also a Research Fellow for the International Institute for Studies in Race, Reconciliation, and Social Justice at the University of the Free State, as well as Adjunct Professor of Comparative Religion at McGill University. She has published a number of articles and book chapters, is the author of *The Birth of Moses and the Buddha: A Paradigm for the Comparative Study of Religions* (Sheffield: Sheffield University Press, 2007) and co-editor with Jane Marie Law of *Imagining the Fetus: The Unborn in Myth, Religion, and Culture* (Oxford: Oxford University Press, 2009). Her interests continue to be focused around religious hagiography, children and childhoods, as well as ordination for women in Theravāda Buddhism, and interfaith dialogue.

Kristin Scheible earned a Ph.D. from Harvard University in 2006, is Assistant Professor of Religion at Bard College in New York, and mother of Aidan, Elias, and Jasper. Her area of expertise is Theravada Buddhist literature; her work revolves around the genre of historical narrative literature (*vamsa*) in the Pali language, and her current book project is on the Pali Mahavamsa. Her most recent publications include "Priming the Lamp of *Dhamma*: the Buddha's Miracles in the Pāli *Mahavāmsa*," *Journal of the International Association of Buddhist Studies* Volume 33, Number 1–2, 2010 (2011) and "Cultivating Mutual Respect: Lessons from the Buddhist Studies Classroom" in *Teaching Comparison: Pedagogical Perspectives as Comparative Theory in Religious Studies*, ed. Jennifer Rapp (forthcoming, *Teaching Religious Studies* series, AAR/OUP).

Gregory Schopen has an M.A. from McMaster University and a Ph.D. from the Australian National University. His work focuses on Indian Buddhist monastic life and early Mahāyāna movements. By looking beyond the Pali Canon in favor of less commonly used sources such as the Mūlasarvāstivāda-vinaya and Indian Buddhist stone inscriptions, his numerous scholarly works have shifted the field away from Buddhism as portrayed through its own doctrines toward a more realistic picture of the actual lives of Buddhists, both monastic and lay. In this sense, he has seriously challenged many assumptions and myths about Buddhism that were first perpetuated in earlier Western scholarship. In

1985 he received the MacArthur Grant for his work in the field of History of Religion. Many of his articles have been published in three volumes dedicated to his work: *Figments and Fragments of Mahayana Buddhism in India* (Honolulu: University of Hawaii Press, 2005), *Buddhist Monks and Business Matters* (Honolulu: University of Hawaii Press, 2004), and *Bones, Stones and Buddhist Monks* (Honolulu: University of Hawaii Press, 1997). He is now the Rush C. Hawkins University Professor of Religious Studies at Brown University.

Karma Lekshe Tsomo is a professor at the University of San Diego, where she has taught since 2000. She is the author of *Sisters in Solitude: Two Traditions of Monastic Ethics for Women* and *Into the Jaws of Yama, Lord of Death: Buddhism, Bioethics, and Death*, and is the editor of numerous volumes, including *Buddhist Women Across Cultures: Realizations*; *Innovative Buddhist Women: Swimming Against the Stream*; and *Buddhist Women and Social Justice: Ideals, Challenges, and Achievements*. As a founder and past president of Sakyadhita International Association of Buddhist Women, she integrates scholarship and social activism, helping guide the international Buddhist women's movement and coordinating bi-annual international conferences on Buddhist women. As founder and director of Jamyang Foundation, she oversees fourteen education projects for girls and women in the Indian Himalayas and Bangladesh. Her current research focuses on neuroethics, human rights, economic justice, and mysticism from a Buddhist feminist perspective.

Little Buddhas

Introduction

Charting New Territory: Children and Childhoods in Buddhist Texts and Traditions

VANESSA R. SASSON

In his effort to perfect generosity,[1] Vessantara[2] gives his two children away to the evil Jūjaka simply because he is asked to. The children are handed over despite their fervent sobs and heart-wrenching protests. They attempt to escape a few times, once by hiding in the river with their heads hidden under the lily leaves, and a second time by squirming out of Jūjaka's tight grip, but Vessantara is unyielding. He explains to his children that "dearer than my son a hundredfold, a thousandfold, a hundred thousandfold is omniscience,"[3] and he sends them away.

Any reader of this story is certain to feel horrified by Vessantara's interpretation of virtue. Vessantara himself is filled with anguish and appears heartbroken by the decision he is convinced is required of him. After the children have gone, he is repeatedly described as weeping pitifully, hot tears streaming from his eyes, trembling violently. He contemplates running after them, killing Jūjaka and bringing them home, but then calms himself down, remembering that once a gift is given, it should never be

1. Melissa Curley, Amy Langenberg, and Jeffrey Samuels each took time to read over this chapter in its previous incarnations and provided me with helpful comments and suggestions. I am grateful to them for their help.
2. I here refer to the *Vessantara Jātaka* of the Pāli Canon, no. 547. See E. B. Cowell, ed. *The Jātaka or Stories of the Buddha's Former Births* (Oxford: Pali Text Society, 1895), 6: 246–305.
3. *Vessantara Jātaka*, 547

reclaimed. When his wife returns, she finds him incapable of speaking. He snaps at her when she asks where the children are. She falls apart when she cannot find them herself. Meanwhile, the children are being brutalized far from their home. Other than Jūjaka, no one in the story is happy with the shape that virtue has taken.

The *Vessantara Jātaka* is one of the most important narratives in the Buddhist canon. It is frequently depicted artistically and is recited throughout the Buddhist world. Its popularity is likely connected to its layered complexity and the various emotions it evokes in its audience. With regard to children, the emotions are particularly acute and oddly paradoxical. It is clear, for example, that Vessantara cherishes his children: the decision to follow through with his commitment to the perfection of generosity is anything but neutral. The Pāli version is uncharacteristically emotional, depicting its hero wavering with angst about the step he feels required to take. And yet Vessantara insists on giving his children away, seemingly excited about the prospect of perfecting a virtue (despite the obvious fact that it cancels out other virtues in the process). In the *Milindapañha*, Nāgasena tries to alleviate King Milinda's distress about this narrative by suggesting that Jūjaka was old and Vessantara knew he would not live much longer,[4] but this explanation serves only to emphasize the discomfort underlying the narrative all the more. How can a reader not feel exquisitely disturbed by a hero's willingly handing over his sobbing children to a violent stranger for the purposes of his own development?

This is not the only narrative in the Buddhist canon that neglects children in favor of the adults responsible for them. The most famous story in all of Buddhism, the story of the Buddha in his ultimate life, has been repeatedly cited as evidence of Buddhism's negative relationship to children. Just as he is on the cusp of awakening after innumerable lifetimes of effort, moments before his Great Departure, the future Buddha abandons his newborn son for the sake of an abstract ideal. Admittedly, he does not transfer him into a monster's care—his son will grow up in palatial splendor surrounded by loving family members—but he nevertheless abandons his son mere seconds into fatherhood.

The tradition, moreover, is replete with narratives of monastics following the Buddha's lead and abandoning their own children. One of the most shocking narratives of this sort emerges from the *Udāna*, in which the monk Sangāmaji is approached by his recently abandoned wife and their newborn child. She begs him to return to the home life, but he does not react. The wife even places the child at her ex-husband's feet, hoping that the sight of his own child will awaken some sense of family responsibility or emotion, but the monk continues to wait passively

4. Nāgasena provides a long list of justifications for Vessantara's decision, the above being just one of them. See Milindapañha 275–84. For an English translation, see I. B. Horner, trans., *Milinda's Questions* (Oxford: Pali Text Society, 1996), 2: 95–109.

for the scenario to end. When the wife finally does give up and returns home with their child, the Buddha praises the monk for his extraordinary restraint (and condemns the wife for her inappropriate behavior).[5] It is no wonder that Buddhism has been interpreted as anti-family. With celibacy as a central value, the primary hero repeatedly abandoning his progeny from one lifetime to the next, and his fellow monks following suit, not to mention the many stories in the *Therīgātha* in which women seem to require the death of their children for spiritual advancement to become possible,[6] the standard conclusion that Buddhism is anti-family is not difficult to comprehend.

But this conclusion is not the only one at which we might arrive. While these narratives seem to place family relationships well below ideals of asceticism on the ladder of Buddhist hierarchies—one need only consider traditional seating arrangements in almost any Buddhist community—recent scholarship has demonstrated that asceticism is not the only, nor even the most dominant, priority in Buddhist circles. Indeed, even where asceticism dominates the philosophical landscape, issues of progeny and virility nevertheless manifest. The very fact of Rāhula's existence is a case in point: as Kate Crosby has noted in her chapter here, bringing Rāhula into the world immediately before his renunciation may very well have been a statement about the Buddha's virility more than anything else.[7]

Moreover, it bears noting that narratives such as the ones just cited are premised on the assumption that children are cherished. Vessantara's generosity would be meaningless if he did not love his children. And as for the Buddha, the *Jātaka-nidāna* describes him peeking into the room where his wife and newborn son are sleeping before he leaves for the Great Departure. He is inclined to take his son into his arms just once, but he fears the movement will wake his wife. He therefore decides to wait until after he achieves awakening to see him. When he does return to the kingdom many years later, the Buddha gives the son he never held the inheritance he had long been preparing. Far from being cold and distant, the Buddha of the *Jātaka-nidāna* seems to have strong feelings for his son; there is pathos in the depiction of his longing to hold him but resigning himself to let go.

Children are often abandoned in Buddhist narratives, but the very fact of their abandonment reveals a deeper sentiment vibrating beneath the surface. Otherwise the stories would have no impact. Moreover, as many of the chapters in this volume attest, Buddhism is not limited to the *Vessantara Jātaka* or the abandonment of Rāhula when it comes to children. There are many other

5. Udāna 5–6. For an English translation, see F. L. Woodward, trans., *The Minor Anthologies of the Pali Canon, Part II* (Oxford: The Pali Text Society, 1996), 6–7.

6. For discussions of this theme, see Reiko Ohnuma, "Mother-Love and Mother Grief: South Asian Buddhist Variations on a Theme," *Journal of Feminist Studies in Religion* 23 no.1 (2007), 95–116; and V. R. Sasson, "Māyā's Disappearing Act: Motherhood in Early Buddhist Literature" in *Family in Buddhism: Buddhist Vows and Family Ties* (New York: SUNY, forthcoming).

7. See also John Powers, *A Bull of a Man: Images of Masculinity, Sex, and the Body in Indian Buddhism* (Cambridge, MA: Harvard University Press, 2009).

narratives, rituals, and lived realities that tell a different story. There is no question that Buddhism can be read as an anti-family religion. But it can also be read as a religious tradition that understands parental love and makes room for the care of children in a number of (often unexpected) ways.

DEFINING THE TERMS

It has been well noted that a distinction needs to be made between children and conceptions of childhood. As Hugh Cunningham has argued, it is one thing to discuss childhood as an abstract concept, and something altogether different to write about the lives of actual children.[8] In this volume, both approaches are represented, with some chapters dedicated to exploring textual representations of children—in the hope that such representation will reveal something about how real children may have lived in various Buddhist contexts—and other chapters dedicated to examining how contemporary Buddhist communities interact with children, influenced by those same historical documents and yet also products of the innumerable circumstances particular to each context. In other words, the chapters in this book demonstrate that, while "children" and "childhood" are two different categories, they are intimately connected. When one is explored, something of the other is invariably made known.

How does one define "child"? This question has been asked at some point by most of the contributors to this volume. The term in English is ambiguous, shifting in emphasis according to the context. Contemporary language demarcates a number of categories for the various moments that might compete for the title of "child": infant, baby, toddler, boy, girl, youth, teenager, and more recently, tween. The elusiveness of these categories becomes all the more apparent when one considers the fact that many of these terms have been used in contexts not specifically associated with a particular biological age: the term "boy," for example, was once commonly used when speaking with or about an adult in a socially disadvantaged position. One may likewise derogatively or affectionately call someone a "baby" at any point in life. Miriam Levering (in this volume) notes that in Chinese sources, "child" is understood as a relational term—it is not a biological age but has to do with relationships to parents, adults, and seniors of various kinds. Determining what a "child" is therefore inevitably leads to a definition of "adult."

Biological age is evidently not always connected to the term "child" (and by extension, to the term "adult"). Even if we set aside metaphorical uses, the precise meaning of the word nevertheless remains vague. Cunningham suggests that it might be associated with education: "if attendance compulsorily

8. Hugh Cunningham, *Children and Childhood in Western Society Since 1500* (London: Longman, 1995), 2; see also Marcia J. Bunge and Don S. Browning, "Introduction" in *Children and Childhood in World Religions: Primary Sources and Texts*, ed. Don S. Browning and Marcia J. Bunge (New Brunswick, NJ: Rutgers, 2009), 7.

at school marked a person as a child, then childhood has been progressively prolonged as the school-leaving age has risen."[9] The United Nations Convention on the Rights of the Child (UNCRC) decided that a child is anyone below the age of eighteen, and while it is understandable that a definition was required for the proceedings to take shape, the number (18) is itself arbitrary. The term "child" cannot be properly contained within the tight parameters of substantive definitions.

Buddhist discourse suffers from—or enjoys (depending on one's perspective)—similar linguistic limitations. A number of terms in Pāli and Sanskrit might be reasonably translated as "child," such as *bāla* (S. *bāla*), *apacca* (S. *apatya*), *putta* (S. *putra*), and so on, but it is not obvious that any of these is either comprehensive enough or specific enough at all times and in all contexts to help delineate a category for our purposes. In her chapter in this volume, Amy Langenberg uses the *vinaya* to help create a definition of childhood: since full membership in the monastic community begins at the age of twenty, she understands "any young person below the age of twenty" to be a child. In my own chapter in this volume, a study of the Buddha's childhood, I have suggested that if childhood has something to do with development, growth, and transformation, the only real childhood the Buddha may be safely said to have experienced is in his previous lives; "childhood" in his final life story may be represented in the few narratives preserved by the tradition that are associated with his youth, but the notion of a Buddha's childhood remains tenuous.

Research on Buddhism and children is just beginning; there is no doubt that with time, definitions will emerge that will provide more nuance to this discussion. For the time being, I suggest allowing the term to remain fluid. In his influential study on *mizuko kuyō*, William Lafleur faced a similar problem in defining the term "life." Rather than becoming embroiled in a debate about hard lines and limitations, he challenges the very desire to create such lines when great concepts in life defy them by their grandeur. As he says, "Really large concepts will never be boxed within precise definitions, and in hoping they will, we are chasing phantoms."[10] A few lines later, he continues:

> The alternative to precise definition is not irrationality. It is not irrational to recognize that some concepts do not lend themselves to easy definitions: "life," "humanness," even "mind" may simply be fish too large to be caught by our definitions. They always slip off the word hooks we fashion to try to snag them.[11]

9. Hugh Cunningham, *Children and Childhood in Western Society Since 1500*, 174.
10. William R. Lafleur. *Liquid Life: Abortion and Buddhism in Japan* (Princeton, NJ: Princeton University Press, 1992), 14.
11. William R. Lafleur. *Liquid Life*, 15.

I suspect that "children" and "childhood" are likewise too slippery to catch with words. Sometimes a child is someone only a few years old. At other times the term can point to a biological adult with little socially recognized authority. It can be a novice, despite many gray hairs, and it can be a *jātaka* tradition in its entirety.

A REVIEW OF THE LITERATURE AND A CALL FOR MORE

The theme of Buddhist children and childhoods has not garnered much attention in academic circles to date. Although Western Buddhist scholarship has largely moved beyond the limited perception that Buddhism is an exclusively philosophical enterprise dominated by texts, the remains of our textual and philosophical orientation continue to be evident. Children and childhoods are therefore rarely given consideration.

The work has begun, however. A number of sources deserve mention here as the germs of a new subfield in Buddhist Studies. Alan Cole's book *Mothers and Sons in Chinese Buddhism*[12] is perhaps one of the first serious inquiries into the relationship between children and their parents in a Buddhist context. Anne Benkhe Kinney's edited volume, *Chinese Views of Childhood*[13]—although not specifically focused on Buddhism—also belongs to this early phase. Shayne Clarke's doctoral dissertation,[14] Liz Wilson's new edited volume *Family in Buddhism: Buddhist Vows and Family Ties*,[15] and Jonathan Silk's recent article on child abandonment practices[16] have all brought family relationships into focus. Kate Crosby's seminal article, "Only If You Let Go of That Tree: Ordination Without Parental Consent in Theravāda Vinaya,"[17] challenges traditional academic expectations concerning child ordination, while Mathieu Boisvert's work on the *shin pyu*[18] ceremony highlights the association generally made between positive experiences of religion in childhood and continuity of that religion into the future. Margaret Childs's now famous article "Chigo Monogatari: Love Stories or Buddhist Sermons?"[19] and Bernard Faure's elaboration in his book

12. Alan Cole, *Mothers and Sons in Chinese Buddhism (*Stanford, CA: Stanford University Press, 1998).
13. Anne Behnke Kinney, ed., *Chinese Views of Childhood* (Honolulu: University of Hawaii Press, 1995).
14. Shayne Clarke, *Family Matters in Indian Monastic Buddhism* (Ph.D. Diss., UCLA, 2006).
15. Forthcoming.
16. Jonathan A. Silk, "Child Abandonment and Homes for Unwed Mothers in Ancient India: Buddhist Sources," *Journal of the American Oriental Society* 127 no. 3 (2007), 297–314.
17. Kate Crosby, "'Only If You Let Go of That Tree:' Ordination without Parental Consent in Theravāda Vinaya," *Buddhist Studies Review* 22 (2005), 155–73.
18. Mathieu Boisvert, "A Socio-cultural Analysis of the Burmese *Shin pyu* Ceremony," *Journal of Beliefs and Values* 21 no. 2 (2000), 203–11.
19. Margaret H. Childs, "Chigo Monogatari: Love Stories or Buddhist Sermons?" *Monumenta Nipponica* 35 no. 2 (1980), 127–51.

The Red Thread[20] have examined the ambiguous notion of the *chigo* in Japanese history. Monique Skidmore's ethnography of children in Burma identifies children from a specifically Buddhist perspective not simply as insurance against old age or as people whose success "enhances one's own social or karmic position, but as beings unconditionally loved."[21] Todd Lewis[22] and Alexander von Rospatt[23] have shed light on the Newari community and their rites of passage for children, and Jeffrey Samuels[24] and Thomas Borchert[25] have each dedicated time to the issue of children's education in Buddhist monastic contexts.[26]

The most prominent voice with regard to children and Buddhism, however, is Rita Gross, and this precisely because she has been the voice of Buddhism in almost every edited volume on children in world religions that I have encountered to date. She paints her picture in broad strokes, attempting to provide a kind of "theology" of childhood in Buddhist terms. Since she has been alone in this work, her interpretations have dominated the broader academic landscape and therefore require some attention here.

Gross raises questions about who children may be from a Buddhist theoretical perspective, and she is characteristically challenging in her comparative negotiations between contemporary North American ideals and classical Buddhist interpretations. She claims that the first commandment in Buddhism is not to be fruitful and multiply, and that contrary to general contemporary

20. Bernard Faure, *The Red Thread: Buddhist Approaches to Sexuality* (Princeton, NJ: Princeton University Press, 1998), 213ff.

21. Monique Skidmore. "The Future of Burma: Children Are Like Jewels" in *Burma at the Turn of the 20th Century*, ed. M. Skidmore (Honolulu: University of Hawaii Press, 2005), 256.

22. See, for example, his article "Childhood and Newar Tradition: Chittadhar Hridaya's *Jhī Macā*," *Asian Folklore Studies* 48 no. 2 (1989), 195–210.

23. See, for example, his article "The Transformation of the Monastic Ordination (*pravrajyā*) into a Rite of Passage in Newar Buddhism" in *Words and Deeds: Hindu and Buddhist Rituals in South Asia*, ed. Jörg Gengnagel, Ute Hüsken, and Srilata Raman (Wiesbaden: Harrassowitz Verlag, 2005), 199–234.

24. Jeffrey Samuels, "Texts Memorized, Texts Performed: A Reconsideration of the Role of *Paritta* in Sri Lankan Monastic Education," *Journal of the International Association of Buddhist Studies* 28 no. 2 (2005), 339–67; Jeffrey Samuels, "Toward an Action-Oriented Pedagogy: Buddhist Texts and Monastic Education in Contemporary Sri Lanka," *Journal of the American Academy of Religion* 72 no. 4 (2004), 955–71; and Jeffrey Samuels, "When Words Are Not Enough: Eliciting Children's Experiences of Buddhist Monastic Life Through Photographs," in *Visual Research Methods: Image Society, and Representation*, ed. Gregory C. Stanczak (Thousand Oaks (CA): Sage Publications, 2007), 197–224.

25. Thomas Borchert, *Educating Monks: Buddhism, Politics and Freedom of Religion on China's Southwest Border* (Ph.D. Diss., University of Chicago, 2006).

26. There are a few popular sources to consider as well. Some worthy of note include Sumi Loundon, ed. *Blue Jean Buddha: Voices of Young Buddhists* (Somerville, MA: Wisdom Publications, 2001); Phra Peter Pannapadipo, *Little Angels* (Bangkok, Thailand: Post Books, 2001); Kamala Tiyavanich, *Sons of the Buddha: The Early Lives of Three Extraordinary Thai Masters* (Boston: Wisdom Publications, 2007); Sarah Napthali, *Buddhism for Mothers of Young Children: Becoming a Mindful Parent* (NSW,

assumptions, children represent neither a romantic innocence nor a depraved fallen state.[27] On the contrary, she argues that children come into the world with their own karmic inheritance, continuing a journey that has no traceable beginning. Children are not idealized in Buddhist literature as they may be elsewhere, since "growing up is the pre-requisite for becoming enlightened."[28] She advocates for responsible reproduction and against what she calls "mindless pro-natalism"[29] and procreative "consumerism,"[30] going so far as to suggest that reproducing without mindfulness may be tantamount to sexual misconduct.[31]

Gross writes from the vantage point of a "Buddhist constructive theologian"[32] and is concerned primarily with reconstructing Western Buddhism for a "post-patriarchal" world. When she reads Buddhism, she sees in its texts a religion that is neither child centered nor family centered; its deepest goals "are not the worldly continuities so sought and valued by some religious orientations, but the transformation of conventional attitudes into enlightened mind."[33] She sees the meditation hall as the core Buddhist space rather than "the fields, the hearth, the sacramental table, the sacrificial altar, or the bazaar."[34] Although she makes a passionate call for mindful, responsible parenting in which children would be loved and well cared for, she does not see children or parenting as Buddhist priorities.

Gross is one of the champions of Buddhist feminist history in Western academia. Her contributions are part of the building blocks upon which we rely today. But Buddhist studies is not limited to these readings, nor indeed is Buddhism itself limited by an idealized asceticism divorced from human reality. There is no question that the ascetic strain in Buddhism relegates *procreation* to the back burner (although there are exceptions even to this rule), but that does not mean children have no roles to play or responsibilities to carry. Asceticism may be kept rigorously pure as a concept, but ascetics live in the world and invariably have relationships with the people with whom they share that world. Amy Langenberg's chapter tells the story

Australia, 2007); Sarah Napthali, *Buddhism for Mothers: A Calm Approach to Caring for Yourself and Your Children* (NSW, Australia: Allen & Unwin, 2010).

27. Rita M. Gross, *Soaring and Settling: Buddhist Perspectives on Contemporary Social and Religious Issues* (New York: Continuum, 1998), 128.

28. Rita M. Gross. "Scarce Discourse: Exploring Gender, Sexuality, and Spirituality in Buddhism" in *Nurturing Child and Adolescent Spirituality: Perspectives from the World's Religious Traditions,* ed. K. M. Yust et al. (Lanham: Rowman & Littlefield, 2006), 411.

29. Rita M. Gross. *Buddhism After Patriarchy: A Feminist History, Analysis, and Reconstruction of Buddhism* (New York: SUNY, 1993), 237.

30. Rita M. Gross, *Soaring and Settling,* 108.

31. Rita M. Gross. *Buddhism After Patriarchy,* 236.

32. Rita M. Gross. "Child and Family in Buddhism" in *Religious Dimensions of Child and Family Life: Reflections on the UN Convention on the Rights of the Child,* ed. H. Coward and P. Cook (Victoria: University of Victoria, 1996), 80.

33. Rita M. Gross, "Child and Family in Buddhism," 82.

34. Rita M. Gross, "Child and Family in Buddhism," 84. She repeats this view almost verbatim in *Soaring and Settling,* 127.

of Ānanda's concern for his orphaned nephews and how he brought himself to the brink of starvation by giving them the food offerings he himself was meant to receive. Ānanda, in this story, is a perfect example of an ascetic who remained concerned for the children of the family he left behind. The Buddha is another, filling his community with many members of his biological family—including his son. Gregory Schopen's chapter here makes the argument that monks functioned as *protectors* of children in some cases, and Monica Lindberg Falk describes the nuns in charge of the school she examined for this book as doing exactly that: protecting the young girls in their charge when society would have otherwise failed them. The ascetic ideal may theoretically separate family from practice, but in reality such separations probably have been, and continue to be, quite rare.

This review of the literature is by no means exhaustive. The bibliography at the end of this volume demonstrates that research has been conducted and is available on the theme in a variety of contexts, but much more work needs to be done. When scholarship began to take women into consideration, it was expected that a few studies would suffice to capture the role, experience, and impact of women in religious traditions. This expectation, we now know, vastly underestimated the situation. It has been suggested that childhood studies may have a similar impact:[35] a few disparate studies cannot possibly capture the many ways in which children contribute to and experience Buddhist life. We need more voices, more discussion, more creative thinking, and we need the courage to unlearn old assumptions in order to make room for new ones.

CONSTRUCTING CHILDHOODS

Philippe Ariès, in his monumental study *Centuries of Childhood*,[36] is consistently credited with the insight that childhood is a constructed category and, as such, has a history. While many scholars have since challenged Ariès on some of the details of his work, he is nevertheless hailed as having enough vision to recognize that the category itself exists and merits historical analysis. Scholars of European history have been exploring the question of a history of childhood

35. Ada Cohen, "Introduction: Childhood between Past and Present" in *Constructions of Childhood in Ancient Greece and Italy*, ed. Ada Cohen and Jeremy B. Rutter (Princeton, NJ: The American School of Classical Studies at Athens, 2007), 2. Also see Ann Oakley, "Women and Children First and Last: Parallels and Differences between Children's and Women's Studies" in *Children's Childhoods: Observed and Experienced*, ed. Berry Mayall (London: The Falmer Press, 1994), 13–32. This is not to suggest that there is an equation between the situation in which women found themselves at the dawn of the feminist era and children today. The situations are vastly different, but the expectations about the potential fruits borne as a result of bringing in new perspectives merits comparison.

36. Phillippe Ariès, *L'enfant et la vie familial sous l'Ancien Régime* (Paris: Éditions du Seuil, 1973).

ever since. Classicists have similarly explored the history of childhood in great detail,[37] but religious studies scholars have not made the same kinds of efforts. Ariès's work has not yet had the impact on our field that it has had elsewhere, and this fact is particularly surprising given how acutely aware of children religious communities tend to be. As Karma Lekshe Tsomo notes in her chapter here, without children, religion has no future. There will be no one left to appease the dead, perform rituals, or study the texts. Religious *communities* focus on the children in their congregations and scholars in other fields have been exploring the history of children and childhoods in various contexts, most notably in the fields of history, psychology, medicine, and even marketing, but as is noted above, religious studies scholars are just beginning to realize that children and childhoods may be worthy of attention.[38]

A history of Buddhist childhood has yet to emerge from the limited materials available, but I would like to make a preliminary suggestion of where we might look for possible answers: Buddhism is replete with doctrinal attempts at understanding who we are and why we come into the world as we do. By reexamining the development of Buddhist doctrine in light of this theme, a history of childhood will likely manifest. Just as the history of Christianity's Original Sin functions as a piece in the larger puzzle of the Western history of childhood, the history of karma, filial piety, and the *tathāgatagarbha* doctrine (among others) may do the same. Each of these doctrines has its own history of interpretation, and that history may function as a conceptual foundation for the history of Buddhist constructions of childhood.

A history of ideas, however, is not the only route to be considered. In her study of Tibetan medical texts for children in this volume, Frances Garrett concludes that the "material culture of children"—the clothing, adornments, amulets, toys, and the like that are signifiers of children and childhood—might likewise provide a glimpse into the history of the construction of childhood. Technologies of protection and healing may in fact function to empower children "against the dangers around them as part of a process of being socialized into a world of relationships with sentient and non-sentient environments." A history of ritual, of medicine, and quite simply, a history of *things* deserves to be attempted in this voyage toward new understanding.

There is no predicting what we will find as the field develops, but it seems obvious that no matter what is concluded, childhood has some kind of a

37. According to Mark Golden, a 1981 bibliography on ancient childhood listed approximately 1,300 sources! See his book *Children and Childhood in Classical Athens* (Baltimore: The Johns Hopkins University Press, 1990), xiii.

38. Contributions in religious traditions other than Buddhism particularly worthy of note include Marcia Bunge's three edited volumes: *The Child in Christian Thought* (Grand Rapids, MI: Eerdmans, 2001); *The Child in the Bible* (Grand Rapids, MI: Eerdmans 2008); and *Children and Childhood in World Religions (*Grand Rapids, MI: Eerdmans [2008?]; and Susan Ridgely Bales, *When I Was a Child: Children's Interpretations of First Communion* (Chapel Hill: University of North Carolina Press, 2005). Also worthy of recognition is the AAR Childhood Studies consultation, which has been available for almost a decade.

Buddhist history. Melissa Curley's chapter here is a case in point: by examining the history of Ikkyū in Japanese memory and bridging that history with contemporary representations, she has produced a localized history of Buddhist childhood. A broader history of Buddhist childhood merits consideration.

THEMES OF CHILDREN AND CHILDHOOD

A number of revealing themes emerge from the contributions in this volume. The first—and perhaps most significant—has to do with human projections and expectations. Children in all contexts are likely to receive a heavy dose of adult projections and to bear the weight of parental expectations. Indeed, I am not certain it is possible to raise children otherwise. As Neil Postman says, "[C]hildren are the living messages we send to a time we will not see";[39] the value we give to that future inevitably manifests in the shape of our hopes and fears projected onto our children. But Buddhist communities, as a result of the idealism to which they are prone, have taken such projections further than most. Almost every chapter in this volume can be connected to this theme in some way. Thomas Borchert, for example, notes that one of the most basic lessons young monks need to learn is how to "dress the part" and behave in public like the little buddhas they are meant to personify; Jeffrey Samuels describes young monks' having to learn how to sit and where to stand, suggesting a kind of *performed* monasticism. The Buddha's hagiography does not leave much room for the possibility that he had any growing up to do as a child, so he seems to be a master even at his birth. Miriam Levering provides a number of examples of precocious children in Chinese Buddhist sources who seem more like adults in small bodies than what we would consider normal children, and Melissa Curley demonstrates how the values of each subsequent generation are projected onto Ikkyū's person. Elijah Ary's discussion of Tulkus identifies these same projections and the tension that is produced when children have awakening inscribed onto them at such a young age. Winston Kyan's study of the *Sujati Jātaka* presents us with a precocious child who reverses traditional family roles and feeds his parents with the flesh of his own body, and Hillary Rodrigues argues that projections were perhaps at their most extreme in the case of Krishnamurti, who at the age of fourteen was expected not only to manifest awakening and act the part, but to *be* the next Buddha and usher in a new era in human history. Even if Krishnamurti cannot be located within strict Buddhist parameters, the influence Buddhism had on his life and the expectations he was forced to carry during his childhood situates his story squarely within this discussion. All of these studies suggest that Buddhist traditions can place (and have placed) a tremendous weight on the shoulders of some of its children—be it in mythologized narratives or in reality.

39. Neil Postman, *The Disappearance of Childhood* (New York: Vintage, 1994), xi.

An important question to emerge from this volume is, how do Buddhist communities transmit the tradition to their children? Karen Derris surveys the exponentially growing corpus of Buddhist children's books available in the West. While this new market reveals a growing interest in Buddhist books for children, she notes that in most cases the content is stripped of any clear reference to the religion—a telling detail about Buddhism in the West. In many traditional Buddhist countries, however, educational materials are much more comfortable displaying their religious colors. Justin McDaniel provides a wonderful array of cultural examples of Buddhist educational devices for children in Thailand, from the traditional *jātaka* wall paintings, parts of which he suggests are positioned low precisely for children's benefit, to *dhamma* textbooks and thrilling popular films, all of which reference Buddhist values and norms.

Jātaka stories often reappear among the primary educational devices for children in a variety of contexts (Derris notes how often this is the case even in Western Buddhist books for children, although the fact of their being *jātakas* is not usually made explicit), raising the question of whether they were in fact produced with children in mind. Kate Crosby suggests that this may in fact be the case with *suttas* associated with Rāhula—the very disciple who represents childhood: the *Rāhula Sutta*, for example, focuses on the importance of truth-telling and is delivered using simple metaphors that a child can easily understand. Truth-telling, moreover, is an issue that returns repeatedly in parenting. If her interpretation is correct, and McDaniel's assumption about the height of the wall paintings being for the benefit of children is correct, this notion begs the question of what other traditional Buddhist expressions are performed specifically for a child audience. How much are we missing by thinking like adults and seeing exclusively through adult eyes?

Educating children about Buddhism is not the only way to transmit the tradition to the next generation. Equally powerful are the rituals that are performed to enact the tradition. In their study of the *ihi* ritual for Newari girls, Lewis and Emmerich explore a number of competing interpretations, many of which identify this rite as an opportunity to feed the tradition to the child. According to one interpreter of the rite, it is understood as a kind of Buddhist activation, awakening the potential of the child to achieve Buddhist ideals. This rite, and surely many others, is a way of ensuring the continuity of the tradition, something that Karma Lekshe Tsomo emphasizes as a tradition's highest priority where children are concerned.

A surprising discovery to emerge from the studies here comes from the contributions of Gregory Schopen and Amy Langenberg. Both scholars have uncovered evidence of a history of gifting children to the monastery—at times even before the child was born. Gregory Schopen argues that some of these children were relegated to the role of "attending menial," or "servant" (*paścācchramaṇa*) in the monasteries. These were children who were not free but were "owned by the monks to whom they were given." Such a gifting of children for the express purpose of providing monks with servants broadens our perspective of monasticism significantly and reminds us that children are difficult to eliminate from any social equation. Where there are people—even if they are monks—there are likely to also be children. And where there are children, some of them are bound to function as servants.

A more mundane issue to emerge from these pages has to do with food. Feeding children is a regular concern for parents and caregivers around the world, and this concern spills from the pages of this volume more often than I could have anticipated. Food is not necessarily a philosophical issue; it does not make much noise in the lofty corridors of our intellectual expectations about Buddhism, but repeatedly throughout this volume the contributors demonstrate that a leading question troubling Buddhist communities is the very same question troubling the rest of us: what to feed the kids!

Wei-yi Cheng's chapter focuses on the experiences of young women who were ordained as children in Taiwan and eventually disrobed. One of the prevailing difficulties these girls complained about had to do with food restrictions in the monastery. Even with three meals a day (not always the case in Buddhist monastic settings), the girls craved snacks and admit to having snuck out to buy food whenever they could. They even stored some of these treasures in the ceilings of their rooms. According to Thomas Borchert, in the Theravāda community in Sipsongpannā, children are provided with dinner even though this breaks one of the novice precepts precisely because it is understood that "children will be less naughty if they are well fed." Kristin Scheible's chapter on Western Buddhism identifies the many difficulties and challenges Western parents face in attempting to negotiate between the ideals of Buddhist practice and the mundane, time-consuming realities of making dinner or packing lunches.

Buddhist texts are likewise concerned with food and children. According to Amy Langenberg, there is a direct correlation between the age limit for higher ordination and food in the *Mūlasarvāstivāda Vinaya*: in one account, seventeen young boys ordained by Maudgalyāyana were overheard crying in the night due to hunger. The Buddha therefore declared that ordination must be set at age twenty. Those younger than that were not believed to be capable of withstanding the ascetic life with its dietary restrictions and the many other sufferings an ascetic is meant to endure. Feeding children is a concern for anyone who has children in their care; Buddhist monasteries (as well as Buddhist parents) are no exception.

Feeding children not only reflects the weight of responsibility, it is also one of the most obvious ways to nurture and care for others. It is an expression of love and this too emerges in this volume. A number of contributors have made reference to the loving concern monastics tend to exhibit for the children in their care. Thomas Borchert describes the abbot of the monastery in a parental role, writing notes to teachers for his young monastics, for example, and having the teachers contact him if they have a concern. Karma Lekshe Tsomo describes Buddhist monastic communities in the Himalayas as surrogate families for young monks. She notes various ways in which children are showered with affection all the while undergoing rigorous training and discipline. Elijah Ary describes his own experience in the monastery and affirms that the relationship between a child and his parents "is in fact reproduced in the teacher–disciple relationship that is forged from the moment a child enters the monastery." Such affection, moreover, is not limited to the monastic compounds: as Jeffrey Samuels notes, the affection and love that radiate from the laity are equally powerful and help shape the young monks' perception of themselves and their role in the wider community.

This is not to suggest that monasteries can replace biological families: Cheng reports that for some of the young nuns, the experience of having rotating mentors was a factor behind their disrobing. But much of the research to emerge from this volume nevertheless suggests that the monastic community can, in the best of circumstances, genuinely nurture the young monastics in their care. Moreover, families often remain close to their sons and daughters even after they shave their heads, visiting them regularly and maintaining the irreplaceable relationship that is the parent–child bond. Although Monica Lindberg Falk provides an example of a monastic setting in which parental visitations are strictly controlled, in most of the situations described here, parents seem to share—rather than transfer—the precious role of raising their children with the many members of the Buddhist community in their midst. The concept of homelessness and renunciation that so often characterizes Buddhist monasticism is not as clear-cut as we may once have imagined.

* * * * *

There are surely many other themes in this volume—many that I myself cannot see but that will be seen by others—and much more that can be said. I hope this volume serves as a building block in the long project that is education, and that it serves future discussions about who children are and who they might have been in the complex network that is a religious community.

PART ONE

Children and Childhoods in Buddhist Texts

CHAPTER 1

A New Hat for Hārītī

On "Giving" Children for Their Protection to Buddhist Monks and Nuns in Early India

GREGORY SCHOPEN

The Buddhist monastic texts that have come down to us refer to, and appear to authorize, several monastic practices seemingly meant to ensure safe childbirth or to cure sick children. Such references or authorizations are not always as full or detailed as one might like, and sometimes they remain obscure. A curious text in the Pāli *Vinaya*—which has a partial parallel in the *Bodhirājakumāra-sutta* in the *Majjhima-nikāya*—is a good example.[1] In both the *Sutta* and *Vinaya* versions the text opens with Prince Bodhi inviting the Buddha to his newly constructed palace for a meal, and he requests the Buddha to step on the white cloths (*odāta-dussa* or just *dussa*) spread out there, but the Buddha refuses. The prince does not say why he wants the Buddha to do this, but states only that doing so would be for the prince's benefit and happiness for a very long time (*yaṃ mama assa dīgharattaṃ hitāya sukhāya*). It is only in the commentaries that we are told that the prince's request was connected to the fact that he was childless and that he thought that the Buddha's treading on his cloth would have a predictive or causative effect, ensuring or indicating that he would obtain a child (*so kira aputtako tasmā 'sacāhaṃ puttaṃ vā dhītaraṃ vā lacchāmi satthā imaṃ akkamissatī ti cintetva*...).[2] And some

1. Hermann Oldenberg, ed., *The Vinaya Pitakam* (London: Williams and Norgate, 1880) 2: 127–29; Robert Chalmers, ed., *The Majjhima-Nikāya* (London: Henry Frowde, 1898) 2: 91–97—both have been reprinted many times by the Pali Text Society, and this applies to all the Pali sources cited here.

2. See, for example, H. C. Norman, ed., *The Commentary on the Dhammapada* (London: Henry Frowde, 1906) 3: 136–39.

connection with childbirth would seem to be confirmed by the ending in both versions of the text.

The two versions do not end in the same way. The *Sutta* version ends, after a long conversation between the Buddha and the prince, with an exchange between the prince and a young brahmin. The latter notes that although the prince declares the praises of the Buddha and the Dhamma, he does not formally declare that he goes for refuge to the Three Precious Things. The prince denies this charge and says this has already happened, introducing a practice that was the subject of some debate. He says, in Horner's translation:

> my mother, who was with child, approached the Lord...[and] spoke thus to the Lord: "Revered Sir, my unborn child, whether a boy or a girl, is going to the Lord for refuge and to *dhamma* and to the Order of monks. May the Lord accept this layfollower who is going for refuge from this day forth for as long as life lasts."[3]

The practice described here of a mother taking the three refuges for her unborn child is, of course, not unique to Pāli sources. It is also found, for example, in the *Vibhāṣā*, and a reason for undertaking it is explicitly stated there:

> And if a mother or some other persons take the refuges and the discipline for the infant, this is so that the gods and spirits would protect the infant, so that, since he has taken [the refuges], the gods and good spirits who respect the Jewels would protect and watch over the infant so that he would not die or get sick.[4]

But if the association of the Buddha or monks treading on cloth laid out for them and safe childbirth is, in the *Sutta*, not necessarily explicit, in the *Vinaya* version of the text it is quite clear. The Buddha's refusal to walk on the prince's cloth in the *Vinaya* version is in fact first presented as the occasion for the promulgation of a general rule: "Monks, strips of cloth must not be tread upon! Should one tread upon one there is an offense of wrong doing" (*na bhikkhave celapattikā akkamitabbā. yo akkameyya āpatti dukkaṭassā ti*). But immediately after this rule against monks treading upon cloth for any reason has been promulgated, the Buddha then orders (*anujānāmi*) that monks must tread on cloth when they are asked to do so as an auspicious ritual (*maṅgala*) for a layman, and the case that gives rise to this order concerns a request

3. I. B. Horner, trans., *The Collection of the Middle Length Sayings* (London: Luzac & Company, 1957) 2: 283–84.

4. L. de La Vallée Poussin, "Documents d'Abhidharma 2. La doctrine des refuges," *Mélanges chinois et bouddhiques* 1 (1932): 84.

made by an infertile woman or a woman who has had a miscarriage—no other case is mentioned.

> Then again on that occasion a woman who had miscarried (or: was infertile, *apagatagabbha*), after she had invited monks and arranged cloth (*dussa*), said this: "Reverends, you must tread upon the cloth (*dussa*)!"
>
> The monks, being scrupulous, did not tread on it.
>
> "Reverends, you must tread upon the cloth as an auspicious ritual (*maṅgalatthāyā' ti*)!"
>
> The monks, being scrupulous, still did not tread on it.
>
> Then that woman looked down upon them, was offended, and critical, saying, "How is it now that Noble Ones when being asked for an auspicious ritual will not tread upon a strip of cloth (*celapattika*)?"
>
> The monks heard about that woman looking down upon them, being offended and critical. Then those monks reported that matter to the Blessed One.
>
> "Monks," he said, "lay people are given to auspicious ritual (*maṅgalika*). I, monks, order you to tread on a strip of cloth when asked by a lay person for a ritual of auspiciousness!" (*anujānāmi bhikkhave gihīnaṃ maṅgalatthāya yāciyamānena celapattikaṃ akkamitun ti*).

This is not the only instance in the Pāli *Vinaya* where a rule is made requiring monks to participate in auspicious rituals (*maṅgala*)—another occurs ten pages further in the same section and deals with the proper ritual exchange when someone sneezes, another life-threatening event.[5] But our passage alone is sufficient to show that the Pāli *Vinaya* required its monks to participate actively in a ritual meant to ensure or predict safe childbirth. For an equally good example of Buddhist monks engaging in activities meant to cure sick children, we might look at another monastic code.

In the *Kṣudrakavastu* of the *Mūlasarvāstivāda-vinaya*,[6] the son of a Brahmin falls ill and the Brahmin first goes to a physician and asks for medicine. Because, the text says, that physician was devout (*sman pa de dad pa can zhig pas*), he said: "Brahmin, go to the Noble Ones and ask for the water from their bowls, bathe him with that and he will be cured!" (*bram ze 'phags pa rnams kyi drung du bzhud la lhung bzed kyi chu slongs la de khrus shig dang sos par 'gyur ro*). The Brahmin then goes to the Jetavana, where he encounters

5. Oldenberg, *The Vinaya Pitakam*, 2: 139–40. See also O. von Hinüber, *Selected Papers on Pāli Studies* (Oxford: The Pali Text Society, 1994), 131 and the sources cited there. These passages almost necessarily call to mind Aśoka's 9th Rock Edict in which he says "people" (*jana*), especially women, perform "numerous auspicious rituals" (*maṃgala*)—see Jules Bloch, *Les inscriptions d'Asoka* (Paris: Société d'Édition "Les Belles Lettres," 1950), 113–17.

Upananda, and the latter asks him why he has come. The brahmin tells him, repeating the instructions of the physician. Then

> Upananda said: "You have come here only for the water from the bowl?"
>
> "Noble One, that is so, that is the reason."
>
> "If that is so, wait and I will get the water from the bowl." Having said that, he went inside. When he had eaten and he washed his bowl, some bones and bits of meat and fish bones and crumbs of boiled rice and flour and greens and baked bread were floating in it. When he came out, he said: "Brahmin, take this water from the bowl!"
>
> When the brahmin saw it, he said: "Noble One, it would be better for my son to die—to bathe with such impure water is improper."
>
> The Venerable Upananda said: "Only through being possessed of devotion of this sort will you get a cure for your son."
>
> The brahmin began to berate him and the monks reported the matter to the Blessed One. The Blessed One thought: "How could what is a danger appear small, since this is what occurs when monks push to the side the scraps in their bowl? A monk therefore should not push to the side the scraps in his bowl." Having thought this, he said to the monks: "Henceforth, monks, a monk must not push to the side the scraps in his bowl! If he does, he comes to be guilty of an offence. But I also will designate the obligatory rules of behaviour for the monk-who-distributes-the-water-from-the-bowls: The monk-who-distributes-the-water-from-the-bowls must wash the bowls three times, and after he has recited a Verse of the Sage over the water from the bowls, he should distribute it. If the monk-who-distributes-the-water-from-the-bowls proceeds without adopting the obligatory rules of behaviour as designated, he comes to be guilty of an offence."

Here one might emphasize at least two points. We would appear to have not only a Buddhist monastic practice meant to provide the means to cure sick children, but yet another example in this *Vinaya* of a Buddhist monastic practice that has been carefully crafted to accommodate core brahmanical values. The Brahmin's reaction to the water first presented to him is perfectly predictable and clearly expresses the brahmanical "horror" of *ucchiṣṭa*, "food that is left over after a person has eaten," and its preoccupation with "impurity."[7] The further instructions put in the mouth of the Buddha on the handling of the

6. *Kṣudrakavastu*, Derge, 'dul ba Tha 226a.5–227a.3—all citations of Tibetan texts are from *The Tibetan Tripitaka. Taipei Edition*, ed. A. W. Barber (Taipei: SMC Publishing, 1991), and all references are to this reprint of the Derge printing. They will always follow this form: Sanskrit title + Derge + section + volume letter + original folio number(s). When the text concerned is in the *bstan 'gyur* this will be inserted after "Derge." Sometimes references to the corresponding passages in the Peking reprint are added as well.

7. See, for example, Patrick Olivelle, *Language, Texts, and Society. Explorations in Ancient Indian Culture and Religion* (Firenze: Firenze University Press, 2005), 236–37.

water prior to its distribution could only, it seems, have been intended to allay such brahmanical anxieties and to render the ritually transformed water acceptable to brahmanical fastidiousness. There may as well be here some hint of the complex of ideas that came to cluster around the Hindu idea of *prasād*.[8]

A second point to be noted is that the monastic practice of providing a means for curing sick children—and that is the only use for the water that is ever stated—is fully institutionalized in this *Vinaya*. The wording used here to deliver the Buddha's instructions—"I also will designate the obligatory rules of behaviour for the monk who..."—is in fact a standardized formula which occurs dozens of times in this *Vinaya* and is used to establish an official monastic office that is to be assigned to an individual monk and to enumerate the duties of that office. In Sanskrit it would be: the name of the office in the genitive + *ahaṃ bhikṣavo bhikṣor āsamudācārikāṃ dharmāṃ prajñapayiṣyāmi*.[9] In other words, the distribution of the curative water used to wash the monks' bowls was, apparently, considered important enough to be made into a monastic office or official duty to which a monk had to be specifically assigned. A further indication that the practice was fully institutionalized is the fact that it continues to be referred to in medieval Mūlasarvāstivādin *Vinaya* handbooks such as Guṇaprabha's *Vinayasūtra* (and its commentaries), Viśeṣamitra's *Vinayasaṃgraha*, and the *Vinayakārikā* of Viśākhadeva.[10]

A third and final example of monastic practices connected with the well-being of children might be cited here because it may represent a development peculiar to Buddhist narrative literature in Sanskrit—a literature that may turn out to be predominantly Mūlasarvāstivādin—and because it may be particularly germane to the sources that will be the main focus here, and may in fact be part of a narrativization of the rules they deliver. It is at least one example of the stereotyped description of the gift of a child to an individual monk that occurs repeatedly in the *Mūlasarvāstivāda-vinaya* and related literature.[11]

8. See, for example, Manuel Moreno, "Pañcāmirtam: God's Washings as Food," in *The Eternal Food: Gastronomic Ideas and Experiences of Hindus and Buddhists*, ed. R. S. Khare (Delhi: Sri Satguru Publications, 1993), 147–78 and the sources cited. For the "Verse of the Sage" that must be recited over the water see Gregory Schopen, "On Buddhist Monks and Dreadful Deities: Some Monastic Devices for Updating the Dharma," in *Gedenkschrift J. W. de Jong*, ed. H. W. Bodewitz and Minoru Hara (Tokyo: The International Institute for Buddhist Studies, 2004), 169–73.

9. For other instances and references, see Gregory Schopen, *Buddhist Monks and Business Matters. Still More Papers on Monastic Buddhism in India* (Honolulu: University of Hawaii Press, 2004), 139 and n. 54.

10. Rahul Sankrityayana, ed., *Vinayasūtra of Bhadanta Gunaprabha* (Bombay: Bharatiya Vidya Bhavan, 1981), 63.8; *Vinayasaṃgraha*, Derge, bstan 'gyur, 'dul ba Nu 258b.2; *Vinayakārikā*, Derge, *bstan 'gyur, 'dul ba*, Shu 56a.2.

11. For some examples see *Pravrajyāvastu*, Nalinaksha Dutt, ed., *Gilgit Manuscripts*, Vol. III, Part IV (Calcutta: Calcutta Oriental Press, 1950). 28.6–30.22 = E. B. Cowell and R. A. Neil, eds., *The Divyāvadāna. A Collection of Early Buddhist Legends* (Cambridge: Cambridge University Press, 1886) 330.3–332.3 (concerning Saṃgharakṣita); *Kṣudrakavastu*, Derge, 'dul ba Tha 41b.4–44b.6 (Lavaṇabhadrika), Tha 56a.5 58a.1 (Gavāṃpati), Da 193a.4–194b.3 (a nameless brahmin boy given to Śāriputra). Most of the children involved were deformed or had some physical abnormality.

These children are always given to a specific monk to be his *paścācchramaṇa*, or "attending menial"—we might say "servant," and they are not free, but owned by the monks to whom they are given.[12] But while all versions of this stereotyped description explicitly state the function these children were meant to fulfill, it is only exceptionally that there is any reference to the situation of the parents or to the reason behind their gift. The story of Sumanā in the *Avadānaśataka*—a variant version of the form—is one such exception.

The story opens with a very wealthy householder in Śrāvastī taking a wife from a suitable family.[13] They have many sons but—and here is the problem—they all die:

> Now in regard to that house the Elder Aniruddha was one who was supported by the family (*kulopagata*). This thought then occurred to the householder: "This Elder Aniruddha is a mighty personage through the maturation of his actions (*vipākamaheśākhya*). I will supplicate (*āyāciṣye*) him then—if a son is born to me I will give it to him as an attending menial (*paścācchramaṇa*)."
>
> The householder, then, invited the Elder Aniruddha to a meal in his house. When he had presented him with alms, he then supplicated him, saying: "Elder, if a son born to me lives (*sthavira yadi me putro jāto jīvati*), I will give him to the Elder as an attending menial."
>
> The Elder Aniruddha said: "May it be so! But you must remember your promise (*pratijñā*)."

When in due course a son is born and the proper birth ceremonies are performed, the son is named:

> Then when the Elder Aniruddha had been invited to the house for a meal, the boy was presented (*niryātita*). Ocher colored cloths (*kāṣāya*) were then given

12. The term *paścācchramaṇa* has been variously rendered and not yet been carefully studied. Its second element—*śramaṇa*—has often been conflated with *śrāmaṇera*, "novice," but in fact *śramaṇa* means first and foremost "toiling, labouring . . . following a toilsome or menial business," and the following discussion of the story of Sumanā suggests that this meaning remained very much alive. It is one of many Sanskrit terms that seem to indicate a status that borders on "slave." That a *paścācchramaṇa* was not "free" is perhaps most explicitly indicated in the story of Saṃgharakṣita in the *Pravrajyāvastu* (see n. 12. There, after Saṃgharakṣita had been given as a *paścācchramaṇa* to Śāriputra, a group of merchants, who had been his childhood friends, ask him to accompany them on a sea voyage. He, however, says: *nāhaṃ svādhīnaḥ/upādhyāyam avalokayata/*(30.8), "I am not a free man. You must ask my preceptor!" and *svādhīna* would appear here to have its full legal force.

13. J. S. Speyer, ed., *Avadānaçataka. A Century of Edifying Tales Belonging to the Hīnayāna* (St.- Pétersbourg: Imperial Academy of Sciences, 1906–9) 2: 67.1–71.11. For the dependence of the *Avadānaśataka* on the *Mūlasarvāstivāda-vinaya* see Schopen, *Buddhist Monks and Business Matters*, 125–26 and the sources cited there. In her paper in the present volume, Amy Langenberg treats this same story from a different angle and with a different emphasis.

to the boy, and the benediction (*āśīrvāda*) "May you live long!" (*dīrghāyur bhavatu*)

When he was seven years old, then he was given (*datta*) by his mother and father to the Elder.

Although this text does not follow the stereotyped form of the description of the gift of children as menials to monks found in the *Vinaya*, it links with other texts there in interesting ways. It links, for example, with the story of the two Panthakas that has long been known from the crudely excerpted version of it that is now found in the *Divyāvadāna*. That tale too deals with a couple who are childless because all children born to them die. There when another child is born, the midwife instructs a girl to take it to a major crossroad and to say to any passing Brahmin or śramaṇa, "This boy does veneration to your feet" (*ayaṃ dārakaḥ pādābhivandanaṃ karotīti*). She does just that to members of other religious groups (*tīrthya*), to Buddhist monks, and finally to the Buddha himself. In each case they too give a blessing: "May he live long! May he maintain a long life! May he fulfill the wishes of his parents! (*ciraṃ jīvatu dīrgham āyuḥ pālayatu*...). This child, unlike all the others, lives, and the same procedure is followed for their next child, who also lives.[14] The link between the two accounts might well suggest that Aniruddha's benediction was not casually chosen and that in the world of the redactors of these texts it was a common practice for parents in distress to seek from religious figures a blessing for long life for newborn children. A second link might be more surprising.

As in the case of Aniruddha's benediction, it is unlikely that the choice of the verb used to express what the householder initially did in regard to Aniruddha was casual: He "supplicated" or "implored" him—*āyācate*. Although otherwise not common, the verb or forms thereof occurs repeatedly in the *Mūlasarvāstivāda-vinaya* and related literature in two related clichés connected to childlessness. In the first of these clichés it is said: "And this is the popular belief of the world: that sons and daughters are born as a result of supplication" (*asti caiṣa loke pravādo yad āyācanahetoḥ putrā jāyante duhitaraś ceti*). The second starts: "He, being sonless and wanting a son, supplicated Śiva, Varuṇa, Kubera, Śakra, Brahma, and so forth, as well as a variety of other gods...." Here again the verb is *āyācate*.[15] Although our redactors deny the truth of the first statement as well as the effectiveness of the second action, the narrative fact remains that in the story of Sumanā the Buddhist monk Aniruddha takes the place of Śiva, Varuṇa, and others as the object of supplication, and that

14. Cowell and Neil, *Divyāvadāna*, 483.20ff = *Vinayavibhaṅga*, Derge, 'dul ba Ja 61a.4ff.

15. For dozens of occurrences of both clichés in Sanskrit, see Hiraoka Satoshi, *Setsuwa no kōkogaku: Indo Bukkyō setsuwa ni himerareta shisō* (Tokyo: Daizō Shuppan, 2002) 158–59 (C and D), and for a translation of a typical instance from the *Cīvaravastu*, see Gregory Schopen, *Buddhist Monks and Business Matters*, 117.

this supplication, together with its promise of the gift of the child, results in the successful birth of a son.

This text from the *Avadānaśataka*, however, may also tell us a few other things of interest for what we will shortly see. It may, for example, reveal something more about the status of an "attending menial" (*paścācchramaṇa*), at least in texts. Although Sumanā appears to enter the religious life (*pravrajyā*) and quickly becomes an *arhat*, there is no reference to his ever having been ordained, and in spite of his religious attainment, he continues to be represented as performing humble duties such as sewing and fetching water for Aniruddha. Moreover, in ordering him to fetch his water, Aniruddha addresses him as "boy" (*putraka*), not as a fellow monk, and he is twice referred to as a *śramaṇoddeśa*, a term that appears to indicate a low state of subordination even while its precise significance remains to be determined. Finally—again in terms of what we will shortly see—the giving of "ocher cloths" (*kāṣāya*) by Aniruddha to the newborn may be more significant than might at first sight appear. It may have been intended to mark the child's station as the property of a monk even while he remained at home for his first seven years.

The examples seen so far, then, might be sufficient to show that—at least in texts—Buddhist monks are represented as engaging in a number of practices connected with childbirth and the well-being and the health of young children. But what may be an even clearer representation of Buddhist monks, *and nuns*, as the protectors of young children is still a little surprising, if for no other reason than because of where it is found: it is attached to the well-known story of the converted *yakṣiṇī* or "demoness," Hārītī, who herself is said to be the "Protector of Children" but may turn out not to have been. At least any cult of Hārītī may be more complicated than has been thought.

Images of Hārītī, and even independent shrines devoted to her, have been identified with different degrees of certainty at a wide variety of Buddhist monastic sites dating to different periods. Her images appear to have been particularly numerous in Gandhāra and the Northwest,[16] but separate shrines for Hārītī have also been located at Kauśāmbī and Ajaṇṭa,[17] and she may be represented already at Sāñci—she is certainly referred to in the early first-century CE inscription of Senavarman of Oḍi.[18] The story of how this *yakṣiṇī*—who had

16. For some good examples, see Anna Maria Quagliotti, "An Inscribed Image of Hārītī in the Chandigarh Government Museum and Art Gallery," *Silk Road Art and Archaeology* 6 (1999/2000), 51–60.

17. G. R. Sharma, "Excavations at Kauśāmbī, 1949–1955," *Annual Bibliography of Indian Archaeology* 16 (1958), xxxvi-xlv; Richard S. Cohen, "Nāga, Yakṣiṇī, Buddha: Local Deities and Local Buddhism at Ajaṇṭa," *History of Religion* 37 (1998), 360–400.

18. E. Bazin-Foucher, "Une représentation de Pañcika et Hārītī à Sāñchi," *Journal asiatique* (1933), 348–49; Oskar von Hinüber, *Beiträge zur Erklärung der Senavarma-Inschrift* (Stuttgart: Franz Steiner Verlag, 2002), 34 (10c). For some examples of Hārītī outside of India, and some good photographs of some of the Indian material, see Madhurika K. Maheshwari, *From Ogress to Goddess. Hārītī A Buddhist Deity* (Mumbai: IIRNS Publications, 2009), but note that the text here is by no means as good as the illustrations.

the children of Rājagṛha as her regular diet, was converted by the Buddha and made to desist from eating any more of them—is well-known and does not require retelling. It was very well told almost a hundred years ago by Noël Peri on the basis of a number of Chinese sources, the most important of which—according to Peri and virtually everyone else who has come after him—was the Chinese translation of the *Kṣudrakavastu* of the *Mūlasarvāstivāda-vinaya*.[19] Unfortunately, scholars who have followed Peri appear not to have always read him carefully, and no one seems to have bothered to look at the version, or perhaps versions, of the *Kṣudrakavastu* account preserved in Tibetan sources: they raise some problems and they solve some problems—both need to be examined.

It has not always been noticed that the Chinese translation of the *Kṣudrakavastu* account of Hārītī which Peri has translated is not, structurally, a single text but rather three separate texts of unequal length, each with its own *nidāna* or stereotyped introduction. The first text has a full introduction—"At one time when the Buddha was dwelling in Rājagṛha, in the Bamboo Grove..."—and is by far the longest. The Tibetan translation, although it lacks some important elements that occur in the Chinese, corresponds in the main to this first text. But in Peri's Chinese version this long first text is immediately followed by two short texts, each marked by its own abbreviated introduction—"the same setting as above"—and although neither of these two short texts is found in the Tibetan translation, the first is of particular interest here. For the convenience of the anglophile reader, Peri's rendering might be Englished as:

> *The same setting as above.* When Hārītī had received the three refuges and the five precepts from the Tathāgata, she was tormented by the other *yakṣas*. Then she brought all her sons and gave them to the Community. One day, seeing the monks going to collect their food, her sons changed themselves into small infants and followed them. When the women of Rājagṛha saw them, many of them were moved by sympathy and came to take them in their arms. Then they disappeared. The women asked the monks: "Whose infants are these?" They responded: "[They are] the infants of Hārītī." The women said: "Those are the infants of that hateful and very nasty *yakṣiṇī*?" The monks reproved them: "She has completely given up all nastiness, and on account of that the *yakṣas* torment her. This is why for the future she has given these [infants] to us." The women thought: "The *yakṣiṇī* has given up her ill will and has given her sons. Why should we not give ours?" And they gave their infants to the Community. The Community refused to accept them. The women then said: "The venerables have indeed accepted the infants of this very nasty *yakṣiṇī*—why do they not accept ours?" The monks took this occasion to ask

19. Noël Peri, "Hārītī, la Mère-de-démons," *Bulletin de l'École française d'Extrême-Orient* 17 (1917), 1–102, esp. 2–15. The "corresponding" Tibetan version occurs at *Kṣudrakavastu*, Derge, 'dul ba Da 145a.4–151a.1.

> the Buddha. The Buddha said: "You must accept them!" The monks obeyed his instruction. But, although they had accepted the infants, the latter were not supervised, and they went around everywhere to amuse themselves according to their whim. The monks reported this to the Buddha. The Buddha said: "When a young boy has been given to the Community, a monk will accept him, will attach to his head (or: neck) a piece of old *kāṣāya*, and will look after him. If numerous [young boys] have been given, senior, middle-ranked, and junior [monks] will accept them [and divide them up] according to their wishes and look after them as [it was said] above, so that they are not exposed to suspicion. Then the parents came back carrying gifts to compensate [for the expenses occasioned by their infants], and to take them back. The monks did not accept them. The Buddha said: "Accept them!" Later on those infants conceived feelings of affection, and they returned bringing garments which they offered to the monks in recognition of their service. The monks, aware of their feelings, did not accept them. The Buddha said: "You must accept them!"
>
> As the Bhagavat had said that they must accept the gifts offered in redemption of the infants, the [group of] six monks came to ask the total price from the parents. The Buddha said: "You must not ask for the price! You must be content to accept [that which they give you] according to their wishes!"[20]

The citation of such a long passage might be forgiven because of its intrinsic interest, because it has been almost entirely ignored, because it is completely missing from the account of Hārītī in the Tibetan translation of the *Kṣudrakavastu* now found in the Kanjur, and because of what it will allow us to see or recognize in some other sources. But it must also be said that as it stands, there is a certain vagueness in the Chinese text as it is presented by Peri. It seems clear enough that his text, for example, provides a warrant or authorization for the acceptance by Buddhist monks of young children that are given to them, but it says very little about the reasons that lead parents to make such gifts. Hārītī, it is said, gave her children to the monks because after her conversion the other *yakṣas* "tormented" her. This situation would suggest that rather than being the "protector" of children, Hārītī and her children were themselves in need of protection, and this is why she gave her children to the monks—the monks, then, and not Hārītī, would be the protectors. This circumstance, however, is only suggested, never clearly stated, and when the women of Rājagṛha give their children, they do so without any clearly stated purpose. But if the motives of the parents—and consequently the role of the monks—remain vague here, so too does the status of the children within the Community: they are marked with "a piece of old *kāṣāya*" and therefore visually identified, but they are not said to be pupils or anything of that sort, and it is unclear what they are expected to do, or what function they were expected

20. Noël Peri, "Hārītī," 13–14.

to fulfill. From other texts in the *Mūlasarvāstivāda-vinaya*—some of which have been cited above—it might be anticipated that they would do menial chores, but this work is never stated. Nor is the gender of the children ever made explicit. Peri himself notes in one place that the Chinese expression used has only "the general sense of infants," but he insists that it must be restricted to boys. He says, "Hārītī had in effect only given sons, and this example would not be able to authorize the adoption of girls in the monastery, against which in any case all the strict rules of the separation of the sexes, delivered in many places and even in this chapter, would protest."[21] He seems not to have even considered the possibility that girls might have been given to the nuns. These and a number of other uncertain issues here are particularly frustrating in the absence of further material, and the absence of a passage corresponding to Peri's Chinese text in the Tibetan translation of the account of Hārītī not only adds to the frustration, but may raise some suspicions about the textual integrity of the Chinese passage itself. Since it is clear, for example, from Yijing's travel account that he was particularly interested in Hārītī,[22] it might not be unreasonable to suspect that the passage dealing with the gift of children found at the end of his translation of the account of Hārītī, but not in the Tibetan, was an addition to the text that he himself made. Any such suspicion can, however, in this instance be happily put to rest since there is good evidence that—while the passage might be missing in the account of Hārītī in the Tibetan translation of the *Kṣudrakavastu*—something very like it must have been already known in India.

The evidence in question comes from Guṇaprabha's *Vinayasūtra*, which could have been written as early as the fifth century,[23] and from the Indian commentaries on it. It is becoming ever more clear that Guṇaprabha, in digesting the *Mūlasarvāstivāda-vinaya*, sticks very close to his canonical sources. He seems to have added little or nothing: he treats in his *sūtra*s only what he found in the canonical *Vinaya*. This makes particularly interesting a substantial set of *sūtra*s dealing with types of property that Buddhist monks may or must accept: villages, fields, a share of crops, bound laborers (*upasthāyakas, kalpakāras, ārāmikas*), a long list of domestic animals, and, it seems, young children of both genders.[24] The *sūtra*s dealing with the latter will look familiar—in part.

A Sanskrit text of the *Vinayasūtra* is now known to have survived in more than one manuscript, but we do not yet have a critical edition and both of the versions

21. Nöel Peri, "Hārītī," 13 n.1. All this is a little odd, and it may be that Peri has fudged his translation. Shayne Clarke tells me that by his reading of the Chinese, Yijing indicates at least twice that the children were of both genders.

22. Li Rongxi, trans., *Buddhist Monastic Traditions of Southern Asia. A Record of the Inner Law Sent Home from the South Seas by Śramaṇa Yijing* (Berkeley, CA: Numata Center for Buddhist Translation and Research, 2000), 36–37.

23. For the limited material available on the life of Guṇaprabha, see Gregory Schopen, *Buddhist Monks and Business Matters*, 64, 312–13 and nn. 63–64.

24. For the whole set see Sankrityayana, *Vinayasūtra*, 95.29–96.9.

that are so far available are not entirely satisfactory. Both have numerous queried or corrupt readings and need emendation. These problems make their use difficult, as does the very concise character of the individual *sūtras*—these are *sūtras* of the Pāṇinian sort, not the usual Buddhist sort. What is stated once in a *sūtra*, and is to be understood in those that follow, is not repeated, for example. What is given here, as a consequence, is a tentative Sanskrit text, sometimes emended on the basis of the Tibetan translation or the commentaries, but it is probably not far off from what Guṇaprabha wrote.

Vinayasūtra

Sankrityayana (1981, p. 96.6-.9) = TaishōU (p. 114.15-.22)[25] = Derge, bstan 'gyur, 'dul ba Wu 78b.7–79a.2 = Peking, bstan 'gyur, 'dul ba Zu 85b.7-.8
grahaṇaṃ rakṣāyai pratipādyamānānām *apatyānāṃ*[26] samānavyañjanānām |
bsrung ba'i phyir byis pa mtshan mthun pa 'bul ba dag blang bar bya'o/

Children of the same gender that are being given for their protection must be accepted.

āsaktakaṇṭhacīvarakatvam eṣāṃ veṣaḥ | kaṭyāṃ vā |[27]
de dag gi cha lugs ni mgul par chos gos btags pa nyid do/rked par yang ngo/

Their outward appearance is (to be marked by) the presence of monastic robe material fastened around the neck. Or around the waist.

pratipālanam anukampācaritena |[28]
phan gdags pa'i sems kyis so sor bskang bar bya'o/

They must be looked after with practiced compassion.

grahaṇaṃ tatjñātyupasaṃkṛtasya |[28]
de'i nye dus phul ba blang bar bya'o/

What is bestowed by (the children's) relatives must be accepted,

25. TaishōU refers to the *Electronic Text of the Vinayasūtra*, ed. TaishōU University [http://www.tais.ac.jp/related/labo/sobutsu/sobutsu_book/vinayasutra.html]. I thank Shayne Clarke for printing a copy of this so I could use it.
26. *apatyānāṃ* is an emendation. Both Sankrityayana and TaishōU read *apy anyānāṃ*, but this reading results in a *sūtra* that would appear to be incomplete—there would be no clear subject for the passive participle, and *anya*, "other(s)" would follow the wrong declension and would need something that it could be contrasted with. The Tibetan translators, moreover, could not have had a text with this reading. The text they had must have had a noun meaning "children" (*byis pa*)—and this is confirmed by all of the commentaries—so, although *byis pa* is not yet attested as a translation of *apatya* ("child"), this is almost certainly the correct reading, and it is easy enough to see how it could have been misread or miswritten.
27. Both Sankrityayana and Taishō print *kaṭyāṃ vā*, not as a separate *sūtra*, but as the beginning of the following one.
28. Reading with TaishōU.

niṣkrayatvena[29] cānte |
mjug tu rin nyid du yang ngo/

and also at the end [what is given] on account of its being the ransom,

taiś ca kṛtajñatayā |
de dag gis byas pa shes pas kyang ngo/

and (what is given) by them on account of gratitude.

naitan mūlyaṃ yācate |
de'i rin 'da' [v.l. gdab; bda'] bar mi bya'o

A certain price must not be asked for this.

These *sūtra*s might themselves suggest the strong likelihood that Guṇaprabha knew a text very close to that found in Yijing's translation even though there are some informative differences between the two, and even though Guṇaprabha's *sūtra*s do not make any explicit connection to Hārītī. The differences are in fact largely differences in detail, although these are not unimportant. For example, where the motive behind the gift of the children in the Chinese text is, at best, only implied, in Guṇaprabha's text it appears to have been explicit: they were given to protect them. Where in Peri's rendering of Yijing's text the gender of the children was left vague or unstated, it appears to have been addressed in Guṇaprabha's source. The similarities are, moreover, too striking to be inadvertent: the attachment of a piece of monastic robe around the children's neck—although Guṇaprabha also allows it around the waist—and the concluding insistence that a specific price must not be asked for the service done by the monks. Nor can the absence of any reference in the *sūtra*s to Hārītī be given too much weight since Guṇaprabha consistently and systematically excludes all narrative elements from his *sūtra*s. They are found, if they are found at all, in the commentaries to the *Vinayasūtra*. One of these commentaries, the *Vinayasūtravṛttyabhidhānasvavyākhyāna*, is particularly important since it is taken to be—and probably is—an auto-commentary by Guṇaprabha himself. It and the *Vinayasūtraṭīkā* attributed to Dharmamitra are both very useful in this regard, since they frequently cite the actual source text for Guṇaprabha's *sūtra*, and both cite as the source of the *sūtra*s given above a text dealing with Hārītī! But these commentaries also do more than connect our *sūtra*s with Hārītī. They also tell us some important things about how a text like that of Yijing's was understood in India, at least by the monastic elite, and

29. *niṣkrayatvena* is an emendation. Sankrityayana prints *nipā(?)yatvena*, and Taishō has *niṣtrayatvena*, neither of which makes immediate sense. But Tibetan *rin* is an attested equivalent of *niṣkraya* (J. S. Negi, *Bod skad dang legs sbyar gyi tshig mdzod chen mo* (Sarnath: Central Institute of Higher Tibetan Studies, 2004) 14: 6431), which fits the context and is supported by all the commentaries; see further below.

they present a much fuller picture than does Yijing of the practice of giving children to Buddhist monks *and nuns* for the purpose of protecting the children. We might start with Guṇaprabha's auto-commentary.

Vinayasūtravṛttyabhidhānasvavyākhyāna

(Derge, bstan 'gyur, 'dul ba Zu 166a.5-b.3 = Peking Yu 211a.8-b.8)

bsrung ba'i phyir byis pa mtshan mthun pa 'bul ba dag blang bar bya'o zhes bya ba ni dge 'dun nam gang zag gis kyang blang bar bya'o/'dir gzhung ni/bcom ldan 'das la 'phrog ma skyabs su song zhing bslab pa'i gzhi dag la bzhag nas/des bu de dag gnod sbyin gdug pas 'jigs pa bsrung ba'i phyir dge 'dun la phul ba thos nas/de dag 'di snyam du des bsrung ba'i phyir dge slong rnams la bu re zhig 'bul bar byed na bdag cag gis kyang ci'i phyir mi dbul snyam nas/de dag gis bu dbul bar btsams pa dang/dge slong dag mi len nas/bcom ldan 'das kyis bka' stsal pa/blang bar bya'o zhes gsungs pa yin no/

'dir tshul ni rjes su 'gro ba ni dge 'dun kyis blangste/kun dga' ra ba'i g-yog tu rnam par gnas pa yin no/de lta bas na bye brag med par brten pa yin no/

de dag gi cha lugs ni mgul par chos gos btags pa nyid do/rked par yang rung ngo zhes bya ba la/de dag gi cha lugs ni mgul par chos gos kyi tshal bu re re btags pa yin no/

phan gdags pa'i sems kyis so sor bskyang bar bya'o/de'i nye dus phul ba blang bar bya'o/mjug tu rin nyid du yang ngo zhes bya ba la/de'i nye du dag gis mjug tu byis pa phyir len pa'i tshe de'i dus phul ba blang bar bya'o zhes bya bar sbyar ro/de ltar yang de rnams kyis phul bar gyur pa la dad pa'i dbang du byas pa nyid yin pas 'di la log pas 'tsho ba nyid yin par dogs par mi bya ste/de bas na de la 'di bstan pa'o/

de dag gis byas pa shes pas kyang ngo zhes bya ba ni/byis pa de dag gis byas pa shes pas phul ba yang blang bar bya'o/

de'i rin gdab par mi bya'o zhes bya ba ni/dge slon gis byis pa de dag yongs su bskyangs pa'i rin dang rngan pa blang bar mi bya'o//

(1st) In regard to the words "children of the same gender that are being given for their protection must be accepted," (they mean): They must be accepted by the Community (*saṃgha*) or by an individual (*pudgala*). Here is what the (canonical) text says: "When they heard that Hārītī, after she had gone for refuge to the Blessed One and was established in the foundations of training (*śikṣāpada*), being (herself) terrified by dangerous demons (*yakṣa*), had given her children to the Community for protection, they (lay people) thought: 'If she gives so many children to the monks for protection, should we not also give ours?' Having thought that, they started to give their children. But when the monks did not accept them the Blessed One said: "They must be accepted!'"

Here in regard to the method, it is the (same) procedure as for the acceptance and establishing of bound servants (*upasthāyaka*) for the monastic complex (*ārāma*) by the Community. Therefore, they are maintained in the same way.

(2nd) As for the words "their outward appearance is (to be marked by) the presence of monastic robe material fastened around the neck. Or around the waist," (they mean): In regard to their outward appearance single strips of a monastic robe are to be fastened around their neck.

(3rd) As for the words "They must be looked after with practiced compassion. What is bestowed by (the children's) relatives must be accepted, and also at the end (what is given) on account of its being the ransom," they must be taken to mean: What is given at that time when at the end its relatives take the child back must be accepted. Thus, moreover, in regard to what they give, since it is just because it is a matter of their piety there must not be any apprehension that in this case there is a wrong way of getting a living (*mithyājīva*). On that account this is explained here.

(4th)In regard to the words "And (what is given) by them on account of gratitude," (they mean): What is given by the children (themselves) because they are grateful must also be accepted.

(5th) In regard to the words "A certain price must not be asked for this," (they mean): The monks must not accept a certain price or wage for protecting them.

Obviously one of the most important things Guṇaprabha's first comment does is to establish the canonical source for our *sūtras*. He does not say here—as he sometimes does—what section of the *Vinaya* it is found in, nor does he explicitly say that all of these *sūtras* are based on it. This appears to be—as it often is—simply understood, and Yijing's text allows us to see that this is so: Every one of Guṇaprabha's *sūtras* in this series has some correspondence with Yijing's text, and even the verbal correspondence between the two is sometimes almost perfect. The last of Guṇaprabha's *sūtras*—*naitan mūlyaṃ yācate*—for example, is nearly identical to Yijing's concluding rule: "You must not ask for the price!" But equally important, since Guṇaprabha actually quotes his canonical source, we can see that while the account of Hārītī that he knew was close to that found in Yijing, it was by no means identical. It has already been noted that unlike Yijing's text, Guṇaprabha's *sūtras* give an explicit motive for the gift of the children, but Guṇaprabha's quotation of his source text indicates that this motive was already explicit in the canonical account of Hārītī that he knew. His canonical source not once, but twice, says that the children were given "for their protection." Since when they can be checked, Guṇaprabha's quotations from the canonical *Vinaya* are verbatim,[30] it would appear that there were at least three different redactions of the Mūlasarvāstivādin account of Hārītī: the redaction now found in the Tibetan translation of the *Kṣudrakavastu* which knows nothing about Hārītī's gift of her children; the redaction reflected in Yijing's translation; and the redaction known to Guṇaprabha, both of which do.

In spite of what has just been said, however, there might remain some doubt about the source of Guṇaprabha's reference to "bound servants," *g-yog* = *upasthāyaka*. He does not quote enough of his canonical source to make it certain that it contained an explicit reference to the assimilation of the acceptance of children with the acceptance of *upasthāyaka*s, but it is clear that Guṇaprabha understood—or wanted it to be understood—that the acceptance of children

30. For some examples, see Gregory Schopen, "The Urban Buddhist Nun and a Protective Rite for Children in Early North India," in *Pāsādikadānaṃ. Festschrift für Bhikkhu Pāsādika*, hrsg., Martin Straube et al. (Marburg: Indica et Tibetica Verlag, 2009), 370–72.

was governed by the same rules that governed the acceptance of such servants. Since he had already treated these rules in a series of *sūtras* that come almost immediately before ours, he does not—and this is characteristic of his method—repeat them in our *sūtras*. Both the prior series and the passage in the canonical *Vibhaṅga* on which it is based make it a rule that, in accepting such individuals, the monks are under obligation to house them separately, to provide them with food and clothing *if* they do their work, and to attend to them when they are ill.[31] That the children who were given were to be bound servants is also explicitly stated, as we will see, in the *Vinayasūtravṛtti*, a second commentary attributed to Guṇaprabha.

Finally in regard to Guṇaprabha's first comment, note that it does not address—does not even mention—the issue of the children's gender or the phrase "children of the same gender." What the latter means, or its implications, are here left unexplained. They will, however, be treated in Dharmamitra's commentary, and again in the *Vṛtti* also ascribed to Guṇaprabha.

Guṇaprabha's second comment verges on the tautological, but it and the *sūtra* on which it is based are not without interest. The procedure described here might, for example, link up with that described in the story of Sumanā in the *Avadānaśataka* cited earlier where Aniruddha gives to the newborn child that is promised to him "ocher colored cloths" (*kāṣāya*). There there is at least a hint of the prophylactic function of such monastic cloth, and that might well hold here as well. In Guṇaprabha's *Vṛtti* that function is made somewhat more explicit. In addition to having any protective or talismanic function, however, the cloth appears to have been intended to mark the fact that its wearer was at least temporarily and marginally a member of the larger monastic household, and it is possible that this meaning of the cloth is related to—and perhaps the origin of—the otherwise curious pejorative expression, "ocher necks," found in both Sanskrit (*kāṣāyakaṇṭha*) and Pāli (*kāsāvakaṇṭha*) used to refer to an individual who is a member of the monastic community in name only, and only for the purpose of having access to its benefits.[32] In connection with this possibility, note that although the Sanskrit and Tibetan sources for the *Vinayasūtra* consistently use *cīvarika* or *chos gos*, Peri understood the Chinese as "un morceau de vieux kāṣāya." Note too that although Guṇaprabha's *sūtras*—and presumably his source—allow attachment to the waist as an option to the neck, the latter is literally secondary and Guṇaprabha does not even refer to it in his comment.

Both the language of the *sūtra* it comments on and Guṇaprabha's third comment are of interest for what they reveal about the nature of the transaction. It might at first go unnoticed that the *sūtras* being commented on here start by insisting on the purity or nobility of the monks' motive for accepting and looking after the children—who after all would have thought otherwise? But Guṇaprabha's

31. For Guṇaprabha's *sūtras* on *upasthāyakas* see Sankrityayana, *Vinayasūtra*, 96.1-.3, and for the canonical text they are based on see Gregory Schopen, *Buddhist Monks and Business Matters*, 200–202.

comment—and even more Dharmamitra's, as we will see—seem to suggest that someone did, and that the practice was open to, or had been the object of, some unflattering criticism that called the monks' motives into question. Otherwise it is hard to account for Guṇaprabha's assurance that the practice did *not* constitute a *mithyājīva*, "a wrong way of getting a living," a term that Guṇaprabha would not have chosen lightly. The wrong ways of getting a living for monks are commonly grouped together, although the individual items also occur separately. They are, in sum, five fraudulent ways of extracting donations from laymen—"display of behavior designed to stimulate laymen to give gifts" (*kuhana*), "boasting (of one's own religious qualities, to extract gifts from patrons)" (*lapana*), and others.[33] Guṇaprabha in his comment is in effect denying that the practice of accepting children is a form of monastic fraud, but the issue, it seems, would not go away. When Dharmamitra addresses it, his remarks look more like an attempt at reformation than a simple assurance or denial. He says:

> dge slong rnams kyis byis pa de dag la phan gdags pa'i sems kyis so sor bskyang bar bya ste/zang zing dang bcas pa'i sems kyis ni ma yin no/[34]
>
> The monks must protect them with thoughts of benefit directed towards those children, and not with thoughts connected with material goods (*āmiṣa*).

The *Vṛtti*, the second commentary ascribed to Guṇaprabha, likewise suggests an awareness of the possibility that the motives of the monks may not be entirely disinterested.

> byis pa bdag gi gan du bzhag pa de phyis g-yog tu bya ba 'am 'di bcangs kyang bya dga' mang zhig byin du re ba'i phyir ni mi bsrung gi phongs te skyabs tshol ba'i phyir snying rjes brtsi bar bya'o/[35]
>
> He does not protect the child who is placed with him because he hopes that afterwards it will be a bound servant (*upasthāyaka*), or that through his keeping it a great deal of wealth (*dhana—or bhṛti*: a substantial wage) will be given, but, because the child is in need and seeking refuge, he must be affectionate through kindness.

The same sense of uneasiness that seems to be felt here about the nature of the practice is almost certainly also behind the concluding rule in Yijing ("ne

32. Daniel Boucher, *Bodhisattvas of the Forest and the Formation of the Mahāyāna* (Honolulu: University of Hawaii Press, 2008), 233 n. 234; Oskar von Hinüber, *Selected Papers on Pāli Studies*, 92–94.
33. Still the best treatment of the *mithyājīvas* occurs in Wogihara's "Lexikalisches aus der Bodhisattvabhūmi" included in the reprint of Unrai Wogihara, ed., *Bodhisattvabhūmi* (Tokyo: Sankibo, 1971), 21–26.
34. *Vinayasūtraṭīkā*, Derge, bstan 'gyur, 'dul ba Yu 231b.3.
35. *Vinayasūtravṛtti*, Derge, bstan 'gyur, 'dul ba Lu 280b.2.

demandez pas le prix") and in Guṇaprabha and his source ("A certain price must not be asked for this!"). But in spite of these assurances and exhortations, it is again hard to see how Guṇaprabha's, and quite possibly his source's, word choice would have allayed any unease or quieted the critics. The fact remains that the monks were rewarded at several points in the procedure: by relatives at the beginning, by relatives at the end, and by the children themselves still later. More telling still, what the relatives give when they take the child back is called a, or the, "ransom," *niṣkraya*, and a single example of the use of the term, and the verb from which it is formed, in Sanskrit literature points not only to the nature of the transaction, but also to the status of the child. In the *Mṛcchakaṭikā*, a well-known Sanskrit drama, one of the courtesan Vasantasenā's female servants or slaves—she is called a *ceṭī*—is named Madanikā. Her suitor wants to free her from her servitude or buy her freedom. He first says: *madanike kiṃ vasantasenā mokṣyati tvāṃ niṣkrayeṇa*? "Madanikā, will Vasantasenā free you for a ransom?" Later when her suitor is reluctant to reveal the source of some jewelry he has stolen, Madanikā says to him, in the Sanskrit *chāyā*: *yadi me pratyayaṃ na gacchasi tat kiṃ nimittaṃ māṃ niṣkrīṇāsi*? Diwakar Acharya has recently translated this phrase—quite appropriately—as "If you don't trust me, why are you buying my freedom?," and Yves Codet as "Si tu ne me fais pas confiance, pourquoi veux-tu me racheter?"[36] The fact that Guṇaprabha uses precisely the same term for what is given when the child is taken back would seem to suggest, if not confirm, that the child was at least temporarily in a state of servitude and that there was indeed an element of purchase involved.

Guṇaprabha's comments on his own *sutras*, then, are fairly full except for one exception already noted: he does not deal with the issue of the children's gender even though he raises it in his first *sūtra*. For an explanation of the phrase "children of the same gender," one must go to Dharmamitra's commentary on the *Vinayasūtra*, the *Vinayasūtraṭīkā*.[37] Dharmamitra's comment on Guṇaprabha's first *sūtra* reads:

> bsrung ba'i phyir byis pa mtshan mthun pa 'bul ba dag blang par bya'o zhes bya ba ni/khyim bdag gis byin pa khye'u dang bu mo dag bsrung ba'i phyir dge 'dun nam/gang zag la dbul na mtshan mthun pa dag blang bar bya ste/

36. For both text and a translation see Diwakar Acharya, trans., *The Little Clay Cart by Shūdraka* (New York: New York University Press, 2009), 176–77 and 180–81; Lyne Bansat-Boudon, ed., *Théâtre de l'Inde ancienne* (Paris: Gallimard, 2006), 627 and 629. For a well-known Buddhist example, see Cowell and Neil, *Divyāvadāna*, 405.12, where it is said that Aśoka, after having given virtually everything to the Community, *catvāri śatasahasrāṇi saṃghasyācchādanaṃ dattvā pṛthivīṃ antaḥpuram āmātyagaṇam ātmānaṃ ca kunālaṃ ca niṣkrītavān*, "by giving an offering of four hundred thousand to the Community he ransomed [or: bought back] the earth, his harem, his council of ministers, himself, and Kunāla."

37. Little is known about Dharmamitra. A Tibetan colophon connects him with Termez, and Fussman recently dates him to "the 6th century(?)"; see Shakirjan

> dge slong rnams kyis ni khye'u dag blang bar bya'o/dge slong ma rnams kyis ni bu mo dag blang bar bya'o/'dir gzhung ni bcom ldan 'das la 'phrog ma skyabs su song zhing bslab pa'i gzhi dag la bzhag nas/des bu de dag gnod sbyin gdug pas 'jigs pas bsrung ba'i phyir dge 'dun la phul ba thos nas de dag 'di snyam du des bsrung ba'i phyir dge slong rnams la bu dag re zhig 'bul bar byed na bdag cag gis kyang ci'i phyir mi 'bul snyam nas de dag gis dbul bar brtsams pa dang/dge slong dag mi len nas bcom ldan 'das kyis bka' stsal pa/ blang bar bya'o zhes gsungs pa yin no/[38]
>
> In regard to the words "children of the same gender that are being given for their protection must be accepted," (they mean): If a householder gives as a gift male children and female children, for the sake of their protection, to the Community or an individual, they must be accepted by those of the same gender: Monks must accept the male children. Nuns must accept the female children. Here is the (canonical) text: "When they heard that Hārītī, after she had gone for refuge to the Blessed One and was established in the foundations of training, being (herself) terrified by dangerous demons, gave her children to the Community for protection, they (lay people) thought: 'If she gives so many children to the monks for protection, should we not also give ours?' Having thought that, they started to give children. But when the monks did not accept them, the Blessed One said: 'They must be accepted!'"

Dharmamitra does two things of note here. First, and unlike Guṇaprabha in the first commentary attributed to him, he explains the reference to the gender of the children, and in so doing he makes it clear—*pace* Peri—that for him both boys and girls were given and that their gender determines whether they will be accepted by nuns or by monks. Reference to children of both genders will be repeated in Prajñākara's commentary, in the second commentary attributed to Guṇaprabha, and in Viśeṣamitra's *Vinayasaṃgraha*. It appears, therefore, to be all but standard in the Indian scholastic tradition that both monks *and* nuns were expected to accept children for their protection.[39] The second thing he does—this time like Guṇaprabha—is to quote his canonical source, and it is exactly the same passage from an account of Hārītī that Guṇaprabha had quoted. Although neither quotes enough of the canonical source to make it absolutely certain that it explicitly referred to the gender of the children and the participation of nuns, this idea appears to be implicit in both, and especially in Dharmamitra: There the quotation immediately follows his remarks about gender and the role of nuns.

In regard to the remainder of Dharmamitra's comments, his insistence that the children must be protected with "thoughts of benefit," and not with

Pidaev, Tukhtash Annaev, et Gérard Fussman, *Monuments bouddhiques de Termez* (Paris: Collège de France, 2011), 1:17 and the sources cited.

38. *Vinayasūtraṭīkā*, Derge, bstan 'gyur, 'dul ba Yu 231a.6.

39. For a non-Buddhist protective rite for children that nuns were explicitly forbidden to engage in, see Gregory Schopen, "The Urban Buddhist Nun and a Protective Rite for Children," 359–80.

thoughts of material gain, has already been noted. Additionally, he repeatedly glosses "what is given" to the monks with *gos la sogs pa*, "cloth and so forth." But beyond this his remarks are very much in line with Guṇaprabha's auto-commentary, and the same can be said in regard to a third commentary, Prajñākara's *Vinayasūtravyākhyāna*.[40] Prajñākara's treatment of the *sūtras* is in fact by far the most succinct, and his language the most difficult to understand. Since it contains little that is new or not already seen, it can be set aside here. Note, however, that he does refer to children of both genders, although he does not cite his source. In this regard, and in his use of the term *gso ba*, "recovered," "cured," to refer to the children when the parents take them back, his remarks are like those found in our last commentary, the *Vinayasūtravṛtti*, also attributed to Guṇaprabha, and it is to that source that we might turn. But with the *Vṛtti* there is the problem of its attribution.

Apart from the auto-commentary for which there is Sanskrit material—although only partially edited and available—the other three commentaries appear to have survived only in Tibetan translation, and their attribution depends entirely on what is found in the Tibetan tradition. The colophon of the Tibetan translation of the *Vṛtti* in the Derge and Peking printings says simply: *'dul ba'i mdo'i rtsa ba'i 'grel pa chung ba slob dpon mang du thos shing yon tan dang ldan pa yon tan gyi 'od thams cad yod par smra ba pas byas so*, "(this) small commentary on the root text of the *Vinayasūtra* was done by the learned *Ācārya* possessed of good qualities, Guṇaprabha the Sarvāstivādin."[41] This description of course is not very much to work with, and until much more work is done on both the auto-commentary and this *Vṛtti*, their colophons, and the colophons of other work attributed to Guṇaprabha, very little can be said with confidence. At this stage of our ignorance at least two possibilities might be entertained. It is possible that the same Guṇaprabha wrote both the auto-commentary and the *Vṛtti*, and that the *Vṛtti* was referred to as the "small commentary" to distinguish it from the auto-commentary which is very much larger and may quickly have been found too unwieldly, even by Guṇaprabha himself. It is equally possible that the Guṇaprabha who wrote the *Vṛtti* was not the same Guṇaprabha who authored the *Sūtra* and the auto-commentary. The latter is, for example, fairly consistently referred to as a brahmin and a great Mūlasarvāstivādin *vinayadhāra* or "Vinaya Master."[42] No such claims are made for the author of the *Vṛtti* and he is said to be a Sarvāstivādin, although this designation may also just be another indication that the Tibetan tradition—and the Indian tradition that it inherited—understood the designations Sarvāstivādin and Mūlasarvāstivādin as interchangeable names for the same large group. In any case, to have two Buddhist authors with the same name might not be that unusual. In the end, though, the authorship of the *Vṛtti* must remain for now undetermined, even if one other—possibly related—thing

40. *Vinayasūtravyākhyāna*, Derge, bstan 'gyur, 'dul ba Ru 218a.5.
41. *Vinayasūtravṛtti*, Derge, bstan 'gyur, 'dul ba Lu 344a.7.
42. So *Vinayasūtra*, Derge, bstan 'gyur, 'dul ba Wu 100a.5.

seems clear: whoever wrote the *Vṛtti* did not cite the account of Hārītī found in the auto commentary and Dharmamitra as his source, and might have been drawing on yet another source which dealt with the same practice. At least his initial comment seems to be telling a different story. The whole of his treatment of our *sūtras* reads:

Vinayasūtravṛtti

(Derge, bstan 'gyur, 'dul ba Lu 280a.7-b.4 = Peking Su 344b.8–345a.6)
msthan mtshungs pa'i byis pa bsrung ba'i phyir 'bul na blang/khyim pa rtag par bu shi bas phyis bu gcig bdog ste shi nas dge slong gi g-yog tu phul na dge slong gis blangs la gtsug lag khang du gzhag/bu mo na dge slong ma'i gtsug lag khang du gzhag/
de'i mtshan ma mgul bar gos gdags pa yin no/'dregs gis mi khyer bar bya ba'i phyir dge slong gis chos gos kyi tshal bu mgul du gdags/rked par yang ngo/chos gos kyi tshal bu rked par btags kyang rung ngo/

snying rje'i sems kyis bsrung/byis pa bdag gi gan du bzhag pa de phyis g-yog tu bya ba 'am 'di bcangs kyang bya dga' mang zhig byin du re ba'i phyir ni mi bsrung gi phongs te skyabs tshol ba'i phyir snying rjes brtsi bar bya'o/

de'i gnyen gyis phul na blang/byis pa bzhag pa de'i pha ma 'am gnyen gyis spyan gzigs sam gos shig dge slong de la phul na blangs kyang nyes med/

mthar rngan pa yang no/ltag ma ltar byis pa bzhag pa phyis ma shi ste sos nas de'i phyir pha mas dad de nor dang rdzas byin na len du gnang ngo

des drin shes par yang ngo/ltag ma ltar byis pa gsos pa de nyid kyis khyod kyi yin no zhes zer zhing nor 'bul na len du dbang ngo/

rngan pa mi blang/dge slong gis byis pa gsos te ma shi ba rngan pa byin zhes mi bya/

If children of the same gender are given for the sake of their protection, they must be accepted:—if a householder, because a son always dies, later gets another son and, when he is dying, he gives him as a bound-servant to a monk, the monk must accept him and place him in the *vihāra*. If it is a girl, she must be placed in a *vihāra* for nuns.

As its insignia a cloth must be fastened around its neck:—so that it will not be carried away by a haughty one, the monk must fasten around its neck a strip of a monastic robe. Also around its waist:—a strip of a monastic robe might be fastened also around their waist.

They must be protected with thoughts of kindness:—he does not protect the child placed with him because he hopes that afterwards it will be a bound-servant, or that through keeping it a great deal of wealth will be given, but because the child is in need and seeking refuge, he must be affectionate through kindness.

If its relative makes a gift, it must be accepted:—if the father and mother or a relative of that placed child gives foodstuffs or cloth to that monk, there is no offence in accepting it.

At the end also a ransom:—so in addition, if when the placed child does not die and recovers, and on that account its father and mother, being devout, give money and goods, their acceptance is required.

Also what is given when it is grateful:—so in addition, if the recovered child itself gives money saying, "It is yours," it is his to accept.

But a fixed fee must not be accepted:—the monk must not say "a fixed fee must be given for the child who has recovered and has not died."

The *Vṛtti* at first sight appears to be remarkably close to Guṇaprabha and Dharmamitra and yet significantly different. Unlike Guṇaprabha and Dharmamitra, the author of the *Vṛtti* refers to the death of previous children and the imminent death of the child to be given. He also twice explicitly refers to the "recovery" of the child and the others do not. In regard to both of these points it might appear that the author of the *Vṛtti* was following a text similar to the one cited above from the *Avadānaśataka*, which begins with a rich householder who had had sons, all of whom had died. If this was the case, if the author of the *Vṛtti* was following such a text here, since the rest of his treatment follows the rules found in the account of Hārītī, it is possible that there were two accounts that delivered the same rules, one dealing with a householder whose children die, and one dealing with Hārītī. It is also possible that in referring to the death, dying, and recovery of the children, the author of the *Vṛtti* was simply making explicit, or drawing out, what was obviously implied in the account of Hārītī and that there was no other account. A third possibility—one for which we have an interesting parallel or precedent—might be that the author of the *Vṛtti* is conflating two passages, if not practices: one like that found in the *Avadānaśataka*, and the other the account of Hārītī that Guṇaprabha and Dharmamitra drew on. The possible parallel is worth citing in some detail not just because it might provide an example of what our author might have done, but also because it introduces a second set of circumstances in which children might be given to monastic communities. This possible parallel occurs in another Mūlasarvāstivādin handbook, entitled the *Vinayasaṃgraha*, which the Tibetan tradition ascribes to Viśeṣamitra.

Vinayasaṃgraha

(Derge, bstan 'gyur, 'dul ba Nu 162a.6-b.2 = Peking Phu 215a.7-b.3)
sbyin bdag gi bu dang chung ma phul na ci ltar bya ba'i rigs zhes de nyid la dri bar bya'o/gal te skyed cig dang rin thang bdag gis dbul lo zhes zer na/bskyed par bya'o/ de la dge slong gis bskyed na nyes byas so/dge 'dun gyis kyang rin thang bzhin du bda' bar mi bya mod kyi/'on kyang de dga' nas ci byin pa de blang bar bya'o/

ma la sogs pas bu dang bu mo byin na blang ngo/slar slong na sbyin par bya'o/ gal te god pa rnams kyi rin dbul na yang blang bar bya'o/god pa bzhin du blang bar mi bya mod kyi 'on kyang dga' nas ci byin pa de blang bar bya'o/

byis pa de yang dge slong gis chos gos kyi tshal bus rked pa dang mgul bar bcings la bskyang bar bya'o/de dag cher gyur te byas pa shes pa'i phyir 'bul na nye gnas lta bu yin pas na blang bar bya'o/

When the children and wife of a donor are given, and it is said "What must be done?," the donor himself must be asked. If he says: "They must be auctioned off and I will pay the determined price," they must be auctioned off. If a monk bids up (the price) here there is an offence. Although the Community must also certainly not call in in accordance with that price, still whatever the donor wishes to give must be accepted.

When a mother and so forth gives a son or daughter, it must be accepted. When later they ask for their return, they must be given. If they give a sum for expenses, it also must be accepted. Although they certainly must not accept in accordance with actual expenses, still whatever is willingly given must be accepted.

Moreover the monk, binding the waist and neck with a strip of a monastic robe, must also protect that child. When they have grown up and, on account of their gratitude, give, since they are like a co-residential pupil, that must be accepted.

Although it is not difficult to see that the second and third paragraphs here are a very condensed summary of the rules found in Yijing's account of Ḥārītī, as well as in Guṇaprabha's and Dharmamitra's treatment of a similar account, the first paragraph of this passage from the *Vinayasaṃgraha* appears to be unrelated, and almost certainly is. The first paragraph in fact almost certainly is an equally condensed summary of a text now found in the *Uttaragrantha*, the last section of the *Mūlasarvāstivāda-vinaya*, that has no connection with Hārītī but rather describes, and gives rules to govern, a practice narratively initiated by the layman Anāthapiṇḍada at the time of the "Great Festival" or *Mahāmaha*. The Great Festival is one of a cycle of festivals connected with events in the early life of the Bodhisattva Siddhārtha—the historical Buddha before he was the Buddha—that is widely known in the *Mūlasarvāstivāda-vinaya* but little studied. As it is described there, it celebrated the initial occasion when the Bodhisattva "entered into unexcelled knowledge" (*bla na med pa'i ye shes mngon du chud pa*), and was consequently focused on an image of the Blessed One sitting in the shade of the Jambu tree—it was when he was so seated that this knowledge first arose—many examples of which have come down to us. The festival involved taking the image in procession into towns and—again according to the texts—large gatherings of nuns and monks from various regions and very substantial donations.[43] Again as a consequence, this festival gave rise to a significant number of rules governing monastic behavior and practices at such events. The text on which Viśeṣamitra's first paragraph is almost certainly based is one example of these.

Uttaragrantha-muktaka II.10

(Derge Pa 179b.4–180a.1 = Tog Na 259b.1-.7 = Peking Phe 174a.5-b.1)

gleng gzhi ni mnyan du yod pa na ste/khyim bdag mgon med zas sbyin pas dze ta'i tshal du dus ston chen po byas nas bu dang chung ma dge 'dun la yon du

43. See for now Gregory Schopen, *Figments and Fragments of Mahāyāna Buddhism in India. More Collected Papers* (Honolulu: University of Hawaii Press, 2005), 128–37 [note that everywhere in these pages where "a great festival" occurs, this should be corrected to: "the Great Festival"]; and Gregory Schopen, "Taking the Bodhisattva into Town. More Texts on the Image of 'the Bodhisattva' and Image Processions in the Mūlasarvāstivāda-vinaya," *East and West* 55 (2005), 299–311.

phul pa dang/dge slong dag gis ji ltar bya ba mi shes nas/de ltar gyur pa dge slong dag gis bcom ldan 'das la gsol pa dang/bcom ldan 'das kyis bka' stsal pa/ khyim bdag la dris shig/

dris pa dang/pha des smras pa/'phags pa dag rin thang chod cig dang bdag gis glud gsol lo/

drug ste dag gis de la 'gran cing spel ba la zhugs pa dang/de'i nang nas chung ma bu chung du ma can gyis khyim bdag mgon med zas sbyin gyi rkang pa la gtud de jo bo bdag gi bu chung gis bdag ma gtang shig ces smras pa dang/de ltar gyur pa dge slong dag gis bcom ldan 'das la gsol pa dang/bcom ldan 'das kyis bka' stsal pa/dge slong dag sems can gyi nang na bud med las snying chung ba med kyis 'jigs par ma bya shig/de bas dge slong gis bud med kyi rin thang ma gcod cig/bcad na 'das pa dang bcas par 'gyur ro/sbyin bdag gis ji ltar dga' zhing dga' ste byin bzhin du longs shig/

The setting was in Śrāvastī. When the householder Anāthapiṇḍada performed the Great Festival in the Jetavana and gave his children and wives to the Community as a gift, and when the monks did not know what should be done, the monks reported to the Blessed One what had occurred, and the Blessed One said: "You must ask the householder!"

Being asked, the father said: "You, Noble Ones, must determine a price (at auction) and I will give the ransom!"

But the Group-of-Six began to compete and raise the price, and one among the wives who had many young children touched the feet of the householder Anāthapiṇḍada and said: "Please, Lord, do not abandon me with my small children!" The monks reported to the Blessed One what had occurred, and the Blessed One said: "Monks, since among living beings there is no timidity from a (threatened) woman, you must not frighten one! Therefore, a monk must not determine a price (at auction) for a woman! If he does so, he comes to be guilty of an offence. Whatsoever the donor wishes to offer must be accepted!"

With this canonical text from the *Uttaragrantha* in hand, it is clear why there can be very little doubt that Viśeṣamitra's first paragraph is based on it. But since it is almost equally certain that his second and third paragraphs are also based on the account of Hārītī that Guṇaprabha and Dharmamitra knew—an account similar to the one Yijing translated—this similarity would seem to present a clear instance of the conflation or conjoining of disparate texts, and a strong parallel for what the author of the *Vṛtti* might have done. But this example may also do much more than that. Certainly the *Uttaragrantha* passage provides a clear indication that at least in texts children were given to monastic communities not just for their protection when sick and in danger of dying, or not just—as was noted earlier—as "attending menials" for a monk, but they were also given as gifts on the occasion of festivals and then—how much later is not said—redeemed or bought back, thus providing another source of ready cash for the monks. Particularly important for one of the purposes here, however, is the fact that Viśeṣamitra's second and third paragraphs would seem to indicate that he, like Guṇaprabha and Dharmamitra, knew a text that was very much like that found at the end of the account of Hārītī that Yijing translated, even though there is no corresponding text in the Tibetan version we now have. But here too it is worth noting—and that is all that can be done now—that this is not the only thing missing from the Tibetan version of the account of Hārītī in the *Mūlasarvāstivāda-vinaya*: it makes no reference at all to monastic communities' putting aside a portion of each meal to feed Hārītī and her children, and this practice is prominent in both Yijing's translation of the *Vinaya* and in his travel "record," for example, and is commonly presented as a key component of the monastic cult of Hārītī and invoked to explain the presence of images and shrines for Hārītī at monastic sites. But to deal adequately with this issue will require a separate study. Here a few more general concluding remarks must suffice.

Anyone who tries to track the role or fix the character of Hārītī will quickly see that she is an almost hopelessly amorphous figure. Her history is, frankly, unknown. She has merged with or absorbed any number of even more obscure local or regional "minor" female "divinities," or so it seems. This means at the very least that many of the images that have been taken to represent her might represent one or more of these other figures, since there is an overlapping iconography. But even when a given image at a given place can be identified with certainty as Hārītī—and such cases are surprisingly rare—it may still be far from clear what she was doing there, since Hārītī, it seems, wore many hats. Lokesh Chandra, for only one example, lists five: She was, in addition to a "stealer of children," "the giver of children," a "bestower of wealth," a "goddess to ward off ill health, e.g. to prevent smallpox," and a provider of "protection," and while this is a typical list, it is far from complete.[44] Most of the Mūlasarvāstivādin *Vinaya* authorities that have been cited here—Guṇaprabha, Dharmamitra, and Prajñākara, for example—while in one place they present Hārītī as the model for the practice of giving threatened children to the monastic community for their protection, in another place they put her at the top of a list of tutelaries or (usually female) divinities who protect monasteries (*gtsug lag khang gi srung ma, vihārapāla*),[45] and this is the role she still has in Kuladatta's *Kriyāsaṃgrahapañjikā* (*hārītīpramukhā vihārarakṣakā devās*).[46] It is, however, the first of these two roles—Hārītī as an exemplar for anxious mothers and the practice of giving children at risk to the monastic community—that has become clear here, and although it has sometimes been mentioned in passing, this is essentially a new hat for Hārītī that must be

44. Lokesh Chandra, "The Khotanese Mural of Hārītī at Dandan-Uiliq," in *Purābhāratī. Studies in Early Historical Archaeology and Buddhism* (Delhi: Sharada Publishing House, 2006), 2: 243.

45. Gregory Schopen, "Counting the Buddha and the Local Spirits in: A Monastic Ritual of Inclusion for the Rain Retreat," *Journal of Indian Philosophy* 30 (2002), 376.

46. Ryugen Tanemura, ed., *Kriyāsaṃgraha of Kuladatta. Chapter VII* (Tokyo: The Sankibo Press, 1997), 23.9, 24.2, 31.12–34.4, 36.6.

given its due. This is a Hārītī who is *not* the protector of children, but a Hārītī who finds a protector for her own children in the Buddhist monastic community. Buddhist nuns and monks are, then, the real protectors of children, and that of course is a very different story from the one we have been told, but it can now be said with certainty that this was a tale told early and often in Mūlasarvāstivādin sources in India.

CHAPTER 2

Scarecrows, *Upāsakas*, Fetuses, and Other Child Monastics in Middle-Period Indian Buddhism

AMY PARIS LANGENBERG

The assumption that the ancient Indian Buddhist sangha is best described as a community of mature individuals who renounced the world out of a personal desire for awakening,[1] a pragmatic and individualistic institution, one that disregarded caste, rejected the centrality of ritual, and opened its doors to women on principle[2] is not entirely unfounded. Parts of the canonical tradition do support something like this vision of the early sangha.[3] The

1. This version of Indian Buddhist history is explicit in multiple textbooks and general works and implicit in the Buddhist Studies scholarly canon, which has focused disproportionately on Buddhist philosophy and psychology. This phenomenon is noted by Jonathan Silk in his study of administrative roles in Indian monasteries, *Managing Monks: Administrators and Administrative Roles in Indian Buddhist Monasticism* (New York: Oxford University Press, 2008), 12–13. The assumption that individual meditative experience is everywhere and always the central and defining feature of monastic life has been criticized by Robert H. Sharf in his essay "Buddhist Modernism and the Rhetoric of Meditative Experience," *Numen* 42 (1995), 238–83.

2. The pioneering female scholars of Buddhism, Caroline Rhys Davids and Isaline Blew Horner, both looked upon the Buddhist sangha as an unparalleled opportunity for women, one with great humanizing potential. In her preface to Horner's *Women Under Primitive Buddhism: Laywomen and Almswomen* (Delhi: Motilal Banarsidass, 1930, 1989 xiii, Rhys Davids writes, "In the records of women who had joined the Order, we see woman become articulate about herself and her life. She had, as to all social ends, all domestic interests, become not woman, but *homo*."

3. In *The Sociology of Early Buddhism* (Cambridge: Cambridge University Press, 2003. Greg Bailey and Ian Mabbett have put this view of the earliest Buddhist community to good use, arguing that the early sangha is best described as a brotherhood of wandering ascetics who, by virtue of their transcendence of social relationships,

idea that Buddhist communal life was primarily the product of an individualistic commitment to a contemplative life does not pan out particularly well, however, when the full gamut of Indian Buddhist literature and inscriptional data is taken into account. Many compelling studies of the last quarter century are essentially social histories that seek to illuminate Indian monasticism's geographic diversity, institutional complexity, dynamic integration with local social, economic, and religious structures, and reliance on ritual.[4] The topic of children and childhood has so far received scant attention from historians and philologists,[5] but it also challenges idealized or incomplete views of premodern South Asian Buddhist monasticism. Since young children cannot be regarded as autonomous, reasoning individuals, and since their presence virtually defines the householding life, they ought to have no place in an enlightened community of like-thinking adults who have elected to reject the social world in pursuit of spiritual goals.[6] Yet legal and narrative sources give us every reason to suppose that children of practically every age lived in Indian Buddhist monasteries, and from an early period. This chapter explores the institutional structures and ritual practices that allowed for the presence of children in Middle-Period (0–500 CE) Buddhist monasteries,[7] and considers

were able to act as mediators in the culturally diverse, politically and socially fragmented North India of the mid to late first millennium BCE. I do not necessarily pit my interpretation against theirs here. I understand my sources to describe the institutionally mature post-Aśokan Buddhist community of the Middle Period, not the fledgling community of the Buddha's time and shortly after that interests Bailey and Mabbett.

4. See, for example, works by Gregory Schopen, John Strong, Jonathan Silk, and Ronald Davidson.

5. Shayne Clarke has written the only full-length study that considers the question of children in the historical Indian sangha. He is particularly interested in children that are related to sangha members. "Family Matters in Indian Monastic Buddhism" (PhD Diss., UCLA, 2006). Kate Crosby has written one of the only other textual studies on child initiation in ancient South Asian Buddhism: "'Only If You Let Go of That Tree:' Ordination without Parental Consent in Theravāda Vinaya," *Buddhist Studies Review* 22 (2005), 155–73. Phyllis Granoff has explored the ordination of children and the importance of kinship in medieval Jain monasticism: "Fathers and Sons: Some Remarks on the Ordination of Children in the Medieval Śvetāmbara Monastic Community," *Asiatische Studien* 60 no. 3 (2006), 607–33. See also Nalini Balbir, "La question de l'ordination des enfants en milieu jaina," in *Les Ages de la vie dans le Monde Indien*, ed. Christine Chojnacki (Paris: Boccard, 2001), 153–85.

6. In response, perhaps, to the challenge posed by the idea of very young children taking part in the early Buddhist community, Crosby historicizes the phenomenon of child ordination in the Theravāda sangha. She speaks of shifts that include "a move towards childhood ordination, the decision to ordain being a family or collective decision rather than an individual's and family responsibilities continuing after ordination," and that "may seem removed from the original spirit of Buddhist renunciation." See her article, "Only If You Let Go of That Tree," 169.

7. Schopen uses the term "Middle Period" because he wishes to avoid the distortions introduced by referring to this period as "the Early Mahāyāna Period," a more traditional way of periodizing Indian Buddhism. Schopen argues that scholars' dependence on Chinese translations of Indian Buddhist texts has led them to exaggerate the influence of Mahāyāna texts and doctrines in India during this period.

how new insights into monastic practices surrounding children help to nuance the argument for a socially enmeshed, ritually engaged, highly gendered Indian sangha.

First the reader requires a clarification of how the terms "child" and "childhood" will be used in this chapter. Since there is no large published body of work on children in Buddhism, a number of questions regarding definition remain unanswered. For instance, to what degree were monks participating in dominant views of childhood and generally accepted understandings about the socialization, education, and protection of children? To what degree were they overhauling childhood to suit their own program? What we do know is that, according to the *Vinaya*, full membership into the community with all of its attendant rights and responsibilities began at the age of twenty. For the purposes of this chapter, then, a "child" will be taken to be any person below the age of twenty.[8] In defining children in this way, I emphasize their dependent status, limited legal standing in the community, and lack of intellectual and psychological maturity in the eyes of the Buddhist monastic tradition.[9] The younger the children we consider, the harder we press against a narrow view of Buddhist monasticism, so particular attention will be paid to materials concerning children in their first fifteen years of life.

This chapter relies primarily on the Tibetan translation of the *Pravrajyāvastu*, or "Chapter on Going Forth [into Homelessness]," from the Mūlasarvāstivāda *Vinaya*. The Mūlasarvāstivāda *Vinaya*, some of which has survived in Sanskrit, is one of six extant sectarian *Vinayas*, each associated with one of the various Indian Buddhist schools.[10] These sectarian *Vinayas* differ in various important

Gregory Schopen, "The Mahāyāna and the Middle Period in India Buddhism: Through a Chinese Looking-Glass," in *Figments and Fragments of Mahāyāna Buddhism in India: More Collected Papers* (Honolulu: University of Hawaii, 2005), 3–24. In this chapter I follow Schopen's usage.

8. I realize that this is a simplistic approach to the problem of definition and does not take into account the modern distinction between young children and sexually mature adolescents, one that was also drawn in ancient India. Unfortunately, the question of how childhood is defined or "constructed" in ancient India is outside the scope of this paper. It may interest the reader to know that, according to the Buddhist monastic law, age is calculated from conception rather than from birth. *Mahāvagga* I.75.

9. Here, I take my lead from Philippe Ariès, who, in his foundational work on the history of childhood in Europe, notes that biological immaturity and dependence were viewed equally as markers of childhood during the medieval period, giving rise to a situation in which a physically mature but socially dependent twenty-four-year-old could still be referred to as a child. *Centuries of Childhood: A Social History of Family Life*, trans. Robert Baldick (New York Alfred A. Knopf, 1960, 1970), 26.

10. Four of these six—the Dharmaguptaka, Mahīśāsika, the Sarvāstivāda, and the Mahāsāṃghika *Vinayas*—are available in their entirety only in Chinese (though fragments exist in Sanskrit). The entire Mahāsāṃghika-Lokottaravādin *Bhikṣuṇī Vinaya* exists in Sanskrit. For an overview of extant *vinaya* texts see Charles S. Prebish, *A Survey of Vinaya Literature* (Taipei: Jin Luen Publishing House, 1994), and Anālayo, "Vinaya," in ed. W. G. Weeraratne, *Encyclopaedia of Buddhism*, vol. 8, no. 3 (Sri Lanka; Department of Buddhist Affairs, 2009), 647–50.

particulars, but resemble one another broadly in both content and structure.[11] The canonical *Vinayas* comprise a *Sūtravibhaṅga* section (a commentary on the *Prātimokṣa Sūtra,* a list of precepts governing the behavior of individual monks) and a *Skandhaka* or *Vinayavastu* section (an explanation of what are called *karmavācanās,* or rules governing communal life). The *Pravrajyāvastu* belongs to the latter division of Vinaya literature. While only an introductory portion of the *Pravrajyāvastu* (containing material of negligible relevance to this study) is available in Sanskrit, various Sanskrit stand-alone *karmavācanā* texts from the Mūlasarvāstivāda tradition have been found and subsequently edited.[12] In addition, Guṇaprabha's *Vinayasūtra,* its autocommentary, and various other related commentarial works, are available in Sanskrit or Tibetan translation.[13] Also relevant is the Buddhist narrative or *avadāna* tradition, which contains accounts of children admitted into the monastic fold. The Pāli *Vinaya* has been critically edited and translated in its entirety and will serve as a point of comparison with the Northern Mūlasarvāstivāda tradition that is the focus of this study.

Dating the Mūlasarvāstivāda *Vinaya* is problematic, since all the manuscripts and translations are relatively late.[14] Scholarly consensus places it in the early

11. The major textual divisions are largely the same for the Tibetan Mūlasarvāstivāda and Pāli *Vinayas,* although the former is considerably bulkier. The organizational scheme of the Mahāsāṃghika *Vinaya* is apparently anomalous. See Shayne Clarke, in "*Vinaya Mātṛkā*—Mother of the Monastic Codes, or Just Another Set of Lists? A Response to Frauwallner's Handling of the Mahāsāṃghika *Vinaya,*" *Indo-Iranian Journal* 47 (2004), 77–120.

12. We have, for instance a translation of a Sanskrit Mūlasarvāstivāda *Prātimokṣa* text in Charles Prebish, *Buddhist Monastic Discipline: The Sanskrit Prātimokṣa Sūtras of the Mahāsāṃghikas and Mūlasarvāstivīns* (University Park: The Pennsylvania State University Press, 1975). The *Bhiksukarmavākya* is a Sanskrit resension of the Mūlasarvāstivāda ordination ritual discovered at Gilgit and published in Anukul Chandra Banerjee, *Two Buddhist Vinaya Texts in Sanskrit* (Calcutta: World Press Private Limited, 1977). We also have an edition of the *Upasampadājñaptiḥ,* ed. B. Jinananda, Tibetan Sanskrit Works Series, Volume VI (Patna: Kashi Prasad Jayaswal Research Insitute, 1961). For a full account of extant Sanskrit *vinaya* material, see Nobuyuki Yamagiwa, "Vinaya Manuscripts: State of the Field," *Indica et Tibetica* (2007), 607–16. See also works by Jin-il Chung.

13. Rahul Sankrityayana, *Vinayasūtra of Bhadanta Guṇaprabha* (Bombay: Bharatiya Vidya Bhavan, 1981). See also Jayarakṣita, *Sphuṣārtha Śrīghanācarasaṃgrahaṣīkā,* ed. Sanghasena (Patna: K. P. Jayaswal Research Institute, 1968.) Not much is known about this author, and the original *sūtra* upon which his commentary is based has been lost. The editor believes him to have lived between the sixth and eighth centuries. J. Duncan Derrett has produced a translation of this work entitled *A Textbook for Novices: Jayarakṣita's "Perspicuous Commentary on the Compendium of Conduct by Śrīghana"* (Torina: Indologica Taurinensia, 1983), 10–11.

14. The Mūlasarvāstivāda *Vinaya* was translated into Chinese by Yijing in the early eighth century and into Tibetan by a translation team in the ninth century. We have Sanskrit manuscripts of portions of this *Vinaya,* discovered at Gilgit and edited by Nalinaksha Dutt and Raniero Gnoli. Nalinaksha Dutt, *Gilgit Manuscripts* (Delhi: Sri Satguru Publications, 1939, 1984). Raniero Gnoli, *The Gilgit Manuscript of the Saṅghabhedavastu, Being the 17th and Last Section of the Vinaya of the Mūlasarvāstivādin* (Roma: Instituto Italiano per il Medio ed Estremo Oriente, 1977) Dutt (1: 42) dates the manuscripts to the sixth or seventh century. No published

centuries of the first millennium, probably around the time of the Kuṣāṇa emperor Kaniṣka.[15] It is, however, a massive text containing some very old material and is by no means the product of a single era.[16] Real engagement with the issue of chronology lies outside the scope of this chapter, but for our purposes, we will assume that Mūlasarvāstivāda *Vinaya* texts and ancillary Sanskrit Buddhist material reflect debates in the monastery during the first half of the first millennium in the regions of Gandhāra, Kashmir, and Mathurā, keeping in mind that these sources may also relate to the sangha during an earlier (or later) period and over a larger geographic area.

Western-language translation exists for this massive text, though Jampa Losang Panglung has summarized its main contents. Jampa Losang Panglung, *Die Erzählstoffe des Mūlasarvāstivāda-Vinaya, Analysiert auf Grund der Tibetischen Übersetzung* (Tokyo: Reiyukai Library, 1981).

15. Erich Frauwallner, *The Earliest Vinaya and the Beginnings of Buddhist Literature* (Rome: Instituto Italiano per il Medio ed Estremo Oriente, 1956), 37. Here Frauwallner associates the Mūlasarvāstivāda *Vinaya* with the ancient Buddhist community at Mathurā. Etienne Lamotte initially insists that it was compiled "very much later" in Kashmir and argues that "we cannot attribute to this work a date earlier than the fourth–fifth centuries of the Christian era." *History of Indian Buddhism from the Origins to the Saka Era*, trans. Sara Webb-Bonn (Louvain-la-Neuve: Universite Catholique de Louvain Institut Orientaliste, 1988), 196, 727. In a later article he revises this estimate downward several centuries to the Kuṣāṇa period. In his edition of the *Sanghabhedavastu*, Raniero Gnoli confidently places the Mūlasarvāstivāda *Vinaya* in the time of Kaniṣka, though he allows that parts could be even older. See Raniero Gnoli, *The Gilgit Manuscript*, xix–xx. Schopen agrees with Lamotte's revised dating and with Gnoli. Gregory Schopen, "The Bones of a Buddha and the Business of a Monk: Conservative Monastic Values in an Early Mahāyāna Polemical Tract," in *Figments and Fragments of Māhāyana Buddhism in India: More Collected Papers* (Honolulu: University of Hawaii Press, 2005), 75–77.

16. If we believe Erich Frauwallner's *Skandhaka* theory, which posits an Ur *vinaya* text dating back to the fourth century BCE and forming the core of the sectarian *vinayas* we know today, some of the Mūlasarvāstivāda *Vinaya*'s oldest material may date to before the time of Aśoka. Indeed, Frauwallner includes many of the rules relevant to the ordination of children, such as the permitted age of novices and the necessity of parental consent for ordination, in his reconstruction of the theoretical "old *Skandhaka* work" (Erich Frauwallner, *The Earliest Vinaya and the Beginnings of Buddhist Literature*, Rome: Instituto Italiano per il Medio, ed Estremo Oriente, 1956), 65.

Of course, Frauwallner's thesis is speculative and has come in for criticism by Lamotte in his *History of Indian Buddhism from the Origins to the Saka Era*, trans. Sara Webb-Bonn (Louvain-la-Neuve: Universite Catholique de Louvain Institut Orientaliste, 1988),195–97; and Charles Prebish, "Review: Theories Concerning the Skandhaka: An Appraisal," *Journal of Asian Studies* 32 no. 4 (1973), 669–78. Shayne Clarke also critiques aspects of Frauwallner's thesis in his article, "*Vinaya Mātṛkā*." Gregory Schopen argues that agreement among sectarian *Vinayas* on certain subjects may well be the product of a process of homogenization and sharing among schools over centuries rather than an indication of the existence of an ancient core text. See "Two Problems in the History of Indian Buddhism: The Layman/Monk Distinction and the Doctrines of the Transference of Merit," in *Bones, Stones, and Buddhist Monks: Collected Papers on the Archaeology, Epigraphy, and Texts of Monastic Buddhism in India* (Honolulu: University of Hawaii Press, 1997), 25–29.

THE NOVICE INITIATION

Two fundamental institutional features of the Indian Buddhist monastery, the noviciate and preceptorship, both of which are attested in all of the sectarian *Vinayas*, allowed ample leeway for the institutionalization of children. Novices, or *śrāmaṇeras*, a subordinate rank in the monastery, received the *pravrajyā* initiation and kept only ten precepts. They did not participate in certain formal acts of the monastery (such as ruling on a monk who committed an offense, or ordaining new monks) and did not enjoy the full legal protection afforded to ordained monks (*bhikṣu*). In other words, novices could be disciplined or even expelled for delinquency without any formal monastic act.[17] Novices could be as young as seven but could not undergo the higher ordination and become *bhikṣus* until they were twenty. From an examination of the *Pravrajyāvastu* texts that describe the evolution of the ordination formula and the establishment of age rules, it is difficult to avoid the impression that, while the noviciate may have been applied to a variety of individuals (for instance, newcomers, the elderly, or the unambitious), it was especially designed for young monastic candidates.

According to all of the sectarian *vinayas*, the Buddha ordained his original disciples with the simple invitation, "Come, *bhikṣu*."[18] When it became difficult to travel long distances to request ordination from the Buddha in person, however, the Buddha authorized "a single *bhikṣu* to confer *pravrajyā* and *upasampadā* initiations simultaneously by means of the refuge prayer [recited three times] and the four acts [of wearing the robe, approaching the sangha, honoring the elders, and squatting down with hands folded.]"[19] These various utterances and gestures, so carefully itemized and described, were of obvious

17. According to the Pāli *Vinaya*, novices were to be expelled for the following acts: destroying life, committing theft, sexual misconduct, lying, imbibing intoxicants, speaking against the three jewels, holding false doctrinal views to be true, and having sex with a *bhikkhunī*. *Mahāvagga* 1.60. They were to be disciplined for surly, disrespectful, or disruptive behavior toward the *bhikkhus*. *Mahāvagga* 1.57. Apparently, monks were allowed to mete out punishments without consulting the entire community, though they were required to consult the novices' preceptors. *Mahāvagga* 1. 58. Hermann Oldenberg, *Vinaya Texts, Volumes 1, 2, 3* (Forgotten Books, 1881, 2007), 104–5. I haven't located a passage that corresponds to *Mahāvagga* 1.60 in the Mūlasarvāstivāda *Pravrajyāvastu*. Derrett, in his *A Textbook for Novices*, comments on the legal status of novices (10–11).

18. Anukul Chandra Banerjee, *Sarvāstivādan Literature* (Calcutta: Calcutta Oriental Press, 1957), 103. Ria Kloppenborg, "The Earliest Buddhist Ritual Ordination," in *Selected Studies on Ritual in the Indian Religions: Essays to D. J. Hoens*, ed. Ria Kloppenborg (Leiden: Brill, 1983), 158–68. Erich Frauwallner, *The Earliest Vinaya*, 73.

19. Derge 'dul ba Ka 47a.6–7. *bka' 'gyur (sde dge par phud)*, 103 vols., TBRC W22084 (Delhi: Delhi Karmapae Chodhey Gyalwae Sungrab Partun Khang, 1976), http://tbrc.org/link?RID=W22084. Unless otherwise noted, translations from the Tibetan are my own. Anukul Chandra Banerjee, *Sarvāstivādan Literature*, 104. See also Hermann Oldenberg, *Vinaya Texts*, 61.

significance to the Mūlasarvāstivāda ordination tradition. In the Theravāda tradition as handed down in the commentaries of Buddhaghosa, a candidate for ordination also had to perform these four acts and repeat the refuge formula accurately and with correct Pāli pronunciation in order for his initiation to be considered valid.[20]

This simple initiation ritual was eventually augmented, the *Pravrajyāvastu* tells us, by a formal procedure (*jñāpticaturthakarma*) requiring community participation. In this procedure, a motion (*jñāpti*) was put forth requesting the assembled monks to ordain the candidate followed by a threefold repetition of a legal formula (*karmavācanā*). The community was to remain silent if they agreed to the candidate's ordination. In the account of this formal procedure, as in the previous two, the *pravrajyā* and *upasampadā* ordinations occurred simultaneously.[21]

In these historiographical *Pravrajyāvastu* accounts of early ordination procedures, *pravrajyā* does not initially appear as an independent ritual that denotes a distinct status (that of novice) but seems to refer simply to wandering forth in a general sense, a preliminary act which all of the homeless mendicants, Buddhist and non-Buddhist, performed after their own fashion. A further development occurs, however, according to the *Pravrajyāvastu*'s chronology of ordination. Since poorly trained *bhikṣus* were tarnishing the Buddhist sangha's reputation abroad, the Buddha determined that all candidates should report to a teacher (*ācārya*) and a preceptor (*upādhyāya*), from whom the candidates would receive various stages of training before attempting full ordination. The *upāsaka* training (five precepts) and the *śrāmaṇera* training (ten precepts) are both specifically mentioned.[22] With this passage, the novice emerges as a distinct person in terms of ritual and disciplinary obligation. Interestingly, the *Mahavāgga* of the Pāli *Vinaya* only requires candidates for *pabbajjā* initiation to recite the triple refuge but makes no mention of the ten novice precepts.[23] As we know from Buddhaghosa's *Vinaya* commentary, the *Samantapāsādikā*, however, the Theravāda community also accepted the precepts as an essential element of the *pabbajjā* initiation at a relatively early date despite their lack of canonicity.[24]

A series of three rules concerning age limitations for initiation (*pravrajyā*) and ordination (*upasampadā*) further differentiate novices from *bhikṣus* in the *Pravrajyāvastu*. The first rule establishes the minimum age for ordination at

20. Kate Crosby, "*Uddis* and *Ācikh*: Buddhaghosa on the Inclusion of the *Sikkhāpada* in the *Pabbajjā* Ceremony," *Journal of Indian Philosophy* 28 (2000), 461. Oskar von Hinüber, "Buddhist Law and the Phonetics of Pāli," in *Selected Papers on Pāli Studies* (Oxford: Pali Text Society, 1994), 198–232.

21. Derge 'dul ba Ka 47a.7-b.6. Anukul Chandra Banerjee, *Sarvāstivādan Literature*, 104–5. See also Hermann Oldenberg, *Vinaya Texts*, 84–85; Erich Frauwallner, *The Earliest Vinaya*, 73; Etienne Lamotte, *History of Indian Buddhism*, 61–62; and Charles S. Prebish, *A Survey of Vinaya Literature*, 13–15.

22. Derge 'dul ba Ka 47b.6–49b.4. Banerjee, 105–10.

23. *Mahāvagga* I.54, Hermann Oldenberg, *Vinaya Texts*, 103.

24. Kate Crosby, "*Uddis* and *Ācikh*," 471–72.

twenty years.[25] Its genesis is explained as follows: one time when the Buddha was in Śrāvastī, Maudgalyāyana ordained a gang of seventeen local boys of unspecified age, whose ringleader was a certain Upāli. Later, the Buddha heard them crying of hunger in the night and asked Ānanda, "Why were children crying in the grove in the darkness of the early morning?"[26] Ānanda related the relevant information and the Lord subsequently established the rule that novices had to be at least twenty years of age before they could receive *upasampadā*, explaining:

> Ānanda, ordaining [before the age of twenty] should not be done. Why, Ānanda? It is because those who are younger than twenty are naturally unable to accept and endure the irritations of cold and heat, hunger and thirst, flies, bees and mosquitoes, wind and sun, scorpions and venomous snakes, verbal abuse and loutish people, and sufferings of the body that are unbearable, harsh, burning, unpleasant, life-threatening, those unthinkable phenomena that are [always] arising and flowing. [27]

This passage makes it clear that children are not to be considered psychologically or physically equipped for the strenuous life of a *bhikṣu*. Directly following the rule concerning the minimum age for ordination (*upasampadā*) is another that sets the age for initiation (*pravrajyā*) at fifteen years. The events leading up to the Buddha establishing this rule are narrated as follows:

> The Lord Buddha went to Jetavana in Śrāvastī, the grove of Anāthapiṇḍaka. In Śrāvastī, there was a particular householder. He took a wife from a clan of equal rank. They amused one other, enjoyed one another, and caused each other to share in every pleasure. A child was born of their dalliance and they nurtured him and raised him up. Then, at a later time, when his loved ones

25. Derge 'dul ba Ka 73a.6. For an English paraphrase, see Anukul Chandra Banerjee, *Sarvāstivādan Literature*, 167–68. Also found at *Mahāvagga* 1.49. See Hermann Oldenberg, *Vinaya Texts*, 99. This rule also appears in the *Prātimokṣa Sūtra*. It is item 72 of the Prāyaścittika Dharmas in the Mūlasarvsāstivāda *Prātimokṣa Sūtra* and item 65 of the Pācittiya Dharmas in the Pāli *Pātimokka*. See Charles Prebish, *Buddhist Monastic Discipline*, 89; Hermann Oldenberg, *Vinaya Texts*, 33.

26. The Pāli text contains much more detail about the initial conversion of Upāli and his friends and their night-time complaints. According to this version, Upāli overheard his parents discussing his future and settling on the monastery as his best chance at a safe, secure, and comfortable life. He decided to go forth and convinced his friends to join him, and they also obtained the permission of their parents. Unfortunately, the monastery did not turn out to be as comfortable as Upāli's parents had imagined. On the first night, the boys wake up hungry and begging for rice-milk and soft and hard food. Not only do they then make a fuss about their hunger, they also "thr[o]w their bedding about and ma[k]e it wet"! Hermann Oldenberg, *Vinaya Texts*, 99. The same story is repeated in the *Suttavibhaṇga*, Horner, Vol. III, 10–14.

27. Derge 'dul ba Ka 73b.5.

were all gone, his wealth exhausted, and his enjoyments finished, the householder thought: "Because I will no longer be able to acquire wealth in my old age, I will go forth." He told his son, "Son, because I will be unable to acquire wealth in my old age, I will go forth." [His son] replied, "Father, if you go forth, I will also go forth." The householder advised him to "Do that," and they went to Jetavana. Approaching a monk, he said, "Noble one, I desire to go forth." The monk replied, "Is this your child?" "This is my son." "He will also go forth?" "Noble one, he will go forth."

Because of their eagerness, the monk initiated both of them as novices. Over two or three days, he taught them some rules of conduct. He said, "Good people, an animal should not be the nourishment of another animal. Because Śrāvastī is a great land, your homeland, and the land of your fathers, go out and get alms and feed yourself with them." In the morning, [the father] put on his lower robes and picked up his bowl and upper robes and set out for Śrāvastī together with [his son, now a] novice. The novice saw a baker's oven by the side of the road. "Father, please give me a pastry," he said. [The father] said to [the baker] "Kind sir, please give this novice a pastry." He replied, "Noble one, do not ask if you don't have any money. You can buy it for a few coins." "Kind sir, since we have gone forth, how are we to get coins?" "Noble one, did you beget this novice after you had gone forth or as a householder?" "As a householder." "Then give me [some of] the savings belonging to that [period of your life.]" The householder replied, "This novice is extremely hungry as a result of being initiated. Come here," [he said to his son.] He then grasped [his son] by the hand. The boy fell down on his back in a swoon and began to cry.

The two were observed by a large crowd of townspeople. They asked, "Wise one, joyful one, who is this novice?" "He is my son." The townspeople asked disapprovingly, "Did they ordain him [just] because he is of the same blood?" They shouted out insults.

The monks asked the Buddha the reason for this slanderous talk. He thought about the various bad situations that would arise if the monks were to initiate people not yet fifteen as novices. Having thought about that, he said, "People under fifteen should not be initiated as novices. If someone asks to go forth, one should ask him if he is yet fifteen. If one causes a boy to go forth without asking if he is yet fifteen, it will be a transgression.[28]

Here, the *Pravrajyāvastu* text states that the townspeople disapprove of family relationship as a reason for Buddhist ordination. The Pāli version of this story gives a different reason for their disapprobation. There, no baker appears, but the boy accompanies his father on his begging rounds and clamors to be given some of the alms, which makes a bad impression on the townspeople. They think, "These Sakyaputtiya Samanas live an impure life; this boy is

28. Derge 'dul ba Ka 74a.3. Anukul Chandra Banerjee, *Sarvāstivādan Literature*, 169–71.

a Bhikkhuni's son."[29] The establishment of a minimum age for novice initiation may represent an effort to avoid practical difficulties by placing limits on individuals' ordaining with families in tow. Maintaining the sangha's reputation for virtue was also of primary importance, however. As the Pāli text makes explicit, this rule may also have been intended to minimize scandalous talk excited by the presence of young children in the sangha. No specific mention is made of young children's physical and psychological immaturity in this episode, though the *Pravrajyāvastu* version does seem to imply that, yet again, the inability to tolerate hunger is an obstacle to children's wandering forth.

The last item in this trio of rules concerning age restriction on admission concerns what is known as the "crow-scaring" initiation.[30] Here we get closer to the heart of the matter. The Lord was residing at Jetavana in Śrāvastī. Meanwhile, Ānanda's two young nephews were suddenly orphaned in Kapilavastu and, hitching a ride with a merchant's caravan, they arrived at the gate of the Jetavana hoping to be taken in by their well-regarded uncle:

> Ānanda, recognizing the two boys, said, "Boys, what happened to your parents?" The boys answered, "Sir, they were murdered by sinful people." Being affectionate toward his family, Ānanda became choked with tears after hearing about the loss of his relatives. The monks said to him, "Ānanda, who are these two boys of yours?" He said, "I have to go out to beg for alms only to just fill my own belly. Where will I [get food] to give to these two?" [The monks] replied, "If these two make offerings of milk, flowers, and fruit to the monks, the monks will give them the leftovers from their bowls." Thus, the two boys started to offer the monks milk and flowers and fruit they gathered, and the monks gave them [in turn] the leftovers from their begging bowls. The monks gave them their leftovers for a few days, but then stopped. Ānanda went out to beg for alms, which he divided in half, eating half himself and giving half to those two. He became pale and emaciated, feeble, skinny, withered, and had no physical strength. . . . The Buddha addressed the monks: "Monks, why is Ānanda so pale and emaciated, so feeble, skinny, withered, and without physical strength?" They answered, "Because Ānanda's two nephews were abandoned by their parents, having begged for alms to fill his mouth, having divided [the alms] in half, he takes half himself and offers half to those two. Because of this, he has become pale and emaciated, feeble, skinny, withered, without physical strength."
>
> Then the Lord said to Ānanda, "Ānanda, are these two not initiated?" "Lord, they are [intending to] go forth." The Lord said, "I allow offerings of food to novices wishing to go forth in this way." After the Lord announced, "One should offer food to novices wishing to go forth," the monks started to grouse

29. *Mahāvagga* 1.50. Hermann Oldenberg, *Vinaya Texts*, 101.
30. The Pāli term for this is *kākuṭṭepaka pabbajjā*, apparently from *kāka* (crow) with the causative form of the verb *uḍḍeti*, "fly up." See I. B. Horner, *The Book of the Discipline*, vol. IV (London: Luzac & Co., 1938–1966), 99, nn. 2, 3.

after offering [food] for a few days. Then the Lord spoke to Ānanda a second time, "Ānanda, are these two not initiated?" "Lord, they have not yet reached fifteen." "Are they able to drive crows away from the monks' couches?" "Lord, they will take up a rock." "Ānanda, in that case, it is permitted to initiate [a child] of seven years who is capable of driving away crows if he has been abandoned." Ānanda initiated those two.[31]

Many important elements come into play in this interesting text. First, it raises the issue of at-risk children, especially those related to sangha members.[32] Ānanda's two nephews are orphaned and without support, a situation for which both Ānanda and the Buddha feel sympathy. Ānanda is compelled to take responsibility for his nephews, since he is now their closest relative, and the Buddha, the highest monastic authority, finds ways to honor and support Ānanda's keen sense of family duty. The boys' presence raises problems with Ānanda's fellow monks, however, who see no need to provide for the boys and complain about having to share food with children that claim no formal connection to the monastery. In response, the Buddha lowers the age of novice initiation to seven years, provided that child candidates be capable of scaring crows. Thus it becomes possible for these young boys to be initiated. The mention of the boys' ability to "drive crows away from the monks' couches" highlights a typical feature of children's role in the monastery community, one that helps to justify their presence: namely, their usefulness as fetchers, sweepers, messengers, lookouts, attendants, and, in this case, scarecrows.[33]

The reference, early in the text, to offering milk, flowers, and fruit to the monks in return for scraps is reminiscent of an episode from the elder Upagupta's past life in which he is a monkey who makes similar offerings to a forest community of *pratyekabuddhas* and, in return, is supplied with their leftovers (*pātraśeṣa*) and allowed to imitate their meditation posture. In his study of Upagupta in Sanskrit Buddhism, John Strong argues, in reference to this story, for the existence of what he terms a "commensal community" in

31. Derge 'dul ba Ka 84a.1–85a.4.

32. In the Pāli version of this story, the two boys are the orphaned children of devout laypeople who had patronized Ānanda. Hermann Oldenberg, *Vinaya Texts*, 101.

33. According to one source, in the Khmer tradition the maturity of the candidate was measured not by his competence to scare crows, but by his ability to wrap his right arm over the top of his head and touch his left ear, a sure indication that the short-armed, large-headed days of toddlerhood had passed. Mathieu Boisvert, "A Sociocultural Analysis of the Burmese *Shin pyu* Ceremony," *Journal of Beliefs and Values* 21 no. 2 (2000), 204. In his article for this volume, Jeffrey Samuels reports that, according to one of his sources, crow-scaring is an indicator of a boy's readiness to take on agricultural responsibilities in general, not of his physical competence to literally scare a crow. In the *Pravrajyāvastu*, however, crow-scaring does seem to refer to children's ability to rid the monastery of marauding crows at mealtimes. As Vanessa Sasson has reminded me, crows present a formidable psychological challenge to small children. They are large, aggressive, and sinister-looking birds. The ability to confront such an adversary proves a certain level of maturity, toughness, and self-sufficiency.

Buddhist monasticism, which, while "larger than the bounds of the everyday sangha (which comprises only novices and monks), is nonetheless clearly hierarchical."[34] This commensal community would include stray animals and community pets that hang around the monastery, spirits associated with the sangha such as the protectress Hārītī or local *nāgas*, and certain types of laypeople (devout elders and, in contemporary Thailand, servant boys called *dek wat*), all of whom would have access to monastic leftovers. Strong's "commensal community" would have particular relevance to orphaned or indigent children like Ānanda's nephews who might have frequented Buddhist monasteries, performing odd jobs or presenting the monks with small offerings such as tooth sticks or flowers in return for monastic scraps.[35] Our *vinaya* text, with its tale of resentments stirred up when needy children hang about the *vihāra*, could be taken as evidence for the occasional presence of small children in the monastic commensal community.[36] Indeed, the crow-scaring rule seems to represent an attempt to provide a legitimate place for young children within the monastery hierarchy, particularly in the case of orphaned or indigent youngsters.

THE CROW-SCARING CAVEAT

To sum up, the *Pravrajyāvastu* contains a nested series of rules that allow for the initiation of children. First, the dignity and elevated status of the ordained monk or *bhikṣu* is protected by the rule forbidding individuals under the age of twenty to receive the *upasampadā* ordination. Since this rule necessitated any candidate *below* the age of twenty to spend months, years, or even a decade in training before becoming a full-fledged member of the community, it effectively created an institutional vacuum. Inevitably all the traditions and practices incumbent upon the Buddhist novice rushed in to fill that vacuum. Indeed, the novice, a figure that appears often in Buddhist narrative literature and even

34. John S. Strong, *The Legend and Cult of Upagupta: Sanskrit Buddhism in North India and Southeast Asia* (Princeton, NJ: Princeton University Press, 1992), 51.

35. See also Gregory Schopen, "Counting the Buddha and the Local Spirits: A Monastic Ritual of Inclusion for the Rain Retreat," *Journal of Indian Philosophy* 30 no. 4 (2002), 359–88.

36. Jonathan Silk cautions against assuming that the presence of rules in the *vinaya* forbidding a certain behavior means that behavior never occurred. He also cautions against the converse, that the presence of a negative rule implies that the legislated behavior did take place. In a footnote, he adds, "The logic of the rules found in the monastic codes does occasionally seem to resemble a Talmudic argument. We sometimes cannot escape the impression that monks sat around saying to each other, 'Hey, what if *that* happened?! What then?'" (*Managing Monks*, 7 n. 9). Silk's points are well taken, and of course one cannot take the *vinaya* as flatly descriptive of events or behaviors. Still, there is nothing strange, surreal, or ridiculous in the crow-scaring rule. Indeed it deals with fundamental and practical issues such as the fair distribution of food in the monastery, the family responsibilities of monks, and the issue of what to do with very young candidates in a pragmatic and realistic manner.

becomes the object of tracts devoted to his educational needs,[37] would not have achieved a distinct legal and ritual status in the Buddhist community in the absence of the first age rule.

The other two age rules apparently contradict one another. One rule forbids children younger than fifteen to undergo initiation, the other requires that they be seven years old and capable of heaving a rock at a crow. This conundrum is partially resolved in the *Pravrajyāvastu* by introducing the condition that the child be indigent, though in the Pāli verison of the crow-scaring rule the economic and social status of the child candidate is not specifically mentioned. Contradictory rules can sometimes be explained by monastic lawyers' reluctance to remove any material from the *Vinaya*. At least with regard to the *Pāṭimokkha*, Oskar von Hinüber is of the opinion that updating monastic law consisted of adding caveats rather than replacing older material with updated ordinances.[38] Sukumar Dutt extends this principle to the entire *Vinaya Piṭaka*.[39] We might then speculate that the crow-scaring rule is a later amendment. The idea that this rule represents a later development (though still prior to the first or second century of the Common Era) adds heft to Kate Crosby's opinion that the practice of child initiation gathered momentum as the Buddhist community matured.[40]

It is also conceivable, however that both age rules for novice initiation were fully operational from an early period. In fact, the narratives that frame these conflicting ordinances provide clues as to how they might have been simultaneously applied in practice. The rule setting the minimum age for *pravrajyā* initiation at a conservative fifteen years seems to be the more general one. Given the monastic elders' reluctance to involve themselves in childcare, a disinclination expressed by the Buddha himself in the story of Upāli and his homesick band of friends, fifteen would undoubtedly be considered a more desirable age for monastic candidacy than seven.[41] Moreover, the narrative about the father and son's encounter with the baker implies that establishing fifteen as the minimum age for *pravrajyā* was necessary to silence the wagging

37. For instance, Jayarakṣita's *Sphuṣārthā Śrīghanācārasaṃgrahaṣīkā*, dating to the sixth–eighth centuries. A similar Chinese textbook for novices can be found at Taisho 1473 (24), 935b-37a.

38. Oskar von Hinüber, "Buddhist Law According to the Theravāda-Vinaya: A Survey of Theory and Practice," *Journal of the International Association of Buddhist Studies* 18 no. 1 (1995), 14.

39. Sukumar Dutt, *Early Buddhist Monachism 600 B.C.-100 B.C.* (London: Kegan Paul, Trench, Trubner & Co., 1924), 18–19.

40. See n.6 above.

41. In the *Samantapāsādikā*, Buddhaghosa compares a poorly trained novice to a young child in order to express how troublesome he is: " ...so long as he does not understand for himself the precepts in which he should be trained and is not skilful in the wearing of the robes, carrying of the bowl, standing and sitting, nor in the correct method of drinking and eating, he can not be sent to the eating hall, the place of distribution of food tickets, or any other such [public] place; he has to stay close by and be taken care of like a young child ." Translated in Kate Crosby, "*Uddis* and *Ācikh*," 469.

tongues of the public. The story about Ānanda's nephews (the frame story for the crow-scaring rule), speaks, on the other hand, to a felt need to provide an alternative for obviously vulnerable children in extenuating circumstances, especially those with some legitimate connection to a particular monastic community. This rule served to legitimize needy children's place in the monastic soup line, thereby silencing complaining tongues *within* the monastery. Thus, a pragmatic if somewhat grim logic is called into play in reconciling the two age rules for novice admission. Even though the rigors of monastic life may have been viewed as unsuited to the very young, for orphaned or abandoned children even the restricted meal schedule of a novice was an improvement over starvation or garbage picking.[42] Child candidates were recognized to be problematic, but the crow-scaring caveat within the monastic code made it possible for individual communities to accommodate children dependent on sangha members for survival.

Closer examination of the language in the passage setting out the rule itself raises further questions about how it was intended to be put into practice. Unfortunately, a Sanskrit version of the passage in question is not available. The Tibetan reads:

> lo bdun lon pa bya rog skrod nus pa yongs su spangs bas rab tu dbyung bar rjes su gnang ngo[43]

I have translated this as "it is permitted to initiate [a child] of seven years who is capable of driving away crows if he has been abandoned." Banerjee paraphrases this as "the Blessed One enjoined the *bhikṣus* to confer the Pravrajyā ordination even on boys, only seven years old, if they could scare away crows."[44] As both interpretations reflect, the Mūlasarvāstivāda version of the story and the Tibetan translation of the rule itself both indicate that the ability to scare crows should be a condition for initiating underage boys. The Pāli text, however, reads somewhat differently:

> anujānami bhikkhave ūnapannarasavassaṃ dārakaṃ kākuḍḍepakaṃ pabbājetunti[45]

42. Most of the sectarian *vinayas* contain a rule criticizing those who become monks in hopes of easy access to food and requiring that candidates be taught the four *niśrayas* (rag-wearing, alms-eating, dwelling at the foot of trees, and consuming fermented cow urine as medicine). *Mahāvagga* 1.31; Hermann Oldenberg, *Vinaya Texts*, 86–87; Erich Frauwallner, *The Earliest Vinaya*, 74. The Mūlasarvāstivāda *Vinaya*'s *Pravrajyāvastu* does not contain this rule. In any case, ordaining children so they will not starve cannot be compared to ordaining someone who hopes to enjoy sumptuous banquets in the houses of wealthy patrons.

43. Derge 'dul ba 85a.3.

44. Anukul Chandra Banerjee, *Sarvāstivādan Literature*, 179.

45. *Vinaya* I.79.19

Horner translates this as "I allow you, monks, to let a youth of less than fifteen years of age and who is a scarer of crows to go forth."[46] Oldenberg prefers, "I allow you, O Bhikkhus, to confer the *pabbajjā* ordination on crow-keeper boys even under fifteen years of age."[47] Von Hinüber's translation is the most grammatically accurate. He quite properly takes the accusative compound *kākuḍḍepakaṃ* (one who causes crows to fly up) as the predicate of the other two accusatives, *ūnapannarasavassaṃ dārakaṃ* (a boy of less than fifteen years): "I allow, monks, to accept a boy of less than fifteen years of age as someone who scares crows."[48] Von Hinüber's understanding of this passage backlights a subtle difference between the Mūlasarvāstivāda and Pāli versions of the text. While the Tibetan translation takes crow-scaring (and indigence) as a condition of initiation for young boys, the Pāli version indicates rather that crow-scaring is a destination for young boys in the monastery. In other words, they may be admitted into the sangha, but as "crow-scarers," not as ordinary novices. Taking the Pāli text as reflective of the original intent of the rule and the Tibetan version as a slight misunderstanding or mistranslation adds further ballast to the notion that novices younger than fifteen played a special role in the monastery. If it was not meant to lower the minimum age of the novice so much as to add a new category of initiate—that of "crow-scarer"—then the crow-scaring caveat in no way contradicts the rule forbidding children under fifteen to be initiated as novices. Assuming this interpretation is correct, we can further surmise that this type of junior novice, the crow-scarer, did not merit his own intiation ritual but had to make do with the Buddhist initiations already in place: the *upāsaka* and *śrāmaṇera pravrajyās.*

One other factor may help to explain the crow-scaring caveat: the influence of competing ascetic groups, especially the Jains. Phyllis Granoff draws on Jain lineage histories and didactic literature to document the ordination of children in medieval Śvetāmbara monastic communities. Her conclusion is that, for Jains, "becoming a monk as a child may well have been far more the rule than the exception."[49] While some Jain authors forbade the ordination of a child (*bāla* or *dāraka*), age parameters were not always specified. Eventually, Jain commentators agreed on eight as the minimum age for child ordination. Granoff, however, indicates the many examples from Jain literature of children admitted at a much younger age. Although her research concerns a later period, her work does raise questions about Jain influences on Middle-Period Buddhist monastic communities regarding child monasticism. If as Oskar von Hinüber has argued in reference to female monastic orders Jain asceticism sometimes influenced Buddhist practice, it

46. Horner, Vol. 4, 99.
47. Hermann Oldenberg, *Vinaya Texts*, 101.
48. Oskar von Hinüber, "The Foundation of the Bhikkhunīsaṃgha: A Contribution to the Earliest History of Buddhism," *Annual Report of the International Research Institute for Advanced Buddhology* 11 (2008), 8.
49. Phyllis Granoff, "Fathers and Sons," 609.

may be that the Jain's ready admission of children provided a model for child monasticism in Buddhist communities.[50] In order to prove any such connection, however, a careful comparative study of Jain and Buddhist sources would be necessary.

THE PRECEPTORSHIP

As was discussed above, the surprisingly complex institution of the novice is one basic feature of Mūlasarvāstivāda monasticism conducive to the admission of children. The second feature, closely related to the first, is the institution of the preceptor. The *Pravrajyāvastu* introduces this institution with a brief account of *bhikṣus* who were badly dressed, were loud, and did not know how to beg for alms properly, thus drawing the scorn of other mendicants. A further problem arose when a sick *bhikṣu* was left unattended and died. The Buddha ordered, therefore, that, monks should have preceptors (*upādhyāya*) and teachers (*ācārya*) to officiate at the *pravrajyā* and *upasampadā* ceremonies, administer the refuge formula, and teach the precepts.[51] The student (*sārdhaṃvihārika* or *antevāsika*) is bound to his preceptor or teacher by a relationship called *niśraya* or "reliance," since he is completely reliant on him for the required training and for the requisites of monastic life.[52]

The student is expected to live with the senior monk upon whom he is officially dependent and to perform various tasks for him, including preparing his bowl and robes, and keeping house according to his orders. He is not to travel

50. Oskar von Hinüber, "The Foundation of the Bhikkhunīsaṃgha: A Contribution to the Earliest History of Buddhism." Anālayo has refuted von Hinüber's view in "Theories on the Foundation of the Nuns' Order—A Critical Evaluation," *Journal of the Centre for Buddhist Studies, Sri Lanka* 6 (2008), 105–42.

51. Derge 'dul ba Ka 47b.6–48b.1 Anukul Chandra Banerjee, *Sarvāstivādan Literature*, 105–7. The difference between the roles of preceptor and teacher are not clear. The *Mahāvagga* contains parallel passages describing the conditions of the relationship between student and teacher/preceptor in identical terms. Compare 1.25 and 1.32; 1.27 and 1.34; also 1.26.6 and 1.32.1. In the Mūlasarvāstivāda *Vinaya*, as well, both of these roles are defined in terms of caretaking, not teaching, a fact to which Schopen draws our attention (see his *Buddhist Monks and Business Matters: Still More Papers on Monastic Buddhism in India* [Honolulu: University of Hawaii Press, 2004], 8). Perhaps the only really identifiable difference between these two is the role each plays in the ordination ceremony. According to Guṇaprabha, the preceptor examines the candidate, dresses him in his robes, and hears his recitation of the refuge formula. The teacher is the "private examiner" and the one who teaches the candidate about the four "supports" (*niśraya*) of a monk. Compare Guṇaprabha 1.16–20 and 1.24–25. According to Lamotte, the term *sārdhaṃvihārika* ("co-resident") refers to the student's relationship with his preceptor, while the parallel term *antevāsika* ("dwelling near or in") refers to his relationship with the teacher (*History of Indian Buddhism*, 61). This distinction may not have held in practice.

52. Derge 'dul ba Ka 48a.6. Anukul Chandra Banerjee, *Sarvāstivādan Literature*, 107; Guṇaprabha 1.3. In many contemporary monastic settings, however, novices and monks have to pay their own way.

any great distance from the monastery nor recite any religious texts without his preceptor or teacher's permission. Just as the novice is to be nursed by the preceptor or teacher when sick, the preceptor or teacher is also to be nursed by the younger monk should he fall ill. The student should attempt to dispel any sadness or remorse that afflicts the preceptor if possible. He is even required to correct any false views his master might generate and to advocate for him should any legal difficulties arise. The preceptor or teacher, of course, is also required to encourage, correct, and advocate for his pupil.[53] In short, a buddy system is ordained, with master and novice mutually committed and mutually reliant on many levels, their hierarchical relationship to one another notwithstanding.

The institution of the preceptor or teacher and the relationship of *niśraya* would have provided a suitable platform for the incorporation of children into the monastery. In fact, the senior monk was explicitly directed to behave as a father toward his charge, the novice as a son toward his master.[54] *Niśraya* was an adaptable institution, pliable enough to provide for the basic physical, educational, and (if the preceptor was so inclined) emotional needs of all but the very youngest children.[55] More important, it placed children in a situation to be of tangible use to the institution through the performance of a variety of menial or tedious tasks. In fact, Buddhist narratives about novices typically portray them as servants or servant-cum-disciples, not primarily as students. It is certainly possible that the Buddhist noviciate received increasingly greater institutional support because it proved indispensable for providing monks with cleaners, fetchers, and nurses.[56] The rather surprising rule that *sārdhaṃvihārikas* and *antevāsikas* should correct the actions or prod the memories of their seniors may represent an effort to place a modicum of power in the hands of novices as a partial safeguard against abuse.

53. Derge 'dul ba Ka 62b.5–65a.4. Anukul Chandra Banerjee, *Sarvāstivādan Literature*, 140–47. The Pāli Vinaya contains instructions about the duties incumbent upon teacher and student in greater detail, though it does not differ from the *Mūlasarvāstivāda* tradition in its essentials. *Mahāvagga* 1.25–27; Hermann Oldenberg, *Vinaya Texts*, 77–84. *Aṅguttara-nikāya* 5.7.114 describes the ideal following-after-ascetic as one who follows neither too close nor too far, holds the heavy alms bowl when it is full, warns his master should he be in danger of transgression, does not interrupt, and is quick-witted, smart, and clever. E. M. Hare, *The Book of the Gradual Sayings*, vol. 3 (London: Luzac and Company for the Pali Text Society, 1961), 106.

54. "From now on, you should think of your preceptor as a father, and your preceptor should think you as a son. From now on, for as long as you live, you should honor and serve your preceptor." Derge 'dul ba Ka 62b5–7. Anukul Chandra Banerjee, *Sarvāstivādan Literature*, 140.

55. It was also well adapted to the needs of elderly monks in their final days. Gregory Schopen, *Buddhist Monks and Business Matters*, 8–9.

56. Granoff cites evidence for the sale of young children to Jain monks. She also suggests that "surplus children" may have been given to Jain monasteries, just as they were in medieval Europe. See her article "Fathers and Sons," 619–20.

HUNGRY NOVICES: THE CASE FOR *UPĀSAKA PRAVRAJYĀ*

The theme of hunger recurs in the *Mūlasarvāstivāda* explanation of age rules for novice initiation. In the narrative commentary on the first rule setting the age for ordination at twenty, Upāli and his friends wake up in the night crying for food. In the commentary on the second rule, the newly initiated father–son pair from Śrāvastī draw criticism from the townspeople after the child's importuning leads his father to beg pastries from a baker. Finally, the question of how to provide food for Ānanda's orphaned nephews is the central dilemma of the story associated with the crow-scaring rule. These *vinaya* narratives about child initiation exhibit an awareness of the special nutritional requirements of children while betraying an anxiety regarding monastic communities' ability to accommodate physically and psychologically immature boys.

With respect to hunger, the noviciate is no more suited to the needs of children than is full monkhood. It is true that novices, with their ten precepts, are subject to fewer restrictions and depravations than monks. The commonly accepted rules of training for the novice, however, dictate that he should not eat at unsuitable times.[57] As generally understood, this precept forbids eating between noon and dawn of the following day.[58] Technically, then, assuming that the rule about eating out of time applied for Middle-Period Indian novices, only a fewer number of precepts, and not the ten *śikṣāpadas,* would solve this problem of hunger.

Here, we might recall the *Pravrajyāvastu* passage cited above stating the necessity of preliminary trainings for monks and establishing both the *upāsaka* and *śrāmaṇera* levels. Although not typically interpreted as such, the inclusion of the *upāsaka* initiation as a preliminary step in the initiation of novices in the Mūlasarvāstivāda *karmavācanā* literature raises the possibility of *upāsakas* holding only five precepts in monastic settings. Canonical and commentarial literature define the *upāsaka* not as a householder per se but as one who has taken the triple refuge, cultivates five virtues, and has pledged to practice some number of the five *upāsaka* precepts.[59] Granted, the context of these canonical and *śāstric* discussions imply their pertinence to lay devotees. Still, there is nothing intrinsically domestic about the *upāsaka* state. Indeed, according to the *Pravrajyāvastu*'s detailed descriptions of the ordination rituals, a novice postulant must pass through the stage of *upāsaka* before receiving the *pravrajyā* ordination.[60] First he is told about the restrictions to joining the order,[61] then he is initiated as an *upāsaka* by means of a triple recitation of the refuge formula

57. Derge 'dul ba Ka 51a.2–3. Curiously, the Gilgit *Bhikṣukarmavākya* text has dropped the rule about eating at the wrong time, actually listing only nine of the ten *śikṣāpadas.* The text does recognize that there should be ten, however: *anena . . . daśamenāṅgena.* Anukul Chandra Banerjee, *Sarvāstivādan Literature,* 61.

58. Jayarakṣita explains "eating at the wrong time" as eating anytime between one "'hair short of midday" and dawn of the next day. J. Duncan Derrett, *A Textbook for Novices,* 21.

59. Giulio Agostini, "Partial *Upāsakas,*" in *Buddhist Studies,* ed. Richard Gombrich and Christina Scherrer-Schaub (Delhi: Motilal Banarsidass, 2008), 1–34.

in front of his teacher, and is administered the five precepts.[62] At some later point the candidate asks his preceptor for the novice ordination. The exact time interval between these two phases of the *pravrajyā* ordination is not specified. Under ordinary circumstances, they would have been performed consecutively, but there also could have been reasons for performing them days, weeks, or even years apart. The important point is that the text clearly discusses the *upāsaka* vows in the context of candidates intending to shave their heads, wear monastic robes, and wander forth, not in the context of lay devotion.[63]

While almost entirely speculative at this point, the possibility of *upāsaka* renunciant is mentioned here because it represents an institutional niche

60. Derge 'dul ba Ka 48b.1–49a.5 Anukul Chandra Banerjee, *Sarvāstivādan Literature*, 108–9. Guṇaprabha's account of the *śrāmaṇera* initiation also describes the necessity of passing through the stage of *upāsaka*. See *Vinayasūtra* 1.5–6; Sankrityayana 9. So does the *Bhiksukarmavākya* (a Sanskrit recension of the Mūlasarvāstivāda ordination ritual discussed above) discovered at Gilgit and published in Anukul Chandra Banerjee, *Two Buddhist Vinaya Texts in Sanskrit* (Calcutta: World Press Private Limited, 1977), 59. In his descriptions of Buddhist India, the Chinese pilgrim Yijing also speaks of candidates definitely intent on wandering forth passing through the *upāsaka* stage on their way to becoming novices. See John Strong's translation in *The Experience of Buddhism: Sources and Interpretations: 3rd ed.* (Belmont, CA: Thomson Wadsworth, 2008), 76–77.

61. The restrictions concern certain persons who are not eligible to become Buddhist monks, including slaves, criminals, soldiers, hermaphrodites, *nāgas*, and lepers. At the time of *upasampadā*, the postulant is interviewed privately and publicly to verify that no restrictions apply. Derge 'dul ba Ka 53b.3–54b.5. Anukul Chandra Banerjee, *Sarvāstivādan Literature*, 119–22.

62. Derge 'dul ba Ka 49a.4. Anukul Chandra Banerjee, *Sarvāstivādan Literature*, 108. These are listed here as forbidding lying, stealing, sexual impropriety, intoxication, and visiting places of ill repute (*bhag med pa'i gnas*). This list is anomalous. Typically, the five precepts begin with the vow to refrain from taking life and end with the vow to abstain from taking intoxicants. While there is variability across traditions in the manner and order in which the ten *śikṣāpadas* of the novice are listed, the first five are uniform. It is possible that since in the Tibetan text no connecting particle *dang* ("and") separates the precept about intoxicants and the precept about visiting disreputable places, these were meant to be just one item, and that the very important first precept, refraining from taking life, was dropped inadvertently. The Sanskrit *Bhikṣukarmavākya* discovered at Gilgit and edited by Banerjee contains the conventional list starting with refraining from taking life and ending with avoiding intoxicants. The Sanskrit makes it clear that the ban on pubs is part of the ban on intoxicants and not a separate item, since the word for "drinking establishment" is compounded with a series of synonyms meaning "intoxicant": *sur āmaireyamadyapramādasthānaṃ*. Anukul Chandra Banerjee, *Two Buddhist Vinaya Texts in Sanskrit*, 60. For a chart comparing sectarian *vinaya* texts on the precepts and discussion, see J. Duncan Derrett, *A Textbook for Novices*, 20, 7–9. For Pāli reference, see *Khuddakapātha*, ed. Helmer Smith (London: Pali Text Society, 1915), 1–2. For translation of the Pāli, see John S. Strong, *The Experience of Buddhism*, 121–22. For discussion, see Mohan Wijayaratna, *Buddhist Monastic Life According to the Texts of the Theravāda Tradition,* trans. Claude Grangier and Steven Collins (New York: Cambridge University Press, 1990), 166–67.

63. The Newar ordination ritual *bare chuyegu,* still practiced today, provides an interesting example of the Mūlasarvāstivādan *pravrajyā* ritual in action. Alexander von Rospatt writes: "With the intention of taking *pravrajyā*, the Mūlasarvāstivādan

especially well suited to children. The inclusion of the *upāsaka* initiation as a unit within the series of initiatory rituals leading eventually to full ordination would have provided a means of institutionalizing young children and other candidates for whom following all ten of the novice precepts could pose a hardship. In contemporary Burma, young children are accepted into monastic communities at the rank of pre-novice. They wear white and typically head the alms procession, ringing a bell as they walk to announce the monks' approach. But is there any evidence that the *upāsaka* initiation was used in this way historically? We will return to this interesting possibility shortly. For now it will suffice to note that several officially recognized denizens of the monastery did actually hold fewer than ten vows. The Mūlasarvāstivāda *Vinaya* lawyers articulated, for instance, a liminal monastic category called the "shaven-headed householder" to accommodate sick, childless householders in their last days. These partially ordained monks had their heads shaved but were not given the rules of training. They were therefore partially ordained novices, not yet full members of the community but eligible for hospice care from monks nonetheless.[64] Monastic candidates who had previously been members of non-Buddhist religious orders were required to undergo a four-month probationary period called *parivāsa*. According to *Mahāvagga* I.38, such an individual had to shave his head, don Buddhist robes, crouch down with hands folded before the preceptor, and recite the refuge formula thrice. If the community was satisfied with his behavior after four months, he could then undergo *upasampadā*. In his *Vinayasūtra*, Guṇaprabha specifically states that such individuals live as *upāsakas*.[65] Finally, female candidates undergoing the required two year probationary period (*śikṣamānā*) held only six vows.

Of course, it is also possible that very young novices holding ten precepts were simply not required to adhere strictly to all ten. A rule allowing sick monks to

candidate first goes for refuge to the Buddha, *dharma*, and *saṃgha*, vows to the keep the five main rules (*śikṣāpada*), and thus becomes explicitly a lay follower, an *upāsaka*. In a second step of what is *clearly one ritual sequence* [my emphasis], he seeks the *saṃgha's* permission to "go forth," asks for a preceptor, and then has his hair shaved, takes a bath, and in exchange for his lay outfit dons the monk's robes and implements, handed over by the officiating *upādhyāya*." See "The Transformation of the Monastic Ordination (*pravrajyā*) into a Rite of Passage in Newar Buddhism," in *Words and Deeds: Hindu and Buddhist Rituals in South Asia*, ed. Jorg Gengnagel, Ute Husken, and Srilata Raman (Wiesbaden: Harrassowitz Verlag, 2005), 203.

64. Discussed by Gregory Schopen in "The Good Monk and His Money in a Buddhist Monasticism of 'the Mahāyāna Period,'" in *Buddhist Monks and Business Matters* (Honolulu: University of Hawaii Press, 2004), 10–11.

65. *upāsakatāntaṃ caturo māsān parivāsayet saṃgho dattvā parivāsaṃ kramaṇā*, Guṇaprabha 2.106. Another interesting example of a sangha member whose status is qualified or partial is the penitent (*śikṣādattaka*). Shayne Clarke describes this type of monk or nun as occupying "a kind of limbo state between full monkhood and noviceship" but "still bound by the regulations of the Vinaya." See "The Existence of the Supposedly Non-existent *Śikṣādattā-śrāmaṇerī*: A New Perspective on *Pārājika* Penance," *Bukkyo Kenkyu* 29 (2000), 160. Another example is found in the literature on nuns' ordination. Even after a nun had completed the probationary period and undergone procedures within the nuns' sangha, she was understood to have received

consume medicines at any time of day provides a loophole that Buddhist monks have sometimes used to justify eating outside of the prescribed time.[66] Young novices could have been allowed to employ the same loophole. Furthermore, at least in the Pāli tradition, novices were not disciplined or expelled for breaking certain precepts. In fact, only the first five precepts, and not the one governing eating, was included in the Pāli *Vinaya* list of actionable offences for a novice.[67] It is likely that crow-scarers were not politically or institutionally important enough to merit their own ritual category. Rather their teachers and preceptors may have simply tinkered with categories and prescriptions already existing in the tradition, creating a system in which underage novices floated in an institutional no-man's land between *upāsaka* and *śrāmaṇera.*

RĀHULA AND THE CROW-SCARING RULE: INITIATION AS RITE-OF-PASSAGE

Whatever its original intent or primary function, it is almost certainly not the case that the crow-scaring rule was exclusively applied to indigent or needy children throughout the Indian sangha's history. Indeed, one encounters well-off children, fussed over by their still-living parents, being ordained under this rule in Sanskrit Buddhist narratives.[68] The paradigmatic example of such a boy being initiated at a young age is Siddhartha's son, Rāhula.[69] The story of Rāhula's going forth is well-known in the Pāli tradition as the occasion for the establishment of an important rule requiring monks (and nuns) to obtain the permission of their parents before wandering forth.[70] Hearing too late of his grandson's initiation, a saddened Suddhodana makes a poignant speech about the grief of parents whose children leave them. Acting as an advocate for parents, Suddhodana pleads with the Buddha to require parental consent for ordination in the future. The parental consent rule receives a different narrative context in the *Pravrajyāvastu*, but the story of the Buddha's return to Kapilavastu and Rāhula's subsequent initiation are not forgotten, appearing instead in the *Saṅghabhedavastu*.[71] In most of the sectarian *Vinayas*,

only *brahmacaryopasthāna,* "support in pure life." No actual ordination could take place until she appeared before the monks' community. See Edith Nolot, *Règles de discipline des nonnes Bouddhistes* (Paris: College de France, 1991), 533.

66. Mahāvagga 6.1.

67. *Mahāvagga* 1.57–60. See n. 17 above.

68. See, for instance, *Avadānaśataka* 82 and *Karmaśataka* 3, both discussed later.

69. *Mahāvagga* 1.54; Hermann Oldenberg, *Vinaya Texts*, 102–4.

70. See Kate Crosby's article, "Only If You Let Go of That Tree" for discussion of this rule in the Pāli commentarial tradition. See also her contribution in this volume.

71. For the rule concerning parental permission, see Derge 'dul ba Ka 78b.3–79b.5. Anukul Chandra Banerjee, *Sarvāstivādan Literature*, 177. For the story of Rāhula's ordination, see Raniero Gnoli, *The Gilgit Manuscript of the Saṅghabhedavastu*, 2: 30–32. See Strong, *The Legend of Upagupta*, 221–24 for analysis of Rāhula's importance in *Mūlasarvāstivāda* tradition.

Rāhula's ordination is also the occasion for briefly laying out the procedure for novice initiation, though not in the Mūlasarvāstivāda *Vinaya*, which, as we have already discussed, includes separate instructions for the *pravrajyā* initiation in the *Pravrajyāvastu*.[72] The *Mahāvastu*, a *vinaya* text associated with the Mahāsāṅghika-lokottaravādins, contains a detailed version of the Rāhula story structurally similar to the laconic Mūlasarvāstivāda *Vinaya* recension.[73] Since they are both from the Buddhist Sanskrit tradition, are roughly contemporaneous, and resemble one another, both versions will be consulted here.

The *Mūlasarvāstivāda Vinaya* and *Mahāvastu* accounts of Rāhula's ordination contain several interesting elements that are highly relevant to the initiation of young children as Buddhist novices. First, in both texts, the Buddha visits his former family in Kapilavastu six or seven years after his enlightenment. In both texts, Yaśodharā is said to experience an unusually lengthy, six-year pregnancy, so Rāhula's birth coincides with the Buddha's enlightenment. When the Buddha reaches his hometown, therefore, his son is about seven years old, an age that the reader will now recognize as significant.[74]

Both of these stories also contain a passage in which the Buddha's announcement of his intention to initiate his son as a novice prompts Śuddhodana to request a reprieve. In the Mūlasarvāstivāda *Vinaya*, he asks for just one day, in the *Mahāvastu*, for seven. Keep in mind that Rāhula has already committed himself in word and action to wandering forth and, indeed, is specifically described in the Mūlasarvāstivāda *Vinaya* as following along behind the Buddha, an attitude associated with young monastic servants called *paścācchramaṇa*[75] or "following-after-ascetics."[76] The lord grants Śuddhodana his reprieve, and the latter then uses the time to perform several of what appear to be childhood life cycle rites (*saṃskāra*). These are characterized simply as

72. Erich Frauwallner, *The Earliest Vinaya*, 76.

73. *Mahāvastu* 3.254–72. J. J. Jones, trans. *The Mahāvastu* (London: Luzac & Co., 1987), 3: 256–61.

74. This manipulation of chronology is not found in the Pāli tradition, but there also Rāhula appears to be a young child. In the *Nidānakathā*, a version of the Buddha's early life and career from the Pāli *Sutta-piṭaka*, for instance, Rāhula is born before his father's Great Departure; however, the Buddha's visit to Kapilavastu seems to occur quite early in his preaching career, only just after the conversions of Sariputta and Moggallāna. This would make Rāhula a boy of perhaps seven or eight.

75. See Gregory Schopen's discussion of the word *paścācchramaṇa* in his article for this volume. In it, he correctly observes that *śramaṇa*, which can be translated as "toiling or laboring," should be distinguished from *śramaṇera* (novice) when rendering *paścācchramaṇa* into English. Thus, he suggests "menial at the back" as a substitute for the less accurate renderings such as "following-after-novice.". Of course, *śramaṇa* also refers to a mendicant or ascetic and, as Bhikkhu Anālayo has pointed out in a personal email correspondence, is sometimes used as an honoric or alternative for *bhikṣu*. For the purposes of this article, I have chosen to translate this term as "following-after-ascetic" in order to reflect the most common meaning of the term *śramaṇa* in Buddhist contexts. Schopen's observation that the term *śramaṇa* also connotes "toil" or "effort" should be borne in mind, however, especially in view of evidence that young monastic boys acted as peons for senior monks.

76. *rāhulabhadraḥ kumāro bhagavataḥ pṛṣṭhataḥ pṛṣṭhato 'nubaddhaḥ*, Gnoli, Vol. 2, 31.

pūja in the Mūlasarvāstivāda *Vinaya*,[77] but as a birth ritual (*jātikarma*), tonsure (*cūḍākaraṇa*), and what appears to be the ear-piercing ritual (*kuṇḍulavardhana*) in the *Mahāvastu*.[78] Here, then, is an account of a young child pledged to the sangha but undergoing rituals associated with Vedic Hinduism, a pattern we will see below in another example of Buddhist child initiation.

In the *Mahāvastu*, when the time comes for the initiation ritual itself, the Buddha advises Śāriputra to ordain Rāhula "in the way the young wander forth in the noble teaching and discipline [*yathā śāriputra ārye dharmavinaye pravrajya kumārabhūtasya*]."[79] The elder is to have the boy recite the refuge formula three times and accept the five precepts. Rāhula is then to say, "Establish me as an *upāsaka* with these five precepts," followed by a triple recitation of "I, Rāhula, follow into homelessness the Buddha, who has himself also wandered forth." Rāhula is then to state his intention to also follow the novice's ten *śikṣāpada* for as long as he lives.[80] At the conclusion of these recitations, Rāhula's hair is cut and he is led away to a seat of grass (*tṛṇasaṃstaraka*).[81]

This grass seat does not appear in the *Pravrajyāvastu* description of the novice ordination ritual.[82] If this feature is mere literary ornamentation, it is well fashioned. The Buddha himself sat on cut grass during the night of his enlightenment.[83] Furthermore, those who, in wandering forth, have accepted the ascetic resort (*niśraya*) of tree-dwelling can expect no better resting place. The image of the newly tonsured prince gently led by two monastic elders to a grass seat is all the more striking since, according to the *Mahāvastu*, he had only just vacated the soft lap of his mother, Yaśodharā, who drew him to her while attempting to dissuade him from following his father's path.[84] According to Boris Oguibenine, however, this feature is more than literary ornamentation. In Buddhist literature, the arrangement of a seat for a Buddhist convert always precedes his first instruction in the Buddhist teachings. Both the arrangement of a seat for the disciple and the instruction of a disciple are typically indicated by causative forms of the verb *pra* √ *jñā* (to instruct). Oguibenine believes that the curious importance given to the arrangement of a seat for

77. Raniero Gnoli, *The Gilgit Manuscript of the Saṅghabhedavastu*, 2: 32.

78. *Mahāvastu* 3.263. *Jātikarma* and *cūḍākaraṇa* are both mentioned in the Vedic *Gṛhyasūtras*. The ear-piercing *saṃskāra* is referred to as *karṇavedha* in Brahmanic literature. It isn't mentioned in the earlier Vedic texts but appears in the *smṛtis*. Rajbali Pandey, *Hindu Saṃskāras: Socio-religious Study of the Hindu Sacraments* (Delhi: Motilal Banarsidass Publishers, 1969, 1994) 70–110. Pandurang Vaman Kane, *History of the Dharmaśāstra*, (Poona: Bhandarkar Oriental Research Institute, 1974), 2 part 1: 188–267.

79. *Mahāvastu* 3.268. This phrase can also be found at *Mahāvastu* 3.269, where Buddha's instructions and Yaśodharā's pleading are reprised in brief.

80. *Mahāvastu* 3.268. The *Saṅghabhedavastu* states that Rāhula is initiated but provides no detail.

81. *Mahāvastu* 3.269.

82. Nor in the Pāli description, nor in Guṇaprabha's *vinaya* digest, the *Vinayasūtra*.

83. *Mahāvastu* 2.131.

84. *Mahāvastu* 3.264–65. Reprised at 3.269–70.

the initiate in Buddhist narratives, and the linguistic conflation of teaching and seat-arranging, stem from Indian Buddhists' Vedic "patrimony." The Buddhist ritual of arranging a seat for the new initiate recycles and reframes features of Vedic preparatory rituals involving seats.[85]

The progression from candidate to novice is sketched dramatically here. Rāhula is guided through an ordered series of verbal and physical actions. He takes refuge, then accepts the five precepts, then states his intention to wander forth in imitation of the Buddha, then finally accepts the ten precepts, at which point his topknot is shaved and he is escorted to his semantically laden grass seat. If one takes into account Śuddhodana's performance of childhood *saṃskāras* prior to the ordination, Rāhula's ritual journey from being Yaśodharā's child to Śāriputra's novice appears even more graduated and complex, beginning, at least symbolically, at his birth and progressing all the way to monastic initiation. The Rāhula ordination story mixes technical and literary description of monastic procedures and cannot be read as *karmavācanā*. The general understanding of the ordination process implied by this text is, however, crystal clear: many ritual steps, each one rather shallow, mark the progression of a Buddhist boy from infancy to membership in the monastic community. Furthermore, the rituals of ordination are understood to build upon the foundation laid by the childhood *saṃskāras* of the lay householder, to share with them a ritual syntax. In the Rāhula ordination story, the performance of the *saṃskāras* molds an inchoate, impure infant into a pure high-caste boy on the cusp of community membership. His topknot symbolizes his socially and ritually refined status. The ordination ritual picks up the action by initiating this well-prepared boy as a Buddhist monk, removing that same topknot in the process. Yet again, a Vedic ritual feature is made use of by Buddhists to signal a change of status (monastic initiation).[86]

CHILD MONASTICS IN BUDDHIST NARRATIVE: THE BOY ASCETIC WHO FOLLOWS BEHIND

We have seen that the *Pravrajyāvastu* excavates institutional spaces suitable for children. An additional source of information about child monastics from

85. Boris Oguibenine, "From a Vedic Ritual to the Buddhist Practice of Initiation into the Doctrine," in *Buddhist Studies Ancient and Modern*, ed. Philip Denwood and Alexander Piatigorsky (London: Curzon, 1983), 121.

86. The symbolism of the topknot is given special attention in the Mūlasarvāstivāda *Vinaya* tradition and its commentaries, which prescribe that the hair be cut in two stages during the novice ordination. The *upāsaka* sequence requires all but the topknot to be cut. During the second part of the *pravrajyā*, then, the candidate's topknot is removed. Alexander von Rospatt discusses this topic in detail, and in relation to the Newar tradition of temporary novice ordination. See his article "The Transformation of the Monastic Ordination (*pravrajyā*) into a Rite of Passage in Newar Buddhism," 203–6. Guṇaprabha 1.12–14 specifically mentions the cutting of the *cūḍā* as part of the *śrāmaṇeratvopayana*.

the Sanskrit Buddhist tradition is Buddhist narrative literature, especially the *avadānas*. As it turns out, the young "following-after-ascetic" or *paścācchramaṇa* (also referred to in Sanskrit as a *śramaṇoddeśa*), is a common figure in Sanskrit Buddhist narrative, so named because his special role is to walk behind the elder monk on the latter's begging rounds, carrying his bowl. The *avadāna* genre, a story-telling tradition closely related to the Mūlasarvāstivāda *Vinaya* tradition, allows for a free elaboration on this figure of the young monastic assistant. Since the special function of the genre is to dramatize the law of cause and effect (*karman*), *avadāna* stories often depict the *paścācchramaṇa* and master as connected in past lifetimes, their relationship of *niśraya* reinforced and undergirded by shared past-life experiences. In addition, *avadānas* evoke an idealized emotional relationship, one characterized by tender affection and a strong sense of paternal duty on the part of the teacher, grateful and eager devotion on the part of the student. Interestingly, these stories often portray something of the attitude of the young candidates' parents, who sometimes balk at surrendering their beloved children to the monastery. In them we also glimpse the troubles (illness, academic failure, and irrepressible rowdiness, for example) that can visit young monastics.

The most important contribution of the *avadāna* literature to the present study, however, is its portrayal of a pattern of child initiation not directly discussed in the *Pravrajyāvastu*: the prenatal pledging of children to the sangha. The following story about the child initiate Sumanas is from the second-century collection of Buddhist narratives, the *Avadānaśataka*:

> There was a certain very wealthy, very fortunate householder in Śrāvastī, whose house was extensive and large, and who was furnished with wealth that rivaled that of Kubera. He married a woman from a family of equal rank. He frolicked with her, made love with her, and slept alongside her. After frolicking, making love, and sleeping together, sons were born [but they all] died. The elder Aniruddha was a daily visitor in that house. On day, a thought occurred to the householder: "This elder Aniruddha has the reputation of being a master because of the ripening of his past deeds. Therefore, I will ask him for help. [I will tell him] that if a son is born to me, I will give [the child] as a following-after-ascetic (*paścācchramaṇa*)." The elder Aniruddha was invited into the house by the devoted householder. After food was offered, [the householder] asked [Aniruddha] for help: "Elder, if my son, once born, survives, I will give [him as a following-after-ascetic]." The elder Aniruddha said, "Let it be thus, but you must remember your promise."
>
> After that, he frolicked, made love with and slept alongside his wife. After he frolicked, made love, and slept with her, his wife became pregnant. From her body emanated a fragrant scent. After nine months passed, she was delivered. The child, who was extremely beautiful, agreeable to the eyes, amiable and divinely benevolent, was born covered by a garment of celestial flowers. After his family celebrated his birthday festival, he was given the name

"Sumanas." Then the householder respectfully invited the elder Aniruddha to the house, and the child was offered to him. The elder Aniruddha presented the child with red-brown monastic robes and uttered the blessing, "May he have a long life."

When seven years had passed, [the child] was presented to the elder by his parents. Having ordained him, the elder Aniruddha granted him the power of mental attention. Because [Sumanas] applied himself, was completely focused, and worked with great zeal, he achieved arhatship after realizing the unstable nature of this wheel of life with its five hindrances, striking down the stations of all the karmic constituents with [knowledge of] the essential nature of things (which is destruction, death, dispersion, and loss), and destroying all the mental impurities . . . . While repairing his dust-heap robes he approached the eight liberations and returned with every stitch of the needle.

Then, at a later time, the elder Aniruddha said: "Go little son, bring the water of the River Ajiravatī." Then the *śramaṇoddeśa* Sumanas took the pot and went down to the River Ajiravatī. There he bathed and, after filling the pot with water, attained heaven. First the pot went, then the *śramaṇoddeśa* Sumanas.[87]

Children like Sumanas who are pledged while in the womb or before conception are stock characters of the Buddhist *avadānas*.[88] Problems with child

87. J. S. Speyer, *Avadānaśataka: A Century of Edifying Tales Belonging to the Hīnāyāna* (The Hague: Mouton & Co., 1958), 2: 67. The story of Sumanas is also found at *Karmaśataka* 10, available only in Tibetan *Kanjur*, Derge mdo sde Ha 5b.7. For a synopsis in French, see M. L. Feer, "Le Karma-śataka," *Journal Asiatique* 17 (1901), 65–66.

88. There is the *avadāna* of the sick child Pūrṇa. Pūrṇa is recruited by Aniruddha, who seems to have a special gift for helping infertile couples. His story is found at *Karmaśataka* 3. Derge mdo sde, Ha 11a.3 summarized in M. L. Feer, "Le Karma–śataka," 65–67. There is also the tale of a little house dog reborn in the womb of his mistress. The little dog who loves the elder Śāriputra and becomes his following-after-novice after being reborn in his former mistress's womb is found at *Karmaśataka* 2, *Kanjur*, Derge mdo sde Ha 5b.7. Summarized in M. L. Feer, "Le Karma-śataka," 63–64. The story of the two tiger cubs reborn as human twins in the womb of a *brāhmaṇī* occurs in the Chinese *Aśokarājāvadāna*. Upagupta finds the two starving cubs and then causes them to be reborn in the house of a *brāhmaṇa* family. The family pledges one of the twins to Upagupta. The other twin does not wish to be left, however. Upagupta ordains both as novices at eight years of age. Taisho 2042 (50) 121b-22b. Translated in John S. Strong's *The Legend and Cult of Upagupta*, 134. The *Divyāvadāna* contains stories of two elders who were pledged before birth. Saṅgharakṣita's ordination story is found at *Divyāvadāna* 23. E. B. Cowell and R. A. Neil, *The Divyāvadāna: A Collection of Early Buddhist Legends* (Cambridge: Cambridge University Press, 1886), 329–31. Upagupta's story is found at *Divyāvadāna* 26. E. B. Cowell and R. A. Neil, *The Divyāvadāna*, 351–556. See also John S. Strong, *The Legend and Cult of Upagupta*, 75–79. The elder Dhītika, Upagupta's main disciple and successor, was also pledged before birth. His ordination story is found in the *Aśokarājāvadāna*, Taisho 2042 (50): 126a-b. It is translated in John S. Strong, *The Legend and Cult of Upagupta*, 134–35. I am indebted to Strong's scholarship for

mortality or fertility are a notable feature of some such stories.[89] Taken together, available references to the pledging of unborn children in Sanskrit Buddhist literature strongly suggest that, however common, this practice was considered somewhat unorthoprax and may well have been a regional practice peculiar to the Northwest. While included with some frequency as a plot element in the *avadānas*, no *Pravrajyāvastu* texts recognize this type of monastic recruitment, as far as I know. A certain passage from the abhidharma compendium, the *Abhidharma-Mahāvibhāṣa* (which will be discussed in more detail below), does debate, however, the legitimacy of parents taking "refuge and discipline" on behalf of their children, a probable reference to the practice of pledging very young children to the sangha.[90] Unfortunately, the formal process of this type of pledging is not usually described with a high level of detail in the *avadāna* literature. My discussion of the pledging procedure will be based on the above-cited Sumanas story, which is one of the more detailed.

In most of the pledging stories, the senior monk targets a particular family he perceives to be especially ripe for the dharma. He makes a point of visiting alone, thereby signaling his intention to collect a child for the monastery and inviting a response from the householder. The householder always reacts as expected, expressing his surprise that a respected elder of the sangha should travel alone and offering one of his own unborn sons to serve as the elder's attendant. In the case of *Sumanas Avadāna*, however, it is the childless householder who takes the lead by formally inviting Aniruddha for a meal in hopes that this powerful personage might somehow cause a son to be born to him.

Aniruddha arrives at the house and is duly fed. The householder then pledges his firstborn son to the sangha, on the condition that the child survive his infancy. Aniruddha acknowledges this promise and states his hope that the householder will honor it when the time comes. At the time of the child's birth, Aniruddha returns and the infant is formally offered (*niryātita*) to him. He accepts the child by blessing him and making him a gift of robes, and then he departs, leaving the infant in the care of his parents. At a later time, the elder returns to take him to the monastery, where the child undergoes the *pravrajyā* initiation.

There is considerable variation among pledging stories in the avadāna literature regarding the age of the candidate when he is collected and carried off to the monastery. The majority of pledged children whose stories are recounted

alerting me to the topic of prenatal pledging in Sanskrit Buddhism and for some textual references.

89. For a discussion of child-pledging as child protection, see Schopen's article in this volume. My own study of this topic, entitled "Pregnant Words: South Asian Buddhist Tales about Fertility and Child Protection," is forthcoming in *History of Religions*.

90. Louis de La Vallee, "Documents d'Abhidharma, part 2," *Mélanges Chinois et Bouddhiques* 1 (1932), 83–84. Strong (1992) notes this reference in his book *The Legend and Cult of Upagupta*, 59 n. 9, and assumes that it refers to the pledging of unborn children. Schopen also discusses this reference in his article for this volume.

in Buddhist avadāna literature seem to leave home and enter the monastery as children. Some remain with their parents, living the life of a pious householder, presumably an *upāsaka*, until young adulthood. In the *Sumanas Avadāna*, for instance, the child's age is stated to be seven or eight.[91] Sometimes the child is simply said to be collected "at the time of initiation (*rab tu dbyung ba'i dus*),"[92] a reference, presumably, to the crow-scaring rule. In other cases, the pledged child grows to maturity at home before leaving for the monastery.[93]

While most pledging stories narrate only the elder's initial visits to the house before the child's birth, and his subsequent return to initiate the boy and claim him for the monastery, the Sumanas story adds other details, regarding the elder's visit and gift of monastic robes at the time of the child's birth. These events take on some significance in light of the above discussion concerning *upāsaka pravrajyā*. The *Sumanas Avadāna* provides a possible example of the detachment of the *upāsaka* initiation from the rest of the novice ordination. Here, the elder presents a set of monastic robes to a baby, a solemn ritual gesture connoting *niśraya*-type obligations for both parties in the exchange. Obviously, since the infant cannot yet walk or talk or even eat solid food, this relationship is not to be enacted for a number of years. The *Sumanas Avadāna* seems to describe, then, a delay between the preliminary act of commitment and the later act of initiation, a delay necessitated by the physical and psychological immaturity of the candidate. This is exactly the type of delay that I have speculated may sometimes have existed between the *upāsaka* and novice phases of preliminary ordination in the case of very young children.

Taking this passage as evidence that the *upāsaka* vows may conceivably have been administered to semi-monastic children is problematic, however, since the infant Sumanas does not appear to actually become an *upāsaka*, there being no mention of refuge or precepts. This difficulty is mitigated somewhat if we reexamine the Sumanas passage in the context of another relevant passage from yet another text, the important early first-millennium abhidharma compendium from the Sarvāstivāda school mentioned previously, the *Abhidharma-Mahāvibhāṣa*. This passage presents an argument in favor of parents' taking "refuge and discipline" on behalf of babies:

91. See the tiger twins story in John S. Strong, *The Legend and Cult of Upagupta*, 134.

92. *Karmaśataka* 2, Derge mdo sde, Ha 8a.5. *Karmaśataka* 3. Derge mdo sde, Ha 13b.3.

93. For the case of Dhītika, see John S. Strong, *The Legend and Cult of Upagupta*, 135. Upagupta has a career in his father's perfume shop before receiving both levels of initiation by Śanakavāsin as a young adult. John S. Strong, *The Legend and Cult of Upagupta*, 75–79. Saṅgharakṣita also is described as "big" when he departs for the monastery, having grown quickly, "like a lotus in a lake." The story goes on to explain that he, "being in his last rebirth, is given the higher and lower ordinations and taught the four *agamas* by the Venerable Śāriputra." Like Upagupta, Saṅgharakṣita appears to be over twenty when he finally leaves home. E. B. Cowell and R. A. Neil, *The Divyāvadāna*, 330–31.

> It is necessary to take refuge and discipline for an infant, so that later he will be inclined to practice it well. In effect, if, having grown up, he violates the three Refuges and commits bad actions, others could reproach him thus: "When you were still in your mother's womb, or when you were small, you had already taken refuge and discipline. How can you now violate the jewels and commit these bad actions?" Thus averted, he will feel shame, respect the jewels, abstain from bad actions, and take and accept refuge and discipline anew. Since it gives these advantages, one should take refuge on behalf of an infant.
>
> And if the mother or other people take refuge and discipline for the infant, it is also so that the gods and spirits protect the child, so that since he has taken refuge, the gods and the god spirits who respect the jewels would protect the baby and see to it that he doesn't die, that he would not become sick.
>
> What good actions has that infant practiced during previous existences so that before his birth or when he is small, one takes refuge and discipline for him in this way? In his previous existences, that child always took pleasure in the praise of the jewels and pure virtue. He exhorted innumerable myriads to take refuge and practice virtue. He gave necessaries to those committed to refuge and discipline. It is because of this that, in this existence, he obtains the advantages spoken of. As the Sutra says, "Those who take refuge in the Buddha do not fall into negative destinies, are born among the gods or men, and obtain joy and happiness."[94]

This passage's references to taking "refuge and discipline" on behalf of an infant can be referring only to establishing him in the *upāsaka* vows, the first step on the initiatory ladder. It also seems to be a reference to the type of quasi-monastic birth ritual so briefly but tantalizingly mentioned in the *Sumanas Avadāna*. Demonic attack was considered to be the chief cause of infertility, miscarriage, and infant death in ancient India, and the power of the Buddha and his monks to protect children from such attacks was an important motivation for pledging children to the sangha, as in the case of the childless householder, Sumanas's father. It is quite possible, therefore, that this pledging narrative neglects to mention that baby Sumanas was administered "refuge and discipline" because there was simply no need to provide a high level of detail: any Buddhist audience would have understood the full ritual to have taken place, any Buddhist story-teller would have known how to improvise the details. To sum up, if the *Abhidharma-Mahāvibhāṣa* does indeed refer to initiating babies as five-vow *upāsakas* (a disciplinary regime any baby has an excellent chance of upholding), and if the monastic birth ritual mentioned in the Sumanas is indeed a laconic reference to the same practice mentioned in the *Mahāvibhāṣa*, then the Sumanas story provides at least a literary example of

94. Translated from the French of Louis de la Vallée Poussin, "Documents d'Abhidharma, part 2," 83–84.

a child undergoing his initiation into monastic life in well-spaced stages: first *upāsaka pravrajyā*, then *śrāmaṇera pravrajyā*.

The Sumanas story also links an ordinary life-cycle ritual (here called the *jātimaha*) and a preliminary to the act of wandering forth (the presentation of monastic robes). We observed a similar association of what have generally been considered disparate ritual traditions in the story of Rāhula's ordination. After Śuddhodana requests a delay before his grandson's *pravrajyā*, he performs what appear to be life-cycle rituals. Though far from conclusive, these obscure elements in the Sumanas and Rāhula stories raise the intriguing possibility that the childhood life-cycle rites of Buddhist householders were linked up with monastic rituals of initiation, at least in the Mūlasarvāstivāda and related traditions. The weaving together of householder and Mūlasarvāstivāda monastic ritual traditions is, of course, evident in contemporary Newar Buddhism in Nepal, a phenomenon which scholars have generally viewed as characteristic of a Hindu–Buddhist syncretism unique to Nepali religion. The present research suggests that Newar Buddhism may resemble Sanskrit Buddhism in the classical period more closely than was previously imagined.[95]

CONCLUSION: CHILD MONASTICS AS SOCIAL GLUE

A careful reading of the Mūlasarvāstivāda *Pravrajyāvastu* alongside other texts from the Sanskrit Buddhist tradition reveals an ongoing and evolving legal accommodation of all but the very youngest children in the male sangha. While adolescents between the ages of fifteen and twenty were able to join a semi-rigorous noviciate well-fitted to their developmental stage, younger children were provided the status of what I am calling "crow-scarer," a subnovice rank that may or may not have required them to follow all ten rules of training. These younger children may have approached local monastic communities in Middle-Period India for any number of reasons. They may have been indigent like Ānanda's nephews, child-oblates like Sumanas, or, like Rāhula, influenced by some other type of family connection with the Buddhist sangha. Some may

95. Newar child initiation (*bare chuyegu*) is the best example of this blending of the householder and monastic ritual agendas. As von Rospatt has shown, this ritual of temporary novice ordination also functions as a coming-of-age ritual, analogous to brahmanical *upanayana*, in Newar Buddhist society,. Working in the opposite chronological direction, as it were, von Rospatt makes a point similar to the one I make here, namely that Indian Buddhism had adapted to its surroundings, and to the ritual habits of the laity, in a manner similar to what we see in Nepal. He bases his assertion on the fact that an important Sanskrit ritual manual used by Newar Buddhists, the *Kriyāsaṃgrahapañjikā*, is antique enough to reflect the situation in Buddhist India several centuries before Buddhism's supposed demise. Alexander von Rospatt, "The Transformation of the Monastic Ordination (*pravrajyā*) into a Rite of Passage in Newar Buddhism," in *Words and Deeds: Hindu and Buddhist Initiations in India and Nepal*, ed. Astrid Zotter and Christof Zotter (Wiesbaden: Harrassowitz, 2010), 208. See also Lewis and Emmerich's chapter in this volume.

even have approached the monastery independently out of a personal sense of religious vocation. A quasi-monastic, subnoviciate, "crow-scarer" rank would have provided very young candidates with a recognized though subordinate place in the Buddhist monastic community, even if they were incapable of taking full part in monastic discipline and practice. Assuming that the picture presented here of a highly articulated monastic structure able to accommodate candidates of almost any age is accurate, whether monastery-bound children carrying some unspecified number of vows lived at home like Sumanas or in the monastery like Ānanda's nephews would have depended more on finances and logistics than ritual standing.

This chapter does not come close to exhausting the topic of child ordination in Indian Buddhism. In particular, it lacks any discussion about the roles of nuns and the importance of gender in the ordination of children. *Vinaya* texts tell of children born to nuns inside the nunneries. These nunnery-born boys and girls apparently received different treatment by virtue of their gender.[96] Age rules also varied somewhat according to gender.[97] The comparison of female ordination and child initiation is another promising direction for research, since a variety of semi-monastic states seem to have been invented or adopted from other mendicant traditions to address the special status of women and children. Though these topics cannot be dealt with here in depth, I mention them as important examples of monastic lawyers' efforts to accommodate and manage nonmale, nonadult persons in the Buddhist monastic community.

Where it concerned children, monastic practice was a particularly porous site of interface with the lay community. As we have seen, there are several scenarios in which children marked for the monastic life may have occupied a semi-monastic status for many years until they matured. Pledged children, for instance, are described as living at home for an unspecified period of time. Young children, especially those who were indigent, were related to other

96. Derge 'dul ba Da 143a.1 and forward. See Shayne Clarke, "Family Matters in Indian Monastic Buddhism" for an excellent discussion of these rules.

97. The *Bhikṣuṇī Vinaya* contains a puzzling rule about when a person scholars have interpreted to be a "married girl" (Pāli: *gihigatā*; Sanskrit: *gṛhicaritā*) is allowed to be ordained. Scholars do not agree on how to interpret the *Pācittika* rule in question, since the wording is not altogether clear. Some (Edith Nolot, K. R. Norman, P. Kieffer-Pülz) say she must not be less than twelve years of age while others (I. B. Horner, Gustav Ross, Oskar von Hinüber) argue that she must have been married for twelve years (or more). See Gustav Roth, *Bhikṣuṇī-Vinaya: Manual of Discipline for Buddhist Nuns* (Patna: K. P. Jayaswal Research Institute, 1970), 245; and Edith Nolot, *Règles de discipline des nonnes Bouddhistes*, 392–93. Von Hinüber has questioned "married girl" as an adequate translation of *gihigatā*. He argues that the original meaning of this word was "a woman known to householders" and that it referred to wandering female ascetics. *Gihigatī* is just one of several technical terms found only in the *Bhikṣuṇī Vinaya* and not in the *Bhikṣu Vinaya* that appear to derive from non-Buddhist, more particularly Jain, sources. These borrowings suggest to von Hinüber that nuns were a late and controversial addition to the Buddhist *sangha*, accepted only as part of Buddhists' effort to compete successfully with other ascetic orders. See Oskar von Hinüber, "The Foundation of the Bhikkhunīsaṃgha," 7–10.

sangha members, or had been pledged *in utero* may have lived in the monastery and worn monastic robes without actually taking full novice vows. Such arrangements would have increased the likelihood of their eventually joining the monastery as *bhikṣus* and would have enhanced sustaining connections with lay patrons. They also indicate the extent to which lay and monastic communities were mutually intertwined, interpenetrating, and interdependent. Shaven-headed children, tied to lay communities by blood and bone and to monastic communities through solemn ritual and well-established institutions, must have provided an especially powerful impetus for the laity and the sangha to join forces, combine resources, and forge ongoing social connections.

Monastic ritual practices around the initiation of children appear to have been particularly prone to borrowing from the householder's ritual repertoire. In fact, it may be best to view monastic and lay rites-of-passage not as sharply distinguished or opposing traditions but as part of the same Indic continuum of ritual practice. It is not difficult to recognize similarities between Buddhist deity worship and the *pūjas* of non-Buddhists. The ritual practices surrounding child ordination indicate that, surprisingly, Buddhist rites of initiation can likewise be viewed in the context of Vedic Hindu social ritual. In short, much like Newar Buddhists, Middle-Period Indian Buddhists accommodated and even incorporated non-Buddhist social rituals into their own monastic rites-of-passage. I would argue that this phenomenon had less to do with some sort of syncretism at the margins (though frontier communities may well have been less orthoprax) than with the fact that Indian Buddhists never really broke with Indic ritual tradition.[98] The study of children, who provided a vital social link between celibate monastics and fertile householders, brings the interesting Vedic underbelly of Mūlasarvāstivāda monastic practices from the Middle Period into view.

It has become abundantly clear that Indian Buddhist monasteries were not only communities of mature individuals who renounced the world out of a personal desire for awakening, at least not for most of their history, and certainly not during the Middle Period in India. Not all of their members were mature; many did not personally choose the monastic life but rather were chosen for it; and some wandered forth without having all their adult teeth, to say nothing of a developed religious vocation. Of these juvenile monastics, few actually renounced "the world" in any meaningful sense. On the contrary, just like their *brāhmaṇa* counterparts, young Buddhist monastics were engaged in a highly articulated, graduated, and complex form of Indian communal life that was thoroughly enmeshed, socially and ritually, with the world beyond the monastery gates.

98. The ritual obligations of monks is a topic that was addressed quite a few years ago by Gregory Schopen in "The Ritual Obligations and Donor Roles of Monks in the Pāli *Vinaya*," *Journal of the Pali Text Society* 16 (1992), 87–107. Reprinted in *Bones, Stones, and Buddhist Monks*, 72–85. He bases his study on sections from the Pāli, Mūlasarvāstivāda, and Mahāsāṅghika *Vinayas* that discuss occasions when monks are permitted to break the rains retreat. These include attending weddings, deaths, and, apparently, births, though Schopen doesn't present detailed evidence for the latter.

CHAPTER 3

The Buddha's "Childhood"

The Foundation for the Great Departure

VANESSA R. SASSON

human beings are not born once and for all on the day their mothers give birth to them, but... life obliges them over and over again to give birth to themselves.[1]

How does one define "childhood" in the Buddha's case?[2] The modern debate about the concept of childhood notwithstanding,[3] is it possible to talk about a childhood per se for the Buddha? In ancient India, childhood would likely have been classified along the lines of the *saṃskāras* that high-caste males were expected to undergo, but the very idea of childhood assumes a period of development and transformation that is not necessarily applicable to the Buddha's hagiography. For some sources, the Buddha was an exceptional being covered with the marks of a Great Man, surrounded by cosmic announcements of his presence, and requiring the experiences of one last and particularly pristine childhood before buddhahood would be fully actualized. For other sources, however, the Buddha had been perfectly awakened for incalculable lifetimes,

1. Gabriel García Márquez, *Love in the Time of Cholera* (trans. E. Grossman. New York: Penguin, 1989), 165.

2. I am indebted to André Couture, Anant Rambachan, and Amy Langenberg for their invaluable comments and suggestions on earlier drafts of this chapter. I would also like to thank Stephen Batchelor for sharing some of his thoughts with me concerning the Buddha's youth. Some of these recently appeared in his book *Confessions of a Buddhist Atheist* (New York: Spiegel and Grau Trade, 2011).

3. A discussion about the concept of childhood was sparked by Philippe Ariès's seminal work, *L'enfant et la vie familial sous l'Ancien régime* (Paris: Éditions du Seuil, 1973), and has been going ever since. See the introduction to this volume for discussion.

and his childhood narratives function as nothing more than a play for his audience's benefit. Either way, the range of permitted childhood tropes is limited: there is only so much development Buddhist hagiographers will allow when the Buddha is at stake. This limitation renders any discussion of the Buddha's childhood particularly constraining, unless one rereads the *jātaka* tales as the stories of his youth instead. In the *jātakas* at least, the Bodhisattva is presented as being in the process of transformation, working diligently toward perfection from one lifetime to the next. If these past lives ultimately function as a long prelude to the moment of his awakening, they seem to fulfill the role of his childhood best.

Despite this general aversion to the concept of personal transformation in the Buddha's hagiography, the theme of his childhood as it is presented in some of the early Pāli and Sanskrit writings merits consideration. The Buddha's childhood has not stimulated much academic discourse, with André Bareau functioning as the most prominent exception. Bareau produced a tremendous study of the Buddha's childhood, clearly recognizing the importance of the Buddha's early years in his larger hagiography, and yet he concluded with a comment about the limited scriptural materials available on the subject. He argued that such limitations either may be the result of the Buddha's lack of interest in his own youth or may simply be the product of his modesty. Either way, though, Bareau became convinced that, despite the seventy-five pages of analysis he could provide, little could be said about the Buddha's childhood.[4]

Bareau's study is an extraordinary contribution, but his conclusion does not end the discussion. He was, after all, hoping that some historical reconstruction might be possible, something this chapter will not attempt. Rather, this chapter aims to understand why the hagiographies told the stories they did. In other words, this is not about the Buddha so much as about the hagiographical construction of the Buddha. Although Bareau is certainly correct that, compared with the abundant post-awakening narratives available, scriptural material pertaining to the Buddha's youth are few, a rich field of resources nevertheless remains to be explored. Childhood is a transitional period in which the foundation for adulthood is laid. The Buddha's childhood functions as a foreshadowing of the man to come. As we shall see, each hagiography presents the Buddha's childhood in a way that reflects the man the authors imagined the Buddha to have been, ultimately revealing, among other things, their stance in the docetic debate. His childhood, moreover, is particularly significant in that it may be expected to unlock a pivotal hagiographical question: Why did the Buddha leave home? What were the circumstances surrounding his youth that motivated, and indeed even justified, his Great Departure? The Four Sights alone do not answer these questions.

4. André Bareau, "La jeunesse du Buddha dans les Sūtrapiṭaka et les Vinayapiṭaka anciens," *Bulletin de l'École Française d'Extrême Orient* 61 (1974), 267.

PALACE LIFE

In all hagiographical reconstructions, attention must be paid to both the overall picture and the details. The overall picture of the Buddha's youth is unanimously one of royal splendor. The Pāli Canon is generally restrained in its elaboration, particularly in comparison to texts like the *Buddhacarita* or the *Lalitavistara*, but it does refer to the extravagant surroundings of the Bodhisattva's childhood. Consider, for example, the description provided by the *Sukkhamalasutta* of the Anguttara Nikāya:

> I was delicately nurtured, O monks, extremely delicately nurtured. At my father's house, O monks, lotus ponds were made. In one of them, O monks, blue lotuses bloomed, in another, red lotuses, and in another white lotuses, all just for me. I only used sandalwood from Kāsi, O monks. My head dress, jacket, undergarment, and outer robe were all from Kāsi, O monks. A white parasol was continually carried over me, O monks, lest cold, heat, grass, dust, or dew touch me.
>
> I had three palaces: one for the winter, one for the summer, and one for the rainy season. In my palace for the rainy season, O monks, during the four months of the rainy season, I was surrounded exclusively by female musicians, and I did not descend from the palace [during this time]. While in other homes, servants ate porridge of broken rice together with sour gruel; in my father's house, servants ate rice and meat.[5]

The elaborate luxury is here quite evident. He had ponds containing different colored lotus flowers, beautiful clothes, a sunshade held perpetually over him, multiple palaces at his disposal, entertainment in his honor, and even his servants are said to have eaten exceptionally well. The *Mahāvastu* provides a lengthier description of this elaborate childhood, dedicating almost four pages to the details of his luxurious surroundings. Here we learn that not only did he have access to different palaces for the different seasons, but these were furnished with couches made of "gold, silver, and precious stones,"[6] and he was provided with "various means of conveyance, elephants, horses, boats and palanquins."[7]

5. *Anguttara Nikāya* iii 38; a similar description appears in the *Māgandiyasutta* (Majjhima Nikāya i 514).
6. *Mahāvastu* II: 115; for an English translation, see J. J. Jones, trans., *The Mahāvastu* (London: The Pali Text Society, 1987).
7. *Mahāvastu* II: 116.
8. *Lalitavistara* 125; for an English translation, see R. L. Mitra, trans. *The Lalita Vistara: Memoirs of the Early Life of Sakya Sinha* (Chs. 1–15) (New Delhi: Sri Satguru, 1998). For an English translation of the Tibetan edition, see G. Bays, trans. *The Lalitavistara Sutra: The Voice of the Buddha, The Beauty of Compassion,* 2 vols. (Berkeley, CA: Dharma Publishing, 1983).

The most elaborate description of his surroundings, however, belongs unsurprisingly to the *Lalitavistara*. Throughout this text, reference is made to the unyielding pomp and splendor of the Bodhisattva's environment: for example, it takes him four months after his birth to return to the palace because 500 Śākyas had built 500 dwellings for him and they each begged the king for an opportunity to host him;[8] 20,000 young women were commissioned to attend to him, and the king's friends, advisors, and relatives on both sides likewise offered 20,000 young girls[9]—resulting, it therefore seems, in a few hundred thousand serving girls! Moreover, the Bodhisattva is said to have spent his days in a palace

> decorated with all kinds of jewels and beautiful ornaments tastefully set off. Uplifted on it were parasols, flags, and pennants, ornamented with numerous strings of jeweled bells. Hundreds of thousands of silken fabrics streamed all about it. Innumerable jewels were set on it. Garlands of pearls were suspended from it. It was provided with stairs decorated with silken carpets and jewels..

Clearly, no conceivable expense is spared in descriptions of the context in which the young Bodhisattva was raised.

The *Buddhacarita* likewise records an extravagant lifestyle throughout its narrative (similar to the ones noted above), but it includes two groups of details worthy of note. First, according to the *Buddhacarita*, the kingdom was not only extravagantly wealthy, but its subjects formed a peaceful and harmonious community, rendering it a realm "free from famine, from danger and disease."[10] There were no beggars other than "the men who had taken the vow,"[11] and no one was "rude to elders, not generous, untruthful, hurtful, or nonobservant."[12] The people built parks and temples, hermitages and wells "in their love for the dharma,"[13] and husbands were "never unfaithful to wives or wives to their husbands,"[14] so that, "independent, free of theft and such vice, free of enemies and enemy rule, his kingdom was prosperous and peaceful."[15]

Most sources will agree with these statements to some extent, and they may be attributed to various causes: the prosperity may be the result of deity intervention in anticipation of the Bodhisattva's arrival, it may be the product of his accumulated karma or of his family's accumulated collective karma, it may provide necessary contrast with the hardships he endured during his wandering years, or it may simply help explain why the Bodhisattva chose this kingdom for

9. *Lalitavistara* 209.
10. *Buddhacarita* 2:14; for an English translation, see Patrick Olivelle's translation, *Life of the Buddha*, Clay Sanskrit Library (New York: New York University Press, 2008).
11. *Buddhacarita* 2:10.
12. *Buddhacarita* 2:11.
13. *Buddhacarita* 2:12.
14. *Buddhacarita* 2:14.
15. *Buddhacarita* 2:15.

his final rebirth.[16] The *Buddhacarita*'s vision, however, includes a specific explanation for the kingdom's prosperity. According to this text, all of these attributes are directly related to the quality of the king sitting on the throne (i.e., the Buddha's father).[17] The *Buddhacarita*, as we shall repeatedly see, is an unusual text in the vast collection of early hagiographies, as it may be "best interpreted as an apologetic work presenting the Buddhist response to brahmanical attacks."[18] Legend has it that its author was a converted brahmin, and given the brahmanic content of the text, there is likely much truth to that belief. The *Buddhacarita* regularly compares the Bodhisattva with the heroes of the *Rāmāyaṇa* and the *Mahābhārata*, and it is particularly concerned with the issue of dharma (here understood as "responsibility" or "obligation").[19] A case in point is the description of King Śuddhodana, who emerges as a magnificently dharmic king, fulfilling all of his ritual obligations and embodying the ethical standard associated with a just king, thereby inevitably producing natural, social, and military prosperity.[20] The Bodhisattva, therefore, was raised not only in a luxurious environment, but in an equally peaceful, harmonious, and happy one.

The other interesting group of details to emerge from this text has to do with something much more mundane: the Bodhisattva's toys. According to the *Buddhacarita*, the young Bodhisattva enjoyed

> Golden toy-carts drawn by deer,
> Ornaments appropriate for his age,
> Toy elephants, deer, and golden horses,
> Chariots yoked to toy oxen,
> And dolls resplendent with silver and gold.[21]

While the literature consistently portrays the Bodhisattva as having been raised in great luxury, none but the *Buddhacarita* remembers that childhood requires

16. I refer here to his contemplations in Tusita heaven before his rebirth. For a detailed discussion, see Vanessa R. Sasson, *The Birth of Moses and the Buddha: A Paradigm for the Comparative Study of Religions* (Sheffield: Sheffield Phoenix Press, 2007), 95–101.
17. An elaborate description of the king in similar terms can also be found in the second canto of Ashvaghosha's *Saundarananda*. For a translation, see Ashvaghosha, *Handsome Nanda*, trans. Linda Covill. Clay Sanskrit Library (New York: New York University Press, 2007).
18. Patrick Olivelle, "Introduction" in Patrick Olivelle, trans., *Life of the Buddha*, Clay Sanskrit Library (New York: New York University Press, 2008), xxiv.
19. The first to point this out was, surprisingly, not Johnston in his introduction and translation of the text (see E. H. Johnston, *Aśvaghoṣa's Buddhacarita or Acts of the Buddha* (New Delhi: Motilal Banarsidass, 1995)), but Alf Hiltebeitel more recently. See his article "Aśvaghoṣa's Buddhacarita: The First Known Close and Critical Readings of the Brahmanical Sanskrit Epics." *Journal of Indian Philosophy* 34, no. 3 (2006), 229–86.
20. A description of Śuddhodana as a dharmic king can be found in 2:33–2:45.
21. *Buddhacarita* 2:21

toys. This text alone makes reference to the Bodhisattva *as a child* and not just as the axis around which a kingdom declares its wealth—a child who had toys and ornaments, chariots and dolls "appropriate for his age." This text calls attention to the Bodhisattva's childhood as no other text does, allowing the Bodhisattva *to be a child* with toys and thus to *not* be the Buddha just yet.

Two significant objectives are fulfilled by these luxurious and harmonious surroundings. First, they establish the Buddha in a clear royal framework—an essential ingredient for any serious ancient Indian hagiography. It has long been argued that the Śākyas probably controlled a very small territory and were thus a far cry from the powerful and wealthy kingdom recorded by the scriptures.[22] Regardless of historical reality, though, the sources were uncharacteristically unanimous in their agreement that kingship and the Buddha were deeply intertwined. Gonda's now classical study of ancient Indian kingship[23] is unequivocal concerning the association between kingship and divinity. Kings were, in his words, members of "a class of powerful beings, regarded as possessing supernormal faculties and as controlling a department of nature or activity in the human sphere."[24] The Buddha's relationship to kingship is evident throughout the literature and at various points in his hagiography. It is an inescapable element of his story, for without it, he would not have been taken seriously by his audience.

The second objective fulfilled by this opulent inheritance is narrative flow. As was mentioned in the introduction, one of the most important questions raised by the Buddha's hagiography concerns the causes and conditions that gave rise to his Great Departure. Contextualizing his departure is a central concern for the sources, leading them to a wide range of answers. The most common narrative to answer this question is his experience with the Four Sights, but other options also present themselves. According to some texts, his departure was motivated by the sight of the sleeping dancing girls who appeared like corpses[25]; according to others, it was his experience under the rose-apple tree (see next section). Each hagiography (or hagiographic fragment) associates his departure with a particular episode (or combination of episodes) that might explain one of the most pivotal moments in the Buddha's story. The

22. See, for example, E. J. Thomas, *The Life of Buddha as Legend and History* (Delhi: Motilal Banarsidass, 1997), 20; T. W. Rhys-Davids, *Buddhism, Its History and Literature* (New Delhi: Asian Educational Services, 2000), 92; Michael Carrithers, *The Buddha* (Oxford: Oxford University Press, 1983), 13; H. Nakamura, *Gotama Buddha* (Los Angeles: Buddhist Books International, 1977), 11.

23. See his three-part series: J. Gonda, "Ancient Indian Kingship from the Religious Point of View," *Numen* 3 no. 1 (1956), 36–71; J. Gonda, "Ancient Indian Kingship from the Religious Point of View (Continued)," *Numen* 3 no. 2 (1956), 122–55; and J. Gonda, "Ancient Indian Kingship from the Religious Point of View (continued and ended)," *Numen* 4 no. 2 (1957), 127–64.

24. J. Gonda, "Ancient Indian Kingship from the Religious Point of View," 59.

25. Liz Wilson's study is worth mentioning here. See her book *Charming Cadavers: Horrific Figurations of the Feminine in Indian Buddhist Hagiographic Literature* (Chicago: University of Chicago Press, 1996).

cause behind his departure is inextricably linked to the cause of suffering and thus functions as the very fabric out of which Buddhist teachings emerge. The extravagance with which the Bodhisattva was raised—the lavish luxury, beauty, and harmony that surrounded him from the moment of his birth—is directly related to the problem of suffering. Indeed, the *Māgandiyasutta* makes this connection implicit: after describing the luxurious surroundings of his youth, the Buddha draws a parallel between addiction to sensual pleasure and the experience of a leper "with open wounds on his body, being devoured by worms, scratching those open wounds with his nails, and then cauterizing them over burning coals."[26] Although the Sanskrit sources repeatedly clarify that the Bodhisattva does not fall prey to the ravages of this environment, in the Pāli Canon the suggestion is clear: the Bodhisattva has to leave home for a life of homelessness if he is to be cured.

The Bodhisattva's extravagant palace life is therefore understood by some as a shield that protected him from experiencing old age, sickness, and death. According to other sources, however, palace life functioned as an obstacle because it was too hectic and made too many demands. According to the *Mahāsaccakasutta*, home life for the Bodhisattva was "crowded and dusty."[27] According to the *Mahāvastu*, it was "too full of hindrances. The way of the religious life is in the open air. It is not possible for one living at home to live the holy life that is utterly bright, blameless, pure and clean."[28] Whether the Bodhisattva departed from his palace because it represented delusion or because it was too distracting, however, there is no question that his experience as a youth determined his decision to go forth into homelessness.

THE ROSE-APPLE TREE

Bareau's examination of the Buddha's childhood includes a thorough study of the episode under the rose-apple tree.[29] It would not be much of a contribution to repeat what has already been done, but a sketch of the narrative nevertheless merits representation and some points need to be addressed. There are, moreover, a few texts Bareau did not include in his study that provide variant readings worthy of note. For those who are not familiar with the story, it takes place at some point during the Buddha's youth before his departure, during a plowing festival. While everyone is focused on the field, the Bodhisattva immerses himself in meditation. The *Mahāsaccakasutta* describes the incident thus:

26. *Majjhima Nikāya* i 506.
27. *Majjhima Nikāya* i 240.
28. *Mahāvastu* II: 114.
29. Hubert Durt's study of this episode must likewise be mentioned here. See his article "La 'visite aux laboureurs' et la "méditation sous l'arbre *jambu*' dans les biographies sanskrites et chinoises du Buddha" in *Indological and Buddhist Studies: Volume in Honour of Professor J. W. de Jong on his Sixtieth Birthday*, ed. L. A. Hercus et al. (Delhi: Indian Books Centre, 1982), 95–120.

> I remember when my father the Sakyan was plowing the field: I sat in the shade of a rose-apple tree, secluded from sensual pleasures and unskillful mental states; accompanied by reasoning and investigation, I entered and abided in the first jhāna, with rapture and bliss born of seclusion. Could that be the path to awakening?[30]

The episode may at first seem trivial; as Bareau notes, many of the early hagiographic sources eventually discarded it in favor of the story of the Four Sights,[31] and many modern biographies of the Buddha have similarly bypassed it.[32] Upon closer inspection, however, it becomes clear that this moment plays a pivotal role in the Buddha's journey toward renunciation and eventual awakening. While the palatial comforts that the young Bodhisattva was said to have been surrounded by may have served to temporarily cushion his experience of reality, this episode provides the Bodhisattva with the essential insight that liberation is, in fact, realistically attainable. Indeed, it may be understood as the fourth noble truth in narrative form—the good news of the Buddhist story that, while there may in fact be suffering, there is nevertheless an end to that suffering and a way to get there. Moreover, this serendipitous meditation answers a question that is posed by Chakravarthi Ram-Prasad in his study of child-narratives in the Hindu epics and that merits consideration here: "What is the state of youth? Is it one in which the intrinsic qualities... are already present, or is it one in which they are still to develop?"[33] The episode under the rose-apple tree suggests that the intrinsic qualities of buddhahood are already present in the young man, although it leaves some room for the possibility that those qualities require development.

As Bareau points out, this meditation also serves to render the future Buddha relatable to his audience:[34] the Bodhisattva undertakes the Great Departure because he has tasted the possibility of liberation—something universally available to anyone who tries. Of course, the episode develops a more magical twist over time, with the miracle of the sun's shade refusing to leave his side and the flying mystics who are stalled by an invisible force, unable to fly over his head despite having had the audacity to fly over the top of Mount Meru.[35] These anecdotes paradoxically *distance* the Bodhisattva from the reader, functioning as a reminder that, while meditative insight might be universally attainable, the Bodhisattva was not an Everyman; he was cosmically Other. The meditation under the rose-apple tree therefore renders the Bodhisattva relatable and yet completely unrelatable at the same time.

30. *Majjhima Nikāya* i 246.
31. André Bareau, "La jeunesse du Buddha," 266.
32. A noted exception to this rule is John S. Strong's book *The Buddha: A Short Biography* (Oxford: Oneworld, 2001).
33. C. Ram-Prasad, "Promise, Power, and Play: Conceptions of Childhood and Forms of the Divine," *International Journal of Hindu Studies* 6 no. 2 (2002), 152.
34. André Bareau, "La jeunesse du Buddha," 231.
35. See, for example, *Mahāvastu* II: 45 and Lalitavistara 176.

Both the *Mahāvastu* and the *Buddhacarita* provide additions to this narrative worthy of note. The *Mahāvastu* introduces the first meditation with the Bodhisattva strolling through his palatial grounds when a plow suddenly overturns a frog and a snake. A young boy nearby grabs the frog to eat and throws away the snake. The Bodhisattva is "deeply stirred by the sight" and thinks to himself: "Pleasure, the body and life itself are burnt out together. Now I shall attain the deathless release from existence."[36] The episode beneath the rose-apple tree takes place immediately thereafter, suggesting that one must be armed with an insight both into the cycle of suffering and into the possibility of release. The *Buddhacarita* is more elaborate but shares with the *Mahāvastu* a similar variant. In this version, the Bodhisattva has already encountered three of the Four Sights[37] and is now wandering through the woods feeling lost and confused. He comes across the sight of farmers plowing their fields. Insects, worms, and all kinds of tiny dead creatures litter the earth where the plow has passed, and as he beholds this sight, the Bodhisattva "grieved greatly, as if a kinsman had been killed."[38] But the death of the tiny creatures is not the only cause for his grief. Unlike other accounts, the Bodhisattva in this version is also affected by the laborers, "their bodies discolored by the wind, the dust, the scorching rays of the sun, oxen wearied by the toil of pulling the plows."[39] Great compassion overwhelms him as he encounters reality as he has never seen it before.

The Bodhisattva next seeks solitude in order to examine his mind. He finds a rose-apple tree and sits beneath it, immediately achieving "the state of mental stillness."[40] After profound contemplation and his seeing "rightly the evils of the world"[41] without giving in to "dejection or delight,"[42] the gods arrange for him to encounter the last of the Four Sights: the renunciant. With this encounter, the motivations for the Bodhisattva's departure are complete and soon after that he walks away.

A few points are worthy of note with regard to this account: first, unlike in previous versions, the Bodhisattva's perception of the cycle of suffering is not limited to a frog and a snake but extends to a much larger landscape of sentient beings. He sees the insects and the toiling laborers as well as the oxen. He does not identify with any one of them in particular but stands back and witnesses them all at once. The scene also reminds readers of his exceptionally sheltered existence: toiling laborers was surely a regular sight

36. *Mahāvastu* II: 45; Mahākassapa's hagiography likewise includes an account of watching animals turned up from the earth, resulting in an insight into the nature of suffering.
37. The *Buddhacarita* is one of the few early sources to include both the Four Sights and the rose-apple tree incident.
38. *Buddhacarita* 5.5.
39. *Buddhacarita* 5.6.
40. *Buddhacarita* 5.10.
41. *Buddhacarita* 5.14.
42. *Buddhacarita* 5.15.

for most people, but the sight of them manages to shock the Bodhisattva profoundly.[43]

Moreover, according to Alfred Foucher, the association between suffering and agricultural labor is not accidental. The *vinaya* includes numerous regulations forbidding monks from participating in any form of agricultural activities precisely because these necessitate suffering. They also encourage attachment to land and thus represent the antithesis of homelessness. By having the Bodhisattva experience repulsion at the sight of the laborers, he is identified with monasticism long before his establishment of the order.[44] The fact that in other accounts it is his father who is doing the plowing (a ceremonial and ritual act in these accounts) puts him in direct contradistinction with his father and the royal heritage he represents. As Strong notes, "the Bodhisattva is making the specific realization that what entails suffering is the reestablishment of kingship."[45]

The *Buddhacarita* version provides us with another interesting feature: the Bodhisattva does not stumble into contemplation as if by accident. On the contrary, he seeks a quiet space and contemplates with intention. It is as though he has done this before; contemplation is natural for the young Bodhisattva, for his qualities are intrinsic and require the help of new conditions for these to come to fruition. This view emerges in the *Mahāvastu* as well, in a story that takes place not long after his birth. The sage Asita reads the cosmic omens that announce the Bodhisattva's arrival and flies through the air to meet the newborn in person. The king welcomes him into their home and the following exchange takes place:

> Then the king asked, "Lord, what is the reason for your coming?" The seer replied, "I wish to see your son." At that time the boy had achieved a tranquil concentration and they thought he was asleep. "Lord, wait a little. Just now the boy is asleep." The seer replied, "Your majesty, the boy is not asleep." The king went close up in front of the boy and saw that he was awake.[46]

The meditation under the rose-apple tree was not his first—according to the *Mahāvastu* at least. The Bodhisattva had been immersing himself in *dhyānic* states since he was born. The episode of the rose-apple tree simply serves to highlight what had been there all along.

43. I cannot help but note the similarity that this version shares with the biblical story of Moses and the taskmaster. In Exodus 2, Moses encounters the Hebrew slaves as though for the first time. He obviously experiences a level of shock because soon after, he kills a taskmaster that was hitting a slave. The incident becomes known and he is forced to flee Egypt, thereby entering the next phase of his life, where his own version of "awakening" will take place.

44. Alfred Foucher, *La vie du Bouddha d'après les textes et les monuments de l'Inde* (Paris: Payot, 1949), 95.

45. John S. Strong, *The Buddha*, 47.

46. *Mahāvastu* II: 31–32.

THE BUDDHA AND HIS *SAṂSKĀRAS*

Childhood in ancient India was likely structured around a series of *saṃskāras that* high-caste males were expected to undergo. It is not clear how prevalent these rites were in ancient India, nor how consistently they were practiced, and indeed it has been argued that certain areas in the Middle-Gangetic valley were strongly anti-brahmanic during the period of early Buddhism, suggesting a possible rejection of such rites in the Buddha's region.[47] We cannot know whether the Buddha as a historical person ever underwent any of these, but for the fictive person of the Buddha[48] as imagined by the early hagiographers, it is clear that the *saṃskāras* had an important role to play in his story. By their presence or by their absence, the *saṃskāras* articulate a vision of the Bodhisattva that will contribute to our understanding of his Great Departure.

Saṃskāra is commonly translated as "rite of passage"—a moment of transition demarcated by a particular ritual, leading the recipient from one state of existence to another. Brian K. Smith, however, outlines a much more specific definition for the term, reminding his readers that the objective of any *saṃskāra* "is to make the thing or being fit (*yoga*) for its purpose. Fitness is of two kinds—that which arises by the removal of taints (*doṣāpanayana*) and that which arises through the generation of fresh, inner qualities (*guṇāntaropajanana*)."[49] He therefore redefines *saṃskāras* as rituals of healing and construction, which is helpful when considering the role *saṃskāras* play in the Buddha's hagiography. Different texts provide different lists of *saṃskāras*,[50] and it is not obvious which of these, if indeed any, would have applied to a young *kṣatriya* in Māgadha 2,500 years ago. The *śramaṇa* culture of the region may have had no use for these, but the later hagiographers certainly engaged with their reality, either by candidly circumventing them or by having the Bodhisattva undergo them only to transcend their necessity.

For most of the early Buddhist hagiographies, Vedic rites initiating the young Bodhisattva into specific doctrinal realities were deliberately avoided. Many texts, for example, describe great celebrations at the Buddha's birth that we might reasonably assume included *saṃskāra* rites, but the term itself along with the specifics of any particular ritual are nowhere to be found. Amy Langenberg's chapter in this volume demonstrates that, for the authors of the *Mahāvastu*,

47. See especially L. M. Joshi, *Discerning the Buddha: A Study of Buddhism and of the Brahmanical Hindu Attitude to It* (Delhi: Munshiram Manoharlal, 1983), 46 ff.; and D. K. Chakrabarti, "Buddhist Sites Across South Asia as Influenced by Political and Economic Forces," *World Arachaeology* 27 no. 2 (1995), 189–90.

48. I borrow the expression "fictive Buddha" from John Powers in his recent study, *A Bull of a Man: Images of Masculinity, Sex, and the Body in Indian Buddhism* (Cambridge, MA: Harvard University Press, 2009), 7.

49. Brian K. Smith, "Ritual, Knowledge, and Being: Initiation and Veda Study in Ancient India," *Numen* 33 no. 1 (1986), 66.

50. Michaels provides a list of forty traditional *saṃskāras*, with twelve functioning as the most essential. See Axel Michaels, *Hinduism: Past and Present*, trans. B. Harshav (Princeton, NJ: Princeton University Press, 2004), 74.

the traditional *saṃskāras* played a prominent role in Rāhula's life, but in the Buddha's story they are absent. The brahmanic apologetic, the *Buddhacarita*, is one exception. Not only does it make reference to the *saṃskāras*, but it seems to go out of its way to emphasize them throughout the Bodhisattva's youth. He was born, for example, "from the side of the queen consecrated by rites";[51] his father, the king, "performed his son's birth rite as prescribed";[52] and after ten days "filled with supreme joy, he offered divine rites with prayers, offerings, and other auspicious rites."[53] The Buddha was immersed in a world prescribed by Vedic ritual, rendering him a perfect high-caste male and thus fully acceptable to his brahmanic readers. The Buddha could not stand outside the tradition and also appeal to its members; the *Buddhacarita* therefore opts to present him in a brahmanic light (which may have been of particular necessity given the Buddha's stated *kṣatriya* origins) only to then have him transcend it. The superiority of the Buddhist tradition is rendered an inescapable conclusion.[54]

The most important rite—the *saṃskāra* par excellence that ultimately created high-caste status—was without question the *upanayana*. The purpose of this rite was, according to Smith, threefold: (1) to initiate the boy into "human society"; (2) to initiate him into Vedic study; and (3) to initiate him into fire sacrifice "and the life-long process of ritual self-construction."[55] Indeed, the dharmaśāstras repeatedly emphasize that, without this rite of initiation, high-caste status is not actualized.[56] In the words of the *Manusmṛti*, when a man spends his time investigating matters other than the Vedas, "while still alive he is quickly reduced to the status of a Śūdra, together with his children."[57] This is at the very root of why *upanayana* renders a man "twice-born" (*dvija*), for without the rite, a man cannot be said to have come fully into himself and his cultural, religious, and social inheritance. The once-born are *all* only once-born, regardless of their initial technical caste affiliation. The "twice-born" quality of this rite is therefore not merely metaphorical.[58] On the contrary, this

51. *Buddhacarita* 1.9.
52. *Buddhacarita* 1.82.
53. *Buddhacarita* 1.83.
54. This is a central argument in Olivelle's "Introduction." Another biblical parallel must be drawn here: Jesus as the perfect rabbi (particularly in Matthew) only to transcend Judaism with messiahship.
55. Brian K. Smith, "Ritual, Knowledge and Being," 65.
56. Brian K. Smith, "Ritual, Knowledge and Being," 67–68. See also Hartmut Scharfe, *Education in Ancient India* (Leiden: Brill, 2002), 102.
57. *Manusmṛti* 2: 168; see also 2: 172: "Such a man…is equal to a Śūdra until he is born from the Veda." For an English translation of the *Manusmṛti*, see Patrick Olivelle, *Manu's Code of Law: A Critical Edition and Translation of the Mānava-Dharmaśāstra* (New York: Oxford University Press, 2005).
58. For a discussion of the use of womb and rebirth imagery with regard to the *upanāyana*, see Walter O. Kaelber, "The "Dramatic" Element in Brāhmanic Initiation: Symbols of Death, Danger, and Difficult Passage," *History of Religions* 18 no. 1 (1978), 54–76. Also Walter O. Kaelber. "Tapas, Birth, and Spiritual Rebirth in the Veda," *History of Religions* 15 no. 4 (1976), 343–86.

second birth is viewed as a virtual replacement for biological birth, thereby demonstrating its exceptional role in high-caste social consciousness:

> Between the man who gave life and the man who gave the Veda, the man who gave the Veda is the more venerable father; for a Brahmin's birth in the Veda is everlasting, both here and in the hereafter. When, through lust for each other, his father and mother engender him and he is conceived in the womb, he should consider that as his mere coming into existence. But the birth that a teacher who has fathomed the Veda brings about according to rule by means of the Sāvitrī verse—that is his true birth, that is not subject to old age and death.[59]

The question inevitably surfaces: did the fictive Buddha undergo this *saṃskāra*? What are the implications if he did, and what are they if he did not?

The *Buddhacarita* is particularly concerned with direct representation of the *saṃskāras*, and while the *upanayana* is not explicitly referred to, the insinuation is certainly apparent: "he passed through his childhood years in the proper way; he went through initiation at the proper time; in a few days he grasped the sciences that were suitable for his family, that commonly take many years to grasp."[60] It is reasonable to conclude that this text imagines the Bodhisattva as having undergone *upanayana*, particularly given the text's central concern with dharma and the fulfillment of rites. Moreover, Indian literature is replete with examples of divine-like heroes undergoing this rite, such as Rāma,[61] the Pandava brothers, Kṛṣṇa,[62] and even the great battle god Indra.[63] If the Buddha was to have a chance against such competitors and if he was to be properly associated with high-caste status, the *Buddhacarita* had everything to gain by suggesting *upanayana* as part of its hagiography. Furthermore, if *upanayana* provides the necessary prerequisite for renunciation eventually to be possible, the Bodhisattva *had* to undergo this rite; otherwise, his Great Departure would have been performed under *adharmic* circumstances. Given that he left a bride and young child behind, along with an ageing father and an empty throne, the Bodhisattva's adherence to brahmanic dharma requirements was already suspicious. *Upanayana* provides his Great Departure with at least some semblance of technical propriety.

59. *Manu* 2: 146–48.
60. *Buddhacarita* 2: 23.
61. *Rāmāyana* 17:14; for an English translation, see Vālmīki, *Rāmāyana, Book One: Boyhood*, trans. R. P. Goldman, Clay Sanskrit Library (New York: New York University Press, 2005).
62. A reference to this event can be found in Harivaṃśa 79. For a discussion, see André Couture, "Kṛṣṇa's Initiation at Sāndīpani's Hermitage," *Numen* 49 no. 1 (2002), 37–57.
63. J. Gonda. *Change and Continuity in Indian Religion* (London: Mouton, 1965), 230.

Other sources were not as concerned with appealing to brahmanic sensibilities. On the contrary, for most of the rest of the literature, *upanayana* was a direct threat to the Bodhisattva's status and not something that would have raised it—and this for a few reasons. First and foremost, *upanayana* required initiation from a guru. Joel Mlecko's research demonstrates that in literature as early as the Vedas, the guru enjoyed a prominent place in his[64] students' lives. Potentially translated as "dispeller of ignorance," the guru was viewed as "the source and inspirer of the knowledge of Self,"[65] as "the one who blesses and enhances the seeker's spiritual life,"[66] and in many Upaniṣadic passages was equated with divinity, thereby encouraging a student to express "the same *bhakti* for his guru as for God."[67] Were the Bodhisattva to undergo initiation with such a guru, he would have owed him allegiance and veneration for the rest of his life. He would, moreover, become indelibly associated with the particular doctrinal tradition with which his teacher identified, thereby entrenching him in a school of thought and limiting him quite specifically. Most important, though, he would have had to acknowledge having had a teacher, someone to have dispelled ignorance for him and to have shown him the way. *Upanayana*, in other words, would have cancelled his eligibility for buddhahood.[68]

And yet it is well known that the Bodhisattva studied with a number of teachers during his wandering years. What, then, would be the difference? King Milinda posed this very question to the monk Nāgasensa in the *Milindapañha*, asking him how the Buddha can claim to never have had a teacher and yet also admit to having studied under Āḷāra Kālāma, among others. Nāgasena's answer is, predictably, that the Bodhisattva did have teachers prior to his awakening, but that they were merely teachers of "worldly things." For the purposes of "piercing omniscient knowledge in this supermundane Dhamma,"[69] however, the Buddha had no teacher. Nāgasena provides a list of these worldly teachers, the second of which merits attention:

> Further, Mahārāja, when the Bodhisatta's father, King Suddhodana, sent for the brahman called Sabbamitta, who was of good lineage, born of the *udicca*, who was versed in brahmanic scriptures and their interpretations, he dedicated

64. While evidence does present a history of female gurus throughout Indian history, the classical sources generally identify gurus as having been male—hence my use of the male pronoun here. See Patrick Olivelle, *The Aśrāma System: The History and Hermeneutics of a Religious Institution* (New York: Oxford University Press, 1993), 183 ff.
65. Joel D. Mlecko, "The Guru in Hindu Tradition," *Numen* 29 no. 1 (1981), 35.
66. Mlecko, "The Guru in Hindu Tradition," *Numen* 29 no. 1 (1981), 35.
67. Mlecko. "The Guru in Hindu Tradition," *Numen* 29 no. 1 (1981), 37.
68. Indeed, this concern with the role of the teacher emerges even in the *Buddhacarita*. After his awakening, the Buddha exclaims that he has no teacher and that he is "self-existent" with regard to the dharma (*Buddhacarita* 15:4, following Johnston's translation).
69. *Milindapañho* 236.

> water poured from a golden ceremonial vessel, handed over (the Bodhisatta), and said: "Train this boy."[70]

This second teacher is, without a doubt, a guru in the classical sense of the term who apparently initiated the young Bodhisattva into *upanayana*. The teacher is identified as a brahmin of pure lineage who was properly trained in brahmanic scriptures (which presumes the Vedas—*padakaṃ veyyākaraṇaṃ*), and the Bodhisattva's father ritually hands his son over to this teacher with the words, "Train this boy." A clearer and more obvious allusion to the *upanayana* rite could not be found.

This passage is certainly unexpected. While it could be argued that the Bodhisattva's other teachers were teachers of "worldly things," *upanayana* was an initiation into precisely that which was "unworldly." And unlike the case with other teachers, what distinguishes the guru who brings the boy through this particular rite is that the guru becomes the new parent, rebirthing him into the tradition and creating a permanent relationship with his disciple that would have followed the Bodhisattva for the rest of his life. How could Nāgasena propose such an obvious problem for the Buddha's hagiography? It is one thing for the *Buddhacarita* to propose it, but another thing altogether for the *Milindapañha*—a text that does not generally read as a brahmanic polemic. Did the authors of this text not recognize the significance of this rite when they had Nāgasena articulate it? It is difficult to imagine that for a North Indian compilation.

Rather, what we probably have here is evidence of a momentary lapse in Buddhist identity formation: Indian Buddhist authors were regularly caught between their cultural roots and their emerging Buddhist identity, with this conversation around *upanayana* serving as a case in point. This passage in the *Milindapañha* may be understood as one of many moments in Buddhist literature whereby the authors temporarily forget themselves, admitting to cultural norms that they were otherwise attempting to shed.

Buddhist problems with *upanayana* do not end here; if we are to follow Smith's interpretation, *saṃskāras* must be understood as "rituals of ontological creation, construction, and perfection."[71] They render complete that which is incomplete, perfect that which is imperfect. Obviously, most Buddhist hagiographers would have had a problem including such rites of passage into their narratives. The *Buddhacarita* is an obvious exception in this case, with its desire to appeal to a brahmanic audience overriding this concern.[72] It may be that the Bodhisattva had some growing up to do, but it is something else entirely to emphasize the need for "ontological construction and perfection." *Upanayana* in particular transformed a young man into a brahmin as no other rite could. If

70. *Milindapañho* 236.
71. Brian K. Smith, "Ritual, Knowledge, and Being," 66.
72. The *Milindapañha* will have to continue to be understood as having unconsciously revealed its Indian heritage here.

we recall those passages in the Pāli Canon in which the Buddha attempts to redefine the lines of brahminhood (arguing that brahminhood is determined not by birth—biological or otherwise—but by behavior),[73] it becomes clear that a rite such as *upanayana* provides an important challenge to the Buddha's hagiography: it ties him to a caste that buddhahood was apparently meant to transcend.[74] On the whole, then, the Bodhisattva's Great Departure was not only a physical departure from the world in which he was raised, but a departure from (or in the *Buddhacarita*'s case, a transcendence of) the rites and rituals that would have otherwise constrained him. And yet every once in a while those same rites resurface, reminding us of the cultural legacy encasing the Buddhist tradition.

FIRST DAY OF SCHOOL

Upanayana is not the only *saṃskāra* alluded to in the hagiographies. The *Lalitavistara* in particular presents a series of childhood narratives that are likely connected to ancient rites, such as the Bodhisattva first visit to the temple[75] (in which the gods bow at his feet rather than the other way around) and his first ornamentation[76] (in which he is bedecked by the royal jewels and yet magically outshines them).[77] Indeed, it is surely safe to suppose that many of the rites of passage normally associated with high-caste males would have made their way into his early hagiographies to some extent. Of these, one that merits special consideration is the rite surrounding the Bodhisattva's first (and perhaps only) day of school.

According to the *Lalitavistara*, the Bodhisattva's first day of school was determined by "a hundred thousand auspicious arrangements." He then walked to school surrounded by the most extravagant of retinues:

> He was accompanied and followed by ten thousand boys. He was followed by ten thousand cars loaded with food of all kinds, and with gold in the forms of ingots and coins. Whenever on the roads...the procession stopped, or people

73. See, for example, the *Assalāyanasutta* (*Majjhima Nikāya* ii 147–57).

74. This is not to say that caste has no place in Buddhism. On the contrary, caste has an ongoing relationship with Buddhist discourse and social organization. Rather, the point here is that, while on the one hand the Buddha must be identified as a high caste to gain credibility, he must also transcend caste himself on the other. For a good discussion of this inherent contradiction, see Jeffrey Samuels, "Buddhism and Caste in India and Sri Lanka," *Religion Compass* 1 no. 1 (2007), 120–30.

75. *Lalitavistara* 158–60.

76. *Lalitavistara* 163–65; this is most likely a reference to the ear-piercing *saṃskāra*, or the *karṇavedha*.

77. Incidentally, one rite that I do not see in the early narratives is the *cūḍākaraṇa*—the first haircut. I suspect that this is so because the Bodhisattva performs this rite himself when he becomes a renunciant.

> descended from their cars, then eight hundred thousand clarions resounded in harmony. Great showers of flowers were rained everywhere.... Eight thousand celestial maidens were strewing flowers to behold the Bodhisattva. Devas, Nagas, Yakshas, Gandharvas, Asuras, Garuḍas, Kinnaras, and Mahoragas, in semiform shapes, held forth flower garlands and clothes from under the sky. All the Śākyas, led by king Śuddhodana, proceeded in front of the Bodhisattva. With such a retinue did the Bodhisattva proceed to the school.[78]

The schoolmaster is overwhelmed by the glory of his new student, falling to his feet at the sight of him. Obviously there was no need for schooling in the Bodhisattva's case, because everything that can be known was mastered by him "many millions of ages (*kalpas*) ago."[79] To prove the point, the Bodhisattva picks up a tablet and asks the teacher which writing system he had intended to teach him, listing no less than sixty-four different scripts, many of which the teacher admits to never having heard of before. The teacher is "wonderstruck and deprived of all vanity and self-importance"[80] by the Bodhisattva's display. He declares the Bodhisattva to be "the god of gods, the great god, the noblest of all gods, the omnipresent. He is unrivalled, the chief, the unequalled soul of all in these regions."[81] The Bodhisattva then replaces the teacher and delivers a lesson to the students himself, associating a dharma teaching with each letter of the alphabet. In this way, "while the Bodhisattva was in the schoolroom, the minds of thirty-two thousand boys were imbued with the sequenceless perfect knowledge."[82]

This is an important event in the Bodhisattva's hagiography. Just as *upanayana* was generally eliminated because he could not have a teacher to whom he would owe allegiance, so his need for schooling was eliminated for the same reason. Harmut Scharfe's research provides invaluable insight into the nature of early Indian education and the role it would have played in a young man's life. Education, according to Scharfe, was not limited to reading and writing but included a wide range of subjects, such as "treatment of ancestors, arithmetic, portents, dialog, politics [?] [*sic*], treasure search, mythology, knowledge of *brahman*, knowledge of spirits, martial arts, astronomy, knowledge of snakes, and heavenly arts."[83] Its objective was to prepare a young man for complete participation in the social community. It sought to mold character and therefore was concerned primarily "with religious, ritual, and philosophic matters."[84] School in ancient India was not focused on developing a specialty but had much broader objectives.

If Scharfe is correct, we may conclude that school would have been as threatening to the Bodhisattva's hagiography as *upanayana*. Just as *upanayana*

78. *Lalitavistara* 166–67.
79. *Lalitavistara* 167.
80. *Lalitavistara* 168.
81. *Lalitavistara* 168–69.
82. *Lalitavistara* 170.
83. Hartmut Scharfe, *Education in Ancient India* (Leiden: Brill, 2002) 58.
84. Scharfe, *Education in Ancient India*, 47.

functioned as an "ontological birth" that helped construct a young man's identity, so school would have been essential in shaping a man's moral and religious understanding. Neither of these construction aids is welcomed in the Buddha's hagiographical tradition because, for most of the early hagiographies, the Buddha had no need of construction, required no ontological birth—other, that is, than the construction and ontological birth he provided for himself. The *Lalitavistara's* account of his day at school is an obvious reminder of this point: he goes to school only to demonstrate that he does not need it.

A parallel narrative appears in the *Jātaka-nidāna*. While he does not go to school in this text (or indeed in any other Pāli text, to my knowledge), an episode recounted here leads readers to the conclusion that the Bodhisattva's innate mastery rendered the need for instruction redundant. When the Bodhisattva was sixteen, a thread of local gossip reached the king's ears: "Siddhattha occupies himself with play; he is not trained in any of the arts. What will he do if war breaks out?"[85] The king brings this accusation before his son and asks him what he makes of it. The Bodhisattva's response is shockingly confident and straightforward: "My king, I do not require training in the arts."[86] He asks for a public competition to be arranged to demonstrate the truth of his statement and there performs such a dazzling display of natural archery skills that no critic is left standing.

An alternative version appears in the *Mahāvastu*: the king wants to marry the Bodhisattva to Mahānāma's daughter, Yaśodharā. Mahānāma, however, awkwardly admits that he cannot give his daughter to the king's son in good conscience because

> the lad has grown up among the women [and] he has not advanced at all in the arts, in archery, in elephant-riding, in handling a bow and sword, and in kingly accomplishments. In short, the prince has made no progress at all.[87]

This information causes the king great concern. When the Bodhisattva learns of the situation, he gently reassures his father and asks for a public competition in which all arts are welcome, "whether in knowledge of the arts, in archery, fighting, boxing, cutting, stabbing, in speed, in feats of strength, in the use of elephants, horses, chariots, bows and spears, or in argument."[88] The king is thrilled and immediately proclaims the competition, welcoming anyone who dares to go to battle against his son. On the day of the competition, an elephant is killed by Devadatta and is left in the middle of the road. No one is able to move her except for the Bodhisattva, who, with herculean strength, single-handedly hurls her over the seven city walls. He then displays his abilities in the ring and proves that no one is his equal "either in fighting or in

85. *Jātaka-nidāna* 58.
86. *Jātaka-nidāna* 58.
87. *Mahāvastu* II: 73.
88. *Mahāvastu* II: 74.

boxing."[89] He throws his bow into the ground and, foreshadowing King Arthur and recalling Lord Rāma, is the only one who can pull it out. The final competition involves archery with his arrow piercing through his target and dramatically entering the earth.

CONCLUDING REMARKS

Stories of the Bodhisattva's youth do more than simply raise him to superhero status; they also serve to articulate the Bodhisattva's unparalleled independence: without teachers or teachings, the Bodhisattva is still heads and shoulders above everyone else. His independence is marked not only by an absence of teachers, though: it is also highlighted by his mother's death. Sudhir Kakar describes the mother as the "all-important 'Other'";[90] she is at the root of the most profound attachment a young man may ever experience, and in Indian culture in particular is raised to unusually idealistic heights.[91] The mother is superseded only by the guru, who, according to the earliest writings, rebirths the disciple into high-caste status. The guru provides the ontological birth, replacing the biological birth provided by the mother. Both mother and guru are tellingly eliminated in the Buddha's hagiographies: his independence is a foregone conclusion as a result.[92]

Hagiographical anecdotes surrounding the Bodhisattva's youth also serve to raise the question of whether he even was a Bodhisattva at all, or whether he was a Buddha in a child's disguise. Many early hagiographical sources tend toward a presentation of the Buddha that highlights his awakening at his humanity's expense. This is particularly the case with the *Mahāvastu* in which he is a Buddha long before his moment under the Bodhi tree—as a god in Tusita, as a fetus,[93] and consequently also as a child—putting on a play for the benefit of others but not necessarily requiring any of these experiences for his own development. In its section on the attributes of a Buddha, the *Mahāvastu* declares that the Buddha's hunger, thirst, need for medicine, and even his need for a haircut are all said to be performed out of "conformity

89. *Mahāvastu* II: 75.
90. Sudhir Kakar, *The Inner World: A Psycho-analytic Study of Childhood and Society in India*, 2nd ed. (Delhi: Oxford University Press, 1990), 80.
91. This point is all the more significant when one considers that Kakar's conclusions emerge not only from his practice in psychoanalysis, but also as a result of his study of the epics and Purānas. He points to a number of classical narratives in which he believes motherhood is idealized, rendering his analysis contextually relevant to the Buddha's hagiography.
92. This argument is elaborated upon in Vanessa R. Sasson, "Māyā's Disappearing Act: Motherhood in Early Buddhist Literature," in *Family in Buddhism: Buddhist Vows and Family Ties*, ed. Liz Wilson (New York: SUNY, forthcoming).
93. This argument is elaborated upon in Vanessa R. Sasson, "A Womb with a View: The Buddha's Final Fetal Experience," in *Imagining the Fetus: The Unborn in Myth, Religion, and Culture*, ed. Vanessa R. Sasson and Jane Marie Law (New York: Oxford University Press, 2009), 102–29.

for the world" and not because the Buddha ever *was* hungry, thirsty, sick, or in need of a barber.[94] One of the most dramatic statements near the end of the section declares that the Buddha had attained perfection many incalculable eons ago, thereby rendering his childhood (*bālabhāva*) nothing more than a show, performed out of "conformity for the world."[95] This perspective, which is typical of the *Mahāvastu's* Lokottaravādin worldview, renders the Buddha's childhood virtually meaningless.

The *Mahāvastu* is not alone in this perception. As we have just seen, according to the *Lalitavistara*, the Bodhisattva embodied an unparalleled intellectual perfection that rendered schooling redundant. And such perspectives do not belong to the Sanskrit sources alone; the *Jātaka-nidāna* presents us with a herculean Bodhisattva who never trained a day in his life. The *Buddhacarita* is less extreme in this regard, for while it certainly presents an extraordinary young man, the Bodhisattva nevertheless had toys, underwent the traditional rites of his era, experienced suffering at the sight of the laborers, and was compelled to leave home as a result. None of this is presented as a play or performance but appears as a real journey through the stages of youth that eventually lead him to buddhahood. And while the Pāli sources agree that the Bodhisattva was unlike any other being in the universe, the tendency is to simultaneously retain his humanity, with Buddhaghosa eventually condemning strict transcendental readings of the Buddha's hagiography altogether. He argued, for example, that while some might have imagined that the Buddha glided over the earth and was born adorned and omniscient, in reality he was born naked, walked, and was only an ignorant child (*bāladārako*).[96]

This range of interpretations is a clear reflection of each text's reading of the Buddha's person. In those texts with a more transcendentalist approach, the Buddha had no childhood to speak of; he was merely manifesting childhood for the benefit of his audience. The Pāli texts tend to struggle more with the human/transcendental dichotomy, and the *Buddhacarita* is torn between its Buddhist ideals and its Indian, brahmanic roots. Each text tells the story of the Buddha's childhood in its own way. Taken together, a rainbow of views emerges—evidence of a healthy, rich, and stimulating debate in the formative years of the Buddhist tradition. Childhood is a most revealing period in one's life, as it transitions us from our beginnings into our futures. The various narratives surrounding the Buddha's childhood articulate the struggle Buddhism

94. *Mahāvastu* I: 158–77.

95. Jones translates *bālabhāva* as "ignorance" while Paul Harrison translates it as "(foolish) childhood"—both fair translations. See Harrison's article "Sanskrit Fragments of a Lokottaravādin Tradition" in *Indological and Buddhist Studies: Volume in Honour of Professor J. W. de Jong on his Sixtieth Birthday*, ed. L. A. Hercus et al. (Delhi: Indian Books Centre, 1982), 218.

96. Papañcasūdanī Majjhimanikāyaṭṭhakathā 123.23. Gananath Obeyesekere produced a wonderful essay on this debate concerning the Buddha's person. See his article "The Death of the Buddha: A Restorative Interpretation" in *Approaching the Dhamma: Buddhist Texts and Practices in South and Southeast Asia*, ed. Anne M. Blackburn and Jeffrey Samuels (Seattle: BPS Pariyatti Editions, 2003).

has always faced between these two poles of Buddhist reality. Did the Buddha begin in the mud and pierce through the water to open like a lotus flower in his adult years, or was he always a lotus flower, unmoving, undeveloping, perpetually open to the sun? The key to this question is to be found in the representations of his childhood.

BRIEF APPENDIX: THEMES AND QUESTIONS FOR FUTURE STUDIES

Much more can be said concerning the Buddha's childhood. Early artistic representations of the Buddha's youth will yield important findings, and there are many more scriptural sources to explore. Questions of the Buddha's appearance and incomparable beauty likewise deserve examination.[97] Particularly worthwhile are questions about the ancient city of Kapilavastu: its history, its contested location and ongoing archaeological excavations,[98] and especially its pilgrimage traditions (or in most cases, lack thereof). Why, for example, do we find references in the *Aśokāvadāna*[99] and Xuanzang[100] about pilgrimage associated with his youth, but rarely later? Where did Kapilavastu go in collective Buddhist pilgrimage memory?[101] What is the significance of this disjunction in Buddhist history? Does it mean that the Buddha's childhood was more important in the past than it is today, that earlier Buddhist communities actively engaged in conversation concerning the Buddha's youth, but that this tradition eventually came to an end? Where did the Buddhist relationship to the Buddha's

97. See John Powers's recent study *A Bull of a Man*, for an innovative discussion on this theme.

98. A debate continues to stir concerning the location of the ancient city of Kapilavastu, with some scholars situating it in India at Piprāhwā (most vocal in this regard is K. M. Srivastava. See, for example, his article "Archaeological Excavations at Piprāhwā and Ganwaria and the Identification of Kapilavastu," *Journal of the International Association of Buddhist Studies* 30 no. 1 [1980], 103–10) and others opting for the Terai region of Nepal (see Robin Coningham, "The Archaeology of Buddhism" in *Archaeology and World Religion*, ed. Timothy Insoll. [London: Routledge, 2001], 69–70). Consensus has yet to be reached.

99. See John S. Strong's *The Legend of King Aśoka: A Study and Translation of the Aśokāvadāna* (Delhi: Motilal Banarsidass, 1983), 247.

100. *Si-Yu-Ki, Buddhist Records of the Western World: Translation from the Chinese of Hiuen Tsiang (AD 629–645),* trans. Samuel Beal (New Delhi: Asian Educational Services, 2003), 2: 19–24.

101. Toni Huber's recent study of pilgrimage traditions in India aptly demonstrates the ebb and flow that certain sites associated with the Buddha's life have experienced over the centuries; he called this the "shifting terrain of the Buddha" (Toni Huber, *The Holy Land Reborn: Pilgrimage and the Tibetan Reinvention of Buddhist India* [Chicago: The University of Chicago Press, 2008], 17). Kapilavastu does not emerge as a significant pilgrimage site in his study, which is revealing in and of itself. Huber is, however, primarily concerned with Tibetan constructions of Indian pilgrimage sites and notes that by the time of Xuanzang's visit to the region, Kapilavastu is already described as being desolate and in ruins (53).

childhood go? This chapter does not exhaust the theme but aims to open the door to what will hopefully prove to be an exciting conversation in Buddhist Studies. The Buddha left home for a reason, and this reason, be it the Four Sights, his meditation under the rose-apple tree, or his "leper-like" wealth, lies at the very heart of the Buddhist tradition.

CHAPTER 4

The Inheritance of Rāhula

Abandoned Child, Boy Monk, Ideal Son and Trainee

KATE CROSBY

It does not sound like the ideal beginning to a father–son relationship: The father absconds without a word the day of the boy's birth, in flight at the prospect of being trapped by his son's arrival. The father leaves at the end of the first week. The father absconds during the pregnancy, throwing the mother-to-be into a period of self-inflicted abstinence and depression so severe the child is not born until six years later, the mother accused of adultery.[1]

1. The Theravada tradition retains the stories in which the Buddha leaves shortly after the birth. Various northern traditions have the Buddha leave after the conception. In the *Jātaka-nidāna,* the Theravada prelude to the *Jātaka* commentaries, the earliest Pali text to present an in-depth chronological biography of the Buddha, the Buddha leaves the night of the day on which Rāhula is born. The text notes, and dismisses, an alternative story in the *Jātaka* commentaries, that he left on day seven of Rāhula's life (see N. A. Jayawickrama, *The Story of Gotama Buddha [Jātaka-nidāna*] [Oxford: The Pali Text Society, 1990], 83). The six-year term of the pregnancy is found in the *Mahāvastu, Mahāsaṅghikavinaya, Mūlasarvāstivādavinaya,* and other "northern" texts, with Rāhula being conceived on the night of the Buddha's departure (see Bhikkhu Telwatte Rahula, *A Critical Study of the Mahāvastu* [Delhi: Motilal Banarsidass, 1978], 133). For the rendition of the six-year pregnancy of Rāhula's mother as found in the *Bhadrakalpāvadāna* (Nepal c.1400–1650), see Joel Tatelman, "*The Trials of Yaśhodharā: A Critical Edition, Annotated Translation and Study of the Bhdrakapāvadāna II-V,*" vol. 2 (D.Phil. thesis, Oxford University, 1996), 6ff. Tatelman also summarises other versions of this story (ibid. p. 6 n. 29 and p. 20 n. 73.) Tatelman's translation of this episode without the supporting material is also available in his article "The Trials of Yaśhodharā: The Legend of the Buddha's Wife in the *Bhadrakalpāvadāna* (from the Sanskrit)," *Buddhist Literature* 1 (1999), 176–261. For a list of Theravada accounts, see Donald K. Swearer, "Bimbā's Lament" in *Buddhism in*

Such are the stories that surround Rāhula's birth in the various Buddhist traditions, yet the relationship between him and his father, Gotama Buddha, comes to represent the highest ideals of filial piety, the closest of father–son apprenticeships, the model for childhood ordination—the dominant form of entrance into the Buddhist monastic life.[2]

The tensions that we might assume to exist between father and abandoned mother, given this start to their joint parenthood, are not ignored in the texts. In the *Bhadrakalpāvadāna*, in which Upagupta relates the story to the emperor Aśoka, Yaśodharā, thin and ill from her asceticism and grief, cries out to her absent husband:

> Pitiless man! Having abandoned me, where will you go? Remember me in my misery and return. The son sprung from your seed—who will protect him? Remember the child in my womb, and return, you whose [very] essence is compassion.... Best of all-knowing ones! Knowing me to be such a sinful woman, why place in me the seed [born of] your gaze,[3] so difficult to bear? Why do you abandon me, showing all the signs of pregnancy, and wander in the forest?[4]

Tatelman notes, "In the first chapter of the *Wei ts'eng yeou yin yuan ching* (T 754; Péri 21), when Maudgalyāyana solicits Yaśodharā's support for Rāhula's ordination, she positively reviles the Buddha, declaring, among other things, that he abandoned her less than three years after marrying her, that in order to marry him, she had rejected offers from eight different princes and that had he known he would leave her, he should not have married her at all."[5]

In the *Mūlasarvāstivāda* version of the story, Yaśodharā is presented as a temptress trying to use magic to win the Buddha back on his first return to his home town of Kapilavastu after his Enlightenment. When she fails, she attempts to commit suicide by throwing herself from the roof, to be saved by

Practice, ed. Donald S. Lopez, Jr. (Princeton, NJ: Princeton University Press, 1995), 542.

2. Because my focus is the accounts of Rāhula in Theravada Buddhism, I shall use Pali spellings as the default, except in specific references from Sanskrit texts or citations that use the Sanskrit versions. Childhood ordination not only is the dominant form of ordination but is regarded by some as the only proper form of ordination. In Thailand I have heard comments about the ungainliness of those who first become monks as adults, and in Sri Lanka arguments against female ordination because nuns lack the inculcated decorum appropriate to monastics due to a lack (and at the time impossibility) of childhood training as a female novice in Sri Lanka.

3. In this version, Rāhula is conceived from a passionate glance of the Buddha-to-be, following the manner of "'visual intercourse' ...practised by the deities residing in the Tuṣita heaven" (Joel Tatelman, *The Trials of Yaśhodharā*, 20 n. 69).

4. Tatelman, *The Trials of Yaśhodharā*, 2: 17.

5. Tatelman, *The Trials of Yaśhodharā*, 2: 17 n. 62.

the Buddha's superhuman power, and then herself becomes a nun.[6] In fact, her attempts to seduce the Buddha with laced sweetmeats offered by Rahula backfires when Rāhula in turn accepts the sweets from the Buddha and so is compelled to follow him.[7]

The *Jātaka-nidāna*, the earliest continuous biography as such in the Pali tradition, which brings together passages extracted from canonical and especially commentarial texts, does not represent Yaśodharā as plaintive. Although she is embarrassed by the thought of the Buddha's "begging" for food, at her first sight of him she immediately recognizes his glory.[8] Yet later renderings of the same story in the Theravada tradition also emphasize her shame and anger at being abandoned:

> Now he has discarded all signs of his royal status. He wears a monk's robes and goes begging for food like a poor, starving person with no sense of shame. Such behaviour brings disgrace upon me as a royal princess. People will think that my husband has deserted me. Having been abandoned by his father, Rāhula is forced to live only with me. Is it the consequence of some bad karma in a previous life that this has befallen us? Being a wife without a husband is a sorrowful state. I have been deserted and am bereft of merit. Woe is me; my life has surely come to an end![9]

Different traditions try to resolve these apparently discordant notes in the Buddha's relationships in different ways. The *Mūlasarvāstivādavinaya* includes many previous life stories, some of which explain how Yaśodharā and Rāhula were karmically bound to endure these trials.[10] Thus the necessity of Yaśodharā's undergoing a six-year pregnancy is attributed to her allowing her mother to carry a pail of milk six leagues in a previous lifetime. Rāhula, in turn, had to endure six years in the womb—universally accepted as an unpleasant experience in early Indian medical and Buddhist understanding—as punishment for a time when, in a previous lifetime, he as the King Brahmadatta had kept a sage waiting six days.[11] Yaśodharā's attempt at suicide is a reliving of her former *satī* as a *kinnarī* (a mythical beast, half bird, half human) on the death of her husband, the Buddha-to-be, shot by a king out hunting.[12] In the

6. Jampa Losang Panglung, *Die Erzählstoffe des Mūlasarvāstivādavinaya analysiert auf Grund der tibetischen Übersetzung*, Studia Philologica Buddhica Monograph Series III (Tokyo: The Reiyukai Library, 1981), 97–98.
7. Bhikkhu Telwatte Rahula, *A Critical Study of the Mahāvastu*, 134.
8. N. A. Jayawickrama, *The Story of Gotama Buddha (Jātaka-nidāna)*, 120–21.
9. Donald K. Swearer, "Bimba's Lament," 545. This is a relatively late northern Thai text translated by Swearer. Bimbā is one of the alternative names for Yasodharā.
10. While the structure of the *Mūlasarvāstivādavinaya* and *Mahāvastu* differs from that of the Theravada *Vinaya*, in embedding *jātakas* into the main text, the Theravada *jātakas* are also often linked in their introduction to a place in the *Vinaya*.
11. Jampa Losang Panglung, *Die Erzählstoffe*, 99.
12. Panglung, *Die Erzählstoffe*, 98.

Mūlasarvāstivādavinaya, Rāhula's recognition of his father, which he does independently, not prompted by his mother, is a reenactment of his doing this in a previous lifetime. In that lifetime the Buddha-to-be was a thief so cunning that he constantly evaded justice. Eventually, the king set a trap using his own daughter as bait. Although she is on a floating garden, her guards, who initially smash every pot the cunning thief floats toward them, become blasé about floating pots, allowing him to approach with his head under one. He gets her pregnant and disappears again. Now when all men are summoned before the king, the princess's son recognizes his father, the thief, although they had never met. Of course, rather than arresting the thief, the king offers him his daughter in marriage.[13]

The commentarial layer of the Pali tradition, by contrast, recasts the stories to provide a nuance that the reader might have missed, for one of the key functions of these commentaries on the canon is to resolve narratives in which the Buddha might seem to fall short in the attributes of omniscience and compassion.[14] Thus the commentary ensures that when Yasodharā sends Rāhula to demand his inheritance of his father—*dāyajjaṃ me samaṇa dehi*, "Give me my inheritance, monk"—we do not read the episode as an expression of bitterness on her part and pestering on his. The Buddha ignores the pestering child, then finally responds—famously—by giving Rāhula his spiritual "inheritance," that is, by asking Sāriputta to ordain him. The commentary explains that Rāhula is asking for his inheritance only in obedience to his mother. Yasodharā, in turn, is referring to a specific treasure that has been mislaid and that they have been unable to find since the Buddha left, with which they plan to set Rāhula up as a universal emperor.[15] Indeed, the aspiration to be born as the future

13. Panglung, *Die Erzälhstoffe*, 97; and John S. Strong, "'A Family Quest: The Buddha, Yaśodhara, and Rāhula' in the *Mūlasarvāstivāda Vinaya*," in *Sacred Biography in the Buddhist Traditions of South and Southeast Asia*, ed. Juliane Schober (Honolulu: University of Hawaii Press, 1997), 120.

14. A more obvious example of the retelling by the commentary with a fresh nuance is found in the commentary to the *Mahāparinibbānasutta*. The advice the Buddha gives King Ajātasattu allows the king to conquer the Vajjī, a historical event attested in other accounts. Commentator Buddhaghosa is at pains to point out that the Buddha speaks as he does in order to postpone the inevitable, gaining the Vajjīs more time to make merit. For a translation of the relevant section, see Yang-Gyu An, *The Buddha's Last Days: Buddhaghosa's Commentary on the Mahāparinibbāna Sutta* (Oxford: The Pali Text Society, 2003), 16–17. For a discussion of the development, from early canonical through commentarial literature, of the expectations of what it meant to be a Buddha in the Theravada tradition, including developments in what it means to be omniscient, see Toshiichi Endo, *Buddha in Theravada Buddhism: A Study of the Concept of Buddha in the Pali Commentaries*. 2nd ed. (Buddhist Cultural Centre, Dehiwala, 2002).

15. "*passa tāta etaṃ vīsatisahassasamaṇaparivutaṃ suvaṇṇavaṇṇaṃ brahmarūpavaṇṇaṃ samaṇaṃ, ayaṃ te pitā, etassa mahantā nidhayo ahesuṃ, tyassa nikkhamanato paṭṭhāya na passāma, gaccha naṃ dāyajjaṃ yāca, ahaṃ tāta kumāro chattaṃ ussāpetvā cakkavattī bhavissāmi, dhanena me attho, dhanaṃ me dehi, sāmiko hi putto pitusantakassā"ti. Rāhulavatthuatthavaṇṇanā, Samantapāsādikā*. This text taken from http://www.tipitaka.org/romn/,last accessed April 26, 2011.

Buddha's wife or son is emphasized in the late canonical and commentarial layers of Pali literature as a great feat that has itself taken many lifetimes of rehearsal and merit-making following an original key act of good in relation to a previous Buddha.[16] For, by the late canonical period, every Buddha must have a wife and son, as outlined in the *Buddhavaṃsa,* which provides a standard career for all Buddhas, including the names of the wife and son for each.[17] The Pali *jātakas*—the narratives of which are post-canonical—contain a number of stories in which Yasodharā and Rāhula have the same position vis-à-vis the Buddha-to-be in previous lifetimes as well. Rāhula's role in the *jātakas* tends to be small. Thus in *jātakas* 9, 188, and 408 he is merely the son of the *bodhisatta* with no further role, and in *jātakas* nos. 354 and 444, as well as in the apocryphal *Arindama jātaka,*[18] his role is even more passive—he is the dead son of the *bodhisatta.* (They do manage to revive him through truth statements in *Jātaka* 354 and the *Arindama jātaka.*)[19] In a few *jātakas,* Rāhula, again as son, is also briefly the interlocutor of the *bodhisatta* (nos. 172, 173, 250), while in many more, there is a rehearsal of the future abandonment either because the *bodhisatta* renounces (nos. 201, 525, 529, 539, and, famously, 547, the *Vessantara Jātaka*) or because the *bodhisatta* is to be taken off by the king's men to be sacrificed to the gods (no. 542) or as a bride-price (no. 545).[20] The scene in the *Cullasutasoma Jātaka* (no. 525) is particularly moving as the seven-year-old Rāhula-to-be, given a speaking part, takes his turn in trying to prevent his father from leaving home. Clasping his father firmly around the neck, he cries:

16. See my discussion of the *Apadāna,* the texts that identify this "pure root" cause, *sukkamūla,* below.
17. For a translation of the *Buddhavaṃsa,* see I. B. Horner, *Chronicle of Buddhas, Minor Anthologies III* (London: The Pali Text Society, 1975).
18. I. B. Horner and Padmanabh S. Jaini, *Apocryphal Birth-Stories (Paññāsa-Jātaka),* vol. 1 (London: Pali Text Society, 1985), 33–44.
19. "Canonical" *jātakas* are taken from E. B. Cowell et al., trans, *The Jātaka or Stories of the Buddha's Former Births,* 7 vols. (Cambridge: Cambridge University Press, 1895). The truth statements in *Jātaka* 354 are hilarious spoofs of what one expects of a truth statement, for the truths in these statements are not positive: the sage admits that, while he liked the idea of becoming a renouncer at the time, he has long since regretted it; the father admits that, while he is forever feeding renouncers, he resents doing so yet continues for form's sake because his family has always been engaged in hosting renouncers; and the mother admits that she has no feelings for her husband, and has remained faithful only because women in her family aren't in the habit of taking on lovers!
20. The allegory in 542 regarding the king, father of the Buddha-to-be, i.e., Suddhodana-to-be, is interesting. He wants his sons, wives, and so on to be sacrificed in order to attain heaven for himself, even though the notion that heaven can be achieved in this way has been inspired in him by a corrupt brahmin. One could see this situation as a rehearsal for Suddhodana's wanting Siddhattha Gotama and the rest of his family to stay in household life—i.e., on the path to repeated death—for his own future security, rather than allowing them to renounce and seek *nibbāna.*

"My mother lo! is weeping and
my brother fain would keep thee still,
I too will hold thee by the hand
Nor let thee go against our will."[21]

Nevertheless in the "apocryphal" *Narajīva jātaka*[22] and in the *Apadāna*, Rāhula's eventual rebirth as son of the Buddha is explained as the direct result of his positive actions, culminating in his generosity and vow under a previous Buddha. In the *Narajīva jātaka*, Rāhula-to-be participates in the generosity of the Buddha-to-be: "At that moment a young man, with a golden turban, bright with a variety of jewels a thousand-thick, standing at the Lord Padumuttara's feet, made the wish, "Revered sir, in the time when the Buddha appears I would be his son."[23]

The *Apadāna* are regarded as relatively late canonical texts that build on the earlier verses attributed to early enlightened monks and nuns who were followers of the Buddha, contained in the *Thera-* and *Therīgāthā*. Also in verse, the *Apadāna* explain the original good action under a previous Buddha that was the "root" of the eventual good fortune of becoming one of Gotama's disciples.[24] In Rāhula's *Apadāna*, the account of the former lifetime that led to his current state, Rāhula recalls that after he had waited on the Buddha Padumuttara, he received from that Buddha the prediction that he (Rāhula-to-be) would be reborn as the King of the Gods 64 times and as a Universal Emperor (*cakkavattī*) 1,000 times, without intervening births in other positions, culminating in the twenty-first *kalpa* (world age), when he would be reborn as the universal emperor called Vimala, the Spotless, whose capital city Reṇuvatī is particularly wonderful. Padumuttara Buddha then predicts his rebirth as Rāhula:

> In the hundredth thousandth aeon from now, there will be a Teacher in the world, arising in the family of the King Effulgent, called Gotama on account of his clan. Leaving behind his life in the Tusita heaven, impelled by the pure conduct that set this course of events in motion, this man will then be reborn as the son of that Buddha Gotama. If he were to remain a householder, he would become a universal emperor, but it is impossible that one such as he would find delight in domestic life. Rather he will quit his household and go forth, strong in the renouncers' vow. He will become an enlightened *arhat*, known by the name of Rāhula.[25]

21. E. B. Cowell et al., trans, *The Jātaka*, 5: 95.
22. I. B. Horner and Padmanabh S. Jaini, *Apocryphal Birth-Stories*, 170–80.
23. Horner and Jaini, *Apocryphal Birth-Stories*, 174.
24. Jonathan S. Walters, "Gotamī's Story," in *Buddhism in Practice*, ed. Donald S. Lopez, Jr. (Princeton, NJ: Princeton University Press, 1995), 113–14.
25. *Kappasatasahassamhi, okkākakulasambhavo; Gotamo nāma gottena, satthā loke bhavissati. Tusitā so cavitvāna, sukkamūlena codito; Gotamassa bhagavato, atrajo so bhavissati. Sace vaseyya agāraṃ, cakkavattī bhaveyya so; Aṭṭhānametaṃ yaṃ tādī, agāre*

The commentary to this *Apadāna* explains further that it was on seeing the "foremost of those keen for training" (*aggo sikkhākāmānaṃ*) among the Buddha Padumuttara's disciples that Rāhula-to-be formed the aspiration to achieve that position under a future Buddha.[26] Elsewhere, in further renderings of this story in the commentaries to the *Majjhima* and *Aṅguttara Nikāyas*, we learn that Rāhula-to-be formed this resolution when, on the basis of his great merit, he had been reborn as the Nāga king, and that the inspirational novice in question was none other than the Buddha Padumuttara's own son, Uparevata:

> Looking at the newly ordained member of the Sangha, the son of the Tathāgata, known as Novice Uparevata, [the Nāga king] thought, 'It's not surprising that the rest of the disciples have such power, but that this tender young boy should have such power is absolutely astounding' and on so thinking was filled with delight and joy.... It seems that he recognized that the same thirty-two marks of a great man that were visible on the Teacher's body were also visible on the boy's.... After performing a great alms-giving lasting seven days, he made the request, 'Lord, may I, on the basis of this service, become the son of a future Buddha, as Uparevata is yours.' The Teacher, being able to see without any impediment, made the prediction, 'In the future, you will become the son of Gotama Buddha.' He then departed.[27]

In these passages, then, the focus is not on what Rāhula-to-be had done wrong to have such a birth and abandonment, but on what he had done right. Moreover, Rāhula now has the same characteristics—those of a great man or superman (*mahāpurisa*)—and the same options—to become a universal emperor or attain Enlightenment—as the Buddha himself.

ratimajjhagā. Nikkhamitvā agāramhā, pabbajissati subbato; Rāhulo nāma nāmena, arahā so bhavissati. Rāhula Apadāna (Apadāna 6, Sīhāsananiyavagga, vv. 79–82). This text taken from http://www.tipitaka.org/romn/, last accessed April 26, 2011.

26. *Ayampi āyasmā purimajinavaresu katādhikāro tattha tattha bhave vivaṭṭūpanissayāni puññāni upacinanto padumuttarassa bhagavato kāle kulagehe nibbatto viññutaṃ patvā satthu dhammadesanaṃ suṇanto satthāraṃ ekaṃ bhikkhuṃ sikkhākāmānaṃ aggaṭṭhāne ṭhapentaṃ disvā sayampi taṃ ṭhānantaraṃ patthento senāsanavisodhanavijjotanādikaṃ uḷāraṃ puññaṃ katvā paṇidhānaṃ akāsi. Rāhulāpadānatthavaṇṇanā.* This text taken from http://www.tipitaka.org/romn/, last accessed April 26, 2011.

27. *saṅghanavakaṃ tathāgatassa puttaṃ uparevatasāmaṇeraṃ nāma olokento "anacchariyo sesasāvakānaṃ evarūpo iddhānubhāvo, imassa pana taruṇabāladārakassa evarūpo iddhānubhāvo ativiya acchariyo"ti pītipāmojjaṃ uppādesi.... Tassa kira sarīre satthu sarīre viya dvattiṃsa mahāpurisalakkhaṇāni paññāyanti.... sattāhaṃ mahādānaṃ datvā, "bhante, ahaṃ imassa adhikārakammassānubhāvena ayaṃ uparevato viya anāgate ekassa buddhassa putto bhaveyya"nti patthanaṃ akāsi. Satthā anantarāyaṃ disvā "anāgate gotamabuddhassa putto bhavissasī"ti byākaritvā pakkāmi. Aṅguttara Nikāya Atthakathā 14. 3 Rāhula-raṭṭhapālattheravatthu.* This text taken from http://www.tipitaka.org/romn/, last accessed April 26. 2011. For a summary of this and the *Majjhima Nikāya* stories, see G. P. Malalasekera, *Dictionary of Pali Proper Names*, vol. 2 (London: Indian Text Series, 1937–1938), 739 with n. 11.

Given the contrast between these narratives extolling the high honor of being the Buddha's son and those expressing tensions in relation to Rāhula's abandonment by the personification of omniscience and compassion, what purposes does this component of the Buddha's life-narrative serve? The earliest biographical layers of the Pali canon do not contain these stories, which seem to have migrated from narratives about other people. Strong observes, "Only the *Mahīśāsaka Vinaya* develops the harem women scene (which it models on the story of the wandering forth of Yaśas), but it too fails to mention the Buddha's son and wife."[28] Nevertheless, their migration into the Buddha biography means that redactors saw them as fitting there. So why give the crown prince a harem, a wife, and a single male heir? Does this picture, as in the giving up of wife and children by the *bodhisatta* in the *Vessantara Jātaka*, indicate the great sacrifices involved in renouncing the world for all parties?[29] In one Thai version of the story the connection is explicitly made between the Buddha-to-be having to give up his wife as part of his progress to buddhahood and the Buddha's being beholden to her for her virtue: "The Tathāgata remembered that Bimbā [Yasodharā] had accumulated countless virtuous qualities over a hundred, thousand, ten thousand, one hundred thousand lifetimes. 'Before I reached enlightenment I gave up my children and wife as *dāna* (a gift) [a reference to the *Vessantara Jātaka*]. So now I must see Bimbā.'"[30] The sense of the strong bond that may develop between fathers and sons, and thus the difficulty of leaving if he allows his relationship to his son to develop (in the *Bandanāgāra Jātaka*, no. 201, the Buddha-to-be is persuaded to stay because of his wife's pregnancy only for this plan to lead to a second pregnancy), lies behind Rahula's name in the Pali traditions:[31]

> At that time the great king Suddhodana, hearing that the queen, mother of Rāhula, had given birth to a son, sent a message saying, 'Convey my felicitations to my son.' The Bodhisatta on hearing it, said, 'An impediment *(rāhula)* has come into being, a bond has arisen.' The king, who came to hear of it

28. John S. Strong, "A Family Quest," 124 n. 2, drawing on the work of André Bareau. The renouncer Yaśas visits the Buddha shortly after the latter's Enlightenment and describes the repulsion he experienced on seeing his wife. The stories of extended pregnancies are also found in other contexts.

29. For a discussion of the function of the different characters' experiences in the *Vessantara Jātaka* for different members of an audience, rather than an assumption that viewers all identify with the hero, see Jonathan S. Walters, "Communal Karma and Karmic Community in Theravada Buddhist History," in *Constituting Communities: Theravada Buddhism and the Religious Cultures of South and Southeast Asia*, ed. John Clifford Holt et al. (Albany: SUNY, 2003), 9–39.

30. Donald K. Swearer, "Bimbā's Lament," 550.

31. Rāhula is also sometimes called "Rāhulabhadra," the good or lucky Rāhula, as explained in the *Theragāthā:* "They know me as 'lucky' Rāhula, fortunate for two reasons; one that I am the Buddha's son, and the other that I am one with vision into truths." See K. R. Norman, *The Elders' Verses I: The Theragāthā*, 2nd ed. (Lancaster, England: The Pali Text Society, 2007), 37.

on enquiring what his son had said, ordered that thenceforth his grandson should be known as Prince Rāhula.[32]

Pali commentaries interpret the word Rāhula as having the sense of impediment because it means "little Rāhu." Rāhu is the monster who eclipses and so obstructs the sun and moon, i.e., Rāhula is a potential obstruction to his father's glory. The commentary to Rāhula's *apadāna* explains, "The passage should be understood with this purport: [The Buddha-to-be thinks] 'Just as Rāhu, the lord of the titans, tarnishes the radiance of the chariots of the sun and moon as he goes along, in exactly that way his being born seems to create an obstacle to my departure and going forth, etc.'"[33]

In the *Mūlasarvāstivādavinaya*, however, while the name Rāhula does refer to the eclipse, there is nothing sinister in it. The birth takes place six years after Rāhula's conception, that is, six years after the Buddha's renunciation, at the point when all obstacles are overcome by the Buddha. Here, then, the name Rāhula is a reference to the auspicious lunar eclipse which marks the child's birth.[34] On hearing that the Buddha has given up fasting, Yaśodharā herself ceases to fast (she had been engaging in identical austerities to the Buddha). Doing so allows Rāhula to develop fully in the womb. His birth then coincides with the Buddha's own enlightenment. This story has led Strong to suggest that the narratives provide paths for Yaśodharā and Rāhula that parallel that of the Buddha:

> In achieving the goal of renunciation—enlightenment—the Buddha also achieves the goal of lay life—fatherhood. But conversely, in achieving the goal of motherhood, Yaśodharā makes possible the goal of renunciation. This story, then, could serve as a soteriological model not just for monks and nuns at the time of their 'wandering forth' but also for laypersons (both female and male) who, willy-nilly, choose the family life. It implies a parallelism and balance between at least two Buddhist paths, both of which lead to enlightenment: a *śramanic* one involving ordination and a stay-at-home one for householders.[35]

A similar proposition, at least as far as parallel male and female renouncer paths are concerned, has been made by Walters in relation to the story of the Buddha's aunt Gotamī.[36]

Is the fulfillment of paternity an aspect of the Buddha's compassion, to alleviate the grief of those left behind and provide a lineage for the family

32. The Pāli phrase is *rāhulojāto, bandhanaṃ jātaṃ* (*Jātaka Nidāna*; N. A. Jayawickrama, *The Story of Gotama Buddha* [*Jātaka-nidāna*], 81).
33. "*Yathā candasūriyānaṃ vimānapabhāya kiliṭṭhakaraṇena rāhu asurindo upeti gacchati, evamevāyaṃ mama abhinikkhamanapabbajjādīnaṃ antarāyaṃ karontoriva jāto"ti adhippāyena, "rāhu jātoti āhā"ti daṭṭhabbaṃ. Rāhul–apadāna-atthavaṇṇanā.* See N. A. Jayawickrama, *The Story of Gotama Buddha* [*Jātaka-nidāna*], 81.
34. John S. Strong, *The Buddha: A Short Biography* (Oxford: Oneworld, 2001), 58.
35. Strong, "A Family Quest," 123.
36. See his "Gotamī's Story."

and the crown? We see such concerns elsewhere in early Buddhist narrative. The monk Sudinna, the first monk to engage in sexual intercourse, who thus provides the reason for the establishment of the first *pārājikā* rule, does so not out of lust but—after much imploring—to provide his family with an heir, which also ensures that they can retain their property.[37] The *Bhadrakalpāvadāna* also expresses this theme: The Buddha's foster mother Gautamī is delighted on realizing that Yaśodharā is pregnant, and she exclaims:

> That ambrosia, a grandson's lotus-face, shall quell that fire of grief, the separation from my son, which blazes in my heart. How fitting! Now that she is pregnant, Gopā (Yaśodharā) will at long last bear a son for my husband, Śuddhodana, and his subjects, as well as for me. He will dispel an enormous grief as well as preserve the family.... Also, my omniscient son, when the dear boy was abandoning me, said, 'A son like me will be born to your daughter-in-law; therefore, grieve not.'[38]

If through Rāhula the Buddha resolves the tensions between renunciation/abandonment and lay-life/paternity, this balance is disrupted by the ultimate soteriological necessity of renunciation in these narratives. Furthermore, while Rāhula's birth might at first seem to offer a lineage of transmission and a crown prince for the Śakyan throne, his own childhood ordination removes this. His subsequent predeceasing the Buddha places him among the many blood relatives of the Buddha who either die before him (Sāriputta and the Śakyans) or are in some way defective (Ānanda and Devadatta), thus in fact ensuring that there is no biological lineage, an absence of potential rivals and inheritors.[39] Does Rāhula's own ordination ensure or explain the absence of a biological lineage, reaffirming the institutional lineage of teaching and Saṅgha (*dhamma* and *vinaya*) seen in the account of the end of Buddha's life in the *Mahāparinibbānasutta*?[40] Rāhula's own death receives no great attention. According to Rahula, "A Pali commentary incidentally mentions that he passed away while staying in the Trāyaśtriṃśa heaven."[41]

37. I. B. Horner, *The Book of the Discipline* (London: The Pali Text Society, 1938), 1: 121ff.

38. Tatelman, *The Trials of Yaśodharā*, vol. 2, 8–9.

39. Pāsādika, whose entry is based mainly on Theravada accounts, notes, "Tradition has it that Rāhula died before his father." See Bhikkhu Pāsādika, "Rahula" in *Encyclopedia of Buddhism*, ed. Robert Buswell (New York and London: Macmillan, 2003), 711.

40. For the proposition that the *Mahāparinibbāna* and other narratives of absence are a defense of institutional over charismatic leadership, see Reginald A. Ray, *Buddhist Saints in India: A Study in Buddhist Values and Orientations* (New York and Oxford: Oxford University Press, 1994), esp. 337–80.

41. Bhikkhu Telwatte Rahula, *A Critical Study of the Mahāvastu*, 136. I have recently heard of a Thai text containing a fuller account of Rāhula's life, as well as a Shan text of Suddhodana's life, but I have not yet secured a copy of either.

Even in those traditions where Rāhula does not die but remains in life to protect the *Dhamma* until the arrival of the next Buddha, Maitreya, he does so as one of the groups of *arhats*[42] or as a solitary figure, not as a leader. Ray writes:

> The cult of long-lived *arhats* is found not only in scriptural evidence such as the [pre-4th century CE] *Nandimitrāvadāna*, but also in other evidence of Buddhist cultic life in India.... An intriguing glimpse of the cult is provided by [the 7th-century Chinese pilgrim] Hsüan-tsang's description of the cult of Rāhula, one of the sixteen *arhats*. Thus the pilgrim tells us that one day, when he was passing through a certain village, he chanced upon the dwelling of a wealthy and eminent Brāhman.... Some time not long before the pilgrim's visit, a certain *śramaṇa*, with thick eyebrows and a shaven head, had accepted the Brahman's invitation to stay awhile. When in the morning the Brahman gave him some food, the *śramaṇa* took a bit, sighed, and returned the remainder to the donor ... [explaining], 'When I sighed, it was not on account of your offering of rice; for during many hundreds of years I have not tasted such food. When [the] *tathāgata* was living in the world, ... I washed his *pātra* [bowl] in the pure stream of the river—there I filled his pitcher—there I gave him water for cleansing his mouth; but alas! the milk that you offer is not like the sweet water of old.

It turns out that the old renouncer is Rāhula, son of the Buddha, who, in order to protect the *dharma*, has not yet entered *nirvāṇa*.[43] We should observe that Rāhula also continues as a teacher, although, again, not a central one. Bareau writes, "According to certain later texts, the Sarvāstivādins had as teacher Rāhula or Rāhulabhadra."[44] Interestingly, one Theravada group has, exceptionally, identified Rāhula as an important teacher in their tradition, a point to which I shall return below.

Is one function of the story that the Buddha fathers a son to establish his manhood? This point is certainly explicit in the *Mūlasarvāstivādavinaya*, in which the *bodhisattva* decides to have sex with his wife before leaving, "Lest others say that the prince Śākyamuni was 'not a man.'"[45] (Strong relates this incident

42. Reginald A. Ray, "Nāgārjuna's Longevity," in *Sacred Biography*, 133; and Strong, "A Family Quest," 121.

43. Ray, "Nāgārjuna's Longevity,"150–51 n. 39, citing Samuel Beal, trans., *Si-Yu-Ki, Buddhist Records of the Western World: Translation from the Chinese of Hiuen Tsiang (AD 629–645)*. 2 vols (New Delhi: Asian Educational Services, 2003), vol. 2, 42–43.

44. Translation by Sara Boin-Webb taken from her translation, forthcoming, with Hawaii University Press, of Bareau. My thanks to Andrew Skilton for drawing my attention to this passage and making this text available to me in advance of publication. The corresponding passage in the French is in chapter 20 on the Sarvāstivāda Vaibhāṣika. See André Bareau, *Les Sectes bouddhiques du Petit Véhicule* (Paris: L'École Française d'Extrême-Orient, 1955), 134–35.

45. Strong, *The Buddha*, 56; and Strong, "A Family Quest," 114–15.

to the prerequisite for ordination that candidates must be male: "In this light, it may be that this biographical episode, set just prior to the Bodhisattva's wandering forth, serves not only to engender his son Rāhula but also to prove his "maleness," one of the qualifications for the monkhood."[46])

We could suggest that the story serves to establish that the *bodhisatta* chooses renunciation from a position of power more broadly. He is the best at everything to which he turns his hand.[47] He could have the highest goals a man in *saṃsāra* can wish for: a kingdom, wealth, wives, sons. Nothing that a man should achieve is left unachieved. He does not leave out of failure, but in order to choose a higher state of power.

We might further speculate that having a son was one of the several episodes that demonstrate that the Buddha achieved the highest soteriological goals of other available paths in the religious contexts in which the story developed. The Buddha practiced the greatest extremes of asceticism and experienced the highest meditative states that other teachers had achieved, but he found them wanting. He had to seek his unique path, the only one that truly bestowed freedom from death. Olivelle, in his study of the position of women and sons in relation to notions of immortality in early brahmanical religion, points out the signficance of the wife for a man to become complete and a son for attaining immortality. He observes that these beliefs are attested in the earliest layer of Indian religious literature, the *Ṛg Veda*, and continue in the *Brāhmaṇas*, *Gṛhyasūtras*, and early *Upaniṣads*.[48] The son, in this worldview, is not just the provider of a material heir and of ancestral rites, but the literal continuation of the father: "At the outset, this embryo comes into being within a man as semen. This radiance gathered from all the bodily parts he bears in himself (*ātman*) as himself (*ātman*). And when he deposits it in a woman, he gives birth to it."[49] Olivelle points out that "rites and ideologies involving sons and the world of the fathers coexisted and continued to coexist in India side by side with the ideologies of rebirth and liberation,"[50] that is, such understandings of the father–son relationship continued even with the rise of the types of renouncer religion that were predicated upon the belief in *saṃsāra* and the possibility of *mokṣa* or *nirvāṇa*, to which Buddhism belonged. Olivelle then quotes further upanishadic passages which indicate an attempt

46. Strong, *The Buddha*, 56.

47. Summarizing the accounts given in the *Mūlasarvāstivādavinaya*, Panglung writes: "Der Prinz Siddhārtha lernte alle Wissenschaften und Künste von verschiedenen Meistern vollkommen. Was seine Kraf anging, so war er allen anderen überlegen. Als Devadatta mit der Faust einen für den Prinzen Siddhārtha bestimmten Elefanten getötet hatte, trug Nanda den Kadaver weg, der Bodhisattva aber warf ihn in die Luft, sodass er in grosser Entfernung niederfiel. In anderen Sportarten... siegte stets der Bodhisattva." See Panglung, *Die Erzälhstoffe*, 86.

48. Patrick Olivelle, "Amṛtā: Women and Indian Technologies of Immortality," *Journal of Indian Philosophy* 25 no. 5 (1997), 431 ff.

49. Olivelle, "Amṛtā," 432, translating from *Aitareya Upaniṣad* 2.1.

50. Olivelle, "Amṛtā," 442–43.

"to synthesise the differing conceptions of death and immortality," including this from the *Bṛhadāraṇyaka Upaniṣad* (1.5.15):

> Now, there are only three worlds: the world of men, the world of ancestors, and the world of gods. One can win this world of men only through a son, and by no other rite, whereas one wins the world of ancestors through rites (*karmaṇā*), and the world of gods through knowledge. The best of these, clearly, is the world of gods, and for this reason they praise knowledge.[51]

We know that the worldview of the earlier upanishads, such as the *Bṛhadāraṇyaka*, comes close to that of early Buddhism and is believed to be of similar date. This shared worldview is confirmed again here in the prioritization of the gnostic over other religious paths. With the continued notions of the importance of sons, even in bestowing immortality, it seems possible that the story of the Buddha's son does contribute to the picture of the Buddha-to-be, exhausting all the other known options for achieving the deathless state and discarding them as ineffective before finding his own superior path. Even though we know that brāhmanical religious ideas continued to influence Buddhism as it developed, however, the extent to which these specific issues remained important or even visible to the ongoing redactors of the Rāhula narratives must remain speculative: we are unlikely to recover a layer of evidence at which these concerns are any more visible than now.

If we turn from the function that Rāhula fulfils for his father's and—with less emphasis—mother's life stories to his own, that is, to the function his narrative fulfills as that of a child and young man, there is evidence available in the texts, in art, and in accounts of Buddhist practice. This is not to say that Rāhula ever develops a substantial narrative or character of his own.[52] As Rahula (the modern author!) writes, "Apart from the detailed and somewhat poetical accounts of his ordination, we hear very little about Rāhula: a fact which has led scholars to conclude that his *rôle* in the history of Buddhism was not very important. The picture of Rāhulabhadra presented and preserved in the ancient records is definitely that of an ideal personality, particularly with respect to his well-disciplined behaviour and meek obedience."[53]

It is perhaps this lack of a complex narrative coupled with the status of Rāhula as the Buddha's son that allows him to serve as this "ideal personality." In the *vinaya* narratives, as was observed above, he is the model for childhood ordination, which the texts represent as an innovation made directly in response to his relationship to his father. Most texts—regardless of whether

51. Olivelle, "Amṛtā," 443.
52. Malalasekera's entries on Rāhula are rich in detail about relevant narratives and texts. The main entries are "Rāhula Thera," "Rāhula Saṃyutta," and "Rāhula Sutta." See G. P. Malalasekera, *Dictionary of Pali Proper Names* (London: Indian Text Series, 1937–38), 737–41.
53. Bhikkhu Telwatte Rahula, *A Critical Study of the Mahāvastu*, 136.

his birth was before the great renunciation or following the six-year pregnancy—agree that Rāhula was seven years old at ordination,[54] although some advocate ordination only from the age of 15.[55] Although his father is already a monk and will look after his spiritual welfare, Rāhula is ordained by Sāriputta, this providing a model for the dual preceptor, *upajjha/upajjhāya*, who ordains and teacher, *ācariya*, who gives religious guidance.[56] Interestingly in terms of how these roles were viewed, the *Majjhima Nikāya* commentary explains that Sāriputta, in spite of his status as *abhidhamma* expert and sometime stand-in for the Buddha in giving sermons, was unable to provide Rāhula's spiritual guidance in meditation, because he did not recognize the stage that Rāhula had reached.[57] Rāhula's ordination is also the occasion for the laying down of the rule on parental consent. This is done, according to the narrative, at the behest of Rāhula's grandfather Suddhodana, who reexperiences the grief he underwent at the Buddha-to-be's own renunciation. Thus, while the Buddha left his home against his father's wishes, after Rāhula's ordination people were permitted to be ordained only with parental consent, even if they were adults. Indeed even the king himself would need his parents' permission. The few exceptions allowed relate to the inaccessibility of parents (through death, abandonment, or distance) and emergency ordination, where the would-be monk threatens to harm himself or others.[58] The extensions to this rule mean that even non-birth parents who stand in *loco parentis* should be consulted, although it is not a legal requirement in *vinaya* terms, indicating just how important the rule on parental permission is for the Saṅgha's harmonious relations with its host communities. Childhood ordination with parental consent can then become a mainstream religious event for both the child and the parents and binds the Saṅgha close into the religious life of the community. The inclusion for the sake of good Saṅgha-community relations of non-birth parents even paves the way for childless people to develop quasi-parent-child relationships through the sponsorship of the ordination of a particular child.

54. Yoshiharu Nakagawa, "The Child as Compassionate Bodhisattva and as Human Sufferer/Spiritual Seeker: Intertwined Buddhist Images," in *Nurturing Child and Adolescent Spirituality: Perspectives from the World's Religious Traditions*, ed. Karen Marie Yust et al. (Boulder, CO: Rowman & Littlefield, 2006), 34.

55. On the variations see Rahula, *A Critical Study of the Mahāvastu*, 135.

56. It is worth noting that although the *Tipallatthamiga and Abbhantara Jātakas* (16 and 281) identify Mogallāna as Rāhula's *ācariya*, it is the Buddha who assumes this function in the Rāhula narratives.

57. Bodhi writes: "Ven. Sāriputta, Rāhula's teacher, gave Rāhula this advice unaware that he had already been given different meditation instructions by the Buddha." See Bhikkhu Ñāṇamoli and Bhikkhu Bodhi, *The Middle Length Discources of the Buddha: A Translation of the Majjhima Nikāya*. Rev. ed. (Boston: Wisdom Publications, 2001), 1266 n. 642.

58. For a discussion of the rule on parental consent and the related matters mentioned here, see Kate Crosby, "Only If You Let Go of That Tree: Ordination without Parental Consent according to Theravāda Vinaya," *Buddhist Studies Review* 22 (2005), 155–73.

The very different narratives of the Buddha's and Rahula's quitting of lay life leaves us with two contrasting models for ordination—leaving home against family expectations as pursued by the Buddha-to-be, and leaving home in fulfilment of family expectations, indeed even following other ordained family members.[59] I have several times heard Buddhists from Asian backgrounds express attraction to forms of Buddhism that were untraditional for their family, specifically in relation to which of these models is seen as authoritative. In other words, they were attracted to Westernized forms of Buddhism, unconcerned with filial devotion and less familiar with the *vinaya* regulations and life narratives other than that of the Buddha. What this means for the textual tradition, however, is the promulgation of a form of passive resistance to parental reluctance, namely the model of refusing nutrition until the parents concede. Thus Sudinna, the first monk to break the *pārājikā* rule against sexual intercourse, who was mentioned above in relation to the question of providing a male heir although renouncing, had first achieved his reluctant parents' consent for his ordination only by undertaking a hunger strike for seven days until his parents eventually give in following the intercession of his friends.[60]

Another occasion on which Rāhula is the model for shaping *vinaya* rules also offers models for how novices themselves should behave. This is the establishment of the rule that monks must provide adequate accommodation for novices, after the Buddha finds that Rāhula has been living in his toilet. In this story, Rāhula does not use his status as the son of the Buddha to demand better treatment but meekly finds shelter in the one place uninhabited—the Buddha's toilet. The rule is linked to two *jātaka*, the *Tipallatthamiga Jātaka* (no. 16) and the *Tittira Jātaka* (no. 319). Both allow the Buddha to explain how Rāhula was already obedient and keen to learn in previous lifetimes. There are interesting nuances in terms of prescriptive behavior. According to the pre-story of the *Tipallatthamiga Jātaka,* not only did Rāhula not make any special demands on account of his family connections, but he also put up with the cruel attention that this status brought him. Mean monks put out rubbish and brooms as if the novices had not finished their sweeping duty and then accuse him. Rather than protest, he apologizes as if the accusation were valid.[61] *Tipallatthamiga* means "deer in three postures," and the main story relates how in a previous life Rāhula-to-be, a fawn, was brought by his mother to the head stag for education. He was a good student, and on being caught one day in a hunter's trap in the woods, he did just what the head stag (the Buddha-to-be) had told him: he feigned not just death, but decay. He moved the leaves around him so that he could answer the call of nature without being spotted, he breathed only through the nostril on the side he was lying on, keeping his visible nostril closed and still, and he bloated out his stomach. The hunter

59. On the continuation of familial relationships after and through ordination, see Kate Crosby, "Only If You Let Go of That Tree."

60. I. B. Horner, *The Book of the Discipline* (London: The Pali Text Society, 1938), 1: 121 ff.

checking his traps then believed that the fawn had been dead for a few days and had begun to putrefy in the heat. When the hunter unhooked the young deer's leg to start preparing the carcass, the deer scampered off to freedom. He attained freedom from the trap and hunter because he had assiduously followed the Buddha-to-be's advice—a clear analogy for Rāhula's enlightenment under the Buddha in the present lifetime. In the second story *Tittira* means "partridge." There Rāhula-to-be ends up being kept by a hunter as a decoy partridge, allowing the hunter to kill wild partridges. The decoy partridge's attempts to warn the wild partridges off have the opposite effect, attracting them to within the hunter's reach. When he tries to stay silent to avoid this result, the plan is again foiled as the hunter beats him and his squeals once more attract the wild partridges. His scruples lead him, when an opportunity arises, to seek the advice of a sage—the Buddha-to-be. Is the analogy here not only in the partridge's keenness to learn but also in the fact that he was being used in the current life—and other lifetimes where the Buddha-to-be sought to renounce in spite of having a son—as a decoy to ensnare others? Rāhula-to-be wants to know from the sage whether or not it is his fault that the other partridges are caught by the hunter. He is told, no, it is not his fault.

> If no sin lurks in the heart,
> Innocent the deed will be.
> He who plays a passive part
> From all guilt is counted free.[62]

While this answer fits with the doctrine of intentional action and individual responsibility, there are interesting further messages about responsibility: the source of entrapment is not at fault. If we take the analogy further, Rāhula, the child who over lifetimes is an obstacle for his father, is not at fault. It is tempting to see here a statement about the innocence of the powerless child.

Two other *jātakas* tell us a little more about child–parent relationships. One is the ongoing relationship between a son and his mother after ordination.[63] This is very familiar from even modern Theravada practice, but it is found here in Rāhula's going to his *upajjha* Sāriputta for help in securing the right decoction to heal his mother's gastric condition, the framing story for the highly complex and entertaining *Abbhantara Jātaka* (no. 281) about the quest for the "middle mango." The other is the *Mahā-ukkusa Jātaka* (no. 486). While this *jātaka* is another example of Rāhula's filial devotion, it also contains a message limiting the service of a devoted child. The baby turtle (Rāhula-to-be) offers to

61. The importance of accepting criticism from one's superiors even if not valid is also seen in stories concerning Ānanda.

62. Cowell et al., *The Jātaka or Stories of the Buddha's Former Births*, 3: 44.

63. On the ongoing role of the mother in the life of a monk, see Kate Crosby, "Gendered Symbols in Theravada Buddhism: Missed Positives in the Representation of the Female," *Hsuan Chuang Journal of Buddhist Studies* 9 (March 2008), 31–47.

take his father's place on a dangerous mission to prevent troublesome visitors to their island from destroying an osprey's nest. The father-turtle expresses appreciation of his sentiment but rejects his offer because he, with his greater size, will be more effective in the task.

As model student, keen to learn and meek in the acceptance of blame, when the Buddha names individual followers as "foremost of" specific activities and skills, Rāhula receives from him the title of *aggo sikkhākāmānaṃ* "foremost of those keen for training."[64] All the *suttas* addressed to Rāhula are specifically about training, and Rāhula quickly masters the training the Buddha offers him. What is particularly interesting is that they are age and capacity specific. Of course, the Buddha gives the teaching because he recognizes his son's readiness. Yet the age-related nature of the teaching, which the commentaries make explicit, comes across also in the style of the teaching.

The *Ambalaṭṭhikārāhulovāda Sutta* (*Majjhima Nikāya Sutta* no. 61) is taught to Rāhula when he is just seven years old, in the year following his ordination. The teachings are given in relation to very vivid, external metaphors. Thus the Buddha uses the water and water bowl that Rāhula had just provided for washing the Buddha's feet and then a story about two contrasting royal war elephants to teach the importance of truthfulness:

> "Rāhula, do you see this small amount of water left in the bowl?" "Yes, sir." "So small, Rāhula, is the recluseship of those who are not ashamed to tell a deliberate lie." Then the Blessed One threw away the remaining water.... "Rāhula, do you see that water being thrown away?" "Yes, sir." '"Rāhula, those who are not ashamed to tell a deliberate lie have thrown away their recluseship in just the same way." ... "Rāhula, do you see that the bowl is now hollow and empty?" "Yes, sir." "That's how hollow and empty the recluseship is of those who are not ashamed to tell a deliberate lie, Rāhula."[65]

The story of the war elephants is intriguing. One war elephant fights for his rider with every part of his body with the exception of his trunk, which he keeps back. The other war elephant gives everything to killing, including his trunk, and his rider thinks:

> This royal tusker with tusks as long as chariot poles ... performs his task in battle ... [the passage includes much description of the elephant and exactly how he fights] also with his trunk. He has given up his life. Now there is nothing this royal tusker elephant would not do. So too, Rāhula, when one

64. F. L. Woodward, *The Book of the Gradual Sayings (Aṅguttara-Nikāya) or More-Numbered Suttas* (Oxford: The Pali Text Society, 1932), 18.
65. Here I have substantially adapted the Ñāṇamoli and Bodhi translation of this passage (see n. 66 below).

is not ashamed to tell a deliberate lie, there is no evil, I say, that one would not do. Therefore Rāhula, you should train thus: "I will not utter a falsehood even as a joke."[66]

This simile of the war elephants relies on a number of complex issues. It draws on two contrasting but concomitant responses to horror: a young boy's natural delight in gory stories and the real fear of the terrifying war elephants. Even until relatively recent times (the early European period) elephants were used in the Theravada world not just in battle, but to perform horrific executions. By keeping something of himself back, the elephant retains an element of dignity or, we might say, his humanity. He had kept a part of his life as his own. The elephant who uses even his trunk has acquired the taste for killing and his rider realizes there is nothing he would not do. A person who loses his shame at lying has reached the same state: there is nothing he would not do. Managing not to lie, even when surrounded by and having to engage in bad things, allows one to retain some control on one's own life and morality. This element, a way of keeping one's integrity in the midst of horror, recalls the *jātaka* of the decoy partridge related above. Not for the first time such texts prompt me to think that the religious narrative of the Buddha developing in a life of privileged royalty and the scholarly narrative of Buddhism developing in a context of urbanization and affluent merchant patronage have conspired to mislead us into an assumption of a kind of *pax Buddhica* reigning in the Saṅgha camps.[67] To me much of the instruction on morality and meditation is built not on the assumption of a tranquil, civilized life, even if that is something to aspire to through renunciation, but on its opposite: how to carve out such tranquility and civilization within oneself given the inevitable horror and trauma not only of death—the element most focused on in writings about Buddhism—but of life.

According to the commentary, the Buddha teaches Rāhula the water bowl and elephant allegories because he realizes that "Young boys are fond of telling lies." According to the commentary also, he tells Rāhula that novices shouldn't spend their time talking about animals, yet the teaching reflects the interest in

66. Translations from Bhikkhu Ñāṇamoli and Bhikkhu Bodhi, *The Middle Length Discources of the Buddha*, (Oxford: The Pali Text Society, 1932), 523–26. A summary of key points from the commentary and a succinct summary of Rāhula's career is given on p. 1265 n. 637.

67. In other words, the internalization of ethics and doctrine, coupled with realism regarding the external world, which we recognize as key features of Buddhism in theory, need to be seen as more broadly applicable in practice. Many stories set in the Saṅgha indicate the risk of violence and the problem of bullying within the Saṅgha, prevalent not only in narrative but in considerations of how to apply the penalties of the *pātimokkha* to those who refuse its procedures. (For more on this theme, see Andrew Huxley, "The *Vinaya*: Legal System or Performance-Enhancing Drug?" in *The Buddhist Forum*, vol. 4, ed. T. Skorupski (SOAS, London 1996), 141–63.) Neither modern experience nor the narratives of the canon and commentaries can allow us to think that children were easily safeguarded from these problems.

animal stories.[68] The Buddha then asks Rāhula the function of a mirror. Rāhula answers: "For the purpose of reflection, venerable sir,"[69] allowing the Buddha then, through word association, to teach Rāhula to reflect before, during, and after undertaking any physical, verbal, or mental action, as to whether that action would harm himself or others. This teaching offers the child a straightforward definition of wholesome and unwholesome action, a topic that could be highly technical. At each stage of this teaching, which concerns honesty and behaving with due consideration, the Buddha engages Rāhula with simple questions that he can answer.

The next *sutta* in the *Majjhima Nikāya,* the *Mahārāhulovāda Sutta,* begins as a teaching on the lack of "me" and "mine." It is set, according the commentary, when Rāhula "was eighteen years old, for the purpose of dispelling desire connected with the household life."[70] At this age, Rāhula is gaining a sense of pride in his own power and appearance. He is aware of his similarity to the Buddha, hence the appropriateness of his learning that

> Any kind of material form whatever, whether past, future, or present, internal or external, should be seen as it actually is with proper wisdom thus, 'This is not mine, this I am not, this is not my self.' Likewise, the same is true of the other four *khandha* that also make up the individual, 'feeling, perception, formations and consciousness.'[71]

Rāhula decides to work on this opportunity and so stops to meditate rather than going into the nearby town for alms. The *sutta* develops into a meditation on which internal and external aspects are in fact the five elements earth, water, fire, air, and space, and on the importance of developing "meditation that is like earth ... water, etc." since these remain pure regardless of what is discarded into or onto them.[72] The meditation develops further into the *brahmavihāra* (divine abidings beginning with loving kindness), *asubha* (loathsomeness), and *ānāpānassati* (mindfulness of breathing) meditations, cultimating in Rāhula's breathing in and out "contemplating impermanence ... fading away, cessation ... and relinquishment [such that] even the final in-breaths and out-breaths are known as they cease, not unknown."[73] In contemplating giving Rāhula this teaching, the Buddha, according to the commentary, assesses his readiness for it as follows:

68. *daharakumārā nāma piyamusāvādā honti.* and *sāmaṇerena nāma, rāhula, tiracchānakathaṃ kathetuṃ na vaṭṭati*, respectively. Text taken from http://www.tipitaka.org/romn/, last accessed February 9, 2011. My translation.
69. Ñāṇamoli and Bodhi, *The Middle Length Discources of the Buddha*, 524.
70. Ñāṇamoli and Bodhi, *The Middle Length Discources of the Buddha*, 1266 n. 640.
71. Ñāṇamoli and Bodhi, *The Middle Length Discources of the Buddha*, 527.
72. Ñāṇamoli and Bodhi, *The Middle Length Discources of the Buddha*, 528–30.
73. Ñāṇamoli and Bodhi, *The Middle Length Discources of the Buddha*, 532. Bodhi explains this last phrase as meaning "the meditator dies calmly, with mindfulness and awareness"(1267 n. 647).

> The Lord Buddha walking along in front thought, "The skin, flesh and blood of Rāhula's body is now mature. Since the time has come for his mind to take the plunge into the engaging subjects beginning with the basis of form, how is Rāhula in fact spending most of his time?" Then the moment he turned his attention to this topic, the Buddha saw what was going on in Rāhula's mind as clearly as if it were a fish in clear water or the reflection of his face in a clean mirror.[74]

The Buddha recognizes that Rāhula is developing pride and an interest in worldly things, so he provides the teaching outlined above. The *Rāhulasutta*[75] contains a series of verses guiding Rāhula toward being a true renouncer rather than developing a craving toward the monastic requisites, and encouraging him to pursue spiritual friendship (which Buddhaghosa identifies as advice the Buddha gave Rāhula regularly). The *Rāhulasutta* in the section on fours in the *Aṅguttara Nikāya* contains the same teaching on the lack of me (self) and mine in relation to the elements, but excluding the fifth element, space.[76] The *Rāhulasaṃyutta* of the *Saṃyutta Nikāya* also contains meditation topics connected with impermanence and lack of me and mine.[77] These meditation teachings culminate in the *Cullarāhulovādasutta* (*Majjhima Nikāya Sutta* no.147).[78] The Buddha realizes, "The states that ripen in deliverance have ripened in Rāhula." He then takes him to the "Blind Men's Grove"[79] and repeats the teachings on impermanence, no self/lack of me and mine with regard to the five aggregates. "Now while this discourse was being spoken, through not clinging the venerable Rāhula's mind was liberated from the taints,"[80] that is, Rāhula becomes an *arhat*, an enlightened being not subject to rebirth.[81]

While these *suttas* are specifically identified in the canon as teachings for Rāhula, the commentator Buddhaghosa adds to this list of texts "The Boy's (or Novice's) Questions" from the *Kuddhakapāṭha*. This is a counting text in the classic decade format so familiar in European children's literature. Like the

74. *Bhagavāpi purato gacchantova cintesi—"paripuṇṇacchavimaṃsalohito dāni rāhulassa attabhāvo. Rajanīyesu rūpārammaṇādīsu hi cittassa pakkhandanakālo jāto, kiṃ bahulatāya nu kho rāhulo vītināmetī"ti. Atha sahāvajjaneneva pasanna-udake macchaṃ viya, parisuddhe ādāsamaṇḍale mukhanimittaṃ viya ca tassa taṃ cittuppādaṃ addasa.* Commentary to MN62. Text from http://www.tipitaka.org/romn/, last accessed February 9, 2011. My translation.

75. *Suttanipāta* II.11; K. R. Norman, *The Group of Discourses (Sutta-nipāta)* vol. II (Oxford: The Pali Text Society, 1992), 36–37.

76. Woodward, *The Book of the Gradual Sayings*, 171–72.

77. Bhikkhu Bodhi, *The Connected Discourses of the Buddha: A New Translation of the Saṃyutta Nikāya* (Boston: Wisdom Publications, 2000), 694–99.

78. Ñāṇamoli and Bodhi, *The Middle Length Discources of the Buddha*, 1126–28.

79. Ñāṇamoli and Bodhi, *The Middle Length Discources of the Buddha*, 1126.

80. Ñāṇamoli and Bodhi, *The Middle Length Discources of the Buddha*, 1127.

81. Pāsādika points out that the Chinese *Ekottarāgama* account of his Enlightenment describes him engaging in meditation after this advice. "Having received from the Buddha the decisive advice, Rahula practiced mindfulness of breathing, experienced *dhyāna* (trance state), and obtained the three kinds of *abhijñā* (higher knowledges) culminating in penetrating insight." (See Bhikkhu Pāsādika, "Rahula," 711).

teaching on the two elephants mentioned above, it starts from animals in a sense but quickly develops into naming demanding topics related to doctrine:

One is what?—All creatures subsist by nutriment.
Two is what?—Name and form.
Three is what?—Three kinds of feeling.
Four is what?—Four Noble Truths.
Five is what?—Five categories of what is affected by clinging.
Six is what?—Six bases in oneself.
Seven is what?—Seven enlightenment factors.
Eight is what?—The Noble Eightfold Path.
Nine is what?—Nine abodes of creatures.
Ten is what?—He that is endowed with the ten factors is declared an *Arahant*.[82]

It may simply be that it is another text for a novice that leads Buddhaghosa to identify it as a text for Rāhula. On the other hand, as a text that makes the transition from animal imagery to doctrine and provides a basic list of doctrine, it makes an interesting intermediate text between the first and the later, two more sophisticated doctrinal *Majjhima Nikāya* texts taught to the mature Rāhula. Buddhaghosa identifies *The Boy's Questions* as also being taught to Rāhula when he was seven years old and as designed to prevent him from talking about inappropriate things.[83]

Thus, in the *suttas* connected with Rāhula, we have a body of literature that provides a model of what and how to teach novices and young monks at different stages of development, and that underlines the necessity of repeated teaching of encouragement to enjoy the renouncer life and the harder meditation subjects. In the later period of Pali textual development, when handbooks on specific topics were compiled, the Theravada tradition developed this genre further by producing handbooks for neophites, such as the *Bālāvatāra*, "An introduction [to Pali grammar] for boys," or the *Khuddasikkhā*, the brief training [in *vinaya* practice] for new monks (i.e., new *bhikkhu*, usually those in their early twenties). Of course, these canonical *suttas* from the first millennium BCE

82. Bhikkhu Ñāṇamoli, *The Minors Readings, The First Book of the Minor Collection* (Oxford: The Pali Text Society, 1997), 2.

83. Buddhaghosa names the texts associated with Rāhula in a single list with the age and purpose.

Mahārāhulovādasuttaṃ aṭṭhārasa vassasāmaṇerakāle vuttaṃ. Cūḷarāhulovādasuttaṃ avassikabhikkhukāle vuttaṃ. Kumārakapañhañca idañca ambalaṭṭhikarāhulovādasuttaṃ sattavassikasāmaṇerakāle vuttaṃ. Tesu rāhulasuttaṃ abhiṇhovādatthaṃ, rāhulasaṃyuttaṃ, therassa vipassanāgabbhagahaṇatthaṃ, mahārāhulovādaṃ gehassitachandarāgavinodan atthaṃ, cūḷarāhulovādaṃ therassa pañcadasa-vimuttiparipācanīya-dhammaparipākakāle dhammaparipākakāle vuttaṃ.... Sāmaṇerapañhaṃ ayuttavacanapahānatthaṃ, idaṃ ambalaṭṭhikarāhulovādasuttaṃ sampajanamusāvādassa akaraṇatthaṃ vuttaṃ Commentary to MN62. Text taken from http://www.tipitaka.org/romn/, last accessed on February 9, 2011.

are not the earliest texts in the world for children. Early literature for the instruction of children is a common development within religious literature. Moreover, there appear to be texts for children among the earliest surviving body of written literature in the world, from the Sumerian renaissance period (c. second millennium BCE).[84] Yet the texts for Rāhula show a sophisticated regard for age/maturity-specific teaching material.

The ability of the Buddha to take the starting point of his audience as the starting point of his teaching, adapting its level to students' capacity, a characteristic taken to one logical extreme in the famous emphasis on *upāya* (skill-in-means) in some Mahāyāna *sūtras*, is emphasized throughout Buddhology. Yet appreciation of how much this quality in effective teaching has influenced the formulation of the canon is worthy of closer attention in academic scholarship more broadly.[85] We have begun to see an appreciation of how texts may serve female audiences, as feminism has enabled us to see for the first time material that had been staring us in the face. The nuanced psychology in the texts is coming to the attention of those working in the emerging fields of Buddhist cognitive therapy and counseling.[86] Yet the awareness of children as an audience prior to the arrival of Sunday schools and their equivalent in the colonial period has remained very limited. Just as we can reject any simplistic assumption that the more accessible and entertaining material of the canon, that is, the *jātakas*, are designed for lay people and children in the light of their close connection to *vinaya* regulation and monastic deportment,[87] so we can see the presence of challenging material for the child in other parts of the canon through this reexamination of the *sutta* corpus.[88]

84. See Gillian Adams, "The First Children's Literature? The Case for Sumer," *Children's Literature* 14 (1986), 1–30.

85. By academic scholarship more broadly, I mean beyond the monastic academic scholarship which still does not seem to transfer substantially into Buddhist studies outside of that context. As a student in Sri Lanka in the early 90s, I was struck by how much the skill of the Buddha in teaching and the qualities of his voice were a focus of writings by monks. I have not returned to the subject in Sinhala writings to confirm the validity of that impression or the sophistication of the analysis, but—after my initial struggle to feel any enthusiasm for the topic—it made sense to me that those who are placed in the position of spontaneous teaching to a variety of audiences and public recitation would retain a keener awareness of these issues than would those working from the comfort of their personal engagement with the printed page.

86. Personal communication with Maya Shobrok (May 23, 2011), who has worked on the applicability of the concept of *prapañca* to cognitive therapy while based in Sri Lanka at the point when the field was about to expand rapidly, partly in response to the Asian tsunami.

87. The relationship between Theravāda *jātaka* and *vinaya*, which I point out in note 10 above, has been overlooked in recent studies of the genre, as I shall explore in more detail elsewhere. The use of *jātaka* for more general audiences including the displacing of *jātaka* as a genre in Western/modern imagination in this way brings to mind other audience-shifts. An example is the uptake of the *Mūlasarvāstivāda* narrative, including some mentioned here, into the *Divyāvadāna* and later *avadāna* literature, and beyond that into court plays.

88. I shall offer an overview of the canonical and post-canonical Pali texts aimed at teaching the children and the young elsewhere.

Returning to those texts dedicated to teaching Rāhula, we see that the Buddha maintains a vigilant awareness of the traps Rāhula might fall into and the level of maturity he has reached. He then tailors his teaching to avoid such pitfalls and take maximum advantage of the stage of readiness for instruction. The care given in this pedagogy enables the Buddha to fulfill his role as father. As the commentary on the *Māhārāhulovādasutta (Majjhima Nikāya* no. 62) points out, it is in this regard that Rāhula can declare in his *Apadāna*: "As a jay might guard her egg, and a flywhisk clasp its excellent tail of hair, so the wise Lord Buddha, of perfect conduct, closely watched over me."[89]

Perhaps surprisingly, given the pervasiveness of childhood ordination in Theravada countries and Rāhula's being the recipient of the first childhood ordination, current ordination rituals, which enact the prince's leaving the palace, are modeled on the ordination of the Buddha, rather than on that of Rāhula.[90] Yet the connection between Rāhula and the aspiring male practitioner does seem to be present in the depictions of Rāhula in early Buddhist art. Taddei observes that in early Gandhāran art this scene is often paired with that of the *Dīpaṃkarajātaka,* in which the future Buddha, as the young brahmin Sumedho, lays down his hair on the ground for the then Buddha Dīpaṃkara to walk over and receives his own prediction of future buddhahood.[91] He notes the same pairing in Ajanta cave 19 and in an account of the missionary Guṇavarman's cave paintings in the early fifth century CE in China under the patronage of Wen Ti of the Sung. "There he [Guṇavarman] stayed several years in a mountain hermitage, under a lone towering crag that he dubbed—from its similiarity to a famous Indian original—the "Vulture Peak." In a neighbouring temple "on the north wall of the Jewel-moon hall, he painted with his own hand a figure of Rāhula, and the scene of the scholar-youth Rāhula spreading out his hair [on the ground before the Buddha] Dīpaṃkara. When finished, these emitted light every night, and continued to do so for a long time."[92]

In art, then, Rāhula's receiving his spiritual "inheritance" from his father, that is, his ordination and promise of enlightenment, is associated with Gotama receiving his own prediction from Dīpaṃkara. For Taddei this connection is further

89. *Idañ ca pana sandhāya rāhulatthero bhikkhusaṅghamajjhe tathāgatassa guṇaṃ kathento idamāha "Kikīva bījaṃ rakkheyya, cāmarī vālamuttamaṃ; Nipako sīlasampanno, mamaṃ rakkhi tathāgato"ti. (apa. 1.2.83).* Text taken from http://www.tipitaka.org/romn/, last accessed, April 26, 2011. Translation mine.

90. The interpretations I have seen on You Tube of Shan ordinations as reenactments of Rāhula's ordination seem to be a modern interpretation, not one traditionally or widely held. An alternative interpretation by Shan is that it reenacts the ordination of the emperor Asoka's son Mahinda, who took Theravada to Sri Lanka (personal communication with Jotika Khur-Yearn April 28, 2011).

91. A list of Gandharan depictions of the encounter between the Buddha and Rāhula on the former's return to Kapilavastu is found in Maurizio Taddei, "The Dīpaṃkara-jātaka and Siddhārtha's Meeting with Rāhula: How Are They Linked to the Flaming Buddha?" *Annali rivista del dipartimento di studi Asiatici e del dipartimento di studi e ricerche su Africa e paesi Arabi* 52, fasc.1 (1992), 105 with nn. 11 and 13.

92. Taddei, "The Dīpaṃkara-jātaka and Siddhārtha's Meeting with Rāhula," 106, citing A. C. Soper, *Literary Evidence for Early Buddhist Art in China* (Ascone 1959), 43.

supported by the emission of flames in the depictions both of Dīpaṃkara and of Gotama Buddha. The emission of flames from around the Buddha is described in the *Mahāvastu* version of the episode when the Buddha returns to Kapilavastu and meets Rāhula.[93] Taddei points out that "the emission of flames is declared by the *Suvarṇaprabhāsasūtra* to be the aspect Buddhas assume whenever they reveal themselves to Bodhisattvas."[94] Taddei identifies these as stories of lineage:[95] the episodes present the lineage of previously enlightened beings handing down the inheritance to the enlightened of the future. Soper suggests that the missionary Guṇavarman chose these two depictions as representations of eager youth.[96]

These stories and paintings suggest the importance these stories have had for the aspiring young Buddhist, or for the missionary setting out into new territory, given Rāhula's status as the *aggo sikkhākāmānaṃ*, the foremost of those who strive to learn, and they illustrate his trust and security in the Buddha's instruction. Thus it seems that the Buddha–Rāhula relationship offers a structure for the young devotee, particularly the young monk. As was observed above, the tragic stories of separation and abandonment for the children and wife in the Buddha life story and the *jātakas* have been interpreted as allowing for the cathartic expression of such loss in real life. Similarly the happy story of Rāhula's spiritual apprenticeship to the Buddha can be seen as giving expression to the emotions of filial and disciple devotion. The narrative provides a model for the heroic following the path trodden before him by the father, Buddha or senior monk.

It is Rāhula's devoted keenness to train in meditation, specifically, and his gradual progression through higher and higher stages, that make him important in the one tradition today that appears to regard him as an important founding father. This is the *boran yogāvacara kammaṭṭhāna*, the traditional meditation, of the Theravada world.[97] *Borān kammaṭṭhāna* is these days regarded by many as unorthodox because of its method of physically incorporating the outcomes, *nimitta*, of meditation practice along energy centers into the "womb" of the practitioner. Because the tradition was widely believed to bestow various kinds of power, including military power, it was suppressed—under the rhetoric of canonical-based reform—by Mongkut in late nineteenth-century Thailand and Cambodia, a process continued in the latter country by the French in the mid-twentieth century. It was further destroyed under the Marxist agenda

93. J. Jones, *The Mahāvastu* (London: Luzac and Company, 1987), 1: 196; 3: 115–16.

94. Taddei, "The Dīpaṃkara-jātaka and Siddhārtha's Meeting with Rāhula," 106.

95. Taddei, "The Dīpaṃkara-jātaka and Siddhārtha's Meeting with Rāhula," 105.

96. Taddei, "The Dīpaṃkara-jātaka and Siddhārtha's Meeting with Rāhula," 106, citing A. C. Soper, *Literary Evidence for Early Buddhist Art in China*, 239.

97. For a survey of literature on the subject up to 1999, see Kate Crosby, "Tantric Theravada: A bibliographic essay on the writings of François Bizot and other literature on the *Yogāvacara* Tradition," *Contemporary Buddhism*, Nov. 2000, issue 2: 141–98. The most important work on the subject since then has been Olivier de Bernon's *Le manual des maîtres de kammaṭṭhan: étude et presentation de rituals de meditation dans la tradition du bouddhisme khmer*, PhD thesis, Paris: Institut National des Langues et Civilisations Orientales, 2000, 2 vols. The most recent publication

there and in Laos in the decades that followed. Yet prior to such suppression it had been the practice of choice for royalty and Saṅgharāja, the heads of the Buddhist monastic community, as we can see from texts connected with such figures in Cambodia, Laos, Thailand, and Sri Lanka. Venerable Phra Khru Sittasangvorn Veera Thanaveero is the current master of *borān kammaṭṭhāna* in the lineage of eighteenth-century Saṅgharāja Somdet Suk Kaitheun, and head of the fifth *kaṇa* (Pali *gaṇa*) of Wat Rājasittharām, in Bangkok. Wat Rājasittharām is Somdet Suk Kaitheun's former residence and the home to many of his manuscripts, while Somdet Suk Kaitheun was the heir to the teaching of Ayutthaya meditation masters, several of whom had also transmitted the tradition to Sri Lanka in the 1750s. According to Venerable Veera Thanaveero, the oral tradition, at least as far back as Somdet Suk, regards the Buddha's son Rāhula as the first teacher in the tradition, and Venerable Veera sees this fact as obvious when we look at Rāhula's progressive development in meditation, in contrast to the instantaneous enlightenment of other early practitioners.[98]

Returning to the imagery of the youthful hero following in his father's footsteps and the devoted student who shirks no hardship in his dedication to teacher and training, both themes are important in Indian narrative literature, most familiar perhaps from the narratives of the *Mahābhārata*. On this note, it is interesting to observe the heroic tone of such narratives echoed in the following verses about the relationship between Rāhula and his father. The verses are taken from the commentary to the *Mahārāhulasutta* (*Majjhimanikāya* 62), explored above. While the sentiments expressed here are the occasion for the Buddha to teach Rāhula the lack of self/me and mine in order to guard against potentially dangerous pride, they are nevertheless also a celebration of Rāhula's coming of age and recognition of his power as he becomes more like his father. The text takes the opportunity, in commenting on the phrase "Now it happened that venerable Rāhula, having dressed early and taken his bowl and outer robe, was following closely behind the Buddha"[99] to celebrate the potential of Rāhula in his closeness and similarity to the Buddha. Far from being an obstacle to his father, he is the "good" or "fortunate" Rāhula, and the lines give expression to another powerful human sentiment—the yearning of a father for his son to be a little version of himself:[100]

the subject is Kate Crosby, Andrew Skilton and Amal Gunasena, 'The Sutta on Understanding Death in the Transmission of *borān* Meditation from Siam to the Kandyan Court', *Journal of Indian Philosophy* 40.2 (2012), 177--98.

98. Interviews September 1 and 2, 2011, conducted by Andrew Skilton and Phibul Choompolpaisal under the research project "Revealing Hidden Collections" (Bodleian Library, Oxford) as part of the Traditional Theravada: Continuity and Diversity programme sponsored by Dhammakaya International, UK.

99. *Āyasmāpi kho rāhulo pubbaṇhasamayaṃ nivāsetvā pattacīvaramādāya bhagavantaṃ piṭṭhito piṭṭhito anubandhi*. Text from MN62 *atthakathā* from http://www.tipitaka.org/romn/, last accessed February 9, 2011. Translation mine.

100. My thanks to Vanessa R. Sasson for pointing out this last point, that the yearnings of fathers, perhaps of the redactors themselves as fathers, is expressed here. While recent scholarship, as was explored above, identifies the expression of

In this passage, when it says that Rāhula followed closely behind the Buddha, it means that he didn't lose sight of him but made his own movement seamless with his, following right behind, emulating his every gesture. For as the Lord Buddha walks gracefully just ahead, placing one foot after the other, so Rāhula[101] comes right on his heels, following in his footsteps.

There shines the Lord Buddha in the middle of the forest of blossoming Sal trees like a prime bull elephant in rut come out to wallow on a good patch of ground,[102] and there's the good Rāhula, like the elephant calf gone out after that marvellous bull.

At eventide the Lord Buddha comes out of his crystal cave like a maned lioned pacing his territory and out comes the good Rāhula like the lion cub following that lion, lord of the beasts.

The Lord Buddha is like a great tiger, strong in tooth, from a grove in the glorious forest of the crystal mountain, and the good Rāhula like the cub following up at the rear of that tiger king.

The Lord Buddha is like the Sovereign of the Garuḍa birds[103] coming out of a grove of silk-cotton trees, and the good Rāhula is like the Garuḍa fledgeling coming out behind that Sovereign of Garuḍas.

The Lord Buddha is like the regent of the golden swans soaring up into the sky from the resplendent-peaked[104] mountain, and the good Rāhula is like the cygnet soaring after that lord of the swans.

The Lord Buddha is like the golden ark fathoming the depths of the Great Lake, and the good Rāhula is like the companion vessel that follows on behind that golden ship.

The Lord Buddha is like the Universal Emperor advancing across the surface of the sky thanks to the power of the treasure that is his universal-discus, and the good Rāhula sets out after him is like the treasure that is the crown prince to that emperor.[105]

The Lord Buddha is like the Regent of the Stars tracking his way across the heavens shedding all clouds, and the good Rāhula is like the pure medicine star,[106] tracing the path of the lunar Lord.

the female experience in Buddhist narrative, especially that of mothers, wives, and would-be *arhats*, I have seen no exploration of paternal sentiments.

101. The text describes Rāhula as a *thera* in this line, presumably retrospectively, since he is still a novice at this point.

102. Apparently this is what elephants and other animals that experience rut do (my thanks for Andrew Skilton for this explanation). The Pali phrase allows for a dual reading, for animal or for Buddha, in which case *bhūmi* could refer either to physical ground or to spiritual state, "entering into an excellent level."

103. A *garuḍa* is a mythical, divine bird.

104. Malalasekera explains that this mountain range in the Himalayas, home to the golden swans, is so-called because "it is composed of all kinds of precious metals" (Malalasekera 1937–38: 809).

105. A king or emperor traditionally has seven "gems" or treasures, including his advisor or eldest son.

106. i.e., Venus, but the feminine connotation of "Venus" makes use of the name inappropriate here.

The Lord Buddha is born in the line of the King Great Elected, first ever to be elected, and in the lineage of his descendant King Effulgent, so too the good Rāhula.

The Lord Buddha is born into the family of the warrior caste, by birth as utterly pure as fresh milk poured into a conch shell, so too the good Rāhula.

The Lord Buddha gave up his kingdom to renounce, so too the good Rāhula.

The body of the Lord Buddha is adorned with the 32 marks of a great man like the soaring gemmed gate-tower to the cities of the gods, breath-taking like the celestial coral trees, a whole mass of full-blown flowers, so too the body of good Rāhula.

So it is that these two, both complete in their perfection, both regal renouncers, both refined princes of warrior stock, both golden in complexion, both bearing the marks of great men, processing along the one path, shine forth competing in splendour with the great celestials Indra, Great Yāma, the gods of the Santusita heaven of contentment, the beautifully formed Sunimmita gods, the power-wielding Vasavatti gods and the mighty Brahmā gods, outdoing the gods' splendour with their own; theirs is the spendour of two moons, of two suns, as they pursue their single course.[107]

107. Text slightly adapted from *Majjhima Nikāya sutta* 62 *atthakathā* from http://www.tipitaka.org/romn/last accessed 9 February 2010. The text is as follows, the translation my own.

Tattha piṭṭhito piṭṭhito anubandhīti dassanaṃ avijahitvā gamanaṃ abbocchinnaṃ katvā pacchato pacchato iriyāpathānubandhanena anubandhi. Tadā hi bhagavā pade padaṃ nikkhipanto vilāsitagamanena purato purato gacchati, rāhulatthero dasabalassa padānupadiko hutvā pacchato pacchato.

Tattha bhagavā supupphitasālavanamajjhagato subhūmiotaraṇatthāya nikkhantamattavaravāraṇo viya virocittha, rāhulabhaddo ca varavāraṇassa pacchato nikkhantagajapotako viya. Bhagavā sāyanhasamaye maṇiguhato nikkhamitvā gocaraṃ paṭipanno kesarasīho viya, rāhulabhaddo ca sīhamigarājānaṃ anubandhanto nikkhantasīhapotako viya.

Bhagavā maṇipabbatasassirikavanasaṇḍato dāṭhabalo mahābyaggho viya, rāhulabhaddo ca byaggharājānaṃ anubandhabyagghapotako viya.

Bhagavā simbalidāyato nikkhantasupaṇṇarājā viya, rāhulabhaddo ca supaṇṇarājassa pacchato nikkhantasupaṇṇapotako viya.

Bhagavā cittakūṭapabbatato gaganatalaṃ pakkhandasuvaṇṇahaṃsarājā viya, rāhulabhaddo ca haṃsādhipatiṃ anupakkhandahaṃsapotako viya.

Bhagavā mahāsaraṃ ajjhogāḷhā suvaṇṇamahānāvā viya, rāhulabhaddo ca suvaṇṇanāvaṃ pacchā anubandhanāvāpotako viya.

Bhagavā cakkaratanānubhāvena gaganatale sampayātacakkavattirājā viya, rāhulabhaddo ca rājānaṃ anusampayātapariṇāyakaratanaṃ viya.

Bhagavā vigatavalāhakaṃ nabhaṃ paṭipannatārakarājā viya, rāhulabhaddo ca tārakādhipatino anumaggapaṭipannā parisuddhaosadhitārakā viya.

Bhagavāpi mahāsammatapaveṇiyaṃ okkākarājavaṃse jāto, rāhulabhaddopi.

Bhagavāpi saṅkhe pakkhittakhīrasadiso suparisuddhajātikhattiyakule jāto, rāhulabhaddopi.

Bhagavāpi rajjaṃ pahāya pabbajito, rāhulabhaddopi.Bhagavatopi sarīraṃ dvattiṃsamahāpurisalakkhaṇapaṭimaṇḍitaṃ devanagaresu samussitaratanatoraṇaṃ viya sabbaphāliphullo pāricchattako viya ca atimanoharaṇaṃ, rāhulabhaddassāpi.

Iti dvepi abhinīhārasampannā, dvepi rājapabbajitā, dvepi khattiyasukhumālā, dvepi suvaṇṇavaṇṇā, dvepi lakkhaṇasampannā ekamaggaṃ paṭipannā paṭipāṭiyā gacchantānaṃ dvinnaṃ candamaḍalānaṃ dvinnaṃ sūriyamaḍalānaṃ dvinnaṃ sakkasuyāmasantusitas unimmitavasavattimahābrahmādīnaṃ siriyā siriṃ abhibhavamānā viya virociṃsu.

CHAPTER 5

The Precocious Child in Chinese Buddhism

MIRIAM LEVERING

WHAT IS A CHILD IN CHINA? WHAT IS CHILDHOOD? WHAT IS A PRECOCIOUS BUDDHIST CHILDHOOD?

A large cultural gap looms between the habitual thinking of the modern or postmodern, Western-educated scholar of childhood in China and the thinking of members of earlier periods of Chinese culture. As a postmodern Westerner, I tend to think of the category "child" as referring to a chronologically early period in the development of a person. My first question about childhood in China is, "At what age did members of this culture understand childhood to end?" In China prior to the twentieth century the first questions about childhood have always been, "What are the obligations of a child, particularly an adult child, to his or her parents and family lineage? How do elders ensure that the (adult) child feels and fulfills those obligations?"

Chinese culture during its long evolution provided some answers to these questions. In general, traditional Chinese culture held in ritual and legal contexts that a boy is a child until age twenty, while a girl is a child until thirteen or whenever she gets married. According to the Han dynasty legal texts, boys became adults at fifteen (equal to fourteen by Western reckoning), at which time they were required to pay the taxes levied on adults; other criteria suggest that boys were not regarded as men until they reached age twenty (equal to nineteen by Western reckoning).[1]

1. See Anne Behnke Kinney, "The Theme of the Precocious Child in Early Chinese Literature," *T'oung Pao* 81 (1995), 1–24. Kinney cites "*Lunheng*, chap. 36, "*Xie duan*"; Huang Hui, annotator, *Lunheng jiaoshi* (Taipei: Taiwan shangwu yinshuguan, 1964), 1: 570. Also see Lien-sheng Yang, *Studies in Chinese Institutional History* (Cambridge, MA: Harvard University Press, 1961), 109. According to ritual texts, a boy received

In ritual texts, boys were to be "capped" at a certain age, while girls were to be "pinned" at an earlier age; capping and pinning were symbols of passage into readiness for marriage and adulthood. In legal texts, if not in ritual texts, ages varied with time and place over the long span of rulers and dynasties. Likewise, in pediatric texts, in writings on early education, and in biographical and autobiographical writings, one finds the word "young [person]" used to refer to a stage in the development of a person.[2] In biographical and autobiographical writings, one finds the expression "when I (or she) was very young (*you*)."

Thus a chronological sense of "childhood," "being young (*you* or *xiao*)," does exist throughout the history of Chinese culture. However, one could argue that, at least prior to the seventeenth century, the "discovery of childhood" that Phillipe Ariès wrote about as happening at a particular moment in Europe, the realization that childhood is a significant and separate stage in the life cycle, did not occur outside of medical texts.[3] My own survey of works in many Chinese Buddhist genres makes clear that it definitely did not happen in Chinese Buddhism, at either the elite or the popular level.

Chinese Buddhist texts display almost no interest in childhood as a significant developmental stage. Biographers of monks and nuns give very little space to the subject's childhood. The authors move on quickly to focus on the subject's monastic career. In what little they say of childhood, biographers portray their subjects as not having a childhood like that of others. They were not interested in play, or, if interested, they played at Buddhist rituals. Their play always presaged their future interests and showed their precocious insight into Buddhism.

In the stories and plays that found a wider audience among ordinary people, future Buddhist saints appear as children, but these children likewise demonstrate a remarkable early commitment to the Buddhist path and behave throughout like small adults. At both the elite and the popular levels, the stories of Buddhist children who are destined to be saints or monastics reflect the motif of "the precocious child" that was already evident in Chinese elite

the cap of virility at age twenty *sui*; during the Han he was required to perform military service sometimes at age twenty *sui* and at other times at twenty-three *sui*. See *Liji*, *"Nei ce,"* in *Shisanjing zhushu*, *juan* 28, 243b; *Han shu* 5, 141; and *Yantie lun*, chap. 15, "Wei tong" in *Sibucongkan zhengpian*, *juan* 3, 17: 8b–9a.

2. Ping-chen Hsiung, *A Tender Voyage: Children and Childhood in Late Imperial China* (Stanford, CA: Stanford University Press, 2005), 21.

3. Phillipe Ariès, *Centuries of Childhood: A Social History of Family Life*, trans. Robert Baldick (New York: Alfred A. Knopf, 1970). Wu Pei-yi argues that in China never before the sixteenth century do events of childhood other than those reflecting precocity or filial piety, events that were not exemplary or even typical but were crucial to the destiny of one unique person, claim a place in the autobiographical subject's story of maturation and development. See his *The Confucian's Progress: Autobiographical Writings in Traditional China* (Princeton, NJ: Princeton University Press, 1992), 145.

4. Ping-chen Hsiung, *A Tender Voyage*, 21. I have changed the romanization of the Chinese words from Wade-Giles to *pinyin* in this passage.

culture in the Han dynasty (206 BCE –220 CE.), that is, in the period prior to the spread of Buddhism in China, and that also entered China from India along with Buddhism.

One reason the discovery of childhood did not occur in Chinese writing generally or in that of Chinese Buddhism is that Chinese culture focuses a much greater attention on what one could call "the social child," particularly the social child as adult. The term "social child" refers to the junior position held by both children and adults in relation to his or her family (or fictive family) elders, ancestors, and others in a hierarchically superior position. Ping-chen Hsiung writes that a child *(zi)* is in a subordinate, inferior, humble, and subservient role in relation to seniors. "In this sense, as long as one's parents were alive, or whenever speaking or acting vis-à-vis the elders in the house, any offspring at whatever age always assumes the position of a child *(zi)*. This was the "child" that most Chinese ritual texts, such as the *Record of Rites (Liji)*, referred to when mentioning the word. It is also the meaning most of China's philosophical references, family instructions, and legal documents adopt in consideration. Socially speaking, that is how *zi* was meant to be read in such important contexts as the *Twenty-four Stories of Filial Piety (Ershisi Xiao)*. The broad, social meaning of *zi* as a relative status gave it a role with clear obligations and definite rules regardless of age, a key point in the concept of the "child" in its premodern context.[4]

When I undertook this research into childhood in Chinese Buddhism, I looked first at the many well-loved filial piety *sūtras*, most of which were written in China. I was disappointed to find that all of the characters in these *sūtras* are children *(zi)* in the social sense but adults in the Western chronological and developmental sense. Buddhist Chinese filial piety *sūtras* are filled with "children" who are at the same time adults. They are "children" in relation to their parents throughout their lives. For example, in the *Sutra of the Past Vows of Earth Store Bodhisattva*,[5] the following story is told: During the Dharma Semblance Age there was a brahman daughter who had much merit from former lives and was respected by everyone.[6] Knowing that when her mother was in the world she had not believed in cause and effect, the brahman daughter realized that, in accordance with her karma, her mother would be reborn in the states of woe. Thereupon she sold the family house, procured incense, flowers, and other items, and performed a great offering in the Buddha's temple.[7] The Buddha then offered to show her the place of her mother's rebirth.[8] On seeing her mother in torment and hearing her mother's voice, the brahman daughter suddenly leaped up and fell back, breaking all her limbs.

5. Heng Ching, trans., *Sutra of the Past Vows of Earth Store Bodhisattva*, rev. by Heng Ch'ih, polished by Heng K'uan, certified by Master Hsuan Hua (New York: Buddhist Text Translation Society, The Institute of Advanced Studies of World Religions, 1974).

6. Heng Ching, trans., *Sutra of the Past Vows of Earth Store Bodhisattva*, 76.

7. Heng Ching, trans., *Sutra of the Past Vows of Earth Store Bodhisattva*, 80.

8. Heng Ching, trans., *Sutra of the Past Vows of Earth Store Bodhisattva*, 82.

In the Chinese version of this text, the word translated as "daughter" could also be translated as "woman" or "girl": "daughter" is the primary meaning. It would be just as correct to translate it as "woman," but incorrect to translate it as "girl," because the story makes clear that the protagonist is in a position to sell property; she is a legal adult. At the same time, as a daughter, she has the concerns, actions, and feelings of a "social child"*(zi)*.

Because "child" is a relational term, an unmarried son or daughter is always regarded as a child, since he or she always belongs to and is thought to be dependent on the parents' household. In contemporary Chinese communities at the New Year's festival adults give children "red envelopes" containing money. Chronologically adult but unmarried children receive red envelopes, but once they marry they are no longer children and thus give red envelopes themselves to children. Once a person is ordained as a Buddhist monk or nun, he or she is understood to be no longer a child of the natal family, but rather a "son of the Buddha" in a new fictive family.[9] Because monks and nuns are no longer children in their parents' household, natal family elders do not give them red envelopes.[10]

REBIRTH AND CHILDHOOD

Buddhist cosmologies and teachings on rebirth in China also have an effect on the importance given to children and childhood. In the biographies and hagiographies of the Song dynasty (960–1279) and the twentieth century, for instance, one can easily find references to a male who had been a famous and widely admired monk from a previous age and was now reborn. How much credence was given to these statements is hard to judge from this distance, but since they were supported by teachings about rebirth, in which all Buddhists believed, it is possible that they were taken very seriously. Even in this present era of scientific education, Chinese Buddhists still like to speculate about the previous births of individuals.

Buddhist teachings on rebirth make it impossible to imagine that a child is a *tabula rasa*. Instead, every child comes with endowments from former lifetimes. When these endowments are favorable to encountering and understanding truth, they are called "good roots" or "good faculties" *(shan gen)*. Precocity of a spiritual sort is thus explained. Precocious talent for worldly matters is also understood as a fruit of past karmic actions.

Children also come with tasks and missions that originate in former lifetimes. The story of Sakyamuni's birth, discussed below, provides a well-known

9. The Chinese Buddhist sangha is organized into lineages in which teachers are fathers and their disciples are sons. In the Chinese Buddhist sangha only male relational terms are used.

10. In modern and contemporary times monks and nuns do receive and handle money, which they need to provide themselves with medicine and other needs.

example. My non-Buddhist hostess in Taiwan, one of the first graduates of the Beijing Normal University and the wife of a famous modern educator, offered this explanation when her servant lost her first child shortly after childbirth: The servant should understand that this child had been born in order to cause the maid suffering. The cause of the maid's suffering lay in her actions in a previous lifetime in a relationship with the now reborn child. The maid should accept what had happened as what it clearly was: a karmic retribution. The strong bond between parent and child is created over many lifetimes, as texts from the Song and other dynasties also aver.

CHINESE BUDDHIST MONASTIC LIFE AND CHILDREN

In Buddhist monastic codes and in China's legal codes in the Song dynasty (960–1279), to take one example, in order to leave home and become a postulant in a temple or monastery, a boy had to be at least nineteen and a girl fourteen years of age. A postulant could then be ordained as a novice through examination, by imperial favor, or through the purchase of ordination certificates. The minimum age for full ordination was twenty. These rules accord with the rules for renunciants of the pan-Buddhist world.

However, when one looks at the biographies of Chan monks in the Song dynasty, it appears that the minimum age requirement for becoming a postulant as well as for ordination as a novice was never enforced. The age at which a person left the householder's life varied widely. Some indeed were reported to have passed the examination for ordination (for males, reading 500 sheets of the *Lotus Sutra* or reciting from memory 100 sheets; for a female, reading 300 sheets or reciting from memory 70 sheets) and been ordained as novices at the age of nineteen, the minimal legal age for postulants. But this was by no means the norm. Chun-fang Yu reports that Jiangshan Canyuan, a descendent of the famous Chan figure Fu Dashi, "left the householder's life at three and became ordained at seven."[11] Perhaps this case was unusual, but there are also in the Chan *Transmission of the Lamp* collections accounts of children who became postulants at seven, nine, eleven, thirteen, and fourteen years old, or became ordained at the ages of fifteen, sixteen, and seventeen.[12]

One would think, then, that the subject of children in Chinese monasteries in premodern China would reward a scholar of children in Chinese Buddhism.[13]

11. *Chan-lin seng-pao chuan* 27: 0547.

12. Chun-fang Yu, "Chan Education in the Sung: Ideals and Procedures" in *Neo-ConfucianEducation: The Formative Stage*, ed. William Theodore de Bary and John W. Chaffee (Berkeley and Los Angeles: University of California Press, 1989), 79–80.

13. For the early twentieth century, see the work of Holmes Welch, *The Practice of Chinese Buddhism, 1900–1950* (Cambridge, MA: Harvard University Press, 1967). Welch draws on extensive interviews of Chinese monks who left the mainland for Hong Kong and Taiwan during and after the Chinese civil war that ended in 1949. In one section he focuses on the life cycle of Chinese Buddhist monks, many of

However, except for brief normative prescriptions in monastic codes ("Rules of Purity," *qinggui*), very little can be found in existing documents about children in monasteries. The following autobiographical account by the Chan monk Zuqin (1216–1287) gives more detail than most and provides something of the flavor of the way children were included in monastic life at young ages:

> When I was five years old I entered a temple. As a footboy to the abbot, listening to his conversations with visitors, I came to know that there was "such a matter" [i.e., awakening as understood in the Chan school] and believed I could achieve it. I studied "sitting-in-meditation." But on account of my obtuseness all my life I have suffered repeatedly and bitterly. I was ordained a monk at sixteen and started traveling at eighteen, determined to get to the bottom of "this matter."[14]

Another source for reflection on Chinese Buddhist views of children and childhood is elite and popular Buddhist stories. The first and most fundamental story is that of the Buddha's birth and infancy. This story appealed to both elite and popular audiences, set a pattern for later Buddhist stories of precocious children, and was incorporated into Chinese Buddhist life through many media. We will first consider its treatment in Chinese Buddhism in monasteries and festivals as well as its treatment in the Chinese Chan school, the source of Korean Son, Vietnamese Thien, and Japanese Zen. Then we will look at two stories from *sütras* and popular texts that have been immensely popular in Chinese Buddhist circles since the Song dynasty. These stories are significant in forming Chinese notions of Buddhist children, because the protagonist is a child. I will present a description of the child hero or heroine in the *sütra* stories and also describe an indigenous rendering or renderings of the story in Chinese popular texts. The first story is that of the child bodhisattva pilgrim Sudhana (Ch. Shancai) in the *Gandavyuha* section of the *Huayan sütra*, and the second is that of the daughter of the Naga/Dragon King Sagara in the *Lotus Sutra*.

From these stories, we will see how precocity in Buddhist children was understood in China. To understand how Buddhist notions of precocity fit into Chinese notions of precocity that predated the entry of Buddhism into China, we will look first at the story of the Chinese cultural hero Hou Chi that appears prior to the Han dynasty (206 BCE–220 CE), when Buddhism was imported into China, and then at the notions of precocity during the Han dynasty itself. Patterns were set in this early period that continued throughout the centuries that followed. And to understand the limits of Buddhist biographical stories

whom, in the context of the pillaging of the countryside by warlords after 1911, were given to the monastery by their families at a very early age.

14. *Xueyan heshang yulu* (The Sayings of Master Zuqin), in HTC, 122: 512. Translation from Pei-yi Wu, *The Confucian's Progress*, 77, with minor changes.

for the study of Buddhist childhood, we will look at two examples of Buddhist biography and autobiography.

CHILD PRODIGY IN EARLY CHINA

Stories of the birth and infancy of the precocious child are found before the second century BCE. In the second oldest stratum of the *Book of Odes(Shijing)* is a poem called "Sheng min." One half of this eight-stanza poem is devoted to the culture hero Hou Chi's conception, birth, and infancy. It relates that Hou Chi's mother "fulfilled her months" and the firstborn then came forth. "There was no bursting, no rending, no injury, no harm, thus manifesting the divine nature of it."[15] When Hou Chi is abandoned and exposed to the weather, he wails loudly. He is then protected by oxen, then by woodcutters, and then by birds. But when the birds fly away, he is forced to rely on his precocious abilities to feed himself. He learns to crawl, stand, and gather food. Finally he manifests his divine knowledge of agriculture by planting beans and grain. The fact that he does this as an infant intimates that Hou Chi's wisdom was inborn, and thus a divine gift, as does his special birth. And the fact that even during his birth he caused his mother no pain can be interpreted as signifying Hou Chi's filial nature. A feature of his story that was important in early China is that he suffered considerably before manifesting his divine gifts.

With the growth of Confucian influence in the Han dynasty, learning became important to one's career. Scholar-class child prodigies in the Former Han dynasty were capable of remarkable feats of learning; as the dynasty continued, these precocities are reported as occurring at increasingly earlier ages. Later the *History of the Later Han (Hou Han shu)* is the first work to note clearly the precocious emergence of the moral dispositions of contemporary figures. Thus Chang Pa (fl. c. AD 89–105) is described as understanding the virtues of yielding and filial piety at age two,[16] and Zhou Xie (fl. c. AD 124) is said to have displayed the virtues of yielding and incorruptibility three months after he was born.[17] These accomplishments must be considered against a background of other, more traditional conceptions of the moral development of children in China, according to which a child began to learn the virtue of yielding at age seven.[18]

Confucius said that the highest type of person is the one who is born wise.[19] Furthermore, according to the *Analects*, only the wisest and the most stupid do not change.[20] To claim that a child was born wise, and therefore good, was

15. Kinney, "The Theme of the Precocious Child in Early Chinese Literature," 2–3.
16. Fan Yeh, et al., *Hou Han shu* (Beijing: Zhonghua shuzhu, 1965), 36, p. 1241.
17. *HouHan shu*, 53, p. 1742.
18. *See Liji, "Neice,"* in *Shisanjing zhushu, juan* 28, p. 243a.
19. *Analects* 16: 9; *Shisanjing zhushu, juan* 16, p. 66b. Traditional commentaries to the *Analects* suggest that "one who is born wise (or:knowing)" refers to the sage.
20. *Analects* 17:3; *Shisanjing zhushu, juan* 17, p. 68b.

subtly to suggest that he was at also incorruptible, because a child born with a superior natural endowment could not be changed and thus tainted by even the most impure environment. Thus the manifestation of moral traits in a child only three months old may have served as evidence of his inborn goodness and, by extension, as an indication of his imperviousness to corruption.

The *Lienu zhuan, Biographies of Exemplary Women,* provides the sole example of female precociousness in the pre-Han period.[21] This is the "niece of Zhuang" who eventually married King Qingxiang of Chu (r. 298–263 BC). As with other precocious children from the Warring States period, her great talent is exhibited in her intelligent political advice and rhetorical skill.[22]

One important motif found in the myth of Hou Chi, that of a miraculous conception, seems to have been reserved in the Han dynasty for use only in the life histories of emperors and sages of ancient times. On the other hand, the more general motif of a special gestation and birth appears frequently in Han biographies. Anne Kinney notes, for example, that "an inscription on the tomb of Feng Sheng, a precocious boy who died at age twelve, remarks on the peaceful gestation and easy delivery of this child. Like the painless birth of Hou Chi, Feng's behavior in utero and at birth serves as early evidence of the child's virtuous nature."[23]

As was mentioned earlier, the ode "Sheng min" is also notable for its dearth of childish behavior in the portrayal of Hou Chi's early career. The account of Teng Sui's life as found in the *Hou Han shu* serves as another example of how Han biography tends to omit all childish traits of prominent individuals. The tendency to discount all childish tendencies, a fondness for play in particular, becomes most extreme in Han times, when biographers repeatedly make the claim that specific historical figures passed through childhood with a distinct dislike of play, or that these individuals engaged in play only of a very specialized variety.[24] Wang Chong (c. AD 27–97) utilizes this formula in his autobiography, stating that as a child, when his friends "would entrap birds, catch cicadas, play for money, and gambol on stilts, [he] alone declined to take part in their games." Wang Chong further states that at age six he "was grave, earnest and very quiet, and had the will of a great man." These are themes that we will find in later Buddhist biographies and in the stories discussed below.[25] Other Han biographical accounts of childhood, while allowing that the child played, attempt to show how the play presaged mature sensibilities or accomplishments. Thus when the biographer of Chen Shi (d. AD 87) mentions that Chen played as a child, he hastens to add that even while amusing

21. *Sibu beiyao*, vol. 104, *juan* 6, p. 12.
22. Kinney, "The Theme of the Precocious Child in Early Chinese Literature," 10.
23. Kinney, "The Theme of the Precocious Child in Early Chinese Literature," 19–20
24. For the earliest example of this motif, see *Zuo zhuan*, Duke Xi, year 9, in *Shisanjing zhushu, juan* 13, 99b. Also see *Hou Han shu*, 82B, 2730. Wu Pei-yi also discusses Wang Chong's autobiographical writing in detail in his *The Confucian's Progress.*
25. Wang Chong, *Lun heng*, chap. 85, "*Ziji.*" Huang Hui, *Lun heng jiaoshi*, 2: 1180, trans. Alfred Forke, *Lun Heng*, 1: 64–65.

himself, the boy was careful to observe the rules of social hierarchy and ritual distinction.[26]While we have seen that adults are still "social children," here we see that precocious children are portrayed as adults!

STORIES OF THE BUDDHA'S BIRTH IN INDIA AND CHINA

Legends of the Buddha's birth were translated from Sanskrit into Chinese as early as the Later Han dynasty. Although originating in India, stories of the Buddha's conception and birth demonstrate his extraordinary origins and destiny, as well as his precocity, and fit well with the genre of Chinese attributions of divine birth and precocity found before and during the Han. His mother, long without children, dreams of a white elephant entering her side and subsequently finds she is pregnant. The Buddha is born from her side without pain to her, as Hou Chi is born. As soon as the Bodhisattva is born, he stands upright without support, takes seven steps, gazes out over the four directions, and makes a proclamation about who he is, pointing with one hand to the heavens and the other to earth. His father takes the infant Bodhisattva to visit a sage, Asita, who predicts that he will grow up to be either a world-uniting ruler *(cakravartin)* or a renouncer of household life who will save all beings.

Let us review in a bit more detail the stories of the Buddha's birth as they were handed down in China. The very first *sütra* in the current Japanese version of the Chinese Buddhist canon, the *Dirgha Agama* or *Long Agama*, tells the story of the Buddha's birth; it is only one of many texts translated into Chinese to do so. The earliest accounts of the Buddha's birth in Chinese may be in two translations made no later than the third century by the translator Zhi Qian.[27] Most texts say that the Buddha's mother, Maya, stopped in a grove of *sala* trees at Lumbini on her way to her family's home. Feeling birth pangs, she grasped a tree and, standing, gave birth to the Bodhisattva from her hip or side. Either he descended to the ground, or one of several figures named in different versions of the story caught him before he could touch the ground: the god Indra, or four gods, or two Brahma gods. Two Naga kings poured water down on him, offering him a cold stream and a warm stream, even though his birth was free of the usual fluids that would need to be washed off; he was already spotless. He stood on the earth without needing any support, took seven steps to the north, gazed out to the four cardinal directions, and proclaimed, as recorded in the *Mahapadana sutta* (Discourse on the Great Legend): "I am chief in the world, supreme in the world, eldest in the world. This is my last birth; there will be [henceforth for me] no re-becoming."[28]

26. *Hou Han shu*, 62, p. 2065.
27. T.184 and T.185. Zhi Qian's translations have been studied recently by Jan Nattier.
28. The *Mahapadana sutta* is found in the Pali *Digha Nikaya* and its Sanskrit parallel text translated and included in the Chinese canon the *Dirgha agama* (Ch. *Chang ahan jing*, T.1).

The infant Bodhisattva's proclamation is perhaps the part of the story that most indicates the extraordinary nature of his precocity: few infants could make such a statement at such a time. The Chinese version of the future Buddha's proclamation took on a slightly more all-encompassing flavor than the somewhat grandiose-sounding statement in the *Mahapadana sutta*. In the Chinese translation produced by Zhi Qian, the future Buddha says: "In the heavens above and below the heavens, I am the world's most honored one. I will free all beings from birth, old age, sickness, and death." The apparent meaning of the first part of that proclamation was that he was and deserved to be more honored than the gods and goddesses *(devas)* above and the earth goddess *(devi)* below, not to mention all the inhabitants of the earth who ranked lower than *devas*. Scholars have suggested that this episode is connected to pre-Buddhist Vedic cosmogonic traditions, as well as to Indian rituals of royal consecration (*abhiseka*). In taking the seven steps, the infant Buddha is accompanied by a flywhisk and umbrella, symbols of sovereignty, and later biographical traditions had him actually walk in all four directions, a reenactment of the *cakravartin* king's claim to universal sovereignty.[29] In the Chinese versions of the story, the two Naga kings often became nine dragons; *naga* indicates "water snake" in South Asia but was translated into Chinese by the word for dragon.

The cycle of episodes in the story of the Buddha's birth was widely represented in art in China in every period. Early depictions of the Buddha's life are described in textual accounts and can be seen in sculptures from the Wei dynasty at the famous Yunmen caves and elsewhere as well as in murals preserved in the caves at Dunhuang, the religious center and waystation on the Silk Road.[30] The period from the Sui Dynasty through the middle of the Tang is rightly considered a high point of Buddhist art in China. There was generous patronage from the ruling elite as well as involvement of the best creative artists, whose names were famous. Late Tang accounts by Duan Chengshi (843) and Zhang Yanyuan (847) give us a good idea of what the subjects of temple-sponsored Buddhist painting were in the Tang. Jataka tales virtually disappeared, but illustrations of Shakyamuni's life, though less frequent than before, were mentioned a number of times by Zhang Yanyuan. The imperially ordered persecution of Buddhist establishments from 845 to 846 brought about a large-scale destruction of temples in China proper, and with them, their murals. The Tibetan occupation of Dunhuang through 846 preserved the caves from destruction. A ceiling painting of "Scenes from the Life of the Buddha" from Dunhuang Cave 290 serves as a good example of Tang-period paintings on this subject that survived at Dunhuang.[31] Although outside Dunhuang the persecution soon ended and temples were reconstructed, the chaos of the late

29. John Strong, *The Buddha: A Short Biography* (Oxford: Oneworld, 2001), 40.
30. Julia K. Murray, "The Evolution of Buddhist Narrative Illustration in China after 850," in *The Latter Days of the Law: Images of Chinese Buddhism 850–1850*, ed. Marsha Weidner (Honolulu: University of Hawaii Press, 1994), 125–50.
31. Published in Julia K. Murray, "What Is 'Chinese Narrative Illustration,'" *The Art Bulletin* 80 no. 4 (Dec. 1998), 603.

Tang meant that they were not rebuilt on the same scale or with the same level of generosity as before.

Nonetheless, murals of scenes from the life of Sakyamuni continued to be painted in the Song and Jin dynasties, and especially often during the Ming dynasty. Among the rare extant temple murals from the Song and Jin dynasties are some remarkably fine paintings on the walls of Yanshan Monastery in Fanzhi, Shanxi province, painted in the Jin dynasty circa 1167. Patricia Karetzky suggests that this temple was on the pilgrimage route to Mount Wutai, a Buddhist center receiving many pilgrims in the spring and fall, and was also an important temple for the celebration of the Buddha's birthday on the eighth day of the fourth month.[32] A painting of scenes from the life of the Buddha on the west wall is one of the major paintings in Yanshan temple.[33] An extant twelfth-century relief from the Song dynasty period at Baodingshan in Dazu in present day Chongqing City shows the infant Siddhartha being bathed from above in real spring water pouring through the mouth of a sculpted dragon.[34]

The theme of the life of Sakyamuni was quite popular in the Ming dynasty.[35] Extant Ming paintings of this subject are found at the Jueyuan Monastery in Jiange county in Sichuan province, Qutan monastery in Ledu, Qinghai province, Chongshan Monastery in Taiyuan, Shanxi province, and Duofu Monastery outside Taiyuan in Shanxi province.[36] Especially interesting is a wall painting of nine dragons bathing the baby Buddha in the corridor of Qutan monastery in Ledu, Qinghai province. Here the dragons definitely pour water on a standing infant, Sakyamuni who is pointing to Heaven and to Earth.

The story of the extraordinary birth of the precocious Sakyamuni appears in Daoist scriptures that tell the story of Laozi traveling to India to take birth as Sakyamuni. The point of these stories is of course to claim that Buddhist

32. Patricia Eichenbaum Karetzky, "The Recently Discovered Chin Dynasty Murals Illustrating the Life of the Buddha at Yen-shang-ssu, Shansi," *Artibus Asiae* 42 no. 4 (1980), 245.

33. Karetzky, "The Recently Discovered Chin Dynasty Murals." See also Ellen Johnston Laing, "Chin 'Tartar' Dynasty (1115–1234) Material Culture," *Artibus Asiae* 49 no. 1/2 (1988–89), 73.

34. See Angela Falco Howard, *Summit of Treasures: Buddhist Cave Art of Dazu, China* (Boston: Weatherhill, 2001), 21.

35. Marsha Weidner, "Imperial Engagements with Buddhist Art and Architecture," in *Cultural Intersections in Later Chinese Buddhism*, ed. Marsha Weidner (Honolulu: University of Hawaii Press, 2001), 135. Julia Murray includes an early Ming woodblock of the birth of the Buddha Sakyamuni, in her article, "The Temple of Confucius and Pictorial Biographies of the Sage," *The Journal of Asian Studies* 55 no.2 (1996), 269–300.

36. Weidner, "Imperial Engagements with Buddhist Art and Architecture," 135–38. The wall paintings at Chongshan Monastery from 1483 are no longer extant, but the monastery has albums of their former wall paintings, including an album of the life of Shakyamuni in 84 episodes. On the wall paintings at the Jueyuan monastery, see also Mu Xueyong, comp., *Jiange Jueyuan si Mingdai fozhuan bihua* (Beijing: Wenwu chubanshe, 1993).

teachings depend entirely on the founder and divine sage of the Daoist tradition, but it is fascinating that the stories of the birth of Laozi as Buddha, which is only one among his many births, follow almost exactly the Buddhist script of birth, seven steps, and proclamation.[37] Stories of the Buddha's birth and life also may have inspired Ming dynasty illustrated books of the life of Confucius, which included a miraculous birth for the Chinese sage as well as stories of Confucius as a boy who was interested only in play that involved performing the rites. The rites are a feature of the Chou dynasty culture of Confucius's time whose importance Confucius and Confucians emphasized.[38] It is also possible that stories of Confucius's extraordinary birth and childhood originated independently of, and for the same reasons that, the Buddha's birth and infancy stories originated: the worldwide tendency to imagine great religious figures as having extraordinary births.

The ritual observance of bathing the Buddha was and is widely practiced in China, as well as Japan and Korea. The ritual focuses on a small statue of the baby Buddha, in modern times usually in his proclamation posture, one arm and hand pointing toward heaven, the other toward earth. Fragrant water or sweet tea is ceremonially poured over the baby's body, standing on a platform in the middle of a large bowl or basin filled with water. The pourer uses a wooden ladle. This ritual action seems to have no precedent in India. The ritual conflates a reenactment of the episode of the washing of the baby Buddha, an *abiseka* ceremony, with a reenactment of the baby Buddha's seven steps and his proclamation of his mission, nature, and destiny in the current birth. To the believer, this ritual denotes respect and care for the Buddha and also represents the washing away of one's own impurities.[39]

From early times in China there were ceremonies of "bathing the Buddha," but they probably involved bathing all the temple's images and are thus not identical in form to those described above. Rituals featuring an image of the infant Buddha are more familiar from the Song dynasty on. For instance, in a

37. Stephen R. Bokenkamp, "Scripture of the Inner Explanations of the Three Heavens" in *Early Daoist Scriptures,* ed. and trans. Steven Bokenkamp (Berkeley, CA: University of California Press, 1997), 211–12. The "Scripture of the Inner Explanations" comes from the Liu Song dynasty and thus dates from between 420 and 479 CE. One difference in the Buddhist story of the infant Buddha's proclamation is the words spoken. The "Scripture of the Inner Explanations" has: "In heaven above and in the world below heaven, I alone am the honored one. In these three realms all is suffering. How could one delight in anything here?" The text also states, in contrast to the Buddhist accounts of Siddhartha's childhood and youth: "As soon as he was born, he devoted himself to religious austerities."

38. In an essay on Ming dynasty pictorial biographies of Confucius, Julia K. Murray includes an early Ming woodblock of the birth of and standing proclamation by the Buddha Sakyamuni for comparison with the many Ming dynasty depictions of the birth of Confucius, which she suggests may have been inspired by the long history in China of and current interest in depictions of the birth of Sakyamuni. See Julia K. Murray, "The Temple of Confucius and Pictorial Biographies of the Sage," for illustrations of Confucius' conception and birth, as well as the child Confucius at play performing the rites.

record from 193/194 CE about Buddhism in the region of Pengcheng we find the first mention of "bathing the Buddha."[40]

> Whenever there was (the ceremony of) "bathing the Buddha" a certain ruler always had great quantities of wine and food set out for distribution, and mats were spread along the roads for over a distance of several tens of miles *(li)*. (On these occasions) some ten thousand people came to enjoy the spectacle and the food. The expenses (of such a ceremony) amounted to many millions (cash).[41]

Another record from about 332 CE reports of Shi Lo (a half-sinicized barbarian) that on the eighth day of the fourth month of every year he went to the temple, bathed the Buddha, and made a vow on behalf of his foster son.[42]

Also concerning the hold of the bathing of the Buddha on the early Chinese Buddhist imaginary, the *Yezhongji*, a historical work on the Posterior Zhao compiled by a Jin author, tells that the monarch Shi Hu (r. 334–349)

> had his celebrated craftsman Xie Fei make an extremely ingenious four-wheeled wagon, ten feet or so wide and twenty long, of sandalwood. When the wagon moved, nine dragons on it would spurt water to bathe a Buddha image, while [the figure of] a monk rubbed the Buddha's chest with his hand. Ten or so [carved] monks in robes would move in procession around the Buddha; as they passed in front, each would bow in worship and drop incense from his hands into a censer. When the wagon stopped, so would they.[43]

39. In her book *A Tender Voyage,* Ping-chen Hsiung reproduces a painting of "Children Bathing the Buddha" by Su Hanchen (Song dynasty). See Fig. 44, p. 250. Two recent articles, both contained in *The Birth of the Buddha: Proceedings of the Seminar Held in Lumbini, Nepal, October 2004*, ed. Cristoff Cueppers, Max Deeg, and Hubert Durt (Lumbini International Research Institute, 2010) discuss the extant visual representations of the standing infant Buddha, the episode of the seven steps and proclamation, and the episode of the bathing of the Buddha after his birth by two Naga kings or Brahma and Indra, two Deva kings: Nicoletta Celli, "The Birth of the Buddha and Related Episodes as Represented in Chinese Art," 305–20 and 437–51; and Juhyung Rhi, "The Birth of the Buddha in Korean Buddhism: Infant Buddha Images and the Ritual Bathing," 321–44 and 452–58. For more art-historical bibliography, see these two articles.

40. Erik Zurcher, *The Buddhist Conquest of China* (Leiden: E. J. Brill, 1931; 1959), 27–28.

41. Zurcher, *The Buddhist Conquest of China*, 327 n. 53.

42. Zurcher, *The Buddhist Conquest of China*, 182; also chap. 2, n. 53 on "bathing the Buddha."

43. Quoted by Tsukamoto Zenryu, *Shina Bukkyoshi no kenkyu,* volume on the Northern Wei, Tokyo 1947 (2nd. ed.), 65. The putative author of the original was a certain Lu Hui. Translated in Alexander Coburn Soper, "Literary Evidence for Early Buddhist Art in China," *Artibus Asiae Supplementum* 19 (1959), 84.

From records concerning the Later Han we learn that the ruler of Wu from 264 to 280 CE, Sun Hao, performed a blasphemous parody of bathing the Buddha by bathing his image. When a Buddhist image was dug up in the park of the imperial harem, he had it moved to a urinal and personally performed what he called "the ritual of washing the Buddha."[44] The result of his bathing the Buddha in excrement was very unfortunate for him: "his body broke out in great boils, and his private parts gave him such pain that his howls reached the Heavens."[45]

In the *Guang hongmingji juan* 16 we find an essay on the mistreatment of images in his day by the prince who became the Liang emperor Qianwen of the sixth century. In the course of this essay the future Qianwen notes that a temple's images are all displayed on the Buddha's birthday and then afterward are stuffed into closets. He also mentions that worshipping the Buddha [as an infant] as the Nagas did is the true spiritual meaning of possessing images:

> Our meaning is this. In general one may say that the purpose of molding metal, carving jade, cutting out lacquer, and painting tiles is to proclaim reverently the Incarnate Person, and to fix attention profoundly on the Divine Enlightenment; to extol that first dawn when the Nagas [= dragons] from their vials [poured pure water on the newborn babe], and to imitate that last devotion shown in the Heron Grove [when the Buddha passed into Nirvana]. Therefore "to worship the gods as if they were present" is of all ways of worshiping them the most exalted; [and the very fact that] the sages are far removed from us today is the most profound reason for cherishing them.
>
> In our land the temples exhibit their images only briefly, on the day of the Nativity. When that is over, they are shut up in cabinets and boxes. [In the process] the clothing is likely to be stripped from their bodies, or the flame aureoles detached from their heads. Sometimes five or ten figures of saints are pushed into a single shrine; or Bodhisattvas and Buddhas are all stored in the same cabinet. Most certainly this is a case of the heart being at cross-purposes with the fact; one in which appearances are right but intentions are wrong. The wish to glorify the higher [powers] is plentiful, but there are few [signs of] hearts that are advancing spiritually.[46]

Three *sūtras* describing the "Bathing the Buddha" *(yufo)* ritual and the merits one could expect from performing it were translated into Chinese in the third and fourth centuries.[47] Another set of *sūtras* was translated in the early eighth

44. Zurcher, *The Buddhist Conquest of China*, 52. This is described in more detail in Alexander Soper, "Literary Evidence," 6.
45. Soper, "Literary Evidence," 6.
46. *Guanghongmingji, juan* 16, *Taisho* 52, p. 210b; Soper, "Literary Evidence," 78.
47. According to Liu Shufen, these are the *Scripture on Anointing [the Buddha Image] with Wax after Parinirvana* (T. 391); the *Scripture of the Buddha's Sermon on Anointing and Bathing the Buddha Image* (T. 695); and the *Scripture on the Buddha's Sermon on the*

century.[48] In rural areas of north China during the sixth century CE, statuary stele were erected that depicted the miraculous events accompanying the birth of the Buddha.[49] A Buddhist image or stele was essential for the ritual of "Bathing the Buddha" *(yufo)* on the Buddha's birthday.

Images of the baby Buddha standing with both arms at his sides likely originated in China. One of two extant bronze statuettes of the baby Buddha in that postion is arguably datable to the early fourth century CE. A cult of bathing the infant Buddha that did not add the pointing arms, the iconography of his proclamation, thus possibly developed quite early in China.[50] The earliest extant representation of the baby Buddha standing with one arm raised and the other pointing to the earth appears to be a mandorla-shaped stele in China dated to 471 CE.[51] It is unclear whether the free-standing image of the baby Buddha with one arm pointing to heaven and one pointing to earth used in Buddha's birthday rituals today originated in Korea, Japan, or China. Relatively early images that can be seen today are from Korea and Japan.

The festival of bathing the Buddha as practiced with the image of the infant Buddha having one arm raised to point to heaven as described above is clearly visible in Chinese texts starting from the Song dynasty (960–1279). It drew of course on the example of meritorious worship set by the dragon kings. It also drew on the appeal of the story of the Buddha's proclamation, which served to remind worshippers of who this infant was.

For example, in the Song dynasty the practice of giving sermons and washing an image of the infant Bodhisattva was carried out in major Chan monasteries. The earliest extant *qinggui* (Rules of Purity of the Chan school) text from the Song the *Chanyuan qinggui,* from early in the twelfth century, does not mention a ceremony for the Buddha's birthday, but later *qinggui* texts from the Song and Yuan dynasties do specify ceremonial forms to be used for such a ceremony. And in discourse records of prominent masters in the Song, particularly Yuanwu Keqin (1063–1135), Dahui Zonggao (1089–1163), and Hongzhi Zhengjue (1091–1157), there are sermons recorded that are listed as "Bathing the Buddha" sermons (*yufo shangtang* or *yufo shizhong*).

Mahasattva (T. 696). See Liu Shufen, "Art, Ritual and Society: Buddhist Practice in Rural China during the Northern Dynasties," *Asia Major* 8 part 1 (1995), 37 n. 63. The stories of the Buddha's birth depicted the nagas/dragons and/or gods washing the infant Buddha. A *sütra* describing this scene called the *Xiuxingbenqi jing* was translated into Chinese in the late secon or early third century, according to Erik Zurcher.

48. One of these, the *Sutra on the Merit of Bathing the Buddha*, is introduced and translated into English by Daniel Boucher in *Buddhism in Practice*, ed. Donald S. Lopez, Jr. (Princeton, NJ: Princeton University Press, 1995), 59–68. It was translated into Chinese in 710 by Yijing, the famous Chinese traveler to India who spent ten years studying at the Buddhist university at Nalanda. An almost identical *sütra* had been translated in China in 705 by an Indian monk, Manacintana, as the *Sütra on the Merit of Bathing the Image.*

49. Liu Shufen, "Art, Ritual and Society," 32–33 and fig. 2. Liu mentions two, one erected in 543 and the other in 546.

50. Nicoletta Celli, "The Birth of the Buddha," 314.

THE PRECOCIOUS INFANT BUDDHA IN CHAN TEXTS

A story found in so many translated Buddhist texts, painted on so many monastery walls for the edification of the laity and monks, and featured in a major popular festival, the Buddha's birthday, certainly promoted reverence toward the extremely precocious "teacher of gods and humans." But the story was not always received quite so reverently. We find a somewhat different attitude to the precocious Buddha in texts from the Chan school.

One famous Chan comment that may have originated as a "bathing the Buddha sermon" displays a certain iconoclastic approach to the story of the newborn Buddha's precocious standing without support, walking seven steps, and proclaiming that he is the world's most honored one. This is the comment on the nativity story by the late Tang dynasty Chan teacher Yunmen Wenyan (896–949) that is recorded in his discourse record as follows:

> Master Yunmen related [the legend according to which] the Buddha, immediately after his birth, pointed with one hand to heaven and with the other to earth, walked a circle in seven steps, looked at the four quarters, and said: "Above heaven and under heaven, I alone am the Honored One."
>
> The Master said: "Had I witnessed this at the time, I would have knocked him dead with one stroke and fed him to the dogs in order to bring about peace on earth."[52]

Yet not all of the Chan sermons given on the Buddha's birthday were so iconoclastic. The ritual of bathing the Buddha is mentioned in more than one of Hongzhi Zhengjue's sermons for that day. In one such sermon Hongzhi makes perfectly clear that at this day's ceremony those present are bathing the image of the infant Buddha's making his proclamation. He says: "For a long time the Buddha has bathed the assembly of monks; today the assembly of monks pours water on our Buddha."[53]

Hongzhi also mentions Yunmen's comment in the context of a not-so-iconoclastic sermon:

> When the pure water of emptiness of self-nature and the radiant body of the Dharma realm are only faintly distinguished, then this person is born. Without cleansing the dusts from the body, because of this water's wonderful touch he expresses clear realization. I ask you, for many years he has been departed, so how can he return to be near us today? On this day two thousand years ago,

51. Celli, "The Birth of the Buddha," 311.
52. *Yunmen guanglu*, T. 47.1988. 560b16–19. Urs App, trans., *Master Yunmen: From the Record of the Chan Master "Gate of the Clouds"* (New York: Kodansha America, 1994), 218.
53. *Hongzhi Chanshi guanglu*, T.48. 2001.44b.7–8.

> he pointed to heaven and to earth and gave the great lion's roar. Yunmen remained at war while thinking about great peace by saying he would kill the baby Buddha and assuredly feed him to the dogs. This is pointing east and calling it west, making nonexistence into existence. Although I pour foul water on you, don't get angry. Now that I see you, how will you accept it? Buddha said: "Not receiving any sensation is called right receiving." If you practice like this, each drop falls on the same spot.[54]

Here is another Hongzhi sermon, which comments specifically on the infant Buddha's proclamation and his taking of seven steps that is ritually commemorated in bathing a statue of the infant Buddha, and on which Yunmen had commented so trenchantly. This time Hongzhi's sermon is rather iconoclastic, one might say disrespectful, in relation to the infant Buddha:

> This is the completely clear water of the emptiness of self-nature; the perfectly bright, pure wisdom body. Therefore, we do not need to wash the body; right here not a speck of dust exists. So he has become Buddha, overcome Mara, [reached] that other shore, and [departed] this deluded riverbank. This "dada wawa" baby talk was at the beginning, then this random crawling around became the cause [for becoming Buddha]. On this occasion, Sakyamuni Buddha, do not get angry at our pouring foul water on your head. Why don't you "invoke the power of Avalokitesvara Bodhisattva, and then naturally [this injury] will rebound to its originator."[55] Benevolent people, what is it like just when the ladle [for pouring water over the Buddha] is in your hand? Without the cause of [thoroughly studying] a single thing, we cannot develop any wisdom.[56]

In this sermon the words "'dada wawa' baby talk" refers to the proclamation by the infant Buddha, while the "random crawling around" refers to the infant Buddha's seven steps.

54. T.48.2001. 54.a.10–17. Dogen Kigen, the founder of Japanese Soto zen, quotes Hongzhi's sermon as recorded in his Eihei koroku. It is translated by Taigen Dan Leighton and Shohaku Okumura in their *Dogen's Extensive Record: A Translation of the Eihei Koroku* (Cambridge: Wisdom Publications 2010), 3: 236–37. I have used their translation.

55. This sentence reflects a passage in chap. 25 of the *Lotus Sutra*, "The Universal Gateway of the Bodhisattva Regarder of the Cries of the World." The translation accords with that in Gene Reeves's recent translation, *The Lotus Sutra: A Contemporary Translation of a Buddhist Classic* (Cambridge: Wisdom, 2008), 377: "Or if someone tries to hurt you with curses or poisons, Keep in mind the Cry Regarder's powers and the harm will revert to its originator."

56. Hongzhi Chanshi guanglu, T.48.2001. 47c24–48a2. Dogen Kigen, the founder of Japanese Soto zen, quotes Hongzhi's sermon as recorded in his Eihei koroku. It is translated by Taigen Dan Leighton and Shohaku Okumura in their *Dogen's Extensive Record*, 3: 249–50.

Hongzhi's contemporary Dahui Zonggao also alludes to Yunmen's statement in the context of a sermon Dahui gave on the Buddha's birthday. Dahui said in a *yufo shizhong*, a message to the assembly on bathing the Buddha[57]:

> Before [Sakyamuni] left the Tusita Heaven, he had already descended to the royal palace. Before he had come forth from his mother's womb, his ferrying of humans [to the other shore of Nirvana] was already finished. When he was born, the quaking moved the net of all the worlds. Then with one hand pointing to heavens and one hand pointing to earth, he gave the great lion's roar and said: "In heavens above and on the earth below, I am the world's most honored one. For the sake of the one great cause [for which Buddhas appear on the earth], I will open the knowledge and vision of the buddhas, show the knowledge and vision of the buddhas, awaken to the knowledge and vision of the buddhas, and enter the knowledge and wisdom of the buddhas."
>
> As you should know, a few thousand years later he incurred [the wrath of] a lame-footed monk [that is, Yunmen] who wanted to kill him with one blow and feed him to the dogs in order to bring about peace on earth.[58]
>
> What was old Sakyamuni's fault? Was it pointing to heaven and earth and opening his big mouth? Was it messing with people's sons and daughters? Was it opening the knowledge and vision of the buddhas, showing the knowledge and vision of the buddhas, awakening to the knowledge and vision of the buddhas, and entering the knowledge and wisdom of the buddhas? If you think along those lines, you will not only insult Sakyamuni, you will also nullify [lit., treat as nothing] Yunmen's [kind instruction].[59]

Here Dahui poses a dilemma to his students: The Buddha's precocious actions and proclamation were not wrong. But neither was Yunmen's comment. How can this be so?

What is the point of all this iconoclastic, noniconoclastic, and both iconoclastic-and-not iconoclastic Chan talk about the canonical story of the infant Buddha's proclamation? I leave it to the reader to interpret these comments on the Buddha's proclamation, and suggest only that this discourse is not intended

57. In Dahui's discourse record *(yulu)* in 30 *juan*. This passage begins at T. 1998A.47.0842c08.

58. The notion that Yunmen had a lame foot came from a story that his teacher Muzhou had pushed him out the door and slammed the door on his foot. The earliest extant passage that mentions the foot injury is in the *Zutingshiyuan (Collection of Topics from the Garden of the Patriarchs)* of 1108, ZZ 113:1d12–13, written by Muan Shanqing. The Korean CDL might possibly be earlier. Essentially the same story is in the *Chanlin sengbaozhuan*. The "One night" text of the *Biyanlu Blue Cliff Record* has a very abbreviated reference to this episode in Case 6. A fuller account is available in Urs App's dissertation, *Facets of the Life and Teaching of Chan Master Yunmen Wenyan* (864–949), (Ph.D. diss., Temple University, 1989), 230–31 and 264–65, n. 63c-e. The *Zutingshiyuan* predates any *yulu* text for Dahui Zonggao by Dahui's disciples.

59. T.1998A.47.0842c09-c20.

to refute the story of the infant Buddha's precocity and extraordinary nature, but rather to force the listeners and readers, many of whom were members of a Song dynasty elite or monkhood who had heard the orthodox story of the Buddha's birth perhaps once too often, to reconfront the story in an effort to understand just what it was that made the Buddha, any other awakened being, and ultimately oneself, precocious or extraordinary.

EMINENT MONASTICS AS PRECOCIOUS CHILDREN

As is mentioned above, biographies of eminent monks and nuns often mention that the future monk or nun was precocious as a child. Occasionally there is something special about the subject's birth. More typically, he or she lacked interest in ordinary play but liked religious activities. However, biographies usually spend very little time on the subject's childhood, making these sources unrewarding for a study of childhood in Chinese Buddhism.

One limitation of the genre of sacred biography is that the biographer could write only about those childhood traits or actions that confirmed that the subject did not change over the years. In general, Chinese biographical literature is static with respect to personality and character. There is no interest in portraying qualities that appeared late or contrasts between earlier and later behavior. This focus makes a candid portrayal of childhood almost impossible. Consequently, we get depictions of the subject's childhood and youth that presage only later virtues or accomplishments. Precocity is not placed in a realistic context. As an example, here is an excerpt from the best-known early biography of the monk Daoan (312–385 CE). Among Chinese Buddhist biographies this one treats the childhood of the subject in unusual detail:

> Shi Daoan, surnamed Wei, was a man of the Fuliu [district] in Changshan [commandery]. His family for generations had been eminent literati. At an early age he lost the shelter and shade [of family and fortune] and was reared by his elder maternal cousin of the Kong family. When he was seven years old he could read books; by twice looking at them he could recite them by heart. The country folk and neighbors sighed and thought him unusual. When he turned twelve he went forth from his family [to become a Buddhist monk]. He was a genius (*shen zhi*, [he possessed] divine knowledge), quick in understanding, yet in figure and feature he was extremely vulgar, and was not esteemed by his teacher. Forced to work as a menial in the fields and huts for three years, he came forward to labor with diligence, and never flushed in resentment. Sincere by nature, vigorous in advance *(virya)*, in his observance of abstention precepts there was nothing lacking.
>
> After several years he began to beg the scriptures from his teacher. His teacher gave him the *Sūtra on the Discrimination of Meaning* in one chapter of approximately five thousand words. [Dao]an reverently carried the *sūtra* with

> him when he entered the fields and utilized his rest period for reading. At sunset he returned and gave the *sutra* back to his teacher and once more begged for another. His teacher said: "You still haven't read the *sutra* of yesterday and again you beg for one, eh" He replied: "I have already memorized it." Although his teacher thought this odd and did not yet believe it, he gave him [another *sutra*] in one chapter of less than ten thousand words. He carried it with him as he did on the first occasion, and at sundown again returned it to his teacher. When his teacher, holding the sütra, made him repeat it, he did not miss a single word! Vastly astonished, his teacher exclaimed and marveled at him. Afterwards he had him receive all the prohibitions [entailed by full ordination] and permitted his travel for study.[60]

A notable counter-example is the annalistic or chronological autobiography *(nianpu)* written toward the end of his life by the late Ming dynasty monk Hanshan Deqing (1546–1623). In this work Deqing devotes quite a bit of space to his childhood.[61]

According to this autobiography Hanshan Deqing was born to a family surnamed Cai in a district west of Nanjing.[62] His mother, née Hong, deftly guided her precocious son from a very early age to take interest in core Buddhist questions, hold monks in respect, and aspire to the sangha, despite opposition from her husband.

In describing her childhood influences on him and his childhood thoughts, Deqing deploys elements from the standard hagiographies in his chronological autobiography.[63] The very first entry recounts that his mother conceived him in a dream: Guanyin came through her door leading a boy whom the mother embraced. Eventually little Deqing was born wrapped in a white caul—suggesting that he was a child of special destiny "delivered" in response to the mother's unwavering devotion by the White-Robed Guanyin.[64]

60. *Gaoseng zhuan* 5. T. 50. 351c-354a. Translation from Arthur E. Link, "Biography of Shih Tao-an," *T'oung Pao* 46 no. 1–2 (1958), 1–48. I have made two minor changes.

61. This autobiography has been studied by Wu Pei-yi in *The Confucian's Progress;* and by Lynn A. Struve in *Deqing's Dreams: Markers in a Reinterpretation of His Autobiography*, unpublished draft of March 2011. Wu had previously published the chapter about Hanshan Deqing's annalistic autobiography as "The Spiritual Autobiography of Te-ch'ing," in *The Unfolding of Neo-Confucianism*, ed. W. T. de Bary (New York: Columbia University Press, 1975), 67–92.

62. The following narration, unless otherwise specified, is based sequentially on Hanshan Deqing, *Hanshan laoren nianpu zixu shilu (hereafter HNS)*. For more extensive information, see Sung-peng Hsü, *A Buddhist Leader in Ming China: The Life and Thought of Han-Shan Te-Ch'ing* (University Park: Pennsylvania State University Press, 1979).

63. I.e., *nianpu.*

64. *Hanshan nianpu zixu shilu*, 1a. See See Chün-fang Yü, *Kuan-yin: The Chinese Transformation of Avalokiteśvara* (New York: Columbia University Press, 2001), 130–34, on the popularity during Ming times of the belief that children specially bestowed by Guanyin in return for sincere devotion were born with a white caul.

However, Deqing's autobiography contains episodes of a kind that are not often found in earlier texts. According to his account, his first spiritual crisis occurred when he was seven. One day his beloved uncle died and was placed on a bed. When Deqing came home from school, his mother said: "Your uncle is asleep. Why don't you go and wake him up?"[65] Completely puzzled to find his uncle both on the bed and apparently "gone," he began to puzzle about where dead men go. When shortly afterward an aunt gave birth to a boy, he asked his mother: "How did this baby enter into Auntie's belly?" She only asked him a personal form of the same question—how had he himself gotten into his mother's belly?[66]

Deqing was an intellectually gifted child. A clear intimation of his future path occurs when, at age ten, Deqing tells his mother that, rather than become an official who will retire some day, he wants to do something in which his efforts would never end. She replies that if he should have the good fortune to become a Buddhist patriarch, she certainly would give him up.[67] Does this choice reflect spiritual precocity, or is it simply a reflection of the way she has molded his interests?

She does indeed give him up at an early age to a monastic education. When he was eight he boarded with a relative across the river so that he could attend school. One day on a home visit he clung to his mother and refused to go back. She threw him in the river and feigned total indifference to her son in order to prevent his being homesick. [68]

In his twelfth year the young Deqing continued his studies at an imperially founded monastery of the scriptural study category, the Baoensi on the south ern side of Nanjing. There he received the best instruction available in the most commonly studied *sūtras* as well as in the secular curriculum oriented toward the civil service examinations that consisted of historical, literary, and Confucian classical texts. When Deqing was nineteen and tempted to take civil service examinations and begin a secular career as a scholar-official, another intercession occurred, this time from a leading Chan monk, Yungu Fahui (1501–1575),[69] who recommended that Deqing—who according to his autobiography was discouraged by the low social status and poor standards of many monks around him—read literature about eminent monks of the past. Upon reading the collected works of the highly respected Yuan dynasty Chan master Zhongfeng Mingben (1263–1323),[70] he set his mind on a clerical career and

65. Pei-yi Wu, *The Confucian's Progress*, 143.
66. Pei-yi Wu, *The Confucian's Progress*, 143.
67. *HNS*, 1.5b–6a. Pei-yi Wu, *The Confucian's Progress*, 144–45.
68. Pei-yi Wu, *The Confucian's Progress*, 143–44.
69. For Deqing's biography of Fahui, see *HMJ*, 30.673b–674c.
70. See Chün-fang Yü, "Chung-feng Ming-pen and Ch'an Buddhism in the Yüan," in *Yuan Thought: Chinese Thought and Religion under the Mongols*, ed. Hok-lam Chan and William Theodore de Bary (New York: Columbia University Press, 1982), 419–77; and Natasha Heller, "The Chan Master as Illusionist: Zhongfeng Mingben's Huanzhu Jiaxun," *Harvard Journal of Asiatic Studies* 69 no. 2 (2009), 271–308. The full title

soon was ordained. Deqing wrote: "I went through [Fahui's] box of books and got Mingben's *Extensive Record*. Halfway through the book I suddenly became exultant and exclaimed, 'This is what delights my heart!' Thereupon I decided to enter the monastic life and asked the abbot to shave my head."[71]

Despite Hanshan Deqing's general intellectual precocity, it is not clear apart from the very last episode in this story that he was particularly precocious spiritually. He did not seem to manifest the early determination to follow the bodhisattva path shown by Sudhana or the infant Buddha. At nineteen, though unmarried and thus a child in the Chinese view, Deqing was rather old to have failed to make a commitment to monastic life.[72]

The interesting thing to note is that a traditional author of Buddhist biography would have left out some episodes that Deqing included and would have reshaped others. As a result they would have depicted Deqing as intellectually and spiritually precocious in the Buddhist mold. One can imagine a more traditional biography that would mention Deqing's mother as a source of his interest in Buddhist teachings; would narrate briefly the episode of his giving rise to profound questions about birth and death in response to the family events, but without mentioning his mother; would stress his great talent for learning, and would finish with his response to reading Zhongfeng Mingben's record. It is striking that Deqing himself, when telling his own story, placed considerably more importance on his relationship with his mother, on her role in shaping his choices, and on his own uncertainty about his monastic vocation than a traditional Chinese Buddhist biographer would do. Perhaps one can argue that his approach marks a turn toward the discovery of the significance of the events and feelings of childhood, or in other words, the discovery of childhood. Perhaps in the early seventeenth century with Deqing Buddhist writers begin to place importance on the not always ideal steps in one's formation that take place in childhood.

SUDHANA AND THE DRAGON DAUGHTER, PRECOCIOUS CHILDREN IN INDIAN BUDDHIST *SUTRAS*

Sudhana in the *Huayan sutra*

If the stories of Hou Chi and the birth and infancy of the Buddha set the pattern in China, the story of Sudhana (Shancai Tongzi) in the *Huayan sutra*,

of Mingben's collected works (often referred to as the *Zhongfengguanglu*) is *Tianmu Zhongfeng heshang guanglu*.

71. Pei-yi Wu, *The Confucian's Progress*, p. 148. The translation is Wu's except for the last clause.

72. Wu Pei-yi reads Deqing's autobiography as demonstrating that he never really left the more respected Confucian option behind. Lynn Struve, on the contrary, finds many signs in Deqing's autobiography that from the first he had a strong sense of being destined for the attainment of advanced bodhisattvahood.

a massive *sütra* compiled in China from many smaller *sütras*, both reflects that pattern and adds another dimension. The *Huayan sütra*, which is sometimes referred to by a Sanskrit or English name as the *Avatamasaka* or *Flower Garland Sutra*, contains in its final section the saga of a precocious boy's achievement of the highest level of bodhisattvahood in one lifetime.[73] A Sanskrit version of this section, the *Gandavyuha*, has been found. The *Huayan sütra* was the center of practical and philosophical system building by the Chinese Buddhist lineage of scholars known as the Huayan school. The Huayan school's third patriarch, Fazang (643–712), did much to foster the idea that all of that *sütra*'s teachings concerning bodhisattva qualities, stages, and conduct were instantiated in the boy's successive encounters.[74]

The *Gandavyuha* consists largely of a repetitious but also stirring tale in which this "Boy of Good Wealth" (Sudhana is translated into Chinese as "good wealth," *shancai*) is discovered by Mañjuśri and understood (in part because of his extraordinary birth) to have accumulated sufficient merit in past lives to ascend to supreme enlightenment. He is sent off by Mañjuśri to learn the ways of bodhisattvas from a series of fifty-two other "good teachers" or "spiritual benefactors" (Skt. *kalyāṇamitras*), of varied walks and social statuses, culminating in an invitation to the palace of Maitreya bodhisattva, a welcome to the ranks by Mañjuśrī, and conferral of the highest *samādhi* by Samantabhadra (Ch. Puxian).[75]

This story was rendered in Buddhist art and referenced in morality tales (see below) as well as in preaching to the elite by Chan and Huayan masters.[76] Eventually the figure of Shancai Tongzi was adopted into popular Daoism as well. The Song dynasty monk Dahui Zonggao frequently told stories from the *Gandavyuha* to support his teaching on the "suddenness" of awakening.[77] The Ming dynasty Chan monk Hanshan Deqing discussed above (1546–1623)

73. In the 80-scroll translation of the *Huayan jing* (*T* 10, 279), the story of Sancai Tongzi is in the "Rufajie pin" (Skt. name, *Gaṇḍavyūha*), which runs from scroll 62 through scroll 80.

74. See Fazang's *Tanxuan ji*, *T.* 35,1733: 20.490a–b. For a summary and schematization, see Jan Fontein, *The Pilgrimage of Sudhana: A Study of Gaṇḍavyūha Illustrations in China, Japan and Java* (The Hague: Mouton, 1967), 17–20 and Appendix, resp.

75. For a complete English translation, see Thomas Cleary, *The Flower Ornament Scripture: A Translation of the Avatamsaka Sutra* (Boulder, CO: Shambhala, 1984–87), vol. 3. For a summary and brief analysis, see Jan Fontein, *The Pilgrimage of Sudhana,* 5–22.

76. See Jan Fontein, *The Pilgrimage of Sudhana*, chap. 2; and Wilt L. Idema, *Personal Salvation and Filial Piety: Two Precious Scroll Narratives of Guanyin and Her Acolytes* (Honolulu: University of Hawaii Press, 2008), esp. pp. 30–35. See also the sculpture in the collection of the Metropolitan Museum of Art, available online at http://www.metmuseum.org/works_of_art/collection_database/asian_art/pilgrim_sudhana_shancaI_tongzi/objectview.aspx?collID=6&OID=60010287.

In popular literature Sudhana becomes the acolyte of the bodhisattva Avalokitesvara or Guanyin. In the acolyte's role, the boy's name changed homophonously to Shancai Tongzi, "Boy of Good Talent." The other acolyte is the Dragon Daughter, Longnü (Skt. Nāgakanyā).

77. See my "Chan Enlightenment for Laymen: Ta-hui Tsung-kao and the New Religious Culture of the Sung," Ph.D, diss., Harvard University, 1978.

referred frequently to the Shancai Tongziin his writings, speaking of him as an exemplar of strong faith, spiritual courage, commitment to the Path, perseverance all the way to his meeting with the bodhisattva Samantrabhadra (Puxian), and the importance of entering many of the 84,000 doors to buddhahood rather than using just one.[78]

Since the whole story takes place while Sudhana is a child, many aspects of it should interest us here, but the most rewarding is what is said in the *sütra* about Sudhana's birth and about those qualities that caused Manjusri to send him on his journey. The following passage is from the only full English translation of the *Gandhavyuha*, the *Entry into the Realm of Reality* by Thomas Cleary:

> Now the people of the city heard that Manjusri had come and was staying at the shrine in the forest. Having heard this, pious men and women, boys and girls, each a company of five hundred…went from the city to where Manjusri was. [Each group] went to Manjusri, bowed their heads to his feet, circled him three times, and then sat to one side.
>
> Sudhana, an outstanding boy, together with a company of five hundred outstanding boys,…went to Manjusri, bowed to him and circled him, and then sat to one side.
>
> Then Manjusri,…imbued with great analytic intelligence, wishing to expound the truth, observed the outstanding boy Sudhana: "Why is Sudhana called Sudhana, which means 'Good Wealth'? When he was conceived, there appeared in the house sprouts of seven precious substances. Great prosperity appeared in the house by his mere birth.
>
> "Sudhana, furthermore, having served past buddhas and planted roots of goodness, imbued with great zeal and devotion, intent on following spiritual benefactors, impeccable in word, thought, and deed, engaged in clarification of the path of [the bodhisattvas] heading for omniscience, having become a vessel of the Buddha teachings, his course of mind purified, had achieved an unhindered, unattached determination for enlightenment."

Manjusri then praises and teaches him and the great crowd of people. The text says that Manjusri departed, having edified, inspired, sharpened, and delighted Sudhana and the others by his teaching. Sudhana, seeing him go, utters a long verse. Manjusri then, gazing like an elephant, tells Sudhana that it is good that he seeks to serve spiritual benefactors, predicts great things for his future after many eons of practice of the teachings of spiritual benefactors on how to become a bodhisattva, and sends him to Meghasri, the first of 52 benefactors.[79]

78. See, for instance, *HMJ*, 2.471a–b, 3.477a and 479c, 5.493a–b, 9.522a, 21.611a, 31.681b, and 40.756b.

79. *Huayan jing. Dafangguang fo huayan jing*, in 80 scrolls. *T.* 10, 279. Thomas Cleary, *The Flower Ornament Scripture*, 3: 49–56. I have used Cleary's translation, but substituted the word "bodhisattvas" for his idiosyncratic translation "enlightening beings."

Sudhana's birth was marked by a great miracle that explains his name and his significance for his family. The enormous surge of precious substances, jewels and the like, that emerges into his parents' house at his conception and birth from treasuries heretofore buried in the earth is described at length in the *sütra*. In that sense, Sudhana is a filial child and one to whom the divine—in this case the deified Earth—responds with showers of gifts. As Hou Chi is to Chinese society's need for agriculture, so Sudhana is to his family: at birth he brings great gifts, which manifest immediately in Sudhana's case and almost immediately in Hou Chi's case. Unlike Hou Chi, Sudhana does not suffer; he is a darling of the gods and bodhisattvas from the first.

As to Sudhana's childhood prior to his meeting with Manjusri, the only thing that is said is that by the time the story begins, having been born with great roots of goodness, he had achieved an unhindered, unattached determination for enlightenment. In Buddhist cosmology, that is of course an exceptional achievement for a child. Sudhana's determination is one of the qualities that attracts Manjusri, and one that inspires Chinese Buddhist readers and illumines for them the requirements of the bodhisattva path. As Buddhist masters in China never tire of pointing out to their followers, great faith and great determination are required for success on the bodhisattva path.

In the course of the long pilgrimage to fifty-three teachers, Sudhana displays no childlike behavior or motivations. He is respectful, appreciative, and dedicated to his quest. His speech is always a model of the kind of eloquence that only a person well educated in the Buddhist tradition could attain. It is very hard while reading the story to sustain the belief that Sudhana is a child. In this way he is like the infant Siddhartha and the precocious children of the Han dynasty biographies. One wonders why the author of the narrative bothered to make him a child.

On reflection, however, making him a child in the story clearly allows the author to stress certain points not made as clearly in other Buddhist literature. It makes clear that, in this lifetime at least, the protagonist is a beginner with respect to the bodhisattva path, a point that could not be so clearly made with a chronologically adult character. To make him a child is also to make clear what he is not. He is not an ordained monk, not because he does not choose to be, but because he is a child. Thus he can be both not a monk and yet not opposed to being a monk. Also, to the Chinese reader it must have been clear that he is not fully independent, for he is in some sense still dependent on his natal family. Further, though not a monk, he is not married; perhaps, being a child, he is an ideal seeker in that he is not yet distracted by sexual desire.[80] In the Indian social frame of the story, his not being married

80. Sudhana shows no attraction when he meets one of his spiritual benefactors, the courtesan Vasumitra, who uses men's desires to awaken them. For discussion about the story of Sudhana's meeting with Vasumitra, see my article "Stories of Enlightened Women in Ch'an and the Chinese Buddhist Female Bodhisattva/Goddess Tradition," in *Women and Goddess Traditions*, ed. Karen King (Minneapolis: Fortress, 1997), 137–76.

means also that he is not yet a householder, as is true in China also. As a child, he has not yet been confronted by this choice.

The message of the *Gandavyuha* seems to be that a child, a beginner who is young, not independent, and not a monk, can achieve the aspiration for awakening and become a bodhisattva. In schools of Chinese Buddhism, which embraced the doctrines of the universal possession of the Buddha nature and the possibility of sudden awakening, Sudhana became an example of a potential that all sentient beings have. Children have this potential, this nature, and can manifest it, at least in some cases. The Buddhist view of a childhood as merely a stage in the endless cycle of rebirth, in which what a child brings to his or her new lifetime varies enormously, comes into play here, of course: Sudhana is a special child. Nonetheless, for those who care about children and their spiritual potential, it is significant that the precocious Sudhana does not have to wait to embark on the full study of the bodhisattva path until he is an adult, as is the case in many other Buddhist texts. It is also important that in the view of Chinese Buddhist interpreters, at the end of the *Gandhavyuha,* Sudhana, still a child, has traversed all ten stages of the progress of a bodhisattva as taught in the *Huayan sütra* and the Huayan school.

The Dragon Daughter

While the story of Sudhana's pilgrimage occupies forty fascicles, the story of the daughter of the Dragon King Sagara, told in the Devadatta chapter of the *Lotus Sutra,* is very short. When the story begins, the exact age of the young daughter is mentioned: she is eight years old by Chinese reckoning; Westerners would call her seven, since she has completed only seven full years. She is unquestionably a child according to Western chronological and developmental thinking. The narrator of the story also regards her as a child, though a part animal/part human rather than a fully human child. Her being a child is part of what makes what is told of her particularly unlikely in the eyes of one of the protagonists of the story, the Buddha's *sravaka* disciple Sariputra.

According to the story, when the Buddha has finished showing that wicked people may attain buddhahood, the Bodhisattva Wisdom Accumulation, an attendant of the Tathagata Abundant Treasures, thinks that the sermon on self-awareness of Buddha-nature is over and suggests to the Tathagata Abundant Treasures that they return to their own land. But the Buddha detains him and tells him to stay for a while to attend to his disciple Manjusri. Immediately the Bodhisattva Manjusri appears from the dragon palace at the bottom of the sea.

The Bodhisattva Wisdom Accumulation greets Manjusri and asks him how many beings he has converted. Manjusri answers that they were countless, but that there must be proof. As he speaks, like a cloud rising from the sea, the splendid bodhisattvas he has converted appear, seated upon beautiful lotus flowers. The Bodhisattva Wisdom Accumulation is struck with admiration and asks what he taught in the sea, to which Manjusri answers, only the Dharma-Flower *Sutra* (that is, the *Lotus Sutra*). The Bodhisattva Wisdom Accumulation presses on:

> Bodhisattva Wisdom Accumulation questioned Manjusri, saying, "This *sutra* is profound, subtle, and wonderful, a treasure among *sutras*, a rarity in the world. Are there perhaps any living beings who, by earnestly and diligently practicing this *sutra*, have been able to attain buddhahood quickly?"
>
> Manjusri replied: "There is the daughter of the dragon king Sagara, who has just turned eight. Her wisdom has keen roots and she is good at understanding the roots/faculties, conduct and karma (deeds) of living beings. She has mastered the dharanis [incantations], has been able to accept and embrace all the storehouse of profound secrets preached by the Buddhas, has entered deep into meditation, thoroughly grasped the doctrines, and in the space of an instant conceived the desire for *bodhi* and reached the level [on the bodhisattva path] of no regression. Her eloquence knows no hindrance, and she thinks of living beings with compassion as though they were her own children. She is fully endowed with blessings, and when it comes to conceiving in mind and expounding by mouth, she is subtle, wonderful, comprehensive and great. Kind, compassionate, benevolent, yielding, she is gentle and refined in will, capable of attaining Bodhi [i.e., the full awakening of the Buddha]."[81]

Having heard this, The Bodhisattva Wisdom Accumulation asks Manjusri how anyone can attain buddhahood without having gone through the long and strenuous career of bodhisattvahood that brought Sakyamuni to full awakening. Before he is finished, the dragon girl appears, bows to and praises the Buddha in a long poem, and then stands to one side. At the end of the poem she speaks the following lines:

> And having heard his [i.e., the Buddha's] teachings, I have attained *bodhi*—
> the Buddha alone can bear witness to this.
> I unfold the doctrines of the Great Vehicle
> to rescue living beings from suffering.

At this, Sariputra, who is not a bodhisattva but rather a *sravaka*, an *arahant*, breaks in and informs the girl that the perfect knowledge of the Buddha took incalculable times and is to be attained only after diligent labor and full practice of the Six Perfections, and that a female who has karmic obstacles in her way can hardly accomplish it. Another crucial passage says:

81. Burton Watson, trans., *The Lotus Sutra* (New York: Columbia University Press, 1993). I have changed "root activities and deeds" to "roots/faculties, conduct and karma" and inserted explanatory material in brackets.

> At that time Sariputra said to the dragon girl "You suppose that in this short time you have been able to attain the unsurpassed way. But this is difficult to believe. Why? Because a female body is soiled and defiled, not a vessel for the Law. How could you attain the unsurpassed *bodhi*? The road to buddhahood is long and far-stretching. Only after one has spent immeasurable *kalpas* pursuing austerities, accumulating deeds, practicing all kinds of *paramitas*, can one finally achieve success.
>
> Moreover, a female is subject to the five obstacles. First, she cannot become a Brahma heavenly king. Second, she cannot become the king Shakra. Third, she cannot become a devil king. Fourth, she cannot become a wheel-turning sage king. Fifth, she cannot become a Buddha. How then could a girl like you be able to attain buddhahood so quickly?'[82]

The girl gives no answer except to present to the Buddha a single pearl she holds in her hand—a jewel worth the three-thousand-great-thousandfold world. The Buddha joyfully accepts her gift. The dragon girl then tells Wisdom Accumulation Bodhisattva and Sariputra that yet more swiftly than the Buddha accepted her pearl will she herself become a buddha, and at once she appears in masculine form as a buddha presenting the teaching of the *Lotus Sutra* in a spotless world far away to the south.[83]

That is the whole story. Clearly the dragon girl has extraordinarily good roots or faculties for attaining wisdom. Thinking about her using the framework of precocity, though, is a bit difficult. Before our eyes she attains more than any other human in the *sütras* has attained, except for the butcher in the Nirvana *sütra* who puts down his knife and attains buddhahood. Manjusri describes extraordinary attainments that were evident to him while he was still in the dragon realm in the sea, but he does not make clear whether she has attained them before he preaches the *Lotus Sutra*, in which case she would be exceptionally precocious, or only after he preaches the *Lotus Sutra*, in which case the message would be that the *sutra* itself is extraordinarily powerful. The passage perhaps deliberately blurs this matter of time in order to stay within the realm of orthodox Buddhist notions of karma and rebirth while emphasizing the power of the *sutra*. When she heard the *sutra* preached, "in an instant" she aroused the aspiration to awakening (the *bodhicitta,* here translated by Watson as "the desire for *bodhi*") that begins a bodhisattva's career. She also, in that same instant, attained the stage on the bodhisattva path of nonregression. The text does not state that she will attain *bodhi* in the future; rather it says, "she can *(neng)* attain *bodhi.*" The auxiliary verb

82. Burton Watson, trans., *The Lotus Sutra*, 188. I have substituted the word "female" for Watson's "woman" in all his sentences but one, and the word "girl" for Watson's "woman" in the last sentence. The Chinese character means "daughter," "girl," "female" or "woman." A translator should choose "female" instead of "woman" since the girl is a nonhuman being, and "girl" in the last sentence, since she is only eight years old.

83. This retelling is taken from Nikkyo Niwano, *A Guide to the Three-fold Lotus Sutra* (Tokyo: Kosei Publishing Company, 1981), 91–92.

"neng" is not marked by tense. Furthermore, in her poem of praise to the Buddha she says that "when she heard [the Buddha's teaching] she accomplished (*cheng*) *bodhi.*" That is, she attained awakening in the dragon palace under the ocean when she heard the *Lotus Sutra* preached.

As Sariputra points out, if her form indicates her karmic burden, as a female she is unqualified to attain liberation and become a Buddha in the current body. Although the *sutra* passage does not state the hindrance offered by her youth, Chinese Buddhist listeners would note that she cannot have practiced the Buddha's teachings in this lifetime for very long, if at all.

What is the point of the story? Surely it is that even a somewhat precocious but also relatively ordinary female child, even one who is not fully human, can swiftly attain buddhahood *if* she has the good fortune to hear the *Lotus Sutra* preached. As one of the characters in the story said, it is the *Lotus Sutra* that makes it possible for sentient beings to attain buddhahood. Speedily.

Perhaps we see here, in sutras received in China, a gendered element in the Buddhist stories of children of extraordinary precocity. Sudhana, a male human child of good family, arrives on this earth with an enormous array of auspicious wealth. Implicit and explicit in the story of Sudhana's successful pilgrimage is that he possessed from the start extraordinary qualifications for awakening. He progresses to the highest bodhisattva stage with the aid of fifty-two spiritual benefactors, *kalyanamitra*. The Dragon Girl is unlikely, by her very femaleness, to possess such extraordinary qualifications for awakening, but definitely she is also exceptionally qualified, though not as qualified as he. She offers to the Buddha enormous wealth, which dragons are known to possess. Unlike Sudhana's, her qualifications are challenged, as is the conception of the bodhisattva path—now strangely short—that Manjusri puts forward. Nonetheless, amazing things happen because she hears the *Lotus Sutra* preached, and she is even more quickly and thoroughly awakened than Sudhana.

Sudhana and the Daughter of the Dragon King Sagara in Popular Literature: An Unfilial Chronological Child

In the popular iconography of the Ming and Qing dynasties, the White-Robed Guanyin (Avalokitesvara) is often accompanied by two young acolytes, Shancai (here the characters mean "Good Talent") and Longnu, Dragon Daughter/Girl.

This triad is not found in any canonical text. The first work that explains how the two of them became disciples of Guanyin is a short sixteenth-century "novel" called the *Complete Tale of Guanyin of the Southern Seas,* in which the story of how Sudhana and the Dragon Daughter came to be with Guanyin occupies but one chapter. From a later (eighteenth- or nineteenth-century) date is another text in twenty-nine *scrolls* that provides a much more developed story told in alternating verse and prose. It is called *The Precious Scroll of Good Talent and Dragon Girl.*[84]

84. Wilt L. Idema, "Introduction," in *Personal Salvation and Filial Piety*, 30–32.

The following is a summary of the latter story: A man named Grand Historian Chen is fated to have no children, despite his great goodness and virtue. He and his wife sincerely and piously beg Guanyin Bodhisattva for a child. She decides to send him an immortal who needs to be reborn as a human before returning to the immortal realm. This immortal, Summoning Riches Lad, served below the throne of the Heavenly Official for Bestowing Riches in the Communing-with-Heaven Office. His mind was set on the Way. Even though he had set his mind on goodness, he distributed too much wealth to people, out of his unalloyed compassion, thereby disrupting the Heavenly Emperor's system of rewards and fines, and in so doing ruined the fruit of his karma. Because of this act, the Heavenly Emperor had been filled with rage, and Summoning Riches Lad had been demoted and sent as punishment to be reborn in the realm of dust.

He is now born to the couple. In a scene reminiscent of King Suddhodana taking the infant Siddhartha (the future Sakyamuni) to see the sage Asita, the Grand Historian Chen consults the court astrologer or diviner, who reports that the child will return to heaven's palace. Grand Historian Chen himself then studies the child's physiognomy, all of which is very auspicious, then notices that the child is breathing like a turtle as immortals do. He worries that this child will achieve immortality and depart, rather than serve at the imperial court, extend the family line, and improve the family fortunes. It is to have an heir to continue the ancestral sacrifices that he has asked for a son. He is tormented by the thought that this is perhaps not to be.

The boy grows, and the narrator says: "With every day [the boy] Chen Lian grew smarter and more intelligent. At the age of three, the little boy could already recite his texts. When he opened his mouth, every word accorded with Truth. Whatever he uttered, whatever he said, was out of the ordinary." We have here the precocious child of the Han dynasty models. But when his elders wanted to send him to school to study the [Confucian or secular] Classics, he said to them: "I don't want to study the Books. I'm too lazy to make the effort. It is not my wish to become an official or to become an officer, but to search for my roots by studying the way of the immortals."[85]

When Chen Lian was five, his mother died. He was completely disconsolate, weeping inconsolably and uttering a long, affecting poem about his loss. At age seven, when he normally would begin studies, he makes it clear again that he has no intention of studying the Confucian classics for the sake of worldly success and the future of the family, as his father wants, but rather will study only those disciplines that would help him transcend this world as an immortal. He has his own version of filial piety. "My father," he says, "I do not belong to the mortal kind of men. I want to ferry my parents back to the land of the immortals."[86]

85. Idema, *Personal Salvation and Filial Piety*, 165.
86. Idema, *Personal Salvation and Filial Piety*, 166.

His father takes him to a teacher who could teach him either kind of learning. Grand Historian Chen asks the teacher to teach his son the classics and the civil and military arts to prepare him for imperial service. After his father leaves, Chen Lian makes clear to his teacher that he wants to study only the way to immortality. He announces to his teacher—promises him, in fact—that he will not return to his father nor learn what his father wants him to learn. His father continues to beg him to study the Classics, but Chen Lian never wavers and refuses his father's invitations to return home for a visit. So his father loses him, both his company and the expectation that his son will give his family any descendants. The son has promised to obey his father but has no scruples about not doing so, because he is determined to reach his goal. His teacher tests his steadfast resolve, finds that he does not waver, and realizes that his determination is that of the brave man who does not fear and of the wise man who is not deluded.[87] It is also, of course, the determination of the Sudhana of the *Huayan sutra* and the infant Buddha, though more inhumanly absolute than that of the young Siddhartha of the later episodes in Indian Buddhist heroic legends.

Good Talent does have a moment of weakness in his unwavering determination to become an immortal. When he is ten years old, his teacher tests him again by leaving him alone on the mountain, telling him to stay and take care of things at the grotto. Fearful of wild animals and increasingly lonely, Good Talent decides to go home for a visit. He remembers that it is his father's sixtieth birthday, a good reason to go home. He never arrives at his home, for before he is completely off the mountain, he foolishly releases a snake spirit, who wants to repay his kindness by eating him. He is powerless to resist and has to be rescued by Guanyin disguised as a young girl. Guanyin takes him directly to her home, the island of Potalaka (*Putuo shan*) off the coast near Ningbo, where he will serve her as a disciple and a fully awakened being.[88] As her acolyte, he is always depicted as a child, the clear symbol of which is his hairstyle.

The snake spirit turns out to be the Naga king Sagara's daughter from the *Lotus Sutra*. Guanyin also takes the snake spirit to Mount Potalaka and gives her an opportunity to reform her mind and heart. When this dragon/snake girl does so after seven years of imprisonment at Mount Potalaka, Guanyin also takes her into her service.[89]

In this story, the child Good Talent is definitely spiritually precocious and intellectually gifted. He has superb spiritual faculties/roots. He shows complete

87. Idema, *Personal Salvation and Filial Piety*, 170.

88. For a study of Mount Potalaka (Puto), see Chun-fang Yu, "P'u-t'o Shan: Pilgrimage and the Creation of the Chinese Potalaka," in *Pilgrims and Sacred Sites in China*, ed. Susan Naquin and Chun-fang Yu (Berkeley: University of California Press, 1992), 190–245.

89. For images of Good Talent as an acolyte of Guanyin, see Chun-fang Yu, "Guan-yin: The Chinese Transformation of Avalokitesvara," in *Latter Days of the Law*, ed. Marsha Weidner, 151–82, and catalog entry 47, plate 23, and figure 24. The latter also includes an image of the Dragon Girl as acolyte.

determination and absolute courage in submitting without demur to years of difficult toil and study under his teacher. He hews without wavering to his desire to become an immortal once again. This behavior is certainly extraordinary in a child.

He is also, while a child, about as nonfilial as it is possible to be, as filiality is defined by his father and by Confucian Chinese culture. He lies to his father and never gives a single serious thought to his father's plans for him. Good Talent's father's destiny of having no son is fulfilled, but at the cost of even greater disappointment, sadness, and pain than he might have known had he never had a son. If the texts about filiality in both Chinese Buddhism and Chinese Confucianism are centered on getting the adult social child to desire to obey the father and make him happy, Good Talent is hopelessly unfilial. He is precocious enough to act like a small adult throughout most of the story; therefore, one would expect him to be filial. There is an endearing exception to his "small adult" behavior, though, when being left alone on the mountain causes him to become fearful and waver. Suddenly we see the child in Good Talent. Guanyin, ever the solicitous mother, rescues him and takes him to serve her as an immortal at her Potalaka, where he is always portrayed as a child.

How can Guanyin reward Good Talent's callous disregard for his father's wishes and happiness? In this story we find a striking illustration of the Chinese Buddhist answer to charges that renunciation of householder life is unfilial behavior. As a result of his suffering, the father ceases to value the world and becomes a Buddhist. Furthermore, seven or nine generations of the Chen family ancestors ascend to the highest heavens. This is the Buddhist answer to the charge of lack of filiality—the true filiality is, like the Buddha, to attain buddhahood and convert and liberate all one's family and ancestors. From the point of view of Chinese Buddhism as it circulated among literate and illiterate classes, one can do this at any age.

Once again in this story we see gender and species differences reflected in the *Precious Scroll of Good Talent and the Dragon Girl*. In this story, the snake spirit who selfishly wants to eat Shancai turns out to be the Naga king Sagara's daughter from the *Lotus Sutra*. Guanyin also takes the snake spirit to Mount Potalaka and gives her an opportunity to reform her "completely poisonous" mind and heart. Only after reforming herself during seven years of imprisonment at Mount Potalaka does Guanyin also takes the dragon girl/snake spirit into her service. Although Shancai and the Dragon Girl both become acolytes of Guanyin, Shancai's selfless courage and determination are held up for admiration from the very beginning, while it is Dragon Girl's capacity for repentance and reform that can win praise. What is striking, though, is that in human form when serving Guanyin the snake spirit is an eight-year-old female. In this story both sets of crucial Buddhist virtues, courage and determination on the one hand and repentance and reform on the other, are represented as fully present in children.

CONCLUSION

Childhood, though hardly represented or discovered in Chinese Buddhist texts about historical people prior to the seventeenth century, or in Buddhist doctrines commonly taught in China, appears in stories of the Buddha's birth and infancy, in ceremonies of bathing the infant Buddha who stands in the posture of proclamation of his real nature and mission, in two *sütras* that are immensely popular in China in part because they portray children in heroic roles, and in indigenous Buddhist tales. Though all the official Buddhist literature about filiality is focused on the adult social child, in popular indigenous literature children can display real filiality as Buddhists understand it. Most important, children can attain the highest stages on the bodhisattva path, as Sudhana does, and buddhahood itself, as the Dragon daughter does. Furthermore, perhaps children, not yet ordained renouncers, not yet sexually active adults, are perhaps the best persons to achieve these universal Mahayana Buddhist goals.

CHAPTER 6

Representing Childhood in Chinese Buddhism

The Sujati Jataka *in Text and Image*

WINSTON KYAN

BUDDHIST FILIAL PIETY?

A familiar trope in Chinese Buddhism is the Buddhist filial child charged with saving his or her family. In texts and images, representations of these paragons repeatedly demonstrate that Buddhist devotion to parents is superior to conventional Confucian forms of filial piety. By extension, this theme of the Buddhist filial child creates a framework for the integration of Buddhist generosity and renunciation into traditional Chinese views of kinship and ancestor worship.[1] Among the best-known of these Buddhist filial children are Syama (Ch. *Shanzi* 睒子), who faithfully gathered food and drink for his blind parents until one day he was accidentally killed by a hunter; Maudgalyayana (Ch. *Mulian* 目連), who saved his sinful mother from the deepest hell; and Avalokitesvara as Princess Miaoshan (妙善), who cured the illness of her cruel father by secretly feeding him her arm and eyes. And although these figures have deep historical roots in the medieval Chinese rhetoric of Buddhist monks and Confucian officials, modern scholars have also studied Syama, Maudgalyayana, and Miaoshan

1. For a discussion of the interaction between Buddhist, Daoist, and Confucian ideals in the construction of medieval Chinese childhood, see Richard B. Mather, "Filial Sons and Spoiled Brats: A Glimpse of Medieval Chinese Children in *Shishuoxinyu*," in *Chinese Views of Childhood*, ed. Anne Behnke Kinney (Honolulu: University of Hawaii Press, 1995), 111–29.

to question conventional understandings of Buddhist family values as rejecting Chinese bonds between ancestors and descendants (in the form of monastic ideals) and as using children to facilitate parental quests for spiritual awakening (in representations of the Vessantara Jataka and the Life of the Buddha).

For instance, Kenneth Ch'en in his landmark study *The Chinese Transformation of Buddhism* (1973) specifically identifies filial piety as the driving force in the "sinicization" of Buddhism and uses the popularity of the *Syama Jataka* to illustrate the process by which medieval Chinese Buddhists extracted *sutras* with filial themes from the vast Buddhist corpus, composed apocryphal *sutras* that espoused filial ideals, and articulated Buddhist concepts of filial piety that superseded those of the Chinese tradition.[2] In the equally important *The Ghost Festival in Medieval China*, Stephen Teiser has demonstrated how Maudgalyayana and the Ullambana Ceremony became a model of Buddhist filial practice by obligating descendants to benefit their ancestors through offerings to the Sangha.[3] Taking Teiser's argument of Buddhist interventions into ancestor worship one step further, Alan Cole has interpreted Maudgalyayana's devotion to his mother in psychoanalytic terms as the eroticized bond between sons and mothers.[4] For Cole, the dual image of the mother as nurturing above the waist and sinful below rendered Confucian filial piety insufficient: only Buddhist filial practices overseen by the Sangha could help, especially since the emphasis of Confucian filial piety on fathers and sons largely ignored the mother–son relationship.[5]

Expanding upon the repertoire of Buddhist filial piety, Princess Miaoshan has also attracted considerable scholarly attention. Unlike Syama, who was a previous incarnation of Shakyamuni, or unlike Maudgalyayana, who was an accomplished disciple of the Buddha, Princess Miaoshan is a manifestation of the bodhisattva Avalokitesvara. And unlike Syama and Maudgalyayana, who have clear roots in Indian Buddhism, the origins of the Miaoshan legend in Chinese texts from the eleventh to twelfth centuries provide rich source material to situate the Buddhist filial child into historically specific and gendered contexts. Beginning with Glen Dudbridge's seminal analysis of Miaoshan as a localized Buddhist myth symbolizing the anxieties of female children caught between family duty and spiritual fulfillment,[6] to Chün-fang Yü's discussion of this figure as representing a crucial stage in the Chinese feminization of Avalokitesvara,[7] to Wilt Idema's recent

2. See Kenneth Ch'en, *The Chinese Transformation of Buddhism* (Princeton, NJ: Princeton University Press, 1973), 18–50.

3. See Stephen F. Teiser, *The Ghost Festival in Medieval China* (Princeton, NJ: Princeton University Press, 1988), 113–34.

4. See Alan Cole, *Mothers and Sons in Chinese Buddhism* (Stanford, CA: Stanford University Press, 1998), 80–115.

5. For a counter view that the mother and son relationship was also a deep Confucian concern during the early medieval periods, see Keith Nathaniel Knapp, *Selfless Offspring: Filial Children and Social Order in Medieval China* (Honolulu: University of Hawaii Press, 1995).

6. See Glen Dudbridge, *The Legend of Miao-shan* (London: Ithaca Press for the Board of the Faculty of Oriental Studies, Oxford University, 1978), and Glen Dudbridge, *The Legend of Miaoshan*, rev. ed. (Oxford: Oxford University Press, 2004).

7. See Chün-fang Yü, *Kuan-yin: The Chinese Transformation of Avalokitesvara* (New York: Columbia University Press, 2000).

reading of the story as a "proto-feminist" guide for female marriage,[8] interpretations of Miaoshan demonstrate the potentiality of Buddhist filial children to illuminate historical and cultural tensions that shape the construction of childhood.

The implications of historical and cultural practice also underscore the investigations of this essay on the construction of childhood, which adds the *Sujati Jataka* to the discourse on Buddhist filial children. More specifically, the following analysis reads pictorial representations of the *Sujati Jataka* from the sixth to eighth centuries at the Mogao Caves, Dunhuang against contemporary Chinese Buddhist translations from the *Sutra on the Wise and Foolish* (T.202, Ch. *Xianyu jing* 賢愚經), and the *Sutra on Repaying Kindness* (T.156, Ch. *Baoen jing* 報恩經).[9] Since both these *sutras* are first listed in the *Collected Notes on the Tripitaka* (T.2145, Ch. *Chu sanzangjiji* 出三藏記), an early Chinese *sutra* catalog compiled by the Liang dynasty monk Sengyou (僧祐) between 501 and 518, these *sutras* provide valuable textual context for the analysis of these images.

Taken together, Buddhist murals painted at a major intersection of the Silk Road and Buddhist narratives translated into Chinese during a time of intense cultural debate on the role of Buddhist filial piety provide a compelling backdrop for an analysis of the *Sujati Jataka* in medieval China, which arguably illustrates more than the perfection of generosity (*dana-paramita*) that is the central message in numerous *jataka* tales.[10] Indeed, the description of a young boy cutting and offering his flesh to his starving parents involve complicated social and cultural issues of self-mutilation, cannibalism, and the parent–child relationship that illuminate the construction of childhood in medieval China. This essay thus considers representations of the *Sujati Jataka* by asking the following questions: What did this narrative mean to its makers and viewers, translators and readers? Why was this story important enough to merit widespread pictorial representation at a major Buddhist site such as Dunhuang? And perhaps most important, what are the implications of representing a child asserting moral authority over his father and reversing the roles of parental responsibility for notions of childhood during this time?

8. Wilt L. Idema, *Personal Salvation and Filial Piety: Two Precious Scroll Narratives of Guanyin and Her Acolytes* (Honolulu: University of Hawaii Press, 2008).

9. The *Sutra on the Wise and Foolish* T.202 (full title: *Sutra on the Wise and Foolish and Cause and Effect*, Ch. *Xianyu yinyuan jing* 賢愚因緣經) contains sixty-nine loosely grouped narratives that illustrate Buddhist principles of good and bad. The *Sutra on Repaying Kindness* T.156 (full title: *Sutra of the Great Expedient Means Buddha on Repaying Kindness*, Ch. *Dafangbianfo baoen jing* 大方便佛報恩經) contains eleven stories divided among nine chapters that demonstrate neither a clear connecting theme nor a clear reflection on the theme of "repaying kindness" that ostensibly serves to link the various narratives. Scholars have taken this lack of thematic coherence as evidence for the apocryphal nature of the *sutra*.

10. For a study of *dana-paramita* and bodily self-sacrifice in Sanskrit, Pali, and Tibetan traditions, see the important work of Reiko Ohnuma, including "The Gift of the Body and the Gift of Dharma," *History of Religions* 37 no. 4 (1998), 323–59; and *Head, Eyes, Flesh, and Blood: Giving Away the Body in Indian Buddhist Literature* (New York: Columbia University Press, 2006).

The methodology employed in exploring these questions acknowledges the importance of visual and textual sources for the study of cultural history; but at the same time I am skeptical of taking images and texts at face value as unmediated reflections of their times. My approach, then, is as attentive to the implicit desires and anxieties embedded in the process of representation as it is to the explicit messages put forward by pictorial and scriptural narratives, and I am as interested in the correlations between texts and images as I am in the discrepancies between them. In the case of Sujati representations, which depict physical sacrifice in an unconventionally gruesome manner, I would argue that analyzing the mechanisms of meaning beneath the graphic depictions of Sujati's sacrifice offers valuable perspectives onto the meaning of childhood both in specific Buddhist communities and in broader cultural views.

EMBODIED IMAGES AND THE CONSTRUCTION OF CHILDHOOD

From the earliest caves cut and decorated during the first decades of the fifth century to the last great constructions undertaken at the end of the tenth century, representations of extreme physical sacrifice have been a staple in the murals of the Mogao Caves, Dunhuang. The violent deeds of royal figures that remove chunks of flesh from their thigh (King Sibi), throw their bodies off cliffs (Prince Mahasattva), and proffer their heads for decapitation (King Candraprabha) appear in vivid contrast to the tranquility of their physical postures and facial expressions. This gap between a willingness to undergo bodily pain and a detachment from the resulting agony indicates the purely motivated generosity practiced by holy personages who have dedicated themselves to the salvation of all beings, even at the cost of extreme personal suffering. Typically, the most demanding bodily offerings are illustrated by a narrative category known as *jataka*, in which the protagonist is a previous incarnation of Sakyamuni Buddha and the self-sacrifice adds to the store of karmic merit needed for enlightenment. But even by the extreme standards of this genre, the cutting and offering of a child's flesh to his parents is intensely disturbing.[11]

Sujati images are also distinguished from other *jataka* pictures in their visual development. That is, while representations of King Sibi and Prince Mahasattva show little variation over the course of several centuries, those of Sujati exhibit significant alterations in iconography and pictorial logic. For example, there is little difference between the images of King Sibi depicted in Mogao Cave 275 dated to the fifth century and in Mogao Cave 85 dated to the ninth century. Although they are separated by roughly four hundred years, both describe how a devout Buddhist king offers his flesh in increasing amounts to substitute for

11. For an introduction to the debates surrounding the practice of filial flesh offerings, see Hubert Durt, "Two Interpretations of Human-Flesh Offering: Misdeed or Supreme Sacrifice," *Kokusai Bukkyōgaku daigaku kenkyū kiyō* (1999), 57–83.

the weight of a dove fleeing from a hungry hawk. In both the early and later example, the narrative relies on the same basic pictorial elements: there is King Sibi, the smaller dove, the larger hawk, and an attendant who cuts flesh from the king's leg.[12] The dove, who is the god Indra in disguise, has magically fixed the scale so that Sibi is forced to give up more and more of his body to match the weight of the dove, thereby testing the depth and purity of the bodhisattva's generosity.

By contrast, images of the *Sujati Jataka* reveal considerable differences between its earliest representation at Mogao in sixth-century Cave 296 and the beginnings of a stable iconographic type in eighth-century Cave 148. How did the multiple scenes in Cave 296—which tells the broader story of Sujati and his parents escaping from their soon-to-be invaded kingdom, journeying to another kingdom for safety, and eventually returning to their kingdom in triumph—become condensed into a narrative centered on a few scenes of Sujati offering his flesh to his parents in Cave 148? How did the minor pictorial role played by Sujati in the earlier image, which merely implies his sacrifice, change into the later image that explicitly depicts Sujati's flesh offering as the focus of the entire composition? In response to these questions, the following analysis compares two visual and two textual representations of the *Sujati Jataka* that circulated in medieval China at the same time. Since my investigation is based on a close reading of these four kinds of evidence, it is as crucial to provide both translations of the *Sujati Jataka* as it is important to offer clear reproductions of the murals from Caves 296 and 148. The resulting close reading and comparison of the evidence arguably sheds new light on Sujati's bodily sacrifice as a mechanism to construct embodied images in Buddhist art and as a lens to analyze shifting constructions of childhood in medieval China.

THE *SUJATI JATAKA* AND THE *SUTRA ON THE WISE AND FOOLISH*

Textual traditions of the *Sujati Jataka* fall into two main categories: a longer version from an apocryphal Chinese Buddhist scripture entitled the *Sutra on Repaying Kindness* and a shorter version from the Buddhist story collection known as the *Sutra on the Wise and Foolish*. I begin with a discussion of the *Sutra on the Wise and Foolish* and the standard account regarding its origins from the *Collected Notes on the Tripitaka*. According to this account by Sengyou, eight Chinese monks went in search of Buddhist scriptures during the reign of Emperor Wen (r. 424–452) of the Southern Song dynasty (420–479), eventually arriving at a large Buddhist convention in the Central Asian city of Khotan. The monks listened to the lectures of numerous religious teachers from the

12. For a discussion of the Chinese version of this story at Dunhuang, see Xie Shengbao, *Dunhuang fojing gushi* (Lanzhou: Gansu shaonian ertong chubanshe, 1992), 107–10.

region and then translated these stories into Chinese as the *Sutra on the Wise and Foolish*.[13] As additional indication that many of the tales in this collection were translated as a group, the tripartite structure of the Sujati narrative echoes other stories of bodily sacrifice in this *sutra:* first, the devotee makes a bodily offering; second, the devotee's sincerity is questioned by the god Indra; third, the devotee is physically restored upon confirmation of his or her sincerity in helping others.

Sutra on the Wise and Foolish: *Sujati Jataka*
(T.202, vol.4, p.356, a14—p.357, a27)

Thus I have heard. The Buddha had been staying in the Bamboo Grove Monastery near Rajagrha when one day he put on his robe, took up his begging bowl, and went into the city with Ananda to beg for food. They came upon an old blind man and woman who were homeless and desperately poor, and who sought shelter beneath the city gates. The old couple also had a seven-year old son who begged on behalf of his parents to nurture them. If the boy ever received anything, he would offer the appetizing portion to his parents and save the unpalatable portion for himself. When he saw this small child, who was respectful and filially obedient despite his extreme youth, Ananda was overcome with emotion.

When the Buddha had finished begging and returned to the bamboo grove, he began lecturing the Buddhist law for the attendees. Ananda knelt down, brought his hands together in prayer, and said to the Buddha, "Just now when we went into the city to beg for food, we saw a small child who was compassionate and filially obedient. He lived with his blind parents beneath the city gates and searched for food everywhere. Whenever he found something good to eat, he would first give it to his parents. Anything that was rank or rotten, he would eat himself. He did this everyday. He was truly a child capable of love and respect."

The Buddha told Ananda, "Whether in monastic or lay life, nurturing one's parents with compassion and filial obedience amounts to superior and immeasurable merit. Who has used this kind of merit before? I remember myself in past ages making offerings to my parents with compassion and filial obedience to the extent of using my own flesh. And I have used the merit from saving the lives of my parents to become a celestial king in heaven and a sage ruler in this world. I have become a Buddha of the Three Realms. The blessings [from this act] were used to achieve all these incarnations."

Ananda said, "I did not know that in past ages the Buddha's compassion and filial piety could forgo life and limb to the point of using one's own flesh to save the lives of one's parents. What can be said about this matter?" The Buddha answered, "Listen and think carefully, and I will speak of it. Many *kalpas* ago on the continent of Jambudvipa, King Deva ruled over the kingdom of Taxila. The king had ten sons, who each ruled his own fief. The land of the youngest

13. For a study of the linguistic and philological origins of this *sutra*, see Victor Mair, "The Linguistic and Textual Antecedents of the *Sutra on the Wise and Foolish*," *Sino-Platonic Papers* 38 (1993), 3–18.

son was particularly prosperous. The king also had a minister named Rahu who served at his side. Unfortunately, feelings of evil and revolt grew in this minister and he murdered the king, dispatched troops to kill each of the princes, and set plans to usurp the throne.

The gods were especially respectful of the youngest of the king's sons and when this prince went for a stroll in his garden a *yaksa* emerged from the ground, knelt down before him, and said, 'Feelings of evil and revolt have grown in the minister and he has murdered the king. He has dispatched an army to kill each of your brothers and these troops are now coming after you. You must think of a plan to escape this tragedy.'

The prince's heart collapsed with terror when he heard this. And although he tried to think of a plan, he just ran away. However, the prince had a seven-year-old son named Sujati, also known as Susambhava, who was dignified, intelligent, and adorable. The prince loved him very much and he had not left the city very far before he rushed back to take his son into his arms, sighing and shedding tears of grief.

His wife saw the panicked comings and goings of the prince and asked, 'Why are you so flustered? You look terrified.' Her husband replied, 'You could not possibly know.' The wife questioned him further, 'Our lives are intertwined. In times of danger, we must follow each other without thoughts of abandoning the other. If there is anything the matter now, you must speak out.'

The prince answered, 'When I recently entered the garden, a *yaksa* guardian spirit emerged out of the ground, knelt down, and said, "Feelings of evil and revolt have grown in the minister, and he has murdered the king. He has also dispatched an army and killed each of your brothers. These troops are now coming to kill you. You must escape if you can." When I heard these words, my heart filled with terror, and I was so frightened by the arrival of the troops that I panicked and tried to escape.' His wife knelt down and said, 'I would rather follow and serve than face abandonment.' The prince then took hold of his wife, put his son in his arms, and left with the intention of reaching the neighboring kingdom.

There were two paths before them: one took seven days and the other took fourteen. In the panic surrounding their departure, the prince managed to prepare just enough food to last one person for one week. Then leaving the city, he took the fourteen-day path by mistake so that the provisions were completely gone after a few days. Dizzy with hunger, the prince could see only one way out of this predicament. Out of love for his son, he decided to kill his wife to save himself and his son. He ordered the wife to carry the son and walk in front. From behind, the prince grasped his knife with the intent to kill his wife. At this moment, the son turned around and saw the father grasping his knife with the intent to kill his mother. Putting his hands together in prayer, he tried to make his father understand that his only wish was that the prince hurt him rather than his mother. This sincere remonstration saved his mother's life.

Sujati then said to his father, 'Do not kill me immediately. Cut my flesh bit by bit and eat it so that it will last for several days. If you end my life now, the flesh will rot and not last long.' So the father and mother decided to cut their son's flesh. Shedding tears of distress, they cut the flesh and ate it everyday until it was almost all gone and only the bones remained. But they still had not yet reached the neighboring kingdom. In a state of extreme hunger, the father took up his knife again to pick the small amount of flesh remaining between each of his son's joints. Soon thereafter, the father and mother were at the point of giving up. The son then thought deeply to himself that since there is not much life left in me, my only wish is that father and mother allow me to offer all the remaining flesh that I have. The parents did not object to this wish, and Sujati gathered the remaining muscles, eyes, and tongue from his body and offered them all to his parents, who then departed in farewell.

The child then set down this vow: 'I have now offered my flesh to my parents and I take hold of this merit to seek the path to buddhahood. I also vow to save all beings of the ten directions and to enable them to leave their collective bitterness and arrive at the joy of nirvana.' As soon as he put forth this vow, six great earthquakes moved the three thousand realms and the gods were thunderstruck. Without explanation, the palace halls shook. Sujati then surveyed the world with the eye of heaven to witness other bodhisattvas offering flesh to their parents and vowing to save all beings through the path to buddhahood. Because of this, heaven and earth gave a great quake and celestial beings descended to form a crowd in the sky, shedding their tears like heavy rain.

At that time, Indra came down to test Sujati by transforming himself into a beggar child who asked for the flesh from his hands, which Sujati gave. Indra then transformed himself into lions, tigers, and wolves that lunged forward as if to bite Sujati. At that moment, the child thought deeply to himself that if these beasts want to eat me, I willingly offer them the bones, marrow, and brain that remain in my body. Without a trace of regret, the thought filled his heart with joy. When Indra realized the child's resoluteness of will, he changed back to his proper form and appeared before the child to say, 'Since you are compassionate, filial, and able to use your body to make offerings to your parents, you may use this merit to become any heavenly emperor or demon king that you wish.'

The child replied, 'I do not wish to seek the happiness of the Three Realms; rather, I hold this merit to seek the path to buddhahood that saves each and every sentient being.' Indra then asked, 'Were you able to offer your body to your father and mother without the slightest regret?' The child responded, 'With total sincerity, I have made offerings to my parents without regret.' Indra continued, 'I see that your flesh is all gone, but you say that you have no regrets—this is difficult to believe.' The child answered, 'If indeed I hold no regrets in my vow to become a Buddha, let my body be restored to its former state.' As soon as Sujati spoke these words, his body was restored, and Indra and all the gods praised Sujati's excellence with one voice.

Later, Sujati's parents along with all the people of the kingdom approached the child and exclaimed that there had never been anything like this. The neighboring king was so overjoyed that he extended numerous terms of congratulations and respect, and made offerings to the child and his parents in his palace. The neighboring king then assembled his army to take Sujati, his father, and his mother back to their kingdom. Rahu was destroyed and Sujati's father was established as the ruler. Eventually, Sujati succeeded to the throne and the country enjoyed great peace and prosperity."

The Buddha then said to Ananda, "The father at that time was also my father in this life; the mother at that time was also my mother in this life; and Sujati was

> one of my previous lives. Throughout the ages, offering one's flesh with compassion and filial piety to save the lives of one's parents generates the effect of this merit. Heaven and earth often produce beings of extraordinary power and unlimited blessings, and this too is the effect of this merit."

THE SUJATI JATAKA AND MOGAO CAVE 296

The Sujati mural in Mogao Cave 296 (Northern Zhou period, 557–81) occupies the entire lower section of the north wall and stretches from corner to corner in a manner not unlike a fully unrolled Chinese hand scroll (Figure 6.1).[14] As the earliest representation of the Sujati narrative at Mogao, this mural offers both an introduction to the image tradition and a foundation to consider how cultural views of childhood emerge from the relationship between texts and images. As a complex representation of sequential events, this image is also suggestive of the use of visual cues to demarcate changes in time and place that restructure and translate a verbal narrative into a visual medium. For example, the rectangular cartouches that punctuate this painting into legible scenes serve as crucial tools in this negotiation between the pictorial and the textual, the temporal and the spatial. Although these cartouches now survive as blank white rectangles, they nevertheless reference the transition from one narrative scene to the next. And regardless of whether or not they once contained written characters, their very presence makes the relationship between text and image explicit.

The complex interaction between time and space conveyed by this pictorial narrative thus necessitates a definition of terms, especially regarding the distinction between "scene" and "event." Accordingly, my analysis uses scene to reference a discrete spatial composition, and event to indicate a distinct temporal moment. Since a spatial scene and a temporal event sometimes overlap, these terms are not mutually exclusive categories but rather indicators of meaning that distinguish my analysis of space (scene) from my analysis of time (event).

Beginning at the far left of the mural, the viewer encounters the first spatial scene of the guardian spirit warning the prince in his palace. This spirit, whose supernatural status is suggested by his larger size, flowing scarf, and half-naked body, presses his palms together in an imploring gesture toward the prince, who is represented as a white-robed human figure that leans back and raises his arms in surprise, a temporal reference to the imminent event of the evil minister Rahu's arrival. Notably, this pictorial scene demonstrates uncanny parallels with textual

14. Other pictorial conventions typical of hand scroll paintings that resonate with this mural include: the reappearance of the same group of figures to give continuity to the sequence of events; hills and trees used to create space cells that distinguish particular narrative moments; and palatial compounds that serve to frame the beginning and ending of the pictorial narrative. See Li Yongning, *Dunhuang shiku quanji: bensheng gushi huajuan* (Hong Kong: Commercial Press, 2000), plates 100–102.

Figure 6.1
Cave 296, North Wall, Northern Zhou Period 557–581 (artwork in the public domain)

descriptions from the *Sutra on the Wise and Foolish*, a relationship first established by the scholar Sun Xiushen.[15] Consider how closely the following passage from this *sutra* (especially in terms of its descriptions of posture and gesture) could have filled in the accompanying cartouche as a caption for this scene (Figure 6.2):

> A *yaksa* [guardian spirit] came up from the ground, then knelt down and told [the prince] about the Minister Rahu. (*Sutra on the Wise and Foolish*, T.202, v. 4, p. 356, b15)
>
> 有一羅刹從地而出。長跪白言羅喉大臣。

Resonances between the Cave 296 mural and the *Sutra on the Wise and the Foolish*, as opposed to other textual sources, become even more apparent when this scene is compared against the relevant passage in the *Sutra on Repaying Kindness*. In this text the spirit is described as an unseen voice rather than a *yaksa* emerging from the ground:

> Once revived, the prince addressed the empty space in a soft voice and said, "Who are you sir?" Although a voice is heard, no form is seen. (*Sutra on Repaying Kindness*, T. 156, v. 3, p. 128, c3-c4)
>
> 乃穌微聲報虛空中言。卿是何人。但聞其聲不見其形。

15. See Sun Xiushen, "Dunhuang Mogaoku di 296 ku Xusheti gushi di yanjiu," *Dunhuang yanjiu* (1992), 1–10.

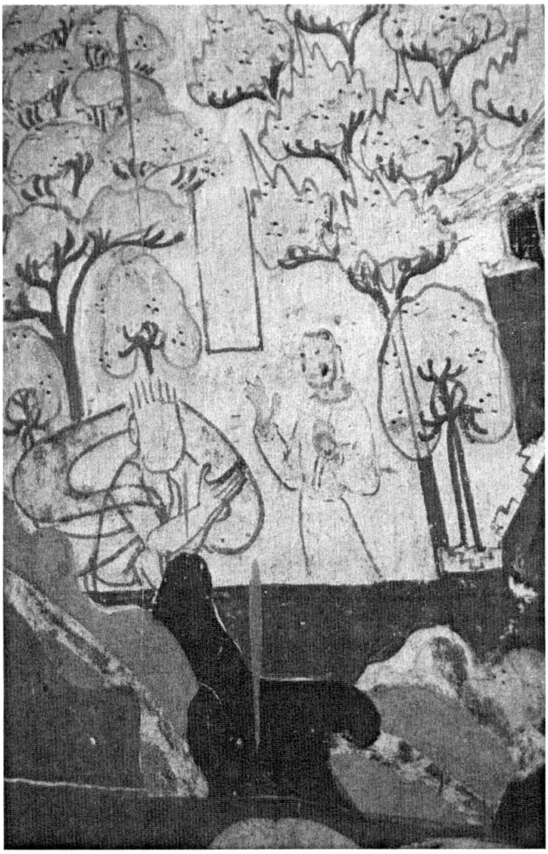

Figure 6.2
Cave 296, Sujati Narrative, Prince Meeting the *Yaksa*, Northern Zhou Period 557–581 (artwork in the public domain)

Clearly, the representation in Cave 296 bears a closer correspondence to the *Sutra on the Wise and Foolish*, which mentions the physical appearance of the *yaksa*, than to *the Sutra on Repaying Kindness*, which notes that the *yaksa* is heard but not seen. Nevertheless, the Cave 296 scene also introduces visual conventions that are absent from both these textual traditions. While textual traditions mention the warning of the guardian spirit *after* Rahu kills the prince's father and elder brothers, this painting leaves out these earlier details and the viewer must understand them through previous knowledge or verbal instructions provided by another party. The second scene in Cave 296 takes place in the courtyard of the prince's palace and comprises two temporal events. To the left, the first temporal event shows the white-robed prince reaching out to the black-robed princess in a touching gesture that communicates his concern over the impending tragedy. To the right, the second temporal event shows the prince and princess in a large palatial hall with the prince gesturing wildly over his panic at Rahu's imminent attack. The third scene shows the two parents and the young child fleeing the palace. Again, a single spatial setting is divided into two temporal events: first, the prince dangles his young son above the raised arms of the princess; second, the prince walks ahead, shouldering a provisions jar and carrying a sword, while the princess follows behind with Sujati on her shoulders.

The fourth scene marks a turning point in the narrative, which from this moment shifts from the actions and decisions of the father to those of the son (Figure 6.3). The prince is shown preparing to swing his large sword at the princess, who now walks with Sujati on her shoulders *ahead* of her husband. At this point, the young boy turns around and raises his hand in a gesture of remonstration. Similar to the scene of the meeting between the *yaksa* and the prince discussed above, this scene of Sujati interceding between his father and mother also corresponds closely with the textual narrative from the *Sutra on the Wise and Foolish*:

> He ordered the wife to carry the son (*er*) and walk in front. From behind, the prince grasped his knife with the intention of killing his wife. At this

Figure 6.3
Cave 296, Sujati Narrative, Sujati Taking Charge, Northern Zhou Period 557–581 (artwork in the public domain)

> time, the son (*er*) turned around and saw the father grasping the knife with the intention of killing his mother. The son (*er*) put his hands together and tried to make his father understand, "My only wish is that the prince kill me and not hurt my mother." His sincere remonstration of his father saved his mother's life. (*Sutra on the Wise and Foolish*, T. 202, v. 4, p. 356, c8—c12)
>
> 令婦在前擔兒而行。於後拔刀欲殺其婦。時兒迴顧。見父拔刀欲殺其母。兒便叉手曉父王言。唯願大王寧殺我身。勿害我母。勤諫父。救其母命。

Beyond the remarkable similarities between representations of the princess and Sujati walking *before* the murderous prince in both text and image, it is important to note that this scene shows Sujati as the most active figure in the family. It is Sujati who confronts his father by pointing his finger like a weapon, and it is Sujati who uses this act to highlight the reversal of conventional family bonds. The viewer no longer sees the three figures as the prince, the princess, and Sujati, but as husband and wife, parents and child. Arguably, the prince's attack on the princess is arresting precisely because it breaks the bonds of husband and wife, and Sujati's intercession is significant because it shows the child protecting his mother from his father.

In short, this scene in Cave 296 signals more than the development of Sujati's moral authority over his parents; it also shifts the narrative point of view from father to son. From now on, the viewer assumes the perspective of the child Sujati rather than of the adult prince.[16] By turning Sujati into a figure of authority, this image also highlights the cultural expectations placed on the shoulders of this child, whose true nature first comes to light with the defense of his mother. Just as important, this image underscores the *sutra*'s message that Sujati's buddhahood ultimately stems from his spiritual rather than his intellectual precociousness—a topic that scholars such as Anne Behnke Kinney and Miriam Levering have discussed in reference to other Chinese and Chinese Buddhist texts.[17]

The fifth scene takes the development of Sujati's spiritual authority to an intensely dramatic level by illustrating the young boy's willingness to save all beings, even at the cost of offering up his own flesh (Figure 6.4). Sujati is shown kneeling between his parents as the prince bends down to his son with a short knife. Notably, the gruesome act itself is implied rather than depicted in this image. Since the pictorial representation of other *jataka* narratives at

16. Mieke Bal has analyzed the shifting quality of narrative points of view through the process of "focalization" and the relationship between presented elements and the vision through which they are presented. See Mieke Bal, *Narratology: Introduction to the Theory of Narrative* (Toronto: University of Toronto Press, 1997), 142–60.

17. Miriam Levering in her chapter in this volume, "The Precocious Child in Chinese Buddhism," argues that Buddhism adds the awareness of spiritual precociousness in children to the long-standing elite Chinese belief that special children were born with intellectual precociousness. For a study of intellectual precociousness in pre-Buddhist Chinese literature, see Anne Behnke Kinney, "The Theme of the Precocious Child in Early Chinese Literature," *T'oung Pao* 81 (1995), 1–24.

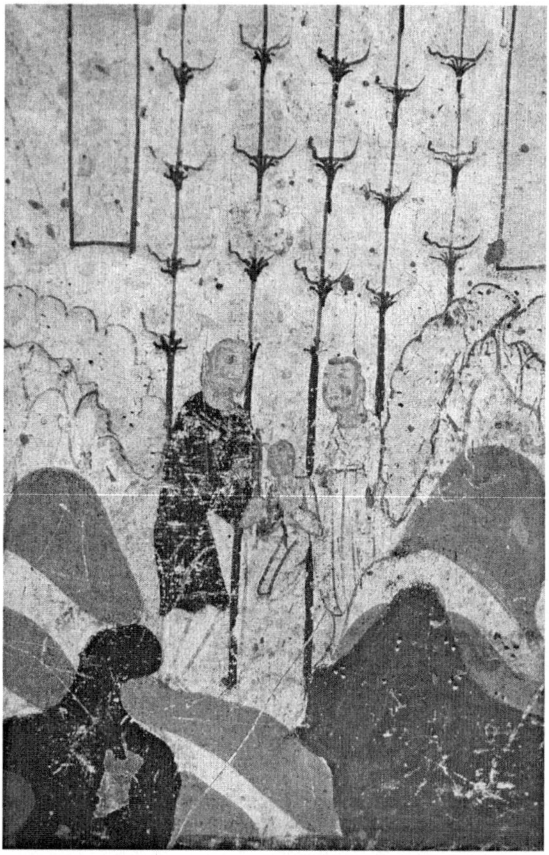

Figure 6.4
Cave 296, Sujati Narrative, Sujati Offering His Flesh, Northern Zhou Period 557–581 (artwork in the public domain)

Mogao shows similar acts of sacrifice in their gory detail, the obfuscation of Sujati's self-sacrifice in Cave 296 requires further attention—especially since Sujati's sacrifice is explicitly represented in examples from later periods at this site. Is this pictorial omission related to the involvement of a child? And if so, what are the implications of this omission for the audience and for concepts of childhood during this time?

I would argue that the narrative clarity of this mural, with its demarcated spatial scenes and temporal events, along with its location at the base of the north wall, provide important clues. Unlike other narrative images from Mogao at this time, which tend to be pictorially convoluted and located higher on the cave walls, the *Sujati Jataka* in Cave 296 is both visually accessible to a child's height and cognitively accessible in its storytelling mechanisms. In other words, a child would not only be able to *see* this mural on his or her own, a child would be able to *understand* it on his or her own. It would be perfectly reasonable, then, to employ the Sujati narrative in Cave 296 to inculcate values of Buddhist generosity and filial piety in a potential child viewer, while protecting this potential child viewer from the distress of seeing a child cutting up his own body. The Sujati narrative in Cave 296 thus conveys a compelling ambiguity toward the precociousness of gifted children who are afforded the moral authority to judge the actions of their parents on the one hand, while simultaneously being shielded from the violence of the narrative on the other. This may explain why almost all pictorial representations of Sujati in the Cave 296 mural show him as bodily whole, even though in textual representations he is whittling away his flesh until there is nothing left. For example, in the following sixth scene, a healthy Sujati sits on his mother's shoulders as the family continues on its journey. In the seventh scene, the prince and princess bid farewell to their still healthy son, who in the texts has now offered up all his flesh and is at the point of death.

Only in the eighth scene, which represents Sujati offering his bones and marrow to lions and tigers, is the boy shown in skeletal form. Since this moment marks the climax of Sujati's generosity in the text of the *Sutra on the Wise and Foolish*, the image of a skeletal child presents a comparably dramatic visual statement that makes the viewer pause and take notice. Notably, this is also the last scene in which Sujati appears in the Cave 296 image, since the final two scenes show, first, the prince and the princess arriving at the city gates of the neighboring kingdom, and second, the couple watching these troops set off to reclaim their own usurped kingdom. While scriptural accounts devote only a few lines to these concluding events, the corresponding pictorial representation in Cave 296 occupies nearly half the length of the mural, far outweighing their importance in textual narratives. Why is so much space given to these two scenes, especially since they have little to do with the actions of Sujati?

I would argue that an important factor is found in the pictorial function of these two concluding scenes vis-à-vis the entire composition. By filling the latter half of the horizontal mural, these scenes effectively push the preceding depiction of a skeletal Sujati to the center of the composition. The focus on the child's ultimate bodily sacrifice for the sake of all beings now occupies the exact center of the pictorial narrative, functioning as the pictorial hinge that connects Sujati's earlier efforts with their eventual outcome. As the images tell it, the child's act of generosity not only saves his mother's life, but also results in the recovery of his father's kingdom. And just as scholars have discussed the importance of *samskaras* (commonly translated as "rites of passage") to structure childhood in ancient Indian high-caste males such as Shakyamuni—I would argue that the representation of a skeletal Sujati is the pictorial equivalent of a child's ritual transition from one state to another.[18] It is precisely in these culturally mandated ritual transitions that the construction of childhood becomes most artificial, symbolic, and at odds with biological development—or at least at odds with cultural expectations of a given biological age. For example, the texts describe Sujati as seven years old—as biologically tender an age as any—yet his success at Indra's interrogation transforms the biological

18. See Vanessa R. Sasson's chapter in this volume.

child into a being of great spiritual maturity, a being that literally sheds his old benighted body for one that is new and enlightened.[19]

THE *SUJATI JATAKA* AND THE *SUTRA ON REPAYING KINDNESS*

The *Sujati Jataka* in Cave 296 survives as an independent visual narrative that does not depend on a broader pictorial context for its formal composition or thematic content. In this regard, this pictorial representation echoes the textual representation in the *Sutra on the Wise and Foolish*, in which the Sujati narrative is one of several independent stories meant to instruct devotees in general Buddhist values. The image in Cave 296 also differs from the majority of Sujati representations at the Mogao Caves in which the story of the self-sacrificing child appears as a subsidiary narrative within larger paintings of the *Sutra on Repaying Kindness*. Within this scriptural context, the *Sujati Jataka* comprises the second of nine chapters and is entitled *Filial Nurturing* (Ch. 孝養). The *sutra* itself opens with an introductory chapter in which the Buddha declares the *sutra*'s purpose as explaining the general merits of filial piety and the specific acts of filial sacrifice that he had done in the past. In the second chapter the Buddha recounts his former existence as Prince Sujati and opens with the standard invocation of dazzling surroundings and vast crowds that accompany all descriptions of the Buddha's lectures. This is followed by a brief exposition of the importance of "filial nurturing" and its relationship to Buddhist ideals of repaying debts, especially those owed to one's parents. After establishing the purpose of his lecture as "explaining the bitter practices of filial nurturing and the principles of cause and effect," the Buddha begins the story of Sujati.

Sutra on Repaying Kindness: Filial Nurturing Chapter
(T.156, v. 3, p. 129, b2—p. 130, a19)

> Countless *kalpas* ago in the kingdom of Varanasi, the Buddha Vipasyin came into the world. The Buddha Vipasyin lived for twelve small *kalpas* and the span of his true law lasted for twenty more *kalpas*. This was followed by a period of his semblance law that continued for yet another twenty *kalpas*. During this period, there was a great king who ruled Varanasi with 20,000 wives, 4,000 ministers, 500 elephant kings, 60 smaller fiefs, and 800 tribes. This king also had three sons who were each granted a small fief at the border regions.

19. The possible connections between Buddhist "acts of truth" (based on sincere vows to save all beings) and Confucian "filial miracles" (based on extreme acts of filial devotion) deserve further attention. On "acts of truth" in Chinese Buddhism, see Kenneth Ch'en, "Filial Piety in Chinese Buddhism," *Harvard Journal of Asiatic Studies* 28 (1968), 81–97. For a discussion of filial miracles in historical and cultural context, see Knapp, *Selfless Offspring*, 109.

This king was intelligent and wise, and he governed with the true law. The force of his virtue ensured that his kingdom was blessed with a favorable climate, abundant crops, and happy people. Unfortunately, the king's powerful minister Rahu allowed evil to rise in his heart and attacked Varanasi with the four divisions of the army, including the elephants, the cavalry, the chariots, and the infantry. Once the king was dead, Rahu dispatched these four divisions to the border kingdoms to kill the eldest and middle princes. He then turned his sights to the youngest prince, who ruled a small border fief. This prince was handsome and dignified, and he also governed with the true law. He never wronged the people, and his fief enjoyed great prosperity. All the gods and spirits loved and respected him. He was also blessed with a son whom he loved dearly—a seven-year-old boy with golden skin and perfect features named Sujati.

As the rebel forces slaughtered the two older princes and their families, the guardian spirit of the palace could not bear to see the same fate befall the youngest one. So he delivered a warning: "Great prince, do you know that evil and perversion have risen in the heart of the Minister Rahu? He now wishes to usurp the throne of the kingdom and has killed your father the king. With the four divisions of the army, he has also captured and killed your two older brothers. These troops and horses will soon be here and you must leave now to escape with your life."

When the prince heard these words, his heart jumped and his hair stood on end. His body began to shake with anger and exasperation, and he could not hold himself straight. He let out a quiet sigh, but he was burning inside and he fainted. Once the shock had worn off, the prince came to and he addressed the empty space in a soft voice: "Who are you that can be heard but not seen?"

"I am the guardian spirit of the palace, and I warn you now because you are intelligent and virtuous, and you govern with the law. Prince, this is the time to make haste, not to cry. The enemy will be here soon." The prince then entered the palace and thought deeply to himself that help from the neighboring kingdom must be sought and that there were two ways to get there—one way taking seven days and another taking fourteen. So he quickly packed enough food for the seven-day path and left the city. He had not gone far when he ran back to the palace and called for the young Prince Sujati, whom he sat on his knee, fixed with his eyes, and hugged tightly.

The prince's wife saw that her husband was intensely disturbed and she asked, "Prince, you look deeply terrified. What is the reason? You are agitated. Your body is covered with dirt, your hair is a mess, your eyes dart back and forth, and your breath is uneven. It is as if you have lost your kingdom and your enemy is about to arrive. Things do not look good."

The prince said, "You have no idea what is happening to me." His wife replied, "You and I are like two forms of the same body. We are like two wings of the same bird, two legs of one person, and two eyes of the same head." At this point, the prince responded, "You have no idea. Evil and perversity have risen in the heart of the Minister Rahu and he has killed my father and two older brothers. Troops and horses are now coming after me, and I must run for my life." With that, he grasped Sujati in his arms and rushed toward the shorter path. The wife followed them from behind.

Desolate and confused, the prince mistakenly took the path requiring fourteen days. The path was dangerous, difficult, and without water or grass. The three were able to proceed for only a few days before the provisions were depleted. Since the prince's original plan prepared only enough food to last one person for seven days, the three mouths quickly consumed the provisions long before they reached the end of the road.

The prince and his wife let out a great cry, and the prince began to wail. "How distressing! How painful! I have never encountered such bitterness in my life. How can I take this? Anguish and tragedy have arrived. I raise my hand to pat my head and only dirt rises in clouds. I raise my body and I only fall to the ground with regret and self-blame. What evil deeds have I done in the past? Did I kill my parents, perfected beings, or arhats? Did I slander the true law or destroy monks and monasteries? Did I hunt animals or catch fish? How should I confront this tragedy that I am suffering? Nevertheless, I am compelled by hunger and thirst to go forward."

The prince and his wife continued to lament their fate until they lost their voices. The prince was so wretched that he let out one last cry before fainting. After a while, he came to and thought deeply to himself that if I do not find some expedient means, the three of us will not escape death no matter how hard we try – given these circumstances, how can I not kill my wife to sustain the lives of my son and myself?"

While pondering this idea, he grasped his knife to kill his wife. At this moment, Sujati noticed that his father had a strange expression on his face and that with his right hand he held a knife poised to kill his mother. Sujati quickly grabbed his father's arm and said, "What do you want to do?"

The prince's eyes filled with tears of sadness and he said to his son in a soft voice, "I want to kill your mother for her flesh and blood so that I can sustain my body and you can continue your life. If I do not kill her, then I will die too. But now it does not really matter whether I live or die—I just wish to kill your mother for your sake."

Sujati then told his father, "If you kill mother, I will not eat her. What kind of son eats his mother's flesh? Since I refuse to eat her, I will die anyway. So why don't you kill me instead to save mother and yourself?"

The prince was so disturbed by his son's words that he fainted. When he came to, he said softly to his son, "You are like my own eyes. What kind of person gouges out his own eyes to eat them? I would rather die than kill my son and eat his flesh."

"Father, my flesh and blood will become corrupt within a few days if I die now. So I ask for only one wish. You must promise to fulfill this wish if you love me."

"I will not refuse your wish. Tell me quickly what you want."

"Father and mother, take pity on your son and put a knife to my body every day. Cut three pounds of flesh and divide it into three portions. I offer two portions to father and mother, and I take one portion for myself so that I can continue to live."

The parents followed their son's words, sliced off three pounds of flesh, and divided it into three portions. They took two portions for themselves and gave one to Sujati so that he could continue to live. In this way, they were able to continue forward for two days before Sujati's flesh was completely depleted and only bones and marrow held his body together. Sujati tried to relieve himself with what little life remained in him, but he only managed to collapse to the ground.

His parents now proceeded forward while carrying Sujati and crying out in grief, "We have perversely eaten your flesh and have inflicted bitter suffering upon you. The road ahead still stretches far ahead and your flesh is already gone. Now all we can do is try to keep your bones together."

Sujati softly remonstrated with his parents, "You have traveled this far eating your son's flesh, but there remains more than a day's journey. I abandon my life here since I can no longer move my body. Father and mother, if you pity me, do not refuse this last request: cleanly cut what little is left between the joints of my body and use it to save yourself for the journey ahead." His parents followed these instructions and took the small amount of flesh remaining between the joints of Sujati's body. They divided it into three parts, gave one portion to the child and ate two portions themselves. When they finished eating, the father and mother left in farewell.

Sujati stood up and fixed his gaze on his parents as they cried loudly and continued down the road. Eventually, they disappeared from sight. But Sujati still yearned for his parents, and his eyes followed after them without wavering. After a long while, he collapsed on the ground with his body fragrant with the scent of fresh blood. Swarms of flies and mosquitoes began to bite and suck. The pain was beyond words.

With the little life that remained in him, Sujati established a vow: "In order to wash away all my bad deeds from past and present, I have offered my body for the salvation of my parents. I wish upon them all forms of happiness and safety in each of their waking and sleeping moments, and I wish upon them the protection of heaven and the love of the people. I also wish for the removal of corrupt officials and thieves, and the prosperity of all beings. My remaining flesh and blood I give to the flies and mosquitoes. Let me become a Buddha in my future existence, because when I become a Buddha I vow to use the law to eliminate the miseries of hunger and thirst, birth and death."

At the completion of Sujati's vow, heaven and earth quaked, the sun became dark, and the birds and beasts scattered in all directions. The waves of the sea surged and Mount Sumeru rose and fell into the ocean. And from the highest realm of Mount Sumeru presided over by the god Indra, deities descended to the world of men. These deities assumed the form of lions, tigers, and wolves that glared and roared at Sujati to frighten him.

Sujati looked at these fierce beasts and softly said, "If you want to eat me, then go ahead and take what you want. I am not afraid." Indra then responded, "We are not in fact lions, tigers, or wolves. I am the King of Devas and the others are gods who have come to test you in disguise." Sujati was overjoyed when he heard this.

Indra then said, "You have been able to relinquish that which is most difficult. You have given your flesh and blood to your parents and this kind of merit proves that you are as worthy as Mara, Brahma, Mahabrahma, and Cakrarartiraja to ascend to heaven. Sujati replied, "I do not wish to be any of these. I only wish to seek out the supreme true path and save all beings."

"You are very foolish. Perfect universal enlightenment is achieved only after suffering great bitterness. Tell me, how can you tolerate this kind of suffering?"

"Even if a hot iron wheel spins on my head, I will never abandon the supreme path because of this bitterness."

"Your words are empty. Who should believe you?"

Sujati responded with this firm vow: "If I have lied to the King of Devas, let incurable sores cover my body. But if what I have said is true, let my former body return to its former state and let my blood turn as white as milk."

Sujati's body immediately became as healthy, handsome, and dignified as before. He bowed before Indra and paid his respects. Indra sighed and said, "Excellent, excellent, I am not your equal. You will go forward with bravery and will quickly reach enlightenment. When you reach enlightenment, I hope you will extend salvation to me first." Indra then disappeared into the air.

Meanwhile, the prince and his wife had finally arrived at the neighboring kingdom. The king there came out to welcome them, and he supplied them with all their necessities. The prince recounted what had happened and concluded, "My son has filially nurtured his father and mother with his very own flesh."

The neighboring king heard this and realized that Sujati was able to relinquish that which is most difficult. He was so moved that a son would offer his flesh and blood to his parents out of filial love and nurturing that he gathered together the four divisions of his army and sent a punitive expedition against the usurper Rahu.

While accompanying the army, the prince and his wife passed the spot where they had left Sujati. The prince said to himself, "My son must be dead now. I must try to collect his bones so that they can be buried in his homeland." He wailed with grief and searched in vain for his remains.

Then in the distance, they suddenly saw their son perfectly restored to his handsome and dignified state. With mixed joy and sadness, they ran toward him and shouted, "You are still alive!" Sujati told his father and mother what had happened, and the reunited family returned home on an elephant. Because of Sujati's virtue, they were able to recover their country and the young boy was immediately crowned the new king.

The Buddha told Ananda, "The prince then is my father Suddhodana now. The mother then is my mother Mahamaya now. And Sujati is none other than myself now."

THE *SUJATI JATAKA* AND MOGAO CAVE 148

Arguably, the earliest image of the Sujati narrative based on the *Filial Nurturing* chapter of the *Sutra on Repaying Kindness*, translated above, is found in Cave 148, dated to the years 766–770 by a commemorative stele that once stood outside the cave.[20] This painting, which appears on the ceiling of the entrance

20. For a discussion of the dating of this cave, see Yin Guangming, *Dunhuang shiku quanji: Baoenjing huajuan* (Hong Kong: The Commercial Press, 2000), 248.

Figure 6.5
Cave 148, Sujati Narrative, Tang Period 766–770 (artwork in the public domain)

passage, is condensed into four scenes that are each accompanied by a large, blank cartouche (Figure 6.5). Reading from top to bottom, these begin with (1) Sujati stopping his father from attacking his mother, (2) Sujati offering his flesh to his parents, (3) Sujati in a loincloth attacked by tigers (that are in fact gods in disguise), and (4) Sujati fully dressed before a being that is presumably Indra. This contrast between the stripped body in the third scene and the clothed body in the fourth scene effectively underscores Sujati's loss and recovery of bodily normalcy following his ultimate vow. The following analysis focuses on the first two scenes and their implications for the construction of childhood authority.

The first scene shows the prince rushing with sweeping violence toward the princess, who reacts by covering her face in horror. Standing between them, Sujati takes hold of his father's sword and pushes him away, a gesture that injects a new level of physical authority in the struggle between father and son. In contrast to the close correspondence between representations of the *Sujati Jataka* in Cave 296 and the *Sutra on the Wise and Foolish*, the *Sujati Jataka* in Cave 148 closely corresponds with the text of the *Sutra on Repaying Kindness*:

> [The prince] grasped his knife to kill his wife. At this moment, his son (*zi*) Sujati noticed that his father had a strange expression on his face and held a knife poised to kill his mother in his right hand. Sujati quickly grabbed his father's arm and said, "What do you want to do?" (*Sutra on Repaying Kindness*, T.156, v. 3, p. 129, a15—a18)

即拔刀欲殺夫人。其子須闍提見王異相右手拔刀欲殺其母。前捉王手語父王言欲作何等。

The physical aggressiveness attributed to Sujati in the textual passage is depicted precisely in the image of Sujati pushing his father away. The next scene is even more remarkable in its explicit representation of Sujati's bodily sacrifice. The young boy presents his bare leg to his father, who kneels to slice the flesh from his son's thigh. The mother stands to the side and hides her face in distress. Below these figures, three pieces of vivid red meat are placed on a tray. Again, the enumeration of *three* pieces of flesh closely matches the text from the *Sutra on Repaying Kindness*, which clearly mentions Sujati's instructions to his parents to cut *three* pounds of flesh from his body each day:

> Father and mother, now for the sake of taking pity on your son (*zi*), you may each day take a knife to your son's body. Cut three pounds of flesh and divide it into three portions. Two portions I offer up to father and mother. One portion I take back to eat myself so that I can continue living. At that time, the father and mother followed their son's (*zi*) words, sliced off three pounds of flesh and divided it into three portions; two portions for the father and mother, and one portion [for Sujati] to eat and sustain bodily life. (*Sutra on Repaying Kindness*, T.156, v. 3, p. 129, b4—b6)
>
> 父母今者爲愍子故。可日日持刀就子身上。割三斤肉分作三分。二分奉上父母。一分還自食之以續身命。而時父母即隨子言。割三斤肉分作三分。二分父母。一分食以支身命。

The physical details in these two scenes are certainly dramatic and graphic; however, I would argue that their significance runs deeper than mere sensationalism. Indeed the textual specificity of referring to Sujati as *zi* 子 in the *Sutra on Repaying Kindness* rather than *er* 兒 as in the *Sutra on the Wise and Foolish*, in addition to the visual specificity of cutting flesh from Sujati's thigh in the Cave 148 image, provide important perspectives onto the construction of childhood authority in medieval China.

Among the many Chinese terms for child, the most commonly used characters are *er* and *zi*. Although both characters are typically translated into English as child, the nuances vary from period to period. In terms of the medieval Chinese context between the fifth and tenth century, nuanced distinctions are evident in *Sutra on the Wise and Foolish* with its repeated reference to Sujati as *er* and in the *Sutra on Repaying Kindness* with its repeated reference to Sujati as *zi*. For example, the passage discussed above from the *Sutra on the Wise and Foolish* that describes the prince ordering the princess and Sujati to walk ahead refers exclusively to the child Sujati as *er*. In contrast, the passage discussed above from the *Sutra on Repaying Kindness* that narrates Sujati offering his flesh to his parents refers to Sujati exclusively as *zi*. What are the differences in meaning, if any? Miriam Levering's chapter in this volume provides some important insights, especially in view of her argument that precocious children in Chinese Buddhism are seen as relational rather than chronological. As Levering puts it:

> When I undertook this research into children and childhood in Chinese Buddhism, I looked first at the numerous famous and well-loved Chinese Buddhist filial piety sutras, most of which were written in China. I was disappointed to find that all of the filial or unfilial characters in these sutras are children (*zi*) in the social sense but adults in the Western chronological and developmental sense. Buddhist Chinese filial piety sutras are filled with "children" who are at the same time adults. They are "children" in relation to their parents, as they will be all their lives, but they are not chronological or developmental children.

Along the same lines, Ping-chen Hsiung writes that a child (*zi*) is in a perpetually subordinate role in relation to seniors and that "as long as one's parents were alive, or whenever speaking or acting vis-à-vis the elders in the house, any offspring at whatever age always assumes the position of a child (*zi*)."[21]

I agree with Levering and Hsiung that Confucian commentaries and Chinese Buddhist filial piety *sutras* such as the *Sutra on Repaying Kindness* define childhood as a state of perpetual subservience to parents and elders. Indeed, this fact is corroborated by the image of Sujati in the Cave 148 mural, which I have argued is based on the *Sutra on Repaying Kindness* and its references to the child as *zi*, and who is represented here as a full-fledged adult despite textual descriptions that Sujati is only seven years old. Moreover, the Cave 148 mural is found high on the ceiling of the entrance passageway, a location that is not visually accessible to the height of a chronological child. Taken together, the high placement of the mural in Cave 148, its representation of Sujati as an adult, and the consistent use of *zi* in the *Sutra on Repaying Kindness* (upon which this mural is likely based) support concepts of childhood as forever relational to one's parents, even when the child demonstrates great spiritual or intellectual precociousness. The eighth-century example in Cave 148 is thus markedly different from the sixth-century example in Cave 296, which is painted low on the north wall, represents Sujati as a small-bodied child, and is based on the *Sutra on the Wise and Foolish* with its consistent reference to Sujati as *er*. What might explain these differences?

In a detailed study of children in medieval China, Annika Pissin has identified several age-marking characters for children that provide a counterpoint to the notion that children were defined primarily as social beings within the context of family relationships. On the basis of a study of a wide array of textual sources, Pissin situates the child into a number of discourses beyond that of the family, including those of the law, taxation, medicine, and education, and discovers over thirty individual characters and binomes that divide medieval Chinese childhood into astonishingly precise categories.[22] Pissin identifies terms

21. Ping-chen Hsiung, *A Tender Voyage: Children and Childhood in Late Imperial China* (Stanford, CA: Stanford University Press, 2005), 21.
22. Annika Pissin, *Elites and Their Children: A Study in the Historical Anthropology of Medieval China*, 500–1000 AD (Ph.D. diss., University of Leiden, 2009), 34.

that not only distinguish the genders of children, but also situates these gendered terms into specific stages of prebirth fetuses, infants, youths, coming-of-agers (fifteen for girls and twenty for boys, respectively), and children who have died prematurely.[23] In regard to the *Sujati Jataka*, Pissin's study sheds light on crucial nuances between differing uses of *er* and *zi*, as well as on the peculiar importance placed on the seventh year of age in medieval Chinese texts.

For example, the most frequently used character for persons between birth and age seven in official documents from medieval China was *er*. This character was typically used with a prefix or suffix to indicate greater specificity, such as *yinger* 嬰兒 (infant), *youer* 幼兒 (youth), and *erzi* 兒子 (son). Notably, the character *zi* occurs much less frequently in these official documents, suggesting that its relational connotations rendered it less suitable for use in official documents than the more objective and chronological meanings of *er*. In this sense, the use of *er* to reference Sujati in the *Sutra on the Wise and Foolish* is appropriate, since the Cave 296 painting that relates to it emphasizes chronological children both in its implied viewership (painted low on the wall) and in its representation (Sujati as a small childlike figure).

Pissin also discusses age-specific terms used for children, which during the medieval period almost always reference the tufted hairstyles carried by children around the age of seven, including *zongzjiao* 總角, *guan* 丱, and *tiao* 髫. Another age-specific term used during this time is *chen* 齔, which also references the loss of baby teeth believed to occur at age seven.[24] And although legal documents indicate that children were to be treated as adults from age fifteen onward, age seven was considered equally significant as the time from which children were believed to have a consciousness of self-responsibilities.[25] For instance, the official *Histories* invariably focus on age seven as the year when intellectual precociousness was first demonstrated by gifted children in the memorization and composition of difficult texts; less mention is made of such abilities at later ages, presumably since such skills then were no longer considered exceptional.[26] It is therefore significant that Sujati is identified as age seven in both the *Sutra on the Wise and Foolish* and the *Sutra on Repaying Kindness*, which arguably sets the stage for elite Chinese understandings of Sujati as a precocious child, even if his demonstration of authority is ultimately more spiritual than intellectual.

Given the numerous close relationships between texts and images discussed above, it is critical to ask whether discrepancies between textual and visual representations of the *Sujati Jataka* are equally suggestive of the construction of childhood during this time. For example, consider that scriptural sources do not mention the slicing of a specific body part, while the mural in Cave 148 clearly shows the father cutting his son's thigh. Why the thigh? Why does it appear in the mural and not the scripture? Is the selection of this body part a random artistic act, or is the focus on the thigh a deliberate reference to

23. Pissin, *Elites and Their Children*, 35.
24. Pissin, *Elites and Their Children*, 35.
25. Pissin, *Elites and Their Children*, 40.
26. Pissin, *Elites and Their Children*, 42.

broader cultural practices at this time? In many ways, these questions implicate important ties between the cutting of thigh flesh, the therapeutic properties of cannibalism, and shifting structures of filial piety in medieval China that I have investigated in detail elsewhere.[27] For the purposes of this essay, which focus on text and image relationships as an index for the construction of childhood, the following eighth-century medical reference offers useful contextualization for the eighth-century representation of thigh cutting in Cave 148.

> During the Tang, Chen Zangqi wrote the *Corrected Materia Medica*. He said that human flesh cures one from wasting away. From this, the folk have taken parental illness as cause to frequently cut thigh flesh and offer it. (*New Tang History*, *juan* 195, p. 5577)
>
> 唐時陳藏器著本草拾遺，謂人肉治羸疾，自是民間以父母疾，多割股肉而獻

Although the original text of Chen Zangqi's (陳藏器) *Corrected Materia Medica* (本草拾遺) is now lost, information about the work, such as its attribution to Chen Zangqi during the Kaiyuan Era (開源 713–741), survives in Li Shizhen's (李時珍 1518–93) *Classified Materia Medica* (*Bencao gangmu* 本草綱目) of 1602.[28] In any case, the association of Chen Zangqi with the medicinal offering of thigh flesh is significant for inaugurating an "origin theory" for the practice of filial flesh feeding, and one that underscores a distinction made between the erudite theories of medical authorities such as Chen Zangqi and the folk practices of the masses.[29] That is, while Chen Zangqi merely claimed that generic human flesh had curative properties, it was left to "the folk" to wildly elaborate this prescription into the actual cutting and feeding of thigh flesh to cure sick parents.

Li Shizhen's citation of Chen Zangqi does not mention the age of those who "have taken parental illness as cause to frequently cut thigh flesh and offer it." Presumably, Chen is referring to adult children. Nevertheless, it is notable that the most complete medical references to childhood health from medieval China appear in the seventh and eighth centuries, just as paintings of the Sujati narrative based on the *Sutra on Repaying Kindness* establish their iconographic conventions. These authors include Chao Yuanfang (巢元方 550–630), Sun Simiao (孫思邈 581--582), and Wang Tao (王濤 c. 752).[30] And although these authors discuss primarily the ailments of adults—and in particular the reproductive

27. Winston Kyan, *The Body and the Family: Filial Piety and Buddhist Art in Late Medieval China* (Ph.D. diss., University of Chicago, 2006), 107–61.
28. Li Shizhen also mentions Chen Zangqi's belief in the curative properties of human blood, human bones, and even human afterbirth. See Qiu Zhonglin, "Buxiao zhi xiao," *Xinshixue* 6 (1995), 1–48.
29. Note that Li Shizhen mentions Chen Zangqi in a negative context and blames him for establishing false credence in the medicinal properties of human flesh rather than exposing it as a fallacy. See Michibata Ryōshū, "Chūgoku Bukkyō to shokunin-niku no mondai," in *Jikaku Daishi kenkyū*, ed., Fukui Kōjun (Tōkyō: The Association for the Tendai Sect for Buddhist Studies, 1964), 391–404.
30. See Pissin, *Elites and Their Children*, 57–60.

health of women—they also address illnesses specific to children. Belief in the child's body as a distinct physiological category reflects more than an awareness of childhood as a biological stage different from adulthood. Indeed, this awareness of childhood as requiring special care from adults further highlights the role reversal depicted in Sujati images, in which the child is shown feeding, caring for, and nurturing his parents. Arguably, the depiction of the child reversing established models of authority is as arresting as scenes of flesh cutting, and as indicative of alternative views of spiritually mature biological children that expand notions of perpetually subservient relational children rooted in traditional values of filial piety.

CONCLUSION

This study has read image against text, image against image, and text against text to explore the relationship between the *Sujati Jataka* and the construction of childhood in medieval China. Arguably, these comparative readings shed light on two key aspects of the development of this narrative between the sixth and eighth centuries. First, there are two distinct pictorial traditions: an earlier type that corresponds with the *Sutra on the Wise and Foolish* and a later version related to the *Sutra on Repaying Kindness*. Second, these images develop pictorial conventions that take Sujati's body as the primary site for pictorial modifications. These bodily cues include Sujati's increasingly physical interactions with his father, and the use of his denuded and mutilated body as an index for spiritual attainments. If these depictions of Sujati's body are situated into the cultural crucible of medieval China, when tensions between Buddhist ideals of renouncing the family and Confucian imperatives of filial piety were particularly intense, it is not surprising that alternative views of the parent–child relationship should emerge from these representations of the Buddhist filial child. Taken together, the passages from the *Sutra on the Wise and Foolish* and the *Sutra on Repaying Kindness*, along with the murals from Cave 296 and Cave 148, reveal an understanding of childhood in which chronological (and not merely relational) children have the authority to feed parents, to surpass their parents in parenting skills, and to claim the prerogative and miraculous powers of filial flesh feeding. In this sense, the growth of a child's authority involves the decline of adult influence, and representations of the *Sujati Jataka* demonstrate that the construction of childhood has the potential to change concepts of adulthood.

ACKNOWLEDGMENT

I am indebted to Wu Hung for guiding my initial research on the Sujati narrative and to Vanessa Sasson for shepherding earlier drafts of this essay into its current iteration.

CHAPTER 7

"What Children Need"

Making Childhood with Technologies of Protection and Healing

FRANCES GARRETT

This chapter will explore the care of children in Tibetan culture, as expressed through several works on the medical and ritual treatment and defense of children. These texts describe a remarkably broad range of technologies aimed at healing and protecting children, recommending the feeding of pills, soups, butters, beers, or texts to children, parents, or deities; physically manipulative techniques, such as surgery, washing, anointing, fumigating, or massaging; the wearing of all manner of amulets, talismans, strings, papers, ointments, or letters; and the theatrical staging of elaborate hospitality or ransom dramas. Some of the texts examined here are old, but all of them are in use today, in some way, each having been recently reprinted in one or more editions. None of this material is therefore obscure or extremely esoteric. Anyone who has spent time around small children in Tibetan parts of Asia, particularly in rural areas, will have observed ample evidence of the kinds of therapeutic technologies described in these texts: amulets hanging from children's necks, mantras and diagrams posted on household doors, ransom effigies left at dusty intersections. An examination of the making and use of these therapeutic and protective objects can illuminate a material culture of childhood that may in turn tell us a bit about the child as a category.

We will begin with a Tibetan-language medical school textbook entitled *Healing Children*. It is part of a multivolume textbook series named "Textbooks Establishing Education in the Real Science (*dngos tshan*) of Tibetan Medicine for the 21st Century" that is used by Tibetan medical schools in China. The volume on children's health bears a title that might typically be translated as "pediatrics" (*byis pa gso ba*), since it provides the curricular focal point for treating children's disorders. Given the youth of pediatrics as a biomedical specialty, however, I will use the more literal title, *Healing Children*. The Tibetan word *gso ba* refers quite broadly to a range of attitudes or practices, including not only "healing" but also "nourishing," "rearing," or "raising"; indeed, as we will see, this textbook addresses far more than the healing of manifest illnesses. In this chapter, following a brief study of the contemporary textbook, we will examine several old but recently republished Tibetan works on caring for children that similarly intertwine a wide range of therapeutic technologies, from herbal concoctions, to bloodletting, surgery, massage, mantras, and a variety of ritual processes. The implementation of these technologies on, in, and around the bodies of children is an important—perhaps the most important—component of the material culture of childhood in Tibet, and it may also reveal something about the making of children.

HEALING CHILDREN

The contemporary medical school textbook *Healing Children* is divided into three main parts, corresponding to chapters 71, 72, and 73 of the third book, the *Instructional Tantra*, of the *Four Tantras*,[1] which comprise the chapters on the care of children in that seminal Tibetan medical corpus. The book's table of contents, translated in an appendix at the end of this chapter, provides a comprehensive survey of the topics addressed in the work. The first section of *Healing Children*, on "What Children Need" (*byis pa nyer spyod*), is subdivided into four sections, covering the care and protection of children in the first year of life. The second and longest section, comprising just over seventy percent of the textbook, addresses the diagnosis and treatment of children's diseases (*byis pa'i nad*). The third section, comprising just over twenty percent of the book, addresses the treatment of conditions caused by specific types of nonhuman spirits, called *dön,* that harm children (*byis gdon*). An appendix offers sections from several short classic texts on related topics.

The technique of delivering "what children need," the topic that is the subject of the textbook's first section, is succinctly defined on the book's first page as "A method of fostering the condition for developed intelligence (*blo gros*), great perseverance (*'bad rtsol*), long life, freedom from illness, and physical health (*bde thang*)" from the moment of birth.[2] The section begins with a presentation

1. The *Four Tantras* (*Bdud rtsi snying po yan lag brgyad pa gsang ba man ngag gi rgyud*, known in short as the *Rgyud bzhi*) is considered the principal text in Tibetan medicine. The text consists of four parts or "books": the *Instructional Tantra* (*Man ngag rgyud*) is its third book. The origins of the text are murky, but it is likely to have been arranged by the Tibetan physician, G.yu thog yon tan mgon po (1112–1203), who is therefore often considered the work's "author."

2. ed. Dri me 'od zer, *Byis pa gso ba*, Dus rabs 21 pa'i bod lugs gso rig dngos tshan slob gso'i 'char 'god slob deb (Pe cin: Mi rigs dpe skrun khang, 2004), 1.

of the signs and procedures of childbirth, which is followed by discussion of a series of protective methods to be performed soon after birth. In the first several weeks after birth, the text explains, parents should diligently worship deities (*lha gsol ba*), create ransom effigies (*gta' gzugs pa*), perform protective rituals (*srung ba'i cho ga*), and offer food to deities (*zla phud btang ba*). In the section on protective rituals, for example, it is suggested that children wear the herbal substance sweet flag (*shu dag nag po*) in an amulet on their hands or throat. Food offerings (*gtor ma* and *bshos bu*) should also be made to deities, and ransom effigies (*chung glud*) should be offered to malicious *dön* spirits (*gdon*) on astrologically auspicious dates. For the first year after birth, ritual offerings should continue to be made to household deities.[3]

Such procedures are echoed in other contemporary publications on child care in Tibetan traditions, indicating their widespread practice today. In one of the few articles devoted to the topic, for example, exiled Tibetan doctor Thupten Sangay begins by summarizing ritual methods that encourage labor. He proposes making nine small indentations on a pat of butter, reciting a mantra and blowing onto the butter, then giving it to the mother to eat, after which birth will proceed quickly. This procedure can be performed by a Buddhist practitioner or, if such a person is not available, by a doctor, father, or uncle. Alternatively, he says, a small piece of butter can be fashioned into a fish, and again a mantra should be recited and blown onto the butter; after the mother swallows this, a peacock feather and bear hair should be burnt, and the mother should swallow the ashes mixed with mantras in water. Thupten Sangay affirms that birth will come quickly after this procedure. While he describes only these two techniques, he confirms that "there are other rituals, but they are too numerous" to describe, a state of affairs we will examine further below.[4]

After a successful birth, Thupten Sangay concurs with our contemporary textbook and other sources, the syllables *hrīḥ* or *dhīḥ* should be drawn on the baby's tongue to give it "the power of wise speech," and the baby should be fed musk water "to protect it from the earth gods."[5] Not long after that, to ensure its intelligence and clear memory, the baby should be fed a particular medicinal compound, after which fire offerings should be performed and the house should be fumigated with incense.[6] At an astrologically auspicious point soon after birth, a tantric practitioner should be called to perform an elaborate protective ritual, involving the manufacture out of dough of a series of deities and a multistoried residence for the deities. The residence should be decorated with arrows (in the case of a male child) or a spindle made from

3. Ibid., 11. See Thupten Sangay for the same advice.
4. Thupten Sangay (trans. Gavin Kilty), "Tibetan Traditions of Childbirth and Childcare," *Tibetan Medicine* 7 (1984), 8.
5. Sangay (trans. Gavin Kilty), "Tibetan Traditions of Childbirth and Childcare," 9. Interestingly, Sangay notes that the *dhīḥ* was mandated by the thirteenth Dalai Lama using a wooden seal with the syllable on it.
6. Sangay (trans. Gavin Kilty), "Tibetan Traditions of Childbirth and Childcare," 9–10.

sticks and strings (for a female), and the child's "life energy" should then be ritually placed in that residence, with the deities, for safekeeping. A protective thread will also be wrapped around the child's neck or waist, as well as an amulet containing protective medicinal materials.[7] Clothed with this defensive armor, even babies are given power over harmful forces. The complex and expensive ritual technologies harnessed by a family to guard its young make clear the significant investment of household resources that can be devoted to small children, as we will see.

Another topic explained in *Healing Children*'s section on caring for children in the first year of life, entitled "Behavioral rules" (*spyod lam bslab pa*), provides parenting guidelines on proper ways of holding an infant and of protecting its head and eyes from bright lights and its ears from cold winds. Parents are warned to be careful with small children around fire, river banks, wild birds and other predators, and are advised to massage their babies with oil and gently warm them in the sun.[8]

The lengthy middle section of the textbook outlines the types of diseases most commonly found in children, divided into three major types, and discusses their diagnostic signs and treatments. The diseases named can be found translated in appendix to this chapter; here we only briefly make note of the kinds of remedies prescribed in the second part of this section. As the text moves through a discussion of each disease condition, remedies (or "antidotes" or "cures," *gnyen po*) are organized by type under the headings food (*zas*), behavior (*spyod lam*), medicine (*sman*), and manipulative or surgical intervention (*dpyad*). A short section on follow-up practices (*rjes gcod*) and prevention (*sngon 'gog*) may follow. Therapies are also organized according to three periods of early childhood. When a baby is taking only breast milk, the prescribed food, behavioral, or medicinal recommendations are typically applied to the mother. When a baby still nurses but also eats some food, these recommendations may apply to both mother and child. Once the child has stopped nursing, then it is he or she who is the sole object of treatment. None of the remedies included in this section of the textbook involve ritual practice of any significant type, or of a type that might be called "religious." Specific foods and drinks are to be emphasized or eliminated from the diet. Behavioral recommendations include, for example, advice on staying warm, or avoiding cool drafts or too much activity. Medicinal therapies describe certain pill or decoction preparations, and manipulative interventions may include such practices as massage or bloodletting. Follow-up and preventative recommendations in this section of the textbook are not ritual in nature but are similar to the behavioral advice provided elsewhere. The configuration of remedies selected for this section of *Healing Children*, despite its extensive reliance on source material from notable authors of religious works, such as Mipham, whose work on

7. Sangay (trans. Gavin Kilty), "Tibetan Traditions of Childbirth and Childcare," 11.
8. Dri me 'od zer, *Byis pa gso ba*, 10.

this subject we will look at below, is nevertheless devoid of explicit religious practice. This orientation will change significantly in the textbook's next section.

The third main section of the medical textbook, which particularly explicates the *Instructional Tantra's* seventy-third chapter, focuses largely on therapeutic reactions to or protection against children's ailments caused by malicious *dön* spirits. As other scholars have discussed, *dön* is a large category that includes a variety of spirits, including those known by Sanskrit names *nāgá, asura, preta, gandharva, rākṣasaḥ* and those known in Tibetan as *klu, sa bdag, rgyal po, bdud, ma mo, lha,* and many more.[9] In Tibetan medicine, *dön* are said to be among the most common disease-causing agents for persons of all ages, and *dön*-caused illnesses in adults receive a significant five chapters' attention in the *Instructional Tantra*, chapters 77–81, grouped by *dön* class (covering *'byung po'i gdon, smyo byed kyi gdon, brjed byed kyi gdon, gza' yi gdon,* and *klu'i gdon,* respectively). Chapter 73, focusing on *dön* diseases of children, is the subject of *Healing Children*'s third major section.

Healing Children's discussion of *dön* that afflict children begins with a summary of several ways of classifying the various kinds of *dön*, citing a range of organizational schemes from such works as the Indian Āyurvedic commentary *Moon Beam*, the influential *Four Tantras* commentary, *Transmission of the Elders*, by Zurkhar Lodrö Gyelpo (1509–1579), the *Four Tantras* commentarial writings of prolific Kagyü author Pema Karpo (1527–1592), and the widely used *Thread-cross Rites for the Fifteen Great Dön*, by Karma Chagme (1613–1678) from Kham.[10] Following this is a long section on identifying the signs of *dön* affliction, each *dön* type manifesting differently, and a short section on identifying whether the affliction will be easy or difficult to treat. The remainder of the chapter addresses methods of healing *dön* affliction using "peaceful" (*zhi ba*) or "wrathful" (*drag po*) techniques.

The primary types of "peaceful" remedies are described as the offering of ritual objects called *yé* (*yas*), *lü* (*glud*), and *torma* (*gtor ma*). These rites have been little studied in secondary scholarship and the terms are difficult to translate precisely. Roughly, *yé* refers to a variety of small offering objects,

9. Ivette Vargas-O'Bryan, "Disease, the Demons and the Buddhas: A Study of Tibetan Conceptions of Disease and Religious Practice," in *Health and Religious Rituals in South Asia: Disease, Possession and Healing,* ed. Fabrizio Ferrarri, Routledge South Asian Religions Series (London: Routledge, 2011), 81–99; Geoffrey Samuel, *Civilized Shamans: Buddhism in Tibetan Societies* (Washington, DC: Smithsonian Institution Press, 1993), 161–63.

10. The *Moon Beam* (*Zla zer*) is a widely cited Indian medical work included in the Tibetan Tengyur, medical texts of which have been published in the four-volume collection *Gso ba rig pa'i rtsa 'grel bdam bsgrigs—bstan 'gyur nang gi gso ba rig pa'i skor gyi dpe tshogs,* Mi rigs dpe skrun khang gi rtsi 'khor, 1996. On this work and also the *Transmission of the Elders* (*Mes po'i zhal lung*) by Zurkhar Lodrö Gyelpo, see Frances Garrett, *Religion, Medicine and the Human Embryo in Tibet,* Critical Studies in Buddhism (New York: Routledge, 2008). The *Thread-cross Rites for the Fifteen Great Dön* will be further discussed below; Karma chags med, "Byis pa'i gdon chen bco lnga'i mdos bzhugs so," in *Gto 'bum* (Thimphu: Kunsang Topgay, 1978).

sometimes (but not always) shaped out of dough using a wooden mold (*zan par*).[11] *Lü* is typically a dough-sculpted object that substitutes for the afflicted person in a ransom ritual, sometimes referred to in English as a "ransom effigy" or "scapegoat."[12] *Torma* is often translated as "ritual cake" but is also widely known by the Tibetan term itself; it too is shaped out of dough and used in a wide variety of ritual practices, as a food offering to placate malevolent deities, for instance.[13] In its discussion of the primary types of peaceful therapies, *Healing Children* refers readers to both Bon and Buddhist textual sources on a range of ritual practices for which there are no simple translation equivalents, broadly described as variants of *yé* and *lü* offering practices (*yas stags*, *mdos yas*, and *glud yas* or *yas glud*).[14] Three primary rituals are said here to be especially helpful for children's *dön* affliction. The most elaborate kind of procedure is the offering of a "thread-cross" (*mdos gtong ba*), a highly ornate and often very large structure created from sticks and thread and decorated with various ritual objects, which is used to guard the life force of a child or to carry malevolent spirits away from an afflicted child; we saw such a structure described above for the protection of infants. A procedure of intermediate complexity (called *glud bskyal ba* or *glud bsngo ba*) involves the creation of a "ransom effigy" (*glud*) out of dough, also used to escort malevolent spirits away from the vicinity of an afflicted child. Finally, the simplest sort of protective or therapeutic procedure is a *yé* offering (*yas bsno ba*), presenting specialized but relatively simple ritual objects to afflicting spirits in order to appease their anger, thereby easing the child's affliction.

These are the key technologies for protecting children, used in either peaceful or wrathful manners, and they will be described further below. *Thread-cross Rites for the Fifteen Great Dön*, which is today one of the most commonly used sources for children's rituals in Tibetan communities, is a source cited by *Healing Children* in this context. This work describes three techniques to deal with the fifteen *dön* who are associated with childhood ailments. In the first option, using clay mixed with precious substances, the practitioner should mold an elaborate four-level Mount Meru, with castles at each of the four corners, decorated with a thread-cross structure (*nam mkha'*), umbrellas, banners, and other decorations. The practitioner should then fashion small *lü* forms that are meant to represent the *dön* themselves; the forms are personified as animals

11. Rene De Nebesky-Wojkowitz, *Oracles and Demons of Tibet: The Cult and Iconography of the Tibetan Protective Deities* (The Hague: Mouton, 1956), 371.

12. Ransom or scapegoat rituals using *lü* effigies are discussed throughout Rene De Nebesky-Wojkowitz, *Oracles and Demons of Tibet*. Also see several articles in José Ignacio Cabezón, ed., *Tibetan Ritual* (New York: Oxford University Press, 2009).

13. On the uses of *torma* for healing illness in particular, see Frances Garrett, "Shaping the Illness of Hunger: A Culinary Aesthetics of Food and Healing in Tibet," *Asian Medicine: Tradition and Modernity* 6 (1): 33–54. On *torma* offering practices as elaborate dramas of hospitality, see Frances Garrett et al., "Narratives of Hospitality and Feeding in Tibetan Ritual," *Journal of the American Academy of Religion* (forthcoming).

14. Dri me 'od zer, *Byis pa gso ba*, 136–38.

and are stamped onto dough using wooden molds (*zan par*). After creating this elaborate structure, the ritualist should coax the afflicting spirits away from the child's body and into the corresponding animal form, following the text's instructions. The form is then removed from the home.[15]

In addition to these primary ritual methods, *Healing Children* describes seven additional "peaceful" techniques: avoiding harmful spirits by isolating the child in a place where there are no *dön*; washing the child with medicinal water; applying protective medicinal ointments; affixing protective amulets filled with medicinal substances to the throat, hands, or top of the head; burning medicinal incense; relying on medicine alone; and offering *torma* while moderating food intake following ritual prescriptions.

In the last part of this section of the medical school textbook, a single page is reserved for the destructive tantric operations (*mngon spyod kyi las*) that must be performed if peaceful remedies have been ineffective. These may involve hurling threatening ritual objects at the *dön* (the *dön* being represented by a proxy effigy), burying the *dön* in a faraway place, burning the *dön* in a ritual fire during a ceremony at which a wrathful deity has been propitiated, or adorning the child with objects similar in type to those described above but created in a ritually "wrathful" manner. These procedures are not described in any detail in this chapter, but below we will look briefly at two texts prescribing wrathful methods for treating children. The textbook stresses that peaceful remedies should always be attempted first, explaining that:

> If you were to treat [the child] first with wrathful techniques (*drag po'i las sbyor*), such as burying and burning, the most powerful kinds of *dön* would only increase in savagery and anger, and the child's life-force would be endangered. Therefore, if you begin by satisfying the harmful *dön* with whatever they want—ritual objects (*yas stags*), thread-cross rites (*mdos*), or ransom effigies (*glud yas*)—with the exception of a few extremely antagonistic ones, for the most part you can mollify their hostility. When you calm down their cruel and malevolent behaviors, you also drive out the damage they've done.[16]

TECHNOLOGIES OF PROTECTION: FEEDING, MANIPULATING, WEARING, STAGING

A very wide range of technologies may be applied to the healing and protection of children. Feeding therapies involve offering pills, soups, butters, beers, or texts to children, parents, or deities. Physically manipulative techniques recommend washing, anointing, fumigating, massage, or surgery. Wearing protective objects, including amulets, talismans, strings, or ointments, may be advised in some cases. Finally, the theatrical staging of elaborate hospitality or ransom

15. Karma chags med, "Byis pa'i gdon chen bco lnga'i mdos bzhugs so."
16. Dri me 'od zer, *Byis pa gso ba*, 136.

dramas is among the most highly structured and complex approaches to caring for children. Before examining a few of these technologies in somewhat greater detail, we will first contextualize the methodological breadth of *Healing Children* with a look at three other Tibetan works that display a similar range of approaches. Each of these has been recently reprinted in volumes edited by the Arura Medical Group, a Tibetan organization based in the Western Chinese city of Xining (in Qinghai Province), focused on research, education, and business objectives through its interlinked Tibetan medical college, pharmaceutical factory, hospital, museum, publication series, and research division.[17] The republishing of classic medical texts is one of Arura's founding aims, with nearly a hundred volumes in print, and the availability of these works gives them a broader readership than ever before. Arura's selection of texts for reprinting in their series on medical literature also provides an important perspective on how the category of medicine itself may be defined, as we will see below.

The first of the three works is a collection that reproduces works from the Drangti (Brang ti) medical training lineage of the Sakya court in the thirteenth century. *A Measure of Gold, a Measure of Silver*, published in the Arura book series in 2004, contains two distinct texts. The second of these, entitled *A Measure of Silver: Exceptional Instructions from the Sakya Medical House*, is organized into 419 healing procedures,[18] twenty-one of which are focused in some way on children; the largest number and the lengthiest of these are aimed at easing childbirth or treating complications in childbirth, the most often mentioned complication being difficulty in expelling the placenta. Three operations are methods of birth control.

A Measure of Silver's relatively thorough treatment of child delivery demonstrates its editorial approach: the work records numerous remedies for each condition. Within a given entry there may be several remedies described, suggesting that a healer could try a range of treatments in the search for one that is effective. For example, several remedies are described in the section titled "Methods for extracting a child and placenta that won't come out [in the context of explaining] common women's diseases." The first set of them,

17. For more on Arura, see Vincanne Adams, Renqing Dongzhu, and Phuoc V. Le, "Translating Science: The Arura Medical Group at the Frontiers of Medical Research," in *Studies of Medical Pluralism in Tibetan History and Society (Proceedings of the 11th Seminar of IATS, Bonn 2006)*, ed. Sienna Craig et al. (Halle: International Institute for Tibetan and Buddhist Studies GmbH, 2011), 111–36.

18. The Arura reprint, *A Measure of Gold, a Measure of Silver* (*Gser bre dngul bre*), contains two texts. The first, entitled *A Measure of Gold: Doctor Drangti's Precious Treasury of Instructions* (*Brang ti lha rje'i man ngag gter mdzod rin po che gser bre ma bzhugs so*), is divided in this edition into nine chapters, which altogether contain fifty-one distinct healing remedies or operations. The second collection is *A Measure of Silver* (*Sa skya sman grong ba'i man ngag thun mong ma yin pa dngul bre ma bzhugs so*). *A Measure of Gold* includes no writings explicitly aimed at treating children and so will not be examined here. Brang ti dpal ldan rgyal mtshan, "Sa skya sman grong ba'i man ngag thun mong ma yin pa dngul bre ma bzhugs so," in *Man ngag gser bre ma dang dngul bre ma zhes bya ba bzhugs so*, Bod kyi gso ba rig pa'i gna' dpe phyogs bsgrigs dpe tshogs (Mi rigs dpe skrun khang, 2004).

attributed to Yuthok Yönten Gönpo (G.yu thog yon tan mgon po, 1112–1203), are organized by whether the child is extracted alive or dead. Ingredients for making pills, to be given after the evening meal, are listed. Bloodletting points are offered. Another set of pill ingredients are proposed, to be consumed with beer while a set of mantras are recited. To expel a deceased child, a different set of ingredients may be combined and consumed with beer, or still another may be mixed and burned as incense. If the child still does not come out, a doctor may reach in and pull it out; failing that, special surgical instruments may be used. Following this set of options, still more techniques are identified from various other sources. Similar in format, elsewhere in the *Measure of Silver* a section entitled "Therapeutic techniques for a human or animal child or placenta that will not come out" reads in its entirety as follows:

> Gather seven white mustard seeds (*nyungs dkar*) and seven grains (*'bras bu*), recite 100 mantras for each, and enclose them in white butter. Give it [to the mother] as before, putting it on the top of her head, navel and lower body. For animals, make a substitute (*dod*) of butter with food (*zan*). As for the mantras, say "*Om ka ka ma*, open the pathway! *Sho na ma*, open the pathway! Open the pathway of the four elements! Open the door!" By saying that, [the fetus] will come out [even from] a large sheep.[19]

Yet another short section in *A Measure of Silver* entitled "Therapeutic techniques for a child or placenta that will not come out" simply advises, "Write this protective diagram and attach it to the crown of [the mother's] head."[20] And another, "Methods for extracting human or animal placenta," says "Recite [the mantras] *Om a kar ba, mi kar ba, bhi kar ba* into some white butter, insert it [into the vagina], and cover her rear."[21] Another section with the same title recommends that a series of mantras be written on a paper and attached to the mother's right ear, after which "the child and placenta that hadn't come out, will now come quickly."[22]

Only four sections in *A Measure of Silver* address the protection or healing of children who have survived birth. The segment called "Protective methods for children" lists three such techniques, the first two involving making pills that are fed to the child, and the third advocating reciting mantras while massaging the child. A short remedy entitled "Healing children's lung illness" lists nine common medicinal ingredients and recommends that they be mixed and

19. Brang ti dpal ldan rgyal mtshan, "Sa skya sman grong ba'i man ngag thun mong ma yin pa dngul bre ma bzhugs so," 146.
20. Brang ti dpal ldan rgyal mtshan, "Sa skya sman grong ba'i man ngag thun mong ma yin pa dngul bre ma bzhugs so," 167.
21. Brang ti dpal ldan rgyal mtshan, "Sa skya sman grong ba'i man ngag thun mong ma yin pa dngul bre ma bzhugs so," 222.
22. Brang ti dpal ldan rgyal mtshan, "Sa skya sman grong ba'i man ngag thun mong ma yin pa dngul bre ma bzhugs so," 289.

consumed. Another short remedy, entitled "Healing methods for little children's vomiting," recommends modestly that one "grind white aconite (*bong dkar*) into a powder, mix it with white honey, and feed it [to the child], and vomiting will cease."[23] A fourth section, "Mantras to halt little children's crying," reads as follows:

> Recite the mantras *Om ka pi swaha* 100 times, seal [the mantras] in water, and wash the little child's body with [that empowered water]. With that water then make dough (*zan khu*) and fashion a little child's form out of it. If there is crying in the evening, put the form on the door lintel; at dawn, put it under the door; and if the child cries all the time, put the form under the bed.[24]

These passages from the thirteenth-century *Measure of Silver* make evident what a variety of therapeutic and protective technologies were available to the healer, and how fluidly such a healer might combine "herbal" and what we today might call "religious" or even "magical" remedies. Some therapies involve consuming medicinal substances prepared as pills, and other remedies use surgical or manual operations, mantra recitation, effigies, or talismans; often several of these are meant to be used together. As other sources confirm, the time of childbirth or the period soon after birth are the times of greatest concern, although children must continue to receive specialized protective care throughout their youth.

An Arura publication of a type similar to *Measure of Gold, Measure of Silver* was released in 2008 under the title *A Volume on Healing Mantras [Drawn] from an Assortment of [Tantric] Actions*.[25] This volume reprints six independent texts, two of which address children's healing: one is *The Indispensable [Rites for] Healing Children*, by Yuthok Yönten Gönpo, which we will examine below, and the other is a compilation of remedies by the great "nonsectarian" (*ris med*) movement figure, Mipham ('Jam mgon 'ju mi pham rnam rgyal rgya mtsho, 1846–1912), entitled *Mantras [Drawn] from an Assortment of [Tantric] Actions: A Good Treasury from which Emerges Everything Needed and Desired*.[26] Mipham's

23. Brang ti dpal ldan rgyal mtshan, "Dngul bre ma," 18.
24. Brang ti dpal ldan rgyal mtshan, "Dngul bre ma," 232.
25. *Las sna tshogs pa'i sngags bcos be'u bum*. Bod kyi gso ba rig pa'i gna' dpe phyogs bsgrigs dpe tshogs (Pe cin: Mi rigs dpe skrun khang, 2008). In addition to the work by Mipham and *Indispensable [Rites for] Healing Children*, introduced below, the book includes texts by 'Jam dbyangs mkhyen brtse'i dbang po (1820–1892) and three consecutive texts by an Amdo scholar Chos dbyings stobs ldan rdo rje (1785–1848). Note that several of these texts are also recently published by the Ngagmang Institute in the collection, Hum chen and Nyi zla, eds., *Sngags bcos be'u bum phyogs bsgrigs*, Sngags mang dpe tshogs (Pe cin: Mi rigs dpe skrun khang, 2006).
26. Mi pham, "Las sna tshogs pa'i sngags kyi be'u bum dgos 'dod kun 'byung gter gyi bum pa bzang po bzhugs so," in *Las sna tshogs pa'i sngags bcos be'u bum*, Bod kyi gso ba rig pa'i gna' dpe phyogs bsgrigs dpe tshogs (Pe cin: Mi rigs dpe

work is similar in format to Drangti's, above: it contains sixty-four sections, each addressing a particular concern or practice. Of the four sections on children, some contain a number of remedies addressing distinctive concerns. These four sections and their own subsections all together, therefore, cover a range of topics, including methods to protect against premature birth for humans or animals, methods for increasing fertility, methods for ensuring that a child will be a boy, methods to protect against repeated stillbirth, and a method to treat crying. Again, as was the case in *A Measure of Silver*, most of this material is not concerned with children beyond the fetal stage but is focused more directly on treating pregnant women or prospective parents. However, a few remedies do directly address young children's needs. Take the following example:

> To protect against crying in children: Write the letters *Om ma tri ni tsu du tro dzo swa ha* in block printing script, and consecrate them with 100 mantras; by attaching [the paper to the child], crying will become impossible. This is a really profound way to protect against children's night crying. Alternatively, on a paper arranged right side up, write [the mantras above] in clockwise order around the circumference; inside [the circle of letters], smear vermillion and the child's urine. Attach [the paper to the child] without his seeing it and with that, night crying and fear will be quieted, there is no doubt.[27]

A section entitled "Survival techniques for [a fetus] in the womb and 'navel changing'" is especially long and detailed, offering a number of remedies for a range of issues,[28] including several recommendations for the protection of small children, mostly against harmful spirits. The following are excerpts:

> A *ḍākinī* tradition of healing children (*sri'u*), according to the Revelation (*gter ma*): Knot mantras into a red protective thread; visualize a hooked knife and vajra rosary, and recite [mantras]. Attach the thread to the child's body, and [demons] will be subdued.
>
> Or, for protecting little children: Offer food (*zan*), a ransom effigy (*glud*), and 100 *torma* to the four directions. Combine a peacock feather with feces and say [mantras]. If you feed this [to the child], his stomach will digest

skrun khang, 2008). Mipham's text has been studied in Bryan J. Cuevas, "The 'Calf's Nipple' (Be'u Bum) of Ju Mipham ('Ju Mi Pham): A Handbook of Tibetan Ritual Magic," in *Tibetan Ritual*, ed. José Ignacio Cabezón (Oxford and New York: Oxford University Press, 2010), 165–86.

27. Mi pham, "Las sna tshogs pa'i sngags kyi be'u bum," 279.

28. "Navel changing" refers to rituals that may convert a girl fetus to that of a boy. Note that this operation is classed under women's protective methods in the edition of this text published in Hong Kong Mi pham 'jam dbyangs rnam par rgyal ba, *Las sna tshogs kyi be'u bum bzhugs so* (Zhang kang then ma dpe skrun khung zi, 1999), 56. On such rites, also see Garrett, *Religion, Medicine and the Human Embryo in Tibet*, 71–76.

> it and he will grow big. Without being harmed by demons (*'dre*), the child (*sri'u*) will be protected (*'tsho ba*). This comes from the *Tantra of all (Magical) Operations* (*Las thams cad pa'i rgyud*).
>
> In a text by Jampel Pawo, it is said that all the following operations may be done using the eleven-syllable *Om a ma ra na* mantra: Drink the water that is consecrated [with that mantra] and you'll be protected against pox diseases (*'brum pa*); if you recite it all the time, you'll live a hundred years even if your [natural] lifespan has been exhausted (*tshe zad pa*); if a woman whose son has died washes in water that has been blessed [with the mantra] 108 times, she'll have a live son; if you attach it written on birch bark to [a woman's] neck or upper arm, her fetus (*mngal*) will be protected. Not only that, but [the mantra] will pacify unbearable poisons, fierce epidemics, harmful wounds, and all demons (*gdon*), such as ghosts, flesh-eaters, or brahmans. By empowering or purifying knots [in protective threads] and medicines with the mantra, you'll be freed from all illnesses. You can protect against all injuries (*rnam par 'tshe ba*) with [such] mantra-[empowered] knots. You can pacify all harmful agents (*gnod pa*). Those who remember [the mantra] are victorious in battle.[29]

As was the case in *A Measure of Silver,* Mipham's work offers a spectrum of therapeutic and protective technologies, including feeding therapies, physically manipulative techniques, the wearing of protective objects, or the staging of hospitality or ransom rituals. In the next section, in order to see how therapies like these may also be described in a somewhat more extensive way, we will look at a slightly longer text dedicated to healing and protecting children.

INDISPENSABLE [RITES FOR] HEALING CHILDREN

In addition to Mipham's work, the 2008 Arura volume, *A Volume on Healing Mantras [Drawn] from an Assortment of [Tantric] Actions*, also includes a short but particularly important thirteenth-century work entitled *Indispensable [Rites for] Healing Children*, with the colophonic subtitle, *What Children Need*. This text has been reprinted at least five times in Western book format, since Lokesh Chandra's publication in the Śata-Piṭaka Series in 1968, a publication run that is indeed indicative of the work's significance.[30] The text is found in an early

29. Mi pham, "Las sna tshogs pa'i sngags kyi be'u bum," 332–34. I am not certain about the identity of the name in the last entry: "Jam dpal dpa" bo could be the treasure revealer Bde chen chos 'khor yongs 'dzin (1720–1780).

30. G.yu thog gsar ma yon tan mgon po, "Sri'u gso ba med thabs med pa bzhugs so," in *Sngags bcos be'u bum phyogs bsgrigs* (Pe cin: Mi rigs dpe skrun khang, 2006); G.yu thog gsar ma yon tan mgon po, "Sri'u gso ba med thabs med pa bzhugs so," in *Cha lag bco brgyad*, ed. Blo bzang and Bkra shis rdo rje (Kan su'u mi rigs dpe skrun khang, 1999); G.yu thog gsar ma yon tan mgon po, "Sri'u gso ba med thabs med pa bzhugs," in *Yuthok's Treatise on Tibetan Medicine*, ed. Lokesh Chandra, *Śata–Piṭaka*

collection of medical works known as the *Eighteen Additional Practices*, a historically valuable anthology that includes some of the earliest indigenous Tibetan medical works still extant.[31] The *Eighteen Additional Practices* anthology is typically attributed to Yuthok Yönten Gönpo himself, although its individual texts appear to have been authored by his students or teachers, dating the collection to a period of two generations from the mid-twelfth to the mid-thirteenth century.[32] The colophon of the *Indispensable [Rites for] Healing Children* itself, however, attributes the work to Vairocana, one of the "founding fathers" of the Buddhist Nyingma tradition and a key player in the formation and early development of the medical tradition. Also evidence of the work's importance is its recent extraction from the *Eighteen Additional Practices* and reprinting in two other collections, both by research, education, and publication organizations located in the Eastern Tibetan region of Amdo, based in Qinghai Province: first in 2006, in a volume of "magical" operations published in the Ngakmang Institute's series of important tantric works, and then in 2008 in the Arura volume. The inclusion of *Indispensable [Rites for] Healing Children* by both groups in its anthologies is interesting, since it identifies the work, at least bibliographically, as both "medical" and "tantric."

Like the texts described above, *Indispensable [Rites for] Healing Children* describes rituals for the treatment and protection of young children using a wide range of techniques, including feeding *torma* of various types to beneficial or malevolent spirits, burning incense, reciting mantras extensively for the empowerment of ritual procedures and objects, and staging elaborate exorcism dramas to entice demons away from children. The primary practice described in this text is a wrathful one, aiming to lure afflicting spirits away from vulnerable children. The spirits are drawn from the afflicted child's body into prepared *torma* decoys, which are referred to as "horses" (*rta*); that is, the *torma*, or decoy effigy, becomes a horse that carries the spirit away from the child. (Note that the term "horse" is used also in a more ordinary sense in Tibetan to refer to a medicinal excipient, a "medicine horse" [*sman rta*]; an excipient is a pharmacologically "inactive" substance that serves primarily as the carrier of

Series (New Delhi: International Academy of Indian Culture, 1968); G.yu thog gsar ma yon tan mgon po, "Sri'u gso ba med thabs med pa," in *Cha lag bco brgyad ces bya ba bzhugs so*, Bod kyi gso ba rig pa'i gna' dpe phyogs bsgrigs dpe tshogs (Mi rigs dpe skrun khang, 2004); and G.yu thog gsar ma yon tan mgon po and Others, "Sri'u gso ba med thabs med pa," in *Las sna tshogs pa'i sngags bcos be'u bum* (Pe cin: Mi rigs dpe skrun khang, 2008).

31. On the *Cha lag bco brgyad* collection, see Frances Garrett, "Buddhism and the Historicizing of Medicine in Thirteenth Century Tibet," *Asian Medicine: Tradition and Modernity* 2 no. 2 (2007), 204–24.

32. The authorship of each of the texts has been discussed in Barbara Gerke, "The Authorship of the Tibetan Medical Treatise "Cha Lag Bco Brgyad" (twelfth Century AD) and a Description of Its Historical Background," *Traditional South Asian Medicine* 6 (2001). Sangye Gyatso discusses the texts' authorship at Sangs rgyas rgya mtsho, *Gso rig sman gyi khog 'bugs* (Dharamsala: Tibetan Medical & Astro Institute, 1994), 277–78.

active substances.) The core protective rites (*'phyong*) in this work are summarized in three overall types: healing rites focused on the twelve demons who affect children, the strategically protective placement of auspicious symbols on children's bodies, and medicinal treatments as might be needed.

The central ritual practice recommended in this text begins with the manufacture of an elaborate *maṇḍalic* structure decorated with numerous *torma* sculptures, anthropomorphically molded figures adorned with powerful drawings, and a copious supply of rare and luxurious material substances. The practice is described as follows:

> As preliminary actions, recite the five types of *dhāraṇī*, make water-offerings (*chu gtor*), offer a children's ransom effigy (*chung glud*), offer the golden libation (*gser skyems*), perform the truth-telling [liturgies] (*bden pa bdar*), and carry out pacifying rituals.
>
> The main practice is [as follows]. At an auspicious place make a *maṇḍala*, draw four lotus petals, and put a glorious *torma* (*dpal gtor*) in the center, with the sky-horses (*gnam rta*) as three small *torma*-morsels (*bshos bu*) in the east. Fasten life-supporting turquoises at each of the five joints of a bamboo shaft, and [at the top, make] an umbrella of paper and white silk. [Erect this in the centre of the *maṇḍala*.] At the south [side of the *maṇḍala*], put the advice-horse (*gdams rta*), a man-like body with a bull's head and a wheel (*'khor lo*) [drawn on paper] inserted inside its torso. In the west, place the earth-horse (*sa rta*), which protects the three realms (*kham skyong kha gsum*), [arranging it together with piles of] royal materials such as silk ribbons, tiger cloth, leopard cloth, and a "bat's anklebone" stone, ogress (*srin mo*) materials such as *tha rams* [grass], *na rams* [grass], snake, and *dpal dreg*, and *nāgá* materials such as the three whites, three sweets, and juice-medicine (*rtsi sman*). Mix these [all together around the form], and cover it with a wheel (*'khor lo*) [drawn on paper]. In the north, place the intermediate-horse (*bar rta*): [to make this,] draw a *linga* on the top of the horse's skull, and on its forehead draw a swastika. Then, scatter materials at the four corners: the medicinal offering (*sman phud*), blood (*rakta*), beer (*tshe*), and water (*brab pa*).
>
> Then, empower (*bsgrubs*) [the *maṇḍala* and its horse-excipients] for five, seven, or nine days. Bury the binding-horse (*bsdam pa'i rta*) at the gate threshhold [of the child's house]. Hide the earth-horse under [the child's] bed. Put the intermediate-horse in an eastern window. Hang the sky-horse and the best parts of the scattered materials above [the child's] pillow.

With the afflicting spirits tamed by this ritual, they may remain near the child without danger. If the spirits are too ferocious to be tamed by this first option, however, the text provides two alternative procedures.

> Offer three morsels (*bshos bu*) of the sky-horse as incense. Bury the binding-horse at the intersection of a wide path, and also leave a

substitute-effigy (*dod po*). Put the intermediate-horse in front of you, invite [the demon afflicting the child] into the *lingu*, and perform the warning ritual (*bab gdab*) [to demand that the demon stay away].

[Or in the worst case,] if all [the demons are especially] bad (*rdugs*), [do this instead:] Make five effigies out of buckwheat, pea-flour and wheat. Inside their hearts put [papers with] the vital-heart (*srog snying*) [mantras], from *om ma ra* up to *swaha*, and tame them [by putting them] in a box (*'grub khang*) upside down and [throwing] mantra pills (*sngags ril*) [at them]. After they're tamed, offer medicine-*torma* and morsels (*bshos bu*), and put [the box of effigies in which the demons are tamed] behind the house to the east. Put three morsels on the roof. Bury the earth-horse to the north. Bury the binding-horse at the intersection of a wide road. Carry the intermediate-horse and the earth-horse to a mountain in the east.[33]

The text then lists a series of wrathful mantras, which are to be written on paper and affixed onto, or stuffed inside, a substitute figure or effigy. While saying the mantras, the practitioner should offer *torma* to the afflicting spirits and say, "May this little child be protected and preserved until age 100! May the parents care exceptionally for the child!" The practitioner should also promise, "I'll offer you morsels at the first of each month for a year, and next year, I'll give you a thanksgiving service!" After that exchange, the dough effigies into which the afflicted spirits had been enticed, should be buried.

In this single text we can see an array of elaborate procedures, with options provided to accommodate one's convenience or the severity of affliction. The basic format of each procedure involves creating a figure out of dough, typically adorned in some way with mantras and possibly other special materials. If the figure has been made to embody a protective deity, it is then placed near the child's residence as a protective device. Conversely, an afflicting demon may be lured into the dough figure so that it may be physically expelled from the child's vicinity, abandoned on a distant hill or buried underground. Some spirits are offered foods, in the form of *torma*, and then commanded to protect the child; others are offered *torma* and asked to stay away. On a practical level, the multiple technologies enabling these intricate interactions with the nonhuman world clearly require a substantial commitment of time and resources. The significant attention devoted to such procedures suggests that a child's presence in a family is highly influential; with generous resources directed toward their protection and healing, the material impact of children on adults is quite evident.

Finally, we will look at a text specifically aimed at protecting or healing children (*sri'u gso ba*), coming from an eleven-volme collection of teachings of the Shangpa Kagyu tradition organized by Kalu Rinpoche (1905–1989). Despite its brevity, this text describes several protective techniques: two kinds of arrow

33. G.yu thog gsar ma yon tan mgon po, "Sri'u gso ba med thabs med pa bzhugs so," 13–14.

that can be placed near children, protective threads that can be wrapped around children's bodies, and the feeding of *torma* to protective deities. The entire text, called *Instructions for Healing Children* (*Sri'u gso ba'i gdams pa*), is as follows:

> From the perspective of this protector [tradition], if you want to care for [vulnerable] children (*sri'u gso ba*), there are life-horse (*tshe rta*) and life-span (*tshe thag*) protective techniques, and there are protective techniques by means of deposit (*gta'*) and *torma*.
>
> First, [the life-horse technique]: In the middle of an intricate knot [wrapped around] a teak dagger that is eight or twelve finger-[widths long], write a *hūṃ*. Contemplatively generate the protector there, apply a pristine awareness to it, and offer *torma*. Recite "*Om badzra ma hā kā la khrim khre ta bignan bi nā ya ka hūṃ hūṃ phat*. Protect this child!" one hundred times. Imagine [empowered substances traveling] "from the protector's mouth to my mouth, and from my heart to the protector's heart," and urge [the deities] to act (*'phrin las bcol*) [on the child's behalf]. Fasten [the dagger] on a pillar, or somewhere else [near the child], and leave it there [as a protective device].
>
> Second [the life-span technique]: Bind together three life-span cords (*tshe thag*), at least one that is blue, and say twenty-one mantras over each knot, making either five or seven knots. Imagine that the child is thereby encircled by five or seven protectors, and thus it is said that he will be protected.
>
> Third, [deposit techniques]: On an arrow [decorated] with unburned vulture feathers, affix a hand-sized cut-out of black silk, and write the mantras above, together with the verses above on three of the feathers. If you've already done initiatory practices (*bsnyen pa*), just write the middle [part of the] ritual [verses]. Then, establish the protector in the arrow and say, "This [arrow] is made as your support, and so protect the life of this child [with it]! Each year I give you a great thanksgiving ritual. Rest now in a safe place."
>
> [Fourth,] with *torma*, protection is guaranteed [by the deity].[34]

From the preceding examples, it is clear that the topic of caring for children is an especially rich arena for investigating how medical and religious concerns and practices are intertwined throughout history, and still today. These protective and therapeutic technologies have been little studied in secondary scholarship and they are indeed complex from any point of view, so their study is particularly difficult. Nevertheless, the presence of such elaborate rituals not only in these recently republished medical/tantric classical texts, but also in the state-sanctioned medical training manual for Tibetan doctors in China, *Healing Children*, with which this article began, makes clear the nonnegotiable centrality of such practices to the act of caring for small children in Tibet. Their

34. Karma rang byung kun khyab [Ka lu rin po che], "Sri'u gso ba'i gdams pa bzhugs so," in *Dpal ldan shangs pa'i chos skor rnam lnga'i rgya gzhung* (Sonada).

presence is not uncontroversial: Ivette Vargas-O'Bryan comments that "at the medical college [in Lhasa], students are taught that [malevolent spirits] *klu* and *gdon* either do not really exist or are mental projections of some kind" and that "*gdon* and *klu* diseases must be treated physiologically, and not spiritually," meaning that medicinal and dietary therapies are taught instead of ritual practices.[35] Vargas-O'Bryan's observation of pedagogical practice provides a different picture of medical training than does the published curriculum of medical colleges in China, however, as our study of *Healing Children* and other works from which it draws suggests. Although ritual therapies are excluded from seventy percent of the textbook, where the bulk of children's diseases and therapies are discussed, in fact neither that textbook nor its companion textbook, *Healing Dön Diseases* (*Gdon nad gso ba*), focused entirely on *dön* affliction in adults and covering the topic much more extensively, discount the "reality" of *dön* in favor of an interpretation modeled after biomedicine. To the contrary, the author of *Healing Children* explains that *dön*-caused illnesses exist and must be treated, and he insists that even biomedicine recognizes some of these conditions under the classification of those psychological disorders (*sems khams nad*) that cannot be detected by modern, scientific diagnostic equipment.[36]

SUGGESTIONS FOR FURTHER RESEARCH

A thorough study of children or childhood in Tibet has not yet been attempted in secondary scholarship. For readers of English, there is a scattering of works from multiple disciplinary perspectives that are relevant to a study of children in Tibetan communities. A few scientific articles, for example, focus on high-altitude adaptation from the points of view of medicine, biology, and ecology.[37] Social scientists have addressed children through an interest in kinship models and fertility, with a significant focus on practices of polyandry and infant mortality.[38] Ethnographic accounts that address

35. Ivette Vargas-O'Bryan, "Legitimising Demon Diseases in Tibetan Medicine: The Conjoining of Religion, Medicine, and Ecology," in *Studies of Medical Pluralism in Tibetan History and Society: Proceedings of the Eleventh Seminar of the International Association for Tibetan Studies, Konigswinter 2006*, ed. Sienna Craig et al. (Halle: IITBS GmbH International Institute for Tibetan and Buddhist Studies, 2011), 389–90.

36. Dri me 'od zer, *Byis pa gso ba*, 147.

37. Yangzong et al., "Childhood Asthma under the North Face of Mount Everest," *Journal of Asthma* 43 no. 5 (2006), 393–98; Andrea S. Wiley, "A Role for Biology in the Cultural Ecology of Ladakh," *Human Ecology* 25 no. 2 (1997), 273–95; Yeshe Yangzom et al., "The Dietary Habits of Non-Asthmatic Schoolchildren in Lhasa, Tibet," *Journal of Asthma* 44 4 (2007), 317–24; Nancy Harris et al., "Nutritional and Health Status of Tibetan Children Living at High Altitudes," *New England Journal of Medicine* 344 no. 5 (2004), 341–47.

38. Wiley, "A Role for Biology in the Cultural Ecology of Ladakh."; Geoff Childs et al., "Tibetan Fertility Transitions in China and South Asia," *Population and Development Review* 31 no. 2 (2005), 337–49; M. C. Goldstein, "Stratification, Polyandry, and Family Structure in Central Tibet," *Southwestern Journal of Anthropology* 27 (1971),

children in passing include Geoff Childs's *Tibetan Diary*, which looks briefly at early childhood and adolescence in a Himalayan village in Nepal.[39] There are a couple of surveys of childbearing and childrearing practices in Tibetan communities, such as *Tibetan Art of Parenting*, which provides anecdotal and sometimes romanticized descriptions of conception, gestation, birth, infancy, and early childhood, based on the authors' exposure to Tibetans in exile in India,[40] or a shorter survey of cultural practices in Ladakh.[41] Written by a contemporary exile Tibetan doctor and translated into English for publication in the journal *Tibetan Medicine*, Thupten Sangay's "Tibetan Traditions of Childbirth and Childcare," cited above, provides a brief summary of topics such as conception, pregnancy, birth practices, postnatal care, naming and infancy, early childhood rituals, and pediatrics.[42]

Of note also are a few English-language works by Tibetans themselves, writing from within China. *A Tibetan Girl's Hair Changing Ritual* documents a thirteen-year-old girl's rite of passage during which her hairstyle is altered; no equivalent ceremony exists to mark boys' entry into sexual maturity and readiness for marriage, making this tradition especially interesting. The ceremony that is the focus of this detailed ethnography is no longer practiced in many Tibetan regions, making this book, which details the rite as practiced in a farming village in Amdo, all the more valuable.[43] In an article by another young Tibetan author writing in English from a nearby region in China, another childhood ritual is described in which a child's "soul" leaves its body and is called back by the child's mother. The author reports that souls leave children, typically before the age of ten,

64–74; M. C. Goldstein, "Fraternal Polyandry and Fertility in a High Himalayan Valley in Northwest Nepal," *Human Ecology* 4 (1976), 223–33; M. C. Goldstein, "New Perspectives on Tibetan Fertility and Population Decline," *American Ethnologist* 8 (1981), 721–38; B. N. Aziz, *Tibetan Frontier Families: Reflections on Three Generations from D'ing-Ri* (Durham, NC: Carolina Academic Press, 1978); S. R. Schuler, *The Other Side of Polyandry* (Boulder, CO: Westview Press, 1987); Nancy Levine, "Differential Childcare in Three Tibetan Communities: Beyond Son Preference," *Population and Development Review* 13 (1988), 281–304.

39. Geoff Childs, *Tibetan Diary: From Birth to Death and Beyond in a Himalayan Valley of Nepal* (Berkeley: University of California Press, 2004).

40. Anne Hubbell Maiden and Edie Farwell, *The Tibetan Art of Parenting: From before Conception through Early Childhood* (Boston: Wisdom Publications, 1997).

41. Helena Norberg-Hodge and Hazel Russell, "Birth and Child-Rearing in Zangskar," in *Himalayan Buddhist Villages: Environment, Resources, Society and Religious Life in Zangskar, Ladakh*, ed. John Crook and Henry Osmaston (University of Bristol, 2001), 519–32.

42. A similar article authored by a Tibetan doctor inside China, with comments on basic care of the birthing woman during and right after birth, is Lhun grub rdo rje, "Bod lugs gso rig las byis pa'i bde srung skor bshad pa," *Krung go'i bod kyi gso rig* 3 no. 2 (2009).

43. This ritual is also described in the article 'Brug mo skyid et al., "Stag Rig Tibetan Village: Hair Changing and Marriage," *Asian Highlands Perspectives* 6 (2010), 173–82. From this publication series also see the autobiography by Tsering Bum, *A Northeastern Tibetan Childhood* (Xining City: Plateau Publications, 2007).

when they fall or are frightened or shocked; the lost souls will then wander the region and may cause harm.[44]

None of these sources comment on Tibetan cultural attitudes toward children or the period of childhood more broadly, however. The corpus of work on the social and cultural construction of childhood, now exhibited in a wide range of disciplines, has still not touched the field of Tibetan Studies at all, despite the presence of a few articles on children. In thinking about how this path might be charted, several potentially fruitful avenues of approach come to mind. A text-historical study of Tibetan children or childhood might usefully draw on children's literature and textbooks, legal texts, or biographical sources, none of which has been investigated for information on children. An increasing number of Tibetan textbooks aimed at children have been published recently, such as the 2010 *General Knowledge for Children* (*Byis pa'i rab byed*), a selection of prose and poetry on aspects of Tibetan culture for middle-school students.[45] Legal texts would be another source for information on societal attitudes toward children or childhood; Rebecca French's work, for example, cites the age of eight as the threshold of legal culpability, noting how law codes distinguish classes of people according to their capacity to perform as legally responsible members of society.[46] (It appears from a number of sources that the age of eight in Tibet, as was the case in medieval Europe, may be a key marker of childhood's end.[47]) Biographies may also be a rich source for information on children's lives; however, like their counterparts in China, biographical accounts of religious figures in particular typically "foreshadow the nature of the adult personality,"[48] rather than describe childhood in a realistic manner, and there are few girls to be seen in this body of literature. Nevertheless, such texts may be our primary sources for depictions of children in history themselves. We have not considered here these kinds of sources, focusing instead on a range of therapeutic and protective technologies

44. Libu Lakhi, Charles Kevin Stuart, and Gerald Roche, "Calling Back the Lost Namuyi Tibetan Soul," *Asian Highlands Perspectives* 1 (2009), 70. Other articles from Plateau Publications document traditional children's games, considered by some to be an especially vulnerable area of cultural heritage. For a contemporary discussion of traditional children's games in Tibetan, see Chab 'gag rdo rje tshe ring, ed. *Yul srol* (Lan kru'u: Kan su'u mi rigs dpe skrun khang, 2006), 42–45.

45. Bcod pa klu rgyal and 'Brug mo byams, *Byis pa'i rab byed*, Blo 'byed klog deb dpe tshogs (Kan su'u mi rigs dpe skrun khang, 2010). A related genre would be books on children's education and morality translated from Chinese into Tibetan, such as *Byis pa'i shes bya'i mdzod chung*, trans. Bkra shis sgrol ma (Si khron mi rigs dpe skrun khang, 2000).

46. Rebecca Redwood French, *The Golden Yoke: The Legal Cosmology of Buddhist Tibet* (Ithaca, NY, and London: Cornell University Press, 1995), 162–63. According to the seventeenth-century Ganden Podrang Code, for example, "small children, being innocent, can't differentiate between good and bad; being foolish, they do not understand"(163).

47. Eight years old is also an important milestone ritually: the blood, skull, or flesh of an eight- year-old child is one of the coveted secret tantric ingredients. For example, in English see Nebesky-Wojkowitz, *Oracles and Demons of Tibet*, 344–45.

48. Kenneth De Woskin, "Famous Chinese Childhoods," in *Chinese Views of Childhood*, ed. Anne Behnke Kinney (Honolulu: University of Hawaii Press, 1995), 2.

aimed at children. From the sources surveyed in this chapter, it is clear that the topic of raising young children illuminates a remarkable cross-section of ritual technologies in Tibet. Children may be healed or protected by feeding of their mothers, deities, or themselves. Children's bodies may be physically manipulated for therapeutic purposes, as with bloodletting, washing, anointing, fumigating, or massaging. Children are adorned with all manner of protective and therapeutic amulets, talismans, strings, papers, ointments, or letters. Children's ears are filled with mantras, and their bodies (or replicas of their bodies) play roles in the staging of complex hospitality or ransom dramas requiring the manufacture of elaborate structures. What we see in the technologies examined here, I suggest, is a "making of childhood" that is strongly focused on the child's body. In this activity of making through ritual (taking technology itself to be "the capacity to make"[49]), we see the making of children's bodies. It is here that we may also see a material culture of children or childhood. Following Sharon Brookshaw, I suggest that the material culture of children is comprised of "objects made, modified, used by, and associated with children." As "signifiers of children and childhood," therefore, Brookshaw continues, these objects "should reveal aspects of the culture of this group."[50]

Some researchers have noted that because many children's objects are shared by adults, as is generally the case with most ritual objects described in this chapter, it can be difficult to interpret just how they may be signifiers of childhood. They may more readily be understood as the material culture of parenthood, since it is often parents who impose their use upon children. In response, we might draw on science studies and medical anthropology to consider "the constitution and transformation of physical bodies and individual identities through technological practices"[51] and ask whether children are something more than passive recipients of the technologies of protection and healing that we have seen in this chapter. As contemporary North American medical technologies are understood, by some, to provide agency (and not repression) to both the "physical bodies and individual identities" with which they interact, can we similarly see therapeutic and protective technologies to empower and provide agency to Tibetan children?

Perhaps so. Perhaps as children engage in the bodily techniques described here—specialized eating of elaborately prepared and empowered substances, performative wearing of valuable amulets filled with exoticized texts and rare materials, or imaginative participation as subjects of ransom dramas—it may be that with these material forces they are themselves also empowered against the dangers around them as part of a process of being socialized into a world

49. Paul Richards, "Dressed to Kill: Clothing as Technology of the Body in the Civil War in Sierra Leone," *Journal of Material Culture* 14 no. 4 (2009), 507.

50. Sharon Brookshaw, "The Material Culture of Children and Childhood," *Journal of Material Culture* 14 no. 3 (2009), 367–68.

51. Alberto Cambrosio, Allan Young, and Margaret Lock, "Introduction," in *Living and Working with the New Medical Technologies: Intersections of Inquiry*, ed. Margaret Lock, Alan Young, and Alberto Cambrosio (Cambridge University Press, 2000), 11.

of relationships with sentient and nonsentient environments. Indeed, as the textbook *Healing Children* states on its very first page, the technologies presented in works on healing and protecting children are offered as methods of empowering children: for developing their intelligence and perseverance, and for ensuring a long and healthy life. The amulets and protection cords worn by small children are much more than simple fashion accessories. As Paul Richards suggests in his study of clothing as part of the technology of war, the special adornments covering children's bodies may be "less a wrapper than a second skin, through which the performative agency of the wearer is protected and enhanced."[52] We may think of children's bodies as empowered by ritually strengthened medicines, foods, objects, and actions that identify them as able to interact appropriately and safely with their environments, not unlike functions served by the partly practical and partly symbolic, or even "magical," components of military combat uniforms. I hope to suggest here in the most preliminary way the importance of considering children's material culture, as an initial step to understanding the category of the child, in Tibet or elsewhere, and to recommend the conjoined technologies of medical and religious practices as an especially rich source for investigating this topic.

ACKNOWLEDGMENT

I would like to acknowledge the substantial contributions to this essay by Khenpo Kunga Sherab.

APPENDIX: TABLE OF CONTENTS FROM *HEALING CHILDREN*

1. What children need (*byis pa nyer spyod*)
   - A, What is needed at the time of birth (*btsa' dus kyi nyer spyod*)
     - i. Signs of birth (*btsa' ba'i rtags*)
     - ii. Techniques of birthing (*btsa' ba'i thabs*)
   - B. What is needed—initial [section]
     - i. Signs of good luck (*bkra shis pa'i rtags*)
     - ii. Signs of poor luck (*bkra mi shis pa'i rtags*)
     - iii. Auspicious sayings (*bkra shis brjod pa*)
     - iv. Methods of cutting the navel (*lte ba bcad thabs*)
     - v. How to do auspicious signs (*rten 'brel bya thabs*)
     - vi. Methods of nursing (*nu ma bsnun thabs*)
   - C. What is needed—intermediate [section] (*bar gyi nyer spyod*)
     - i. Offerings to deities (*lha gsol ba*)
     - ii. Pledge effigy offerings (*gta' gzugs pa*)
     - iii. Protection rites (*srung ba'i cho ga*)

52. Richards, "Dressed to Kill," 504.

iv. Food offerings (*zla phud btang ba*)
v. Naming (*ming gdags pa*)
vi. Ear piercing (*rna ba dbug thabs*)
vii. How to give food and medicine (*zas sman bsten tshul*)
viii. Behavioral rules (*spyod lam bslab pa*)
D. What is needed—final [section] (*tha ma'i nyer spyod*)
i. Dispelling teething pain (*so skye'i nad bsal ba*)
ii. Methods of offering pledge effigies (*gta' bkrol bya thabs*)

2. Children's illness (*byis pa'i nad*) [pages 13–124 (111 pages)]
A. Causes and conditions [of illness] (*rgyu rkyen*)
i. Causes
ii. Conditions
a. Conditions in the mother (*ma rkyen*)
b. Conditions in the child (*bu rkyen*)
B. Classification (*dbye ba*)
i. Classification of hereditary diseases (*lhan skyes nad*)
ii. Classification of sudden diseases (*glo bur nad*)
a. Coarse diseases (*rags pa'i nad*)
b. Subtle diseases (*phra ba'i nad*)
c. More subtle diseases (*zhib tshags nad*)
C. [Diagnostic] signs (*rtags*) [pages 17–62 (45 pages)]
i. General signs
ii. Particular signs
a. Diagnosis of the 8 coarse diseases
1. Chest disease (*brang nad*)
2. Lung disease (*glo nad*)
3. Liver disease (*mchin nad*)
4. Diarrhea (*'khru ba'i nad*)
5. Vomiting (*skyug nad*)
6. Contagious disease (*rims nad*)
7. Navel disease (*lte ba'i nad*)
8. Stone disease (*rte'u'i nad*)
b. Diagnosis of the 8 subtle diseases
1. Head swelling (*mgo skrangs*)
2. Blocked pharynx (*gre 'gags*)
3. Spleen disease (*mtsher pa'i nad*)
4 Bile disease (*mkhris pa'i nad*)
5. Stomach disease (*pho ba'i nad*)
6. Intestinal disease (*long ga'i nad*)
7. Earth eating disease (*sa zos nad*)
8. Disease from breastfeeding (*zho ras nad*)
c. Diagnosis of the 8 more subtle diseases
1. Eye disease (*mig nad*)
2. Ear disease (*rna ba'i nad*)

3. Mouth disease (*kha yi nad*)
4. Skin ulcers (*rmen bu'i nad*)
5. Life channel disease (*srog rtsa'i nad*)
6. Worm disease (*srin nad*)
7. Meat disease (*sha nad*)
8. Blister disease (*phol nad*)

iii. A clear view of life and death (*'tsho 'chi'i kha dmar gdags pa*)
a. Signs that [a disease] will be difficult to survive (*'tsho dka' ba'i rtags*)
b. Signs that [a disease] will be easy to survive (*'tsho sla ba'i rtags*)

D. Therapeutic techniques for children's disease (*byis nad kyi bcos thabs*) [pages 63–124 (61 pages)]
i. General therapeutic techniques
a. Healing in the three periods [of childhood]
b. Healing with the four antidotes: food, behavior, medicine, and surgery
ii. Particular therapeutic techniques [in the sections below, each disease is enumerated, as above]
a. Therapeutic techniques for the 8 coarse diseases
b. Therapeutic techniques for the 8 subtle diseases
c. Therapeutic techniques for the 8 more subtle diseases

3. Children's demons (*byis gdon*) [pages 125–143 (18 pages)]
A. Identifying children's demons (*byis gdon ngos bzung ba*)
i. Divisions of kinds of demons (*gdon rigs kyi dbye ba*)
ii. Signs of demon affliction (*gdon gyis zin pa'i rtags*)
a. General signs
b. Particular signs
iii. Signs of that which is difficult to heal (*gso dka'i ba'i rtags*)
iv. Signs of that which is easy to heal (*gso sla ba'i rtags*)
B. Therapeutic techniques (*bcos thabs*)
i. Peaceful therapeutic techniques (*zhi ba'i bcos thabs*)
a. Brief teaching
b. Extended teaching
ii. Wrathful therapeutic techniques (*drag po'i bcos thabs*)

4. Appendix [pages 144–160 (16 pages)]
A. A supplementary appendix on healing children's spirit[-caused diseases] (*byis gdon gso ba*)
B. An appendix with some points from the *Rust-free mirror of flesh, clearly reflecting the diagnostic practice of ear divination in children* (*Byis pa'i rma phra brtag pa gsal snang sha yi me long g.ya' bral*)[52]
C. *Mirror of water, the diagnostic practice of milk divination* (*Sho pra brtag pa chu yi me long*)[52]
D. Methods of diagnosing [the causes of] crying (*ngu skad brtag thabs*)[52]

CHAPTER 8

Picturing Buddhism

Nurturing Buddhist Worldviews through Children's Books

KAREN DERRIS

SHARING STORIES

A gift of the picture book *Zen Shorts* received at the birth of my second child started my search for picture books about Buddhism. Initially this interest was primarily personal: as I read aloud to my children I hoped to nurture in them a Buddhist worldview as they encountered and explored the world. Silently, I also read these books as a scholar of premodern Buddhist narrative traditions. Looking for patterns of continuity and change—the most basic pattern for the historian of religion—I found many examples of both forms of engagement with Buddhist traditions.

Storytelling has served as an important resource for cultivating children's religious and ethical worldviews in Buddhist cultures across Asia. Quite naturally, children growing up in Buddhist societies hear stories from their parents and grandparents about the Buddha, (in)famous monks and nuns, and Buddhist legends.[1]

My thanks to Benjamin Derris Murphy and Rebekah Derris Murphy for their assistance in the research for this chapter.

1. Ranjini Obeyesekere captured this practice of ordinary life when she wrote movingly of her childhood in Sri Lanka, listening to her grandparents' narrations of Buddhist stories drawn from Buddhist canonical and commentarial texts. Hearing these stories, Obeyesekere reflected, taught her how to be a Buddhist. Ranjini Obeyesekere, *Jewel of the Doctrine* (Albany: SUNY Press, 1991), x.

The importance of narratives for Buddhist traditions developing in Western cultural contexts has been minimally charted.[2] This is not surprising, as Buddhist narrative literature has been largely underexamined in scholarship of Buddhist traditions in Asian cultural contexts. In recent decades, however, a growing number of scholars have begun to take seriously the importance of Buddhist narratives as sources for historical, ethical, and philosophical thought and practice.[3] Children's literature is an important starting point for considering how Buddhist narrative traditions are beginning to develop in Western cultural contexts. As we will see, children's books are becoming one important line of transmission of Buddhist narratives into English and other Western languages.

While it is certainly a generalization, there is some degree of truth to the assessment that a significant percentage of converts to Buddhism engage primarily with Buddhism as a philosophical system or contemplative practice. Without knowledge or investment in Buddhist narrative traditions, adults and children alike may be encountering Buddhist stories for the first time through children's books. These stories introduce their readers, children and adults, to Buddhist worlds and being in the world with a Buddhist worldview.

A considerable number of children's Buddhist storybooks have been published in English by both commercial presses and Buddhist organizations. Several important books were written in the first half of the twentieth century, notably Noor Inayat Khan's *Twenty Jātaka Tales* (1939) and Elizabeth Coatsworth's *The Cat Who Went to Heaven* (1930), and they remain in print today.[4] Other books were written sporadically in the intervening years, such as James van de Vettering's *Little Owl: An Eightfold Buddhist Admonition* (1978), but the proliferation of children's books on Buddhism began in the late 1980s and gained considerable momentum in the last twenty years with the publication of over five dozen Buddhist picture books.[5] Popular interest in Buddhism increased in Western countries in the same time period. These books are easily accessible from on-line book sellers, public libraries, and specialty Buddhist or "new age" bookstores, but it is still rare to find them at mainstream bookstore chains. That is, these books are readily available to those who wish to look for them, but they have yet to become a part of mainstream children's culture.

2. Charles Johnson, *Turning the Wheel: Essays on Buddhism and Writing* (New York: Scribner, 2003); Jeff Humphries, *Reading Emptiness* (Albany: SUNY Press, 1999); John Whalen-Bridge and Gary Storhoff, eds., *The Emergence of Buddhist American Literature* (Albany: SUNY Press, 2009).

3. In addition to Ranjini Obeyesekere, Charles Hallisey, Anne Hansen, Frank Reynolds, John Strong, and Jonathan Walters have made foundational contributions to the study of Buddahist narrative traditions.

4. Elizabeth Coatsworth, *The Cat Who Went to Heaven* (New York: Aladdin Paperbacks, 2008); Noor Inayat Khan, *Twenty Jātaka Tales* (Rochester, Vermont: Inner Traditions International, 1983).

5. Janwillem van de Wetering, *Little Owl: An Eightfold Buddhist Admonition* (Boston: Houghton Mifflin Company, 1978).

Many of these storybooks retell traditional Buddhist narratives, primarily the *jātakas* and the Buddha's biography. Others craft new stories based upon Buddhist teachings and practices. While some books in this latter category make explicit connections to Buddhist concepts and themes, many make only vague allusions that indicate these stories are inspired by or linked to Buddhist traditions. This chapter explores texts in each of the categories just described, but this genre is already too large to survey it comprehensively in its entirety.

The exploration here of these children's books is guided by three sets of interrelated questions: First, what does Buddhism look like in these stories? What kinds of vantage points do these books offer for seeing Buddhist worlds? Second, how do these stories encourage children to understand and live in the world? That is, what kinds of worldviews do they nurture for children raised with a relationship to Buddhism in the West? Third, what do these books teach us about children? How are children and childhood conceived and depicted in these books?

Unlike traditional practices of retelling Buddhist narratives to children from authoritative texts (whether canonical, commentarial, or apocryphal), this new story literature is written expressly for children; adults are a secondary, instrumental audience which begins as reader but need not be limited to this role. These storybooks offer points of reflection for both child and adult to consider the capacities and challenges of children in the world.

My explorations attempt to move inside the world created in and between these children's books;[6] although what we find there can suggest a great deal about the worlds outside of the one in which these books live. While I am not attempting to construct a sociological analysis of the authors and readers of these books and the relationships they may have with Buddhism, I do make the basic assumption that the readers are English speakers who encounter Buddhism primarily in an English-speaking cultural context. This is not to assume that English is the primary language of author or reader, nor do I assume that the child and adult readers are Buddhists, by whatever criteria that identity may be judged. Rather, I cautiously assume that readers are at minimum Buddhist sympathizers, a category introduced by Thomas Tweed as "those who have some sympathy for a religion but do not embrace it exclusively or fully."[7] Books on Buddhism are a central point of encounter for many sympathizers, a subcategory Tweed describes as "night-stand Buddhists" who keep a book or two on Buddhism by their bedside for night-time reading. Here, I focus on what I'll affectionately term "bedtime story Buddhists," that

6. I mean to indicate the world inside the text as suggested by Umberto Eco, *Six Walks in the Fictional Woods* (Cambridge, MA: Harvard University Press, 1994), 27–45.

7. Thomas A. Tweed. "Nightstand Buddhists and Other Creatures: Adherents, Sympathizers and the Study of Religion," in *American Buddhism: Methods and Findings in Recent Scholarship*, ed. Duncan Ryuken Williams and Christopher Queen (Richmond, Surrey: Curzon Press, 1999), 74.

is, children whose engagement with Buddhism is formed in part by the stories that might be read to them as a part of their bedtime rituals.

JĀTAKA PICTURE BOOKS: ENGLISH BECOMES A NEW BUDDHIST VERNACULAR

Retellings of the *jātakas*, the birth stories of the Buddha's previous lives as a bodhisattva, form one of the largest categories of picture books drawn from pre-extant Buddhist material. As one of the most popular genres in traditional Buddhist societies, the *jātakas* were a generative narrative tradition: while plots and characters remained fairly stable in different versions of these stories, narrative details were reimagined, as were the groupings of *jātakas* and the genres of texts in which *jātakas* were included, such as *sutras*, chronicles, and anthologies.[8] As popular literary traditions, *jātakas* were translated from canonical languages into vernaculars, and new apocryphal *jātakas* were also authored in vernacular languages, creating regionally specific story traditions. The fluidity within the ongoing history of the *jātaka* tradition continues with the retellings of the *jātaka* stories in the modern English versions.[9]

While many scholars of Buddhist traditions have long recognized the popularity of the *jātakas*, they have often largely dismissed this narrative tradition as merely simplistic folk tales for teaching basic morals without significance for understanding Buddhist doctrine and ethics. The scholarly legacy of underestimating this literature seems to be connected to the designation of children as the primary audience for the *jātakas* in Western cultural contexts. Limiting the appropriate audience for the *jātakas* to children misjudges both the richness of these narratives and the astuteness of children as readers.

In an issue of the Buddhist magazine *Tricycle*, which focused upon childrearing in Buddhist families and communities, Gyokuko Carlson and Domyo Burk of Dharma Rain Zen Center explained the natural tendency to turn to *jātaka* stories for educating children, but shared their concerns about the usefulness of these stories for meeting this aim in an American dharma context:

> The teaching should be illustrated by engaging stories and rich imagery, and there are a growing number of resources. Many people trying to share the dharma with children have looked to what seems an obvious source of ready-made material in the *Jātaka* tales.

8. For example, see R. E. Emmerick, trans., *Sutra of Golden Light* (Oxford: The Pali Text Society, 1970); N. A. Jayawickrama, trans., *The Sheaf of Garlands of the Epochs of the Conqueror* (London: The Pali Text Society, 1978); Peter Khoroche, trans., *Once the Buddha was a Monkey* (Chicago: Chicago University Press, 1989).

9. I employ the term "traditional" here quite loosely to indicate premodern Buddhist societies of regional specificity throughout Asia rather than the universalist ideals of modern Buddhism in Asia and the West.

> These are ancient Buddhist fairy tales that recount former lives of the Buddha, most of which date back to when Buddhism thrived in India. However, most people ultimately find the *Jātaka* tales to be of limited usefulness in teaching dharma to children. For one, they are dated and as culturally flavored as European fairy tales, so there is often a cultural gap to bridge. Second, though there are many *Jātaka* tales, the virtues demonstrated in them are limited in scope and number: kindness, honesty, loyalty, and more loyalty.[10]

My aim here is not to disprove their assessment but to offer another perspective on the value of the *jātaka* stories that emerges when we consider the broader historical and literary context of this narrative tradition. First, from a performative perspective, picture books are an ideal form for the transmission of the *jātaka* tradition into an English vernacular, as word, sound, and image are all experienced as the *jātaka* picture books are read aloud to a child. The multisensory experience of reading or listening to a *jātaka* picture book distantly echoes the traditional experience of hearing a *jātaka* in a temple adorned with mural paintings of the stories, since *jātaka* are one of the most popular themes in Buddhist art and were intended for adult and child visual audiences.[11] As adults read the *jātakas* to children, they obviously encounter the *jātakas* too, perhaps for the first time, and they too are rewarded by the rich multisensory experience of word, image and sound building a narrative experience.

While the *jātaka* stories are individually coherent, the richness of their meaning is found in the total narrative structure encompassing the hundreds of individual *jātakas*.[12] This larger frame identifies their single narrator: the Buddha Gautama Śākyamuni, who recounts his previous lives to his disciples. Each story is woven into this metastructure by framing passages: as an introduction, each story is preceded with a description of the occasion when the Buddha told the story of this particular lifetime, and then at its conclusion the Buddha identifies who he and others were in the story. Together, the *jātakas* narrate a significant portion of the bodhisattva path, as well as foundational doctrines of karma, rebirth, and the continuities of relationships over lifetimes.

Authors and illustrators of *jātaka* picture books engage with the metanarrative structure of the *jātakas* in a variety of ways. In *Kindness: A Treasury of Buddhist Wisdom for Children and Parents*, Sarah Conover follows the traditional pattern of the frame passages, locating the Buddha as narrator and

10. Gyokuko Carlson and Domyo Burk, "The abc's of Enlightenment," *Tricycle: The Buddhist Review* (Fall 2008), 117.

11. Richard Gombrich, *Theravada Buddhism: A Social History from Ancient Benares to Modern Colombo* (London: Routledge, 1988), 156.

12. While the Pāli canonical tradition contains 547 *jātakas*, this number varies in Buddhist historical-cultural contexts.

the conditions that lead him to tell the story of his previous life, and then she concludes each story with a final summation of the meaning.[13] Her retellings emphasize the Buddha's agenda of narrative as didactic device, particularly on the workings of karma. Unmentioned, however, is the identification of the Buddha himself and others with the characters in the *jātaka* story. Those identifications emphasize rebirth and the continuity of relationships over lifetimes. Those dimensions of the *jātaka* tradition form the frame story of *The Giant Turtle*, published by the Buddhist Text Translation Society.[14] The illustrations by an unnamed child begin and end with a picture of the Buddha in meditation posture, aglow with golden light. The final brief passage is the only one in a picture book, to my knowledge, that makes the across-lifetime identifications: "After telling this tale, the Buddha said, 'I was the king turtle and the people who lived on my back became my disciples.'"[15] With this simple sentence, the important ideals of continuity of care over lifetimes is succinctly expressed.

Jeanne Lee's *I Once Was a Monkey* innovates with the *jātaka* tradition by creating a new frame story of the Buddha's narration of his previous life stories.[16] In this collection of six animal *jātaka* stories, a statue of the Buddha in a ruined temple—illustrated to evoke a ruined Khmer temple in Angkor—becomes animated and recounts his previous lives as animals and a tree to an assemblage of animals. With each story the Buddha statue explains why he took each particular rebirth and the lesson to be taken from each story.

Other authors retelling *jātaka* stories remove the frame stories from the stories altogether. The only reference to the greater narrative structure of the *jātaka* tradition is relegated to a preface or an author's note. For example, in Noor Inayat Khan's collection, *Twenty Jātaka Tales*, the following passage precedes the jātaka stories:

> And while the Buddha sat, and all around him listened, these are the stories he told. "My children," he said, "I have not come now among you as your Buddha for the first time; I have come many times before; sometimes as a child among the little children, sometimes among the animals as one of their kind, loving them as I love you now; sometimes in Nature, among the flowers, I traced a way for you and you knew it not.[17]

In Khan's narrative setting the Buddha directly addresses an assemblage of children, who replace the adult monastic and lay disciples who surround the

13. Sarah Conover, *Kindness: A Treasury of Buddhist Wisdom for Children and Parents* (Spokane: Eastern Washington University Press, 2001).
14. Buddhist Text Translation Society, *The Giant Turtle* (Burlingame, CA: Dharma Realm Buddhist Association, 2000).
15. Buddhist Text Translation Society, *The Giant Turtle*, 49.
16. Jeanne Lee, *I Once Was a Monkey* (New York: Farrar, Straus and Giroux, 1999).
17. Noor Inayat Khan, *Twenty Jataka Tales*, 11.

Buddha in the traditional *jātaka* frame stories. Here, the Buddha's storytelling is an act of nurturing and care; he is telling these stories in order to display his continuity of care and love across lifetimes. Regardless of time or place, all children are a part of the Buddha's loving concern.[18] While the idea of rebirth prefaces the entire collection of stories, this central theme of the *jātakas* is not repeated within each story. Without this repetitive, rhythmic pattern interweaving the *jātakas,* the totality of the bodhisattva path is easily lost. Much of the soteriological and ontological meaning in the *jātakas* is lost as well.

In other *jātaka* picture books, explanations of the *jātaka* tradition and the workings of the *jātaka* literary form is limited to the authors' notes preceding or following the story. Intended to explain the historic and present-day didactic function of these stories to an adult reader, the authors' notes almost uniformly cast the *jātakas* as virtue stories. For example, Tarthang Tulku says in his introduction to the Dharma Publishing *Jātaka* picture books: "As an embodiment of great compassion, the Awakened One reappears in many forms, in many times and places to ease the suffering of living beings."[19] The absence of the *jātaka* frame story in these *jātaka* collections largely erase the workings of karma, the concept of past and future lives, and the possibility the *jātaka* narratives generate of watching people and relationships evolve over lifetimes. The emphasis on virtues, while valuable, is disconnected from other soteriological and ontological themes.

The majority of *jataka* picture books retell the animal *jātaka* stories. Mark McGinnis explains the attraction of the animal *jātakas* in the introduction to his collection, *Buddhist Animal Wisdom Stories*: "Employing animals to illuminate the basic human condition is a universal device for pointing out human foibles and virtues with clarity and humor."[20] The *jātakas* are often funny, sometimes very much so, making for entertaining reading. The retellings of the *jātaka* stories in picture books offer other possible readings in addition to embodied actions of Buddhist virtues—these readings are not, of course, limited by the authors' guidance. In his biography of the Buddha, John Strong argues that the *jātakas* are shaped by several "biographical thrusts" that explain the working of karma in the Buddha's life, the bodhisattva path, and the Buddha's ethical attainments as well as ethical failings.[21] These readings suggested by Strong and other possible interpretations require engagement going beyond the clear or surface meaning. Child readers, as we saw above, are capable of meeting such a challenge.

18. While "children" may reference all human beings, since this book is written for children, they may be the intended audience in the imagined narrative setting.

19. For example, Rosalyn White, *The Rabbit in the Moon: A* Jātaka Tale (Oakland, CA: Dharma Publishing, 1989).

20. Mark W. McGinnis, *Buddhist Animal Wisdom Stories* (Boston: Weatherhill, 2004), 7.

21. John Strong, *The Buddha: A Short Biography* (Oxford: One World, 2001), 15–34.

For example, here is one interpretation that emerges from the collection of animal *jātakas* in picture books. Many of the animal *jatakas* in these collections depict the interaction between noble animals and less noble human beings. While the human beings have greater power, the animals have great capacities to understand the world and to care for others. This imbalance is particularly well seen in the "Monkey Bridge" *jātaka*, one of the most popular *jātaka* stories, found in several *jātaka* picture books.[22] In this *jātaka* story a wise and brave monkey king knows that he must keep secret the most delectable fruit of the tree housing his monkey clan from greedy human beings who would destroy their home in order to have the fruit for themselves. When the feared event does in fact occur, the monkey king sacrifices his own life by making himself into a bridge for his monkeys to climb over and escape the human beings' weapons. In this act, the monkey king teaches the human king about real leadership, care, and bravery. What strikes me as particularly powerful about this and other *jātakas* of this kind, such as the "Banyan Deer," is that those with lesser power, who must bend to the dictates of others, are shown to have great capacities for ethical life. Empowered, a child reader of this category of *jātakas* might recognize that while they too are subject to the power of others, most notably their parents, they might see that like these animals, they too have much to offer even in their vulnerable condition.

THE BUDDHA'S LIFE STORY

Another significant category of picture books tells the life story of the Buddha Śākyamuni. Like the *jātaka* picture books, some of these are retellings of traditional Buddhist sources and others are new narratives. All offer the opportunity to explore two foundational, complex questions: Who is the Buddha? Where can we encounter the Buddha? As would be expected, the variety of nuanced answers is dependent largely upon the perspectives of the Buddhist tradition that is inspiring or informing each story. When these texts are read together, another pattern also emerges that differentiates two present-day perspectives on the Buddha: one that sees the Buddha as extraordinary as demonstrated by the supernatural aspects of his biography, and another that sees the Buddha as identifiable with every person, a perspective that erases the mythical aspects of the Buddha's life story.

Picture books that transmit the extraordinary experiences of the Buddha's life are rich with cosmological details of a traditional Buddhist worldview. In *Buddha*, the author-illustrator Demi creates a Buddhist landscape of interpenetrating realms of the cosmos where *devas* (celestial beings) peer down at the

22. Mark W. McGinnis, *Buddhist Animal Wisdom Stories*, 99–101; Noor Inayat Khan, *Twenty Jātaka Tales*, 13–21; Rafe Martin, *The Monkey Bridge* (New York: Alfred A. Knopf, 1997).

action in the human world from their lofty homes above the sky.[23] This intermingling of the *devas* and human beings is presented most fully in her illustration of the Buddha's Awakening as a sky full of heavenly beings appear above the heads of human beings with offerings for the Buddha on a lotus throne. Demi describes the effect of the Buddha's Awakening on the world with traditional images and phrases: "Suddenly, the dry rivers began to flow, the still animals began to dance; the birds began to sing, and all the flowers bloomed. Radiant light flooded the land to reveal spirits, angels, and heavenly protectors. The scent of incense filled the air and ten thousand worlds quaked."[24] From the first pages of this picture book, Prince Siddhartha (who will become the Buddha in adulthood) is always marked as more than human. In the moments following his birth the Buddha is drawn taking his magical steps in all directions marking his unique presence in this world.[25]

In stark contrast, Jonathan Landaw's *Prince Siddhartha: The Story of Buddha* relates many of the same episodes from the Buddha's biography as does *Buddha*, yet this is a modern biography with all mythical and magical elements stripped away.[26] The newborn prince causes feelings of peace, but there are no other extraordinary signs or events at his birth. The *devas* who play an important role in traditional biographies of the Buddha, such as revealing the four signs to the prince, are totally absent. This is the story of a remarkable child, but a child who lives in a world that appears to work in much the same ways that a present-day reader would expect. The universal relevance of the Buddha's life story is the final message of the picture book, as the narrator implores the reader to use this book to reflect upon the purpose of her own life:

> Everyone, in every country, no matter what he or she believes, can learn from these teachings of the compassionate Buddha. By following them properly, we can get rid of all selfishness, hatred and greed. We can conquer all fear and

23. Demi, *Buddha* (New York: Henry Holt and Company, 1996).

24. Demi, *Buddha*, 22. The same scene is described in the *Jataka-nidana*: "The great ocean eighty-four thousand *yojanas* deep turned into sweet water. Rivers ceased to flow. Those blind from birth were able to see objects. " N. A. Jayawickrama, trans. *The Story of Gotama Buddha (Jātaka-nidāna)* (Oxford: The Pali Text Society, 1990), 100.

25. A similar image can be found in Z. A. Lu, trans., *A Pictoral Biography of Śākyamuni Buddha*, (Taiwan: The Corporate Body of the Buddha Educational Foundation, 1997), 5. Importantly, both books tell this important narrative detail only in images, but not in words. Readers would have to know the story in order to interpret what they were seeing. The baby's steps are described in the *Buddhacarita* in this way: "As he took seven steps that were steady, lifted up evenly and straight, stretched out wide and firmly set down." Patrick Olivelle, trans., *Life of the Buddha by Ashvaghosa* (New York: Clay Sanskrit Library and New York University Press, 2008), 7.

26. Jonathan Landaw, *Prince Siddhartha: The Story of Buddha* (Boston: Wisdom, 2003). There are several interesting modern biographies of the Buddha for adult readers that share this demythologized narrative. See, for example, Hammalawa Saddhatissa, *Before He Was Buddha: The Life of Siddhartha* (Berkeley, CA: Seastone, 1998).

> reach the same peace and understanding that Prince Siddhartha found under the Tree of Enlightenment. In the same way that he did, we can each become a buddha, an awakened one. We can bring the same happiness to others that he did.[27]

Buddhahood is a potential for all human beings, according to this perspective, and yet modeling one's own life on the actions of Prince Siddhartha is quite a tall order. How should a child see herself in the life of the Buddha? Thich Nhat Hanh uses narratives not only to explain the answer to such questions, but to sympathetically understand how confusing these questions can be.[28] In *A Pebble for Your Pocket*, a collection of teachings for older children, Hanh tells the story of a young Vietnamese monk who peeked in at the Buddha statue on the alter in his temple every night expecting the Buddha to reach out and eat the fruit offerings that had been left for him. When the statue remained a statue, he searched for the Buddha elsewhere, but others told him that the Buddha was in a pure land far distant from our world. Hanh offered this confused child an alternative universal perspective on who a Buddha is, and where a Buddha is to be found: "Anyone can be a Buddha. Do not imagine that the Buddha is a statue or someone who has a fancy halo around his or her head or wears a yellow robe. A Buddha is a person who is aware of what is going on inside him or her and has a lot of understanding and compassion."[29]

But is a statue or painting of the Buddha always just a statue or a painting? Is the Buddha (as a reality other than one's own potential) still present in our world? And if so, does the Buddha's presence transform the ordinary world of our perceptions through these qualities of wisdom and compassion? Readers of Elizabeth Coatsworth's*The Cat Who Went to Heaven* encounter a Buddha as a distinct and present reality in the world regardless of where or when one lives. The story set in a vague "once upon a time" in Japan tells of a young, poor painter who is commissioned by a temple priest to paint a picture of the death scene of the Buddha. Before he begins to paint, he spends several days recollecting the life of the Buddha and his previous *jātaka* lifetimes. His composed little cat is always by his side devotedly joining her paws together in front of the Buddha altar.[30] The completed painting is miraculously transformed during the first night it is hung in the temple: the Buddha no longer lies supine, in his death position, but reaches out a hand to bless a cat, the painter's own pet, who has now moved from the margin of the painting to sit directly in front of the Buddha.[31]

27. Landaw, *Prince Siddhartha*, 143.
28. Thich Nhat Hanh, *A Pebble for Your Pocket* (Berkeley, CA: Plum Blossom Books), 3–6.
29. Thich Nhat Hanh, *A Pebble for Your Pocket*, 6.
30. Elizabeth Coatsworth, *The Cat Who Went to Heaven*, 28.
31. Coatsworth, *The Cat Who Went to Heaven*, 85–87.

The Buddha, this book suggests, still acts with compassion in the world in miraculous ways. More precisely, the Buddha responds to those who contribute to his living presence in the world through their devotion, recollections of his life, and embodiment of his teachings. While the magical conclusion of the story might be amazing and fantastical to the intended English language audience, it is not unusual for Japanese tales to recount the animated movements of statutes and paintings in response to the needs of their devotees.

Buddha in the Garden gives another vantage point on the meaning of the Buddha that synthesizes these two perspectives, emphasizing the Buddha as an internal potential or the Buddha as an external, extraordinary reality.[32] In this picture book, a young boy is left orphaned at the gate of a Chinese monastery where he is raised to become the temple gardener. When he is left alone in the monastery with only one blind monk, this old man tells him over and over: "The Buddha is in the garden." Searching for the Buddha, the young boy comes to observe the same signs in nature that precipitated the Buddha's own departure from the palace, named here as sickness, illness, death, and then his own enlightenment.[33] The boy vowed that he would never leave the peace that he found in the garden, and through this vow, it seems, the boy turns into a beautiful statue of a buddha. When the other monks return to the monastery, they receive the same message from the old, blind monk: "The Buddha is in the garden"; seeing the statue of the young boy, now buddha, the monks are said to "see what they have been seeking all their lives: peace and fulfillment."[34]

Who is the Buddha? Where is the Buddha? These are not simple questions, and thus there are no simple or singular answers. As *Buddha in the Garden* and all of the picture books focused on the Buddha suggest, the answer to these questions is always relational. For some, like the garden boy, the Buddha is an internal potential he realizes, and in turn he becomes an actual manifestation of a buddha for the monks who find him as a statue in the garden. He is both boy and statue, both boy and Buddha. Picture books on the life of the Buddha offer a variety of buddhalogical positions ranging from the extraordinary to the demythologized and others in between. Who is the Buddha? It depends on which picture books you read, or how many.

CREATING NEW NARRATIVES: CHILDREN'S CAPACITY TO SEE THEIR WORLD ANEW

Picture books serve not only as sites for transmitting and transforming received Buddhist literary traditions; they are also a generative narrative form for the

32. David Bouchard, *Buddha in the Garden* (Vancouver: Raincoast Books, 2001).
33. Bouchard, *Buddha in the Garden*, 12–24. In traditional biographies of the Buddha, the fours signs encountered by Siddhartha are a sick person, an old person, a corpse, and a renunciant.
34. Bouchard, *Buddha in the Garden*, 28.

innovation of new stories on Buddhist themes. As is true of all Buddhist vernacular literary traditions, the topics of these stories vary widely. There is a recurring theme of children's openness to Buddhism as it enters their world, and they have the capacity to learn new ways of being in the world through these encounters.

Jon Muth's picture books about Stillwater, the Zen panda, and his friends, the siblings Addy, Michael, and Karl, are arguably the best known of all Buddhist picture books.[35] In this series, Buddhism is clearly a foreign religion not of the suburban American neighborhood, and yet these children, because of their open hearts and minds, quickly embrace the lessons their Buddhist friend offers. In the first of Muth's books, *Zen Shorts*, the youngsters straightforwardly accept the arrival of a panda in the children's yard after a brief moment of amazement. The littlest one, Karl, tells his brother that a bear is outside. "A what?" His brother asks; but three pages later our narrator explains that big sister Addy introduces Karl because "Karl was shy around bears he didn't know." As I read Muth's books, being an animal has a particular significance of signaling Other-ness, and Buddhists are Others in the Stillwater series. One can easily substitute "monk" for "bear" in the dialogue above (Karl tells his brother there is a monk outside. "A What?" his brother asks?) Stillwater is most decidedly not like the children. Stillwater is foreign; "he spoke with a slight panda accent," sharing his vague East Asian culture of paper parasols, kimonos, and calligraphy with these suburban American children. On the one hand this "Otherness" may be an ethnic one: Stillwater is Asian and the children are Euro-Americans; on the other hand, the Stillwater character suggests that Buddhism *qua* Buddhism is "Other," foreign, and imported into ordinary American life. Anything associated with it is distinct from the ordinary, and yet it can quickly transform the ordinary for the better.

In the course of *Zen Shorts,* Stillwater tells each child a story, and these stories are retellings of traditional Zen and Taoist stories, as Muth explains in his "Author's Note" addressed to the adult reader.[36] The illustrations accompanying Stillwater's stories portray all of those characters as animals as well. They too are foreign, Buddhist–Others. Stillwater avoids a heavy-handed, didactic telling of the stories. He shares a story and lets it sit with the child, only gently making the connection between the message and the child's experience. In *Zen Shorts*, Stillwater uses narratives to nurture children as they learn about themselves and others. As this book is read aloud, as well as the stories retold within it, adult reader and child listener together replicate this sharing of stories. While reading *Zen Shorts*, the attentive adult learns a method of *how* to read, of *how* to tell a story, to a child.

35. Jon J. Muth, *Zen Shorts* (New York: Scholastic Press, 2005); Jon J. Muth, *Zen Ties* (New York: Scholastic Press, 2008); Jon J. Muth, *Zen Ghosts*(New York: Scholastic Press, 2010). Of all the books discussed in this chapter, Muth's books are the only ones that can reliably be found in mainstream commercial bookstores.

36. Muth, *Zen Shorts*. Muth's approach to retelling traditional stories within the context of his innovative narrative mirrors traditional patterns in pre-Buddhist literary culture of anthologizing received narrative traditions in new compositions.

The three children in *Zen Shorts* are friendly, curious and playful, but they also fight with one another; they are real children. We never catch sight of their parents—even the family portrait hanging in their home is only of the children.[37] The children's independence is stressed: their relationships with Stillwater and their encounters with Buddhism are solely of their own choosing. In the second Stillwater book, *Zen Ties*, their panda friend teaches them how to be in a relationship with an adult, and once again their parents don't get in the way. It is Stillwater who teaches the children to be compassionate toward an elderly neighbor whose cross temperament has scared them and made them keep a wary distance.

In his postscript, Muth makes the story's lessons explicit for the adult reader (who may not be as good a reader as a child, and Muth has deep respect for children as quick and astute learners) that "it's (also) a gentle reminder that we are all connected and interdependent whether we recognize our neighbor's face or not."[38] Children are not only observant, but ready to trust their perceptions, capacities all too easily lost in adulthood. Making a humorous connection to the earlier *Zen Shorts*, *Zen Ties* begins with an almost identical dialogue: 'Mom! There's a bear over there!' Said the little girl. 'A what?' asked her Mother. 'A big panda bear!' Said the girl. 'What's he doing?' asked the little girl's mother. 'He's...sitting.'[39] Unlike the brothers in *Zen Shorts,* who go together to meet the bear, the little girl's mother never looks up from her newspaper to see Stillwater seated in zazen. If adults would only look at what's right in front of them, see what they might learn. A child's capacity to live in and with the present moment is most fully represented in Koo, a child panda visiting his uncle Stillwater. Koo speaks only in the poetic form of haikus ("Hi Koo"): "Tea was very good/my cup holds emptiness now/where shall I put it?"[40] Each of Koo's haikus are expressions of the simple experiences he shares with his uncle and the children, but in his articulation of those moments we see that the ordinary moments in a child's day—like drinking tea or picking an apple—are opportunities for deepening awareness. While Stillwater, the adult panda, is guiding the children toward compassionate actions, it is a child who expresses the meaning of these actions.

Muth's books invite his readers to make their own meaning in his story worlds.[41] Children might feel especially empowered to do so as the children

37. Muth, *Zen Shorts*.
38. Muth, *Zen Ties*.
39. Muth, *Zen Ties*, 1–2.
40. Muth, *Zen Ties*, 5.
41. Muth's respect for children as sophisticated readers is clearly evident in his recollection of an exchange with a girl at one of his readings who made a connection between characters in his different books that Muth himself had not intended: "There was a little girl who came up to me after I had done a presentation and she said to me, she held *The Three Questions* up and she said, "So is the little panda that gets rescued in *The Three Questions*...is that Stillwater?" I said, "Yes, it is!" But I hadn't thought of it before that. I love the things I get from my readers, I really do. I think they tell me much more than I could know about what it is that I'm

in his books consistently shape the worlds around them. In Muth's *The Three Questions*, a boy lives out the answer to his own questions ("What is the best time to do things? Who is the most important one? What is the right thing to do?") when he responds to the present moment to help those in need in the ways they need aid at that very moment.[42] In Muth's book *Stone Soup*, a little girl is the only person in a Chinese village willing to respond to three monks' requests for contributions to make a stone soup.[43] Trusting others, she alone is capable of being generous to others. When the monks give her the opportunity to do so, she becomes a model for the others in the village, who follow her example, initially out of curiosity but later from the reawakening of virtues in themselves. *Stone Soup* is the only one of Muth's books explicitly set in a Buddhist culture, and interestingly, the most recognizable Buddhists in this story, the monks, are human characters rather than the animal ones they are in his other books. In an Asian setting, Buddhists are not "Other," as they are when they enter Western worlds.

Muth's third book in the Stillwater series, *Zen Ghosts*, illustrates increasingly interconnected worlds inhabited by Buddhists and "bedtime story Buddhists." Stillwater becomes a part of the children's world by wearing a Halloween costume and handing out candy. In turn, the children become active participants in Stillwater's Buddhist stories, no longer only the outside interpreters listening to his narratives. As is the case in all of Muth's picture books, when Stillwater tells the children a story it is illustrated with animal characters in a distinct style from the primary narrative frame—the frame that bounds where the children live. Barriers are crossed in *Zen Ghosts*, however, as the girl Addy appears in the illustrations of the Buddhist "ghost story" as herself in human form. She has entered into Stillwater's narrative Buddhist world, just as he has become a resident in her's.

Children imaginatively travel between cultural worlds through these stories and others like them. These movements can circle the globe in complex patterns.[44] Does a Buddhist world have boundaries? How does one live in the world as a Buddhist?

NARRATIVE AS WINDOW INTO OTHER BUDDHIST WORLDS

Several of Thich Nhat Hanh's books for children as well as the books written by those in his Tiep Hien, Order of Interbeing (also known as the Unified

doing." From "An Interview with Jon Muth."*Reading Rockets*. http://www.readingrockets.org/books/interviews/muth/transcript.

42. Muth, *The Three Questions* (New York: Scholastic, 2002).

43. Muth, *Stone Soup* (New York: Scholastic, 2003).

44. Muth's *Three Questions*, for example, was inspired by a story told by Thich Nhat Hanh (also published by Hanh as *The Hermit and the Well)* that is itself a retelling of Leo Tolstoy's *The Three Questions*. See "An Interview with Jon Muth." *Reading Rockets*.

Buddhist Church), are new stories created to introduce the experiences of Buddhists in Vietnam to English-speaking children and their adult readers. In Hanh's *The Hermit and the Well* the narrator tells a story about his life as a boy in North Vietnam.[45] The story interweaves aspects of Vietnamese culture with universal childhood experiences. A field trip into the mountains would be less familiar to a child in an English-speaking context not for the activity, but for the goal of finding a hermit who lives high above the children's homes. Their efforts are frustrated, however, by finding an empty hut. The boy comes to realize that this is what he was searching for—anything, even a well that satiates his thirst, can be the Buddha. The expectation to find a hermit in the mountains arises from living in a Buddhist landscape. Buddhism is infused in this world in a way that isn't readily available to the children reading this book. In some way, the reader sees her world not only as different, but as less-than this one, and thus there is great value in employing one's imagination in order to encounter Buddhism in that narrative world. At the same time the story encourages children to consider that the Buddha is found anywhere and everywhere that there is awareness of the earth's responsiveness.

The life of Tinh, protagonist in Carolyn Marsden's *The Buddha's Diamonds*, a book for older children, is anything but familiar to most children reading this book.[46] This ten-year-old boy works on his father's simple fishing boat struggling to help his family survive storms, illness, hunger, and the remnants of war that dangerously litter the ground with hidden mines. Forced by circumstances to grow up very quickly, Tinh finds strength by worshiping the Buddha statue in his village temple and by praying to Phat Ba Quan Ahm, the female bodhisattva of compassion. But he is also still a boy: he would like to join in the soccer games with his friends on the beach, but he knows he has little time for play.

Tinh's life of deprivation contrasts with another boy in the village, who has soccer balls and toy cars sent by an uncle who immigrated to the United States.[47] The children reading this book live in that prosperous world, but it is also a world where Buddhism is not as richly present as it is in Tinh's village. Tinh's Buddhism is a devotional Buddhism where amulets and images of the Buddha and bodhisattvas are a part of everyday life. Unlike the vast majority of English-language picture books emphasizing meditation and awareness, the devotional Buddhism of *The Buddha's Diamonds* illustrates a less-known traditional way that children live their lives as Buddhists in a different part of the Buddhist world.

The realities of war in a Buddhist landscape are among the most challenging issues in children's books. While this is gently broached in *The Buddha's Diamonds*, the issue of war and the ever-present possibility of peace is the focal

45. Thich Nhat Hanh, *The Hermit and the Well* (Berkeley, CA: Plum Blossom Books, 2003).

46. Carolyn Marsden, *The Buddha's Diamonds* (Cambridge: Canlewick Press, 2008).

47. Marsden, *The Buddha's Diamonds*, 10–11.

point of Thich Nhat Hanh's *The Coconut Monk*.[48] In the depoliticized context of Western Buddhist communities, discourses around peace tend to focus on the development of inner states that may contribute generally to creating a more peaceful world. *The Coconut Monk* describes the reality of the warfare, violence, and social suffering found in many Buddhist societies, as is true not only for the recent history of Vietnam, but also Laos, Cambodia, Thailand, Myanmar, Sri Lanka, and Tibet. When children learn about this aspect of Buddhist histories, discussions of the connections between inner peace and creating peace in the world move beyond ideals to lived realities. Hanh respects children's capacities to engage with such difficult realities as necessary education for contributing to peace. As Hanh describes in the biographical afterword, the Coconut Monk was a real person, Dao Dua, who lived through the Vietnam War and was often jailed, as is narrated in this story.[49] By drawing its reader into its world, the narrator challenges her to face the hard realities of working for peace in a time of war.

The story begins with a tangible act of transforming the instruments of war into ones for peace, as the Coconut Monk takes the metal from bombs and bullets and melts them into a bell that he rings from his perch in a coconut tree, speaking this intention: "You have been playing the game of war. Now you can help create peace,"[50] The Coconut Monk lives atop a coconut tree with a cat and mouse that are constant, loving companions. These animals exemplify the always-present possibility of peace in spite of any degree of difference. The Coconut Monk voluntarily leaves his quiet island village in hopes of sharing this possibility with politicians. Arrested for his message, the monk and his animal companions are put in jail, where their survival is even further endangered, but their commitment to lovingkindness, generosity, and peace remains unassailable. If the cat and mouse can transforms their natural roles of predator and prey into friendship, this picture book suggests, then human beings, who arrogantly assume a greater capacity of self-control over baser instincts, should be able to refrain from hurting one another as well.

MEDITATION FOR CHILDREN: BUDDHIST PRACTICE WITHOUT BUDDHISM

In Western cultural contexts, people with a generalized awareness of Buddhism often assume that Buddhist practice is synonymous with meditation. While this assumption is short on nuance, it is not an inaccurate description of the emphasis placed upon meditation practice in many Buddhist communities of convert practitioners. This prioritization of meditation is perhaps of a greater

48. Thich Nhat Hanh, *The Coconut Monk* (Berkeley, CA: Plum Blossom Books, 2009).
49. Thich Nhat Hanh, *The Coconut Monk*.
50. Thich Nhat Hanh, *The Coconut Monk*, 9.

degree, or a more exclusive kind, than in Asian contexts, but it is better described as a characteristic of modern Buddhism rather than being peculiar to Western Buddhism.[51] For children in Buddhist families, particularly families that have *chosen* a Buddhist identity rather than being born as Buddhists, meditation is likely a defining aspect of the family's life as Buddhists.[52] Further, the origin of meditation in Buddhist traditions is often deemphasized, since this practice is presented as universal and in some sense, contextless.

Picture book presentations on meditation suggest the value placed on it for shaping everyday life regardless of age. In *Peaceful Piggy Meditation*, Kerry Lee MacLean playfully describes meditation and its benefits as a self-care practice that need not be entangled with Buddhism as a religion.[53] She makes no reference to the Buddhist context of meditation in the story itself, although in the book's apparatus she identifies her role as a children meditation teacher associated with Shambhala in Colorado, and in her acknowledgements she thanks her own meditation teacher, Mipham Rinpoche.[54] Functioning much like premodern colophons and opening dedications in traditional Buddhist texts, these frames surrounding the book proper suggest the context of her vision of meditation: it has a source tradition and a lineage of teacher–student relationships, but these are not directly transmitted to the children who read her book. With no context meditation is presented as a universal method for developing emotional well-being and humanistic values. Cute piggies meditating are certainly approachable for children but they are also nonthreatening characters for both child and adult readers: these pigs don't have ethnic, national, or religious identity—anyone can and should try this practice. Even their gendered identity (indicated in the opening pages by pigs in clothing, jewelry, and gendered toys—soccer ball for him, ballet slippers for her) is stripped away when the piggies are meditating. When piggies meditate, they are their truest selves, their best selves that seem to transcend any differentiation of identity.

Each Breath a Smile by Sister Susan, a nun in Thich Nhat Hanh's Tiep Hien order, also suggests that meditation can be practiced by anyone, but here, while also emphasizing that age is not an impediment, it acknowledges meditation as a vital part of personal identity.[55] Unlike the anthropomorphizing of meditating pigs, the illustrations by Nguyen Thi Hop and Nguyen Dong in *Each Breath a Smile* depict children of a variety of racial backgrounds practicing meditation first with a Buddhist nun who, as teacher, addresses the children with an invitation: "Dear Little Ones, let us sit very quietly and listen."[56] The

51. Donald S. Lopez, Jr., ed. *A Modern Buddhist Bible: Essential Readings from East to West* (Boston: Beacon Press, 2002), xxxvii–xxxix.

52. For a description and discussion of teaching meditation to children, see Peter Doobninin, "Tough Loving Kindness," *Tricycle: The Buddhist Review* (Fall 2008), 74–77.

53. Kerry Lee MacLean, *Peaceful Piggy Meditation* (Morton Grove, IL: Albert Whitman & Company, 2003).

54. MacLean, *Peaceful Piggy Meditation*.

55. Sister Susan, *Each Breath a Smile* (Berkeley, CA: Plum Blossom Books, 2001).

56. Sister Susan, *Each Breath a Smile*, 1.

universal quality of meditation is envisioned differently here: meditation originates in Buddhist tradition, but its practice can create a universal sangha, or community. As the pages turn, children cultivate awareness through focusing upon their breathing and they gain the capacity to see the true nature of all things—true natures that are virtuous and beautiful.

As children listen to or read *Each Breath a Smile,* they are addressed alongside the children in the book and invited to engage in the breathing meditation. As they read the book, a child can have the experience of practicing this kind of meditation. The ability of a child to control his or her breath as a means to deepening awareness is presented as a natural process that needs only a gentle introduction and guidance. The narrative of the Buddha's spontaneous experience of meditation under the rose apple tree as a young child provides the idealized, traditional model of child meditator. In his collection of essays for older children, *Under the Rose Apple Tree*, Thich Nhat Hanh includes this story from the Buddha's biography. Nestled within this book, the story of Siddhartha's first experience of meditation in his final lifetime, is the example of meditation as a way to "return to the here and now" and to "touch the Buddha inside of you."[57] Thich Nhat Hanh's version of the story emphasizes Siddhartha's youth (nine years old), his great sensitivity to the suffering of small animals caused by the annual plowing ceremony performed by his father, the king, and the understanding of what he had witnessed through his meditation under the rose apple tree at the edge of the plowing field.

> Siddhartha was still absorbed by what he had seen in the field, when the King and Queen passed by. They were surprised to see Siddhartha sitting with such deep concentration. His mother was moved to tears when she saw how beautiful Siddhartha looked. When she approached Siddhartha, the boy looked up and said, "Mother, reciting the scriptures does nothing to help the worms and the birds."
>
> Later, when the Buddha had been practicing for a long time, he thought back to when he was nine years old and sat in meditation for the first time beneath the cool shade of a rose apple tree on the day of the year's first plowing, and recalled how refreshing and peaceful those moments had been![58]

Directly after telling this story, Thich Nhat Hanh encourages his readers to meditate because it makes them happy. In many of his writings, Thich Nhat Hanh expresses his deep joy at sharing meditation with children: "I love to sit close to children because of their freshness. Every time I hold the hand of a child and practice walking meditation, I always benefit from his or her freshness. I might be able to offer the child my stability, but I always benefit from

57. Thich Nhat Hanh, *Under the Rose Apple Tree* (Berkeley, CA: Parallax Press, 2002), 14; 2.
58. Thich Nhat Hanh, *Under the Rose Apple Tree*, 16–17.

his or her freshness."[59] This reciprocal relationship of adult and child sharing meditation practice together is illustrated in the pictures of *Each Breath a Smile* of parents and children sharing meditation practice together. There is a strong, consistent message that family life can sustain and even be a benefit for Buddhist practice.

In Gail Silver's *Ahn's Anger*, a young boy uses his breathing meditation as a way to transform his anger.[60] The story begins in a way that is deeply familiar to both child and adult: Anh doesn't want to stop playing with his blocks when his grandfather calls him for dinner. His emotions quickly escalate into a full-scale tantrum. Anh's grandfather responds in a way that adult caretakers would hope they could emulate when their child has just told them they hate them: "'You're upset,' said Grandfather. 'Please go to your room and sit with your anger.'"[61] A monster appears to Anh who turns out to be his anger. Anh and his anger decide to play, a play that could also be described as a tantrum, as they howl, pound the ground with their fists and feet. Eventually he sits in a meditation posture together with his anger monster. As they sit, the expression on Anh's face becomes happier and the monster's features soften, eventually turning into a smile as he slowly shrinks into a tiny, happy doll-sized friend. Finally when Ahn and his grandfather gently sit together, Anh's anger has been transformed into a smiling flower and his green tongue has become the flower's stalk.

Anger is accepted as a part of you, but it is an emotion that must be tended to. This teaching on anger and the instrumental role of breathing meditation as an effective means of caring for one's anger is told without Buddhist teachings being directly addressed, as is common with picture books that present meditation as a universal practice usable in any cultural-religious context. Anh's sitting posture is recognizably Buddhist but not explained as such. Anh and his grandfather are recognizably Asian, but nothing in the stylized collage illustration identifies them as a Buddhist family. While the book does not explicitly make the connection, its message expresses Thich Nhat Hanh's teachings on anger, as he discusses in another book for older children, *A Pebble for Your Pocket*. *Anh's Anger* tells us in story and image Thich Nhat Hanh's words:

> Our anger is a part of us. We should not pretend that we are not angry when in fact we are angry. What we need to learn is how to take care of our anger. A good way to take care of our anger is to stop and return to our breathing.... When we take care of our anger like this, we are being "mindful." Mindfulness acts just like the rays of the sun. Without any effort, the sun shines on everything and everything changes because of it. When we expose our anger to the light of mindfulness, it will change, too, like a flower opening to the sun.[62]

59. Thich Nhat Hanh, *Under the Rose Apple Tree*, 3.
60. Gail Silver, *Anh's Anger* (Berkeley, CA: Plum Blossom Books, 2009).
61. Silver, *Anh's Anger*.
62. Thich Nhat Hanh, *A Pebble for Your Pocket*, 24–25.

These books empower children by teaching them not only how to control their anger, but also how to accept themselves even when they experience emotions that are typically cast as negative or bad. They also encourage readers to see meditation as a humanistic practice they can claim as their own. Meditation requires only the commitment to sit and calm the breath and thereby focus the mind. It doesn't require a commitment to be a Buddhist. Meditation becomes an ageless practice, not limited by a person's age or historical location. While the virtues described in broad strokes in these books could be easily identified with specifically Buddhist categories, meditation, as a contextless practice, is seen as the source for generating humanistic values.[63]

READING INTO THE FUTURE

Will "bedtime-story Buddhists" grow up to read these stories to their own children? Will any of the books discussed in this chapter or the many others beyond its scope become children's classics approaching the cultural import of *Curious George*, *Hello Moon*, or *Frog and Toad*? Maria Tatar, the theorist of folklore and children's literature, argues that the power of children's literature is not only in the original moments of discovering these narratives, but in the enchantment born from nostalgia for childhood stories as these narratives are reencountered throughout life.[64] For the adult readers of the picture books discussed here, this nostalgic reunion with cherished childhood stories is not yet possible. The newness of this genre means that children and adults are encountering these narratives together for the first time. The ongoing longevity of these picture books and others like them is yet to be seen. As I've argued here, picture books communicate a nuanced and multidimensional Buddhist worldview to children. One can imagine that a child's understanding of rebirth would be developed by reading and remembering *Samsara Dog*,[65] or that a child would consider what it means to take care of neighbors through the actions described in *Zen Ties*. These picture books may well become the stories Western Buddhists carry through life, both in boxes of childhood treasures and as memories that shape how one lives in the world.

Time will also tell if narratives, beyond but including children's literature, come to form an important part of cultural practices in Western Buddhist communities. At present the number of children's picture books far outweighs adult literature about Buddhism or inspired by Buddhist concepts. Charles Johnson's works are the most notable literary works building a foundation for

63. These values rooted in care for self and others are articulated in many contexts on Buddhist contributions to humanistic ethics. See, for example, H. H. 14th Dalai Lama, *Ethics for the New Millennium* (New York: Riverhead Books, 1999).

64. Maria Tatar, *Enchanted Hunters: The Power of Stories in Childhood* (New York: W. W. Norton & Company, 2009), 19–23.

65. Helen Manos, *Samsara Dog* (San Diego: Kane Miller, 2007).

an English vernacular literary tradition.[66] While the success of the children's picture book genre might be read as an optimistic sign for those who value literary practices in Buddhist traditions, it might also have a stilting effect if narratives are dismissed as valuable solely for children.

This exploration of the multiple categories of children's picture books on Buddhism and inspired by Buddhist ideas or practices suggests that narratives for children can be sophisticated expression with nuanced meanings when children are respected as capable readers. By considering these stories in the broader framework of Buddhist literary traditions, one can better see these deeper levels of meaning, such as the soteriological significance of the *jātakas*. Further, just as vernacular literatures throughout Buddhist Asia have been rich sites of producing particular Buddhist cultures, so too might we look forward to an English Buddhist vernacular tradition that imagines ideal readers of all ages.

66. Charles Johnson, *Middle Passage* (New York: Scribner, 1998); Charles Johnson, *Dreamer: A Novel* (New York: Scribner, 1999); Charles Johnson, *Soul Catcher and Other Stories* (New York: Mariner Books, 2001); Charles Johnson, *Oxherding Tale: A Novel* (New York: Scribner, 2005).

PART TWO

Children and Childhoods in Buddhist Traditions

CHAPTER 9

Ordination (*Pabbajjā*) as Going Forth?

Social Bonds and the Making of a Buddhist Monastic

JEFFREY SAMUELS

It was an unusually cool morning in the small village situated about ten kilometers from Kandy, Sri Lanka. It was approximately 6:00 A.M. on January 1, 2000, and the drone of chanting monks as they finished the all-night protection (*paritta*) ritual had finally ended. The crowd of 150 to 200 laypeople who had gathered in the preaching hall of the temple that night to receive blessings for the new millennium had largely dispersed. Those laypeople still residing at the temple abandoned the hall in hopes of finding a secluded corner where they might catch a few minutes' rest. Although most would be returning to the preaching hall in several hours, they were doing so for a very different reason: an ordination ritual. The candidates—thirteen boys ranging from eight to eighteen years of age—were about to partake in a "lower" or initial (*pabbajjā*) ordination ritual. By doing so, they would become Buddhist novices (*sāmaṇeras*). The audience—made up of patrons of the temple and the family members of the initiates—would also be there. For the former, the ritual would be another way to make merit, which would presumably help them in this life and the next. For the parents, the ritual would symbolize something else: giving away their sons to the Buddhist monastic order.

This chapter examines the processes by which boys become novices. Focusing largely on an ordination ceremony I attended in Sri Lanka, it provides an in-depth description of the ritual from the perspective of one of the thirteen initiates, a boy whom I will call Piyananda.[1] This chapter, however,

1. Piyananda is a pseudonym.

is more than a simple description of an ordination ritual; by briefly assessing the factors that led Piyananda to become a monastic, my aims are twofold. First, I seek to highlight the role that social relationships and affective bonds play in the recruitment and socialization process. Here I challenge the tendency found in some secondary scholarship on Theravāda monasticism to view entry into the monastic order as a means for upward social and economic mobility. Although some scholars[2] have begun considering the range of religious and nonreligious factors that may prompt a young boy to become a Buddhist monastic, the tendency to reduce these to a single factor such as education or social mobility remains somewhat prevalent in Theravāda studies since the publication of David Wyatt's influential essay in 1966.[3]

Second, in highlighting the social matrices that are often behind monastic recruitment and ordination, I will question the very literal understanding of ordination (*pabbajjā*) as "going forth from home into homelessness." Building on the works of some scholars who have maintained the need for social bonds between members of the sangha and the laity,[4] I highlight the role that affective bonds play in monastic culture. Rather than reducing the bonds between the laity and the sangha to economic (for monastics) and religious (for the laity) needs, I argue that such bonds are essential to the maintenance of Buddhist communities in contemporary society. Thus, far from representing an act of going forth from society or a move from home to a life of homelessness, monastic ordination is ritual through which one's ties and social bonds become altered and expanded as they begin to embrace new communities of people, monastic and lay. Before turning to Piyananda and the factors that led him to the sangha, however, it might be helpful to discuss briefly the types of Buddhist ordination rituals in South and Southeast Asia.

2. See, for instance, Y. Hayashi, *Practical Buddhism Among the Thai-Lao: Religion in the Making of a Region* (Kyoto and Melbourne: Kyoto University Press and Trans Pacific Press, 2003), 106.

3. See, for example, Jane Bunnag, *Buddhist Monk, Buddhist Layman: A Study of Urban Monastic Organization in Central Thailand* (Cambridge: Cambridge University Press, 1973); Craig Reynolds, *The Buddhist Monkhood in Nineteenth-Century Thailand* (Ph.D. Dissertation, Cornell University 1972); Stanley J. Tambiah, *World Conqueror and World Renouncer: A Study of Buddhism and Polity in Thailand Against a Historical Background* (Cambridge: Cambridge University Press, 1976); Melford E. Spiro, *Buddhism and Society: A Great Tradition and Its Burmese Vicissitudes*. 2nd ed. 1970 repr. (Berkeley: University of California Press, 1982); Gananath Obeyesekere, "Child Monks: Good or Bad?" *The Sunday Times*, July 8, 2001, Plus Section; and Gananath Obeyesekere, *Medusa's Hair: An Essay on Personal Symbols and Religious Experience* (Chicago: Chicago University Press, 1981).

4. See, for instance, Jane Bunnag, *Buddhist Monk, Buddhist Layman*; and Ilana Friedrich Silber, *Virtuosity, Charisma, and Social Order: A Comparative Sociological Study of Monasticism in Theravada Buddhism and Medieval Catholicism* (Cambridge: Cambridge University Press, 1995); and Ilana Friedrich Silber, "Dissent Through Holiness: The Case of the Radical Renouncer in Theravada Buddhist Countries," *Numen* 28 no. 2 (1981), 164–93.

TYPES OF MONASTIC ORDINATION RITUALS

Traditionally, Buddhist ordination comprises a two-step process: an initial (*pabbajjā*) ceremony, in which the candidate becomes a novice (*sāmaṇera*), and a second (*upasampadā*) ceremony, in which the candidate becomes a monk (Pali: *bhikkhu*; Skt: *bhikṣu*).[5] Although both *pabbajjā* and *upasampadā* ceremonies confer ordination on a candidate, they are quite different.[6] First, while *upasampadā* is bestowed on candidates who are at least twenty years of age,[7] the minimum age for participating in the *pabbajjā* ceremony is fifteen (*Vin.* I.50), though there are certain exceptions.[8] Since most novices have not yet reached adulthood, they are required to have parental consent before entering the sangha, a rule imposed by the Buddha after the acceptance of his own son, Rahula, in

5. For a more complete discussion of monastic ordination in Theravāda Buddhism, see J. R. McRae, "Ordination," *Encyclopedia of Buddhism*, ed. Robert E. Buswell (New York: MacMillan Reference, 2004), 614–18; J. F. Dickson, "The Upasampadā-Kammavācā Being the Buddhist Manual of the Form and Manner of Ordering of Priests and Deacons," *Journal of the Royal Asiatic Society of Great Britain and Ireland* 7 (1874), 1–16; and S. Htun Hmat Win, *The Initiation of Novicehood and the Ordination of Monkhood in the Burmese Buddhist Culture* (Yangon: Department of Religious Affairs, 1986).

6. Originally, it appears that there was no division between ordination ceremonies, since the Buddha merely accepted his first students without any type of formal ritual. Shortly after the death of the Buddha, the two terms began to be used in reference to two different Buddhist initiation ceremonies.

7. The age of twenty is first mentioned in the Mahavagga (I.49; Rhys Davids and Oldenberg, trans. [1968]) section of the *Vinaya Piṭaka*, where the Buddha purportedly decrees: "Let no one, O Bhikkhus, knowingly confer the *upasampadā* ordination on a person under twenty years of age." However, later in the same text the Buddha (drawing on the example of the monk named Kumārakassapa) qualifies that requirement by allowing his monks to calculate a candidate's age from conception and not from the moment of birth (Mv. I.75): "When, O Bhikkhus, in the womb the first thought rises up in the nascent being], the first consciousness manifests itself, according to this the [true] birth should be reckoned. I allow you, O Bhikkhus, to confer the *upasampadā* ordination on persons that have completed the twentieth year from their conception [only]."

8. An exception to this rule was subsequently offered when Ānanda intervened on behalf of two boys who were orphaned at a young age and purportedly asked the Buddha how they can be helped. In response the Buddha proclaims that they can go forth so long as they can "scare away crows" (*Vin.* I.51), an age generally interpreted to be about eight years old (see Amy Langenberg's contribution in this volume). One monk I spoke to in Sri Lanka about this rule suggested that the reference to scaring away crows appears to have more to do with the age at which boys are given certain agricultural responsibilities (and thus must protect the fields against crows), than merely being physically strong enough to pick up a rock and throw it at a crow. From my own research with over sixty monks and novices in Sri Lanka, it appears that the average age of ordination is somewhere between ten and twelve.Unlike in Thailand or Sri Lanka, in Burma the acceptable age for entering the sangha as a *sāmaṇera* is as young as two years. In these cases, it is not unusual for the young boy's father to stay in the temple with his son. For a fuller account of the *pabbajjā* ceremony in Burma, see Htun Hmat Win, *The Initiation of Novicehood and the Ordination of Monkhood in the Burmese Buddhist Culture*.

the sangha caused the Buddha's father, Suddhodana, much grief.[9] Another difference between the *pabbajjā* and *upasampadā* ceremonies pertains to the number of precepts that must be followed; while novices keep ten precepts,[10] fully ordained monks must abide by the 227 rules listed in the *Pāṭimokkha* section of the *Vinaya Piṭaka*.

In terms of the options for becoming a monastic, Sri Lanka is different from the other Theravāda countries (e.g., Myanmar, Thailand, Cambodia, and Laos). Unlike those countries, there is no widely accepted system of temporary ordination in Sri Lanka.[11] Although there have been several movements to introduce such a system—such as at Kanduboḍa International Meditation Center outside of Colombo, Gaṅgārāma temple in Colombo, and, most recently, at Dekanduvala Meditation Center in Horana[12]—the monkhood in Sri Lanka (for both novices and fully ordained monks) is still perceived to be a lifelong commitment,[13] an idea that goes back to the *Vinaya Piṭaka* (I.58), in which

9. This rule was discussed in M. Wijayaratna, *Buddhist Monastic Life: According to the Texts of the Theravada Tradition*, trans. Claude Grangier and Steven Collins (Cambridge: Cambridge University Press, 1990), 14; Kate Crosby, "'Only If You Let Go of That Tree': Ordination Without Parental Consent in Theravāda Vinaya," *Buddhist Studies Review* 22 (2005), 155–73; and Amy Langenberg in this volume. In the Mahāvagga (I.54) section of the *Vinaya*, the Buddha—after being confronted by his own father, Suddhodhana—decreed: "Let no son, O Bhikkhus, receive the *pabbaggâ* [or *pabbajjā*] ordination without his father's and mother's permission." In Sri Lanka, it is incumbent upon the head monk to ensure that a candidate for ordination has his parents' consent; the Sri Lankan government does not require formal consent.

10. These are outlined in *Vin* I.55 and will be discussed below.

11. In many of these countries, every male is expected to become a monk for a short period of time. In Thailand, the system of temporary ordination is usually applied to young men who are at least twenty years old. The reason is because of the greater merit that can be gained: if a monk ordains at twenty, he is able to partake in the *upasampadā* ceremony, thereby accruing more merit for himself and his family. In Burma, however, the same system is usually applied to pubescent and prepubescent boys. For instance, in Spiro's sample of sixty boys seeking temporary ordination in Burma, the mean age was eleven (Melford E. Spiro, *Buddhism and Society*, 235). I should also note that although most people in Sri Lanka (e.g., Amarasiri Weeraratne. "Vinaya—Rules and the Sangha," *The Island*, August 19, 2003, Features) continue to view ordination as a lifelong commitment, a small minority do see a system of temporary ordination as serving a good purpose in society, since it would create a more moral and honest society (see, for instance, Candra Wickremegamage,. "Tavakalika Paevidda Ratata Yahapatak [Temporary Ordination Is Better for the Country]," *Lankadipa* December 27, 1999; and Ruwanthi Herat Gunaratne. "From Layman to Monk in Two Weeks." *Sunday Times*, February 3, 2002, Plus).

12. In these temples, the temporary ordination system is directed toward the upper, often English-speaking, elite, unlike the more inclusive models in Thailand and Burma.

13. While Gombrich has remarked that "there is no stigma attached to leaving [the monkhood] before receiving the higher ordination," (Richard Gombrich, "Temporary Ordination in Sri Lanka," *Journal of the International Association of Buddhist Studies* 7 no. 2 [1984], 45) my research at two *sāmaṇera* training centers indicates otherwise. As will be shown below, there is a certain degree of stigma attached to leaving the sangha as a novice, especially for those who come from rural areas.

candidates seeking to enter the sangha are told that ordination is for the rest of their lives (*yāvajīvaṃ*).

I should also note that the categories of temporary and permanent are ideal, canonical types. With the lifelong ordination system in Sri Lanka, for example, we must bear in mind that although there might be social pressure to remain in the order, society's acceptance of former monks is varied and the rate of leaving the order remains quite high.[14] While the rural population is still noted for chiding and even harassing monks who have recently left the order, returning to lay life is more accepted among the urban populations, who regard well-educated monastics who have left the sangha as being able to contribute to society. My conversations with several well-educated former monks living in and around Kandy revealed that even though monks expected to be criticized by the laypeople around them, they were in fact treated quite well and welcomed back into lay society. Despite the increasingly tolerant attitudes toward disrobing in urban centers, most young initiates from villages around the ancient capital of Anurādhapura took part in the ordination ritual with an awareness that they would not be welcomed back as laypeople. This was certainly the case for Piyananda: after seeing his older brother return home to the anger of his father after spending six years in robes, it was clear to him that ordination should not be taken lightly.

Finally, as this study concerns monastic ordination in the Theravāda tradition, it may be helpful to point out the obvious: that the different views concerning ordination—that is, that it is either a lifelong commitment or something that could be quite temporary—clearly suggests that the very notion of "a" Theravāda tradition is problematic. Although the term "Theravāda" may function as a convenient tool for Theravādins to imagine themselves as part of something greater—or by others to highlight differences between most Buddhists living in South and Southeast Asia from those living in other regions—there is no unitary "Theravāda" tradition.

When we turn to individual "Theravāda" countries such as Sri Lanka, Burma, Thailand, Laos, and Cambodia, we encounter a similar problem. Although we can speak about Sri Lankan or Thai Buddhism, we should bear in mind that even at the national level, there is no single institutional entity called Theravāda. In Sri Lanka, for instance, one finds three different sects of Buddhists; while all three adhere to a common monastic disciplinary code—the Pali *Vinaya*—each sect (including many of their subsects) have particular injunctions (e.g., how to wear the robe, what type of umbrella to carry, whether or not to shave the eyebrows, and so on). Thus, while there may be 37,000 Theravāda monastics in Sri Lanka today,[15] the very ideas about what it means to be a monk or novice vary

14. There are no statistics on the percentage of monks leaving the order. However, from the perspectives of the older monks with whom I spoke, the rate of leaving may be as high as 80–90 percent.

15. C. R. de Silva, "Categories, Identity and Difference: Buddhist Monks (*Bhikkhus*) and Peace in Lanka," *Lines* (2003), 4. The 37,000 may be broken up according to sect or Nikāya as 18,000 (Siyam), 12,000 (Amarapura), 7000 (Rāmañña).

considerably between those who restrict ordination to Sri Lanka's high Goyigama caste, and those who do not; between those whose main source of support may come from fields rented out to cultivators, and those whose land holdings are quite small and who must rely regularly on the generosity of the laity; between those who believe that monks should have a place in politics, and those who feel that a monastic should confine his service to the people's social and religious needs; between those whose primary efforts are oriented toward the practice of meditation, and those whose efforts fall largely under the category of study or the so-called burden of the book (*granthadhura*). This contrast becomes even more dizzying if we consider that while almost all young monastics study in a monastic college or *piriveṇa* where they follow a national curriculum issued by the Ministry of Education, their training and socialization is often left in the hands of their own teachers and head monks, who—through a system of advising, rewarding, and punishing—instill in their students particular visions of monastic life and what constitutes an acceptable vocation.

IMPETUS FOR BECOMING A NOVICE

Piyananda became a Buddhist monastic at the age of twelve after living in a temple as an ordinand for several months. When I asked him who first came up with the idea of becoming a monastic, he immediately replied "Father." As I have discussed more fully elsewhere,[16] after hearing about the forthcoming ordination ritual at the temple in Kandy, Piyananda's father approached his son and suggested that he become a monastic. The decision to direct his son to a temple did not come from nowhere. Two years earlier, Piyananda failed to pass the fifth-grade scholarship exam; although not passing the exam carries no negative repercussions, it caused Piyananda to lose faith in his abilities as a student. Preferring to hang out in the village and watch television rather than focus on his studies, Piyananda's father saw his son's ranking in school become lower and lower. After watching his son struggle for two years, Piyananda's father decided to circumvent what he saw to be a harmful path down which his son was traveling by directing him toward the temple. Piyananda was also clearly aware of what was going on; thus, when his father approached him about ordaining, Piyananda readily agreed, understanding that if he stayed at home, he would surely become a "wretch," like a number of other children in the village who gave up on their studies.

In many ways, Piyananda's case study supports a view of monastic recruitment that scholars have sometimes advanced: that many "join the monkhood to get a free education and the prospect of later employment."[17] Indeed, for

16. Jeffrey Samuels, *Attracting the Heart: Social Relations and the Aesthetics of Emotion in Sri Lankan Monastic Culture* (Honolulu: University of Hawaii Press, 2010).
17. Gananath Obeyesekere, *Medusa's Hair, An Essay on Personal Symbols and Religious Experience* (Chicago: Chicago University Press, 1981), 43.

Piyananda and his father, the sangha itself provided the means to obtain numerous educational opportunities as well as a way to curtail what they saw as harmful behavior.[18] At the same time, however, it became increasingly clear to me as I began to reflect on my conversations with Piyananda and his father that while the temple provided the boy with certain educational opportunities, the choice of becoming a monastic was also based on other factors, including social ties that often extended well beyond the walls of a single family concerned with upward mobility. The close bonds that the family had formed with monastics not only prompted Piyananda's father to consider the possibility that his son should become a monastic,[19] but also led Piyananda to evaluate his father's idea in a positive manner. When I asked Piyananda why he agreed to become a novice, he explained: "I associated with monks in the temple to a great extent (*bohō durața*). They helped us to learn. They gave us books and such when we went there. We were treated well. They were affectionate to us. They used to call us "younger brother" (*mallī*). When I went to the [temple's] dharma school (*daham pāsäla*), I wasn't really interested in learning. I went there waiting for the young novices to come. They were really affectionate to me. They liked me very much.... Even the head monk kept a plate of rice for me when I returned from school." Such replies suggest to me that while becoming a monastic provides one with certain opportunities, the decision itself may be prompted by a whole range of social and emotional factors; any single theory about recruitment may overlook other "situational variables" that—more often than not—play a crucial role in the recruitment process.[20]

THE ORDINATION RITUAL AND TEMPLE PRETRAINING

Piyananda arrived at the temple on October 10, 1999. Less than three months later, on January 1, 2000, he became a novice. He lived by a temple in Anurādhapura and attended his elder brother's ordination when he was quite

18. See also P. P. Pannapadipo, *Little Angels* (Bangkok: Post Publishing, 2001), 183–99.

19. When I asked Piyananda how he ended up at a temple so far from his home in Anurādhapura, he explained: "When my father comes to this temple, [the monk] Dhammadassi used to treat him well. The other reason is that those young novices who are in this temple always visited us during the new year and [school] vacation[s]. They brought sarongs and gifts for my father. Father also treated them well when he had the means to do so.... My father looked after Dhammadassi like his own child when Dhammadassi used to come to our home for the new year....Dhammadassi used to bring clothes to father. Father likes Dhammadassi. We too like him."

20. This notion of situational variables is discussed in Stark and Bainbridge's excellent essay on religious recruitment. See Rodney Stark and William Sims Bainbridge, "Networks of Faith: Interpersonal Bonds and Recruitment to Cults and Sects," in *The Future of Religion: Secularization, Revival and Cult Formation*, ed. Rodney Stark and William Sims Bainbridge (Berkeley: University of California Press, 1985), 323.

young; nonetheless, he—like most of the other twelve boys becoming novices on that day—had little understanding of the meaning and content of monastic life. While their lack of knowledge would seemingly precipitate some form of premonastic training for the ordinands, there was a complete absence of any formal training. Conversations with senior monastics suggest that such a pre-training was in place when they were ordinands; however, as many of them pointed out to me, there has been an increasing tendency to ordain initiates with little or no preparation.[21] Despite the existence of several types of novitiate handbooks (e.g., the *Sāmaṇera Baṇadaham Pota* and the *Śāsanāvataraṇaya*), the head monk at the temple where Piyananda ordained felt that using a handbook would be futile since many of the boys were unable to read well enough. In lieu of a more formal training, the head monk felt that just living in the temple and spending time alongside other monastics would sufficiently prepare the initiates for the beginnings of monastic life:

> It is not my own advice that is important. The thing I do here is put them into the group. For example, take a trained group of hunting dogs. If you put another dog among them, the newcomer will be trained automatically. The newcomer doesn't know what to do but by being in a group, he automatically learns. I cannot approach the ordinands so easily because I am older than they are. They have their own age groups so I cannot be with them. They do it [among] themselves. The method I am using here is like that. It is more important than the teachings I give them. My teaching is secondary.[22]

By potential candidates being placed in the same dormitory rooms as similarly aged novices from identical regions or villages, close bonds naturally begin to form. As newcomers tag along with their new monastic-friend(s) and start imitating their behavior and deportment throughout their daily activities and

21. Commenting on this particular change, Välamiṭiyāvē Kusaladhamma, the head of Vidyālaṅkāra Piriveṇa in Colombo, noted: "I became a monk after being in the temple for four years. I was a boy for four years in the temple and then became a monk. During that [ordinand] period, I became aware of my teachers. I became aware of the activities of a temple. I became aware of the devotees who were connected to the temple. I became close to the temple. Then I became a monk. Now, that method no longer exists. Now they bring boys, keep them for one month, ordain them, and send them to a monastic college [or *piriveṇa*] after one month.... They don't teach them about the life of a monk." As I have mentioned elsewhere, it was such changes regarding monastic training that led to the creation of a new monastic training institution in 1992, the Sāmaṇera Bhikṣu Puhuṇu Madhyasthāna (Sāmaṇera-Bhikkhu Training Institute). See Jeffrey Samuels, "Establishing the Basis of the Sasana: Social Service and Ritual Performance in Contemporary Sri Lankan Monastic Training," in *Approaching the Dhamma: Buddhist Texts and Practices in South and Southeast Asia*, ed. Anne Blackburn and Jeffrey Samuels (Seattle: BPS Pariyatti Editions, 2003), 105–24; and Jeffrey Samuels, *Attracting the Heart*.

22. Quoted in Jeffrey Samuels, *Attracting the Heart*, 64.

duties, the newly recruited boys naturally become adjusted to and learn about monastic life.[23]

The day before the ordination ceremony, the head monk assembled all of the initiates on the roof of a building that was under construction, to prepare them for the following day's events. He demonstrated how he wanted them to line up for the ceremony and how to sit properly in the squatting position. Lining the boys up according to their height, the head monk explained: "Tomorrow you have to line up like this. I cannot remind you tomorrow morning how to arrange yourselves. There will not be enough time. So, you have to remember the people who are on both sides of you now." Then, telling Piyananda and the other boys assembled how to sit in the squatting position, the head monk continued:

> Keep in mind the following procedures which are to take place tomorrow: I will tell you the verses and then I will tie the belt around your neck. At that time, you have to recite the verse recollecting the use of the robes. Since you have not learned it by heart, I will recite it and you should repeat it. Then we will go out of the room and I will help you put on your robes. At that time, I will recite other verses of recollection and you will have to repeat them. Once dressed, you will come back into the hall in robes. I will then recite [more verses and]...you should repeat them. Then I will give you the [ten] precepts.
>
> ...Do you still remember now how to line up? You have to be ready by 8:00 A.M. to have your head shaved. Before tomorrow morning, you have to bathe. Wash your clothes and do not forget to clean your teeth properly. Be ready by 8:00 tomorrow morning. By tomorrow you should be ready to go ahead with the ceremony. Keep in mind that from tomorrow, I will be strict with you and there will be more rules and regulations. If you cannot follow them, you should leave now. It is no problem. You should not play today. Do not run here and there. If you break your legs or hands, you cannot partake in the ceremony tomorrow.
>
> ...If you have an extra pair of good trousers, you can give them to the others who do not have any. If you have extra clothes in your bags, take them out and give them to the others who might need them. Do not keep the extra clothes in your bag. There will be no one to wear them after tomorrow.

As I began to reflect on the *pabbajjā* ritual and the days leading up to the event, I began to realize that while not much consideration was given to the

23. I have referred to this type of training as an "action-oriented pedagogy" in "Toward an Action-Oriented Pedagogy: Buddhist Texts and Monastic Education in Contemporary Sri Lanka," *Journal of the American Academy of Religion* 72 no. 4 (2004): 955–71. For further work on this form of training and education, see Jean Lave and Etienne Wenger, *Situated Learning: Legitimate Peripheral Participation* (Cambridge: Cambridge University Press, 1991); and Anna M. Gade, *Perfection Makes Practice: Learning, Emotion, and the Recited Qur'an in Indonesia* (Honolulu: University of Hawaii Press, 2004).

content and meaning of ordination and life in the sangha—including the actual precepts that the boys will be required to follow—a large amount of attention was given to what might be called an "aesthetic" of ordination, something that Borchert also discusses at length in this volume. In other words, rather than teaching his students what the Pāli-language verses that they will soon recite actually mean (as none of the boys knew Pāli), the head monk was curiously preoccupied with how the ordinands behaved and, more important, how they looked: being clean, well-dressed, with brushed teeth, and physically restrained. Moreover, the desire to order the initiates in terms of their physical height rather than their age or their seniority as initiates points to further examples of the importance given to the aesthetics of monastic ordination. Finally, during the same morning as the head monk's advice, the ordinands were also asked to prostrate in front of their parents as soon as they arrived and to inquire after their well-being, again pointing to the importance of proper behavior and discipline.

Piyananda's parents arrived on December 31 at approximately 4:00. Although his brother who was previously a monastic at the temple did not show up, his parents, uncles, aunts, and other siblings were there to share in the festivities. Piyananda was anxiously awaiting his family's arrival most of the afternoon. As they began to make their way up the steep driveway leading to the temple, he walked briskly over to meet them. After they exchanged greetings, Piyananda brought his family over to meet with the temple's head monk.

The remainder of the afternoon was spent catching up. When Piyananda's parents dashed out of the temple to buy some last-minute items, he hung out with his younger brother, showing him around the temple and introducing him to his new temple-friends.[24] All in all, the mood at the temple that afternoon and evening was quite jovial, reminiscent of family weekend at a sleep-away summer camp.

Ordination day began at 6:00 A.M. Piyananda, washed his face and brushed his teeth, as did the other ordinands and their family members. Then, as usual, it was time to venerate the Buddha (*Buddhapūjā*) in the image house (*piḷimagē*). The ordinands followed the novices and, once inside the image house, sat alongside them. Piyananda and several other novices who had already learned some of the verses by heart chanted with the monks and novices. A quick breakfast followed. Too excited to eat, Piyananda had only several mouthfuls of food.

At approximately 8:30, the head monk and his deputy rounded up the ordinands and brought them over to the bathing tank that sat opposite the row of toilets. There, the novices were asked to line up in the order they were shown the day before. As they approached the head monk, he cut a short lock of their hair. Piyananda was fourth in line. His own lock of hair was placed in his hands. He was beaming as he stood there with his lock of hair cupped carefully in his hands, which were held closely at his waist.

24. Several years after Piyananda's ordination, his younger brother also became a monastic at the same temple.

As his turn approached, Piyananda was led to the bathing tank, where his mother—with tears streaming down her cheeks—rinsed and shampooed his hair. Then, with shampoo still in his hair, an older novice approached and began shaving Piyananda's head. During the shaving, Piyananda was supposed to recite, to himself, the five Pāli words, *kesā, lomā, nakhā, dantā, taco* (head hair, body hair, nail, teeth, skin), that make up the skin pentad (*tacapañcakakamaṭṭhāna*) of the thirty-two objects of mindfulness that pertain to the foulness of the body (*kāyānupassanā paṭikūlamanasikārapabbaṃ*).[25] This was supposed to be Piyananda's first lesson on mindfulness of the body (*kāyānupassanā*), but he was unable to focus his mind on the verses amidst the excitement and the jostling for space at the bathing tank.

Once Piyananda's head was shaven, he was brought back to the bathing tank, where his mother washed and rinsed him. He was then led to a space right beside the tank, where his mother tied a white sarong around him, removed his shorts, and placed an upper white sash over his left shoulder.[26] When all of the other initiates were dressed in white as well, they were lined up and led to the lower residence hall. There, Piyananda and the others were given a cup of tea. Several sets of parents took photographs of their sons; Piyananda's father did not have a camera with him that day.

Once everyone finished their tea, oil was rubbed into their heads, presumably to prevent their heads from becoming dry and irritable. Then all the family members and patrons were asked to go to the nearby preaching hall At that point, the head monk asked the boys to line up once again. Following the three boys standing in front of him, Piyananda—and those behind him—began walking toward the preaching hall. As the initiates waited at the entrance to the packed hall, four fully ordained monks (i.e., those who had gone through the *upasampadā* ritual), made their way through the hall and, facing the crowd, sat down on cloth-covered chairs that were placed in the front of the room.[27] Before the initiates entered the room, straw mats were laid out on the floor directly in front of the chairs where the elder monks sat.

At the head monk's signal, the initiates began filing into the room to the audience's approving cries of "*sādhu, sādhu, sā*" (It is good, it is good, it is good).[28] Once they were in front of the room, the head monk asked the boys to turn around (so as to face the audience) and sit down. While the boys were

25. This is outlined in M I.57 and D II.293f.; for further commentary, see Vism. VIII.49ff.

26. Several older monks mentioned to me that when they became ordinands in a temple, they were always dressed in white, a sign of their purity as a monastic-in-training. In more recent times, however, white clothing is not commonly worn by ordinands, because it would be difficult for them to keep it clean. During all of *pabbajjā* rituals I attended, the ordinands were dressed in white robes only on the actual day of their ordination.

27. Later the four elder monks were joined by two more.

28. This is a customary phrase said when a beneficial or meritorious action is being performed. The work *sādhu* may be translated as good, virtuous, and/or meritorious.

seated, the parents of each initiate was asked to come forward and stand in front of their sons. As their parents stood in front of them, the initiates prostrated at their parents' feet. There was nothing unusual in seeing a child show respect to his or her parents by prostrating; what marked this particular act was that this would be the last time that any of the initiates would do so. Indeed, as monastics are the most respected members of Sri Lankan society, all people—including the prime minster and president—must prostrate themselves in front of members of the sangha. Although many of the boys did not yet catch the significance of this fact—though they would as soon as they put on their robes—it was clear that several crying parents clearly comprehended the significance of their sons' actions.

With the boys facing the seated monks again, the head monk announced: "Today is an historic day. Today we end 1999 and enter into 2000. We have all gathered today to make merit. We are now going to chant *pirit* [protection verses] to bless the boys who are going to ordain in a little while." The seated monks then recited a number of discourses (*suttas*) and protection verses to bless and protect the initiates: the *Ratanasutta, Maṅgalasutta, Karaṇīyamettasutta, Aṭavisi pirit,* and *Mahājinapañjarasutta.*[29]

The recitation lasted approximately twenty minutes. Once finished, the boys were asked to stand up and face the audience again. Parents were then requested to come forward to offer robes to their sons. Although most parents, like Piyananda's parents, purchased the robes themselves, several who could not afford the cost of new robes were given a set from the temple. As the parents came forward, the initiates unfolded a small, white, square piece of cloth and placed it over their forearms. As the parents placed the robes on the outstretched cloth, the audience once again responded with shouts of *sādhu, sādhu, sā.*

The boys faced the monks and sat down with their palms joined together at chin level and their new robes placed on their forearms, close to their chest. Prompted by the head monk, the initiates recited a Pāli verse asking permission to go forth.[30] Following this verse—which none of the boys understood, since it was in the ancient language of Pāli and not Sinhala—the boys were prompted to recite another Pāli verse: "Leaving behind all suffering [and] seeing with my own eyes enlightenment, please, oh reverend sir, having taken this yellow robe, ordain me." As soon as the boys recited this verse three times, the head monk and his assistant took the robes from the initiates and stacked

29. This last discourse is quite unique in the Theravāda tradition. If the *sutta* is recited, it is believed, a cage (*pañjara*) of protection made up of Buddhist arahants is built around one's body. For a more complete description of this discourse, see Roger Jackson's article, "A Tantric Echo in Sinhalese Theravada? Pirit Ritual, the Book of Paritta and the Jinapanjaraya," *Journal of the Rare Buddhist Texts Research Project* 18 (1994), 121–40.

30. The Pāli verse is:
Okāsa ahaṃ bhante pabbajjāṃ yācāmi.Dutiyampi okāsa ahaṃ bhante pabbajjāṃ yācāmi.Tatiyampi okāsa ahaṃ bhante pabbajjāṃ yācāmi..(I ask permission to go forth, oh reverend one.)

them on their laps. Now, with their palms joined together again, the boys were prompted to recite another verse which, with the exception of replacing the words having taken (*gahetvā*) with having given (*datvā*), was identical to the previous one. Heeding the initiates' request, the head monk asked each boy to come forward and assume the squatting position. Then, after checking his watch for the right or auspicious time at which to "ordain" the children, the head monk suddenly began tying the belt of the robes around each initiate's neck to symbolize the act of ordination. As each belt was tied, the audience cried out *sādhu, sādhu, sā*.

With their belts tied around their necks, the boys began filing out of the hall toward an adjacent room. There, the head monk and more senior novices helped them put on their new robes. Although monastics who have been in robes for some time are quite comfortable with their robes draped around them, the initiates appeared awkward. Piyananda, after having his robes put on him, began fidgeting as he adjusted and readjusted the robes and his own posture to keep his robes from falling off his shoulder.

It took approximately twenty minutes to dress the thirteen initiates. In their absence, cloth and blankets were strewn over the straw mats where the postulants had sat earlier. Since the boys were about to become monks, their seats had to resemble those of monastics, and this was accomplished by covering them with a cloth. Once the boys were ready, the head monk and the other senior monks entered the room and took their seats. The initiates then entered the room in single file. Their arrival was met by even louder cries of *sādhu, sādhu, sā*, lasting from the first moment they entered the room to when the last initiate sat down. Although Piyananda experienced some conflicting emotions throughout the event, he had a beaming smile as he entered the room.

As soon as the new initiates sat in place and their robes were properly adjusted, the head monk called the first (tallest) boy to sit directly in front of him with his palms joined together. Holding the boy's forefingers, he began reciting verses about the impermanent constituents of the body. Each boy, in succession, repeated the verses while sitting in front of the head monk.[31] After doing the same for each initiate, the head monk prompted them, by having them repeat another Pali verse, to ask for the ten precepts with the triple refuge.[32] While remaining in the squatting position, the boys recited the triple refuge formula three times: "I go to the Buddha [for] refuge, I go to the dharma [for] refuge, I go to the sangha [for] refuge." After taking refuge, the

31. This is the same verse that was recited when the boys were getting their heads shaved: "*kesā, lomā, nakhā, dantā, taco* (head hair, body hair, nail, teeth, skin)." This time, however, each boy, following the lead of the head monk, recited the verse in a forward, backward, and forward order.

32. The verse in Pāli is: *ōkāsa ahaṃ bante tisaraṇena saddhiṃ pabbajjā dasasīlaṃ dhammaṃ yacāmi anuggahaṃ katvā sīlaṃ detha me bhante* (I, going forth, ask for the ten precepts with the triple refuge. Please, oh reverend sir, give me the precepts).

head monk administered the ten precepts: (1) not to take life, (2) not to take what is not given, (3) not to engage in sexual relations, (4) not to lie, (5) not to take intoxicants, (6) not to eat after midday, (7) not to watch shows or listen to musical performances, (8) not to wear garlands or perfumes, (9) not to sleep on high beds, and (10) not to accept gold and silver.

Some lay people follow the same ten precepts when observing full moon or *poya* day celebrations. The ten precepts that the novices vowed to follow, while not different in content, was different in meaning. When a layperson takes the ten precepts (or the five or eight), he or she recites *sikkhāpadaṃ samādiyāmi* ("I undertake the precept") after each one. Thus for a layperson the precept regarding refraining from taking life would be: *pāṇātipātā veramaṇi sikkhāpadaṃ samādiyāmi* (literally, "I take on myself (*samādiyāmi*) the precept (*sikkhāpadaṃ*) of refraining (*veramaṇi*) from taking life (*pāṇātipātā*)." When the precepts were administered to initiates, however, the *sikkhāpadaṃ samādiyāmi* was omitted after each precept. It was only after all ten precepts were taken that the novices were prompted to say: *imāni pabbajjā dasasikkhāpadāni samādiyāmi* (I take upon myself these ten precepts of one who has gone forth). Even though the difference between saying *sikkhāpadaṃ samādiyāmi* after each precept or waiting until the end to say one *sikkhāpadaṃ samādiyāmi* appears quite inconsequential, the change is significant. Implied in the difference is that all ten precepts are bound together with a common "undertaking." In other words, for members of the sangha, all of the precepts form one great precept so that when one precept is broken, all the others are deemed null and void.[33] Novices, thus, are supposed to be particularly careful about upholding all of the precepts.[34]

The boys prostrated themselves in front of the seated monks. This time, the newly ordained novices placed an ocher-colored cloth down on the ground in front of them before prostrating, so when they bent their heads forward, their heads would touch the cloth and not the ground. As the boys prostrated themselves, the seated monks blessed them. The newly ordained novices then faced the audience and the head monk asked the mothers of the initiates to come forward. The mothers came forward and prostrated themselves in front of their sons while their sons blessed them. Some with tears running down their cheeks, some crying quite heavily, and others, somewhat unemotional, gave gifts (e.g., suitcases, sandals, umbrellas, pillows, and so on) to their newly ordained sons, many of whom, like Piyananda, were uncomfortable seeing their parents prostrated before them. After the women gave the gifts, the head

33. This interpretation was offered to me by the head monk officiating at the ritual. A similar explanation was also offered to Tessa Bartholomeusz by a monk officiating at the ordination of novice women. See her *Women Under the Bo Tree: Buddhist Nuns in Sri Lanka* (New York: Cambridge University Press, 1994), 167.

34. At this point, initiates are typically assigned to a spiritual guide (*upajjhāya*) and teacher (*ācariya*). During this ceremony, however, this part of the ritual was omitted. When I later asked the head monk why he decided to pass over this part of the ceremony, he said that the monks were getting restless and, as a result of the large number of boys partaking in the ceremony, it was already getting close to the time when the monks were supposed to eat their midday meal.

monk asked the men to come forward to offer their newly ordained sons the eight monastic requisites (*aṭapirikaraya*): lower robe, upper robe, under robe (vest), needle, bowl, water strainer, belt, and razor. As each male carried the *aṭapirikaraya* to the boys, the audience exclaimed: *sādhu, sādhu, sā*.

Before the end of the ceremony, the head monk gave a speech in which he praised the children, their relatives, and the patrons of the temple. Although the speech itself lasted fifteen minutes, I am including the following segment which, I believe, captures the general sense of the head monk's speech:

> I decided to ordain several boys to commemorate the twenty-fifth year of my [own] ordination.... The boys came a short while ago. After staying here in the temple, receiving the donors' affection and love (*ādaraya*), and the great sangha's compassion, they took part in a wonderful opportunity by becoming novices this morning. Becoming a disciple of the Buddha is a very important occasion. It is invaluable. To receive it, you have to wish for it from an early birth in *saṃsāra* and continue to wish for it birth after birth. It is not easy to acquire....
>
> This group ordained, leaving aside their parents' affection, their relatives, their friends, and the lay life that they enjoyed a lot. They have sacrificed all that to enter into the religion of the perfectly enlightened Buddha. My own teacher is here. He is ninety years old and he has been serving the religion for seventy years. I hope that the small novices will also have the strength to do a long service to the religion. They have to have great determination and they have to do well to win the hearts and impressions of the donors and fulfill the respect of their parents and the head monk. They have to be determined to protect the respect of all their brother-monks. They have to be determined to become fruitful monks to the religion by doing all religious activities and all temple duties.
>
> I would like to remind the parents and the relatives who came from afar that the donors are the ones who feed the monastics. The donors protect the young novices like their own children. Sometimes they care for the novices when they are ill, just as if they were their own children. The devotees in this temple are compassionate and affectionate and they are kind not only to the young novices but to the older monks as well. I think that it is difficult to find a group of devotees who are so kind and so very loyal to the religion, even if you search all over the country.
>
> Today these young monks have received the compassion and the concern of the devotees. These young monks will not miss their parents, because they will have many mothers and fathers.... Parents, you must be happy that you have selected the best place in the whole country for your sons.

At the end of the speech, which will be discussed further, everyone—monastic and lay—began clearing out of the assembly hall. As the monks were getting prepared, the laity began transforming the preaching hall into an alms-giving hall. With tables, benches, plates, and cups in place, the monastics began filing into the hall once again. They took their places, in order of their seniority, at the tables circling the room. For many of them, it was just another alms-giving ritual. For thirteen boys, it was their first meal as Buddhist monastics.

The meal was followed by several hours of mingling and comparing, among themselves, the gifts they received. At 3:00 Piyananda's family, like so many others, began trickling out of the temple. For some novices, seeing their parents leave was quite upsetting. Several of them asked to go home with their parents; others, like Piyananda, were accustomed to life in the temple. For them, life in the temple resumed, though with one difference: they were wearing saffron robes. Indeed, for many of the novices, putting on their monastic robes was the most significant part of the ordination ritual. As the most palpable symbol of their new status as Buddhist monastics, the saffron-colored robes had a clear impact on the manner in which the newly ordained viewed themselves as well as how others viewed and treated them.

Because the post-ordination training of novices has been explored elsewhere,[35] I will not discuss it in depth here. I would like to reiterate, however, that even though most novices began a more formal course of study at a monastic school or *piriveṇa*, most newly ordained novices I spoke with, including Piyananda, felt that they learned as much as or even more about being a monastic through working alongside their peers and participating in monastic rituals and events. Indeed, by becoming members of what might be called "communities of learning and practice," many novices came to learn about what is expected of them and how to conduct themselves as monastics.

What also became quite evident from my conversations with several newly ordained novices is how the budding relationship between them and the temple's donors affected the novices' views of themselves. When I interviewed Piyananda approximately two months after the ordination ceremony about the changes he perceived in himself, he said that while he was just interested in studying beforehand, he now wants to become a head monk in order to serve Sri Lankan society. When I asked him what contributed to that change, he replied: "After seeing the donors here, hearing them talk about us, and seeing how close they are to us, I began to understand that the donors are good [people]. They come to the temple and look after us. They bring us meals and make sure that we are well. So, I want to serve them."

ORDINATION AS A GOING FORTH? SOCIAL BONDS AND THE MAKING OF A BUDDHIST NOVICE

The Pāli term that is often used to designate the lower ordination ritual is *pabbajjā*. The term—which is derived from the prefix *pa* plus the verbal root √*vraj*— literally, means to go (*vraj*) forth (*pa*). Etymologically, then, the term

35. Jeffrey Samuels, *Attracting the Heart*, chapter 4.

pabbajjā may be understood as an act of going forth.[36] Given the literal meaning of the term, it is not surprising that some scholars[37]—focusing on the literal meaning of *pabbajjā* as "leaving the world" or drawing on the characterization of Buddhism as a form of otherworldly asceticism—have tended to view worldly monks with suspicion.[38]

Despite its literal meaning, most scholars recognize that the survival of the sangha is founded upon establishing and maintaining harmonious ties with society. This is most clearly articulated in Rupert Gethin's introductory text where he aptly surmises that "the basis of the renouncer's lifestyle lies in two things: (1) renunciation of the household life for the sake of the religious life, and (2) dependence upon the generosity of the population at large for the provision of material needs—food, clothing, and dwellings."[39]

Although the relationship between the sangha and society is often portrayed as one of reciprocal exchange (in which the members of the sangha receive material support in exchange for religious teachings, the performance of rituals, and the opportunity to make merit), it is clear that the ties are based not only on economic and religious exchange. Even though the head monk's speech about the affectionate and supportive temple patrons may be understood as a form of flattery to ensure a continuous flow of goods from the village to the temple, I believe that his speech reveals something more about monastic training and life in saffron robes.

In my conversations with Piyananda and other novices, it became increasingly evident that just as affectionate ties between groups of monks and the laity facilitate monastic recruitment, so too do such bonds play a role in the socialization process. By drawing connections between the parents of the newly ordained novices, the temple donors, and the head monk's own teacher, the head monk presiding over the ceremony sought to instill in the novices a particular vision of their role in the sangha. Rather than distracting one from the so-called "path of renunciation," social bonds and experiences of affection and love shape and even increase the newly ordained novices' commitment to their roles as Buddhist monastics. Given the importance of such bonds, then, it is should not be surprising that the head monk also emphasized the importance of being clean and well dressed prior to the ordination ritual; seeing something beautiful has the potential to facilitate the building of close bonds.

36. T. W. Rhys Davids and William Stede, *Pali-English Dictionary* (London: The Pali Text Society, 1972), 414.
37. See, for example, Max Weber, *The Religion of India: The Sociology of Hinduism and Buddhism* (Glencoe, IL: The Free Press, 1958), 267–301; K. E. Wells, *Thai Buddhism: Its Rites and Activities* (New York: AMS Press, 1960), 136; K. Malalgoda, *Buddhism in Sinhalese Society 1750–1900* (Berkeley: University of California Press, 1976); Melford E. Spiro, *Buddhism and Society*, 246; and H. L. Seneviratne, *The Work of Kings: The New Buddhism in Sri Lanka* (Chicago: University of Chicago Press, 1999).
38. This notion of leaving the world is offered in the Pali-English Dictionary.
39. Rupert Gethin, *The Foundations of Buddhism* (Oxford: Oxford University Press, 1998), 85.

Along with the ties between monastic and the laity, the ties among monastics are also important. My discussions about monastic training with more seasoned monastics as well as with several newly ordained novices revealed the importance that such bonds play in the socialization process. By working alongside others, the newly ordained novices feel part of a community and, in the process, learn how to act, dress, and carry themselves as members of that community.

Far from representing an act of going forth from society or a move from home to a life of homelessness, monastic ordination is a ritual through which one's ties and social bonds become expanded as they embrace new communities of people, monastic and lay. Novices continued to see their own biological families from time to time; however, with their ordination completed, the families of novices expanded to include new sets of parents (e.g., head monks, senior monks, and the temple's patrons) and an ever-increasing number of brothers (e.g., other monastics). Just as parents ideally care for, educate, socialize, and protect their children, so the novices' new parents and brothers play a vital role in the training, education, and development of young boys into full-fledged members of the Buddhist monastic community.

CHAPTER 10

Monk and Boy

Becoming a Novice in Contemporary Sipsongpannā

THOMAS BORCHERT

LEARNING HOW TO DRESS AS A MONK

Monks in mainland Southeast Asia often act very differently within the temple compound compared with how they act outside the monasteries.[1] In public, they are often somber faced and walk with a certain measure of dignity. Inside the monastery, they move differently. They are often quicker, more playful, dressed in just two of the three robes that make up a Theravāda monk's full outfit. The outer robe is often kept aside for several reasons: the layer adds to the heat, or there is a desire to keep it neat and fresh-looking, or simply because it is easier not to have a third robe to wear. When going outside the monastery, or when meeting a layperson inside it, a monk usually very carefully pulls his outer robe (*sanghita*) into folds and then drapes it around his body, pulling it tight so that he looks neat and tidy. Although there are different ways to wear the robes, reflecting different schools or lineages of Theravāda Buddhism, what is important is that the robe be folded properly.[2]

There are other ways of being in public, though. On a trip to Sipsongpannā in September 1998 I encountered a large group of novices playing on their temple grounds. There were ten boys, all between the ages of seven and eleven, and

1. This paper is based on fieldwork conducted between 1998 and 2009, with the greatest portion of the research taking place between March 2001 and June 2002. The research has been supported by the University of Chicago, the Fulbright program with the Institute for International Education and the University of Vermont. Of course, it would have been impossible without the good humor and graciousness of the monks of Sipsongpannā.

2. When a monk or novice is to wear all three robes is addressed in Thanissaro Bhikkhu (Geoff DeGraff), *The Buddhist Monastic Code Volume 1: The Patimokkha Training Rules* (Valley Center, CA: Metta Forest Monastery, 1994), 489–95.

Figure 10.1
Novices posing for a formal snapshot, Meng Ce 1998

when I walked up to the temple, they were playing ball and running around, without an adult or even an older novice to be seen. While not quite wild, they were unkempt. Yet, when I asked them if I could take a picture of them, they immediately scurried around, placed their robes into a formal configuration lying neatly on their bodies, and then sat down calmly (Figure 10.1).

While it may seem perfectly natural to want to be at one's best for the camera of a stranger, the need to present oneself in a particular array is of course a learned behavior. Moreover, despite the quotidian nature of dressing, it too is something that these boys have had to learn. This process begins in the months before being ordained as novices, when they learn the forms of the ceremony, shave their heads, and become familiar with monastic robes. Their ignorance about getting dressed, though, is marked quite clearly in the ordination ceremony during which a boy becomes a novice monk. Prior to the event, boys are ceremonially washed by their parents and dressed as little princes or "precious children" (*luk kaew*), after which they are carried on horse, bicycle, or back to the temple where they will be ordained. At a key moment in the ordination ritual, the boys change their clothes. This procedure begins with the boys, who are all wearing button-down white shirts, taking their right arms out of their shirts. Soon after, the monks who preside over the ceremony come over and dress the boys in their new monastic robes, hiding them behind these robes as they take off their "princely" clothes, and redress them in the formal robes of a novice.[3] Unlike the

3. Getting dressed in monastic robes is only one part of the novice ordination. For a more detailed description of the ritual, see Sao Htun Mat Win, *The Initiation of Novicehood and the Ordination of Monkhood in the Burmese Buddhist Culture* (Rangoon, Burma: Department of Religious Affairs, 1986) and Jeffrey Samuels's chapter in this volume.

Figure 10.2
Luk Kaew during ordination to become novices, Jing Hong 2002

Figure 10.3
Monks helping new novices get dressed in their robes, Jing Hong 2002

boys whose picture I had taken three years earlier, these boys did not know how to dress themselves, at least not as monks. (See Figures 10.2 and 10.3.)

Getting dressed is clearly a cultural practice, and this includes the way the monastic robes are put on, and how they are worn once they are put on. It is a practice that must be learned, although it is by no means the only thing that must be learned in order for a boy to be considered a proper monk.

Both groups of boys, those who posed for me after I encountered them playing and those whose ordination I observed, were in the process of becoming proper novices in Sipsongpannā, a Theravāda Buddhist community on China's Southwestern border with Myanmar and Laos. The first group was further along in this process; they had already been socialized to the extent that they knew how to get dressed.

Scholars have long understood that becoming a Buddhist novice, whether Theravāda or another form of Buddhism, is at least as likely to be for cultural reasons as it is for religious ones. Donald Swearer notes that "ordination... may be motivated more by a lad's sense of social obligation to his parents rather than the pursuit of transforming wisdom."[4] Sao Htun Hmat Win, in a study of Shan novice ordination in the 1930s, notes that while ordination reaffirms central religious values, it is also marked by less lofty goals, such as the reassertion of communal solidarity, the revalidation of prestige rankings, and the clear operation of economic transactions and gift exchanges.[5] Hayashi Yukio, moreover, highlights four different types of ordination in Northeast Thailand: "temporary ordination in accordance with custom (*buat taam prapheni*); ordination as an offering to the deceased at their funeral (*buat na sop, buat sung sop*); ordination as a petition or as a "return gift" (*kae bon*) for recovery from illness, practices which are thought to have been influenced by Chinese customs (*buat bun, buat ba*); and ordination in order to study at the temple (*buat rian*)."[6] Two of these are usually thought of as "religious" motivations (*buat na sop* and *buat bun*), but the other two (*buat taam prapheni* and *buat rian*) are less obviously religious. Moreover, scholars have argued that in Thailand, at least, ordination has been a significant source of social mobility. Education in monastic schools provides boys from poor and/or rural areas of Thailand with the opportunity to gain an education, which can serve them well, whether or not they remain "in robes."[7]

These observations are useful in pointing to the multiple motivations that induce young men to ordain as novices, but they also seem to be based on understanding the boys who ordain as rational actors. The problem is that those who are being ordained as novice monks are often between the ages of

4. Donald K. Swearer. *The Buddhist World of Southeast Asia* (Albany: State University of New York Press, 1995), 5.

5. Sao Htun Hmat Win, *The Initiation of Novicehood and the Ordination of Monkhood in the Burmese Buddhist Culture* (Rangoon: Department of Religious Affairs, 1986), 2.

6. Yukio Hayashi, *Practical Buddhism among the Thai-Lao: Religion in the Making of a Region* (Kyoto: Kyoto University Press, 2003), 106.

7. See David Wyatt, *Studies in Thai History* (Chiang Mai: Silkworm Books, 1994) and Dhitiwatana Palanee, "Buddhism and Thai Education," *The South East Asian Review* 7 no. 1–2 (1982), 75–86. In Thailand, the practice of temporary ordination is common. A large portion of Thai men will ordain for as little as a few days, though often for two weeks or a rainy season. There is no social stigma to their disrobing. Within the Theravāda world, temporary ordination is more common in Laos, Thailand, Cambodia and Sipsongpanna in China and less common in Sri Lanka and Burma.

seven and fifteen. While many of them are undoubtedly thoughtful and have made a rational decision, just as many are undoubtedly less clear about why they are entering the sangha (the Buddhist community of monks, nuns, and laymen and women). In contrast to the instrumental motivations noted above, Nancy Eberhardt has recently discussed ordination among young Shan men in Northern Thailand in a somewhat different way, as a part of the "life course" of boys in northern Thailand. In her discussion, the important questions are not about why a Shan boy decides to become a novice, but rather how they anticipate and experience the event, whether with excitement, dread, or some combination of emotions.[8] Eberhardt's attention is on the entire life of people in Shan communities, and so she addresses ordination and its aftermath only in passing, but hers is a useful shift because it puts the experience of ordination, and implicitly of life as a novice or monk, at the forefront of our analysis.

I will follow Eberhardt's lead in focusing on the subjective experience of boys as they become novices, but with a slightly different emphasis. Namely, I want to ask what kind of people are produced in the temples of Sipsongpannā, and how do they understand this process? In Sipsongpannā, it has been commonly pointed out that prior to the 1950s, boys who did not ordain as novices or as fully ordained monks for a time would be unable to get married, a sentiment found in Thailand in the recent past as well.[9] This was so because this was the place where young men were made into proper adults, turned from raw to cooked (in language used by both Levi-Strauss and Tai Buddhists). Justin McDaniel in his monograph on monastic education in Laos and Northern Thailand notes that "monastic education produces teachers. They are the progenitors of local tradition and arbitrators of translocal prestige."[10] While this is patently true, it is also worth noting that most of the boys who enter into the temples do not become teachers, even though they have absorbed monastic traditions, including traditions of dressing. They become marked by the traditions, becoming supporters or even enforcers of it, but not necessarily active producers of culture (such as teachers). Thus I will pay attention here to the varieties of people who are the product of village temples, at least in Sipsongpannā.[11]

8. Nancy Eberhardt, *Imagining the Course of Life: Self-Transformation in a Shan Buddhist Community* (Honolulu: University of Hawai'i Press, 2006), 171–73.

9. Jane Bunnag, *Buddhist Monk, Buddhist Layman* (Cambridge: Cambridge University Press, 1973), 36.

10. Justin Thomas McDaniel. *Gathering Leaves and Lifting Words: Histories of Buddhist Monastic Education in Laos and Thailand* (Seattle: University of Washington Press, 2008), 21.

11. While there is clearly a great deal of continuity across the Tai communities of mainland Southeast Asia (see, for example, Andrew Turton's edited volume *Civility and Savagery: Social Identity in Tai States* (Surrey: Curzon, 1999)), there are also great distinctions of culture, language, and history as well. These distinctions have become more pronounced with the rise of nation-states in Southeast Asia, and the different experiences that these countries have had in relation to colonialism and the histories of the Cold War.

What is training like for novices? What are they taught, and to what effect? While it may seem obvious, I want to emphasize here that becoming a novice is not a moment, but a process whereby boys are molded into a certain kind of person.

SIPSONGPANNĀ: A KINGDOM UNDER TWO SKIES

Before discussing the life of monastic children, it is necessary to explain some of the factors that condition the practice of Buddhism in the region. Sipsongpannā is a region of Southwest China, on the border of Myanmar and Laos. Like much of the middle Mekong region, it is rich in ethnic diversity and contains (according to the Chinese state) fourteen different ethnic groups (*shaoshu minzu*). Among these different groups, the Dai-lue have been dominant in the region for much of the last thousand years. While relatively powerful locally, the Dai-lue kingdom in Sipsongpannā was subject to the predations of the far more powerful armies of both Southeast Asia[12] and imperial China. Indeed, Historian Pat Giersch has referred to it as a "middle ground," a region where no one group could maintain longstanding hegemony.[13] The *cao phaendin*, the Dai-lue king known as the "lord of the earth," was conceived in some ways as an absolute ruler who owned all of the land.[14] At the same time, not only did his government regularly pay tribute to both the Burmese and Chinese states, but he appears to have been the most powerful of a collection of local lords rather than someone who wielded absolute authority.[15]

In a variety of ways, Theravāda Buddhism provided the central organizing institutions for traditional Dai-lue society. The political system of the Dai-lue in Sipsongpannā, resembled that of other Tai[16] city-states of the middle Mekong region. Polities based around Chiang Mai, Luang Phrabang, and Keng Tung (in what is now Thailand, Laos, and the Shan States of Myanmar, respectively) worked on the logics of patronage and moral authority that were based on

12. See Ratanaporn Sethakul, "Tai Lue of Sipongpanna and Müang Nan in the Nineteenth Century," in *Civility and Savagery: Social Identity in Tai States*, ed. Andrew Turton (Richmond: Surry: Curzon, 2000), 319–29.

13. C. Patterson Giersch, *Asian Borderlands: the Transformation of Qing China's Yunnan Frontier* (Cambridge, MA: Harvard University Press, 2005), 7–9.

14. Laohasirinadh Natchā, *Sipsongpannā: Raat Carit* [Sipsongpannā: a Traditional State] (Bangkok: The Thailand Research Fund/Foundation for the Promotion of Social Sciences and Humanities Textbook Project, 1995), 60.

15. See Ann Maxwell Hill, *Merchants and Migrants: Ethnicity and Trade among Yunnanese Chinese in Southeast Asia* (New Haven, CT: Yale University Press/Center for Southeast Asian Studies, 1998).

16. There can be some confusion between "Tai" and "Thai." "Tai" usually refers to ethnolinguistic communities that are spread around mainland Southeast Asia. "Thai" is an adjective referring to the nation-state Thailand. The Thai citizens of Thailand are themselves members of a Tai ethnic group, as are the Lao, the Shan, and the Dai-lue.

Theravāda Buddhist notions of moral rulers.[17] Moreover, the sangha was the key institution for the maintenance of culture. Boys ordained for a period; some remained for life, and though most did not, they had learned the Dai-lue language, how to participate in religious rituals, and other types of knowledge, such as medicine or astrology.[18] As was noted above, time in robes was understood as essential for young men to be considered true members of society and marriageable. For the most part, prior to the mid-twentieth century, the Dai-lue defined themselves in relation to other Tai, Theravāda Buddhist groups of Southeast Asia, with whom they shared a number of cultural forms as well as ties of kinship that grew out of both trade and religious networks,[19] rather than identifying with modern nation-states.

Politically, while Sipsongpannā was a semi-independent kingdom until the end of the nineteenth century, since then it has been recognized as a part of China and thus subject to the political shifts that have taken place over the course of the sixty years of the People's Republic of China (PRC). The region was recognized as a part of China in the 1896 Franco–British treaty which divided up Southeast Asia,[20] but it was not until the People's Liberation Army entered the regional capital of Jing Hong in 1953 that the process of integration into the PRC began. This process has been uneven and bumpy. While the Dai-lue leadership was generally integrated into the local Chinese Communist Party (CCP), Dai-lue culture was greatly damaged by being incorporated into the PRC.[21] This was particularly true during the Cultural Revolution (1966–1976). During this period, traditional cultural forms were deemed to be detrimental to the creation of a modern society and so were banished, often violently. Buddhism in the region was largely eliminated: monks were either forced to

17. Anne Hansen, *How to Behave: Buddhism and Modernity in Colonial Cambodia, 1860–1930* (Honolulu: University of Hawai'i Press, 2007).

18. For some understanding of what was learned in monasteries prior to the early decades of the twentieth century, see Justin Thomas McDaniel, *Gathering Leaves and Lifting Words*, and Kamala Tiyavanich, *Sons of the Buddha: The Early Lives of Three Extraordinary Thai Masters* (Boston: Wisdom Publications, 2007).

19. Hsieh Shih-chung, "On the Dynamics of Tai/Dailue Ethnicity: An Ethnohistorical Analysis," in *Cultural Encounters on China's Ehnic Frontier*, ed. Stevan Harrell (Seattle: University of Washington Press, 1995), 301–28

20. Charles Keyes, "Who Are the Lue Revisited? Ethnic Identity in Laos, Thailand and China" (Working Paper, Center for International Studies. Cambridge: MIT, 1992).

21. Dai-lue incorporation into the political economy of the PRC is a complicated century-long process that has been described in Susan McCarthy's *Communist Multiculturalism* (Seattle: University of Washington Press, 2009) as well as Hseih's "On the Dynamics of Tai/Dailue Ethnicity: An Ethnohistorical Analysis." Giersch (*Asian Borderlands*) and Hsieh have both argued that over the centuries, the Dai-lue political elite engaged in a strategy of accommodating more powerful armies to the north and south, and in particular the decision to welcome the People's Liberation Army into the region in 1953 should be seen in this light (though Hsieh also argues that in the current period this accommodation is self-defeating for the perpetuation of a Dai-lue identity—an argument echoed in Grant Evans, "Transformation of Jing Hong, Xishuangbanna, PRC," in *Where China Meets Southeast Asia*, ed. Grant Evans, Christopher Hutton, and Kuah Khun Eng [Singapore: Institute of Southeast Asian Studies, 2000], 162–82).

flee to Theravāda polities of Southeast Asia or to disrobe; village temples were converted to other uses and Buddha images and texts were either destroyed or buried (and thus for the most part lost). The practice of Buddhism (like religion around China) was once again legalized in the early 1980s with the beginning of the reforms of Deng Xiaoping. The Dai-lue people of Sipsongpannā returned to Buddhism with great energy, particularly for the next decade. Despite this energy, the long-term consequences of the Cultural Revolution continue to be felt. Because ordination was essentially prohibited from the early 1960s until the 1980s, an entire generation's worth of knowledge has been lost, a fact important for understanding the conditions (and opportunities) for young men who have ordained since that time.

The other aspect of politics that is important to understand here is that the Chinese government has categorized the Dai-lue as an important group within the *Daizu*, one of the fifty-five minority nationalities (*shaoshu minzu*) of China. Groups that make up China's minorities comprise less than ten percent of the population, but for the most part they inhabit the sparsely populated, mineral-rich border regions of the nation-state.[22] The impulse to categorize these different groups of peoples was (and is) multifaceted. Above all else, it stemmed from a desire to control the border regions of the nation-state. This desire for security was matched with a concern to help these groups attain modern forms according to Marxian criteria. In tension with this, though, was the argument that these groups should be allowed to develop "autonomously," according to their own culture and conditions.[23]

There are two important, if contradictory, consequences of Chinese minority policies for the experiences of the Dai-lue novices. The first is that, because these boys are minorities, they are allowed to be ordained at an earlier age than boys who are members of the majority nationality (the Han). Chinese government policy generally does not permit children under eighteen to receive a religious education.[24] However, for certain minority groups in which religion is deemed to be an essential part of the culture (such as the Dai-lue or the

22. Colin Mackerras, *China's Ethnic Minorities and Globalization* (London: Routledge/Curzon, 2003).

23. There has been a lot of excellent work published in the last two decades on the minorities of China. Among the many topics addressed are state efforts to create minority identities that fit official notions of proper citizens and the different ways minority groups have responded to these efforts. Among the best works are Louisa Schein, *Minority Rules: The Miao and the Feminine in China's Cultural Politics* (Durham, NC: Duke University Press, 2000) and Dru Gladney, *Muslim Chinese: Ethnic Nationalism in the People's Republic* (Cambridge, MA: Harvard University Press/Council on East Asian Studies, 1991). For a useful review of some of this literature, see Susan D. Blum, "Margins and Centers: A Decade of Publishing on China's Ethnic Minorities," *The Journal of Asian Studies* 61 no. 4 (2002), 1287–310.

24. It should be obvious that I am focusing on the experience of boys here. While girls and women actively participate in the Buddhism of Sipsongpannā, there is no tradition of female renunciation in the region. To my knowledge, there has been no research specifically focused on Buddhist practices and beliefs among Dai-lue girls in Sipsongpannā (Anne Hansen addresses these issues tangentially in her book *How*

Tibetans), some allowance is made for the ordination of children.[25] The second point is that, ironically, these boys often know about their own minority group largely through the eyes of the Chinese state. Over the last sixty years a large bureaucratic-academic system has grown up to create knowledge about China's minority groups (often in the service of the politics of the nation), and the knowledge that this apparatus has produced filters into school curricula. Because of the knowledge lost in the generation gap produced by the Chinese Revolution, for many Dai-lue, even the ordained, the public schools are the place where they learn about their own history.

LIFE IN THE VILLAGE TEMPLES OF SIPSONGPANNĀ

Life in the village temples of Sipsongpannā can be quite varied, and in part depends on where the novices are in the "life-cycle" of a monk. Boys are considered to be "little novices" (*pha noy*) until they are fifteen or sixteen, after which they are usually referred to as "senior novices" (*pha long*). They retain this status until (and if) they take the higher ordination, between nineteen and twenty-one.[26] While boys will occasionally ordain after they have studied in junior high school, most who ordain do so while still of elementary school age, often between the ages of ten and thirteen. The law states that no one under eighteen may ordain, but as is noted above, exceptions are made in the case of national minorities for whom ordination has historically been an important part of the culture. Moreover, because public education is supposed to be compulsory at least through elementary school, since the end of the 1990s it has been increasingly common for novices to attend public school run by the Chinese state at the same time that they are living in the temple. This practice

to Behave and Modernity in Colonial Cambodia, 1860–1930 [Honolulu: University of Hawaii Press, 2007]). The higher ordination of women within Theravāda Buddhism ended sometime in the first millennium CE., though there have been efforts to revive it over the last several decades.

25. It should be noted that this allowance does not seem to be formally ratified. Rather, it is an informal policy, so that when the government determines that allowing young children to be ordained destabilizes the local situation, it can easily reverse the policy. For an example of this, see Melvyn Goldstein, "The Revival of Monastic Life in Drepung Monastery," in *Buddhism in Contemporary Tibet*, ed. Melvyn Goldstein and Matthew Kapstein (Berkeley: University of California Press, 1998), 15–52.

26. The Pāli Vinaya notes that boys are not to take the higher ordination (*upasampadā*) until they are twenty. This is the rule as promulgated in Sipsongpannā (see Thomas Borchert, *Educating Monks: Buddhism, Politics and Freedom of Religion on China's Southwest Border* (Ph.d. Dissertation, University of Chicago, 2006), 258), but there are cases where boys will either take the higher ordination a little before their twentieth birthday, or alternatively be treated as if they have taken the higher ordination because there is no one else to act as an abbot, a result of the generational gap produced by the Cultural Revolution. In these cases, the preceptor and the temple committee are often more influential than they might otherwise be.

has been actively supported by senior monks within Sipsongpannā, and in general it has not been opposed by local school board administrators.

The public schools have been something of a mixed bag for novices. For those who continue to attend elementary school after ordination, their experience is in many ways only a little different from that of their fellows. They are likely to attend the same village school, and they seem to interact with their fellows much as they did prior to ordination. It becomes different if they are attending junior or senior high school; most of these schools are in other towns, and the novices must either board at the school (where usually they share rooms with other novices) or commute daily. Perhaps because of this necessity, the boys in junior high school seem to be more likely to spend time with other novices than are the elementary school students. This seems to be a relatively natural function of a desire to spend time with people who share one's interests (or status), and few of the novices I interviewed thought that the simple fact of their being novices caused them any problems. To the contrary, most of these novices report that they generally liked going to school. If they do drop out, they do so usually because of financial strain or the challenge posed by placement tests for secondary school.[27] Related to this view, the public school teachers I spoke with suggested that novices tended to work harder than their lay classmates.

Monastic education in contemporary Southeast Asia can be usefully divided into two types: apprentice and curricular education.[28] Apprentice education is best defined by the centrality of the relationship between the master and the apprentice. In most cases in Sipsongpannā the master is a monk, though occasionally it might also be a senior novice or even (if there is no abbot, or the abbot is particularly young) a former monk, known in Sipsongpannā as a *khanan*. Because it is the relationship that is of greatest import, apprentice education takes place essentially wherever monks and novices interact. The curriculum is not standardized, though it is not random. Rather, it is the product of whatever the master was taught by his own master, and it can be generally understood within local traditions and lineages.

Apprentice education can be usefully contrasted with "curricular education." In contrast to apprentice forms, curricular education can be characterized by a

27. I explore these issues more fully in chapter 2 of my dissertation, *Educating Monks: Buddhism, Politics and Freedom of Religion on China's Southwest Border* (Ph.D. Dissertation, University of Chicago, 2006).

28. The distinction between apprentice and curricular education made here is discussed by Anne Blackburn, following a suggestion by Charles Hallisey. See Anne Blackburn, *Buddhist Learning and Textual Practice in Eighteenth-Century Lankan Culture* (Princeton, NJ: Princeton University Press, 2000), 45. I discuss the distinction with greater detail in *Educating Monks*. Monastic education in village temples is also sometimes referred to (uncritically) as "traditional" education, as in Yoneo Ishii, *Sangha, State and Society: Thai Buddhism in History* (Honolulu: University of Hawaii Press/Center for Southeast Asian Studies Kyoto University, 1986), 25; or Zhao Shilin and Wu Jinghua, *Daizu Wenhua Zhi* (A Cultural History of the Dai Nationality) (Kunming: Yunnan Minzu Chubanshe, 1997), 319.

Figure 10.4
Novices studying at a dharma school

formal setting, where the students sit at desks. The teachers may be monks, but the relationship between the monk and the novice will generally be more distant (Figure 10.4). The curriculum itself is standardized by system administrators, who may be either lay or monastic officials. The monastic education system varies according to the country, but in countries such as Thailand and Sri Lanka, Buddhist high schools are part of the formal educational projects of the state and in turn are governed by their respective ministries of education. Curricular education in Sipsongpannā, by contrast, exists outside the public school system. Because of this, the system is quite small, and indeed within Sipsongpannā, most boys' experience of monastic education is within the context of apprentice education.

While temples can be run differently, there are a number of consistencies to the daily routine of village temples. Novices tend to get up between six and seven in the morning and chant a morning service. If they are *pha noy* and still in school, they will eat breakfast and go to school. They might return to the temple for lunch, but they are just as likely to go home and eat lunch with their families. Similarly, in the afternoon after school they may return to the temple, but they are just as likely to head home. Both *pha noy* and *pha long* will be responsible for doing chores around the temple in the late afternoon, but for the most part these are not onerous and include sweeping the living quarters and courtyard of the temple, doing light gardening and/or feeding the chickens, dogs, and cats that may live on the temple grounds, and generally keeping things tidy. In the early evening the boys may eat a light

Figure 10.5
A novice gardening to maintain the upkeep of the temple

meal,[29] and then they go into the *wihan* to chant the evening service. At some time during the day, usually in the late afternoon or in the evening after the evening service, the boys will also study how to read and write the Dai-lue alphabet (Figure 10.5). There are some important differences between the days of older and younger novices to which I will return below.

Just as they cannot dress themselves, boys cannot read Dai-lue when they enter the temple (and they may or may not be able to read Mandarin Chinese). In part because of the way that the Dai-lue ethnicity has been defined and shaped by the Chinese state, learning to read and write has become among the most important things that boys can learn. For the most part, the way they learn is through the modeling of the monk. For example, every night the *pha noy* goes into the *wihan* (worship hall) to chant with the monk. However, when he first enters into robes, the boy does not know any of the words he is to chant, he does not know the letters (and so manuals do him no good), and he

29. It should be noted that this breaks the precept against eating after noon, one of the ten precepts boys accept when they are ordained as novices. In Sipsongpannā, most people whom I have spoken with (lay and monastic) tend to express the view that novices are growing boys and they are less likely to be naughty if they are well fed. Often they refer to this meal as a snack or noodles rather than dinner (as in, "Are you going to eat dinner?" "No, just noodles"). While the novice precepts are standard throughout Buddhist Southeast Asia, I would suggest that this rule in particular is unevenly enforced. See Phra Peter Pannapadipo, *Little Angels* (Bangkok: Post Books, 2001).

may not know the tones. He might know how to sit properly, partly because his parents have probably been taking him to a temple since he was very young. It is also likely that he spent four to eight months observing how the monk and novices spent their days in preparation for his ordination. Regardless, his job is to learn what the monk is chanting and the way to chant it properly, which is done by imitating the monk. In one village temple I visited, during the evening service the monk and a senior novice both had liturgical notebooks during their chanting. The monk, who was in his early twenties, rarely looked at the book, whereas the novice consulted it more often. There were three other novices, all *pha noy*, none of whom had books (they couldn't read and so would not yet need the liturgical handbooks). Over the course of the twenty or so minutes that they chanted, these boys would alternatively chant, mumble, and listen depending on what part of the liturgy and whether they knew it. The same process is evident when novices learn the Dai-lue alphabet. For the most part this knowledge is achieved by repeating after the monk (or the senior novice or the *khanan*, depending on who is teaching the novices). Most temples that I visited had a blackboard that was used to teach the boys how to read and write. Initially, the monk writes a set of letters on the board. To teach, he simply points at a letter, says its name, and the novices repeat after him. As the novice gains knowledge, more letters are added until the boys learn the forty-four letters and thirty-plus vowels, and then words. Eventually the monk writes on the board lines from *sutras* the boys are to learn (thereby also aiding the process of learning the morning and evening services). The process of teaching the boys how to fully read and write takes a number of months. Indeed assuming that the boys are still in elementary school when they ordain, it can take over a year to learn how to read the alphabet fluidly, a fact that a number of abbots complain about resignedly (Figure 10.6).

The relationship between the abbot and the novice is a complicated one, particularly when the novice is still a *pha noy*.[30] The abbot certainly does not replace the parents in anyone's eyes, but the boys do sleep at the temple, and in many ways it is the abbot who is responsible for the their well-being (a fact attested by the parents of newly ordained novices that I interviewed). The abbot is responsible for ensuring that the boys are well-fed, learn about Dai-lue culture and Buddhism, and get to the public school. Indeed when novices were to miss school because of responsibilities or events at the temple, it was the abbot of the temple who wrote to ask permission. Moreover, when novices get into trouble at school, I was told, the teacher is as likely to contact the student's abbot as his parents. This relationship is not always easy or loving, though. Monks (or senior novices) can inflict corporal punishment on novices who are naughty. I was told by one novice that, "When I first became

30. Sipsongpannā has about five hundred village temples (*wat*), approximately one for every Dai-lue village. It should be noted that as of 2007, there were about 600 fully ordained monks. This means that that the vast majority of temples had only one fully ordained monk.

Figure 10.6
Blackboard at a village temple

a novice, it was a little difficult. I was very small when I ordained. Everyday the older monks made me do things. If I didn't do them, they would hit me and swear at me."[31]

Despite the fact that novices and monks in Theravāda Buddhism are traditionally described as having "gone from home into homelessness," in many ways the novices of Sipsongpannā have not left home at all. The village temples are usually within about five minutes' walk of their home, and as noted above, it is not uncommon for novices to go home to eat a meal with their family, particularly when they are younger. Although the monk can act *in loco parentis* with regard to the school, it is still the parents who pay the tuition fees, not the monk (indeed most monks in Sipsongpannā are relatively cash poor, though well supported by their villages). Moreover, when one sees novices with their families, it is clear that the relationship has not really changed, especially the parent–child relationship. Over the course of my research, I ate meals with the parents of several novices. One night I was eating with the parents and cousins of a novice. The novice did not eat dinner with us, but he was in and out of the room where we were eating. At one point he

31. This discipline is, I suspect, generally supported by the local community. Mendelson relates a story of a mother adding to a bruise already inflicted by a monk. See Michael E. Mendelson, *Sangha and State in Burma: A Study of Monastic Sectarianism and Leadership*, ed. John P. Ferguson (Ithaca, NY: Cornell University Press, 1975), 157.

came over to his father and grabbed a one *yuan* note out of his father's shirt pocket (about twelve cents, enough to buy some ice cream). As he did this, he said to his father, "You went out to play today; you should give me this because I didn't get to go." The father laughed at his "naughty" son and gave him the money. "He's my son," he told me later, "I'll do what I can for him." Clearly, despite the son's changed status vis-à-vis his family, both father and son remained enmeshed in a familial relationship.

REASONS FOR ORDINATION

The fact that these novices are still eleven year-old boys interacting with their parents raises one of the key questions about ordination in this time and place. It is clear both from the anthropological literature and from my own research that in places like Thailand ordination remains a natural part of the life cycle of young men. Most of the Thai men express a desire to be ordained if they have not yet had the chance. Even among urban elites within Bangkok, who are far less likely to ordain than other groups of Thai men, there remains a residual feeling that ordination is something that they should do (even if they never will). When I have asked middle-class urban Thai men if they have ordained, their answer is usually, "not yet" rather than "no." Moreover, while Buddhism is not the official state religion, for many Thai men, being Thai and being Buddhist are closely related.

However, in Sipsongpannā, this is no longer the case. It is difficult to know what percentage of the Dai-lue population of Sipsongpannā has ordained, because records are either not kept or not available publicly.[32] My best estimate, based on official demographics and those reported by the Buddhist Association, is that in 2000, roughly fifteen to sixteen percent of the eligible male population was a novice. While it is difficult to interpret this relatively static number, it is also not an insignificant portion of the population. But then if it is no longer absolutely necessary for young men to ordain, why does a sizeable group still become ordained?

Boys are ordained for a variety of reasons. Many boys themselves told me that it is the custom of the Dai-lue people to ordain. One boy told me, "Why [did I become a novice?] I also don't know. It is because it is the Dai custom. When we arrive at the right age, and we are over ten, then we want to become novices." Some boys framed this custom in terms of the opportunity to study, particularly to study the Dai-lue language/writing system. Another told me, "Dai [boys] become novices in order to study the Dai language." Others put their decision in relation to Buddhism. One told me he had ordained "so that Buddhism would not be lost," while another wished to "Carry Buddhism to

32. I have been told by people in the local government of Sipsongpannā that these statistics are not kept. This may be true, or it may be that they did not want share those statistics with a foreign researcher.

greater glory!" There were still others who understood that the temple was the place where novices became "cooked." One particularly articulate novice said:

> Because ordaining as a novice is one of the traditional customs of we Dai people. [When] boys reach a certain age, they come to the temple to ordain as novice monks. Because ordained novices can study many things, people also greatly respect novices and monks. If you don't come to ordain as a novice, the people then might say that you are a savage (*ye ren*), that you are a boy who doesn't understand things. Therefore I came to ordain as a novice.[33]

Far more common, though, were the boys who could not articulate clear reasons for why they had decided to enter into robes. Many boys, particularly the younger ones, told me that they had ordained because they "felt like it" (*xiang dang heshang*). Conversely, others who had not ordained, had "not felt like it." Most of the boys who expanded beyond the answer of "feeling like it" told me that some of their friends had ordained and so they decided to do so as well. Thus the decision to ordain seemed to come in clear cohorts. One or two boys in a village might decide to ordain and their friends would be likely to join them, and so suddenly a village might have eight to twelve novices. As the novices decided to disrobe, the numbers would gradually decrease, but there might not be another ordination in the village for five to ten years.[34] The vast majority of boys did not choose to ordain in order to follow in their father's footsteps. Indeed, for most of the boys with whom I spoke their fathers could not have become monks because the Cultural Revolution would have made their ordination impossible. Indeed, this response suggests that, in Sipsongpannā at least, ordination is at least partially a peer-driven decision.

Parental involvement in the decision is hard to gauge. Mette Hansen reports that most parents she talked to told her that the decision to ordain was made by their sons alone, a point that she finds hard to believe given the age of many of the boys who are ordaining.[35] Most of the boys whom I talked to about the decision to ordain told me that doing so was their own idea—or rather it was their own decision (since they might have been following the lead of a friend—although some said that the decision had been made by their parents. However, there is a strong ethos that boys enter into the temple voluntarily. Indeed, in theory at least, one cannot be forced to enter

33. Most of these statements come from questionnaires that were filled out by the students at one of the formal Buddhist schools in Sipsongpannā, May 2002.

34. It is worth noting that, while the one-child policy remains in effect within China, most Chinese minorities, including the Dai-lue, are allowed to have two children. Moreover, the policy went into effect only at the start of the Reform Era (1979 to present), so that people over the age of thirty, regardless of ethnicity, are far more likely to have siblings.

35. Mette Halskov Hansen, *Lessons in Being Chinese: Minority Education and Ethnic Identity in Southwest China* (Seattle: University of Washington Press 1999), 112.

robes. I think that where parents are more heavily involved in the decision, it is as often as not through suggestion rather than through coercion. Phra Pannapadipo tells the story of a boy in Thailand whose father suggested he ordain when he started to get into trouble because he was trying drugs.[36] It may seem banal to put it this way, but parents can encourage children to do their bidding in a variety of ways.

Most boys told me that their parents supported their decision to ordain, but perhaps more interesting were the cases where the parents did not support ordination. Some boys told me that their parents eventually came around when they saw how serious the boys were. Others ordained, despite continued parental resistance, only through the help of the monk in the temple. Several of the parents that I talked to were deeply ambivalent about the whole process. The parents of the novice who took the money from his father's pocket told me that he and his wife had resisted their son's desire to ordain and had relented only when he persisted in his desire. They were concerned about the amount of pressure on the boys, needing to learn both Dai culture and Chinese culture. Other parents were concerned that if their son ordained he would not be able to succeed in the Chinese public schools. This ambivalence of the parents, a desire to foster the future possibilities of their sons without denying the importance of Dai-lue culture, was reflected in the father who said of his son, "We were very happy when [our son] ordained. If he also goes to junior high school and high school, we will be very happy with that as well."

THE FUTURE LIVES OF BOYS WHO ARE NOVICES

A novice can become one of three things: he can take the higher ordination and remain a monk for life, called a *dubi*; he can take the higher ordination and disrobe, being referred to as a *khanan* in Sipsongpannā; or he can disrobe while still a novice, from which he will be referred to as *ji noy*. These figures, *dubi*, *khanan*, and *ji noy*, have a descending degree of status in traditional Dai-lue society. While this remains the case to a certain extent, the world of contemporary Sipsongpannā is more complicated. The boys who ordained in the first decade of this century are in a complicated dance of shifting expectations: of who they should be as Dai-lue men and of how the Dai-lue fit into China. These shifts are changing the way men and women view the space of ordination within contemporary Dai-lue society.

This attitude can be seen with regard to the issue of marriage. Whereas once ordination was a necessary prerequisite for getting married, the current situation is more complicated, as seen in Mette Hansen's research among Dai-lue girls in junior middle school and high school in Sipsongpannā. She has shown that there is a clear shift in the attitudes of Dai-lue girls depending on the amount of time they have spent within the Chinese public school system.

36. Phra Peter Pannapadipo, 61.

Those who are just beginning their secondary school education are much more likely to consider prior ordination to be a desirable trait for a future husband than those who have completed this public education.[37] The older girls have received a deeper and richer set of messages regarding the inferiority of the *Daizu*, and they themselves are also more upwardly mobile within the broader Chinese national-economy. To these older girls, ordination is an indication of laziness or stupidity, rather than of being an upstanding member of society. Ironically, one can see a comparable devaluation within novices who are attending high school.[38]

So the question remains: what is the value of ordination for most boys? I would suggest that there are two different tracks for novices in Sipsongpannā (becoming *dubi, khanan, ji noy* notwithstanding). The most common is for the boys without ambition or direction. While the life of "little novices" can be quite stressful between attending elementary school and learning to read and write in Dai-lue, by the time most boys are sixteen or seventeen, their lives are generally quite the opposite. They have already learned to read; most are no longer in school, and they have relatively few religious responsibilities at the temple. It's not uncommon to see novices like this drifting through the days until they become bored enough to disrobe. Once they have done so, they become peasants or run small businesses just as their families have done (indeed, this is essentially all they are qualified for). Like the novices who ordained because "they felt like it," most of these ultimately disrobe because they "feel like it" (or perhaps because there is a girl involved). For the majority of these boys, even if they become fully ordained monks for a short time, the temple remains a relatively benign place to pass their teenage years.

The second set of novices is more ambitious. Regardless of whether or not they attend middle school, they end up in a more advanced educational setting (the curricular mode of monastic education discussed above). After studying for three years in one of the formal monastic schools of Sipsongpannā, they are likely to go to a Buddhist institute either in China or in Thailand. After studying, particularly in Southeast Asia, these novices express a desire to come back to Sipsongpannā and serve as teachers. They are more likely to be inculcated into an ethos where they have a responsibility for the well-being of the sangha, of the Dai-lue people, and of Buddhism in general.[39] This attitude puts them in a position to become local leaders, but only insofar as they remain within the sangha. Once they disrobe, their status falls significantly.

37. Mette Halskov Hansen, *Lessons in Being Chinese,* 147–49.

38. The role of the Chinese public schools in the attitudes of novices in Sipsongpannā is an important one, though beyond the scope of this paper. I elaborate on these issues in my dissertation, "Educating Monks."

39. I have referred to the Buddhism developed within curricular education in Sipsongpannā as "subnational Buddhist revivalism." Thomas Borchert, "Worry for the Dai Nation: Sipsongpanna, Chinese Modernity and the Problem of Buddhist Modernism," *The Journal of Asian Studies* 67 no. 1 (2008), 107–42.

CONCLUSION: BOYS WILL BE BOYS, EVEN WHEN THEY ARE IN SAFFRON

In the end, most of the boys who ordain at nine or ten eventually disrobe when they become young men. Most do so for prosaic reasons: they are bored; their parents need them to work in the fields; they are interested in girls. This latter is indeed especially important. Many of the older novices I have spoken with have "girlfriends." While the boys are a bit cagy about the subject, my sense is that these are relatively innocent relationships. These are girls with whom they have swapped phone numbers and with whom they flirt, but not much more. The boys know that there is a (sexual) line that they are not supposed to cross, and they reach that line far before they commit a *parajikā* offense and have sex.

One could take this observation and suggest that in the early twenty-first century this is the way that monastic discipline is degraded in Sipsongpannā. However, I think a different thought is more appropriate. Novices have always been young men who are growing up in a context that is highly confining. I suspect that in most places in the Theravāda world, the majority of them do what they can to act appropriately, but they can also be naughty. They tease and joke; for the most part they listen to their abbot, but they also like to watch television, talk about sports, and flirt.[40] These young men clearly learn something of social value when they live as monks for several years. Moreover, as Eberhardt notes,[41] this experience conditions the possible futures young men imagine. Yet even as they are being shaped and molded, their subjective experience and understanding of being a monk is not necessarily the same as that of adult renunciants. Indeed, at a fundamental level, we should remember that they are boys.

40. The famous Thai monk Buddhadasa talks about learning how to box while a novice. See Kamala Tiyavanich, *Sons of the Buddha*, 49–54.
41. Nancy Eberhardt, *Imagining the Course of Life*, 172.

CHAPTER 11

Buddhism as a Vehicle for Girls' Safety and Education in Thailand

MONICA LINDBERG FALK

This chapter addresses children and Buddhism with special focus on Thai girls who study at a Buddhist *samnak chii* (female Buddhist "temple").[1] In Thai society, Buddhism plays an important role in the socialization process and for centuries Buddhist temples have been an important aspect for boys' education. Buddhist temples have provided a safety net for poor boys by offering them free education. Girls from low-income families have not had the same opportunity. It was not until 1990 that the first school for girls was opened by Thai Buddhist *mae chiis* (female ascetics),[2] and since then Thai girls have been able to obtain free education through a Buddhist-ordained community.[3]

The Thai education system has recently been reformed, and today free basic education with nine years of compulsory schooling is provided to all Thai boys

1. I would like to acknowledge Khun Mae Prathin, the *mae chiis*, teachers, and students at the Dhammajarinee School for generously sharing their knowledge and experiences with me. I would also like to thank my assistant, Nantana Pidtong, who worked with me in 2009. I am very grateful for Vanessa Sasson's constructive comments on the text.

2. *Mae chii* is the Thai term for women who shave their heads and brows, wear white robes, and reeive ordination as eight- or ten-precept Buddhist female ascetics. *Bhikkhuni* is the Pali term for a fully ordained female Buddhist monk in the Theravada tradition. The Thai sangha is still not open to women.

3. See earlier texts about the Dhammajarnee School: Monica Lindberg Falk, *Making Fields of Merit: Buddhist Female Ascetics and Gendered Orders in Thailand* (Copenhagen/Washington: NIAS Press/University of Washington Press, 2007); "Thammacarini Witthaya: The First Buddhist School for Girls in Thailand" in *Innovative Buddhist Women: Swimming Against the Stream*, ed. Karma Lekshe Tsomo (Richmond, Surrey: Curzon Press, 2000), 61–71; and Monica Lindberg Falk, *Making Fields of Merit*, 110, 125, 162, 204, 207, and 212–18.

and girls. The reform has decreased the gender gap that previously favored boys' education over girls', but it has made other disparities more visible. One example is that the poorest children are overlooked, since educational services are unavailable to them. Many of these children are from the hill minorities, the Deep South, and immigrant families.[4] For some, the Dhammajarinee School (Buddhist school for girls) in central Thailand has come to the rescue. The increasing popularity of this school rests on the uniqueness of its location in an entirely safe female space, which has attracted a growing number of Thai girls to the school.[5] The Dhammajarinee School is a boarding school where girls from low-income families can live and study free of charge. Formerly an unaccredited school, it has become accredited and has increased its number of students from about fifty in 1998 to more than three hundred in 2009.

This chapter explores why a Buddhist school for girls, which was established at a *samnak chii* as a response to a lack of educational opportunities for poor girls, had to expand its educational responsibility when the Thai government's educational reform gave girls and boys equal access to nine or twelve years of free education. The school highlighted in this chapter has for more than two decades, prior to the educational reform, provided secondary education for girls who otherwise would not have had a chance to study more than four and later six years' primary education. Contrary to what was expected, the demand to study at the Buddhist school increased after the educational reform was implemented. This chapter investigates who the students are, why they have chosen to study at this school, and how teaching, living, and learning at the *samnak chii* are experienced by them and their teachers. The ethnography here is based on material collected between 1997 and 2009 and the methods used for gathering information are participant observation and interviews with *mae chii*s, lay teachers, *dhammajarinee*s (former students who observed the eight Buddhist precepts), and contemporary students.

GENDER AND EDUCATION

The important role played by Buddhist institutions in education might explain the unusually high rate of literacy among Thai men. However, both laywomen and *mae chii*s in premodern Siamese society were excluded from text-based knowledge.[6] Educational level is a crucial factor in Thai girls' and women's lives.[7] Many young women who could not afford education began working while

4. Alain Mounier and Phasina Tangchuang, eds. *Education & Knowledge in Thailand: The Quality Controversy* (Chiang Mai: Silkworm Books, 2010), 303–4.

5. Names and titles are romanized according to established convention, and personal names follow the preferences of the persons concerned.

6. Charles F. Keyes, ed., *Reshaping Local Worlds: Formal Education and Cultural Change in Rural Southeast Asia*, Monograph 36/Yale Southeast Asia Studies Yale Centre for International and Area Studies, 1991, 94.

7. See John Knodel, "The Closing of the Gender Gap in Schooling: The Case of Thailand," *Comparative Education* 33 no. 1 (1997), 61–86.

very young in poorly paid jobs, and many have sought employment in urban areas to help support their families. The new Thai education system, making it mandatory for all Thai children to have a minimum of nine years of education, gives girls access to learning beyond primary education.

Formal Buddhist education has been the exclusive privilege of monks and a few Thai Buddhist *mae chii*s who have acquired Buddhist education from the Thai Buddhist institutions. Many *mae chii*s of the older generation have had only four to six years of primary education, and as a result, there has been a shortage of female Buddhist teachers. There are many skilled Thai female meditation teachers, since meditation is considered a suitable vocation for the *mae chii*s. In contrast, Buddhist education is obligatory for monks. Even though education has been the key factor enabling the *mae chii*s to act as religious specialists and also serve as teachers, many *mae chii*s have had difficulties accessing Buddhist education, More recently the Thai Buddhist institutions have opened up more opportunities for women's Buddhist education, and there has been a positive effect on women.

Thus the legal obstacles to a fair education have finally been removed for girls in Thailand since the reform was initiated by the government in 1999. Still it has been a lengthy process to implement this reform throughout the country. The basic education system (enacted in 2003) is divided into six years of primary schooling (*pathom* 1–6) followed by three years at lower secondary (*mattayom* 1–3), and three years at upper secondary (*mattayom* 4–6). These nine years of compulsory education and twelve years of free basic education are guaranteed by the constitution. The pre-primary school is for children between three and five years old, primary school (grades 1–6) is for children between six and eleven years, lower secondary school (grades 7–9) is for children between twelve and fourteen years, upper secondary school (grades 10–12) and vocational and technical education are for children between fifteen and seventeen years.[8]

GENDER ASPECTS ON CHILDREN IN RELATION TO BUDDHISM AND EDUCATION

Buddhism in Thailand has had a pervasive influence on shaping Thailand's social hierarchy in which monks are supreme moral agents. Theoretically, Buddhism is open to everyone regardless of caste, class, race, or gender, and according to the Buddha, women and men have the same spiritual potential to reach the final goal. However, Thailand does not fully conform to those views, and females in Thailand have no recognized authority in the Buddhist sangha, which embraces only male monks and male novices.[9]

8. For information about the education system in Thailand, see www.onec.go.th.
9. Falk, *Making Fields of Merit*, 23–25, 227–28, and 236–45; Falk, "Gender and Religious Legitimacy in Thailand" in *Gender Politics in Asia: Women Manoeuvring*

Thai society is noted for relatively egalitarian gender relations arising from women's roles in finance, land ownership, kinship structures, and the labor market.[10] Yet Thailand is in many ways a highly androcentric society, not least ideologically. In the dominant discourse of Buddhism there, maleness is ranked above femaleness in both cosmology and social praxis. Generally, Thai people are ambivalent about women who abandon traditionally accepted social roles, and they do not encourage women to renounce the world and receive *mae chii* ordination. The *mae chiis*' role is ambiguous and somewhat vague. Thai women who have received *bhikkhuni* ordination have not been ordained by the Thai sangha, since only men are allowed ordination by Thai monks and there has never been a *bhikkhuni* order there. However, for centuries there have been women renunciants and there are many notable women ascetics.[11]

Buddhism plays an important role in children's socialization. For example, Thai children are taught to respect their parents, and all children have a moral debt of gratitude to their parents for giving them life and raising them. The *bun khun* obligation of repaying debts is commonly met by a son through his ordination, by which he creates and ritually transfers merit to his parents, especially to his mother. Being ordained into the monkhood is a man's major merit-making act.[12] Thai children have a special moral obligation to their mothers, who are personified as loving, sacrificing, and the main caregivers and whose goodness is to be repaid with obedience and respect.[13] Daughters are not expected to repay their debts through ordination; instead, they are required to help support their parents and siblings. A daughter's lifelong obligation to look after and, if necessary, support her natal family is considered one reason some women from poor areas engage in sex labor.[14]

within Dominant Gender Orders, ed. Wil Burghoorn, Kazuki Iwanaga, Cecilia Milwertz, and Qi Wang (Copenhagen: NIAS Press, 2008), 95–120; and Chatsumarn Kabilsingh, *Thai Women in Buddhism* (Berkeley, CA: Parallax Press, 1991).

10. See, for example, Jane Monig Atkinson and Shelly Errington, eds., *Power and Difference: Gender in Island Southeast Asia* (Stanford, CA,: Stanford University Press, 1990).

11. See, for example, Steven Collins and Justin McDaniel, "Buddhist 'nuns' (*mae chi*) and the teaching of Pali in contemporary Thailand," *Modern Asian Studies* 44 no. 6 (2010), 1373–408; Falk, *Making Fields of Merit*; Martin Seeger, "'Against the Stream': The Thai Female Buddhist Saint Mae Chi Kaew Sianglam (1901–1991)" *South East Asia Research* 18 no. 3 (2010), 555–95; and Kamala Tiyavanich, *Forest Recollections: Wandering Monks in Twentieth-Century Thailand* (Honolulu: University of Hawaii Press, 1997).

12. Thomas A. Kirsch, "Buddhism, Sex-Roles, and the Thai Economy," in *Women of Southeast Asia*, ed. Penny Van Esterik. Southeast Asia Monograph Series (Dekalb: Northern Illinois University, 1996), 21.

13. Darunee Tantiwiramanond and Sashi Ranjan Pandey, "The Status and Role of Thai Women in the Pre-Modern Period: A Historical and Cultural Perspective," *Sojourn* 2 no. 1 (1987), 130.

14. See Pasuk Phongpaichit, *Rural Women in Thailand: From Peasant Girls to Bangkok Masseuses* (Geneva: International Labour Office, 1980); and Sukanya Hantrakul, "Prostitution in Thailand," in *Development and Displacement: Women in Southeast Asia*, ed. Glen Chandler, Norma Sullivan, and Jan Branson. Monash Papers on Southeast Asia, no. 18 (Clayton, Melbourne: Centre of Southeast Asian Studies, Monash University, 1988), 115–36.

Thai girls are commonly treated more strictly than boys and they are socialiszd to be neat and tidy and, in contrast to boys, are assigned tasks that require responsibilities.[15] A "good" woman should be equipped with proficient culinary skills, speak pleasant words, and be cautious in all matters—skills and characteristics that are reinforced by teachers.[16] Fongkaew states that the Thai feminine stereotype is characterized by gentleness, weakness, dependence, emotionality, and responsibility for taking care of the house and children. The masculine stereotype, on the other hand, is characterized by accomplishment, leadership, and responsibility as head and financial provider of the household.[17] Daughters are socialized to stay at home, carry out household chores, and take care of their brothers and sisters, while sons are socialized to participate in the wider society. Parents fear that if daughters are given too much freedom, they risk being involved in premarital sex, which would affect not only the moral standing of the daughter but the reputation of the parents as well. There are no such restrictions in the socialization of sons; boys are given more freedom to be with friends and entertain themselves.[18] Paradoxically, as is mentioned above, daughters should not risk involvement in premarital sex, and yet since those in low-income families are encouraged to contribute financially to their natal homes, they risk involvement in prostitution.

Baker has found that parents now value their children's education more than before, and thus they are required to work less, both in household chores and in the paid work force, and are able to focus on their schooling. As a result, children's economic benefit to their parents has declined,[19] and for poor families the children's education can become burdensome. Baker states that education is seen as a means of reducing "child labor," and he has found that the level of parents' education influences whether or not children enter the work force. He has also discovered that education can increase children's awareness of their rights, which can protect them against potential exploitation. He declares that the most important factor for the children is that they are physically in the classroom, which reduces their opportunity to work.[20]

Most parents consider education as the means to a better life for their children. Baker's research reveals that parents do not want their children to end up as farmers because they feel that it is a hard and unrewarding occupation.[21]

15. Warunee Fongkaew, "Gender Socialization and Female Sexuality in Northern Thailand," in *Coming of Age in South and Southeast Asia: Youth, Courtship and Sexuality*, ed. Lenore Manderson and Pranee Liamputtong (Richmond, Surrey: Curzon Press, 2002), 151.

16. Fongkaew, "Gender Socialization and Female Sexuality in Northern Thailand," 151.

17. Fongkaew, "Gender Socialization and Female Sexuality in Northern Thailand," 151.

18. Fongkaew, "Gender Socialization and Female Sexuality in Northern Thailand," 151.

19. Simon Baker, *Child Labour and Child Prostitution in Thailand: Changing Realities* (Bangkok: White Lotus, 2007).

20. Baker, *Child Labour and Child Prostitution in Thailand*, 147.

21. Baker, *Child Labour and Child Prostitution in Thailand*, 165.

I received similar responses from Thai parents that I have interviewed over the years. Those who work as farmers, fishermen, or carry out other types of tough manual work do not want their children to suffer the same hardships they endured. Most parents want their children to benefit from a more rewarding livelihood and therefore make great efforts to provide them with a good education.

A BUDDHIST SCHOOL FOR GIRLS

The Dhammajarinee School was established in 1990 at an autonomous Buddhist *samnak chii* and was the first school for girls in Thailand established by *mae chiis*. The *samnak chii* is located in the southern part of central Thailand approximately 120 kilometers south of Bangkok in Ratchaburi province. Ratchaburi has a mixed population with several ethnic groups and is close to the Burmese border. The initiative to set up a *samnak chii* independent from the Buddhist monks' temples came from the national Thai Mae Chiis' Institute. Ratburi Samnak Chii was the fourth *samnak chii* founded by the Institute.

In 1978 Khun Mae Prathin Kwan-Orn had just completed her Master's degree in India when she and her friend Khun Mai Sumon accepted the difficult task of establishing and running the *samnak chii*. From the very beginning they wanted to provide educational facilities for impoverished girls. Therefore setting up a school for girls was one of the incentives for the two *mae chii*s in establishing the *samnak chii*. Khun Mae Prathin saw the lack of educational opportunities for Thai girls as a fundamental problem; otherwise girls risked being exploited in poorly paid jobs while very young or, even worse, recruited into the sex industry. Boys have always had easier access to education than girls.[22] Boys from poor families have commonly been ordained as novices and lived at the Buddhist temples, where they learn both secular and Buddhist subjects; but a similar opportunity had not been open to girls from low-income families until the Dhammajarinee School opened. Education is still open to boys through the monasteries and is financially supported by the government.

I conducted fieldwork at the *samnak chii* in 1997 and 1998 and at that time there were approximately fifty-nine *mae chii*s and forty-seven *dhammajarinees*. There were always a number of temporary ascetic women who stayed for various amounts of time at the *samnak chii*. The *dhammajarinee*s studied secondary education and Buddhism at the Dhammajarinee School. The schoolgirls came from different parts of Thailand and they stayed for either two or four years at the school. Also, older *mae chii*s had a chance to study secondary education at the school.[23]

The Dhammajarinee School was unaccredited for fourteen years, during which time the *mae chii*s taught most of the subjects. In 2004 it became

22. Keyes, *Reshaping Local Worlds*.
23. See Falk, *Making Fields of Merit*, 213–15.

an accredited school and, since the majority of the *mae chii*s did not have the required teachers' training certificates, they were qualified only to teach Buddhist subjects. Nevertheless, the *mae chii*s are now working at administration and the lay teachers work under their supervision. The *mae chii*s at the *samnak chii* keep their monastic lifestyle and follow the same regulations and daily routines as they have always done. However, the school has gone through major changes. The girls had been studying only secondary education at the *samnak chii*. In 2004 the Dhammajarinee School opened a preschool and primary school. Since the accredited schools' curriculum covers more subjects than that of the uncredited schools, the girls do not have as much time as before to work on vegetable gardening or with handicrafts.

Khun Mae Prathin, who is still the director of the school at the time of this chapter (2011), considers it the school's mission to provide education for deprived girls, since society still does not support low-income girls in the way that the government supports poor boys at the temples. The situation is difficult for deprived girls. The *mae chii*s state that they must help those who have very little and in this way are also practicing *dhamma* (teaching of the Buddha). Khun Mae admits that helping these girls is not an easy task and the *mae chii*s must be patient. She states that it is important to think ahead, stressing that they are helping society by offering these girls an education.[24]

For the first five years, the Dhammajarinee School survived from donations by laypeople, individual monks, and *mae chii*s. The government gave some financial support in 1995 but not during the years of financial crisis.[25] The school is still dependent on private donations, but the government contributes more than it did when the school was unaccredited. The amount of money they receive is based on their number of students. The support from the government covers about 25 percent of the expenses, and the remaining 75 percent comes from private donations.[26]

It is costly to run a boarding school, but the school has become well-known over the years and more people are making donations. The donors are not only funding the cost of running the school but also financing the construction of various buildings. With more students than before, the cost of running the school has risen significantly. According to Khun Mae, a particularly important expense is the lay salaries.

The Dhammajarinee School also has expenses for the special care of girls with disabilities. Khun Mae refers to a father who is a single parent of two daughters with mental health problems and learning disabilities. On request from the father, who had been in contact with the social welfare workers, the *mae chii*s decided to take care of the girls and send them to a school in a neighboring province with special education. Such arrangements are usually carried out with the social care system and it is the *samnak chii* who pays the cost.[27]

24. Interview, May 2009.
25. Falk, *Making Fields of Merit*, 212.
26. Interview, August 2009.
27. Interview, August 2009.

Khun Mae highlights the importance of the *mae chiis*' work and engagement in the Dhammajarinee School. She says that the *mae chiis* represent continuity and sustainability and that they are imperative to the school's existence. According to her, the Dhammajarinee School would not survive without the *mae chiis*' work.

WHO NEEDS THE DHAMMAJARINEE SCHOOL?

Although the government's policy is to provide education for all Thai girls, the Dhammajarinee School run by the *mae chiis* remains a necessity. The number of girls who are studying at the school has increased dramatically during the last decade. Over the years the school has become well known and enrollment has increased. Khun Mae states that poverty is the main reason.[28] Poverty has always been a core problem for the girls at the Dhammajarinee School. While they do have access to a free education, the expenses of books, uniforms, utensils, and travel are a financial burden for many families. Poverty, combined with family difficulties and a government educational system that fails to reach all children inevitably leads to an increase in social and educational challenges.

Khun Mae states that the reasons girls seek education at Dhammajarinee School have changed in nature. Poverty is still a main reason. Moreover, a child who continues studying is not contributing to the family's economy, and all the expenses are beyond what many families can afford. The Dhammajarinee School provides the girls with uniforms, books, and the utensils that are necessary for their studies.

As was already mentioned, the number of girls who study at the Dhammajarinee School has increased dramatically. In 2009 there were more than 300 girls, compared with about 50 girls before the educational reform. Ratburi Samnak Chii runs a nursery as well as a preprimary school and they also provide education at primary and lower secondary levels. They are planning to offer upper secondary education in the near future. The girls who are studying at upper secondary school are doing so at schools in the vicinity of *samnak chii* by means of the *samnak chii*'s expenses.

Information about the Dhammajarinee School has spread through the *mae chiis*' networks throughout the country and through media. The school has a reputation as a safe place for girls to study. Khun Mae and other *mae chiis* from Ratburi Samnak Chii are invited to schools and local Buddhist temples in faraway villages to introduce the Dhammajarinee School. A few years ago a Buddhist monk accompanied a group of thirteen Karen girls who were going to begin their studies at the Dhammajarinee School.[29] When the girls returned

28. Interview, August 2009.

29. About a quarter million Karen live in Thailand; it is the largest ethnic minority in the country. Karen have their own traditional culture, but many today are Christian because of intense Christian missionary activities. Others have become

home, they told their parents and the other villagers about their positive experiences there, and as a result more girls applied to study at the school. In 2009 there were approximately forty Karen girls studying there.

Khun Mae emphasizes the importance of boys' and girls' equal rights to education and she complains that many parents lack this understanding. According to her, a daughter's education is traditionally deemed unnecessary in Thailand. A girl's place is in the home, where an education is believed to have little impact. A son's education, by contrast, is considered more important because they will become the head of the family and be responsible for its economic support.[30] However, in reality, women often become the head of the household and the sole breadwinners. Khun Mae states that women are disadvantaged by the subordination they are expected to embody. She finds that daughters are treated unfairly in many respects—not only in educational matters. She highlights adoption as one example. She says that most parents who would like to adopt a child prefer to adopt a boy. If they adopt a girl, she is commonly assigned the role of a friend to the daughter in the family. Khun Mae says that the impression seems to be that boys possess a future that girls can never have. According to Khun Mae, the unequal treatment of daughters and sons is more predominant in rural areas. In cities parents commonly treat their daughters and sons more equally and consider that both boys and girls have the same right to education.

The transition from unaccredited to accredited has resulted in a number of important organizational changes for the Dhammajarinee School. In the unaccredited school, the *mae chii*s carried out most of the teaching, but in the accredited school most of the teachers are lay persons. Most of the *mae chii*s are not officially qualified to teach secular subjects, and as a result the *mae chii*s have handed over secular teaching to lay teachers and are now teaching Buddhist subjects. The school strives to have one teacher per ten pupils and in August 2009 twenty-five lay teachers were teaching at the school.

I asked Mae chii Ben, who is a longstanding *mae chii* and has lived at the *samnak chii* for many years, if it is important for the parents that the Dhammajarinee School be a Buddhist school. She answered that the primary parental concern is not about how Buddhist it is, but that the school be completely female. She said that the parents trust that the school is keeping their children safe there, and that this safety issue is paramount. Khun Mae emphasises that only female teachers and staff work at the *samnak chii.* This insistence upon an all-female educational environment arises in conjunction with a number of scandals to have emerged from the monasteries in recent years, resulting in a loss of trust among laypeople. Monks' misdeeds have shaken the Thai Buddhist community and weakened the moral authority of the monks.

Buddhist, and in Thailand they practice together with Thai people. The province where Dhammajarinee School is located and the neighbouring province Kanchanaburi have a large Karen population.

30. Interview, August 2009.

Cases of monks who have broken their vows of celibacy have been publicly broadcast. Phra Bhavana Phuttho, a well-known monk in central Thailand, was arrested in 1995 and forced to leave the monkhood on charges of having raped several under-age ethnic minority girls who were being cared for at his monastery.[31] This means that the safety of the children is to some parents more important than is Buddhist learning.

CHILDREN AND THE BUDDHIST PRECEPTS

When the Dhammajarinee School was unaccredited, students were required to observe the eight Buddhist precepts: to abstain from killing, stealing, sexual activity, lying, taking intoxicants, eating after noon, beautification or entertainment, and sleeping on thick mattresses. When the school transitioned to an accredited primary school, the students were required to observe only the five precepts, namely: to abstain from killing, stealing, sexual misconduct, lying, and taking intoxicants. The change was made because the school accepted younger girls than they had before and the *mae chii*s did not think it was healthy for them to fast.

Mae chii Ning has been ordained and has lived at the *samnak chii* for more than twenty years.[32] Her impression is that the *mae chii*s were more present in the girls' daily lives when all who lived at the *samnak chii* observed the eight precepts. She notices that most of the girls today are less confident when they participate in the Buddhist ceremonies: they are very silent when compared with the *dhammajarinees*' performance; they have learned how to chant properly and are thus confident enough to ask for their precepts in a loud voice. Mae chii Ning concludes that the *dhammajarinees* act with more self-assurance in Buddhist settings than do the regular students and are proud of their skills.[33]

Mae chii Ning has also noticed that over the years the girls generally have more difficulty concentrating, which makes them absent-minded and less successful in keeping to the five precepts. She says that they manage to observe only two precepts well: the one concerning alcohol and the one concerning sexuality. She explains that they violate the first precept (against killing) often by unintentionally killing insects because of a lack of mindfulness, and they violate the second precept (to abstain from stealing) by acting impulsively. They see something that they like and they cannot resist taking it. The fourth precept, concerning speech is for many of them likewise difficult to observe. However, lying to the *mae chii*s frightens them because they believe that they will be

31. Peter A. Jackson, "Withering Centre, Flourishing Margins: Buddhism's Changing Political Roles," in *Political Change in Thailand: Democracy and Participation*, ed. Kevin Hewison (London: Routledge, 1997), 81–82.

32. The *mae chii*s' and the girls' names are fictitious.

33. Interview, August 2009.

punished by Nature (like a lightning strike). This belief is something that they have learned, from home and has not been instilled by the *mae chii*s.[34]

Mae chii Ning, as a Buddhist teacher, begins her lesson on the precepts by explaining wrongdoings (*benjasil*) and then focuses on how a person should act (*benjatham*) in order to be in line with the Buddhist precepts and develop into a good person. She explains the importance of *metta* (lovingkindness), right livelihood, not taking advantage of others, how to curb sexual impulses, and how to act in honest ways.

Several *mae chii*s complained that the teachers do not have the same authority over the students as they once had. Most of the *mae chii*s consider media in general, and especially the use of the Internet, to be responsible for the changing attitudes toward teachers' authority. The girls still listen to the teachers' advice but they ultimately seem more concerned with popular trends. Another contributing factor is the increase in lay teachers. Buddhism is not as central to the pedagogy as it was when only *mae chii*s were teaching.

Mae chii Ning starts every lesson with five minutes of meditation. She tries to convince the girls that if they meditate for only a short moment—as long as it takes for a snake to stick out its tongue or for an elephant to wave its ears—they will still receive *bun* (Buddhist merit). She wants the students to feel that they can meditate and feel proud of their achievement. She says that the girls at the Dhammajarinee School still have better opportunities than other girls to learn how to become good Buddhists.[35]

A REFUGE FOR GIRLS

The Dhammajarinee School is still a refuge for girls. Near the end of the 1990s the majority of the students came from poor villages in the northeastern and central provinces, and they stayed at the *samnak chii* for either two or four years. In 1998 secondary education was still out of reach for girls without financial means, and the Dhammajarinee School became the only chance for them to continue their education. Girls who had finished primary education and were eleven or twelve years old were then welcome at the school.

The Dhammajarinee School was initially strict about not allowing young children to stay at the *samnak chii*, because they considered that taking care of little children would create attachment for the *mae chii*s and go against their Buddhist rules.[36] Now, many laypersons are working at the *samnak chii* and the school has changed this policy. For the past few years the school has accepted children as young as three years old, most from the nearby village. They are taken care of in the nursery at the *samnak chii*. Both girls and boys are accepted at the nursery, but from grade one only girls are admitted to the

34. Interview, August 2009.
35. Interview, August 2009.
36. Falk, *Making Fields of Merit*, 127–29.

school. The majority of the children at the nursery are there only during the daytime. It is only under certain circumstances and at the request of the parents that children can board at the *samnak chii*.

The current lay teachers have made it possible for the school to admit young children. One significant reason for the demand to accept young children at the *samnak chii* is Thai girls' responsibility for their siblings. This custom became explicit by the many younger sisters that accompany older sisters to the Dhammajarinee School. Some parents require the older daughter to take care of her younger sister/s studying at the same school. For some girls, doing so is a prerequisite for being able to study. Khun Mae says that they do not want these girls to lose their opportunity to study, recognizing that if the Dhammajarinee School rejects them because of the girls' responsibility toward their younger siblings, they would probably find it difficult to finish school. Therefore, they opened a nursery to take care of children from three years old so the older sisters would have the opportunity to study. Ten years ago when the *samnak chii* was strict about not allowing little children to stay at the *samnak chii,* there was no demand for a nursery. The need arose after the education reform was implemented with mandatory secondary education, and as the school became more widely known.

The *mae chii*s state that it is difficult to take care of small children. More staff are needed and it is also more costly to nurse small children. Khun Mae considers that it is best for small children to stay with their parents, and therefore she thoroughly investigates whether or not the families can support their children. The younger children commonly miss home, and if the family can support them, they should do that instead of handing over the responsibility to the *samnak chii* and to the *mae chii*s who run the nursery with employed laypeople. Khun Mae is concerned about the increasing number of small children arriving at the *samnak chii*.

Like the situation in the 1990s when the school was established, many of the girls come from the northeast of Thailand, and today the monks at the local village temples are also important for introducing the Dhammajarinee School to the girls and their families. However, one striking difference is that now many of the students at the Dhammajarinee School belong to ethnic minority groups and the majority belong to the Thai-Karen and the Thai-Mon groups. Most of the Karen and Aka girls come from the north of Thailand and the Mon girls are from a district in Rachaburi province, the same province where the *samnak chii* is located. The education that the government provides is out of reach for many Thai children, and one *mae chii* explains that accessing the education that the government offers is an obstacle for children who live in outlying regions. Many minority girls who live in remote areas cannot reach the school bus in the mornings because they would have to walk at night in order to do so, and this would be too dangerous.

Khun Mae and the other *mae chii*s talk with appreciation about the Karen and Mon pupils—their interest in learning and the good results that they achieve. According to the *mae chii*s, the majority of the Karen girls are eager to study, they learn quickly, and they have good manners and are respectful to the teachers. The teachers assign these characteristics to those who live in the countryside far away from cities. The *mae chiis* use the word "pure" when they describe these girls.

The conditions at the Dhammajarinee School are better than what many of the girls have at home. Some of the girls have experienced difficult problems, and their lives are safer at the Dhammajarinee School. Security for young girls is a theme that is frequently brought up in my conversations with both lay teachers and *mae chiis*. They are all concerned about the vulnerable circumstances in which many girls are placed. Khun Mae says that the better-known the Dhammajarinee School becomes, the more children in vulnerable situations are brought there. Khun Mae considers the school's mission to take care of these children and to find ways to finance their living costs. In Khun Mae's view, doing this is important not only for the children and their families but also for the very future of Thai society.[37]

For those girls coming from stronger economic conditions, the primary explanation provided for their enrollment is a need for discipline. Many parents are concerned that they are losing authority over their daughters: the girls do what they want, when they want. Parents fear that such lack of discipline will eventually jeopardize their future, and they look to the Dhammajarinee School to instill Buddhist values into them. The hope is that they will eventually become calmer and less argumentative. Girls who constantly argue or exhibit disruptive behavior are challenging for the *mae chiis*, but they try to help the girls, and those who continue living at the Dhammajarinee School must be willing to change their behavior. Khun Mae says that the parents are relieved when their daughters' behavior improves and they achieve a calmer state of mind.[38]

RULES AND DAILY ROUTINES

The very young children who live in the nearby village are brought to the *samnak chii* and taken back home every day by their parents or older siblings. All girls in grade one must also live at the *samnak chii* if they come from the village. The parents' visits are restricted and the school does not allow the parents to visit their daughters during weekdays. The *mae chiis* say that such visits would distract the girls from their studies and would disturb the girls who do not receive visits from their parents. They are strict about the rules but Khun Mae says that some parents do not understand the importance of the visiting regulations and they wish to visit their daughters when it is convenient for them.[39]

37. Interview, May and August 2009.
38. Interview, August 2009.
39. Interview, August 2009.

Being away from home is difficult for the girls, especially when they are new to the school. One of the girls explained to me that they are not allowed to go home on weekends but she visits home during semester breaks. However, during the semesters, they are allowed to go home if their parents are sick. Previously, her parents came to visit her twice a month but now can manage only once a month because they have to work longer because of financial difficulties.

Rules at the Dhammajarinee School

1. Pupils must follow the five Buddhist precepts and the daily routine at the *samnak chii*.
2. Pupils are not allowed to keep or spend money, keep a cell phone, or have any unnecessary belongings.
3. Parents should not visit their daughter for the first three months at the school. It is important that the girls adjust to the school routine.
4. Parents are encouraged to visit their daughter at least once a month, but they should not bring any food or any unnecessary things. Any goods the parents bring to the school will be for public use.
5. Parents or visitors are not allowed to meet the students in the dormitory.
6. Pupils are allowed to go home once a year. The school will send a letter to the parents and inform them when they can come and collect their daughters.
7. If a pupil violates any of the school rules, the school will inform the parents. If the pupil breaks the school rules more than three times, the school will consider sending the pupil back to her parents.

Not all of the girls who are accepted to study at Dhammajarinee School can adjust to life at the school. The *mae chii*s and staff help them to settle in but, as Khun Mae explains, their ability to adjust and stay at the Dhammajarinee School depends on their background and how motivated they are to study. The *mae chii*s stress the importance of the parents' role.

The girls who study at the Dhammajarinee School come from diverse backgrounds, and occasionally conflicts arise. Dorm rooms accommodate seven girls each. The girls need to keep things tidy, so they create their own rules and determine what kind of punishment they receive if they break them. One girl says that she did not follow the rules in the beginning of her stay—she was often noisy and late for class and was subsequently punished by being assigned cleaning duties.[40]

40. Interview, August 2009.

Students' Daily Schedule

04.45	Wake up
05.00	Physical exercise. Cleaning the school building
06.30	Breakfast
07.45	National anthem. Pay respect to the national flag.
08.00	Chanting (*suadmon*) sitting meditation.

The school day starts.

11.00	Lunch
12.30	Meditation (rest)

The school day continues.

15.30	Vocational training
18.00	Dinner
19.45	Homework, chanting (*suadmon*) and sitting meditation.
21.45	Bedtime

GIRLS' EXPERIENCES OF THE SCHOOL

Siri undertook her primary schooling at a government school and began her secondary education at the Dhammajarinee School. She was fourteen years old and had studied at Dhammajarinee School for more than a year when I met her in 2009. She belongs to the Thai-Mon minority group and is from the province where the school is located. She became interested in studying at this school after listening to one of the leading *mae chii*s who was invited to her school to speak. She knew that her parents would not give their consent for her to study away from home, so she phoned her aunt and asked her to contact her parents and ask for permission. [41]

She was right about her parents' initial disapproval, since the family needed her help to take care of her younger brother and her older sister's daughter. When the parents learned that these children could accompany Siri to the Dhammajarinee School, they gave their consent to let her study there. She says that otherwise it would have been difficult for her to continue studying. When her brother reaches the age of six he will return to his parents' home and go to the primary school in the village. Their parents visit them regularly at the school and now believe that studying there is the best solution for them.[42]

Fah is a ten-year-old girl from Roi Et province in northeastern Thailand. Her parents were positive from the beginning about her studying at the Dhammajarinee School. She is one of three sisters and brothers and is at the Dhammajarinee School with a sister, who is four years older. She

41. Interview, April 2009.
42. Interview, April 2009.

explains that her family does not have the economic means to support their studies and could not even afford to take their daughters to the Dhammajarinee School. It was the abbot at the village temple who paid for their travel. Fah says that she had no difficulties adjusting to life at the *samnak chii* and she liked the Dhammajarinee School from the very beginning; she is happy there.[43]

Not all girls who come to study at the Dhammajarinee School adjust to the school's routines and regulations. In 2009 fifty girls left the school during the first month because they felt homesick or had difficulties adjusting. Luaknam, from the Thai-Mon ethnic group, is one of them. Initially she did not want to stay at the school because she missed home, but she decided to give it a try and to her surprise, before long she was enjoying herself there. She thinks that several of her classmates, who are from the same ethnic group, have contributed to her well-being at the school. The fact that they speak the Mon language helps them to feel at home. The school encourages the girls to use Thai, but Luaknam and other girls from minority groups feel that it is important to use their mother tongue.[44]

The girls say that they spend their leisure time differently at the school than they do at home. They follow the school's rules and regulations, and they do not have the same freedoms that they have at home. At home, many of them mainly watch TV, but at the school TV is limited to twice a week. Interestingly, the girls do not seem to miss watching TV when at the school because there are so many other things they prefer to do.

Many of the girls are used to working and helping out in the home, so they do not complain about the additional responsibilities at the Dhammajarinee School. Some of them say that they initially felt that life at the school was too regulated and circumscribed. Others, however, find the structure helpful, keeping them focused on their schoolwork. In addition to the schoolwork, all the girls are assigned special tasks. One of Luaknam's responsibilities is to accompany the *mae chii*s on the daily alms round and she says:

> Every day during the two years I have been here, I and two of my friends have walked together with the *mae chii*s on their alms round. The *mae chii*s walk in three different groups in three directions, and the *mae chii*s and my friends and I walk without shoes. If I get sick, another girl will replace me. I very much enjoy assisting the *mae chii*s on the alms round. Sometimes it starts raining while we are walking but we continue walking. The rain can be very heavy but we always go on the alms round because we do not want to disappoint the villagers. If the *mae chii*s for some reason have to cancel their daily alms round, they always inform the villagers in advance.[45]

43. Interview, May 2009.
44. Interview August 2009.
45. Interview, August 2009.

The girls say that in many respects the Dhammajarinee School is similar to the schools they studied at previously, but there are also differences. For some of the girls the main reason they want to study at the Dhammajarinee School is that it is a school for girls and they feel safe there. Moreover, those who have experienced other schools appreciate the freedom from financial pressures. Their relationships with classmates are remarkably more relaxed given the fact that they are forbidden from using money—an otherwise obvious stratifying factor. One of the girls said that "At Dhammajarinee School, everyone is equal."[46]

Near the end of the 1990s the *dhammajarinee*s lived in dormitories with approximately thirteen students to a room.[47] The housing capacities have improved since then and today seven girls share a room. Taking into consideration that many girls are living together and every girl has only a small space for her belongings, it is necessary that they cooperate and keep their possessions in order. The girls say that when quarrels occur, it is often over trivial matters that are soon resolved. The girls learn to solve problems through Buddhist values. Teachers urge them "to use *sati* [mindfulness] rather than power." One girl explains: "When I quarrel with somebody, I must think about what I have done and not only blame the other person. If it is my mistake, I will apologize. If it is not my mistake, I will forgive."[48]

Many of the girls say that studying Buddhism is important to them. One girl says that she appreciates that she learns more about Buddhism here than she would have in an ordinary school, and she states that the best thing about that is that it makes her calm and she learns about life. On a question about what she likes most, she answers that she especially likes chanting and meditation practice. In ordinary schools Buddhism is more integrated into other social subjects but here she says she studies Buddhism with more depth. She seems to have a sincere interest in Buddhism and is voluntarily taking evening classes in Buddhism and has passed Naktham Tri (*dhamma* scholar elementary level).[49]

Ooy also has a special interest in Buddhist studies. She is fourteen years old and has been studying at the Dhammajarinee School for one year. She says that her mother has inspired her to study Buddhism in order to be happy and successful. She stresses that it is most important to act in a noble way, and she is especially interested in learning how to be a good person by studying Buddhism. She explains that it is important to understand that no person is alone and we must support each other; we must take care of ourselves first and then we should also support others. At the Dhammajarinee School the girls learn the value of giving, both from Buddhist studies and also from lay teachers. Ooy says, "We learn to be givers and through that we will get good

46. Interview, August 2009.
47. Falk, "Thammacarini Witthaya."
48. Interview, August 2009.
49. The *naktham* levels are *tri, tho,* and *ek* (3, 2, and 1). The three levels of *naktham* studies are the foundation of the Buddhist education system in Thailand.

results, but we should not wish to get rewards because if we do that we will not get them."[50]

Ooy says that studying Dhamma has made her much calmer than she was before. She especially likes to study the Buddha's life. She is not fond of the practice of meditation, because it makes her feel sleepy. Her friend Siriporn is also fourteen years old and she says that when she was younger she did not believe that the Buddha existed. It was only when she saw photos from the places where the Buddha lived that the Buddha and Buddhism became relevant to her. Both Ooy and Siriporn are eager to learn more about *dhammic* principles and they say they want to understand the arguments and reasons behind the Buddhist way of living. At the Dhammajarinee School the girls learn to take care of themselves, which they say makes them more independent and confident.[51]

IMPROVED CURRICULUM

The education reform was created to motivate teachers and children to accelerate the learning process. However, the new system burdened the teachers' workload dramatically and, to their disappointment, administrative work and report-writing have put a strain on their teaching. The government gave long-serving teachers the opportunity to take early retirement, which became an attractive option for older teachers. The result has been a decreased number of teachers and an increase in the number of students: the many vacancies in the schools opened up possibilities for new teachers to be employed at government schools. The *mae chiis* and other teachers that I have spoken to are concerned about young and inexperienced teachers who lack older experienced colleagues to guide them. The *mae chiis* say that the requirement that teachers at governmental schools write extensive reports (which is time-consuming) in order to get a promotion has badly affected the quality of the teaching, and that is one reason why many girls apply to the Dhammajarinee School. Khun Mae says that more students than previously have insufficient knowledge in basic subjects such as writing and reading and she ascribes that situation to the fact that teachers are spending less time with the students.

The Dhammajarinee School follows the general curriculum in the Thai education system. The *mae chiis* say that the curriculum at the school has improved as a result of the external evaluation.[52] Those who teach there must have graduated in one major subject and must have a teaching certificate. There is also a requirement to work full time. According to the *mae chiis*, it is generally not difficult to find teachers, since there are many recent graduates but it is difficult to find qualified, experienced teachers.

50. Interview, August 2009.
51. Interview, August 2009.
52. Interview, April 2009.

One major change in the curriculum is that the school places more emphasis on meditation than it did before. Meditation was not a part of the curriculum until 2008, when it became mandatory. Previously it was practiced daily but on a voluntary basis. Nowadays, two hours of daily meditation is compulsory, and the girls practice with instructions from meditation teachers. The course is divided into three levels—basic, intermediate, and high—and the pupils must qualify for the different levels. The *mae chii*s say that the reason for making meditation mandatory is to improve the girls' mindfulness (*sati*) and calmness. Through meditation they can improve their concentration and that in turn has positive results on their studies.

Music is another new subject in the curriculum. The girls learn about Thai music and also learn to play instruments. However, the *mae chii*s who study at the school cannot participate in the music classes since doing so is against *mae chii* rules. The school has its own orchestra, which plays the national anthem every morning before the school day starts. The girls line up outside the school buildings while they hoist the Thai flag and the orchestra plays. The same procedure is performed in all Thai schools in the mornings. In the past, when the Dhammajarinee School did not have its own orchestra, they used to switch on the radio to hear the national anthem being played at eight every morning.

Khun Mae has observed that meditation has a positive effect on the girls, and she says that the girls seem to be happier in their daily life and are less aggressive.[53] A lay teacher, who has extensive teaching experience and has taught at the Dhammajarinee School for approximately a year, says that it is sometimes challenging to teach at the school because the girls have such diverse backgrounds. However, she states that daily meditation practice and chanting have a positive influence on the girls and that living and studying at this Buddhist school gradually brings about improvements. She does not think that the girls at the Dhammajarinee School are much better than students in other schools, but they definitely learn much more about morality and Buddhism than other students do and she considers that feature to be also beneficial for their studies.[54]

GIRLS' DESIRE FOR ORDINATION

At the unaccredited Dhammajarinee School, the *mae chii*s were involved in almost all the teaching and they served as role models for the *dhammajarinees* (students following the eight precepts), and today the *mae chii*s remain important role models for the girls. The girls say that they think highly of them, and many have their own favorite *mae chii* that they especially admire. The schoolgirls praise the *mae chii*s for their high moral standards, wisdom, good manners, honesty, and straightforwardness. The *mae chii*s also bestow on the

53. Interview, August 2009.
54. Interview, April 2009.

girls a sense of security, and the girls subsequently become more attached to the *mae chii*s than to the lay teachers, a bond that has not altered over the last decade. The girls and the *mae chii*s live at the *samnak chii* and also have a lot of contact outside the classroom. The special relationship of trust between the students and the *mae chii*s is different from the teacher-student relationship the girls have with the lay teachers, who do not live at the *samnak chii* and so do not have much contact outside the classroom.

Something that has changed between 1998 and 2009 is that many more girls today are interested in receiving *mae chii* ordination.[55] Every year on Khun Mae's birthday on June 2, the *samnak chii* organizes an ordination ceremony. Those girls who are interested can apply and the *mae chii*s determine whether or not they are mature enough and able to follow the precepts to lead an ordained life. In 2009, fifty girls applied to be ordained; twelve passed the screening and were accepted to become *mae chii*s. Five of those who received ordination belong to the ethnic minority groups.

The newly ordained young *mae chii*s continue to study together with the same classmates as when they were laypersons. However, their status has changed and their lay classmates have to treat them with veneration and address them with the honorific *khunmaechii*. These young *mae chii*s can no longer play with their classmates and they have to move out of the dormitory and live with the other *mae chii*s in their quarters. Their daily routines are likewise altered, since they now have to carry out additional ceremonial responsibilities.

One *mae chii* who teaches several subjects says that she is especially impressed by the young *mae chii*s who belong to the minority groups. They had experienced difficult living conditions in remote mountainous areas and at home they depended on cooperation. The *mae chii* says that their earlier lifestyle has probably helped them to develop stamina and a willingness to help out. These young *mae chii*s were planning to visit their village later in 2009; they were proud of being ordained and were eager to meet their parents in their new presence.[56]

SOME EDUCATIONAL RESULTS

Mae chii Ben is a longstanding *mae chii* and a highly appreciated teacher at the Dhammajarinee School. Previously she taught several disciplines, but now she teaches primarily Buddhist subjects. Mae chii Ben emphasizes the importance of girls' learning about Buddhism. She explains that Buddhism is especially important for girls because most of them will become mothers and, in effect, their children's first teacher. If mothers know about Buddhism, the children will learn. She states that society has changed but Buddhism remains relevant. Mae chii Ben declares that the girls must learn about the processes of life and

55. Falk, *Making Fields of Merit*, 92–98.
56. Interview, August 2009.

about the body—we are born, we get old, sick, and finally die. She says that Buddhist teaching is important for all stages of life and teaches one how to be happy. She thinks that it is important for the girls to learn how to support themselves through a livelihood that is in line with Buddhist teaching. She teaches fundamental Buddhist principles about true happiness and how to be free of suffering.[57]

For Mae chii Ben, is it important that teaching and practicing go hand in hand, and she says:

> [We] teach about morality and about the Buddhist precepts and we must live and act accordingly. We want to help them to be free from defilements (*kilet*). Our teaching is not only academic. We also teach them how to live peacefully together with others. We want the girls to develop lovingkindness (*metta*), forgiveness, and the willingness to help each other.[58]

High school students (grades 7–9) study the three Naktham grades; the content of the three levels of Naktham studies was more extensive before than it is now. When the Dhammajarinee School was unaccredited, the students had more time for their Buddhist studies; Mae chii Ben says that they came to her with their assignments and wanted her comments, or they had memorized something that they wanted to recite to her. She says that that seldom happens today, but the girls still learn and apply their knowledge in their daily lives.[59]

Since the girls live for several years at the *samnak chii,* they are also taught how to cook, clean, and carry out certain duties that they would otherwise have learned, at home. Mae chii Ben is one of the *mae chii*s who teaches them these skills, and she incorporates Buddhism in all her teaching as well as in her cooking classes. Commonly, the girls are initially extremely motivated in these classes but are unaware of the amount of work required or how time consuming it is to cook. Mae chii Ben teaches the girls about vegetables, and they collect plants and learn about different ingredients. She teaches them how to prepare the ingredients and everything is done manually. The girls commence with simple cooking and gradually learn to cook more difficult dishes. Mae chii Ben says that the girls are very satisfied when they visit home and show their skills, cooking for their parents and family.

The girls practice patience in mediation, but patience becomes an embodied practice during their cooking lessons. They have to develop their concentration, and Mae chii Ben says that cooking is a good way to develop mindfulness (*sati*). Mae chii Ben does not teach cooking as often as she did before accreditation, because of the greater number of subjects on the schedule. The number of

57. Interview, August 2009.
58. Interview, August 2009.
59. Interview, August 2009.

formal subjects and the time spent practicing sitting meditation have increased at the expense of manual work such as growing plants and cooking. However, Mae chii Ben stresses the importance of practicing mindfulness firsthand.[60]

Currently, Mae chii Ben teaches 107 girls. In her Buddhist classes she teaches girls from the age of twelve. She has noticed that they often interpret the Buddha's life mythologically. Showing the students the geographical places in India and Nepal where the Buddha lived and taught, showing the pilgrimage sites associated with the Buddha's life, and explaining how Buddhism spread throughout Asia and eventually reached Thailand renders the Buddha's story more concrete for the students. Mae chii Ben also teaches the Jātaka stories (*Maha Chadok*), explaining that it would be otherwise too difficult for the girls to understand karma, rebirth, and the eventual attainment of Buddhahood.

Mae chii Ben says that Buddhist teaching is of great importance for the girls because it prepares them for life. Some girls are very interested in learning about Buddhism but not all, so she tries to find ways to make Buddhism interesting. The young students commonly find the Jātaka stories entertaining and an excellent introduction to teaching them about karma and the importance of the precepts. She tells them that keeping the precepts will protect them throughout their lives. Her teaching concerns living and dying, and she exemplifies the law of karma by using plants, trees, and animals at the *samnak chii*.

The *samnak chii* has a considerable number of dogs, and she uses their behavior as examples. Recently she described a dog that tried to take its own life. That dog was weak and had an infected wound after being injured by a bird. It suffered constantly and tried to drown itself by jumping into one of the ponds at the *samnak chii*. The *mae chii*s rescued the dog, but the dog jumped into the water several times until it finally succeeded in drowning itself. Mae chii Ben uses this event as a starting point for exploring the meaning of suffering, death, and intentional actions that create merit and demerit (*kham*).

The Buddhist classes also include learning about the *bhikkhuni sangha,* and the girls become upset when they learn about the special rules (*garudhamma*) that subordinate the *bhikkhuni*s' (fully ordained female monks) to the monks. They do not think it is right that a *bhikkhuni* who has been ordained for many years should pay respect to a newly ordained male novice or monk. However, the girls have also seen that some *bhikhsuni*s (female monks ordained in the Mahayana tradition) are flexible about the rules. The girls were surprised when they met a *bhihksuni* who was ordained in Taiwan and noticed that she wore a watch and had a meal in the afternoon. The girls compared that conduct with that of the *mae chii*s who never use watches, never eat after twelve, and drink only water, all of which caused discussions about the value of the precepts. Because the *bhikhsuni*s did not adhere to the precepts as the *mae chii*s did, the *bhihksuni*'s status as ordained was puzzling to the girls.

Lay teachers who have had experience teaching in the Dhammajarinee School as well as elsewhere appreciate the Dhammajarinee students' etiquette

60. Interview, August 2009.

and good behavior, which the teachers attribute to the daily Buddhist practice and Buddhist lifestyle at the school. The teachers say that they feel that the Dhammajarinee School students have greater responsibilities than those in other schools where they have taught. The students are far away from home and sometimes the lay teachers and often the *mae chii*s become substitute parents. The girls' heterogeneous background is a challenge for the teachers, and they emphasize that since the girls live at the school it is significant for them that they learn more than the set school subjects.[61] Therefore the *mae chii*s teach the girls cooking, gardening, sewing, and similar subjects that they would normally have learned at home.

CONCLUDING REMARKS

The Dhammajarinee School was established at an autonomous Buddhist *samnak chii* in May 1990 with the aim of helping impoverished girls attain a better future. Women's exclusion from the sangha made it a male privilege to attend monastic schools; it was through the Dhammajarinee School that girls could first receive education through the ordained (*mae chii*) community. Access to Buddhist instruction, as well as to secondary and higher education, has long been an important issue for many *mae chii*s. Education has been singled out as a key factor for generating better circumstances for poor women and children, and the *mae chii*s had long wanted to provide schooling for girls who had no chance to further their education otherwise. When the Dhammajarinee School was first established, many Thai girls with only primary education entered the workforce while they were very young, and they had to cope with poor working conditions, leading many to be recruited into the sex industry. The leaders of the Dhammajarinee School hoped that educating these young girls might help prevent that course of events.

The school reform that has recently been implemented in Thailand aims to give both girls and boys access to free education. However, many girls, especially in remote areas, still have difficulty gaining admission to government schools and that is one reason for them to leave home and study at the Dhammajarinee School. The leading *mae chii*s at the school explain the increase in student applications there as resulting from a combination of societal problems, poverty, and family difficulties. Some parents, especially from the city, are worried that their daughters might drop out of school because of a lack of motivation and discipline problems. The moral training in combination with a good quality education and the disciplined life at a *samnak chii* led them to apply for their daughters to study at the Dhammajarinee School. This study has found that the most important matter for the girls and their families is that the Dhammajarinee School is strictly female. The safety these parents seek

61. Interviews, April and August 2009.

for their daughters translates into an apparently very enjoyable educational experience for the daughters themselves.

In Thailand, notions of the "good" and the "bad" girl/woman are defined in terms of their relationship to the institution of the family. Being a "good" girl/woman implies a steadfast loyalty to the family, being a dutiful daughter, a faithful wife, and an all-giving mother. Thai children are taught to respect their parents, and throughout their lives children have a moral debt (*bun khun*) to their parents. Boys' ordination as novices for a short period of time before they marry is a highly valued form of repaying those debts.[62] Girls are not expected to ordain and instead are required to start their domestic responsibilities in their early childhood, something boys are exempted from. Daughters' *bun khun* relationship to their parents makes them responsible for their siblings, and this duty explains why small children accompany their older sisters to the Dhammajarinee School. Continuing to take care of their younger siblings while they are studying is today a prerequisite for more girls studying at the Dhammajarinee School than it was a decade ago. This study concludes that in the 1990s, before the educational reform was implemented, parents would not send their daughters to Dhammajarinee School if they had the responsibility of taking care of younger siblings. Their daughters would have remained at home and in many cases would probably not have studied at all.

Education is expected to solve social and individual problems and is seen as the vehicle for attaining a desirable future. The curriculum at the Dhammajarinee School follows what the educational reform prescribes. In addition, the school holds onto traditional schooling that values moral knowledge and discipline, and it emphasizes the importance of Buddhist teaching. To achieve basic education, instill good Buddhist manners, and become a good person are perceived as an individual's safeguard, completely in line with traditional Thai social values of what is considered necessary for creating a peaceful and trouble-free society. In Thailand, educational levels, social prestige, and age can sometimes outflank gender inequalities. I got the impression that the girls at the Dhammajarinee School did not feel excluded from taking up any profession as long as they had received proper education. Police work, law, and the armed forces were frequent answers that I received when I talked with the girls about what they dream of doing in the future if they have a chance to study further. This response demonstrates that a child's education instills hope for the future. The improvement of quality of education and equality of the education system is the source of a community's future.

62. Charles F. Keyes, "Ambiguous Gender: Male Initiation in a Northern Thai Buddhist Society" in *Gender and Religion: On the Complexity of Symbols*, ed. Caroline Walker Bynum, Stevan Harrell, and Paula Richman (Boston: Beacon Press, 1986), 66–96.

CHAPTER 12

Superheroes and Slapstick

New Media and the Teaching of Buddhist Children in Thailand

JUSTIN MCDANIEL

Recently a significant number of new texts, films, songs, websites, and posters designed for educating Buddhist children have appeared in Thailand. This chapter will focus on a new generation of Buddhist texts and films for children. There is an abundance of sources. Indeed, these stories are much more popular than didactic and systematic Buddhist lessons. However, until now they have been ignored by scholars. To this end, this chapter serves as a descriptive introduction to new Buddhist pedagogical material for children in Thailand.

Even though Buddhist comic books and films in Thailand are modern media, and their contents are often quite shocking, instead of concentrating on their "newness" and unorthodox teachings, it may be more fruitful to see them as continuations of traditional Buddhist narrative traditions in Thailand. Thai vernacular Buddhist literature, murals, and dramas have always adapted and localized, enhanced, and changed Indic stories or created entirely new Buddhist tales. Dozens of creative adaptations of Indic Buddhist literature can be seen in the *Paññāsa Jātaka* collection, from which stories are often requested by lay people at religious ceremonies and family events (weddings, funerals, house blessings, tonsure ceremonies, and the like).[1] Secular texts such as *Sangthong*, *Lilit Phra Lo*, *Samut Ghot Kham Chan*, *Khun Chang Khun Paen*, *Aniruddha Kham Chan*, *Lilit Ong Kan Chaeng Nam*, *Pakṣi-pakaraṇam*, and *Yuan Pai* all are romance

1. For a discussion about the lasting popularity of the *Jātakas* in Thailand and Laos, see Patrick Jory, "Thai and Western Scholarship in the Age of Colonialism: King Chulalongkorn Redefines the Jatakas," *Journal of Asian Studies* 61 no. 3

or adventure tales that incorporate Buddhist themes and characters. They are publicly performed and have long been part of the education of young Buddhist children in Thailand.

Some of the most creative adaptations of Indic Buddhist texts are seen on Thai murals. These are some of the first places children are introduced to Buddhist narratives. Even though murals are often overtly sexual or violent, the most explicit scenes are on the lower registers of temple walls and often at the eye level, of children. Being literate is not a requirement for viewing murals. For example, the murals of Wat Kho Kaeo Suttharam in Petchaburi Province (among many others, including royal first-class monastery Wat Rakhang) depict the cosmology of heavens and hells from the *Traiphumikāthā*, unlike any cosmological depiction in Sanskrit or Pāli. The murals in the *wihan* of Wat Ratchaorot contain scenes from the Chinese epic romance *Sam Kok*. Wat Suwandararam in Ayutthaya has murals depicting the life of King Naresuan, with brahmin priests *ṛṣi* casting spells over fires, bloody battles, and prison torture. Some murals at Wat Suthat depict scenes of women being plucked from trees like fruit, as well as Westerners arriving on ships to Bangkok.[2] In the depictions of the Himavanta forest from the *Vessantara Jātaka* at Wat Khian in Angthong Province, there are depictions of Chinese physicians drinking rice whisky and Persian warriors groping mythical *makkaliphon*. In the murals depicting the Lao epic poem *Xiang Miang* (known in Thai as *Srithanonchai*) at Wat Pathumwanaram in Bangkok, Thai soldiers are wearing colonial American military uniforms and on the pillars there are paintings of two *bhikkhunī* (fully ordained nuns), Brachabodhi and Bathacara, even though there is no evidence that there were ordained *bhikkhunī* in nineteenth-century Thailand or sixteenth- century Laos (approximately the era the *Xiang Miang* was compiled).[3] The inscriptions of the names of these two nuns are written in Khom script. Therefore, in one set of Thai murals in a Bangkok monastery you have a Lao epic that depicts men in American dress, and Cambodia (Khom/Khmer) script labeling Indian nuns. Time and space are collapsed according to the whims of the artist and the patron. Buddhist children in Siam/Thailand have been

(2002), 892–96 and 911–13. There are dozens of studies on the use of *Jātakas* in art and drama. For an overview, see Justin McDaniel, *Invoking the Source: Nissaya Manuscripts, Pedagogy and Sermon-Making in Northern Thailand and Laos*, Ph.D. Dissertation (Cambridge, Harvard University, 2003), 128–43. Bosaenggam Vongtala et al., *Vannakhati Lao* (Vientiane: Kaxuang Seuksa, 1987), 208. Vernacular epic poems that do not have any particular religious themes, like the *Thao Hung Thao Cheung* and *Xin Sai*, are also often chanted at Buddhist ceremonies in Laos. See Khongdeuane Bunyavong, *Thao Hung Thao Cheuang* (Vientiane: Toyota Foundation, 2000), Introduction.

2. Similar scenes are depicted at Wat Suwannaram in Thonburi. I thank Donald Stadtner for pointing these out to me.

3. See No Na Paknam, *Wat Pathumwanaram* (Bangkok: Muang Boran, 2539 [1996]). See tdm.sas.upenn.edu, where I have posted a large number of photographs I took of these murals and the monastic grounds.

exposed to creative adaptations of Buddhist narratives in popular stories and in visual depictions for centuries.

TEXTS AND WEB-BASED BUDDHIST CHILDREN'S MATERIAL

Although there have been Thai Buddhist pedagogical printed texts designed for children since the late nineteenth century, they were almost sponsored by Thailand's Supreme Patriarch (*Sangharat*) Prince Wachirayan and intended primarily for male novices residing in monasteries. There were some basic etiquette guides for lay children, but little else. Two of the most common texts for children for decades were the *Navakowat* (see below) and the *Buddhasāsanāsubhāsit*, a selection of short, pithy Buddhist proverbs from the canon; a Buddha biography; and a guide to the *Vinaya*. However, in the past twenty-five years there has been an explosion of new creative texts for children.[4] Previously, Buddhist texts for children were designed for novice boys and included primers for learning the ten precepts, the *Jātakas*, the *Chet Tamnan* (*Sattaparitta*) liturgical chants, and the life of the Buddha. Most were in the vernacular with short explanations of Pāli words.[5] With the expansion of Buddhist Sunday schools (*Rongrian Wan Athit*) for lay children, the variety of books expanded to include

4. The prince also instituted three grades of *nak dham* (student of the Dhamma), which remain relatively unchanged today. Novices can take these examinations beginning as young as seven or eight years old. However, they are taken mostly by students in their late teens or older. These examinations are in Thai and were prerequisites for the Pāli examinations. Most of the examinations are on commentarial texts like the *Dhammapada-Atthakathā*, *Maṅgala-atthadīpanī*, and the *Visuddhimagga*, and on Thai handbooks and anthologies, not on canonical texts themselves. *Nak dham* examinations and essays do not involve exact word-for-word translation or memorization and are not based on Pāli language texts. Before monks and novices can enter monastic universities, they study at primary and secondary monastic schools. There are 31,071 monasteries in Thailand, but only a small percentage of these actually run schools. The largest number of monastic students in modern Thailand study in *Pariyatidhamma* secondary schools, which have three major divisions: *Paliseuksa* study (Pāli language, liturgy, and texts), *Dhammaseuksa* (ethics, general Buddhist history and teachings), and *Samanaseuksa* ("common," secular). Most schools teach only Buddhist subjects, but some also teach *garuhat* (householder or lay subjects). See further: Phot Saphianchai (the former Secretary of the National Ministry of Education]) *Sabhap Kan Seuksa Khong Khana Song Thai* (Bangkok: Samnakngan Khana Kammakan Kan Seuksa Haeng Chat, 2523 [1979]), and Sawana Phonphatkun, *Kan Seuksa lae Kan Damrong Samanaphet Song Thai*, and Phra Mahasuk Suwiro, *Khwam Sonchai to Kan Seuksa Phra Pariyatidham khong Phra Song Seuksa Karani Phra Nisit Mahachulalongkorn Rachawithyalai* (Bangkok: Ph.D. Diss., Thammasat University, 2539 [1996]). For more information on the history of these schools, see Justin McDaniel, *Gathering Leaves and Lifting Words: Histories of Monastic Education in Laos and Thailand* (Seattle: University of Washington Press, 2008), chap. 3.

5. For more information on Buddhist liturgical guides that are used by children in Thailand see Justin McDaniel, "Liturgies and Cacophonies in Thai Buddhism," *Aséanie* 18 (2007), 119–50.

multiple volumes of primers with descriptions of the lives of famous disciples such as Sāriputta, Kisa Gotamī, and Visakha, as well as short lessons drawn from *Vinaya* commentaries, *Dhammapada* commentaries, and *Sutta* texts.[6] In the mid-1970s, Danai Chaiyotha, through the textbook division at Mahamakut Buddhist University in Bangkok, published a six-volume series in Thai and in English (to be used in English grammar courses at Buddhist schools) called "Buddhism for Young Students."[7] It included a wide variety of subjects divided into chapters such as "Buddhism and Democracy," "The Roots of Akusala and Kusala," "The Four Iddhipāda," Kathin Ceremony," and "Causes of Destruction of a Wealthy Family." This mix of ritual instructions, social commentary, and didactic lessons began a trend in Buddhist didactic publishing for children.

Recently, though, advances in printing and packaging technology have led to a much greater variety. There are dozens, especially at high-end bookstores in Bangkok and Chiang Mai, of expensive books replete with glossy images and creative fonts for children. Phra Wachiramethi, Phra Phayom, and Phra Mahasompong have written several. They have cartoonish covers and explain basic Buddhist ethics in simple vocabulary. Many often use English words as well in an attempt to make the books seem more modern. For example, Phra Mahasompong in 2008 published a book for children called "Dhamma Delivery." Even though the text is in Thai, half of the title is in English. The cover is a cartoon of a monk delivering a pizza to a child's door, and inside the pizza box are Buddhist teachings! In a similar style, Suddasa Onkom (a female student of Luang Pho Charan) wrote the popular *Sat lok Yom Ben Pai Tham Kam,* which is largely lessons she learned from her teacher.

One of the most creative new texts for children consists of a "lunchbox." Instead of holding snacks and juice, the box holds five books either that children can use themselves or families can donate to needy monasteries.[8] The five books all have glossy cartoon covers. The first is the well-known *Navakovat*, which was composed in the late nineteenth century by Prince and Supreme Patriarch Wachirayan. This text was originally designed to be a Buddhist ethics

6. In 1958, "Buddhist Sunday Schools" (*Rongrian Kanseuksa Buddhasāsanā Wan Athit*) were introduced formally to Thailand at Wat Yuwanajaransristi in Bangkok. They are usually funded by private donors who are dissatisfied with the government purely secular education. These schools design their own curricula, set schedules, hire their own teachers (usually monks or lay volunteers), and provide their own materials. There are 1,239 registered Sunday schools in Thailand. These schools continue to grow as government schools become less accessible, less funded, and more crowded. Of the 59,000 students in monastic Sunday schools, most are not novices or monks. In fact, lay girls (31,434) under eighteen make up the largest percentage of the students in monasteries. They are served by 1,787 teachers (about three for every 100 students). Of these teachers, 1,329 are laypeople. Only 2,233 go on to higher-school-level monastic education (~4 percent).

7. Danai Chaiyotha, *Buddhism for Young Children*, six vols. (Bangkok: Mahamakut Buddhist University Press, 2519 [1976]).

8. Lay students can study at monastery schools in Thailand. However, the vast majority take "culture" classes at government-funded public schools. These culture classes discuss basic Buddhist ethics and history.

primer based upon his reading of canonical texts. It largely explains the basic precepts and provides helpful hints of how to memorize certain Pāli liturgical phrases. This version of this handbook emphasizes in bold letters and cartoonish writing that *thong sanuk cham ngai brayok chai nai chiwit bracham wan!* (Memorization is fun! Remembering is easy! It is very useful for everyday life!). The second book is the *Sasana Phithi*, which explains basic Buddhist rituals and holidays. The short explanations are accompanied by cartoons depicting lay children sweeping, chanting, giving gifts to monks, and the like. The third book is the *Thesana Wa Rai Di*, which is a series of short sermons composed by Phra Phicitthammaphathi (Chaiwat Thammawatthano). These also have cartoons and are largely sermons about home and family life, including sermons about motherhood, etiquette, the importance of reading, and even explanations about death and end-of-life concerns in families. The fourth is the *Phra Kaeo Morakhot*, a history of the Emerald Buddha, the national palladium and most sacred Buddha image in Thailand. It emphasizes the connection between the Emerald Buddha, the royal family of Thailand, and the history of the movement of the image, and how it ended up at the Grand Palace in Bangkok. This text reinforces the connection between the nation and Buddhism for children. Finally, the largest book is the *Monphithi,* which is one of the more common liturgical handbooks in Thailand. It includes the Pāli and vernacular for many common Buddhist chants.

Most of these books are not well distributed outside of the major cities in Thailand and are prohibitively expensive for most families. However, there are popular and inexpensively produced comic books for children that are more widely available. These books generally are not didactic lessons for children, like those of Phra Wachiramethi and Phra Mahasompong; instead, they are adventure stories drawn from *jātakas* and the lives of famous monks in India, China, and Thailand. These have rather garish covers. For example, the cover of the comic book, *Phra Chikong: Thong Yomlok* depicts a Chinese monk (Chikong) with a long beard walking through the flames of hell surrounded by green-faced demons and suffering naked and bleeding women.[9] The contents are gruesome and many of the illustrated cells depict people in hell being tortured with hot irons, being crucified, and having their tongues pulled out. This is part of a series of comics on Buddhist heroes by So Thammabot and published by Phutthapucha Tun Thamma in Bangkok.

One of the most popular and frequently distributed by a number of large presses is the *Mahājanaka Jātaka* (Thai: *Phra Mahachanok*). This *jātaka* tale (#539

9. There have been a large number of Chinese Buddhist comic books for children printed in Thailand recently. These books, written in Thai, are adventure stories about Kwan Yin (*Avalokiteśvara*; Thai: *Guan Im*). Phutthabucha Press publishes many of them. They also publish adventure stories about Indian princes as well and are not exclusively a "Chinese" press. Indeed, the lines between Brahmanism, Chinese religions, and Theravāda Buddhism are not rigid. There are also posters depicting good and bad actions in the form of cartoons for children sold in Buddhist bookstores and comic book shops.

in the canon) is well-known throughout South and Southeast Asian Buddhism. It is a story of brotherly rivalry, war, and betrayal and features powerful goddesses, complex riddles, and miraculous rescues. However, presently in Thailand it is not simply a popular story; it is associated with the king, Phummiphon Adunyadet (Rama IX). The king composed a version of the story starting in 1977 but not published until 1996. When the comic book version of the king's edition was published in 1999 (Amarin Press, original artwork by Chai Rachawat), the story became popular with children.[10] There have been a number of reprintings as well as unofficial versions produced by other presses trying to profit off the popularity of the tale.[11] It is read by most schoolchildren and has reached the level of near compulsory reading in primary education. The Amarin Press edition now has an accompanying English translation which is used to teach English to secondary school children in Thailand. There is also an on-line edition. The king's version emphasizes the difficult decisions a monarch must make and the values of restraint, perseverance, and self-sufficiency. For obvious reasons, the role of the monarch and his pithy wisdom takes center stage, whereas in the original *jātaka* the ascetic life of Mahājanaka is emphasized. The story is also updated and the drawings make it seem as if the original story took place in Bangkok. There are Thai-style palaces, Buddha images, and monasteries throughout.

Another way new Buddhist material for children is reaching those living outside of Bangkok is through the internet. Many small towns in Thailand now have internet cafés (where children play on-line video games or use "instant messenger" and social networking programs to chat with friends), and internet is slowly becoming common in the homes of even very small villages. Some sites that are designed to teach Buddhism to children are (1) http://www.dmc.tv/index.php (a very professional site run by the "Dhamma Media Channel" which includes videos of lay children at Buddhist fairs, Buddhist cartoons, and testimonials from children and adults about the value of Thai Buddhism in their lives); (2) http://board.palungjit.com (run by the Palungjit group, which has a Thai message board where Thai Buddhists can ask questions, view videos, and read stories about famous Thai Buddhists, and submit their own videos); (3) http://www.buddhistelibrary.org/cpg1420/index.php?theme=thai&lang=thai (this is the Thai section of the Buddhist e-library, which has resources for children and short stories about different aspects of Buddhist practice); (4) http://www.dhammajak.net/board/viewtopic.php?p=8147&sid=55421fb3916731211598b6b6455cf865 (this is the Dhammajak site, which is less impressive than the others but has a popular /discussion section). These are just a few of the Thai Buddhist websites that have material for children. These sites focus largely on Thai Buddhism as part of a global Buddhist movement and are relatively well funded. They do not focus on local Buddhist issues and most of the participants on the web-boards are elite Thais living in Bangkok, Singapore,

10. Phrabat Somdet Phra Chao Yu Hua Phummiphol Adunyadet, *Phra Mahachanok chabab kartun* (Bangkok: Amarin, 2542 [1999]).
11. See especially Phutthabucha Press's multiple editions.

Taiwan, California, or Hong Kong. While they have material for children, they are designed for parents to learn more about bringing Buddhist education into their home. Most of the comments on the blogs connected with these sites are written by adults. Children certainly read Buddhist comic books, study Buddhist textbooks in school, and also attend sermons, go to temple fairs, and watch Buddhist movies (see below), but a robust engagement of children with Buddhist pedagogical websites has not been researched to date.[12]

NEW BUDDHIST FILMS FOR CHILDREN

The Thai film industry is one of the most developed in the Buddhist world and certainly the largest in southeast Asia. The production value, acting, and special effects of Thai films are world-class. Not surprisingly, perhaps, is that Buddhist themes and stories are a major part of Thai films. Moreover, scenes that have monasteries as their backdrops and actors playing monks are common. Many of the new films in Thailand are marketed to children. Instead of offering didactic ethical lessons or systematic teachings, they are ghost stories, adventures, or comedies. They depict monks struggling with difficult situations or battles between the ghostly and human worlds. A few of these films are described below.

Nak

Several recent Thai films for children tell Buddhist adventure stories. Many of these are local stories with no Indic equivalent. *Nak is* a very popular film about Thailand's most famous ghost—"Mae Nak Phrakhanong" or "Mother Nak of Phrakhanong District" (currently on the southern edge of Bangkok). The story of Mae Nak has been told and retold by Siamese of all classes for more than a century. It is about a young woman who dies in childbirth in the 1860s. She misses her husband and children so much that she fools them into believing that she is still alive. Anyone who tries to tell the husband and child that Mae Nak is actually a ghost, she kills.

In most versions of the story, Mae Nak is pacified by the famous monk Somdet To and goes on to her next life. Over time, this story has taken on a life of its

12. Many monasteries hold an annual festival/carnival, often seven to ten days long. One of these, the "annual monastery festival/fair" (*ngan wat bracham pi*), is a raucous and fun event. Usually there are Ferris wheels, carnival games, beauty contests, several stages with bands and small dramas (often these are amateur Chinese-style romance operas or Thai puppet shows), magicians, Pāli and vernacular chanting blasted through loudspeakers, variety shows with comedians, dancers, and short humorous skits, and the like. Children run around, monks shout out winning lottery or raffle numbers, there are food vendors and fireworks, and the entire monastery is lit up with multicolored florescent light tubes hanging from trees, gates, and eavesMuch money is generated for the monastery at these festivals and it is a good way for children and families to get together.

own. Mae Nak is no longer seen as a murderous ghost, but is a symbol of dedication and love. She deserves compassion. She is actually worshiped at several monasteries in modern Thailand and has become a type of patron saint of widows and the lovelorn. There are many versions of the story, with different characters and names. It has been a novelette, a play, a poem, many radio programs, and an opera. After the 1950s it became a popular comic book and graphic novel, as well as the most popular genre of ghost films (more than twenty versions) in Thailand, leading up to the 1997 blockbuster hit *Nang Nak,* the 2003 *The Ghost of Mae Nak* (in 3D), and the 2005 *Ghost of Mae Nak,* the last written and directed by a British national, Mark Duffield. The following discussion is on the very popular 2008 digitally animated version, called, simply, *Nak.*[13]

Nak opens with a narrator stating that in the past in Thailand people were kind and offered gifts to monks and to ghosts. The ghosts and monks were happy, and society ran well. However, in the modern world, people have forgotten the ghosts and so the ghosts cause havoc in society. Some ghosts, though, like Mae Nak, still want to protect humans and so the good and the bad ghosts battle, and their battlefield is the world of the living. Unlike most didactic Buddhist textbooks, this film doesn't ignore the prevalent belief in ghosts in Thai society. Indeed, here the ghosts and the monks are on equal standing; they are both worthy of gifts and both ensure that the world is free of disease, violence, and chaos. These ghosts need to be propitiated. Nak becomes the hero who saves modern Thai society from the ghosts who have turned on humans.

This film is visually sumptuous. The colors are vibrant, the production value is high, and the soundtrack is memorable. It was very popular for six- to twelve-year-olds in Thailand when it was released. Nak, who in most versions is a beautiful but unassuming and humble young woman, has become in the animated version a very buxom and sexy, red-headed teenage girl who can fly, stretch her arms out 50 or 60 feet to save children from falling, and stand up to the most menacing of evil ghosts. She is a superhero. She is backed by a team of other ghosts that are popular in Thai folklore—a legless (and also sexy) floating maiden, a giant blue *preta* (a hungry ghost who is condemned to the world of the undead because of his greed and gluttony), a loyal ghost dog, a small green ghost child, and a flying and goofy nymph-like ghost. Led by Nak, they all, protect Thailand from local, but especially foreign ghosts like Dracula, the Grim Reeper, a Jack-o-Lantern-headed flying ghost, a Western style red devil, skeletons who wear modern army helmets, and even the long-haired young girl ghost (Sodako) from the international popular Japanese film *The Ring.*[14] There are some evil local ghosts like an old woman whose entrails

13. I thank Arthid Sheravanichakul for sending me news of the musical's premiere. See http://www.your-bestweb.com/video_4DBOm_o5wrc.html for more information. See also http://entertainment.th.msn.com/news/entertainment/article.aspx?cp-documentid=2607571 and http://www.thaiticketmajor.com/performance/maenak_the_musical.php.

14. I thank Adam Knee for a number of fruitful conversations about various versions of the film. I thank him, Pimpaka Towira, and Arnika Fuhrman for agreeing

hang out of her chest cavity, but most bad ghosts are foreign. The nationalist overtones in the film are coupled with scenes of the Thai flag behind the good ghosts as they battle foreign ghosts, and the not-so-subtle suggestions throughout the film that foreigners have led Thais astray. They need good, traditional ghosts to remind them how to behave properly. In this film, it's the good ghosts that protect Thailand, not Buddhist monks.

Arahant Summer

This is a delightful film (Premium Digital Entertainment, directed by Phawat Phanangksiri, 2008) about a group of eight- to ten-year-olds who are forced by their parents to spend one summer ordained as Buddhist novices.[15] The film is in Thai but uses an English word in its title.[16] In the film, six boys ordain for their school break. Two of them stand out as the stars and the others provide comic relief. Namo (*dara*) is quite intelligent and impresses adults and the senior monks by being able to see patterns in complicated sentences, number strings, and shapes. He is also a promising young meditator, a skill that will come in handy later in the film. Khaoban, his close friend, is also very bright, but unlike the case with Namo, whose parents care for him, Khaoban's father abandoned him and so his mother had to save money by putting him in robes. Both Namo and Khaoban are linked by their love for comic books and especially Chinese kung-fu stories. These two are accompanied by Pu, a funny kid who loves kickboxing and whose mother is a money-grubbing merchant in their town. Khunthong is a very tall and oafish child who dreams of being a kung-fu master and hates being ordained. Namchup is an obese child who is always sneaking food after noon (novices are permitted to eat only between dawn and noon). Namchup's father is a drunk and always lets the novices watch television and eat candy in a small shop he owns; the novices often

to speak at the film festival and colloquium "The Supernatural in Southeast Asia," held at the University of California (Riverside) on Halloween Weekend, 2008. The festival and colloquium were organized by Tamara Ho, Lan Duong, and myself.

15. Although the location of the small town is not discussed, it was filmed in the province of Kanchanaburi, about two hours from Bangkok, and anyone who has spent time in Thailand will recognize that the backdrops are of Wat Tham Seua, a somewhat famous local monastery in that region near the Burmese border. Other backdrops in the film include Wat Wang Wiwek and other small monasteries dotted along the road from Amphoe Muang, Kanchanaburi, and the town of Sangkhlaburi.

16. This reflects how the modern "school calendar" in Thailand has changed the ways in which children ordain. In the past, they would begin their ordination period at the beginning of *pansa* (Pāli: *vassa*), the traditional three-month rains retreat observed thoughout the Southeast Asian Buddhist world (following the lunar calendar, this retreat usually takes place between July and October) as a time for novices, nuns, and monks to reside in their monasteries and spend their time dedicated less to public service and pilgrimage and more to meditating and studying. However, in modern Thailand, the public school break doesn't overlap with the rains retreat, and so students often ordain on their school's summer break (often in April and May).

sneak away from their monastery to go there. Nokiang is a young girl who loves playing with the boys and is disappointed that they have to be novices for the summer. Her older sister (about eighteen years old) has a secret crush on the boys' teacher, a monk in his early twenties who only goes by "Luang Phi" (venerable older brother).

Temporally, the film goes back and forth between the "*arahant* summer course" in 1983 and present-day (2008) Suvannabhumi Airport. In the present, Khaoban has become a long-haired and unkempt drug dealer, wearing sunglasses and trying to smuggle drugs through the airport. He knows the police are on to him and he finds a seat in the corner of the departure lounge to hide from them. His life is miserable and he is paranoid. Namo, who remained a monk, is about to leave for to another country to practice as a *thudong* (Pāli: *dhutaṅga*) wandering monk. He smiles, is calm, and seems not to have a care in the world. Namo and Khaoban recognize each other at the airport and Namo reminds Khaoban of all the experiences they went through that summer twenty-five years previously. Namo's face is still young and fresh, but Khaoban's is rough and aged.

In 1983, the children are very angry with their parents that they have to become novices; they want to play soccer, read comics, and watch television.. They cry when their heads are shaved. They can't sit still, so one has his ear accidently slashed by the razor. After they are ordained, they are lazy. They argue with each other and stay up late at night playing practical jokes on each other. They sing, dance, and clap. They belch and pass gas while eating. They gossip. They are petty. Overall, they act like who they are—children. There are lots of slapstick jokes replete with silly sound effects. The film is particularly irreverent when depicting the children studying Buddhist texts. They sleep or yawn during lessons. When the teacher is writing on the blackboard and his back is to them, they sneak outside to play soccer or run away. One time, the teacher catches them, yells at them, and then spanks one with a bamboo stick. To escape another lesson, they sneak into the forest and pretend to be Chinese kung fu masters and mock-fight each other. The only book in the monastic library they are interested in reading is a Chinese comic book they found. They shuffle their feet during meditation, and instead of reading *suttas*, they sneak away to watch television at a local shop. They even steal candy on alms rounds.

The scenes with the children don't just show their irreverence; they also show their loneliness and force the viewer to question the value of this type of education for children. They are afraid of ghosts and tell ghost stories, which causes several of the children to miss their parents and they sob in their beds at night. When they see their mothers and fathers, they rush to hug them even though they are still in robes and despite the fact that this type of affection is not permitted for novices. However, the children slowly change, especially Namo and Khaoban. They get better at meditation. Khaoban in particular spends time with the teacher even when other novices run off to play. He asks the teacher why he should study *dhamma* (Buddhist teachings). The teacher states that *dhamma* is actually very simple—suffering and happiness are in you. There is no need to pray to gods, you only need to look inside yourself—*dhamma* helps you understand yourself, nothing else. This lesson comes right before the climax of the film. One night, Khaoban is kidnapped by two thieves whom he catches stealing from the monastery's donation box; they want to eliminate all witnesses. While he is being dragged away, two sisters, Nokiang and her older sister, try to rescue them, but they are kidnapped too. The thieves take them to an old abandoned farm storage house and mill. The thieves do not know how to write and so the smart young novice and the two girls write the ransom note for them, but put a secret code in the note which reveals where the hideout is. While waiting for their teacher, the monk Luang Phi, and the police to rescue them, they happen upon a ghost in the old mill. The ghost doesn't hurt them because Khaoban uses his powers of meditation to keep them safe. The ghost, however, scares the kidnappers and they run out of the mill to be captured by the police.

The final scene, twenty-five years later in the airport, shows Namo reminding Khaoban of his heroics how meditation saved him and the girls. Khaoban realizes how he has gone astray and, as the film ends, the viewer is led to believe that Khaoban will start a new and better chapter in his life. The message given to the audience is that monastic life is ideal.

Luang Phi Teng

Luang Phi Teng was the biggest box office draw in Thailand in 2005, watched by several million families (Phra nakhon Films, directed by Note Choem-Yim, 2005). Just as the boys in *Arahant Summer* loved to practice kung fu, the protagonist of *Luang Phi Teng* is a fighter as well. Luang Phi Teng, it is shown, was a very good Muoy Thai (Thai Kickboxing) street fighter, as well as a former drunkard, thief, and liar. He becomes a monk to make up for his past and he goes to a small village that doesn't have any monks. He is surprised that the monastery is occupied by lazy and clumsy drunks. He is also surprised that nearby a lay magician, named Than Poem (Master Poem), has been exploiting the villagers by setting up a fake fortune telling business and forcing his daughter, a beautiful young woman named Paniang, to be a fake medium for a powerful spirit. He also sells fake love potions (*nam man sane*), frequents prostitutes, hosts cockfights, and sponsors explicit dance shows.

Slowly, the new monk, through his clever teaching, jokes, and guidance to young children, starts inspiring the villagers to join him. He uses simple reasoning to convince them that their belief in numerology, spirits, and other superstitions are irrational. For example, when a local mafia boss, named Pattana, asks the monk to help him get #9 as his registration number when he wants to illegally run for local political office, Luang Phi Teng asks him why he wants #9. He states that #9 is lucky. Luang Phi Teng askes why it is lucky. The mafia head states that it is lucky because everyone thinks it is and #13 is unlucky. When asked for proof, the mafia boss can't provide any. So Luang Phi Teng asks him, "If someone gave you a choice between a gift of 9 million baht and 13 million baht, which gift would you take?" The mafia head says, "13 million, of course!" Then Luang Phi Teng says, "Aren't you afraid of bad luck from having 13 million!" While this pithy wisdom might seem quite different from the open acceptance of superstitions in *Arahant Summer*, this film entertains Buddhist children in another way—it depicts the protagonist as a comedian (indeed, the actor who plays Luang Phi Teng, Pongsak Pongsuwan, is one of Thailand's most popular stand-up comedians), who defeats his rivals with his wit and wisdom.[17] With the clever use of flashbacks to a time when Luang Phi Teng was a street fighter, the film suggests that the monk could easily defeat his enemies with his fists but chooses not to. In this way, the audience is entertained by violent fight scenes but learns the importance of wisdom over violence. Indeed, there is much physicality and even slapstick humor in this film. People laugh at the naked monk when his robe is pulled off by a taxicab door and when he jumps into a river to save Poem, his supposed enemy, from drowning. He experiences diarrhea and is often clumsy. It also shows, like *Arahant Summer* and a number of other films and Thai vernacular stories, that monks are attractive to young women. In Luang Phi Teng, the beautiful woman who plays the medium falls in love with the monk. He resists her urgings, but this element in the film certainly adds a touch of romance and intrigue. These scenes combined with the flashbacks humanize the monk and garner sympathy from the audience.

This film shows that Thai monks do not have to be calm, reverent, and reserved to be effective teachers. It also shows monks as defenders of their congregation, not just as preachers who do not involve themselves in local politics and economic disputes. For example, he talks a suicidal villager off of a ledge. The man had lost all of his money betting on Liverpool in a soccer match. Luang Phi Teng, instead of citing Buddhist texts, states that the man should have bet on team Arsenal and can do so next time. Furthermore, if he dies, then his pretty wife will marry someone else. Jealousy over his wife and the hope for future gambling victories convince the man to come off the ledge. In other scenes, Luang Phi Teng doesn't criticize rituals and the belief in mediums or ghosts. He even shows that he is afraid of ghosts sometimes, but he preaches that ghosts are not physically harmful because they don't have bodies. He doesn't ask his congregation to give up believing in local spirits, mediums, and amulets, but he does tell them to beware of people practicing trickery (*lok luang*).

The Life of the Buddha and The Adventures of Milinda Panha

Finally, two animated films were recently released in Thailand which, unlike the previous films, are set not in Thailand but in India during the time of the

17. In the sequel, *Luang Phi Teng II*, the protagonist is played by the famous Thai hip hop artist, Joey Boy (original name: Apisit Opsasaimlikit). In this film, Luang Phi Teng uses his rhyming skills to teach the village and to get out of trouble. *Luang Phi Teng III* was just released in late 2010, but I have not had the chance to see it.

historical Buddha. Whereas earlier Thai films have not emphasized Buddhist history or its Indic origins, these two films attempt to teach the Pāli Canon creatively to children. This does not mean that they deemphasize adventure, romance, and magic; indeed, they depict the Buddha, the monk Nagasena, and King Milinda as swashbuckling heroes. While English versions (usually read in excerpts in Introduction to Buddhism textbooks or as parts of anthologies of Asian scripture textbooks) emphasize the ascetic choices and the ethical lessons of Nagasena and the Buddha, these animated films feature lengthy battle scenes, struggles between the Buddha and an evil snake, the Buddha performing miracles, as well as the miracles surrounding his birth. While all of these elements are found within different Sanskrit and Pāli versions of the story, here they take center stage (as they may have taken in orally delivered versions in India two millennia ago). Moreover, like the comic book version of King Rama IX's *Phra Mahachanok*, even though the stories are set in India, the backdrops often feature Thai architecture. Moreover, as one critic pointed out, there are no nuns featured as there may have been at the time of the Buddha, and there is one scene of a monk reading a manuscript composed in Khom script (a type of Khmer script commonly used for premodern manuscripts and modern yantra and tattoos in Thailand).[18] Anachronisms like this are common in these films. The production value of the two films is very different though. *Milinda Panha* was conceived as one film originally but is sold in six volumes on DVD. The animation is relatively simplistic and I have found it sold only in monastic bookstores. *The Life of the Buddha* (Thai: *Phra Phutthachao*), on the other hand, was a major motion picture which cost its producer, Wallapa Phimtong, over 100 million baht (3 million USD), a huge amount for a film in Thailand.[19] In the end, she even had to sell her automobiles and home to fund the film. The animation reminds one of a Disney children's film, and its epic nature certainly is influenced by American animated films such as *The Lion King* and *Ice Age*. Unfortunately for Wallapa Phimtong, the film, despite its sumptuous animation, did not do very well at the box office. Even though both *Milinda Panha* and *The Life of the Buddha* are adventure stories, it appears that Thai children prefer films set in modern Thailand over ancient India.

OK Baytong

The film *OK Baytong* is not for children, but it depicts children and novices. It was directed by one of Thailand's most avant-garde directors, Nonzee Nimibutr.

18. Eisel Mazard, "Be warned: Thai film: "The Life of Buddha," March 1, 2008, http://www.prachatai.com/english/node/461.

19. There were several newspaper stories and critical reviews of this film in Thai newspapers. English readers see Parinyaporn Pajee, "Drawing on faith: The producer of the first animation about the life of Lord Buddha searches for funds to finish it," *The Nation*, July 1, 2007; and, Kong Rithdee, "Taking the middle path: Animated Thai Buddha epic proves far from timeless," *The Bangkok Post*, December 14, 2007.

It is about a monk named Phra Tham who has to return to his hometown of Baytong after his sister has been killed in a terrorist bombing. After being very depressed and realizing after the funeral that he must take care of his orphaned and half-Muslim neice, Mariya, he decides, reluctantly to disrobe. Mariya's father, a wealthy Malaysian Muslim businessman, had left her mother and returned to Malaysia. Phra Tham does not adjust well to lay life. He had become a novice when he was just eight years old and then later ordained as a monk, and so he had never experienced adult life as a layman. He is befriended by a dancing girl named Fern who is always trying to tempt him with sex and alcohol; he falls in love with a woman who is secretly engaged to a Muslim terrorist; and he is forced to work at a hair salon, where he constantly has to listen to rock music and hang around hormonally charged young men and women! Throughout the film he retreats to his room to be alone. He speaks to himself in the mirror, and the image he sees there is himself dressed as a monk. His monk-self uses Pāli phrases and offers him pithy Thai Buddhist advice about attachment and discipline. However, the struggle to live a life of discipline as a layperson is too much for Phra Tham and he often breaks down in tears. One thing he can't understand is why he is constantly getting erections and can't seem to control himself.

As the film progresses, the person speaking to him in the mirror changes from being dressed as a monk to being dressed as a hairdresser, a meditator, etc. He struggles emotionally throughout the movie and is often crying. The director was trying to show that the monk's problem was not that he didn't have discipline, but that he was actually too attached to the monastic life. The film even starts off with the Pāli phrase *sabbe dhammā nālaṃ abhivesāya* and Thai translation: *sing thang buang mai khuan yeut man kheu man* (nothing is permanent and we shouldn't be attached to anything), or, more simply, "embrace change." Once Phra Tham embraces change, he learns how to be a good hair stylist and, accepting the fact that Muslims are struggling to survive in a Buddhist country, he gives up his hate for them and thoughts of vengeance for his sister. He also convinces Mariya's father to reunite with his daughter. He realizes while in Malaysia (Penang) visiting Mariya's father, that Muslim society actually is what he longs for—no public drinking, not many nightclubs, no scantily clad women coming into his hair salon, and the like. He wonders why he is attracted to the Muslim lifestyle. Slowly he loses his attachment to both the monastic life and the very idea of being a Buddhist. At the end of the film he finds balance, he works as a hair stylist during the weekdays, and on weekends he dresses in white and gives tours of Buddhist temples. He is not overjoyed, but he no longer openly struggles with lay life in Thailand.

This film shows how a man grows up in a monastery from a child but then, when forced to live an adult life, is unequipped emotionally, intellectually, and financially to do so. It shows that a Buddhist monastic education has strengths and can be an effective guide for children, but influence from the secular world is not necessarily a bad thing. Buddhist children need to learn to adapt to the changing and diverse world around them.

CONCLUSION

New texts and films for Buddhist children in Thailand focus, as most children's literature does, on adventure, struggles between good and evil, and bigger-than-life heroes and villains, intermixed with a healthy dose of slapstick humor. They are neither prescriptive moral tracts nor descriptions of ideal ethical standards. Buddhist Studies scholars and orthodox devotees might argue that the ethical messages are lost amid the fistfights, magical incantations, and bathroom jokes. Instead of lamenting the ways in which modern Thai children are being presented with Buddhist and Buddhist-inspired stories (as dozens of modern urban Thai and ex-patriot internet bloggers and newspaper editorials in Thailand do), we might return to the discussion of murals in Thailand. Indeed, anyone who studies premodern Buddhist murals in Thailand or reads Thai traditional Buddhist stories will know that these texts and murals are often focused on battles, magic, miracles, and adventure. Indeed, live stage dramatic depictions of local and canonical *jātaka* tales in Thailand are often presented as tales of violence and romance more than didactic ethical lessons related calmly by saffron-robed sages.[20]

Certainly the rise of cheap modern printing, film making, and the internet has increased parents' and children's access to Buddhist educational materials, but this change has been in degree more than in kind. Narrative still dominates the way in which Thai children learn about Buddhist history, ethics, esthetics, and ritual. A detailed study of children's reactions to these new materials remains a desideratum. It is too soon to tell if these films, comics, and other texts which poke fun at monks or question their ethical motivations will slowly erode children's desires to enter the monkhood or if parents will see ordaining as meritorious in and of itself. However, for centuries children growing up in Thailand have seen narrative as a presentation of choices rather than of an ideal. Therefore, I doubt that these new media alone will weaken the importance of Buddhist monkhood in the eyes of parents or children. Still, their massive popularity among children is undeniable. It is hoped that we can encourage future studies that take children's literature and film as a subject of serious scholarly inquiry.

20. This is actually similar to modern Evangelical Christian and Muslim media for children in which animation and adventure stories are used to depict religious history and teachings.

CHAPTER 13

Once We Were...

Former Child Nuns in Taiwan Reflecting Back

WEI-YI CHENG

I had known her for two years; she seemed a devoted Buddhist who maintained a strict vegetarian diet and often voiced Buddhist apologetic opinions. But she was chic and stylish, and nothing in her behavior suggested "monastic" to me. I was surprised to learn later that a young woman like her had been a Buddhist child nun.

This chapter focuses around her, whom I will code as "Apple," and her friends from the same monastic order ("*sangha x*" hereafter). Apple was a central informant in this research project, for she introduced me to other former child nuns. They had all once been child nuns at sangha x and were interviewed between February and May 2009. Each interview ranged from thirty minutes to more than two hours. Follow-up questions were conducted through on-line chats and social outings. To encourage them to speak freely, I promised them confidentiality of their and their sangha's identities. I will therefore use only pseudonyms here.

This research is concentrated on former child nuns for three reasons. First, child monastics are rare in contemporary Taiwan. The fact that sangha x once ordained a significant number of children is itself interesting. It provides us with a view into what life might be like in a Buddhist child monastic community. Second, former child nuns who had already disrobed were interviewed rather than those who were still in robes, because I believe that they provide particular insight into the child monastic experience. Divorced from monastic identity, they no longer carry the burden of having to represent Buddhist monasticism. Their retelling of their monastic experience is done more freely, it is hoped, less daunted by the concern of stigmatizing one's community. Above all, these former child nuns may answer an important question: "What does monasticism mean for children?" Since child monastics are rare in Taiwan, I was relatively unaware of them until 2002, when I conducted fieldwork in Sri Lanka and encountered many nuns who had entered sangha at a young age. I was astounded to see children living in a monastic community and began to wonder what life might be like growing up as a monastic, especially when so much has changed since the founding of the Buddhist monastic order in ancient India. I am grateful to Apple and her friends for providing me with the opportunity to explore this question.

BACKGROUND

Statistically speaking, Buddhism is not the predominant religion in Taiwan. A survey conducted in 2004 reveals that only about 25 percent of the total population identified itself as Buddhist.[1] Nevertheless, Buddhism wages significant influence on the culture of Taiwan,[2] for Buddhist doctrines and practices are diffused into the wider cultural spectrum.

In the last two decades of the twentieth century, Taiwan went through a series of political and social transformations. The lift of Martial Law in 1987 paved the way for religious freedom. Notably, BAROC ("Buddhist Association of the Republic of China," a quasigovernmental organization) was no longer able to maintain its grip on Buddhist affairs in Taiwan, and Buddhist groups became free to organize their own monastic ordination ceremonies.[3] The result was a strong religious resurgence. Sangha x was part of this religious resurgence. Founded only in the 1980s, sangha x has quickly grown into one of the largest Buddhist monastic communities in Taiwan. On its official website, accessed in April 2009, sangha x boasts of over one thousand members worldwide and claims authentic Ch'an lineage. It is a mixed sangha,[4] consisting of both male and female monastic members. Although at the time of this research, sangha x no longer ordains children, it once had a sizeable child monastic order, more than forty during its peak.

1. "Taiwan Minzhong Xinyang Leibie De Bianqian," *Taiwan Shehui Bianqian Quanjilu*. Taipei: Institute of Sociology, Academia Sinica, online data: http://www.ios.sinica.edu.tw/TSCpedia/index.php/%E5%8F%B0%E7%81%A3%E6%B0%91%E7%9C%BE%E4%BF%A1%E4%BB%B0%E9%A1%9E%E5%88%A5%E7%9A%84%E8%AE%8A%E9%81%B7, accessed on May 8, 2009.

2. For more on religion in Taiwan, see Philip Clart and Charles B. Jones, eds., *Religion in Modern Taiwan: Tradition and Innovation in a Changing Society* (Honolulu: University of Hawaii Press, 2003). Gary Marvin Davison and Barbara E. Reed,*Culture and Customs of Taiwan* (Westport, CT and London: Greenwood Press, 1998).

3. Previously, BAROC was the only organization allowed to conduct monastic ordination ceremonies. For details, see Charles B. Jones, *Buddhism in Taiwan: Religion and the State: 1660–1990* (Honolulu: University of Hawaii Press, 1999), 178–83. See also Richard Madsen, *Democracy's Religious Renaissance and Political Development in Taiwan*. (Berkeley: University of California Press, 2007).

Table 13.1 BACKGROUND INFORMATION OF THE INFORMANTS

Code	Age at interview	Age at ordination	Age at disrobing	Current occupation
Apple	25	10	19	shop clerk
Bael	23	11	18	student
Cherry	24	11	15	insurance salesperson
Duku	23	11	18	student
Emblic	20	10	13	student
Ficus	24	12	21	unemployed
Grape	24	12	18	shop clerk
Hackberry	19	6	18	student
Imbe	27	14	18	student
Jambul	20	7	15	student

As Table 13.1 shows, all the women interviewed for this research were in their twenties. They may have entered the sangha at a tender age but none stayed in robes for more than a decade.

ENTERING SANGHA

Buddhist child monastics are rare in Taiwan. Not only have I never seen a Taiwanese child monastic in person, but I know of no Taiwanese scholarly work on the subject. It is ironic considering that no law prevents or regulates child monasticism in Taiwan.[5] It seems to have sunk into oblivion along with the ever-decreasing birth rate, which I suspect to be a contributing factor, since there are now fewer children to enter sangha.[6] This is not to say, however, that child monastics do not exist in Taiwan. Around the time of my writing this chapter, an eleven-year-old *śrāmanera*, Zhan Jie, caught the attention of the Taiwanese media. Reports were generally positive, focusing on Zhan Jie's childishness (using words such as "sweet" and "cute"), his ability to recite Buddhist sutras, his claim to be the reincarnation of Nāgārjuna, and the fact that he was ordained on his own accord.[7] The attention Zhan Jie received highlights how unusual child monastics in Taiwan are at the moment.

4. Mixed sangha, with both female and male monastic members, is common and noncontroversial in Taiwan despite sex segregation being required of Chinese Buddhist monasticism. For more, see Wei-yiCheng, *Buddhist Nuns in Taiwan and Sri Lanka: A Critique of the Feminist Perspective* (London: Routledge, 2007), 149–66.
5. At least I could not find any such law or regulation through my own search on *Law and Regulations Database of the Republic of China*, http://law.moj.gov.tw/Index.aspx, accessed on March 23, 2010.
6. For the birth rate in Taiwan, see *Statistical Yearbook of the Republic of China 2008*, online edition: http://eng.dgbas.gov.tw/public/data/dgbas03/bs2/yearbook_Eng/y009.pdf, accessed on March 24, 2010.
7. For example, Xiaoshami Zhanjie, "Woshilongshupusazhuanshi." *Liberty Times*, April 1, 2009(http://www.libertytimes.com.tw/2009/new/apr/1/today-life13.htm), accessed on April 28, 2009.

Is Poverty a Factor?

When Welch conducted his research on Chinese Buddhism in the first half of the twentieth century, he found that Western opinions toward Chinese Buddhist child monastics were generally negative. "Sold into the sangha" was the Westerners' common view toward child monastics in Chinese Buddhism.[8] However, Welch went on to suggest that this stereotypical view could not fully explain the existence of child monasticism:

> This customary popular respect for monks and monasteries is the thread that runs through most of the explanations that I have been given by monks [. . . .]. It suggests that monkhood was correlated less with poverty than with attitudes. There may be a certain parallel in the number of Massachusetts Irish who have entered the priesthood. Poverty has been one factor, no doubt, but probably a more important and pervasive reason has been that it was an approved career.[9]

In other words, even when poverty matters, the cultural factor of a favorable attitude toward child monasticism must exist.

My finding is consistent with Welch's; namely, none of my informants claimed that she was "sold" to the sangha. With the sole exception of Duku, whose ordination was undertaken as a result of parental pressure, all of them entered sangha more or less willingly. Duku was the only one among my informants who spoke bitterly about her ordination:

> My father told me to [enter the sangha]... My father was really strict when I was a child and I never dared disobey him. He wanted to enter the sangha himself, so he asked my younger sister [Emblic] and I whether we wanted to go along with him. I don't know if my younger sister really wanted to [enter the Sangha] or did not understand the whole thing. But me, simply because my father told me to.... People said that our Old Master[10] is really advanced in spiritual practice and he could read minds. Back then, we must request for ordination. When I went to him, I kept saying in my mind, "Please do not agree. Please do not agree." Yet he said, "Okay, you can come." I was shouting in my mind, "How could you not listen to what I said?"

Duku's father and younger sister, Emblic, also entered sangha at the same time. Emblic's recollection of her ordination was a blur, however. She simply said that she entered sangha because it "felt good." All three had subsequently disrobed. Given that Duku's father ran a successful business at the time of ordination, poverty was unlikely the main factor behind her decision to enter sangha.

8. Holmes Welch, *The Practice of Chinese Buddhism: 1900–1950*(Cambridge, MA: Harvard University Press, 1967), 248–49.
9. Welch, *The Practice of Chinese Buddhism*, 257.
10. Referring to the founder monk of sangha x.

After inquiring about my informants' family background, I decided to accept their claims that poverty was at least not the *main* factor for their ordination. What emerges from the interviews is the weight of parental influence. Parents' contact with Buddhism and/or sangha x acted as an initiative for many of my informants' ordinations.

PARENTAL FACTOR

It has been pointed out that family is the prime agent for children's religious socialization.[11] Jeff Samuels in this volume also notes the importance of social relations (i.e., family's acquaintance with sangha) for recruiting child monastics in Sri Lanka. Hence, it is no surprise that parental influence emerged as the most significant factor for my informants' ordinations.

Generally speaking, my informants encountered Buddhism and/or sangha x because their parents had already been devotees. It was usually the parents who initiated the children's contact with sangha x. For example, Ficus recalled how her mother encouraged her to join a meditation retreat run by sangha x:

> I had just finished elementary school, and then my Mom told me to join this seven-day meditation retreat [with sangha x].... After that, I did another two seven-day meditation retreats and an eight-precept retreat. Well, I quite enjoyed our Old Master's sermons and wished to stay in the monastery forever... Yes, my Mom was a Buddhist. My family is a Buddhist family.... I felt very happy.... Maybe because the monastery provided a tranquil environment and I like that tranquility a lot, so I decided to join sangha after the meditation retreat.... Since we were very little, Mom and Dad had always taken us to visit Buddhist sanghas and we also knew some Dharma Masters.[12]... Children are naïve and think that to obtain Buddhahood, one must enter sangha... On several occasions, I saw a Dharma Master walk by. She looked very elegant and I wanted to become like her, so spiritual and mindful.

Without exception, every one of my informants had at least one devoted Buddhist parent. Long before their ordination, their Buddhist parents introduced them to activities at the various local branch temples of sangha x or encouraged them to join meditation retreats/summer camps hosted by sangha x. Seemingly, their parents had high regard for Buddhist monasticism before their daughters' ordinations. It is consistent with Welch's observation that cultural reverence toward monasticism is an essential factor for children's ordination.[13] It is also

11. Meredith B. McGuire, *Religion: The Social Contest* (Belmont, CA: Wadsworth, 1997), 54–56.
12. Referring to Buddhist monastics.
13. Welch, *The Practice of Chinese Buddhism*, 257; statement quoted earlier.

consistent with other findings that parental influence is the strongest among all factors determining a child's religiosity.[14]

While I did not find any statement by the founder monk of sangha x in regard to child monasticism, an online article reveals his view on monasticism in general. In it, he says that although both monastics and householders can advance positively on the spiritual path, monasticism is like a full-time profession; only monastics can devote themselves wholeheartedly to the spiritual path while householders face many more obstacles.[15] A young nun[16] ("*N1*" hereafter) who was a child nun together with my informants and was still in robes at the time of the interview mentioned the benefit of earlier ordination: "Old habits die hard. As one gets older, one develops more and more habits that are harmful to spiritual practice. So entering sangha as a child is good."

Monasticism is positively propagated by sangha x's founder monk; if N1's opinion voiced the general opinion of sangha x, then child monasticism is also perceived positively. Moreover, popular Chinese Buddhist culture is filled with myths of how parents' salvation is achieved through the merit of their monastic children.[17] Buddhist parent(s) of my informants were exposed to rhetoric that revered monasticism, thus their willingness to encourage their daughters into monasticism.

In the cases of Duku, Emblic, and Grape, because their fathers had wanted to enter sangha themselves, they pressed for their daughters' ordinations. Grape, whose father was still in robes at the time of the interview, said:

> It was partly because I wanted to, and partly... because my father wanted to enter sangha. He thought it's better to send his children to a good environment and then he could be content enough to enter sangha himself.

Similarly for Hackberry and Jambul: they were sisters and their mother and grandmother were still nuns at sangha x at the time of their interview. Hackberry, who had disrobed only six months earlier, told me:

> Papa died when I was very little. Because of Papa's death, our family came into contact with Buddhism. We couldn't accept it at first. Then gradually, Mom and Grandma accepted [Buddhism] and became nuns.... [My sister and I] had lived in the monastery before we donned the robes [because both Mom and Grandma were there].... There were many little monastics. We were together with them. After awhile, it seemed not bad to us. That kind

14. Ralph Hood Jr., Bernard Spilka, Bruce Hunsberger, and Richard Gorsuch, *The Psychology of Religion: An Empirical Approach* (New York: The Guilford Press, 1996), 74–78.

15. Official website of sangha x, accessed on May 12, 2009.

16. Age twenty-seven ordained at the age of twelve, still in robes and with sangha x.

17. For examples, see Alan Cole, *Mothers and Sons in Chinese Buddhism* (Stanford, CA: Stanford University Press, 1998); and Chun-fang Yu, *Kuan-yin: The Chinese Transformation of Avalokiteśvara* (New York: Columbia University Press, 2001), 293–351.

> of lifestyle seemed pretty good. Then I thought... I was very little! Quite naïvely, I wanted to be ordained. That's because [members of] my family had entered sangha.

Since there was no adult left in the family to look after the sisters, Hackberry and Jambul were brought to live in the monastery and eventually received ordination themselves.

But not all Buddhist parents were happy about their children's ordination. Both of Apple's parents were devoted Buddhists but her mother was distressed by Apple's wish to don the robes:

> So, I called my Mom and said, "Mom, do you have time tomorrow?" That was late in the afternoon. I said, "Can you come to the Monastery tomorrow? You need to sign my permission form." [She] was shocked. Then she asked why. I said, "I want to enter sangha." She said, "We'll need to talk about it." Two days later she came with my Dad and a friend [...]. Then we talked for a long time. They kept luring me by promising to take me to Disneyland, Shin Kong Mitsukoshi Tower. [My Mom] wanted to lure me to go back home. But I would give her some Dharma talks that I had just heard. And she would say, "Do you really understand?"... Back then, I honestly believed that I understood [the Dharma talks] and was not just repeating.... The key person was my Dad. My Dad told my Mom not to stop being in the way of somebody's spiritual practice. I think that's because they had been practicing Buddhism for many years. My Dad also told my Mom to respect my choice.

Overall, parental influence appears to be the most significant factor behind Buddhist child monasticism in contemporary Taiwan. Children are socialized into Buddhist religiosity before they take the step to become monastics.

LIVING IN SANGHA

Curiously, none of my informants recalled their initial period of living in sangha negatively. Even Duku, whose ordination was pressured by her father (see above), did not complain about this period "But sangha was fun. There were many kids and I thought that it was not too bad."

I discussed this issue with Apple and Ficus in post-interview meetings,[18] and they replied that their memory of their initial days in sangha x was generally a happy one. Perhaps because they entered sangha of their own volition, they remembered those days as "fun" and "exciting." Since I did not pursue this issue further, it has to wait for future research.

As much as Apple and Ficus may have found their initial days in sangha x fun and exciting, they also found their time there "like living in a military

18. Personal conversation, June 8, 2009.

school." "Strict lifestyle" was how my informants described their life in sangha x, for there were precepts/rules to observe and a rigid schedule to follow. According to Imbe:

> Our daily schedule required waking up at 3.45 A.M., and the morning devotion had to be conducted at 4.20 A.M.[19] Because I was living at the Academy [see Table 13.2], we had lectures after that. The subjects included Chinese Literature, Dharma, *Vinaya* and so on. The lectures would go on for the whole day. Then around ten in the morning we had meditation for about forty minutes. Lunch was at 11.30 A.M. Then at 1:00 P.M. we resumed study until about 4 P.M... 5.30 P.M. was to take medicine [*yaoshi*, referring to evening supper]. It was bath time around 8 :00 P.M. After that was study time. Ten o'clock was bedtime.

The daily schedule in sangha x does not seem to deviate too much from Welch's observation of the daily life of Chinese monastics in the early twentieth century.[20] But there is one main difference: my informants had to go to secular school outside of the monastery. I will return to this point later.

In addition to adjusting to a strict lifestyle, my informants also had to adjust to a life without their birth family. In Chinese Buddhist monasticism, the role of parents might be replaced by one's tonsure master (preceptor-monastic).[21] Similar caretaking relationships of the adult preceptor can also be found in ancient Indian Buddhist literature as discussed by Amy P. Langenberg in this volume. In a sense, in Buddhist monasticism, preceptor-monastics are expected to play the parental role to junior monastics, especially child monastics. Nevertheless, sangha x was a massive organization; the founder monk, being the only tonsure master[22] in sangha x, could not possibly look after all of his disciples on a daily basis. A system of "minder-master" (*jiaoshoushi*) was thus created for its child monastics. That is, child nuns were assigned to an adult nun as their "minder-master" to look after their daily matters. According to Ficus, sometimes one minder-master might have to look after more than forty child nuns. This was a heavy responsibility, so perhaps it is of little wonder that my informants' relationship with their minder-masters often turned sour.

One cause for the failed relationship could be attributed to the frequent change of the minder-masters. Jambul said:

> Our relationships with our minder-masters were not always good. There were conflicts. For example, there were some trivial issues. For example, we were

19. I would like to point out that it is customary in Taiwan to take a long nap at noon. This might explain why none of my informants complained about sleep deprivation.
20. Welch, *The Practice of Chinese Buddhism*, 53–87.
21. For more on the tonsure custom in the Chinese Buddhism, see Welch, *The Practice of Chinese Buddhism*, 276–81.
22. He did not allow other monastics of sangha x to give higher ordination, making himself the only preceptor/tonsure master at sangha x.

> not allowed to listen to music! Not even to look at photos of pop stars! If you got caught, you would be punished .... Every two or three years we got a new [minder-master]. And then we had to readjust!

On average, a minder-master was replaced every two or three years. This cycle caused psychological strain for my informants—every one of them complained about the high turnover. Grape explained: "[. . .] the minder-master kept getting replaced. Personally, I think the minder-master had great impact on us. She would affect everyone's emotional state."

My informants also attributed the failed relationship to the minder-masters' youth and lack of parenting experience. Duku pointed out:

> [T]he minder-masters had to look after some little menaces, children who were not even [theirs]. The point is that they were also super young. Our minder-masters were only in their twenties. How can you look after children? You were yourselves children! It was difficult for them too.

Accordingly, because sangha x assigned young inexperienced adults to look after the child nuns who were themselves constantly rotating, none of my informants found her relationship with her minder-masters easy.

FOOD

Amy P. Langenberg's chapter in this volume mentions stories of hunger experienced by growing child monastics in Indian Buddhist literature. Those ancient stories are echoed in the modern-day experience of my informants, though with some variation.

First, Langenberg discussed how sangha in ancient India must deal with the *Vinaya* rule, which prohibits taking solid food after noon. As accounts cited by Langenberg testify, this rule posed a problem for children living in sangha, since growing children are likely to become hungry later in the day. At first glance, abstaining from food after noon should not be a problem for my informants, since the Chinese Buddhist sangha had long abandoned the rule by using the loophole in the *Vinay*a and terming the evening supper as "medicine" (*yaoshi*) to legitimatize it. In addition, since going on alms rounds is no longer practiced in Chinese Buddhism, Buddhist monastics in Taiwan have to prepare their own meals. At sangha x, child monastics had to take turns in the kitchen and had to follow a strict schedule for meals. Bael remembered:

> Our life was very disciplined. So disciplined... it's difficult to describe. We must wake up at a certain time, eat breakfast at a certain time, and then do some cleaning, and then go to school. After school, we could take a little break but then we must do the evening prayer. After the evening prayer, it was the medicine time [*yahosho*].

Regular meals at sangha x seemed bountiful, for Ficus said:

> The cooks were really good, and they always made delicious meals.... I remember when I first moved to the monastery at the age of twelve, I was thin and small. But because the meals at the monastery were so delicious, I changed from snack-only to one big bowl of vegetables, two bowls of rice, and one bowl of soup every meal every day. I grew from tiny to taller and stronger.

It would seem that, unlike children in the accounts cited by Langenberg, longing for food would not be an issue for my informants. Yet they still recalled how they longed for food. Apple vividly remembered the temptation of snacks:

> Back then, we would be very excited whenever someone's family came to visit and brought us pizza, stinking tofu, or a soft drink cocktail. Sometimes we would use these opportunities to "sack up" [snacks], and use the opportunity for medical care to leave the monastery.... Just "by chance," there would be a whole bunch of us in need of medical attention: some needed a new pair of glasses, some had knee problems, some needed to see a Chinese herbalist. There would be like ten child nuns. Before we left, we would sort out a "to buy" list: sometimes we had to buy Ferrero Rocher, sometimes Pringles chips.... At times, when we did not have our own private lockers, we would buy snacks from a supermarket in town, put them in a plastic bag, and hide them in the space between the ceilings, where we also hid our novels.... After school and before the bus arrived, we would run to the grocery shop to buy soda or apple pie .... In my fifth grade [...] the monastery gave each of us a phone card.... Then some younger child nuns who did not have any money used the phone card to exchange for snacks with the shop owner!

Apple's recollection is very interesting, not only because it confirms that stories in ancient Indian Buddhist literature as discussed by Langenberg remain relevant today, but also because it draws a vivid picture of natural hunger by growing child monastics. Strict mealtimes as prescribed in the *Vinaya* or by Chinese Buddhist monastic protocol seem incapable of satisfying ordinary child monastics' hunger. Thus, it is little wonder that, as Langenberg shows in her article, consideration for children's hunger was sometimes the precondition for setting down a *Vinaya* rule. By limiting the age of ordination, children living in sangha were allowed to consume food at hours forbidden to adult monastics.

MONASTIC EDUCATION

Although my informants might complain about the minder-masters or the severity of their daily routine, they all praised the excellent monastic education provided by sangha x. Imbe said:

> At the beginning, I did not think about having a [government- recognized] degree because I felt that I learned more from the sangha than from the secular school.... We used to emphasize only Chinese literature and Dharma. But after we began to attend secular school, the Old Master said that worldly knowledge is important too and he made a new curriculum. We had courses in Chinese painting, pottery, English, and Japanese. It was wholesome and rich. I loved it! I really loved the courses in the Academy. Besides the knowledge from the books, I thought that classes in calligraphy, pottery and painting were just awesome!

From sangha x's website, it seems that monastic education is a major focus in sangha x. This is not unusual, for since the turn of the twentieth century, monastic education has been seen by Chinese Buddhist reformists as essential to the survival of Buddhism. For example, Chinese reform monk Taixu (1890–1947) advocated a new vision of monastic education as a way to prevent Chinese Buddhism from further decadency. His vision was carried over to Taiwan (and modified) by other monastics and affected Buddhism in Taiwan profoundly.[23] Another more recent example was a conference organized by Luminary nuns[24] in May 2009 with the theme devoted to Buddhist nuns' education.[25] Hence, the great attention given by sangha x to monastic education is not unusual in the context of Buddhist discourse in Taiwan.

According to the official website of sangha x,[26] the educational establishments at sangha x were multifarious, ranging from adult and children's Dharma/meditation classes at its branch temples to a multilingual secular school (not yet established during my informants' stay) near its headquarter monastery. For its monastics, a seemingly comprehensive program was planned (see Table 13.2). "Postgraduate Institute" and "Academy" refer to different training grounds at the headquarter monastery. Once a child monastic enrolled in the Academy, he or she was physically moved out of the children's dormitory and into the facilities at the Academy. Even though sangha x gives its educational institutes titles such as "postgraduate" or "Academy," none of these institutes is recognized by the state. Additionally, since sangha x was founded only in the late 1980s, its monastic education program as shown in Table 13.2 was not well established during my informants' stay in sangha x. There seemed to be a lack of training consistency, for timetables, facilities, curriculum, and so on often changed. Sometimes

23. Don A.Pittman. *Toward a Modern Chinese Buddhism: Taixu's Reforms* (Honolulu: University of Hawaii Press, 2001), 229–36, 262–92.

24. "Luminary nuns" refers to a *bhikkhunisangha* in Taiwan that places great emphasis on the education of Buddhist nuns. For more, see Wei-yi Cheng, *Buddhist Nuns in Taiwan and Sri Lanka*, 43–47. Or the official website of Luminary nuns: http://www.gaya.org.tw, accessed on June 13, 2009.

25. *2009 International Conference for Buddhist Sangha Education — Exploration on Education for Contemporary Female Sangha*, Taipei: Maojia Long Shan Temple Banqiao Wenhua Guangchang, May 30–31, 2009.

26. Accessed during April–June 2009.

Table 13.2 MONASTIC EDUCATION

monastic education		Programs	Duration
	Postgraduate Institute		3 years
	Academy	Degree Level	2 years
		Senior Level	3 years

Source: sangha x official English website, accessed on April 21, 2009.[i]
[i]My informants told me that there used to be a pre-Academy school for its child monastics, but since sangha x no longer ordains children, it has been abolished.

the child monastics were asked to drop out of secular school to attend the Academy as full-time students; other times, they attended monastic training at the Academy only during evenings, weekends, and school holidays. Nevertheless, monastic education was considered superior to secular education by the adult members.

The value placed upon this monastic training program can be seen from a statement of nun N1, who now lives at a branch temple in Australia. In response to whether she gave Dharma talks at the branch temple where she lodged, she replied, "No, I only help out in sermons. I have not completed the Academy, so I am not qualified to preach." Apparently, N1 considered the completion of the program (Table 13.2) a necessary condition for preaching Dharma. This was a widespread idea among my informants.

According to my informants' accounts, the Academy provided a relatively rich curriculum. In addition to Buddhist courses such as *Vinaya* study and sutra study, other courses included classical Chinese literature, English, visual arts, and calligraphy. The instructors included some well-known artists and calligraphers. Duku, Ficus, Imbe, and Jambul held part-time jobs in graphic design at the time of the interviews, and they credited their artistic ability to the training they received at sangha x.

Supposedly, monastics at sangha x would take at least eight years to be trained in this program. However, for one reason or another, none of my informants successfully completed the program. Each one had a different reason for dropping out of the Academy earlier. For Jambul, her difficult relationship with her minder-master played a role:

> I retorted back to my minder-master. That was really not my fault, but still... I didn't want to apologize to my minder-master, and so it happened that a group of us did not want to stay at [the pre-Academy school]. We told the minder-master that we wanted to go to the Academy .... At the Academy? Really stressful! I was at the age of junior high school but I ended up at the level of senior high school. We got to learn senior-level Chinese literature, senior-level Dharma. I couldn't handle it .... I was the youngest there. I was only fourteen .... So I didn't stay there for long, only for about half a year.

Although Jambul left the Academy early because of her inability to handle the curriculum, her failed relationship with her minder-master was the cause for her premature enrollment there. After leaving the Academy, Jambul did not go back to the pre-Academy institute but was transferred to a branch temple in another county.

Imbe was another one who did not complete the program because of conflict with her minder-master:

> Yes, I was really angry. That minder-master was of the opinion that I asked too many questions .... I thought the minder-master was wrong. She favored another student... I almost finished [the senior level of the Academy]. The new minder-master who replaced her was even worse. There was a time when I was transferred to a branch temple. That was no-study-but-work-everyday life. [I was there] for about a half-year .... Then I returned to the Academy. The minder-master thought I used the measure of the branch temple to challenge the system of the Academy.... I adjusted to the life in the Academy well but the minder-master kept pressuring me to leave.

For others, leaving the Academy came in the form of a natural disaster. On September 21, 1999, a devastating earthquake with a magnitude of 7.6 on the Richter scale struck central Taiwan.[27] The earthquake hit sangha x hard and many of its buildings collapsed. Unable to house all of its members, many monastics had to move away, including my informants Apple, Cherry, Grape and Imbe. Once moved out, none of them ever returned to the Academy.

GOING TO SCHOOL

Whether my informants were living in the monastery or elsewhere, the government required that they attend secular school. Compulsory education in Taiwan began in 1919 when a formal educational system was introduced. In 1943 a six-year compulsory education system was implemented, and by 1968 it was extended to nine years.[28] Before the founding of sangha x's own secular school,[29] its child monastics had to attend secular school outside of the monastery, as required by the state.

The first challenge was the inevitable conflict that arose between the Buddhist monastic ideal and popular youth culture. Cherry recalled:

27. Jang, Li-ju, *The 921 Earthquake: A Study of the Effects of Taiwanese Cultural Factors on Resilience* (Ph.D. Dissertation submitted to the Faculty of the Graduate School of Social Work, University of Denver, 2005), 17–18.
28. Chou, Chuing Prudence and Ho Ai-Hsin, "Schooling in Taiwan" in *Going to School in East Asia,* ed. Gerard A. Postiglion and Jason Tan (Greenwood eBooks: http://ebooks.greenwood.com/reader.jsp?x=GR3633&p=344&bc=EGR3633,2007), accessed on May 12, 2009, 346.
29. Sangha x's own secular school was founded only recently, and none of my informants had the chance to attend.

> Trivial things could be big issues when we are young. For example, pop music! Pop music, novels, and comic books were popular among kids. When we were young, we liked to play video games. But those were banned in our [sangha]. If we got caught, we would be punished.

In postinterview gatherings the informants joked about how they used to hide snacks and comic books in their dormitory ceilings and how they used to watch movies on their laptops behind adult monastics' backs.[30] Apparently, resisting pop culture was not easy for the child monastics.

Secular school also confronted the child monastics with non-Buddhist values, namely Confucianism. Confucianism influences many areas of Taiwanese life.[31] It is unsurprising that my informants came across teachers or schoolmates who, influenced by Confucian values, could not appreciate Buddhist monasticism. Ficus recalled one such teacher:

> It's not that he targeted us. But he would say, "Why did you want to enter sangha? You haven't had fun, haven't experienced life; why renounce the secular world? Haven't you ever thought about your parents?"[...] "The country and society need talents like yours. How dare you [renounce] at such a young age?"

The teacher's comments reflect Confucian ethics in which one's duty toward the state and parents are deemed paramount.[32] He seemed to suggest that by entering sangha, the child nuns neglected their duties as citizens and daughters. Imbe, too, met an unfriendly teacher:

> Actually, we [child monastics] were assigned different classes. Every class had a different homeroom teacher .... [My homeroom teacher] was like, "You should not have entered sangha." The government scheme of school lunch was already available at that time, so the school would prepare lunch for the students. The teacher would say to us that we could eat lunch with them. That contained meat!

For the teachers to tempt the child monastics with meat is very telling. Vegetarianism is so integral to Chinese Buddhism that meat-eating is sometimes employed by Christian missionaries as a signifier of a new convert's

30. Fieldwork note, 22/3/2009 and 15/5/2009.
31. For example, see Philip Clart, "Confucius and the Mediums: Is There a "Popular Confucianism?" *T'oungPao*89 (2003), 1–38; Douglas C. Smith, "Foundations of Modern Chinese Education and the Taiwan Experience," in *The Confucian Continuum: Educational Modernization in Taiwan*, ed. Douglas C. Smith (New York: Praeger, 1991), 1–61.
32. Rujia Zhang and Yuhai Zhang, "Zhongguo Chuantong Renlunguan Jiqi Xiandai Qishi," *Journal of University of Science and Technology Beijing* 23 no. 4 (2007), 157–61.
33. Eric Reinders, "Blessed Are the Meat Eaters: Christian Antivegetarianism and the Missionary Encounter with Chinese Buddhism," *Positions* 12 no. 2 (2004), 509–37.

religious commitment.[33] By tempting the child monastics to eat meat, the teacher was in fact questioning the legitimacy of their religiosity.

Imbe's experience might be interpreted as a cultural remnant of the imperial past; imperial literature often portrayed Buddhist nuns as corrupt, lustful, and wicked, indicating male authors' anxiety of not being able to confine them (Buddhist and Daoist alike) to the captivity of their patriarchal home setting.[34] While insults against nuns were common in the popular literature of that era and might influence Taiwanese public perception about Buddhist nuns today, my nun students from university told me that such insults were rare in their experience (although not completely unheard of). They viewed them as being the product of ignorance. Since Buddhism is not the predominant religion in Taiwan, some people simply did not know how to interact with Buddhist nuns. This point is exemplified in Grape's recollection of her days as the only monastic student in a secular high school in a rural area:

> Hey, I was the center of attention! When the principal came for inspection round during the lunch hour, he would specifically inquire about you. And the school's military officer and student affairs officer would want to know more about you. They would ask, how were you? Are you okay here? And they would want to take photos with you. . . . They were curious about sangha life. . . . They would ask about Buddhism, or why you want to be a vegetarian? They would say something like "Are plants vegetarians too?" Something sarcastic.

Fortunately, the secular school did eventually become accustomed to their monastic students and most teachers learned to respect their religious decisions and lifestyle. One of the younger informants, Hackberry, did not experience disrespectful teachers the way her older counterparts did. She said, "No, the same [treatment from the teachers as to other students]. I felt that the teachers were very good to us. They took good care of us." Bael, who later attended an occupational school in another city, also said:

> People were curious about you. But there had been monastic students in earlier years, and my year also had quite a number of monastic students. My classmates understood [about our religiosity]. At least they had seen monastics before. I was lucky, because all my teachers and classmates were great.

The statements of Hackberry and Bael suggest that the teachers' and schoolmates' prior acquaintance with Buddhist monastics was the key to a respectful attitude. This point seems reasonable when one considers the experiences of other informants.

34. Chen, Yuhneu, "Mingdai Funu Xinfo De Shehui Jinzhi Yu Zizhu Kong Jian," *Chengda Lishi Xuebao* 29 (2005), 121–64.

For example, as was mentioned earlier, Buddhism is not the predominant religion in Taiwan and not every Taiwanese has the opportunity to become acquainted with Buddhist monastics. When my informants were removed from the area near the monastery, their schooling experience could become traumatic. Apple, Cherry, Grape, and Imbe had to move out of the monastery because of the infrastructural damage caused by the 9/21 earthquake. Cherry was transferred to a branch temple in a rural area, where she experienced traumatic school bullying. She said:

> The teachers were good to me. But I would not tell the teachers about the male classmates' bullying. They were very over. For example, we all brought lunch boxes to school and heated them in the steamer. Sometimes they brought hot dogs. They would repeatedly eat hot dogs in an obscene manner right in front of me! They would do some acts and say something to me. They scolded me... I dared not tell anyone what they did to me. How would I dare? It's the first time that I am telling anyone about this, and it's because you want me to give you an example.

The fear of retribution stopped Cherry from telling anyone about the school bullying that she suffered. Grape, who was transferred to a rural school, suffered similar bullying:

> Yes, it's a mixed class. Most classmates were boys. I didn't know how to... interact with the classmates as a monastic. Sometimes if I talked too plain, without much polishing, they would think that I disrespected them.

Thus even though sangha x offered its child monastics a rich monastic education, the need to attend secular school could be very challenging. Not only did the child monastics often encounter different values at their secular schools, but the lack of familiarity with Buddhist monasticism on the part of their teachers and schoolmates led to difficult personal experiences for many. Although none of my informants directly attributed their disrobing to these experiences, education was very much on their mind when they considered disrobing.

LEAVING SANGHA

In Janet Jacobs's research on deconversion from charismatic religious movements, she finds that it does not occur on the basis of one incident.[35] My finding is similar in that none of my informants claimed their disrobing to be the result of one event. Imbe's disrobing, for instance, required almost a year of deliberation:

35. Janet Jacobs, "Deconversion from Religious Movements: An Analysis of Charismatic Bonding and Spiritual Commitment," *Journal for the Scientific Study of Religion* 26 no. 3 (1987), 294–308.

> After I left the Academy [I began to think about disrobing]. Back then, we were not allowed to continue our [secular] education as monastics. If we wanted to continue [secular] education, we must disrobe .... I only discussed this with the monastics of the same age, never with adults .... And I had never experienced the world. I had left the secular world for too long. So besides the desire to continue education, I also wanted to see the world.

Jacobs's study finds that the first step toward deconversion occurs when one is disillusioned with the social aspect of the religious affiliation. During this stage, the potential deconverter's reverence toward the group leader remains.[36] Similarly, all of my informants retained a certain degree of reverence toward the founding monk ("Old Master") of sangha x and all still identified themselves as Buddhists at the time of the interviews. They attributed their disrobing to their dissatisfaction with the middle-level hierarchy.

The most common reason given by my informants for disrobing was their disagreement with adult authority regarding their education. Even though sangha x provided the child monastics with a good monastic training program, the monastic Academy was not a government-recognized institute, and its degree has no credential in society at large. It created consternation in the minds of these child monastics who were already unhappy about their relationship with their minder-masters. Apple recalled one argument:

> The minder-master who I absolutely hated even told me to drop out of secular school. Why keep telling me to drop out? I asked her the question too. She said that [secular education] is not important and we should stay in the sangha to concentrate on our spiritual practice, to help out in the kitchen, and to seek enlightenment. So I said to her: "If secular education is not important, why do [sangha x's monthly magazines] always run articles about who graduated from university? And in every single issue!" She was speechless.

Imbe also noticed the contradiction between the said value of secular education and the actual value placed upon it by adult monastics:

> They always said secular education was not important, and all we needed was to attend the Academy. But in fact, you could see [contradictions]. I will give you an example. There was a nun in our sangha and she had double M.A. degrees. She was ordained later than me, but soon after her ordination, she became a teacher-master. In just one year!

Therefore, although adult monastics of sangha x hailed monastic education as superior to secular education, my informants noticed that adult monastics in fact held more respect for those with higher secular education. Consequently, some child monastics (i.e. my informants) sought to pursue secular education that was not encouraged by sangha x. It was the case with Duku:

36. Jacobs, "Deconversion from Religious Movements," 298.

> I left sangha x because I wanted to continue my education.... In fact, we youngsters left sangha x because we wanted to continue our education. Most people thought it was not a good idea. Perhaps I was thinking like a layperson. For example, wouldn't it be a shame that we don't even have a junior high school diploma?... They said that it's not necessary to go to outside school because the outside world would pollute us.

Duku left the monastery to attend senior high school in a city. Throughout her three years of attending, she lived alone (financially supported by her mother) and went to school as a Buddhist nun. After graduating from senior high school, she. along with Apple, decided to disrobe upon entering university. They reasoned that the new environment would ensure the anonymity of their monastic past and enhance their assimilation into secular society. That they deemed this an advantage is significant; they were obviously looking for a way out, and university provided it.

Not all of my informants disrobed because of the desire to pursue secular education. Emblic did so because of an emotional bond with her mother:

> Once I went home to visit my mother. She told me that she missed me and this and that. She told me to return home. I didn't particularly want to stay in the robes or to disrobe.

Ficus disrobed because of her concern about being a perfect monastic:

> I set high standards for myself. Ever since I was a kid, I set high standards for myself .... The vice-abbot even told me to take it easy, don't think of myself as worthless and don't be so demanding [of myself] all the time. After my higher ordination, I became even more demanding [of myself]. I thought that being a *bhikkhuni* is different and I should be more mature and grown up. So I had to be even more vigilant about the ways I interacted with people. The more I demanded of myself, the less I could accomplish.

Uncertain of whether she could be a good monastic, Ficus decided to disrobe.

LIFE AFTER SANGHA

In his study of the adjustment of Western ex-Buddhist monks, Mapel finds that the initial experience of disrobing is often a mixture of the sense of freedom and excitement with feelings of "insecurity and anxiety of having one's

37. Tim Mapel, "The Adjustment Process of Ex-Buddhist Monks to Life After the Monastery."*Journal of Religion and Health* 46 no. 1 (2007), 23–24.

identity, points of reference, and structures removed in an instant."[37] Some of my informants did experience such feelings of insecurity and anxiety. For example, Imbe said:

> I cried every day. I couldn't face anyone. I locked myself in my room..... It was like I must face a new life. I lost contact with everyone, because at that time only very few of us had left the monastery to attend school elsewhere. I couldn't find anyone.

Cherry also mentioned the difficulty of adjusting to lay life:

> In the beginning it was like, not exactly the feeling of inferiority, but something like that. I didn't know anything at first. I didn't know how to dress myself, well, almost everything. In fact, there were a lot of things that I didn't know. We spent more time chanting and in meditation.

But not everyone experienced such insecure and anxious feelings. Hackberry, who had disrobed only six months prior to the interview, seemed to have adjusted well to her new identity as a laywoman, in spite of the fact that she grew up in the monastery: "Actually, I think that I am okay in every aspect. Some people may not feel they fit in when they first return [to secular life], but I am fine. My ability to adjust is quite okay."

Perhaps age is a factor. Mapel's samples were middle-aged at the time of disrobing, whereas most of mine disrobed in their late teens. My informants probably did not experience as much "lack of development and missing out" as Mapel's samples did.[38] For example, one cause of Mapel's samples' resentment toward their monastic past was their inability to find employment and the financial destitution that followed. My informants were young enough to apply for student loans and return to school. Their continuing education acted as an interim for adjustment before the eventual challenge of finding employment. This may explain why none of my informants expressed resentment toward their monastic past; on the contrary, they seemed grateful for their monastic experience. For example, Bael said:

> Sometimes an unwholesome thought might arise, and [I] remind myself of the karmic consequences. Then there is the right thought. Oh, yes, [the eight years as a child nun] was a precious experience for me. No, [no regret] at all! I am very glad that I had those eight years [of living as a child nun]. I cherish those years!

Ficus also credited the monastic experience for helping her to be more mature and independent:

38. Mapel, "The Adjustment Process of Ex-Buddhist Monks to Life After the Monastery," 28–32.

> Just like I said, you grew up in a group and you learned to be independent. Unlike some young people I know… as far as I know, if girls my age still live at home, they would still let their parents do their laundry and clean their rooms. But for me, because I grew up in that kind of environment, I know how to take care of myself.… I can think more, consider things more deeply. People my age don't usually use their brains.

Even Duku, who expressed the most resentment toward sangha x, did not denounce her monastic experience entirely:

> I think they have a management problem. How should I put it? It's not that I don't like sangha life. If you tell me to live in sangha again, I am okay with it. For I think sangha life is not bad! But I won't join [sangha x] again.

As for my informants' relationship with sangha x after disrobing, it varies widely, from Duku, who wanted nothing to do with sangha x, to Hackberry and Imbe, who actively participated in the activities of sangha x. But their active involvement with sangha x did not occur at first, for the initial period of disrobing was usually filled with uncertainty about one's relationship with the sangha. It took a tragedy for my informants to reconnect and even to reassociate with sangha x. In 2005 one of the ex-child nuns died in a car accident. Her funeral brought other ex-child monastics together. Soon after the funeral, an online social group[39] was set up enabling them to reconnect and stay in touch with one another. Through it, they made arrangements to meet from time to time, and even to participate in activities of the monastery or its branch temples.[40] This eventually led to some of their (e.g., Hackberry, Imbe) reinvolvement with sangha x. Evidently, social networks and emotional support were crucial for my informants' emotional well-being after sangha. Their experiences differ considerably from those of Mapel's samples, who lack this social and emotional support. This fact might explain the discrepancy of adjustment to secular life between the two groups.

CONCLUSION

Talking to former child nuns offered a glimpse into the life of child monastics in contemporary Taiwan. The fact that they openly critiqued their monastic past is very revealing, for it shows that they were not passive vessels and quite capable of assessing child monasticism by themselves. Although they may have been molded by their monastic pasts and may have appropriated many of its values, they were also critical of monastic authority and searched for ways

39. They insisted that the online social group is "insider (i.e., ex-child monastics of sangha x) only" and refused to give me access to it.
40. Fieldwork note 25/5/2009.

to reconcile themselves with their monastic childhoods. Certainly, not all child monastics at sangha x disrobed: I also talked to N1, whose statements were briefly cited earlier, and two other nuns of sangha x who were still in robes. My informants represented those for whom child monasticism failed, but their recollections reveal the virtues and shortcomings of child monasticism with clear hindsight, as opposed to those who still carry the burden of representing Buddhist monasticism.

What does monasticism mean for children?. First of all, it means communal life and growing up fast, for child monastics must adjust to a life without parents and a life of discipline and expectation. It also means maturity and independence. I found my informants to be more independent and forward-thinking than most young people of their age. As child monastics, however, they had to face particular challenges while growing up. Institutional incompetency at sangha x was one problem they frequently cited. For example, the frequent rotation of minder-masters meant a lack of constant adult role models and subsequently led to emotional upheavals in their monastic childhoods. Another challenge for my informants was the conflict between social values and Buddhist monastic ideals. These young people did not live in ancient India or contemporary Sri Lanka where Buddhist monasticism was presumably understood and respected; they lived in a society where Buddhist monasticism was often frowned upon. They had to attend secular school, where their monastic identity was often ridiculed. They also had to struggle between the lure of pop culture and monastic discipline.

My informants may have failed to stay in robes, but their stories provide important insight into the experience of child monasticism.

CHAPTER 14

Zen-Boy Ikkyū

MELISSA ANNE-MARIE CURLEY

The fifteenth-century Zen priest Ikkyū Sōjun (1394–1481) is the subject of several important portraits: not only the famous painting by his disciple Bokusai (d. 1492) now hanging in the Tokyo National Museum, but also two memorial sculptures, one held at Shinjuan, on the grounds of the Daitokuji complex in Kyoto, and the other at Shūon'an, in the small city of Kyōtanabe. These portraits show us Ikkyū as an old man, with unkempt hair and a downcast expression—so downcast, in fact, that in a review of the fourteen types of facial expressions, the statue at Shūon'an is selected as the emblematic representative of "the expression of antagonism or displeasure."[1] We know that Ikkyū himself signed off on Bokusai's portrait[2] and so must have thought that, despite his high rank and fine reputation, he was best depicted as scruffy and miserable. Donald Keene writes approvingly that if Ikkyū as depicted here is not exactly the picture of dignity, the portrait does give us "the face of an individual, as striking, strange, and unorthodox as Ikkyū's life and poetry... From the life, from the poems, and from this portrait we know that this is what it means to be a man."[3]

On the grounds at Shūon'an, however, we find a statue representing a quite different version of Ikkyū—not a man at all, but a cheerful young novice holding a broom, with a clean-shaven head and a smile on his face. The plaque on the statue indicates that this is a portrait of Ikkyū-san. Ryūichi Abé has noted in passing that Ikkyū is one of just three Japanese Buddhist saints referred to with the fond suffix *-san*, indicating "affectionate respect."[4] This particular

1. Shirakabe Yukio et al, "Expressions of Faces in Sculptures and Paintings as Seen from an Anatomical Viewpoint," *Aesthetic Plastic Surgery* 5 (1981), 331.
2. Donald Keene, "The Portrait of Ikkyū," *Archives of Asian Art* 20 (1966/1967), 58.
3. Keene, "The Portrait of Ikkyū," 65.
4. The others are Kūkai (or Kōbō-san), the founder of the Shingon school, and the poet Ryōkan; see Ryūichi Abé, "Introduction," in *Great Fool: Zen Master Ryōkan*,

depiction of Ikkyū-san, however, points not to a generalized affection for Ikkyū Sōjun, but to a very specific vision of Ikkyū as a child—the cute, bald-headed, broom-wielding child who appears on the cover of children's story books, in the pages of children's *manga*, and, most influentially of all, in the opening credits of the Tōei Corporation's long-running animated series *Ikkyū-san*. The child Ikkyū-san is all over Kyōtanabe—holding his broom outside the train station, prancing across the bottom of tourist maps for the city, appearing on stickers on the supermarket's automatic doors and the banner on the overpass urging drivers to proceed with caution. At Shūon'an—the last place where the historical Ikkyū lived and the site of his mausoleum—cartoon images of characters from the Tōei series decorate the main hall and the stands outside where visitors tie the wooden plaques on which they have written requests to the powers associated with the temple.

This vision of Ikkyū has considerable currency not only in Kyōtanabe but across Japan, and the invoking of that vision—produced outside of Buddhist systems of representation—within the precincts of Shūon'an seems to function as a way of reconciling Ikkyū Sōjun and Ikkyū-san by suggesting that the happy child Ikkyū grew up to become the old man Ikkyū. Tōei too positions *Ikkyū-san* in this way: although the series focuses almost exclusively on the child Ikkyū, it is described as the "story of a great man"; we are thus prompted to understand that this very child would eventually become Japan's famous "high Zen priest."[5]

But the relationship between Ikkyū-san and Ikkyū Sōjun is not actually this straightforward. I will try to show, first, that the child Ikkyū-san is the product of the adult Ikkyū Sōjun and not the other way around—that is, it was the adult who eventually became the child—and, second, that the relationship between the fifteenth-century adult and the twentieth-century child is marked by both important continuities and a dramatic rupture: the sudden appearance in the nineteenth century of childhood itself.

THE MUROMACHI IKKYŪ

Ikkyū Sōjun was born in 1394 in the midst of the political and cultural upheavals of the Muromachi period (1338–1573). In some respects, the Muromachi was a time of flourishing for Japanese Zen, which had emerged as an independent school only a century before, organized under a framework borrowed from China called the Gozan or Five Mountains system. When the Ashikaga family came to power at the beginning of the Muromachi period, they expanded this system, developing ranked lists of five temples apiece in both Kyoto and Kamakura,

trans. with essays by Ryūichi Abé and Peter Haskel (Honolulu: University of Hawaii Press, 1996), xi.

5. "Ikkyu-san," Toei Animation, accessed April 23, 2011, http://corp.toei-anim.co.jp/english/film/ikkyusan.php.

with a single temple, Kyoto's Nanzenji, positioned above all ten to function as a kind of interface between the Zen institution and the administrative center in Kyoto's Muromachi district. A handful of smaller, lower-ranked temples identified as *jissetsu*—literally "Ten Temples"—formed a second tier beneath the Five Mountains. At the suggestion of the Rinzai monk Musō Soseki, whose own line controlled the top temples in the Kyoto Five Mountains, the Ashikaga family also sponsored *ankokuji*, or "temples for the peace of the state," in every province.[6] The strategically located *ankokuji* were to serve as "military fortifications and centers of surveillance," and their spread, as Jeffrey P. Mass argues, "provides an index of the growing authority of the Ashikaga and of their claim to exercise benevolent rule over the whole of Japan."[7]

Because they were so profoundly implicated in the efforts of the Ashikaga to extend their reach in the provinces, Zen institutions involved in the Gozan system had little autonomy, but they did enjoy unprecedented economic support and political and cultural influence. Within Gozan Zen during this period, then, we see an efflorescence of Zen aesthetics, in such diverse modes as poetry, painting, drama, flower arrangement, gardening, and tea. We do not see an efflorescence of Zen thought, however, at least not in the Five Mountains. Akamatsu Toshihide and Philip Yampolsky say bluntly that "Although the Gozan temples remained politically powerful throughout the Muromachi period, the Zen content of monastic life declined markedly. By the Higashiyama period [beginning in the latter half of the fifteenth century] little or no Zen of any variety was being taught in the Gozan."[8]

There were also Zen temples outside of the Gozan system, however. These had little traction with the imperial court, relying instead on popular patronage. In 1431 Kyoto's Daitokuji, a Rinzai temple in the line of Daitō Kokushi (1282–1337), lost its status as a *jissetsu*, and joined the ranks of these extra-Gozan temples, eventually finding patrons among the merchants and artists of the free city of Sakai on Osaka Bay. During the fifteenth century, Daitokuji developed a reputation as a serious place for serious monks, attracting those "who did not take to the bureaucratized organizational structure or the stultifying literary atmosphere" of the Gozan system.[9] Ikkyū was for a time the abbot of Daitokuji and is perhaps the paradigmatic example of just such a monk.

The *Ikkyū oshō nenpu* (Chronicle of the High Priest Ikkyū), a hagiographical account of Ikkyū's life attributed to Bokusai, suggests that Ikkyū's mother

6. Martin Collcutt, *Five Mountains: The Rinzai Zen Monastic Institution in Medieval Japan* (Cambridge, MA: Harvard University Asia Center, 1981), 107.

7. Jeffrey P. Mass, *The Origins of Japan's Medieval World: Courtiers, Clerics, Warriors, and Peasants in the Fourteenth Century* (Stanford, CA: Stanford University Press, 2002), 289.

8. Akamatsu Toshihide and Philip Yampolsky, "Muromachi Zen and the Gozan System," in *Japan in the Muromachi Age*, ed. John Whitney Hall and Toyoda Takeshi (Berkeley: University of California Press, 1977), 317.

9. Collcutt, *Five Mountains*, 125–26.

was a member of the aristocratic Fujiwara family and a consort of the young Emperor Gokomatsu (1377–1433), widely believed to be Ikkyū's father; in his indispensable study of Ikkyū's life and work, *Zen-Man Ikkyū*, James Sanford notes that the poems in Ikkyū's *Kyōunshū* (Crazy Cloud Collection) indicate that Ikkyū too believed himself to be Gokomatsu's illegitimate son.[10] In 1399 the six-year-old Ikkyū is sent to a temple referred to in the *Chronicle* simply as Ankokuji,[11] and in 1406 he leaves Ankokuji to study with a poetry master from Tenryūji, the first-ranked temple in the Kyoto Gozan.[12] By the time he is a teenager, he is demonstrating a censorious streak: the *Chronicle* records an incident in 1409 when, overhearing the deputy abbot bragging about his lineage, Ikkyū is said to have "covered his ears and fled the hall," writing two poems castigating the monastery for harboring such scoundrels.[13] The following year Ikkyū leaves Tenryūji—and the Gozan system—for the small hermitage of Saigonji, where he studies under Ken'ō Sōi (d. 1415), a disciple in Daitō's line.[14] The *Chronicle* records an incident in 1411 in which Ikkyū brazenly defies the will of the shogun,[15] and another in 1412 in which he informs a teacher from Daitokuji that despite their rigorous reputation, the monks of Daitokuji—aside from the abbot, Kasō Sōdon (1352–1428)—were really "just so-so."[16]

Ikkyū attains realization in 1420, at the sound of a crow's cry; his awakening is certified by Kasō himself.[17] But as his reputation grows, his unorthodox behaviors continue apace—he leaves Kyoto for Sakai and seems to begin developing his own idiosyncratic style as a teacher: in 1435 he makes waves by parading through the streets of the city brandishing a wooden sword, characterizing the Zen of his day as, like his sword, having the appearance of wisdom but lacking killing power;[18] in 1437, he is said to have gone to the trouble of retrieving the certificate of dharma transmission given to him by Kasō, only to tear it to pieces and throw it into the fire;[19] and in 1440, having been coaxed into serving as abbot at a subtemple of Daitokuji, he quits in disgust after just a week and a half, leaving behind this poem:

> *Only ten fussy days as an abbot,*
> *And already my feet are tangled up in red tape.*
> *If, someday, you want to look me up,*
> *Try the fish-shop, the tavern, or the brothel.*[20]

10. James Sanford, *Zen-Man Ikkyū* (Chico, CA: Scholar's Press, 1981), 10.
11. Sanford, *Zen-Man Ikkyū*, 73.
12. Sanford, *Zen-Man Ikkyū*, 74.
13. Sanford, *Zen-Man Ikkyū*, 75.
14. Sanford, *Zen-Man Ikkyū*, 76.
15. Sanford, *Zen-Man Ikkyū*, 77.
16. Sanford, *Zen-Man Ikkyū*, 77.
17. Sanford, *Zen-Man Ikkyū*, 84.
18. Sanford, *Zen-Man Ikkyū*, 91–92.
19. Sanford, *Zen-Man Ikkyū*, 93.
20. Sanford, *Zen-Man Ikkyū*, 94 and 48.

Ikkyū's thirties and forties are marked by a constant back and forth between Kyoto and Sakai, or between the monastic institution and city life, until finally in 1452 he settles down in his own hermitage, Katsuroan.[21] Sanford remarks that the following decades see Ikkyū enter a period of "stability and productivity—a sort of prolonged, late maturation," during which time Ikkyū flourishes as a writer and an artist.[22] Throughout this period of calm, however, his work continues to record his contempt for the Zen practitioners of the time, whom he castigates as leprous, poisonous, and perverted. Ikkyū saves particular scorn for a fellow disciple, Yōsō Sōi (1376–1458), who had succeeded to the position of abbot at Daitokuji, calling him "a putrid fellow" and his Zen "a Zen of fame and profit."[23] Despite his rigorously anti-institutional stance, Ikkyū is persuaded to return to Daitokuji once more in 1474, this time to serve as head abbot—he ultimately ends up commuting from his new hermitage at Shūon'an. Much of the temple complex had been burned down during conflicts stemming from the Ōnin War, and Ikkyū was charged with rebuilding, enlisting the support of lay disciples in Sakai to do so. By the time of his death in 1481, Daitokuji is thriving as a monastic and cultural center; a century later Daitokuji is under the patronage of the warlord Toyotomi Hideyoshi (1536–1598) and is poised to surpass the Gozan monasteries in terms of power and influence.

While he is savaging the Zen institution, Ikkyū is also representing himself as a drunken, libidinous, precept-breaking good-for-nothing, "a demon in Daitō's line."[24] If some poems find Ikkyū praising himself—"For thirty years I have shouldered the load; I alone have borne the burden of Sung-yüan's Zen"[25]—others suggest struggle and uncertainty:

Come this far; and no sign of Buddhahood yet.
Though Hell begins to show itself all about.
At every bend and every step, always the passions
Darkness at the corner; and beyond, sharp, Hellish trees.[26]

Though a precept-breaking monk for eighty years,
I am ashamed of Zen that tries to sweep karma aside.
Still if this illness is the fruit of past actions,
Will it ever come to an end?[27]

21. Sanford, *Zen-Man Ikkyū*, 100.
22. Sanford, *Zen-Man Ikkyū*, 56.
23. See Sanford, *Zen-Man Ikkyū*, 135–37. Martin Collcutt says of Yōsō that he "seems to have been everything that Ikkyū was not: a gentle, sober, monk administrator who devoted his energies to training Daitokuji monks and restoring the monastery. For some reason Ikkyū developed a violent dislike of Yōsō and took every opportunity to denounce him as a counterfeit Zen master"; see "Zen and the *Gozan*," in *The Cambridge History of Japan: Medieval Japan*, ed. Kōzō Yamamura and John Whitney Hall (Cambridge: Cambridge University Press, 1990), 614.
24. Sanford, *Zen-Man Ikkyū*, 185.
25. Sanford, *Zen-Man Ikkyū*, 130.
26. Sanford, *Zen-Man Ikkyū*, 154.
27. Sanford, *Zen-Man Ikkyū*, 158.

This kind of self-representation is consistent with images of the ideal Chan monk that develop in Song-period China within the context of a ritualized iconoclasm through which performances of unorthodox behavior become institutionally licensed;[28] it likewise anticipates later Japanese Rinzai masters such as Hakuin, who will assume the posture of an outsider, speaking of the Zen institution in withering terms while nonetheless working hard to revive said institution. However genuine Ikkyū's own understanding of himself as a precept-breaker and reprobate may have been then, we should acknowledge that within a Zen system of representation, this is a way of asserting his *bona fides*—his positioning of himself as the demon in the lineage is a way of asserting his status as the true lineage holder.

The *Chronicle*, however, develops a somewhat different picture of Ikkyū than do his own writings, by selecting for only certain kinds of antinomian behavior. His scathing critiques of Gozan Zen and Yōsō's Daitokuji remain, but some of his own scandalous behavior is excised. Rumors about other people's sexual dalliances are dutifully recorded—in the winter of 1454 Yōsō "joyfully moved to a newly built retreat...There was some gossip about man and woman stuff there"[29]—but Ikkyū's own relationship with the blind singer Mori, which Ikkyū himself treats as one of the signal events in his religious life, is not mentioned. The Ikkyū of the *Chronicle* is unconcerned with impressing the Ashikaga but is unfailingly loyal to the imperial family; it is implied that on his deathbed Emperor Gokomatsu acknowledges Ikkyū as his son, and Ikkyū is later said to assure Emperor Gohanazono, "This humble seeker is but a citizen of Your Majesty's realm."[30] In its closing passage, the *Chronicle* reiterates Ikkyū's antipathy toward the Zen teachers of his day—"he hated the kind of Zen that was spooned out by masters who treated their disciples like so many pet birds"—but also describes Ikkyū himself as an unimpeachably good person:

> His kindly character was seen in all his undertakings. He made no difference between high and low and happily mixed with artisans, merchants, and small children. He treated unknown monks and old followers alike and without favoritism. Children could follow him about and play with his beard. Birds came to eat out of his hand. He gave things cheerfully: what he received in one hand, he immediately gave out again with the other.[31]

In short, Ikkyū is to be remembered as kind and respectful to everyone, except for those who plainly didn't deserve it.

28. Morten Schlütter, *How Zen Became Zen: The Dispute Over Enlightenment and the Formation of Chan Buddhism in Song-Dynasty China* (Honolulu: University of Hawaii Press, 2008), 15–16.
29. Sanford, *Zen-Man Ikkyū*, 102.
30. Sanford, *Zen-Man Ikkyū*, 98.
31. Sanford, *Zen-Man Ikkyū*, 116.

The *Chronicle* thus draws us toward the conclusion that Ikkyū's antinomian behavior was in fact only an *upāya* undergirded by moral flawlessness. It ascribes to Ikkyū virtues that resonate powerfully with the popular values of the Muromachi period: he is egalitarian in his dealings with members of his own institution, warm and generous in his dealings with various representatives of the underclass—artisans, merchants, small children—and unconcerned with his own fame and profit.[32] At the same time, he is recognized as virtuous by those monastic and imperial authorities that the *Chronicle* identifies as respectable themselves. This all functions to undercut the danger of Ikkyū's antinomian behavior by assuring the reader that his wildness was well controlled, operating in concert with a recognizable popular ethic. Beneath his unconventional appearance, Ikkyū is understood as possessing the self-control and moral clarity of any orthodox Buddhist hero.

This is true even when he is a child. Sanford notes that the *Chronicle* skips the period between Ikkyū's birth in 1394 and his arrival at Ankokuji in 1399; it likewise skips from 1399 directly to 1405, when Ikkyū makes an appearance at a public lecture on the Vimalakīrti Sūtra. This means that the *Chronicle* give us scarcely any information about Ikkyū's life before the age of eleven (or twelve by the Japanese count), the period we might most readily understand as his childhood. The brief notes in the *Chronicle* do, however, give us some indication of how Ikkyū's disciples imagined their teacher as a child: even as a newborn, the *Chronicle* tells us, "Our master bore the signs of a dragon or a phoenix. But the wider world knew nothing of this";[33] in the audience at the lecture in 1405, "Everyone noticed him and said, 'That youth has the looks of an elder. His future seems limitless.'"[34] Here the child Ikkyū is important because he bears the marks of the man he will become—the impression he makes is that of an adult, despite his young age. In effect, then, even when discussing Ikkyū as a child, the *Chronicle* does not represent him as a child. Ikkyū's childhood is not a period in which he is less than the man he becomes; he is simply born a master. His youth is thus not a period of maturation, but one of holding himself in reserve: when he leaves the Tenryūji training hall in disgust as a teenager, Botetsu is said to have told him, "In another thirty years your words will take effect. You must bear up until then."[22] The young Ikkyū of the *Chronicle* is not a youth at all—he is a mature adult biding his time.

THE TOKUGAWA IKKYŪ

Ikkyū Sōjun is able to restore Daitokuji in the aftermath of the Ōnin War, but the Ashikaga shogunate is not so successful—the civil war marks the beginning of Japan's Warring States period, which sees the Ashikaga family ousted

32. See Amino Yoshihiko, *Muen, Kugai, Raku* (Tokyo: Heibonsha, 1978).
33. Sanford, *Zen-Man Ikkyū*, 73.
34. Sanford, *Zen-Man Ikkyū*, 74.

by the warlord Oda Nobunaga (1534–1582). Nobunaga's successor, Toyotomi Hideyoshi (1536–1598), is a supporter of Daitokuji, but his tenure as warlord is brief; when he dies, Tokugawa Ieyasu (1543–1616) embarks on a five-year campaign that ends in 1603 with the crushing of Hideyoshi's supporters, securing Ieyasu the position of shogun. The Tokugawa family rules Japan for the next 250 years.

As Nam-lin Hur has explained, the relationship between Buddhism and the state during the period of Tokugawa rule is deeply ambivalent: in some ways the Tokugawa regime is rigorously secular, making no attempt "to incorporate Buddhist ideas or rituals into its governing principles";[35] at the same time, local and state governments remain on guard against potential efforts on the part of Buddhist institutions to acquire an undue amount of economic and social power, trying "to contain, control, and even in some cases, suppress Buddhism."[36] The religion which is most vigorously suppressed during the Tokugawa, however, is Christianity, and this suppression, Hur argues, is congenial to the development of a "public custom" requiring that every household patronize a Buddhist temple, by way of proving that they are not Christian; this public custom is, in short order, integrated with the Tokugawa administrative system in such a way that Buddhist temples come to serve as a kind of census bureau. The fact that the Tokugawa regime is not interested in joining with Buddhist institutions in cultural production means that we do not see an elite Buddhist culture arise during the Tokugawa that can compare with that of the Muromachi. On the other hand, we do see an unprecedented expansion of Buddhist popular culture accompanying the growth of the patronage system: "Buddhism permeated daily life during the Tokugawa period, and Buddhist temples stood in every corner of the country.... Almost no village in Tokugawa Japan was without a Buddhist temple and few people were untouched by the activities of Buddhist monks."[37]

Twentieth-century historians have sometimes advanced the view that the Tokugawa period was a time of institutional or clerical degeneration (*kinsei bukkyō darakuron*).[38] Scholars of Tokugawa Zen, however, have vigorously disputed this view, with Duncan Williams, for instance, insisting that "Buddhism was as full of vitality during the Tokugawa period as in any previous era, if not more so,"[39] and Janine Sawada holding that "popular Zen" is among the innovations of the Tokugawa period.[40] It is in the context of popular Zen that we see the transformation of Ikkyū from high priest to folk-hero.

35. Nam-lin Hur, *Death and Social Order in Tokugawa Japan: Buddhism, Anti-Christianity, and the Danka System* (Cambridge, MA: Harvard University Asia Center, 2007), 1–2.
36. Hur, *Death and Social Order*, 2.
37. Hur, *Death and Social Order*, 1.
38. For a thorough study of the roots of this theory, see Orion Klautau, "Against the Ghosts of Recent Past: Meiji Scholarship and the Discourse on Edo-period Buddhist Decadence," *Japanese Journal of Religious Studies* 35/2 (2008), 263–303.
39. Duncan Ryūken Williams, *The Other Side of Zen: A Social History of Sōtō Zen Buddhism in Tokugawa Japan* (Princeton, NJ: Princeton University Press, 2005), 6.
40. Janine Anderson Sawada, *Confucian Values and Popular Zen: Sekimon Shingaku in Eighteenth-Century Japan* (Honolulu: University of Hawaii Press, 1993), 23.

The Muromachi Ikkyū is an important source of inspiration for Tokugawa-period thinkers who are working on bringing Buddhist thought to a mass audience, and—like Ikkyū himself—concerned with critiquing the contemporary Zen institution as corrupt and inauthentic. The relationship between the Muromachi Ikkyū and the Tokugawa Ikkyū is made ambiguous, however, by the production of apocryphal texts attributed to him, and the circulation of folktales about him—the Ikkyū of the Tokugawa is, Sawada implies, a kind of construction: "Along with Mujū, Musō Soseki, and other medieval popularizers, through his writings 'Ikkyū' continued to transmit a simplified, accessible form of Zen throughout the Tokugawa period."[41] Sawada concurs here with Sanford's suggestion that the Ikkyū who emerges in the Tokugawa-period tales is invented in part to serve the immediate purposes of Buddhist priests—"these lively tales make the messages of the *kana hōgō* slide down as easily and tastily as a bowl of sweet, fried eel"[42]—and in part to serve the changing ideology of the time, which required new heroes to represent a legacy of indigenous Japanese individualism.

There are two elements of the Tokugawa-period tales that are of particular interest to us. The first is their emphasis on wit as one of Ikkyū's defining characteristics. In tales describing encounters between Ikkyū and his fellow monastics, this wit is sometimes on display just to demonstrate Ikkyū's superior insight, as when he bests a fine-looking monk in a dialogue on the reason for Bodhidharma's having come from the west, despite being so drunk "he couldn't tell up from down."[43] Sometimes, though, Ikkyū's wit has a polemical (and scatological) edge. In one tale, for instance, he encounters a boastful *yamabushi* who demonstrates his power by causing magical flames to emanate from an image of Fudō Myōō; Ikkyū extinguishes the flames by urinating on them.[44] And sometimes his wit is put to use in service of the people, as in another of the tales translated by Sanford in which Ikkyū prepares a petition on behalf of a group of farmers who are being heavily taxed by the representative of a provincial lord; Ikkyū's petition is terribly impertinent, but the lord is impressed by his daring—"No one else would try something like this in this day and age"—and good-naturedly lowers the taxes.[45] In the tale literature, then, Ikkyū's wit can have a satirical function and reflect a populist orientation.

The second interesting element of the Tokugawa tales is their use of Ankokuji as a setting, and the invention of incidents said to have occurred during Ikkyū's childhood. Here the story-tellers had a free hand in some sense—these stories could be made up out of whole cloth, given the paucity of detail provided in the hagiographies of the Muromachi period. At the same time, the story-tellers were still serving the same interests that shape the development

41. Sawada, *Confucian Values and Popular Zen*, 23.
42. Sanford, *Zen-Man Ikkyū*, 247; Sawada, *Confucian Values and Popular Zen*, 22.
43. Sanford, *Zen-Man Ikkyū*, 261.
44. Sanford, *Zen-Man Ikkyū*, 281.
45. Sanford, *Zen-Man Ikkyū*, 265–66.

of the Tokugawa's adult Ikkyū. It is thus no surprise that the child Ikkyū too is largely defined by his wit.

This wit is sometimes exercised in opposition to the authority of the institution in which the young acolyte finds himself. In one tale, when Ikkyū is just nine or ten, he comes upon a fellow novice in tears over having broken a cup much loved by the master. Ikkyū offers to take the blame—in return for some bean jelly—and heads to the meditation hall to wait for his master's return, with the pieces of the broken cup concealed in his sleeve. When he sees the master, he goads him into giving a discourse on the teaching of impermanence, forcing him into affirming that the enlightened person would "understand that when things break, it is because their time is up, and one should not be upset by it"; once the master has agreed that this is quite right, Ikkyū presents him with the broken cup. The master ruefully concludes the story by wondering if Ikkyū is so clever already, "What will you turn into? Probably a headache to generations yet unborn."[46]

In another tale, his master acquires a jar of syrup and, wishing to keep it all for himself, tells the young monks in his charge that it is poison and that any child who eats it will die. Ikkyū—now twelve or thirteen—thinks it over, realizes this must be a lie, and at the first opportunity rummages through the master's things until he finds the syrup and eats it all up. Then he takes the master's treasured jar and smashes it to pieces. When the master returns to the temple, he finds Ikkyū sobbing mightily. He asks what the trouble is, and Ikkyū explains that he broke the jar and, thinking he would rather die than live with the shame, ate the poison in order to kill himself. Despite eating all the poison, unfortunately, he has found it impossible to die. The head priest, caught in a lie, says nothing (though he cannot help but smile on the inside).[47]

Like the adult Ikkyū, then, the child Ikkyū is clever in a way that allows him to flout the law and gain the upper hand in every situation. Although the stories are framed in a way that may suggest that the child anticipates the adult—"From childhood," we are told, "Ikkyū was an exceptionally bright and inventive person—different from ordinary people"[48]—in fact of course the reverse is true: the adult Ikkyū of the Tokugawa, half-remembered and half-imagined, is the pattern for the creation of this child Ikkyū. Given the number of stories that circulate about the child Ikkyū, it seems fair to conclude that there was something about this particular representation that was appealing to Tokugawa audiences, but we should also note that the child Ikkyū of the Tokugawa tales is, in a number of ways, marked as a grown man: he is presented as cleverer than the other acolytes, which cleverness he uses to protect the young acolytes from punishments, taking on the role of patron; he engages authority figures in dialogue as an equal (and ultimately proves to

46. Sanford, *Zen-Man Ikkyū*, 250–54.
47. Mikame Tatsuji and the Zen Bunka Kenkyūjo, eds., *Ikkyū banashi shūsei* (Kyoto: Zen Bunka Kenkyūjō, 1993), 340–41.

be their better); and with both mother and father entirely absent, he has no ties to the private sphere of family life. The stories of the child Ikkyū also regularly depict him as a transgressor—not only gobbling up the high priest's syrup, but also eating fish, threatening to beat up a parishioner, and in perhaps the most famous (and most literal) example, crossing a bridge in direct defiance of a signpost prohibiting such a crossing by exploiting an ambiguity in the wording of the sign itself. The child Ikkyū of the Tokugawa tales, then, does not seem to have been appealing because of his innocence or sweetness—on the contrary, he is characterized by knowingness and craftiness.

I would suggest that the Tokugawa representations of Ikkyū as a child serve the same purpose as the representations of Ikkyū as a drunkard: they create a narrative situation in which our hero's triumph over his opponent can come as a surprise within the framework of the story, while at the same time prompting the audience to permit and even enjoy transgressive behavior. In other words, childishness, like drunkenness, licenses Ikkyū's antinomian behavior, but just as the drunken Ikkyū ultimately reveals himself to be more clear-headed than his sober interlocutors, the child Ikkyū ultimately reveals himself to be more sophisticated than his adult interlocutors. The child Ikkyū no more needs to grow up than the drunken Ikkyū needs to sober up—both conditions mask Ikkyū's perfect self-mastery and make his transgressive behaviors permissible. Given this, the continuity between the child Ikkyū and the adult Ikkyū in the Tokugawa tale literature is unsurprising: although the image of Ikkyū as a child is more richly developed in this context, Ikkyū's character is, as it was in the *Chronicle*, always that of the fully formed man.

THE TWENTIETH-CENTURY IKKYŪ

If the Muromachi Ikkyū inspires the Tokugawa Ikkyū, the Tokugawa Ikkyū inspires the twentieth-century Ikkyū-san. Sanford suggests in *Zen-Man Ikkyū* that Ikkyū-san is "a fairly direct reincarnation of the cranky Ikkyū of the Tokugawa popular stories."[49] He is undoubtedly right to suggest that there are important continuities between the Tokugawa's cranky Ikkyū and the twentieth-century Ikkyū-san. For one thing, both position cleverness as Ikkyū's defining characteristic—as the refrain to the Tōei theme song puts it, "He's witty! He's wily! Nothing gets to him! Nothing gets to him, no, nothing gets to him!" (*tonchin kanchin kinishinai, kinishinai, kinishinai*). But it is also noteworthy that the twentieth-century Ikkyū-san is specifically inspired by the child of the Tokugawa tales and is sold to a contemporary audience of children. There are many Ikkyū-sans available to the child of the late twentieth century: some more or less reproduce the Tokugawa materials; some—most notably Tōei's *Ikkyū-san*—use the Tokugawa-period material as an anchor for what amounts

48. Sanford, *Zen-Man Ikkyū*, 255.
49. Sanford, *Zen-Man Ikkyū*, x.

to an elaborate animated historical melodrama; and some insert the figure of Ikkyū-san into quite novel situations (like the young adult mystery novel *Secret Room of the Golden Temple,* in which detective Ikkyū is summoned to investigate a murder, or the animated series *R.O.D.,* in which Ikkyū—or, more precisely, a clone of the historical Ikkyū Sōjun—leads a terrorist squad attempting a mass cull of the human race).[50] However, the dominant image in material for children is that of the child Ikkyū, to the exclusion of the adult man. I would suggest that this emphasis on the child Ikkyū is at least partly the result of a profound change in the meaning of childhood that in fact requires the effacing of the adult Ikkyū.

It is useful to understand the twentieth-century reappropriation of the Tokugawa Ikkyū in the context of a larger movement that drew on premodern folk literature as an inspiration for modern children's literature. In Japan, as elsewhere, this required a rewriting of the folk literature—which was not particularly intended for the edification of children—and with it, a reimagining of the historical context in which that folk literature emerged. Through this reimagining, the premodern appears as modernity's innocent, uncorrupted other, just as childhood appears as adulthood's innocent, uncorrupted other. This alignment of childhood with premodernity and adulthood with modernity allows writers of the romantic school to register a critique of modernity by privileging childhood: "The more adults and adult society seemed bleak, urbanized, and alienated, the more childhood came to be seen as properly a garden, enclosing within the safety of its walls a way of life which was in touch with nature and which preserved the rude virtues of earlier periods of the history of mankind."[51] Like their European fellows, Japanese writers who identified with the romantic school insisted that childhood must be accorded a special status. One consequence of this was the creation of a new literary genre: *dōwa bungaku,* or children's literature, a movement spearheaded by the romantics.

Karatani Kōjin goes so far as to argue that the romantics are in fact responsible for the invention of the child: "Although the objective existence of children seems self-evident, the 'child' we see today was discovered and constituted only recently"—it was the "writers of the romantic school, such as Ogawa Mimei, who discovered 'the child.'"[52] Mimei (1882–1961) is sometimes said to have inaugurated modern Japanese children's literature with his 1911

50. Kujira Tōichirō, *Kinkakuji ni hisokamuro: tonchi tantei no Ikkyū-san* (Tokyo: Shōdensha, 2002); "R.O.D. (Read or Die)," Sony Music Corporation, accessed June 8, 2010, http://www.sonymusic.co.jp/Animation/ROD/archive/media/ovaindex.html. I was alerted to the existence of these unconventional depictions of Ikkyū by Chiaki Sakai.

51. Hugh Cunningham, *The Children of the Poor: Representations of Childhood Since the Seventeenth Century* (Oxford: Blackwell, 1991), 43.

52. Karatani Kōjin, *Origins of Modern Japanese Literature,* ed. Brett de Bary (Durham,NC: Duke University Press, 1993), 115 and 116.

53. Joan E. Ericson, "Introduction," in *A Rainbow in the Desert: An Anthology of Early Twentieth-Century Japanese Children's Literature,* trans. Yukie Ohta (Armonk, NY: M.E. Sharpe, 2001), xii.

book *Akai fune* (The Red Ship). In Mimei's work we see a clear identification of the child with a pastoral premodernism—his decision to devote himself to children's literature was informed "by a desire to recapture lost innocence and simplicity, embodied by premodern customs, when childhood was both natural and indistinguishable from nature."[53] This vision of childhood as a benignant state of nature rests on an understanding that there is a necessary discontinuity between childhood and adulthood—here growing up means losing one's natural goodness, which the romantic writer longs to recapture. Children's literature written in this mode is thus a deeply nostalgic form, and as such a somewhat conservative.

Because of the way childhood and premodernity are intertwined here, it makes sense to draw on premodern material as a source for children's stories.[54] And Ikkyū is an attractive subject: as a child, and a monk, living in a period vaguely conceived as "long ago" (*mukashi*), and in a place vaguely conceived as a pastoral countryside, his innocence is overdetermined. What's more, he comes with a set of stories ready for retelling.

Tales of Ikkyū Sōjun's life based on the Tokugawa materials appear in *otogibanashi* (nursery story) collections as early as the turn of the century.[55] These collections are sometimes framed as inspirational tales of a great historical figure—a 1939 volume from Sekibunkan Shōten titled *Great Men and Heroes* (*Ijin to eiyū*), for instance, treats the lives of Ikkyū, George Washington, nineteenth-century agricultural reformer Ninomiya Sontoku, and the Russo-Japanese war hero Nogi Maresuke. As a fifteenth-century Buddhist priest, Ikkyū is in several ways the odd man out in this group, but by emphasizing his knowledge (*chishiki*) and sincerity (*magokoro*), the volume effectively positions him as possessing the qualities that characterize an educated modern Japanese man. This treatment seems perfectly in keeping with Sanford's suggestion that Ikkyū represents an indigenous way of doing modern individuality.

Even here, however, where Ikkyū is explicitly identified as one of Japan's great men, the focus is on his youth; six of the volume's eight chapters on Ikkyū's life are devoted to events that took place before his eighteenth birthday. By midcentury, collections focusing more narrowly on the child Ikkyū-san were appearing as well, and the relationship between the child Ikkyū-san and the adult Ikkyū Sōjun was becoming more abstract. In 1938 Kōdansha published a picture book titled *Ikkyū-san,* by Miyao Shigeo, in which Ikkyū appears as a child monk with perfectly round eyes and a sweet expression[56]; a 1949 storybook from Nihonbunka Shuppan, also titled *Ikkyū-san*, presents stories of Ikkyū as a child, an adult, and an old man, but the illustrations on the cover,

54. Ericson, "Introduction," ix.

55. Wada Tokutarō, *Rekishi sōdan: shūshingadan*, vol. 9 (Tokyo: Shun'yōdō, 1898), 6–7; Iwaya Sazanami, ed., *Kaitei shūchin nihon otogibanashi* (Tokyo: Hakubunkan, 1911), 160–86; Dōwa kenkyūkai, ed., *Ijin to eiyū: kyōkundōwa*, vol. 2 (Osaka: Sekubunkan Shōten, 1925), 95–203.

56. Miyao Shigeo, *Ikkyū-san* (Tokyo: Dai Nihon Yūbenkai Kōdansha, 1938).

frontispiece, and title page show us only the child monk, now with a perfectly round head to match his perfectly round eyes.[57]

This cute representation of the child Ikkyū seems to be a recognizable precursor to Tōei's *Ikkyū-san*, which first aired in Japan in 1975. The series remained in production for almost seven years, airing 298 episodes, two one-hour specials, and two short films. Tōei's *Ikkyū-san* was exported across Asia and beyond, with dubbed versions broadcast in Chinese, Thai, Russian, Arabic, and Italian. Nintendo has released a video game featuring the Ikkyū-san characters, and the Anime Hero *kyūjon* series of characters includes one that fuses Tōei's Ikkyū-san and the Kewpie doll. Tōei's Ikkyū-san, with his distinctive blue head, seems also to be the inspiration for even cuter iterations of the Ikkyū stories from the Mukashi Banashi and Anime Fantasy series, in which Ikkyū appears less like a child and more like a toddler. In these widely circulated representations of Ikkyū-san, there is only the barest trace of Ikkyū Sōjun.

There is a considerable historical and ideological distance between the romantic writers working at the turn of the century, for whom childhood is a garden, and the children's media conglomerates producing popular versions of Ikkyū-san during the latter half of the century, for whom childhood is a market. However, the overwriting of Ikkyū Sōjun by Ikkyū-san in these later mass market materials is a predictable effect of the romantic vision of childhood as a state of innocence. Further, it is bound up with a romantic interest in Ikkyū as the representative of an indigenous premodern childhood sociality—in other words, as precisely the opposite of an indigenous way of doing modern individuality. It is in this overwriting that the modern child saint Ikkyū-san emerges out of the Tokugawa tales.

This process requires considerable creative effort on the part of modern mass market producers. On the one hand, like the romantics, they continue to mine the Tokugawa tales as source material for stories of Ikkyū-san. On the other hand, a great majority of the Tokugawa tales about Ikkyū are totally unsuitable for children, if we understand the protection of childhood innocence to be paramount. Narrowing the focus to stories of Ikkyū's childhood is one way that the Tokugawa tales come to be edited for children's consumption; such a focus immediately eliminates most of the sexual and scatological material. But this in itself does not always seem to be sufficient: sometimes the childhood stories too are rewritten in small but significant ways. Let's consider three retellings of the story of the pilfered syrup and the broken jar, from Mukashi Banashi, Tōei, and Nihon Mukashi Banashi.

In the Mukashi Banashi version, the story of the pilfered syrup and the broken jar is combined with the story of the broken teacup. In the retelling, the story unfolds as follows: Ikkyū and a gaggle of his friends spy the head priest eating a spoonful of syrup; he tells them that it is poison and they must not eat any. The following day one of Ikkyū's friends accidentally breaks

57. Ōtsubo Sōjirō, *Ikkyū-san* (Tokyo: Nihonbunka Shuppan, 1949).

something belonging to the temple—here it is a vase rather than a teacup—and although everyone else is terribly upset, Ikkyū just smiles and tells them that he will take care of everything, inviting them all to join him in feasting on the forbidden syrup. When the head priest returns and finds Ikkyū alone with the empty syrup jar, Ikkyū tearfully explains that he broke the vase and ate the jar of poison to punish himself, but he just cannot seem to die. The head priest is flabbergasted; the other young acolytes, hiding behind a screen, are delighted.

The way in which the two stories are combined allows for a number of small narrative interventions that position Ikkyū-san as childlike in the sense of being sweet or innocent. In the Tokugawa version of the pilfered syrup story, Ikkyū intentionally breaks something belonging to the head priest and eats all the syrup himself, and in the Tokugawa version of the broken teacup story, Ikkyū's motivation for taking the blame for the broken cup is selfish—he exacts payment in the form of the bean jelly. In the retelling, however, nothing is intentionally broken—the pretext for taking the syrup is the accidental breaking of the vase, in which Ikkyū plays no part. And Ikkyū here is quite unselfish: seizing an opportunity, he invites his friends to share the syrup with him, but he takes the blame for the broken vase alone, while his fellows hide and watch. If there is a certain naughtiness at work here, it is a naughtiness without calculation: this Ikkyū-san is clever but not crafty. And there is no threat of punishment—the retelling ends with laughter, not with a scolding.

The Tōei retelling seems to share this impulse toward the elimination of conflict from the sphere of childhood. In Tōei's *Ikkyū-san* episode, the head priest is given the jar of syrup as a gift from a patron, the horrible Yayoi. Here it is Yayoi who tells the acolytes that the syrup is poison and they must not eat it; she proceeds to falsely accuse Ikkyū's little friend Sayo-chan of stealing her hair comb, and when Ikkyū shows her up, she storms off, returning some time later to drop off another gift for the head priest—an inkstone which she has broken and then carefully put back together, intending to get Ikkyū in trouble. Another monk picks up the inkstone and mistakenly believes that he is the one who has broken it; he begs Ikkyū for help, and we see Ikkyū picture the cruel Yayoi in his mind before he comes up with a scheme of eating the syrup, pretending to believe it is poison. When Yayoi and the head priest come upon the young acolytes lying prone in the training hall waiting for death, Yayoi is furious, but the head priest is tickled by Ikkyū's cleverness. In this retelling, everyone other than Yayoi has perfectly good intentions and every effort is made to indicate that Yayoi's punishment is richly deserved, foregrounding the moral correctness of Ikkyū's actions. Here the bad action of intentionally breaking the inkstone is clearly done by the villain of the tale, and Ikkyū eats the syrup and takes the blame for the broken inkstone not in search of some reward—there is little indication that he even has an appetite for the syrup—but in service of some kind of moral integrity.

A third retelling of the story—this one from the Nihon Mukashi Banashi series and aimed at an even younger audience—gives us a relatively straightforward version of the story, with one striking intervention. Here Ikkyu and his friends eat all the syrup while the head priest is away; when he returns, Ikkyū confesses to eating the syrup, as punishment for having broken the head priest's inkstone. The head priest confesses in turn that he has done a bad thing by lying to the young acolytes, whereupon Ikkyū reveals that he has not broken the inkstone at all—it has been hidden up his sleeve the whole time. Both master and disciple dissolve in laughter and affirm to each other that the moral is that one ought not tell lies. Here nothing gets broken, nobody gets angry, and nobody gets punished—in the version of the story intended for very young children, there is really no conflict at all.

This elimination of conflict is consistent with an understanding of childhood as a protected state, and with a particularly modern way of structuring the lives of children in order to, as Patricia Holland puts it, maintain "a firm *institutional* separation" between adults and children and ensure that children are "confined to spaces designed especially for them."[58] Michel Foucault likewise notes that childhood as we know it is constructed through institutional reforms that "made it possible to form around children an unreal, abstract, archaic environment that had no relation to the adult world"; one of the chief functions of this environment is that of "preserving the child from adult conflicts" (while at the same time exposing the child "to a major conflict, the contradiction between his childhood and his real life").[59] In the Ikkyū-san world, Ankokuji serves as the unreal, abstract, archaic world of children, with the adult head priest typically appearing as a bumbling, benevolent, and easily outsmarted grandfather figure, and Ikkyū-san himself effectively in charge. Even in the Tōei version, which as a long-running series requires some conflict to drive the narrative, the story is structured so that the bringer of conflict—the adult Yayoi, serving as the representative of the world outside of Ankokuji—is continually cast out of this world of children. But if, as Foucault argues, one of the consequences of eliminating adult conflict from the world of children is to highlight "the distance that separates, for a man, his life as a child and his life as an adult,"[60] then this judicious editing of the tales of the child Ikkyū serves to widen the gap between Ikkyū-san and Ikkyū Sōjun, even more than the wholesale excising of the tales of the adult Ikkyū, with the consequence that it becomes increasingly difficult to represent Ikkyū-san and Ikkyū Sōjun together—only one can be in focus at a time.

58. Patricia Holland, *Picturing Childhood: The Myth of the Child in Popular Imagery* (London: I.B. Tauris, 2004), 17.
59. Michel Foucault, *Mental Illness and Psychology*, trans. Alan Sheridan (Berkeley: University of California Press, 1987), 80–81; see also Karatani, *Origins of Modern Japanese Literature*, 127.
60. Foucault, *Mental Illness and Psychology*, 80.

FORGETTING IKKYŪ SŌJUN

Keeping Ikkyū-san in focus while allowing Ikkyū Sōjun to drift out of focus has several interesting effects. For one thing, if we want to understand Ikkyū Sōjun as a moral exemplar for twentieth-century children, who can model what it means to be a good student and a good citizen, it is very useful to have only a vague picture of him as a great man who lived in the distant past. Some of the more recent children's material we have considered does gesture toward a connection between the child Ikkyū-san and the great Muromachi priest: the Mukashi Banashi series ends with the suggestion that the clever child whose adventures we have just seen eventually "became the very eminent priest" Ikkyū Sōjun, and the Tōei catalogue entry, as is noted above, describes the *Ikkyū-san* series as the story of a great man. This kind of coda seems intended to suggest that reading these tales of the young monk's wit will prove edifying, and indeed the Tōei catalogue describes the series as one that leaves "an unforgettable impression on the souls of young people." It continues in this vein:

> Needless to say, it can play a great part in their character development. This television series depicts the pure life-style of the high Zen priest affectionately known as "Ikkyū-san" as well as his noble teachings and beautiful paintings. The program tries to present humorous and enjoyable anecdotes about him to children. The production has, in fact, been planned to serve as a good friend to children and to nourish their hearts.[61]

Here it is apparent that the connection between the child Ikkyū-san and the Muromachi priest Ikkyū Sōjun is meant to elevate the cartoon aesthetically and morally, but this only works if one does not know any of the details of the real Ikkyū Sōjun's "life-style." Maintaining an extremely abstract sense of Ikkyū Sōjun's historical significance is required if we are to understand the tales of the child Ikkyū-san as playing a positive role in the character development of modern children in any normative sense.

A second, related effect seems to be that the Buddhist content of the Ikkyū-san stories is rendered similarly abstract. At first glance, we might be tempted to suggest that these materials—produced by mass market publishers, without particular ties to any Zen institutions—are just secular, without any Buddhist content. This conclusion, I think, would be too hasty. On the one hand, in some instances the Tokugawa tales are rewritten in such a way that their Buddhist content is edited out—we see this in the way that the reworking of the broken teacup story results in the elimination of the dialogue on impermanence that is the centerpiece of the Tokugawa version. On the other hand, some of the more recent children's material takes considerable pains to

61. "Ikkyu-san," Toei Animation, accessed April 23, 2011, http://corp.toei-anim.co.jp/english/film/ikkyusan.php.

explain the details of life at Ankokuji—showing Ikkyū-san doing *kōan* with the head priest, for instance, and pausing the narrative to explain *dokusan* practice. This suggests that the Buddhist setting is felt to be important in some way. At the same time, these materials demonstrate an unsteady grasp of the details of that setting—there is little to suggest that a novice in a fifteenth-century *ankokuji* would have been doing regular *kōan* practice. Another vivid and charming example of this vague appreciation of the Zen tradition comes from an episode of Tōei's *Ikkyū-san* in which the head priest's receiving room is depicted complete with the famous ink painting *Six Persimmons* hanging on the far wall. *Six Persimmons*, by the Chinese artist Muqi, is identified these days as among the finest pieces of Zen art—Graham Parkes, for instance, suggests that it would not be unreasonable to characterize it as a "consummate expression of profound Buddhist ideas in the arts of East Asia"[62]—and although it might be slightly out of place in a small *ankokuji*, the real thing has been held by Daitokuji since the seventeenth century, which gives it some kind of connection to Ikkyū Sōjun. The key difference between the real *Six Persimmons* and the *Ikkyū-san* version? The *Ikkyū-san* version has just four persimmons. The way in which Muromachi Zen is evoked in these kinds of materials—with approval but without precision—has the effect of producing what I will call, paraphrasing Fredric Jameson, an atmosphere of Zen-ness, signaling that *Ikkyū-san* is a period piece. Again, enjoying this historical pastiche requires that we know something about Zen, but not too much. Quite unlike the Tokugawa tales in which the narrative elements allowed for the Buddhist content to be more readily appreciated, here the Buddhist details allow for the narrative to be more readily enjoyed.

A final effect of this careful focus on the conflict-free world of the child Ikkyū-san is that the satirical force of Ikkyū's wit is dissipated. In the *Chronicle*, Ikkyū's sharp wit is clearly directed against those he and his disciples understood to be slanderers of the dharma; similarly, in the Tokugawa tales his wit is directed against the representatives of state and institutional power (as well as those other popular Buddhist figures—like the poor *yamabushi*—who may have been in competition with the Zen story-tellers). This Ikkyū, whether in his guise as a drunk or in his guise as a child, thus represents the possibility of resistance. And the childhood stories in particular seem consistently to play with the theme of resistance through excessive obedience: Ikkyū escapes punishment for the broken cup by insisting on a rigorous adherence to the doctrine of impermanence; he escapes punishment for the pilfered syrup by playing at an extreme form of self-punishment; and he makes it across the bridge by reading the sign too literally. In each case, Ikkyū subverts the intention of the law by scrupulously—indeed, excessively—adhering to the letter of the law. In the Tokugawa tales, then, the wit of the child Ikkyū is put to use

62. Graham Parkes, "The Role of Rock in the Japanese Dry Garden Landscape Garden," in François Berthier's *Reading Zen in the Rocks: The Japanese Dry Landscape Garden*, ed. (Chicago: University of Chicago Press, 2000), 137.

in the calculated, deliberate refusal of the law.[63] When the modern versions of these stories shift the setting to the unreal environment of childhood, such antinomianism largely disappears—Ikkyū-san's wit cannot stand in resistance to the laws of the real world, because as a modern child he does not participate in the real world. In the modern representations, Ikkyū-san's transgressive quality is replaced by a wholesome, anodyne morality based around the values a modern society seeks to inculcate in children. We have a striking example of this approach in the way Tōei's Japanese-language catalogue entry on *Ikkyū-san* reinterprets the tale of the bridge-crossing: in the Tokugawa version Ikkyū crosses the bridge for no reason other than his own willful desire to best the townsman who has put up the sign, whereas in the Tōei version his motivation is said to be that of a lonely child desperate to return to his mother's home in the city—as he crosses, the onlookers are all said to praise him aloud, wondering in admiration what kind of mother such a wonderful child must have.[64] It is difficult to understand this representation of Ikkyū-san as registering a political or economic critique in a context where childhood is properly understood precisely as freedom from political and economic engagement.

It is likewise difficult to grasp the relationship between the cute child Ikkyū-san and the wild man Ikkyū Sōjun as a concrete one. The short books and animated films can treat Ikkyū Sōjun in an abstract way, by mentioning him only in a preface or an afterword. In the Tōei series, where by virtue of serialization more is done to build up Ikkyū-san as a character, we see a different choice made about how finally to deal with the relationship between the child and the adult. The final episode of the series (titled "Mother! Friends! Ankokuji! Goodbye!") finds young Ikkyū-san deciding to leave Ankokuji to become a traveling monk. This departure is treated as a tearful leaving home—long scenes depict the weeping and wailing that accompanies the goodbyes between Ikkyū and the head priest, his fellow monks, his young friend Sayo-chan, his erstwhile enemy Shin'emon, and his mother, with the implication being that while everyone else remains in the pastoral world around Ankokuji, Ikkyū will be going into a new life as a mature, self-sufficient, independent man. The final frame shows us Ikkyū striding off purposefully into the sunset, which is rendered in a style that mimics premodern Japanese gold-leaf paintings. On one level, this image suggests the start of Ikkyū's new life, in which we are meant to imagine that he grows up and becomes the great priest Ikkyū Sōjun. On another level though, the backdrop of the golden sunset and purple clouds evokes classical depictions of the Western Paradise, suggesting—weirdly—that Ikkyū has died. But perhaps it is reasonable enough to assert that this is the

63. This sense of Ikkyū's wit as marked by an excessive interpretation of the law still has currency, as we see in Tawada Yoko's characterization of a Tokyo school's decision to protest a bylaw mandating the raising of the Japanese flag at assemblies by raising 110 other flags alongside it as part of "an Ikkyū-san competition"; see Tawada Yoko, "Is Europe Western?" *Kyoto Journal* 61 (2005), accessed April 23, 2011, http://www.kyotojournal.org/kjselections/Tawada_Europe.html.

death of the child Ikkyū-san, and that the death of the child is required for the birth of the adult man.

CONCLUSION

Although the modern Ikkyū-san borrows heavily from the Tokugawa tales, the child saint of the twentieth century exists in an ambiguous relationship with the wild Ikkyū of the premodern imagination. Only with careful rewriting of the earlier folk material does a representation of Ikkyū suitable for children's consumption emerge, and this representation requires a near-total—but never complete—forgetting of the older Ikkyū. Nonetheless the recirculation of the Tokugawa tales through these popular modern representations can be at best imperfectly controlled by producers. As Karatani puts it, "Even when rewritten as *dōwa*, or nursery tales, these stories retain cruel and absurd elements"[65]; in the Ikkyū stories, that cruel element is Ikkyū's wit, and so in any story of Ikkyū's cleverness or cunning there is the potential for cruelty to resurface, and with it the antinomian strain of the earlier material.

To take just one example of a different representation of Ikkyū-san, consider a 1976 picture book aimed at young readers, with text by Teramura Teruo and drawings by Hise Kunihiko. In many respects, this book is like the others we have considered—the same title (*Ikkyū-san*), the same exclusive focus on the child Ikkyū, and the same reliance on the Tokugawa tales as source material.[66] The chief difference is that in rewriting this material for a contemporary audience, Teramura makes none of the interventions that we have seen elsewhere. This Ikkyū-san intentionally breaks a vase from the altar as a pretext for stealing the jar of syrup while his fellow monks look on aghast, and then he reports to the head priest that the poison has so far failed to kill him, so might he please have some more? This Ikkyū-san walks confidently across the bridge, urging on the head priest, who is chattering with fear. This Ikkyū-san negotiates a reward for besting the shogun in a battle of wits and filches red bean buns from the altar where they were placed as a devotional offering. The head priest is repeatedly shown to be furious with Ikkyū, and Ikkyū in turn is repeatedly shown to be openly laughing at his distress. Hise's illustrations, in keeping with the tone of the text, show Ikkyū with a misshapen head, laughing eyes, and an upturned nose, his expression by turns

64. Toei Animation, "Ikkyu-san," accessed April 23, 2011, http://www.toei-anim.co.jp/lineup/tv/ikkyu.

65. Teramura Teruo, *Ikkyū-san* (Tokyo: Akane Shobo, 2009).

66. Strikingly, however, Teramura's afterword both provides more information about the life of the historical Ikkyū Sōjun than is usual, and distinguishes his Ikkyū-san from Ikkyū Sojun, explaining that not very much is known of Ikkyū Sōjun's childhood and that the stories in the book are based on Tokugawa folktales invented long after Ikkyū Sōjun's death.

malevolent and gleeful. Rather than excising the conflict from the Tokugawa tales, this *Ikkyū-san* amplifies it, producing a positively devilish representation of the child monk.

Set against the cute Ikkyū-sans that dominate the popular materials, Teramura and Hise's cranky Ikkyū seems to be a revenant of the antinomian impulses of the Tokugawa. At the same time, this cranky Ikkyū speaks to a conception of children that exists in tension with the romantic image of childhood as a garden—namely of childhood as a jungle, and children as wild, uncivilized animals. The cruel and absurd elements of the Tokugawa tales here might be thought to appeal to some cruel and absurd elements of the child's person. In this intersection of antinomian premodern Ikkyū and the antinomian modern child, we see a way of conceptualizing the child which is neither nostalgic nor conservative, and so the possibility of a different kind of politics of childhood.

As Ikkyū-san becomes caught up in contemporary concerns around the meaning of childhood, he becomes less and less reliable as a representation of the historical Ikkyū Sōjun. By the same token, however, he reveals more and more clearly the ambiguous way in which the modern adult conceives the child and, by extension, the way the modern subject conceives the premodern past. Just as Sanford argues for a careful reading of the Tokugawa-period Ikkyū tales as having the potential to tell us "a great deal about the ideals of the Japanese culture of post-Ashikaga times,"[67] a careful reading of the Ikkyū-san stories—however slight they may seem—has the potential to tell us a great deal about how a break with the Tokugawa period is negotiated through a misremembering of those tales, and the rebirth of a Zen man as a Zen boy.

ACKNOWLEDGMENTS

I had the opportunity to present early versions of this paper at the 2009 meeting of the American Academy of Religion and at a brown bag session organized by the Center for Asian and Pacific Studies at the University of Iowa in the spring of 2010; I am grateful to the many people participating in those sessions whose comments helped me in shaping this final version of the paper, and would like to thank particularly Jeff Wilson, Morten Schlütter, and Philip Lutgendorf. I am also deeply indebted to the University of Iowa's Japanese Studies librarian, Chiaki Sakai, for all of the resources she uncovered for me.

67. Sanford, *Zen-Man Ikkyū*, 246.

CHAPTER 15

Marrying the "Thought of Enlightenment"

The Multivalency of Girls' Symbolic Marriage Rites in the Newar Buddhist Community of Kathmandu, Nepal

TODD LEWIS AND CHRISTOPH EMMRICH

In the late fall of 1997, friends informed me (Todd Lewis) that a family in the Asan Tol neighborhood of Kathmandu, Nepal, was sponsoring an *ihi* ceremony in a Buddhist monastery near to where we were living. They asked if my daughter—then five years old—would like to join the group. We presented this invitation to my daughter as a chance to join some of her new friends "to sit for *pūjā*," and the fun of dressing up in a new sari, wearing golden jewelry, and receiving presents. She agreed. The first American girl ever to sit for the *ihi* life cycle rite (*saṃskāra*) made the local vernacular press; I was involved as never before as a participant-observer in this community, and as the two full days of sitting in the cold courtyard went on, the thrill of new clothes and gold jewelry faded. Special interest in understanding *ihi* further began with this experience of trying to explain to her[1] why all our Newar friends took so much trouble for their little girls.[2]

1. One of Lewis's mentors at Columbia University, anthropology professor Robert Murphy, liked to challenge academics-in-training with the observation that if you cannot explain the key insights of your scholarship to ten year-old children, you probably don't have them clearly in mind.
2. In 2009 she wrote one of her college application essays about this, "her first marriage."

The Newars of the Kathmandu Valley, Nepal, perform *ihi*, one of two life-cycle rites for girls, as a "coming of age" symbolic marriage done before they reach menarche. High-caste families adhering to Hindu and Buddhist traditions seek out Hindu or Buddhist ritualists, respectively, to perform this ceremony for their daughters. For the three days of rituals, it is primarily mothers and aunts who focus on their daughters, overseeing purifications, dressing them up in fine saris and special jewelry, and helping them perform a long series of rituals. The last two days are devoted to making offerings to Buddhist and Hindu divinities, rituals designed to seek their blessing and protections; the highlight comes on day three when each girl's father comes dressed formally to offer his daughter as a gift to the divine as part of a symbolic marriage.

This ritual for girls, along with its sociohistorical context, and the cultural multivalency of children's religious rites is the subject of this chapter. Through a series of accidental yet fortunate events, the co-authors discovered a confluence in their working on this subject in the fall of 2010 and decided to graft our areas of expertise into this single study. Our special focal points are on Hindu-Buddhist cultural contestation, modern interpretations of this rite among contemporary religious leaders, and the variety of understandings the ritualists, parents, and girls themselves derive from their undergoing the *ihi* ceremony.

I. CONTEXT: PLACE AND CULTURE

The Kathmandu Valley's prosperity flowed from the fertility of its soils and the profits from trans-Himalayan trade. This Valley's relative geographical isolation (prior to 1769, the defining area of all "Nepal") enabled it to become a prosperous and independent artistic center of South Asian civilization. The Newar people and their Indic culture have been dominant there for at least a millennium, even though their spoken language is from the Tibeto-Burman family. But beginning as early as 100 CE[3] the formative sociocultural influences have been from the Gangetic region: caste defines the social order, the pantheon from ancient South Asia is found in temples scattered across its towns, inscriptions were made in Sanskrit from as early as 464 BCE. Artists, ritualists, and spiritual masters from all Indic traditions have sustained a vibrant pluralistic culture. Unconquered through its history by North Indian empires—Hindu, Muslim, or British—Kathmandu Valley civilization is noteworthy today for its distinctive urban society and its enduring panoply of Hindu-Buddhist traditions that are still observed in rich multiplicity.

The vitality of Newar culture today derives from the peace and prosperity of the later Malla period (1482–1768), an era that created the magnificent art and architecture in the Kathmandu Valley.[4] In this era, Newar scribes

3. Theodore Riccardi, Jr., "Buddhism in Ancient and Early Medieval Nepal," in *Studies in the History of Buddhism*, ed. A. K. Narain (New Delhi: B.R. Publishing, 1980), 265–81.

4. Mary S. Slusser, *Nepal Mandala* (Princeton, NJ: Princeton University Press, 1982).

also established vast libraries of Sanskrit manuscripts,[5] and the Newars—kings, priests, merchants, commoners—maintained an almost continuous yearly round of festival observances in their three city-states: Bhaktapur, Patan (or Lalitpur), and Kathmandu. Likewise, their priests and monks arranged complex rites to mark all significant events in an individual's lifetime. From conception to long after death, in celebration and in mourning, Indic religious rituals have been integral to the Newar lifestyle, and most elaborately so for the elite classes.

For this study of the Kathmandu Valley's Buddhist girls' symbolic marriage, it is key to introduce the Mahāyāna traditions that underlie them. These reflect patterns of sociocultural development that once characterized other Buddhist communities of south, southeast, and central Asia. Of special significance is the ritual service of the local sangha, the monastic community. For centuries now, most Newar "monks" have been married and sustained by a system of closed patrilineage: a two-section endogamous caste group with surnames Vajracarya[6] and Shakya[7] maintain the "monastic traditions." With their families they inhabit dwellings referred to with the classical term for monastery, *vihāra* (New. *bāhāḥ*) and more than three hundred of these and their affiliated sanghas exist in the Valley today.[8] Thus the modern Newar Buddhist community consists entirely of householders.[9]

The practice of Newar Buddhism is also ordered by an individual's caste birth; only those born as Shakyas, Vajracaryas, or Urāy (a cluster of merchant/artisan subcastes)[10] are deemed eligible to take part in all ritual practices,

5. Brian H. Hodgson, *Essays on the Languages, Literature, and Religion of Nepal and Tibet* (New Delhi: Manjushri, 1972); Eugène Burnouf, *Introduction à l'histoire du Buddhisme indien* (Paris: Imprimerie royale, 1844).

6. Often spelled *Bajrācārya* by modern individuals in this group. The term means "*vajra* master." We adopt the Sanskritized initial *v* for the caste name, without diacritics, but use the spelling authors themselves use for their own names.

7. This is the name of the royal clan of the historical Buddha Śākyamuni. There is no evidence of any connection between Newars and the Buddha's kin beyond proximity and the name itself.

8. David N. Gellner, *Monk, Householder and Tantric Priest: Newar Buddhism and Its Hierarchy of Ritual* (Cambridge: Cambridge University Press, 1992).

9. On the basis of the Mahāyāna ideology that insists that householders can achieve enlightenment and be advanced spiritual beings, the Newar sangha justifies their being respected Buddhist leaders on the basis of their learning Sanskrit, studying sacred texts, engaging in meditation practices, ritually maintaining monastic shrines, and mastering rituals and mantras that still make them worthy of merit-making gifts (*dāna*) from other Newar Buddhists. Their remaining ritually pure is also a significant expectation. Similar "householder monks" are found in the Nyingmapa tradition of Tibet since 900 CE, the Pure Land schools of Japan since 1250 CE, and all Japanese Buddhist lineages since 1880 CE. See also Alexander von Rospatt, "The Transformation of the Monastic Ordination *(pravrajyā)* into a Rite of Passage in Newar Buddhism," in *Words and Deeds: Hindu and Buddhist Rituals in South Asia*, ed. Jörg Gengnagel, Ute Hüsken, and Srilata Raman (Wiesbaden: Harrassowitz Verlag, 2005), 199–234.

10. See David Gellner and Declan Quigley, eds., *Contested Hierarchies: A Collaborative Ethnography of Caste among the Newars of the Kathmandu Valley, Nepal* (Oxford: Oxford University Press, 1995) for a discussion of the groups constituting modern Newar society.

including esoteric tantric initiations.[11] Most Newar Buddhists participate exclusively in the exoteric level of Mahāyāna Buddhism: they direct their devotion to *stūpa* reliquary shrines, make regular offerings at temples dedicated to the celestial bodhisattvas such as Avalokiteśvara and Tārā, and focus their attention primarily on merit-making.

Newar Buddhists provide material support for their local Vajracarya-Shakya sangha who, in return, guide ritual devotions that shape their spiritual destiny in this world and beyond. Newar Buddhist householders support their sangha materially in exchange for the merit they earn from donations and for performing the rituals that protect and empower them throughout their lifetimes.

Despite the anomaly of a caste-delimited married sangha, this exchange is fundamental to all Buddhist societies, and Newar Buddhist householders closely resemble coreligionists in other countries.[12] A vast and complex web of ritual relations link householders such as merchants to their *vajracarya* sangha, who perform Buddhist rituals to benefit them in this lifetime and in future existences. They do recitations of sacred texts, healing rites, site consecrations, and Mahāyāna Buddhist initiations that give access to meditation practices. Especially numerous, and definitive of the Newar Buddhist identity, are life-cycle rituals.

Buddhist Life Cycle Rituals: Applied *Vajrayāna* Buddhism

A modern ritual guidebook, the *Nepāl Jana Jīvan Kriyā Paddhati*, outlines the mid-twentieth-century repertoire of *Vajrayāna* Buddhist life-cycle rites.[13] The number and complexity of Buddhist ceremonies in this community is extraordinary: one handbook[14] lists over 125 "major" rituals (*pūjās*), but some have by now slipped from observance. In this enormous ritual heritage, most life-cycle and other rituals can be broken into core "units" that tend to be assembled in consistent patterns.[15] Still, the cumulative ritual tradition is so vast that even expert *vajracarya* priests must refer to ritual texts to do all but the most common *pūjās*.

The logic of *Vajrayāna* Buddhism underlies Newar practices today. This esoteric tradition that grew in importance from the fifth century CE onward

11. Skt. *dīkṣā* (New. *dekhā*) that direct meditation and ritual to tantric deities such as Saṃvara, Hevajra, and their consorts (*yoginīs*).

12. David Snellgrove, "Buddhism in Nepal," in *Indo-Tibetan Buddhism* (Boston: Shambhala, 1987), 2: 362–80.

13. A full translation and extended discussion of this work is found in Todd T. Lewis, "The *Nepāl Jana JīvanKriyā Paddhati*, a Modern Newar Guide for Vajrayāna Life-Cycle Rites," *Indo-Iranian Journal* 37 (1994), 1–46.

14. Ratna Kāji Vajrācārya, *Yem Deyā Bauddha Pūjā Kriyāyā Halaṃjvalam* (Kathmandu: Saṅkata Printing Press, 1981).

15. Documented in Todd T. Lewis, *The Tulādhars of Kathmandu: A Study of Buddhist Tradition in a Newar Merchant Community* (Ph.D. Dissertation, Columbia University, 1984), 192–98 and 210–27.

influenced all religions in South Asia. The ancient tantra-path Buddhist exponents and exemplars, the *siddhas*, discovered the possibility of immediately harnessing the innate powers of human experience to attain enlightenment.[16] As a corollary, they also composed rituals that applied a master's power to accomplish more mundane goals: health, safety, long life, and accumulating worldly powers. These were inherited by the *vajracaryas* in Nepal, who adopted the bodhisattva ethos[17] and regarded serving the lay community with ritual service as their chief duty.

The context for the domestication of *Vajrayāna* Buddhism in the Kathmandu Valley was a society increasingly dominated by Hindu kings and their brahman ministers, who ruled according to the Hindu law.[18] Caste orthopraxy was the law of the land; proximity to the palace was contingent on maintaining classical norms of purity and pollution. High social status was based on adherence to upper-caste ritual practices specified in the Brahmanical texts. For the Newar *sangha* to exist in the Malla state after 1480, the task was to adapt their Mahāyāna-Vajrayāna traditions to conform to this Hindu socioreligious environment.[19] They did so by remaining loyal to Buddhism through rituals that were outwardly styled on the Brahmanical traditional forms;[20] but instead of ultimate devotion to Viṣṇu or Śiva, Buddhists focused on celestial Mahāyāna deities such as Avalokiteśvara, Tārā, and tantric *yoginīs*.

This pattern of adaptation interjects Buddhist tradition into every conceivable juncture: for relating to divinities, celebrating festivals, moving an individual through his lifetime, and seeking nirvana. Lacking the scholasticism of Tibetan monastic tradition, the "genius" of Newar Buddhism lies in its pervasive orchestration of *Vajrayāna* rituals and teachings which channel blessings, provide well-being, and—for those householders willing to practice—making progress toward enlightenment.

16. Alex Wayman, "Buddhism," *Historia Religionum*: Handbook for the History of Religions (Leiden: Brill, 1971), 2: 443.

17. By the Pala period in northeast India (c. 750–950 CE), this Mahāyāna-Vajrayāna culture was predominant (Sukumar Dutt, *Buddhist Monks and Monasteries of India* [London: Allen and Unwin, 1962], 389) and shaped the development of Buddhism in the nearby Kathmandu Valley. The bodhisattva vows to postpone his own enlightenment to address compassionately the sufferings of others.

18. The *dharmaśāstra*, the most famous of which is the *Manusmṛti*, "Laws of Manu."

19. From the beginning, the Buddha instructed individuals in the sangha to adapt the tradition to the exigencies of the locality. Doing so could entail reinterpreting certain monastic community rules (*vinaya*), adapting to local cultic practices, and making accommodations to societal norms (Sukumar Dutt, *Buddhist Monks and Monasteries of India*, 25ff). The skillful adaptation of the Buddhist tradition, called *upāya* in later Sanskrit texts, is a high virtue in the Mahāyāna tradition.

20. Some scholars, in noting this Newar Buddhist emphasis on ritual and their adherence to pollution-purity norms, have labeled the *vajracaryas* as "Buddhist Brahmins" (Stephen M. Greenwold, "Buddhist Brahmins," *Archives Europeennes de Sociologie* 15 (1974), 483–503). This label in some ways is apt, but it can be misleading in failing to note how the Newar Buddhist elite has carefully crafted rituals that express inversions of and alternatives to Hindu meanings, as will be seen below.

The Buddhist life-cycle rites (*saṃskāras*) outlined in the Newar ritual manuals closely follow the classical paradigms of Indian Brahmanical tradition,[21] marking the key points in a person's life with outwardly similar *Vajrayāna* rituals that remove forces that threaten her passage, empower her, while eliminating pollution. There are no other Buddhist life-cycle rites like this in the Buddhist world, since elsewhere in Asia these are completely outside the purview of the monastic elite.[22]

These Buddhist *pūjās* outwardly follow many ancient Brahmanical ritual procedures but have been transformed with alternative Buddhist gestures *(mudrās)*, ritual implements (*vajras*, *vajra*-bells), incantations *(mantras, dhāraṇīs)*, and meanings. In general, Newar Buddhist ritualists adopted many core components of Brahmanical tradition (caste perceptions, rite organization, *mantra* belief, purity concerns) to design their rituals, but they maintained separate boundaries through transpositions of ritual implements, priestly vestments, mantra formulae, *mudrās*, and theories of ritual empowerment.

While most Newar Buddhists today still utilize their services, few *vajracaryas* in recent generations possess more than the most basic knowledge to explain the philosophical assumptions underlying the rituals; what most can articulate is only the proper sequence of the rites and *mantra* recitations.[23] Nonetheless, many of these traditions are so deeply embedded in Newar life that they continue to survive. Even though many observances have been discarded in the last century, the vast cumulative tradition of Mahāyāna-Vajrayāna ritual remains one of the most distinctive characteristics of Newar civilization. Symbolic marriage is one such example.

II. *IHI:* THE THREE-DAY RITUAL

General Considerations

For Newar families, *ihi* is a necessary rite of passage that marks a girl's transition toward ritual adulthood.[24] It is followed in the future (usually by age ten) by *bāhrācvanegu*, a twelve-day ritual of confinement from the sun and free of

21. Rajbali Pandey, *Hindu Samskaras: Socio-Religious Study of the Hindu Sacraments*, 2nd ed. (Delhi: Motilal Banarsidass, 1969).

22. The only exception is with death rites, in which Buddhist monks have officiated in the last rites and the disposal of the body from ancient times until the present.

23. Lewis. *The Tulādhars of Kathmandu*, 569–73.

24. Though performed by Newars across the Kathmandu Valley, the *Buddhist ihi* ceremony that informs this study is that found in the heart of one of Kathmandu City's oldest bazaars, Asan Tol; here in the capital of modern Nepal resides one of the few remaining merchant groups adhering to Buddhism (Todd T. Lewis, "Buddhist Merchants in Kathmandu: The AsanTol Market and *Urāy* Social Organization," in *Contested Hierarchies: A Collaborative Ethnography of Caste among the Newars of the Kathmandu Valley, Nepal*, ed. David Gellner and Declan Quigley (Oxford: Oxford University Press, 1995), 38–79; Todd T. Lewis. *Popular Buddhist Texts from Nepal: Narratives and Rituals of Newar Buddhism* (Albany: State University of New York Press, 2000). This summary does not cover every specific aspect of every component of the full ritual, which would be too detailed to be of interest to the nonspecialist reader.

contact with any males, a rite before menarche[25] that requires no priest. When both are completed, Newar girls can then marry a human husband. Now it is with this social progression in mind (and mindful of the social consequences for *not* doing so) that upper caste-Newars follow these prescribed rites to this day.

It is noteworthy that it is simply the *completion* of this ritual that is paramount, not strict religious conformity: Buddhist Newars can send their daughters to *ihi* rituals sponsored by Hindu families and conducted by brahman *purohitas* without any social repercussions, and vice versa. Both Buddhist and Hindu versions are fully acceptable even though the respective *pūjās* differ significantly in symbolic and technical ways.

Ihi is called a *saṃskāra* ("life-cycle rite") in the ritual manuals. It is organized on an ad hoc basis under a variety of circumstances. Families may sponsor one so that girls among their extended kin and neighbors of similar caste standing can fulfill this duty; alternatively, families celebrating the old-age *burā jaṃkva saṃskāra* for elders reaching 77 years, seven months, seven days—a relatively rare occurrence—often sponsor an *ihi* group so that the merit for doing so will accrue to the elder being honored. A third avenue to this sponsorship is kin's gathering to build a family Buddhist shrine, called *stūpa* or *caitya*; sponsoring *ihi* is especially meritorious at this time, fitting in with the established rituals for these shrines that themselves are treated as individuals that must be given life.[26] Yet another scenario is *vajracarya* or brahman *purohitas*' organizing an independent ceremony and publicizing it as a service to the community (which will also yield some donation income to them as well). While *ihi* can also be done on a private family basis, nowadays most prefer to avoid the considerable expense by joining larger groups. (In recent decades, the number of girls has ranged from a half dozen to four hundred.) Once a merchant family has a daughter who reaches the appropriate age (five to eleven), her mothers and aunts will be alert to find an *ihi* group that she can join.

The Buddhist *ihi*

For this discussion, we will describe a *vajracarya*-led *ihi*[27] as observed in Asan Tol, Kathmandu, at the time of a *caitya* dedication, and then make some comparative observations regarding the Hindu rite.

Day One. The *ihi* begins with a symbolic purification by a woman of the barber caste, who comes to the family home to cut toenails and fingernails, after which the girls take a bath. The father's sister (*nini*) should gather the

25. Non-Newar Hindus in Nepal and Hindus across most of South Asia do this rite only *after* the first menstrual period occurs. Newars do this before the biological event.

26. Like a statue of the bodhisattva Avalokiteśvara in its yearly birth and death cycle (see below), Newar Buddhists ordain *stūpas/caityas* in human ritualism in order for them to be spiritually alive.

27. It is noteworthy that the different Buddhist communities in the major towns of the Kathmandu Valley have ritual guidebooks that prescribe quite different details in practice. Those described by anthropologist Michael Allen (Michael Allen, "Girls'

nails and deposit them in the Vishnumati River, outside the western wall of the old city. From this point until the feast at the end of the ritual, the girls sitting for *ihi* must abstain from all "*āmay*" foods: meat, fish, duck egg, tomato, eggplant, black lentil, ginger, garlic, onion.

Day Two. On the first day of priest-led ceremony, the girls wear fine clothing and jewelry and come to the site of the ritual with the list of ritual supplies provided by the sponsor. Each holds a ritual tray (*pujābhaḥ*). The girl's mother, along with other adult women in the household, will accompany the daughter, providing gentle support and ritual guidance.

As they enter the site for the ritual (usually a monastery courtyard), one girl (usually related to the organizer) is designated as *nakiṃ*, the girl who leads the group in all collective movements. The organizers provide a formal ceremonial welcome, *laskus,* for each, starting with the *nakiṃ*: the senior sponsor pours a few special auspicious items from a large copper container over every girl's head. As each girl then moves on (nowadays also given a fancy hand-made name tag), she is directed to sit in a line on woven rice-stalk mats next to the others.

With the group now settled, the girls are directed by the *vajracarya* ritualist to do the standard establishing Buddhist preliminary ritual, the *gurumaṇḍalapūjā*.[28] This is the first time in her life that this girl will do this on her own. In it, the *vajracarya* priest (nowadays probably using electronic amplification), assisted by his wife or another experienced senior woman from this caste (*guru-mā*), chants alone in places while directing the girls to make a series of simple offerings to all small *maṇḍala* in front of each. This ritual states the purpose of the event in Sanskrit, as the *vajracarya* asks the deities of the locality to aid in its performance, and it ends in everyone taking refuge in the *triratna*.[29] He then calls upon the bodhisattvas to apply their powers so that the ritual performance will bless the girls and all living beings.

The next activity is further purifications and preparing objects to be used in the central rites on the following day. The purifications are physical through lustrations with pure water and *pañcagavya,*[30] then symbolic with a lighted wick

Pre-Puberty Rites Amongst the Newars of the Kathmandu Valley," in *Women in India and Nepal*, ed. Michael Allen and S. N. Mukherjee [Canberra: Australian National University Press, 1982)], 179–210) in a ceremony in western Kathmandu, and those discussed by anthropologist Anne Vergati in Bhaktapur (Anne Vergati, *Gods, Men and Territory: Society and Culture in the Kathmandu Valley* [New Delhi: Manohar, 1995]) vary from those observed in Asan Tol. A thoroughgoing study of these rituals across the Kathmandu Valley, with attention to both Brahmanical and *vajracarya* variants, has yet to be done. The forthcoming monograph *Buddhist Rituals for Newar Girls: Mimesis and Memory in the Kathmandu Valley*, by Christoph Emmrich is expected to cover further ground in this field.

28. David N. Gellner, "Ritualized Devotion, Altruism, and Meditation: The Offering of the Guru Maṇḍala in Newar Buddhism," *Indo-Iranian Journal* 34 (1991), 161–97.

29. Buddha, Dharma, Sangha. This "taking refuge" is spoken thrice for conversion to Buddhism and begin every Buddhist ritual across the Buddhist world.

30. Five products of the cow, mostly milk, curds, ghee, with urine and dung in minute amounts.

waved completely around each girl to symbolize the removal of bad karma (*pāp*). Purificatory ritual phrases (*mantras*) and tantric texts are also recited. This phase ends with offerings to Gaṇeśa, the elephant-headed deity revered by Hindus and Buddhists, and to Mañjuśrī, the bodhisattva of salvific wisdom (*prajñā*).

The girl must next make an "*ihi* necklace." This is fashioned from a long piece of yellow six-stranded thread as the girls stand up and their mothers wind twenty-one circular lengths of thread according to their height.[31] Once this is done and the thread is securely tied, the *gurumā* provides each girl with ten different spices which they must wrap into leaf pieces, then sew each into the necklace. Once this is made and the necklace is placed in a special clay bowl (see below), then the *vajracarya* comes to each girl and performs the *siphaṃluyegu* rite three times, pouring out *pūjā* items over their heads using his *vajra*-bell; the girls then stand in line to make a series of basic offerings to the *caitya* shrine.[32] The *vajracarya* completes the *pūjā* to it and gives *prasād* to the girls (including a returned flower offering put on her head); the day's rites conclude when their mothers give them milk to break the day's fast and they return home.

Day Three. On this final day the girls must be fasting again; they bathe and then arrive, still fasting, at the astrologically determined time (usually in the morning). Each wears her best finery (ideally bridal red) and ornaments. After the same *laskus* welcome as on Day 2, the girls make offerings and receive the ritually blessed returned offerings (*prasād*) as part of the *vajracarya*'s fire ritual (*homapūjā*) and a large series of new offerings (*mahābalipūjā*) for the *caitya* shrine. Like an adult bride, each girl wears a red *ṭīkā* on her forehead and has her eyes made up with traditional lampblack mascara.

The vajracarya priest now moves down the line, picks up each girl's yellow necklace, and puts it around her neck. Assisted by the *gurumā*, he then fixes on the top of her head a paper which has an image of a special ceremonial flask (*kalaśa*) painted on it. The *gurumā* then applies bright red powder to the girl's hair part.

After the *vajracarya* makes other offerings to the *homa* fire, the girl's father[33] comes to sit with her; he sits down and holds her on his lap. The *gurumā* gently binds the girl's wrists with a short piece of hemp rope after placing a *byāḥ* fruit,[34] betel leaf, a feast leaf, and a rupee note in her hands. The father then rises and carefully guides the daughter (with her hands still bound) in a procession led by the sponsoring family, which moves three times around the *caitya*.

31. Urāy informants said that the twenty-one circles represent the twenty-one Tārās and that the spices are medicines which protect the girls during their fasting. Other ritual manuals specify a different formula: to get the auspicious number of 108 body lengths through the 6 strands x 18 body-lengths = 108.

32. Called *pañcopacārapūjā*.

33. Or some other senior male o£ the family.

34. "Wood apple," *aegle marmelosa*.

Once they are all seated again, the *gurumā* comes to pour the five divine substances (*pañca-amṛta*)[35]on the girl's still-bound hands. The *vajracarya* follows and takes the rupee note and then releases the rope that binds the wrists. All of the objects fall into the special painted large clay bowl, the *ihi salāḥpāḥ*.[36] The *vajracarya* then adds a small dab of *khīr* ("sweet rice pudding") flavored with five spices to the *byāḥ* fruit, which now rests in the bowl.[37] The girls should break their fast by eating a bit of this special food. Each will take home and save this necklace, *byāḥ* fruit, and bowl.

Once the girls give their final *pūjā* offerings and receive *prasād* from the large central rituals done by the *vajracarya,* they sit in line to accept gifts of rice and other presents from their own families, from others who also participated, and from the general public who want to earn good karma (*puṇya*) for these gifts. Once the girls return home, their families present them with a congratulatory ritual welcome snack (*sagaṃ*[38]), new clothes, and other gifts. Most families hold a large feast in the daughter's honor.

Pragmatic Effects of the Ritual

Ihi is the first of two rites of passage for girls as they progress into ritual adulthood. Once this rite is done, she must henceforth observe the adult pollution and purity norms of their caste. This rule applies mainly to eating and accepting water only from caste equals or superiors. Moreover, the girls acquire and now begin to wear their first saris.[39] Most significant in Buddhist terms, this is the moment when many Newar Buddhists reckon that karma accountability and retribution begin in the girl's life.

In this sense, *ihi* is the counterpart to the boy's rite of passage, the *kaytā pūjā saṃskāra* ("loin cloth rite").[40] Significantly, while boys celebrate their ritual by venturing out into the forest alone,[41] *ihi* has girls join other girls in the city. Most prominent in the religious domain is that the girls begin taking part in the domestic Buddhist rituals that they will be doing for the rest of their lives. Taking refuge in the Buddha, doing *pūjās*, and learning short

35. Milk, yogurt, butter, honey, sugar.

36. Or *ihipā*.

37. The *khīr* mixture with the five spices symbolizes *bodhicitta* and the Five Buddhas, respectively.

38. Per Lowdin, *Food, Ritual and Society: A Study of Social Structure and Food Symbolism among the Newars* (Kathmandu: Mandala Point Books, 1998).

39. Some girls become a ritual friend for life (*tvāy*) with another girl in the group, a connection finalized by a short ritual at the end of the *ihi* rites.

40. For this, boys act out the ancient ideal of the student, dressing as an ascetic and going off to the forest to study with an educational and spiritual teacher (*guru*). Today this is for most merely a symbolic exercise, involving a short period of leaving home to visit kin (always under the care of the mother's brother); completing this life cycle rite is essential to make boys into marriageable young men.

41. Sometimes brothers do this *saṃskāra* together in the home.

chants is now open to them. This role will place them closer to the center of family religious activity. Of particular significance here is that they will now be able to take part in the worship ceremonies of their natal patrilineage's deity, *digudyaḥ*. Even though after marriage they will join their husband's patrilineage, this tie to their father's *digudyaḥ* worship and other household rites will be lifelong from the time of *ihi* onward. Indicative of their being made "fully human" through *ihi*, they will only now be given full adult cremation rites if they die.

III. INTERPRETATION OF THE RITUAL: THE (RE-)WORKINGS OF CULTURE

Multivalency: Decoding the Virtuosi's Symbolic Order

Ihi is clearly a symbolic ritual marriage. This point is made clear in the *vajracarya gurumā*'s placing vermillion on the girl's hair part, something that a woman's husband will also do in the marriage rites a few years later. The question for *ihi* then is: "marriage to whom?" The Hindu *ihi* is a marriage to Viṣṇu, a fact spoken of explicitly by brahman *purohita* at the time when the girl's hair part is marked with vermillion and when she gets the paper (or a medal) with an image of this god placed on top of her head. But when the *vajracarya* ritualists perform this gesture and mark the same *byāḥ* fruit with offerings, the meaning has been transformed to conform to Buddhist doctrinal symbolism.

The paradigm for the Buddhist version of *ihi* is found in the comprehensive life-cycle rites, male and female, that are administered each year to the icon of the bodhisattva Avalokiteśvara in Kathmandu's central temple in Jana Bāhāḥ.[42] According to the Jesuit scholar John Locke's documentation, when the *byāḥ* fruit is presented to the sacred icon, the *vajracarya* recites:

> Regard this as the form of *bodhicitta* in which there is no distinction between *śūnya* and compassion. Consider the seed letter in your own heart manifesting itself in the different realms of the world and then proceeding up to the highest heaven. From there, attract it so that it disappears into the *bel* [i.e., *byāḥ*] fruit.[43]

The Buddhist priests, in effect, infuse the fruit with the potency of compassion and the key salvific discernment of all phenomena as ultimately "empty."

42. This is the most important deity, the celestial bodhisattva of compassion, in the Māhāyana Buddhist world since 500 CE until today. Newars refer to this divine figure as Karuṇāmaya ("Compassion-hearted One"), called Guanyin in China, Kannon in Japan, Chenrizi in Tibet.

43. Ritual text in the heavily corrupted Sanskrit as recorded by Locke: *śanyatā* [read: *śūnyatā*] *karuṇābhinnaṃ bodhicittaśvarūpāṃ* [read: °*svarūpaṃ*] *bhārvāyatvā* [read:

Similarly, the binding of the girls' hands is identified in the ritual manual with "the gesture (*mudrā*) of a Buddha."... This makes bright the light of spiritual insight (*prajñā*) and opens proficiency in meditation (*dhyāna-samādhi*)." Similar chants and recitations mark the Buddhist *ihi* for girls.

The placing of a paper image of a *kalaśa* flask on the girl's head conveys how the Buddhist rite makes the *ihi* girls "vessels" who can now fully receive—and become—spiritual beings. The ritual guidebooks further make clear the association of the *byāḥ* fruit with *bodhicitta*, a term that has the dual meaning "enlightened mind" and "the thought of enlightenment." The *vajracarya*'s application of the *khīr* with five spices on the *byāḥ* fruit is similarly mimetic: the spices symbolize the Pañca-Buddhas,[44] and *khīr*, according to Newar tradition, is the food given to Śākyamuni Buddha by the village maiden Sujātā to break his fast, right before his realization of complete enlightenment. When the *ihi* girls eat a small bite of this *khīr* in the ritual, they symbolically become vessels (like empty, receptive *kalaśa* vessels) now capable of being filled with *bodhicitta*.. Buddhist girls thus can be said to "marry" the thought of enlightenment.

The Centrality of Newar Buddhist Merit-Making

The second major theme in *ihi* is merit-making, here in the focal moment of the father's offering his daughter in *kanyadāna*, "the gift of a virgin." In pan-South Asian tradition, this is thought to be productive of great *puṇya* ("merit") for her mother and father. Newar parents also make this offering, not when other groups do it, at the adult marriage, but earlier in life during *ihi*. Significantly, the Nepali Hindus, in contrast, perform *kanyādana* when the human groom fetches her from her home; when she is about to leave, the parents grasp her hands and literally "give her away" to the new husband and his family.

Newar girls are not subjected to this direct "handing over" in their adult marriage rites. They will retain superior status through lifelong connections to their natal homes. Newar marriages are almost always local, so while adult marriage does involve a shift to the husband's household, it does not sever strong, lifelong connections in her natal home. The Buddhist ritual thus ensures that the parents garner merit, but since it is done during *ihi*, their daughters are not ritually turned over to the wife takers by being treated as property.

bhāvayitvā] / *tataḥ svahṛdayastha*[-]*vijākṣaraṃ* [read: °*bījākṣaraṃ*] *nānā lokadhāpusphuritvā* [read: *lokadhātu spharitvā*?] *akaniṣṭhābhūvanaṃ* [read: *akaniṣṭhabhuvanaṃ*] *gatvā tasmādākṛṣya* [read: °*akrṣya*] *śrīphale cintayet* / (John Locke, *Karunamaya* [Kathmandu: Sahayogi, 1980], 216).

44. The Buddhas of the four directions, with the cosmic Buddha Vairocana at the center (Snellgrove, "Buddhism in Nepal,") 365ff.

The Intended Work of Elite Culture

Our third topic is cultural politics. "High culture" in the Newar public arena has been managed by men, from the leadership of the Buddhist priests to those elder men of the merchant castes whose locality and kin organizations (*guthi*)[45] make collective decisions on important issues.[46] In Nepal, where since 1769 the state was dominated by non-Newar brahmins and where Hindu kings enacted laws to limit non-Hindu cultural practices, even life-cycle rites carried political and legal implications. In response, and in order to sustain their own Buddhist identity, Newar Buddhist men devoted careful attention to the management of their own caste groups. Girls' symbolic marriage is one of many cultural creations by the premodern *vajracarya* elite that transposed a Brahmanical ritual into a Buddhist observance.[47]

Over the last century, the *ihi* rite has especially resonated with the aspirations of the nation's Newar Buddhists—a minority in a nation with a large Hindu population—to express proudly their separate religious and ethnic identity. Social, political, and cultural context shapes children's lives, and from this point of view, these Buddhist girls are players in their minority group's proud expression of difference and its determined contestation against sociocultural inferiority.

Receptions of Intended Meaning

Multivalency is important to measure, and account for, in all cultural performances, including those involving children. Especially in urban, literate societies, the researcher should be aware of, and seek out, gendered, elite, and age-based meanings of cultural performances, charting how they connect with others or work autonomously.

The Newar ritual manuals, and the intricate codings of Buddhist philosophical meaning that we have examined, are impressive cultural creations. Any anthropologist who is literate in the local printed literature and works with the most learned informants can join scholars of Buddhism to find the intricate connections the Newar Buddhist *vajracarya* elite of its past created: between spices and Buddhas; the choreographing of a moment when salvific insight (*prajñā*) is opened for each girl; and implanting the thought of achieving enlightenment (literally, *bodhicitta*) in her body, speech, and mind. In ritual gestures, mantra

45. On the Newar institutions that resemble the ancient Indic *goṣṭhi*, see Gérard Toffin. "Études sur les Newars de la vallée Kathmandou: *Guthi*, funérailles et castes," *L'Ethnographie* 2 (1975), 206–25.

46. Lewis, "Buddhist Merchants."

47. The musical analogy is useful here: with the complete change in ritual paraphernalia, ritual utterances, shrine focal points, and esoteric symbolisms, the premodern *vajracarya* masters of ritual changed the "key" of the Brahmanical score to

utterances, and symbolic immersions, ritualists highly proficient in *Vajrayāna* Buddhist thought have created a powerful, exceptionally artful choreography of esoteric Buddhist symbols.

The problem is that this carefully constructed ritual thoroughly imbued with Buddhist meaning has become opaque to merchant parents and their children, and today even to many of the rank-and-file Buddhist priests themselves. In part—and as was true at my (Todd Lewis's) daughter's 1998 *ihi*—this is so because the *vajracaryas* in charge did what many have done in recent decades: skip the ritual guidebook's injunction, "Now explain the meaning of the ritual" and rush through the remainder of the ceremony. Whether from the priest's ignorance or haste, the Buddhist meanings so carefully constructed in the *ihi* ritual tradition by past masters are not evident or transmitted in contemporary priestly performance. What is clear from recent observations is that group impression management and the family's seeking only the most basic instrumental result (marriage-eligible daughters) far overshadow the enculturation of any subtleties in Buddhist content.

IV. *IHI* IN LATE TWENTIETH/EARLY TWENTY-FIRST CENTURY NEWAR BUDDHIST DISCOURSE

The apparent reluctance of priests to talk about *ihi* on the ritual stage seems to be complemented by a growing interest in discussing it on paper and in public speeches during "secular" events, discovering *ihi* as a way to articulate visions of more vigorous forms of Buddhism among the Newars. The last decades have seen a flurry of publications in Newari on Buddhist ritual, with quite a number on *ihi*. Priests, public intellectuals, academics, and hobby folklorists have discussed the rite in monographs, articles, and speeches, offering their reading of the practice and the role children, particularly girls, are supposed to play. We highlight here the contributions of four outstanding contemporary figures of Newar religious life who offer some insight into the role *ihi* plays in the discussions surrounding the varying directions in which Newar Buddhists and, more generally, Newar religious activism may be heading. These four figures, whose interventions span from the late 1960s to the 2010s, are Asha Kaji, Chunda Bajracharya, Baldev Juju, and Naresh Man Bajracharya.[48]

express their Buddhist identity, but allowed their disciples to conform outwardly with high-caste practices.

48. For a more comprehensive treatment of the authors mentioned in this section,, see the discussion in Christoph Emmrich's forthcoming monograph with the working title "Buddhist Rituals for Newar Girls: Mimesis and Memory in the Kathmandu Valley."

Ganesh Raj Vajracharya

Better known as Pandit Vaidya Asha Kaji (1908–1992), Asha Kaji is one of the most respected and influential scholar-practitioners of twentieth-century Newar Buddhism. With a background in traditional medical sciences, this tantric priest had a crucial role in partially "opening up" the Newar Buddhist priestly culture to foreign scholars (e.g., Michael Allen, David Gellner) and research institutions (such as the Nepal German Manuscript Preservation Project), but especially to the modernizing Newars themselves and to Buddhists beyond the Kathmandu Valley in the 1970s and 1980s. His major work, the *Daśakarmavidhi* (*The Instructions for the Ten Rites*),[49] is an overview of the life-cycle rituals prescribed for a Newar Buddhist. Uncharacteristic for this genre of traditional manuals, this book combines ritual prescription, exegetical commentary, historical considerations, and, in its English version, even ethnography-style photographs. The chapter on *ihi*[50] follows the structure of a manual on liturgical proceedings; it includes the verses (*gāthā*) recited at the relevant points in the ritual as well as their interpretation (*arthavāda*) and English translation. The author also supplies the historical derivation (*itihāsa*) of key rites, giving an origin narrative from either local historiography or Sanskrit Buddhist narrative literature.[51] The practice of tying and wearing the yellow thread is connected to a girl called Divyasundarī, who was given in marriage by her adoptive father, the Buddhist sage Bhavabhūti of the town of Sankhu, to the son of king Brahmadatta, whom she adorned with

49. Existing until recently only in its original Newar language manuscript form (Āśa Kāji, Paṇḍit Vaidya (a.k.a. Gaṇeś Rāj Vajrācārya). *Daśakarmavidhi.*) and in possession of the author's family, this text is now accessible in an English version prepared by his son N. B. Bajracharya and edited by Michael Allen (Pandit Vaidya Asha Kaji (Ganesh Raj Vajracharya). *The Daśakarma Vidhi. Fundamental Knowledge on Traditional Customs of Ten Rites of Passage Amongst the Buddhist Newars,* trans. N. B. Bajracharya, edited, annotated, and typeset by Michael Allen (Kathmandu: Mandala Book Point, 2010). I (Christoph Emmrich) am greatly indebted to Michael Allen for sharing with me the manuscript. It may be fair to point out that the English publication is indeed a version rather than a translation, since it considerably abridges, condenses and somewhat reorganizes the original. The discussion here is based on the English version, which is the readily available one and includes occasional references to the Newar source text. For a more detailed analysis of Asha Kaji's manuscript, see my forthcoming monograph mentioned in the preceding note.

50. Asha Kaji, *The Daśakarma Vidhi*, 109–15.

51. Of the four authors discussed here, the form of Asha Kaji's commentary, despite its hybridity, is at the same time still strongly indebted to traditional exegetical forms of ritual going back to the Vedic commentarial tradition initiated with the *brāhmaṇas*. Michael Witzel writes about their commentarial style: "It 'explains,' so to say, a formula spoken in the course of the ritual by pointing out its mythological origin (*itihāsa*): illo tempore, the gods did thus, and therefore humans have to follow suit; this is the message." (Michael Witzel, "How to Enter the Vedic Mind? Strategies in Translating a brāhmaṇas Text," in *Translating, Translations, Translators from India to the West*, ed. Enrica Garzilli. Harvard Oriental Series, Opera Minora, vol. 1 [Cambridge: Harvard Oriental Series, 1996], 168). The other authors we will be discussing have all abandoned this traditional style in favor of alternative, generally modernist ones.

a garland made of yellow thread.[52] This is meant to indicate that the marriage of a Buddhist girl with a Hindu prince forms the historical background to *ihi* and connects it with a figure called Suvarṇa Varṇa, "the Golden-Hued One," or Suvarṇa Varṇa Kumār, "the Golden-Hued Bachelor," the protagonist of the homonymous *avadāna*,[53] who, as Asha Kaji writes, "is represented by the fruit," thereby reading the wedding itself as the expression of the girls' "wish to get married to a handsome and good boy like Suvarṇa Varṇa Kumār."[54] According to Asha Kaji, it is the bodhisattva Suvarṇa Varṇa's mother, Śāntivatī, who immediately before marrying his future father, Divākara, allegedly "practiced this *ihi* system" (or *ihividhi* in the original), just as it was done by another legendary girl called Prabhāvarī, who married a bodhisattva called Jñānāloka.[55] It is not without reservation, yet for due measure, that the author adds: "although some claim that [this practice] was propagated by the Tathāgata."[56] Completing the chapter by giving a series of major titles of Buddhist bibliography as assumed literary sources for the ritual,[57] we have here a narrative that suggests its origins go back all the way to the Buddha himself, drawing on early tantric Buddhist manuals, while at the same time resounding in the deeds of Sanskrit bodhisattvas and Newar heroines.

Referring to the ritual connection between Śāntivatī's *ihi* and her marriage to SuvarṇaVarṇa's father, pandit Asha Kaji's exegesis moves from history to

52. Asha Kaji *The Daśakarma Vidhi*, 93.

53. Sita Ram Roy, *Suvarṇavarṇāvadāna. Decipherment and Historical Study of a Palm-Leaf Sanskrit Manuscript: An Unknown Mahāyāna (avadāna) Text from Tibet* (Patna: K.P. Jayaswal Research Institute, 1971); Tissa Rajapatirana, *Suvarṇavarṇāvadāna, Trans. and ed. together with Its Tibetan Translation and the Lakṣacaityasamutpatti* (Ph.D. thesis, Australian National University, 1974).

54. Āśa Kāji, *The Daśakarma Vidhi*, 114. The ms. has *ihividhi yābale byāphalapūjā yānā suvarṇavarṇakumāra* [fol. 175] *tulya guṇaṃ pūrṇahna purusa jhiputrī yāta lāyumā dhakā āśikā yānā sama totugu khāḥ* (Āśa Kāji, *Daśakarmavidhi*, fol. 174–75).

55. While the manuscript clearly reads Jñānāloka, the English version prefers Gonatoka (Āśa Kāji, *Daśakarmavidhi*, fol. 174). It is also striking that this last reference to a girl named Prabhāvarī and a bodhisattva called Jñānāloka corresponds very closely to the key verse used in the liturgy of *ihi* and borrowed from the *Kriyāsaṃgrahapañjikā*, in which the taking of the hand (*pāṇigrahana*) is performed and which runs: *iyaṃ tatāgatha mudrā jñānāloka prabhākarī gṛhitvā pāṇināpāṇi buddhakṛtyaṃ pravarttatā* (Ryugen Tanemura, *Kuladatta's Kriyāsaṃgrahapañjikā. A Critical Edition and Annotated Translation of Selected Sections* (Groningen: Egbert Forsten, 2004), 197). Here the almost homologous words (*jñānāloka* and *prabhākarī*), however, refer grammatically to the "seal" or tantric partner (*mudrā*), who is described as "producing the splendour of the light of knowledge." One cannot but be tempted to suspect that Asha Kaji here tries to give a popular "itihāsic" explanation of that verse.

56. Āśa Kāji, *Daśakarmavidhi*, 114. The ms. has *gathye dāsā, thva ihi vidhi dhaigu dyagu nhāpājuyā vaṃpiṃ tathāgatapiṃsaṃ bodhisattva juyā coṃbale yānā vaṃgu yāta* [...] (Āśa Kāji, Daśakarma, fol. 174).

57. The *Kriyāsaṃgraha*, the *Kriyāsamuccaya*, the *Abhidharmasamuccaya*, the *Mañjuśrīpārājikā* as well as the *Vajrasattvapārājikā* (Asha Kaji, The *Daśakarmavidhi*, 115). The ms. adds three more texts, the *Śikṣāsamuccaya*, the *Patatipārājikā* and the *Niyamapārājikā* (Āśa Kāji, *Daśakarmavidhi*, fol. 177).

intention: accordingly, while *ihi* may be an act prefigured in the premarriage rites, resulting in the bodhisattva's birth, it is equally read as an expression of the girls' wish to marry somebody like that very bodhisattva, thus inscribing the Buddhist ideal onto whichever marriage candidate the Newar Buddhist girls (really their families) ought to be looking out for. *Ihi* is supposed to evoke within the girls the wish for a marriage that is specifically Buddhist. In a variant reading Asha Kaji expands the aim, moving beyond exclusively Buddhist territory by adding that *ihi* "is performed as a mark of promise to remain a virgin until marriage with a boy."[58] Interestingly, he here takes a position diametrically oppositional to some anthropological speculations that *ihi* is a precondition (and explanation) for an assumed—but unproven—widespread sexual promiscuity among Newar girls prior to marriage.[59]

Ihi, according to Asha Kaji, guarantees that Newar girls remain respectable and meet the preconditions for a liturgically sound marriage to a man in line with the Vedic household regulations prescribing the "gift of the virgin" (*kanyādāna*). Anthropologists such as Allen may have seen strategies of circumventing brahmanical marriage regulations in order to facilitate perceived sexual liberties based on a hypothetical Newar "tribal substrate,"—outsmarting, so to speak, the non-Newar brahmans—this exegesis by Asha Kaji reverses this idea, presenting *ihi* as a ritual that explicitly performs and guarantees that ideal of virginity which the non-Newar brahmanical ritual specialists may claim to be particularly competent to uphold. *Ihi* makes girls not only better Buddhists, but better daughters: more Buddhist, but also more in line with general south Asian norms of personal decency and family honor expected to be upheld by any good daughter. If one reads Asha Kaji's text as instructing interested laypeople—parents, uncles, aunts, and so on—in why they should (and what it means if they) have their daughters perform *ihi*, one may view it as a conversation about what parents are actually making their daughters do and, assuming the parents are not fully aware of them already, the reasons why that is a good thing.

Baldev Juju

We find a similar approach in Baldev Juju, a Kathmandu brahman priest, local historian, and authority in normative questions regarding Newar ritual, who is consulted by priests, laypeople, and government institutions regarding decisions involving religion. In his article *Ihi saṃskārayā abhiprāya* ("The Meaning of *Ihi*

58. Asha Kaji, *The Daśakarma Vidhi*, 114. Instead of the word "virgin" the ms. here uses *jhiputrī* (sic; read: *jhīputrī*), which literally means "our [family's] daughter" and refers to the girl remaining in her own patrilineage until marriage mediates the transfer to that of her future husband (Āśa Kāji, *Daśakarmavidhi*, fol. 175).

59. Allen, "Girls' Pre-Puberty Rites," 203–4; critically discussed in David N. Gellner, "Hinduism, Tribalism and the Position of Women: The Problem of Newar Identity," *Man* (N.S.) 26 (1991), 114–16.

as a Life-Cycle Ritual") published in 1997, Baldev Juju argues against reading *ihi* as in any decisive way connected to marriage and in favor of understanding it as a life-cycle ritual (*saṃskāra*) in its own right. His opening lines show the provenance of his arguments: the interest in establishing a *saṃskāra*, which differentiates the Newars from other ethnically defined Nepalese groups (the Indo-Parbatiyā or *khayṃ*, or the groups of the Terai or *marsyā*) and at the same time helps resist perceived trends toward imitating the "white man" (*bhuyū*, literally "the ash-grey man"). For Baldev Juju, performing *ihi* signifies the girls' emergence as social beings[60] in Newar society. It confers on them a status in which they are compelled to follow Newar societal rules[61] and in which they no longer have the option to act in whatever way they wish.[62] Preeminent among these rules, he writes, are those regarding the handling of food and body (*cipan-ipa*), but also more specifically the gendered duties connected to the running of the household. Baldev Juju effectively isolates liturgical elements to make his point: receiving *sindhūr* in the hair parting is bearing the sign of society, getting one's hands bound while holding the *byāḥ* fruit is having one's hands bound by rules. Equally dexterously, he disconnects *ihi* from marriage: the gift of the girl (*kanyādāna*) is one only by name; since the parents take their daughter back to their own home, the rite is not followed by that of joining (*hvaṃkegu*), which marks marriage between woman and man; it does not invoke the ritual code the girl has to follow after changing from her father's paternal lineage to that of her new husband.[63] By pointing to the absence of a wife-taker's party in *ihi*, Baldev Juju pushes further his view of *ihi* as an introduction into Newar society: he elaborates that on the basis of an assumed Newar understanding (*siddhānta*) of society that is based on the communality of gods and men, *ihi* is an occasion "to invite the ancestral gods (*purkhā dyaḥta*) and all the chosen gods (*iṣṭadevatāta*) inside in order to introduce (*duthyāgu*) one's own girls to society."[64]Baldev Juju equates the gift of one's daughter with that of sharing food: just as Newar "table manners" require of one to set aside an offering to the gods before one may start eating, so does *ihi* arrange girls in the form of an offering to the gods, who then join in the commensality of the religious feast after a relationship with the gods has been established.[65] In this reading it is the ancestral and the chosen gods to whom the girls are presented, and it is the ancestor's and the chosen gods regulatory power over Newar society to which they submit. Through this submission, they become fully Newar.

60. *Ihi yāyegu dhayāgu misāmacātayta samājay duthyākekathaṃ dutahayegu jyā khaḥ* (Bāldev Juju. "Ihi Saṃskārayā Abhiprāya." *Svakvaḥgu Ihi Munejyā. Smarikā*, ed. Javāharabhāi Prajāpati, Gaṅgārāma Prajāpati, and Śyāma Prajāpati. (Yeṁ [= Kathmandu]): Dharmacakra taḥnanī khalaḥ, NS 1118 [1997 CE]), 32.

61. *nevāḥ samājayā sakatāṃ niyamata pālanā yānāḥ* (Bāldev Juju, "Ihi Saṃskārayā," 32).

62. *lāḥlaḥthe yāye majiu* (Bāldev Juju "Ihi Saṃskārayā," 32).

63. Bāldev Juju "Ihi Saṃskārayā," 33.

64. Bāldev Juju "Ihi Saṃskārayā," 33.

65. *dyaḥnāpa svāpū tayekegu lyākhaṃ kanyādānanayā nāmaṃ vidhi yāyegu juyācvaṃgu khaḥ* (Bāldev Juju, "Ihi Saṃskārayā," 33).

Rather than argue in favor of a Buddhist or Hindu idiom of doctrinal exegesis, Baldev Juju conspicuously focuses on ancestor worship as the fundamental, trans- or pre-sectarian ideology of the Newars. In an almost Rappaportian[66] stance, for him, here and elsewhere, *ihi* becomes the ritual that possesses the power for "the making of humanity," inasmuch as it places the individual under the law that governs the interactions between the living, the dead, and the divine. For Baldev Juju, this conception of humanity (and divinity) is Newar. *Ihi* is not only prior to the distinctions between Buddhists and Hindus, it is prior and foundational to the whole ritually ordered world of Newar society, at least as far as girls and women are concerned. In a move not unlike religious movements elsewhere in Asia and beyond, it is the woman emerging out of childhood—through rituals directed by male priests, which bear the burden of making sure that the Newars retain or regain their Newarness. As with Asha Kaji, who rereads *ihi* as the declaration of intention (of virginal future marriage) reflective of a stance (that upholds particular Newar female roles), Baldev Juju abstracts this act even further, severing its anticipatory linkage with marriage, and declares it to be the one on which all future rituals and Newar society itself is based. They both accept the liturgical elements that denote marriage as key to *ihi* but reformulate their implications. What distinguishes Asha Kaji from Baldev Juju is that, for the latter it is the rules enacted by those key performances that make the Newars distinctive vis-à-vis others, while for the former it is the girls' ritual stance that makes the Buddhist girls shining examples of Newar values within Newar society.

Chunda Bajracharya

Chunda Bajracharya, a Buddhist woman and professor of Newar language and literature,[67] proposes another reading of *ihi* which combines Asha Kaji's genealogical-historiographical approach with Baldev Juju's ethnic one, but it is her take on which liturgical element is really crucial in *ihi* that sets her apart from her fellow exegetes. According to her article simply called *Ihi*,[68] the fact that girls are tied to the *byāḥ* fruit and receive the vermillion mark of marriage is not even worth mentioning. Instead, *ihi* is about wearing the sari. She develops her argument by stating that female ornaments are specific markers of ethnic groups and that the bearing of these signs confers to girls both ethnic specificity and peer seniority. In an exegetical move that is similar to

66. "In sum, it is not ritual's office to ensure compliance but to establish obligation." (Roy A. Rappaport, *Ritual and Religion in the Making of Humanity* (Cambridge University Press, 1999), 129–30).

67. Ms. Bajracharya is headmistress of one of the only two Newar-medium schools in the Valley and is considered a feminist by many modern literati.

68. Cundā Vajrācārya, "Ihi," in *Svakvaḥgu Ihi Munejyā*, ed. Javāharabhāi Prajāpati, Gaṅgārāma Prajāpati, and Śyāma Prajāpati (Yeṁ[=Kathmandu]): Dharmacakra taḥnanī khalaḥ, NS 1118 [1997 CE]), 1–7.

Baldev Juju's, Chunda combines life stage and Newar-ness to stress the initiatory character of *ihi* as a life-cycle ritual (*saṃskāra*). Unlike Baldev Juju and Asha Kaji, however, who stress its legalistic aspects implied by rule and vow, Chunda speaks of the recognition of having become part of the community,[69] which comes with the event, and the natural development from childhood to old age that a girl undergoes in the move from one *saṃskāra* to the next,[70] transforming a small girl into a big one (*macā lyāse jula vā macā taḥdhikaḥ jula*). Chunda stresses much more the gradual rather than the sudden in the ritual sequence, referring to further rituals for girls and women, as well as the different life stages and the roles conferred by seniority just as she is much more aware of gender. In fact she points out that *ihi* is meant not only for the recognition of social seniority (*taḥdhikaḥ vā vaiṣkayā mānyatā*), but more specifically about dressing and being dressed in a certain way that is specific to, yet brings together Newar women of multiple generations.

In an interesting turn that seems to counter the more overtly functionalist readings of her colleagues, Chunda claims that "the purpose of the *saṃskāra* is to give the *parsi* to wear,"[71] in exchange for her childhood shirt. Just stopping short of calling *ihi* a "*parsi pūjā*," Chunda stresses gender by pointing out that the *ihi* sari, the *parsi*, is for girls what the loincloth (*kaytā*) is for the boys in the coming of age ritual prescribed for Newar boys called *kaytā pūjā*.[72] Where the male priest Asha Kaji speaks for the girls only as future brides and Baldev Juju seems to level ritual gender differences in favor of the patrilineal Newar ancestors, Chunda argues for regarding *ihi* as "a *saṃskāra* performed only for women"[73] as part of a line of rituals for and by women. In her exegesis, the voice of the male priest remains silent and the historian of Newar woman finds her voice.

In line with Chunda Bajracharya's larger interest in Newar history in general and in a Newar group called the Gopālis or the Gvāla in particular, she points out that instead of a full-fledged *ihi,* this community celebrates the coming of age of their daughters in a ceremony called *sīdu,* in which they combine a five-day fasting period with the gifting to the girls, and then donning the *parsi* (*parsi siṃkyeta*), a garment worn by adult Gopāli women.[74] In her attempt to compensate for the fact that the modern Newar *ihi* does not follow this surmised Gopāli tradition, Chanda views Gopālis as being more archaic Newars. Characteristic of certain tendencies in contemporary Newar historiography, she links the origin of Newar traditions back to the homonymous and legendary early Nepalese dynasty, the Gopālas. Supplying the historical depth that is missing from Baldev Juju's account, Chunda finds in rituals for girls the "ethno-historical" link that

69. *ihi yāye dhune dhāyevaṃ tini sāmājik byavahārakathaṃ misātayta mānyatā jui* (Vajrācārya, "Ihi," 1).

70. *pratyak saṃskāra dune prakṛtinapa svāpu dugu darśana khaḥ. macā, lyāse va burhi manūyā prākṛtik hyūpāḥyā yathārtha khaḥ* (Cundā Vajrācārya, "Ihi," 1).

71. *arthāta saṃskāragata prakṛyāṃ parsiṃ siṃye bī* (Cundā Vajrācārya, "Ihi," 2)

72. Cundā Vajrācārya, "Ihi," 2.

73. *misātayta jaka yāigu saṃskāra* (Cundā Vajrācārya, "Ihi," 1).

74. Vajrācārya, "Ihi," 2.

helps Newars ground their Newarness not in the form of the ritual as observed today but in its female core dating back to the legendary origins of Nepal. What Chunda and Baldev Juju do share is their interest in clearly stripping from *ihi* its Hindu or Buddhist sectarian connotations, removing anything that may smack of brahmanical narrative or ritual traditions and situating core Newar traditions in either ancestor worship or dressing practices.

Naresh Man Bajracharya

The fourth authority in this group is Naresh Man Bajracharya, a tantric priest and Buddhist activist resident in Kathmandu, who is professor of Buddhism at Tribhuvan University. In the last fifteen years he has worked to establish a more accessible and at the same time more assertive form of Mahāyāna/Vajrayāna Buddhism among the Newars. He has vigorously sought to situate *ihi* in its rightful place in the heart of a Buddhist exegesis of ritual and the life cycle, thus reacting strongly against attempts at undercutting its Buddhist content. In doing so Naresh Man goes far beyond what Asha Kaji attempted: Naresh Man[75] sees the originary place of *ihi* in the context of image consecration and old-age ritual, being only relatively recently extrapolated and performed independently as an event exclusively celebrating the girls and their families.

Basing his interpretation of *ihi* on a ritual manual by his teacher Badri Ratna Vajracharya,[76] Naresh Man refers to a parallel liturgy aimed at simultaneously consecrating the image and the girls,[77] two distinct ritual procedures for which he uses different terms: "It is a *pāṇigrahana* for the deity image, it is *ihi* for the small kids and girls." He makes clear that this is not marriage (*ihipāḥ*) in the sense of "a formally sanctioned sexual union between male and female," but a "union of the image with the *prajñā* [...] and also for the girls *ihi* is a union with the *bodhicitta*." The thought of enlightenment as the union of emptiness and compassion is summoned from Akaniṣṭha Heaven by the recitation of the appropriate verse on *bodhicitta* in which emptiness and compassion converge, quoted already above,[78] and "inserted into the *bilva*" or *byāḥ* fruit.

75. As elaborated in an interview with Emmrich on March 15, 2010.

76. Badri Ratna Vajrācārya, *Daśakarma pratiṣṭhā, chāhāyeke vidhi va balimālā* (Yeṁ [=Kathmandu]: Candramāna Mālākāra, Surendramāna Mālākāra, Pradipamāna Mālākāra, Prakāśamāna Mālakāra: Mālākāra prinṭiṅ pres, VS 2045 [1988 CE]).

77. For considerations regarding a shared history of Buddhist *ihi* and consecration rites, if not a relation of genealogical derivation, in whichever direction, see generally Tanemura, *Kuladatta's Kriyāsaṃgrahapañjikā*,10, 91, and 96; Alexander von Rospatt, "The Consecration Ceremony in the *Kriyāsaṃgraha* and Newar Buddhism," in *Hindu and Buddhist Initiations in India and Nepal*, ed. Astrid Zotter and Christof Zotter (Wiesbaden: Harrassowitz, 2010), 197–260; and the above-mentioned forthcoming monograph by Christoph Emmrich.

78. *śūnyatā karuṇābhinnam bodhicitta svarūpaṃ bhāvayitvā tataḥ svahṛdaya bijākṣaraṃ nānā lokadhātu spharitvā akaniṣtha bhuvanaṃ gatvā tasmādakṛṣya srī phalaṃ linaṃ cintayet //* (Badri Ratna Vajrācārya, *Daśakarmapratiṣṭhā*, 24).

The girl holding the fruit is by the recitation of the so-called "wedding verse"[79] then made to perform "not a marriage with a person, but a union with bodhicitta." The verse itself instructs her, as it instructs the image, "to clasp the hand with the hand" (*gṛhitvā pāṇiṃ pāṇināṃ*), which Naresh Man explains as grasping the *byāḥ* with both hands, and to do "what a Buddha has to do" (*buddhakṛtyaṃ*). In this reading the girl becomes a Buddha, "not," as Naresh Man insists, "a bodhisattva, but a Buddha Tathāgata." He is equally adamant in denying the marriage character of this act, not to a Buddha, or to an image or to the *byāḥ* or to any future husband. As understood from the perspective of consecration, which turns an object into a living deity, the girl is not only turned from a passive "baby" into "a complete human being, but [much more than that, the] girl will undertake the Buddha work."

Stopping short of claiming that the girl actually becomes a *female* Buddha, Naresh Man expects the girl to do much more than the child in Asha Kaji's reading, where *ihi* clearly anticipates marriage: she is not expected to take a bodhisattva-like vow to marry a bodhisattva-like husband, but rather to take on the tasks worthy of a Buddha and in the process become a being as perfected as a human being can be. This approach is implicit, he argues, by the same procedure being done for girls as is done to give life to a Buddha image. Apart from the obvious cultural presuppositions which come with a discourse that places itself firmly within the Newar Buddhist ritual cosmos, there is no mention here of an explicitly Newar content. In that sense Naresh Man's reading is less gender-specific and less explicitly ethnic than that of his Buddhist co-exegetes. While Asha Kaji and Baldev Juju see *ihi* as that one liminal event which will make the girls a part of the world of ritual and social norms—be it in their commitment to a future Buddhist husband or to the Newar ancestors of hoary antiquity—Naresh Man comes much closer to Chunda's view of *ihi* as being the beginning of a series of religious activities. In Chunda's case that trajectory was marked by further coming-of-age rites and a movement up the seniority ladder within the community of women.

For Naresh Man, *ihi* is merely an intersection between two series of rituals, that for divine images and that for humans, a series that he, in a Buddhist eschatological fashion and as elaborated in a lecture dating from 2005,[80] depicts as a cycle. If the girl child becomes a complete Buddhist being with *ihi*, she will proceed via a subsequent ritual before menarche, and then after performing marriage rites, to being a fully ritually qualified partner to her husband. She will

79. *iyaṃ tathāgatha mudrā jñānāloka prabhākarī gṛhitvā pāṇināpāṇi buddhakṛtyaṃ pravarttatā yena jñānena satyena prajñopāyatmaṇḍalaṃ kāmātvaṃ paripūrayet* (Badri Ratna Vajrācārya, *Daśakarmapratiṣṭhā*, 25, quoting *Kriyāsaṃgrahapañjikā*, for which see RyugenTanemura, *Kuladatta's Kriyāsaṃgrahapañjikā*, 197).

80. Nareś Mān Vajrācārya "Daśakarma". Paper presented at the IVth Conference on the Buddhist Heritage of Nepal Mandala, Kathmandu, Sept. 7–10, 2005.I refer to this source on the basis of the notes I took during its presentation as well as to the references the author himself made to his presentation in the above-mentioned interview.

then help to conduct all necessary household rites, including the life-cycle rituals for their children as well as optionally serve as tantric consort in the spouses' joint tantric initiation. This full trajectory is organized as the so-called Ten Rites (*daśakarma*), which both humans and deities undergo. It is with human marriage and tantric initiation that the cycle ends in a certain sense and a new one begins with the religiously sanctioned emergence of the next generation, when the adult parents in turn participate in their children's Ten Rites. For Naresh Man it is the performance of the Ten Rites that ensures that the Buddha-work is done and is carried beyond the life cycle of one individual only. *Ihi* is not only the ritual in which the individual girl's religious career coincides and is enacted in unison with a deity's. It is also placed halfway between and thus connects the end of her parents' cycle and the second half of her own.. Thus there is a hierarchy of stages: it starts with a still unenlightened and inactive little Buddhist before *ihi*; after she completes it, the first half of the Ten Rites is performed *for* or *to* her; then the second half of the Ten Rites is performed *by* her, in the sense of its being her Buddha-work for the well-being of all living creatures. Though marriage, reminiscent of Asha Kaji's model, remains a key event in the girl's life which *ihi* eventually leads up to, it is enlarged to become the key element of Newar Buddhist religious life in general, linking not only one generation to the next but one set of Ten Rites to the next. But while marriage is the link and birth is the resumption, *ihi* is thus the culminating point in childhood, the moment in which Buddhist agency is injected into a process that is based in Naresh Man's view, on a regenerational model that draws upon the gender roles assigned to Newar Buddhists. Newar Buddhist men and women are made, and can only be made, not when the process of birth and death starts all over again, but when a child becomes active, and actively Buddhist.

When these four contributions are viewed together it may be useful to look at the times, places, and circumstances in which they were made in order to historicize the attention given to childhood through one particular ritual. With Asha Kaji's text dating in its Newar form back to 1967/68, Chunda's and Baldev Juju's contributions to 1997, and Naresh Man's oral elaborations to 2005 and 2010, the ideas reflect late twentieth- and early twenty-first– century trends in the perception of childhood as part of discussions on Buddhism and Newarness. While narrative embeddings have likely always been part of ways of talking about what religious communities ritually do to their members, the manner in which Asha Kaji conjoins prescription and exegesis is definitely new in writing *ihi* as a ritual text. And while in doing this he may have utilized old material, his publication reflects the need to exegetically comment on the history and function of *ihi* in a form that suggests that the Newar Buddhist community perceives itself as threatened, seeing "traditions" and "heritage" as something to be safeguarded by collecting, systematizing, commenting, and presenting them in new forms.

The various ways *ihi* is explained among the four indicates that there has not been a widely enculturated explanation at all and that—then as now—there was no explanation that has ever been fixed. What seems clear is that all authors, Asha Kaji first among them, react against standard "folk" or brahmanical readings still found today of *ihi* as "mock marriage." Asha Kaji's agenda reflects one lineage common to the 1970s and 1980s to "open up" Newar Buddhism by resuffusing *ihi* with Buddhist doctrinal content, absorbing popular readings of the Golden-Hued Bachelor, and making traditionally strong pronouncements about marriage. Asha Kaji's pedagogical reading is meant to help parents produce good Buddhist daughters. The late 1980s, 1990s, and early years of the new millennium—the time of the Maoist uprising with the Hindu monarchy and as a consequence large domains of institutionalized urban religion in a crisis—saw a marked development of an ethnically conscious Newar activism. This lineage compromised on the sectarian religious exegesis in favor of a more comprehensive Newar identity cutting across the Hindu–Buddhist divide. Chunda's and Baldev Juju's readings move away from the religion of the modernizing temple or monastery and toward a more political pedagogy that can still back Buddhist or Hindu religiosity. Foundational mythologies are developed which tell parents that nothing should come between their daughters and their Newarness and that they should first and foremost be true to their ancient ancestors' rules and their rural female norms and codes. *Ihi* changes from marriage to initiation, be it into the patri- or into the matrilineage, from prescribing a relation between two individuals, the girl and her future husband. These literati authors follow Buddhist role models to prescribe a relation between the girl, who may happen to be Buddhist (or not) and those authentic, archaic forces that mold group solidarity and ethnic identity.

It is with Naresh Man that we return to discussions closer to Asha Kaji's, taken up by the next generation of Newar Buddhist activists. Here we see a second wave of reading *ihi* in a Buddhist way, an increased focus on the ritual textual tradition and its textual-doctrinal heritage. Instead of drawing on *avadāna* narratives, we find here a detailed exegesis of both instructions and prescribed verses, an assertive move to ground rituals in other rituals rather than in the popular Buddhist literary context. It speaks to the time after 2000 when there has been a surge in Buddhist image consecration events and a time when tantric consecration is a central arena in which old forms and norms (especially secrecy and caste restrictions) are being tested and rewritten. The innovations in interpreting *ihi* are consistent with the modernizations in tantric praxis by the school of Badri Ratna and his student Naresh Man Bajracharya.[81] Thus, doing *ihi* for them has shifted from being a marriage to a consecration (via initiation), from making good Buddhist wives to making empowered young Buddhists, with the ultimate purpose of building a stronger, more assertive but also more self-aware generation of Buddhists whose praxis is the Newar way.

81. For some of these see David N. Gellner, "Initiation as a Site of Cultural Conflict," in *Hindu and Buddhist Initiations in India and Nepal*, ed. Astrid Zotter and Christof Zotter (Wiesbaden: Harrassowitz, 2010), 169–73 and 180–81.

V. THE FILIAFOCAL *IHI* EXPERIENCE

It is a truism in anthropology, and a marker of successful fieldwork, that a researcher can not only specify what the formal cultural rules are in a given community and what the cultural elite thinks, but also see how individuals can and do make choices in how they negotiate these norms to live their lives. It is clear in observing the Newar *ihi* ritual that still other hands also shape the experience of *ihi* to achieve familial and personal goals.

To use the fruitful term coined by anthropologist Lynn Bennett,[82] one can discern a "filiafocal moment" created in the best interests of the girls themselves by mothers, fathers, and kin. For the first time, girls are taken as serious actors in family life, becoming the chief focus of a grand ritual, gift giving, and subsequent feasting. This role is consistent with the adult woman's centrality to Newar Buddhist family ritual life, and the group setting of *ihi* is congruent with the norm of women working together. The Newar Buddhist love for their daughters, and the conscious "softening" of the patrifocal brahmanical ritual practices, is clearly discernible in the contemporary *ihi*.[83]

Intended Meanings and Received Experiences

What still remains is to describe and analyze what the girls *themselves* report about their participation in *ihi*. From a modest survey conducted in the spring of 2010 with eleven Newar Buddhist adult women ranging in age from twenty-one to fifty-five,[84] it is possible to make a first attempt.[85] Table 15.1

82. Lynn Bennett, *Dangerous Wives and Sacred Sisters: Social and Symbolic Roles of High–Caste Women in Nepal (*New York: Columbia University Press, 1983), viii.

83. This observation should be taken in comparative terms. While Newar culture provides strong support for its daughters in comparison to other South Asian groups, the elevated status of sons versus daughters is nonetheless still present. In *Jhī Macā*, the popular children's book authored by the great Newar writer Chittadhar Hridaya (1906–1982), a series of characteristic incidents in the life cycle of a Newar child is told entirely from the boy child's perspective (Todd T. Lewis, "Childhood and Newar Tradition: Chittadhar Hridaya's *Jhī Macā*," *Asian Folklore Studies* 48, 2 (1989), 195–210). In Hridaya's great epic poem *Sugata Saurabha*, however, the text includes several passages that specifically call for showing respect for and support of daughters. See Todd T. Lewis, *Sugata Saurabha: A Poem on the Life of the Buddha by Chittadhar Hridaya of Nepal* [with Subarna Man Tuladhar] (New York: Oxford University Press, 2009).

84. Ages when *ihi was* done: Age 4–2; 5–1; 6–1; 7–2; 8–1; 9–2; 10–1; 11–1; Buddhist *ihi*-7; Brahmin Hindu *ihi*-4

85. Although fieldwork on *ihi* and other Newar *saṃskāras* began over three decades ago, the only recent inquiry for this chapter was a short e-mail questionnaire sent out by Professor Nirmal Tuladhar of Tribhuvan University in April 2011. It has many limitations in its scope and sampling, but we include these findings nonetheless because they illustrate points of methodology and interpretation alluded to above. Of course the data summarized here is only very preliminary. Many thanks to Professor Tuladhar for this assistance.

Table 15.1 SUMMARY OF SURVEY RESULTS

Recollection	Number
Toenail cutting	1
Vermillion part	2
First fasting, its difficulty	6
First learning, doing ritual	5
Sitting on father's lap	5
Holding *bel(byāḥ)* fruit	5
Being taught a religious chant	2
Becoming free of widowhood	2
Receiving gifts	4
Getting new clothes	7

records the major themes that were expressed in response to the prompt: "What do you remember about doing the *ihi* rituals?"

In response to the question, "How does this relate to Buddha Dharma?" all but one of the women responded that it "had nothing to do with Buddhism," with the one exception stating: "Ensuring that our children fulfill their duties is a parent's Dharma." Despite the meanings presented by the Newar elite in the local cultural media since 1970 (as discussed in the previous section), none reported seeing *any connection whatsoever* with the complex Buddhist symbols or meanings cited above. Instead, the women looking back on their doing *ihi* felt that they were simply expressing their own cultural identity and fostering their own social development. This emphasis on social status ("becoming a complete woman") and acting out their loyalty to Newar culture ("One does not feel complete as a person without going through these practices") is the dominant meaning derived from doing *ihi,* according to the reminiscences of the adult girls themselves.[86]

However history and tradition have "set up" *ihi* to be a moment of *kanyādāna* enacted by men—a time for focusing on daughters for parental merit-making, and for their group to "make a statement" about Buddhist identity to the Hindu majority and state—the analyses of this and any life-cycle rite must also connect with how the girls themselves experience the ritual acts. The Buddhist ritual is designed to open new spiritual awarenesses and to affect each girl's consciousness by "planting seeds" of future possibility; but these effects and each individual's self-awareness of them is assumed to take time to be manifest, and this ripening of understanding, according to each daughter's

86. Based on other congruent culture patterns, my analysis would be that over the half century, while awareness of Mahāyāna Buddhist doctrine has declined among Newar Buddhist merchants, the performance of the associated rituals continues because of ethnic pride and cultural nationalism.

87. It is perplexing and unfortunate that scholars of Buddhism in context have never, to our knowledge, sought to survey systematically the patterns of belief found

karma, can also vary among individuals.[87] What remains to be understood in a fully human way—today and in earlier history—is how any childhood Buddhist ritual shaped sons and daughters to become men and women, be members of their ethnic group, and be formed as Buddhists. What Newar tradition suggests—for today and in Indic antiquity—is that it is problematic to separate out the thread of Buddhist culture from the interconnected fabric of ancillary sociocultural, reformist, and political meanings.

in Buddhist communities. A modest effort in this domain for merchants in Nepal is found in Todd T. Lewis, "Patterns of Religious Belief in a Buddhist Merchant Community, Nepal," *Asian Folklore Studies* 55, no. 2 (1996), 237–70.

CHAPTER 16

Children in Himalayan Monasteries

KARMA LEKSHE TSOMO

Cherubic young monks smiling impishly against maroon robes and snow mountains have become signature images of Himalayan cultures in film, travelogues, and advertising. Small boys as young as six can be seen memorizing texts, chanting prayers, serving tea, and playing ball in Buddhist monasteries throughout the Tibetan Buddhist cultural region. From Ladakh to Bhutan and far north to the Siberian steppes, thousands of young people make their homes in monasteries, where they receive education, training, spiritual guidance, and nurturing. Apart from photos and film clips, however, little is known about the lives and aspirations of these young monastics. What lies behind the images of these photogenic children? What family dynamics and cultural values enable them to leave their homes at a young age to join a monastery, and what motivates them to do so? Are they coerced into adopting a rigorously disciplined lifestyle or do they naturally aspire to "the pure life"? What happens if a child ultimately decides to leave the monastery?

Until recently, career options in agrarian Himalayan societies were limited. With few of the many career paths open to children in Western societies—doctor, fireman, race car driver, astronaut—the choices for young children in Himalayan societies were generally limited to farming and monastic life, with few exceptions. In these devoutly Buddhist societies, children often expressed a wish to join the monastery, even at a very early age. Monasteries served as community centers where children imbibed learning, values, and practical skills. Instead of Superman or Batman, children were likely to take monks, perhaps an uncle or older sibling, as their role models. Children were welcome in the monasteries and generally had little difficulty moving from their large natal families to the bustling lifestyle of the monastic community. The brightest and best-behaved young boys were often encouraged by their families to become monks, though birth order may play a larger role in determining which children are encouraged to become monks. And, although girls are rarely encouraged to become nuns, if they were determined, then devout parents generally accede to their wishes.

Since the eighth century, with rare exceptions, Buddhism has been at the heart of religious life in the Himalayan cultural region. After the Indian scholar monk Santarakshita established Samye Monastery in central Tibet in 766 CE and ordained the first five Tibetan monks, monastic centers have been central to the survival and flourishing of Buddhism, not only in Tibet itself but also in the vast region of Tibetan cultural influence in India, Nepal, Bhutan, Mongolia, and beyond. In these predominantly agricultural societies, it became customary for boys to stay in these monasteries from a young age to study the texts and traditions that were the repository of the Buddha's teachings that became central to the lives of the people. Once they assimilated the teachings, liturgies, and monastic traditions, they became teachers and conduits for transmitting their knowledge and wisdom to future generations. Children in Himalayan monasteries, especially boys, thus became key to the continuity of age-old Buddhist cultures.

Despite many political upheavals, Himalayan monasteries are still vibrant, esteemed centers of Buddhist learning and practice throughout the Tibetan cultural region. Unlike in the past, however, when Buddhism stood virtually unchallenged as the locus of a constellation of religious sensibilities and institutions, the monasteries are now subject to powerful new cultural influences. As children increasingly attend government schools and take up jobs in government, commerce, and the tourist industry, the fact that fewer boys are entering monastic life has become a matter of vital concern. Without monastics, there will be no one to perform rituals, appease the dead, or ensure the spiritual and material well-being of the people and the land. Consequently bringing children into the monasteries, demonstrating the advantages of monastic life, and training them in Buddhist philosophy, prayers, and rituals is essential to preserving the culture and religious traditions of Himalayan peoples. The continuity of their ancient heritage depends on the children. Unless they are properly directed and taught the beauty and spiritual value of their unique Buddhist culture and tradition, both the continuity and very existence of this ancient heritage are endangered. Without the children, there may no longer be monastics to maintain the heart of the culture and pass it to the next generation.

Himalayan societies have seen many changes in recent years, changes that have transfigured families, communities, and monasteries throughout the Tibetan Buddhist world. This chapter will track the effects of political, social, and economic changes on the younger generation of Buddhists in the Himalayan region. In particular, it will explore the lives and experiences of children who join Himalayan Buddhist monasteries and the changes that are currently transforming traditional expectations and opportunities for these children. Further, it will discuss the social, political, and economic influences that encourage and discourage boys and girls from entering monasteries, past and present, and the importance of children in the continuation of Buddhist culture in the Himalayas.

This chapter depicts the lives of children who enter monastic life, the benefits that accrue to them by virtue of their monastic vocation, and the challenges that children in Himalayan monasteries are likely to face in an increasingly secular society. At the same time as enrollments of boys and young men are declining in Himalayan monasteries, there is an appreciable increase in the number of girls and young women who are attracted to monastic life. Here I reflect on these changes and possible reasons to explain them. These reflections are based on my experience of living in and around monasteries in India, Nepal, Tibet, and the western Himalayan regions of Zangskar, Spiti, and Kinnaur since 1972, and on interviews with monastics, laypeople, and researchers in these regions.[1] As a Buddhist nun trained in the Tibetan tradition, I pay special attention to the experience of girls who become nuns, aware that accounts of Tibetan monastic life often focus on the experience of boys who become monks.

THE HIMALAYAN LANDSCAPE

The Himalayan region is home to a vast range of peoples speaking a variety of languages and dialects, most of which are closely related to Tibetan. The majority of the people are agriculturalists, growing barley, peas, and other staple crops, while some are nomads or traders. The area is largely Buddhist[2] and most homes have a shrine room (*lhakang*) or at least an altar dedicated to the Buddha, including scriptures and a colorful assortment of religious imagery and offerings. Based on the Mahayana Buddhist theory that all living creatures have the potential for enlightenment, human relationships are guided by the principle of respect for all living beings, including children. In actual practice, Himalayan societies are ordered according to age, family background, ordination status, gender, and wealth. These principles and practices are also evident in monastic life in the Himalayan cultural regions, which is a curious mix of egalitarian theory and hierarchical practices, designed to ensure harmonious personal relationships as well as the orderly functioning of the monastery. In the case with a young *tülku* (*sprul sku*, one who is recognized as the rebirth of a realized being), religious status may outweigh all other criteria in gaining public approval and wielding social capital. Assuming they do not behave badly, monastics overall enjoy a privileged status vis-à-vis the laity. Within the monastery ranks, *bhikṣus* (fully ordained monks with 253 precepts) outrank the *śramaṇera* (novice monks with ten precepts), who in turn outrank the *rabjung*

1. This article is informed by the stories and experiences of numerous kind and knowledgeable friends, including Lauren Galvin, Elles Lohuis, and monastics throughout the Himalayas, especially nuns from the monasteries associated with Jamyang Foundation. I am deeply indebted to all of them.

2. There are also important minority communities, including Muslims, Hindus, and Dards.

(those with generic renunciant status who have not necessarily received monastic precepts) and *upāsakas* (Buddhist laypeople with five precepts).

Religious ceremonies punctuate the lives of the villagers and are celebrated according to the lunar calendar. Children typically imbibe their religiosity from their parents:

> Young children participate in numerous religious ceremonies in the villages. Sometimes they attend religious gatherings at the village temple, where they recite prayers and mantras with the villagers, eat together, and later sing and dance. They watch their parents make offerings at the altar in the family shrine room, follow them as they circumambulate Mani walls, shrines, and chortens [reliquaries]. They may also participate in the fasting ritual known as *nyungne*... [and] recite mantras. All these experiences help shape their religious consciousness. Children from more religious families may learn many prayers by heart that they recite throughout the day and throughout their lives.[3]

These ceremonies, performed either at the local temple or monastery[4] or in the home, may last for a single day or for weeks.

Monks are trained in monasteries, often from a young age, to read the scriptures and to perform rituals to ward off malevolent forces, appease the local gods (*yül lha*), and ensure the well-being of the villagers, their animals, and their crops. Families with more than one son might encourage those who are most disciplined and spiritually inclined, especially sons who are second or third in birth order, to join the monastery and train to provide these essential ritual services. The boy's parents will then take him to a lama (spiritual teacher), who will be asked to confirm the decision and provide guidance on which monastery would be most auspicious.

Robes for the young boy and offerings to the monastery are then prepared, either in the form of a monetary donation, a round of tea, or a meal offering to the resident monks. In Tibet, incipient monks were sometimes led to the monastery on horseback, as if to reenact the story of the Buddha's renunciation of household life in ancient India. Well-wishers might offer the new renunciant a white scarf (*kha ta*) as a sign of auspiciousness. Fruits or other items might be offered to create merit, since making offerings to a person with fresh, as-yet-unsullied precepts is believed to accrue merit for the donor. A teacher, often a relative of the new monk, is selected to guide his accultura-

3. Namgyal Lhamo Taklha, *Women of Tibet* (Dehra Dun: Songtsen Library, 2005), 161.

4. Here the word "monastery" (Tibetan: *gon pa*) is used for a monastic community, whether it is the home of monks or nuns, in accordance with both English and Tibetan usage. Somehow the word "nunnery" (Tibetan: *tsun gon*) has a different ring, presumably reflecting gender stereotypes in society at large and sexist preconceptions about who nuns are and what they do.

tion to monastic life and to instruct him gradually in prayers, discipline, and scriptures.[5]

GROWING UP IN THE HIMALAYAS

As in most societies, parents in Himalayan societies love their children and want them to be happy. Children are gradually socialized to be respectful of others and to contribute to the family and the life of the community. Discipline is rather strict, but family relationships are generally loving, especially when children are small. Children may or may not get a chance to go to school, but they generally are free to play and often get into mischief. Although for convenience parents themselves sometimes name their children, often after the day of the week they were born, such as Nyima (Sunday), Dawa (Monday), and so on, it is more common for parents to request a lama to select a name. Since these names usually have Buddhist meaning, they are considered auspicious and a portent of high aspirations for the young child. The lama may give the child a white scarf (*kha ta*) as a blessing or a protection cord on such an occasion.

Social and religious protocols and taboos are introduced during the socialization process of children across the Buddhist Himalayan region. Some pan-Himalayan taboos include prohibitions against urinating near water sources where *nāgas* (Tibetan: *lü*, serpentine beings) reside, placing dirty objects above the hearth or near a shrine, stepping over people or sacred objects, failing to consecrate construction sites, and so on. Children are taught to show respect for elders (especially males), sacred texts and images, and rites of propitiation to family and clan deities. An emphasis is placed on the accumulation of merit, avoidance of demerit, and observance of ritual practices to ensure the prosperity of the family and the community, largely composed of blood relations. Values, protocols, and taboos are instilled in children in their homes and monasteries and are reiterated in the surrounding community.

Families and extended family members are very close, since they must rely on each other to face the extreme challenges of their environment. Sharing all the joys and hardships of life in such harsh terrain with a fragile ecology of climatic extremes and pestilence creates a need for consensus and helps reinforce religious values and beliefs. Inhabitants fear drought in summer and avalanches in winter. The use of water, soil, and stone is protected and strictly regulated for the benefit of the village community. Family members feel protective toward one another and also feel strong obligations to contribute to the family economy and guard against bringing shame to the family. Life in Zangskar revolves primarily around one's own household and household unit (*khang chung*); the willingness to help others is understood largely in relation to blood relationships. The fact that two families are neighbors does not necessarily mean they will assist one another during harvest,

5. Palden Gyatso's experience of leaving home to join a monastery as a young boy is included in *The Autobiography of a Tibetan Monk* (New York: Grove Press, 1998), 19–25.

yet there exist subtle systems of mutual assistance that are not entirely regulated by blood relationships. These small, informally organized groups routinely host each other for *pūjās* and celebrations on a rotating basis, and members of each household within the group are expected to assist each other during busy times, such as the harvest season, or during large gatherings that require a lot of work, such as weddings. Children are always expected to help out in whatever ways they can; helping the family with various tasks, whether household duties, fieldwork, or herding, makes children feel useful and powerful. Even at a very young age, children are instilled with a feeling of responsibility toward the maintenance and flourishing of their own households. As a result, children are generally eager to assist with whatever their parents and other relatives request of them. Of course, there are also children who are stubborn; in such cases, parents must exert much effort to get them to do what they are told. Children who resist socialization in this way are looked upon unfavorably by members of the community and may be subject to marginalization or ridicule. In Zangskar, children known for their bad behavior are called *tulku sokpo* (contaminated emanations). Good behavior, an easygoing attitude, and a propensity for hard work are not only highly valued in children there but expected and rewarded. In a fragile ecology and subsistence economy, children have a very clear sense of the importance of helping others, because they realize that their household will need help in return. Deviating from this normative reciprocity is one way to bring shame to one's natal household and to become the target of social disapproval.

More broadly, the village is a family. It is common to hear Himalayan peoples refer to residents of their villages as their brothers and sisters. Even when there may be no close blood ties, people in the villages are often descendants of common ancestors somewhere along the line. Networks and feelings of affinity extend like waves, starting from the basic household to the immediate sub-villages to the larger village and ultimately to the region as a whole. Children of the village all play together from early on. As children, they do the same work: taking animals to pasture in the morning, shepherding them during the day, corralling them in the evening, collecting water, washing dishes, and so on. Even at a young age, girls are expected to do a bit more work than boys, including washing clothes and caring for younger siblings, but there is no great gender distinction or division of labor. As children start to get older, gender roles become more pronounced: women milk the cows, feed the animals, and look after the house and children, while men do masonry work and weave woolen fabric (*nam bu*). There are also many jobs that are not gender specific, such as fieldwork, grinding grains, and building. The allocation of tasks is a practical matter of getting work done in a timely and efficient way, such that gender roles are often quite fluid. When it comes to parties and gatherings, though, the village segregates: girls with girls, boys with boys, women with women, and men with men.

Children may experience a certain amount of separation anxiety when they go to live in a monastery, but they quickly become absorbed into the monastic community, where they have constant contact with their teachers and senior monks or nuns. Children living at home experience a similar separation anxiety when they go off to school or their parents go off to work, as their mothers work long hours in the fields and their fathers are often away, traveling to distant Indian cities. It is very common in Zangskar for adolescent boys to enter the army, return to Zangskar to get married (so as to maintain their ancestral household), and then leave the valley again, only to return for annual visits. This pattern of migration has repercussions for children, who may see their fathers for only a few months each year.

LIFE IN A HIMALAYAN MONASTERY

Buddhist cultural regions of the Himalayas have an old tradition of accepting and encouraging young children to take up residency in monasteries, even at the age of six or eight. According to the *vinaya* (codes of monastic discipline), a child is allowed to enter monastic life as soon as he or she is able to scare away the crows. This convention has been observed in the Himalayan region for centuries. Occasionally children join the monastery when they are orphaned or one parent dies and the other does not feel adequate to take care of the children. In such cases, the monastery becomes a home, whether temporary or permanent, and the monastic community becomes a surrogate family for the child. Abandoning or leaving children at the monastery against their will is rare.[6] Allowing a child to enter a monastery is a sacrifice, in the sense that the child no longer contributes to the family income and requires some degree of support.[7] When children live in monasteries near their homes and villages, the connections with family remain close, since their parents visit the monastery often. When children are sent to distant monasteries, for example in south India, they may be separated from their parents for years and may consequently experience loneliness, dislocation, or alienation.[8]

Children are given tasks around the monastery and feel happy to be entrusted with these duties. Although they may receive few formal teachings or systematic instruction, they learn primarily by observing and listening to their teachers and senior residents, who take the younger monks and nuns under their wings like apprentices. Although the younger ones may get scolded or even

6. In the two cases I personally witnessed, a young girl in Zangskar and a young boy in Spiti, the children's mothers had died and their fathers were not able to take care of them. In both cases, the children returned to the care of their father or extended family after a few years, having been affectionately raised by the nuns in the interim.

7. Referring to the Sherpa Buddhist community of northeastern Nepal, Sherry Ortner contends that a preponderance of monks and nuns come from wealthier families, since their families "had to be able to absorb this double cost." See her book, *High Religion: A Cultural and Political History of Sherpa Buddhism* (Delhi: Motilal Banarsidass, 1989), 173.

8. The Dalai Lama recounts his initial feelings of loneliness as a child growing up in the Potala, in his memoir, *Freedom in Exile: Autobiography of His Holiness the Dalai Lama of Tibet* (New York: HarperOne, 1991).

hit from time to time if they are careless or act up, childrearing practices still common throughout the Himalayan region, extreme instances of child abuse are rare in the monasteries, or at least not a matter of public record. Children take pride in serving around the monastery and, in the process, become efficient in all the monastic duties. Typical duties for children are fetching cups and other items from the kitchen, serving tea, running messages to the village, helping prepare for rituals, and so on. Children generally find life in the monastery more interesting than life at home, with special events to celebrate, visitors to spy on, and many nooks and crannies to explore. Children feel a sense of belonging to a happy community while enjoying the freedom to play with animals and other children outdoors without supervision. The younger ones bask in the attention and affection of residents and visitors alike, which gives them a sense of security, love, and well-being. Their identity as a monk or nun affords them a respected place in the community and special treatment, such as occasional snacks and small gifts given by relatives or the blessed offerings (*'bza tshogs*) that are distributed at *pūjās* (ritual services). Although hygiene in remote Himalayan regions may not be up to Western standards, children are free from constant badgering about tracking dirt in the house and ruining the carpet. The nuns, though, take special care to keep themselves and their surroundings clean. They seem much more concerned with hygiene and cleanliness than the villagers or the monks.

Monastic training naturally entails discipline, which is regarded as conducive to shaping character and, ultimately, to reducing selfishness and carelessness. This day-to-day training helps cut through arrogance and develops humility. Monastic training also entails education and can be quite demanding. When I asked Pasang, a young man from Zangskar, what kind of training he underwent, he replied: "It was very rigorous. For three years, we were given text after text of the scriptures to memorize. It was a slow process. First, we had to master the Tibetan alphabet. Then we had to learn some mantras, then slowly we were taught the shorter versions of the scriptures, or tantras. Finally we graduated to the long versions." Children are first taught to write with ash on a slate, until they improve to the point where they are allowed to use ink. Except during *pūjās* and studies, however, discipline in Himalayan monasteries is often fairly relaxed. In village monasteries, where ritual training is prized, bright monks sometimes will be selected for education at larger monasteries and, if they do well, may become teachers. Higher studies are not always encouraged, though, since this would deplete the vital workforce of young monks in the monasteries, yet without study programs or similar challenges, young monks may become bored with the daily monastic routine and drop out as they get older.

Discipline in the monasteries encompasses both spiritual cultivation and mundane tasks. Children learn respect for elders, teachers, and Buddhist traditions by making prostrations and offerings before the Buddha, Dharma, and Sangha, and learn core Buddhist values through morality tales and by memorizing scripture passages. Simultaneously, they learn practical matters, such as showing up for *pūjā* on time and performing all the practical tasks of running a monastery. The day's schedule and expectations are very clear, so children do not have to think about mundane matters and can concentrate on their studies, practice, and duties. There are not many choices to be made, so children can relax into a familiar, comfortable routine. Before joining a monastery, young boys and girls have often already learned the basic protocol surrounding shrine rooms and making offerings, since each household usually has its own shrine room. Buddhist traditions are inculcated by parents as soon as children can walk; it is even common to see parents bow their baby's head toward Buddha images and *lamas*. Children learn to make offerings to the Buddha, a time-honored way to develop generosity and a reminder of one's own potential for enlightenment. Children are taught to respect all living creatures, based on the teaching that all have Buddha nature; on the practical level, children are taught to avoid killing any living creature, no matter how small. Based on the well-known Buddhist teachings on compassion and nonviolence, children are taught not to kill any living creature. Like everywhere, if parents are sensitive and kind to their animals, their children tend to be kind, too, but if parents treat animals disrespectfully, their children often pick up these habits. Monastics tend to be more careful and sensitive in their treatment of animals than lay folk, because they are generally more familiar with the Buddha's teachings on kindness toward all living creatures and have more time for reflection on these teachings. Although discipline in the monasteries can be strict, it serves the important purpose of engendering mindfulness and thoughtfulness of others. The monastic discipline for children is relatively relaxed; as long as children fulfill the expected duties and protocols, they are free to play, laugh, and explore at will.

THE RATIONALE

The most common question foreign observers pose is why young children are often found in monasteries in the Himalayas. It is often assumed that the decision is made by the parents, but although this is often the case, it does not mean that children are forced into monastic life against their will. Whereas children in North America may express a wish to be a fireman, policemen, or movie star, children in Himalayan cultures as young as three or four often express a wish to become a monk or a nun. Geshe Rabten, a Tibetan from Kham who joined the monastery when he was seventeen, recalled:

> From the time I was a small child, I met monks in their maroon robes returning from the great monastic universities near Lhasa. I admired them very much. I also occasionally visited the large monastery in our region; and when I watched the monks debating, I was again filled with admiration. When

> I was about fifteen years old I began to notice how simple, pure, and efficient their lives were. I also saw how my own home life, in comparison, was so complicated and demanding of tasks that were never finished.[9]

When a child expresses the wish to join a monastery, the parents usually agree, because they believe it is good karma for the child as well as the family. Himalayan parents' willingness to support children's monastic aspirations contrasts markedly with neighboring Hindu and Muslim communities, in which marriage is the only option. Although, in the past, life in a monastery offered few comforts, a certain mystique has always surrounded religious life, and popular devotion to religion and respect for religious life are strong influences on Himalayan people of all ages. Monastics are admired as exemplars of religious culture and an attractive alternative to the hardships and problems of lay life. In some cases, children try to convince their parents to let them join a monastery but the parents are reluctant. If there is parental resistance, a child may persist in requesting permission until the parents finally agree. To placate the parents, the monastic authorities may ask the child to wait a year; if the child continues to insist on joining the monastery, the parents generally respect the child's wishes and acquiesce. There are cases where parents try to convince children to join a monastery, but children also have ways of expressing their resistance; if the parents insist, the child may misbehave, refuse to study, or run away.

Parents may offer their children to a monastery as an expression of gratitude[10] or in the belief that living the religious life creates continuous merit for the entire family. When parents express the wish that children become monastics, the children usually agree, out of respect for their parents and a wish to repay their kindness, but also because life in the monastery among other children, away from household duties and the watchful eyes of their parents, is freeing and fun. As long as they feel confident that the child will be well cared for, parents believe that the child will have the opportunity to live a meaningful life, progressing steadily toward enlightenment, rather than creating nonvirtue through farming, herding, or other occupations that may harm living beings. Parents who bring children to the monastery are often motivated by the same logic. Monastic life is a respectable vocation, and a family who has one or more children in the monastery is respected in the community. It is believed that having a child in the monastery is a constant source of merit and blessing, benefitting the family line for seven generations past and future. Having children in the monasteries also benefits local communities by increasing the ranks of religious practitioners who will generate merit and preserve

9. Geshe Rabten, *The Life and Teachings of a Tibetan Monk* (Mount Pelerin, Switzerland: Edition Rabten, 2000).

10. The story of a Ladakhi woman who "resolved to offer her daughter to the Buddhist faith" after recovering from a near-fatal illness is recounted in Anna Grimshaw, *Servants of the Buddha: Winter in a Himalayan Convent* (Cleveland: The Pilgrim Press, 1992), 140–42.

Buddhist teachings and practices. If the child does not protest and is willing to stay in the monastery, the parents assume that the child is suited for monastic life. If the child is reluctant or does not immediately take to life in a monastery, the parents may take the child home and try again later. Sometimes children resist the idea of life in a monastery initially but may decide to join later of their own volition.

Children are attracted to monastic life for many reasons. Some feel a natural affinity to monastics and monasteries, which is interpreted as evidence of a strong karmic connection from past lives. Children often hear family members and visitors recount the benefits of Dharma practice and learn that living a monastic life is meritorious. They witness community rituals, such as processions in which monks and community members circumambulate the fields carrying sacred Buddhist texts to ensure a good harvest. Young people may see monastic life, demanding as it may be, as a desirable alternative to back-breaking labor in the fields and the anxieties of looking after parents, grandparents, and herds of animals. Some may prefer to stay in a monastery rather than go to school, simply because it is a fun place to be, with opportunities to learn many interesting things, such as butter sculpture, ritual instruments, and so on. These children enjoy preparing for *pūjās* on auspicious days—the freedom to play with other children, a supportive environment, the affection of older monastics, and a certain status in the eyes of the surrounding community. Children are often the center of attention and playfully teased by older monks or nuns. Young monks, and especially *tülkus*, are "treated like kings."

Considerable prestige attaches to having a respected monk in the family, but also considerable censure if the monk runs away, behaves poorly, or disregards the discipline of the monastery. Typically, the eldest son does not join a monastery, but instead is expected to take responsibility for his parents and the family property.[11] Frequently, a boy's parents will go to a *lama* to request a divination (*mo*) to determine whether the indications are good for the boy to enter monastic life. If the signs are good, the parents are likely to ask which monastery will be most auspicious. The parents will generally provide the first set of robes and basic necessities and preferably take the boy to stay with a monastic relative who will provide guidance and education.

Parents are less likely to encourage a daughter to become a nun, since the same prestige does not attach to it as it does to being a monk. Girls are useful workers around the house and in the fields, and it is generally assumed that they will grow up to marry and have children. Because of these societal expectations, most girls who enter monastic life do so of their own volition. For

11. For example, "Traditionally in Spiti, first sons were responsible for the fields, home, and parents; middle sons were sent to monasteries; and younger sons were encouraged to engage in trade." Margaret Coberly, "Crisis as Opportunity: Nuns and Cultural Change in the Spiti Valley," in *Buddhist Women and Social Justice: Ideals, Challenges, and Achievements*, ed. Karma Lekshe Tsomo (Albany: State University of New York Press, 2004), 204.

many of them, the allure of marriage is weak. Girls are aware of the hardships of household life, especially for women. They see the difficulties their mothers' experience—money, substance abuse, endless work, childbirth. Everyday life in the Himalayas is full of hard work, simply to survive. Girls observe the drudgery that their mothers endure, working from early morning to late at night in the harsh Himalayan climate—hauling water, cooking over a wood fire, slogging away in the fields, caring for children and animals, foraging for fodder, washing clothes in freezing water, and performing numerous tedious household duties—without much help or positive feedback. Young girls also observe the special sufferings of women, including social strictures, disparagement, childbirth without access to modern health care, and domestic violence. After witnessing the terrible sufferings their mothers endure giving birth to one baby after another without anesthesia and losing their children to preventable diseases, it is no wonder that some girls find the monastic life attractive and freeing. Now that education is available in a number of Himalayan nunneries, the opportunity for learning Dharma is also a powerful draw for girls and young women contemplating monastic life.

If a girl has a religious temperament and expresses a strong wish to become a nun, her parents will generally agree, unless she is already betrothed. For example, in Spiti Valley, "All the nuns at Yangchen Chöling have been nuns since they were young. Even as children, most of them expressed such strong interest in religious practice that their parents allowed them to shave their heads and wear robes, and encouraged their interest in religious devotions when they had finished their chores."[12] It is rare for an eldest daughter to become a nun, since eldest daughters inherit their mothers' traditional headdress (*perak*) and jewelry.[13] Girls who are shy are often disinclined to go to school and may prefer to go live in a monastery. There are cases in which parents try to convince children to join a monastery. Now that the status of the nuns is rising, because of support from abroad and improved access to textual and ritual learning, parents increasingly recognize the benefits of monastic life for women over the difficulties of household life. This view is most common when the eldest daughter of the family is already married and the parents have enough household help from other daughters. Although the first daughter is expected to marry, each marriage requires the bride's family to allocate a great deal of material wealth to the husband's household, so provided that the girl's household already has sufficient hands for household chores and field work, having a daughter enter monastic life can be economical for the family.

12. Margaret Coberly, "Crisis as Opportunity," 196–97.

13. Referring to Yangchen Chöling Monastery in Spiti, Coberly reports: "Interestingly, case histories of the nuns reveal that 99 percent of the nuns were middle children and 82 percent were second daughters.... It is likely that families are more willing to allow a second daughter to join the monastery, keeping the elder daughter at home to help with the housework until she is of marriageable age." See her article, "Crisis as Opportunity," 204.

Some women also become nuns after experiencing married life. One young woman in Zangskar got married and lived with her husband for a year, but had such a horrible experience that she ran away, returned to her parents' house, and decided to become a nun. According to her account, she had wanted to become a nun before the marriage but was kidnapped from her home one night by her future husband's friends. The practice of kidnapping women is not uncommon; if a man wants a woman, he may take her from her home and bring her to his own home; in this way, the engagement is considered consummated. If the woman stays at his home, this is generally taken to signify her consent, and the relationship is accepted as a marriage by the surrounding community. Indeed, according to hagiographic tradition, this is the very situation Yeshe Tsogyal is said to have suffered several centuries ago.[14]

When children join monasteries, it is common for them to join the largest one near their home, especially if they can share the living quarters (*shag*) of a relative. If a child has a close relative at a more distant monastery and can be assured of getting a teacher and a living space, he or she may join that monastery. Even without a blood relationship, a child's relationship with his or her teacher is generally loving and supportive, providing the child with security and a sense of identity. Nevertheless, it is not uncommon for children to feel homesick when they first leave their homes for a monastery. Whether caused by environmental or emotional factors, a few informants reported that they got sick when they first joined the monastery.

When children are young, they help around the monastery grounds or kitchen and learn the many important tasks that are necessary for maintaining the grounds and buildings, such as shoveling snow from the rooftops, cooking and serving, and maintaining the annual ritual calendar, such as making ritual offerings (*torma*) and playing the ritual instruments. After a certain age, they take their place on the roster of duties that all resident monastics are required to do. The schedule of rotating duties, while specific to each monastery, commonly includes stints of one to three years as chanting master, storekeeper, financial officer, and shrine keeper.

The teacher–student relationship entails benefits and responsibilities on both sides. The child sweeps, hauls water, makes tea, and, if the teacher is an older relative, may also wash clothes. In return, the child receives living space, food, education, and training. The child learns prayers and rituals, serves the needs of the teacher and community, and still has time to play. Children are expected to learn at least one verse each day, reciting it several times in front of the teacher in the morning, repeating it over and over in the early hours of the morning and throughout the day, then reciting it by memory in front of the teacher in the evening. In the monasteries, it is common to see children reciting the texts loudly while rocking back and forth. It is also common to

14. See the following translation for an account of this part of her life: Gyalwa Changhub and Namkhai Nyingpo, *Lady of the Lotus Born: The Life and Enlightenment of Yeshe Tsogyal*, trans. Padmakara Translation Group (Boston: Shambhala, 2002), 12–22.

see children assessed in terms of their intelligence, typically measured in terms of their ability to memorize texts. If a child is not bright, most teachers are understanding and simply accept this as the child's natural limitation, as long as the daily tasks get done. A close, loving relationship between teacher and student is common and engenders respect, such that discipline can often be maintained with a soft voice.

If a child is recalcitrant or lazy, the teacher may resort to punishment rather than let the child get spoiled. As in many other cultures, discipline in the Himalayan region may be instilled and enforced through corporal punishment. It is very common to hear parents and teachers justify beatings as a means to teach children proper behavior: "If you don't beat them, they won't turn out well." In the monasteries, many senior monks admit that they use corporal punishment to teach the young monks to respect or even fear authority. Although parents and senior monks contend that the beating of children is pedagogically motivated, beatings may also be motivated by anger or frustration. Although disciplinary action may have been warranted, I know two men who left the monastery as young monks because their teachers beat them. Excesses may be exacerbated by circumstances; several monks explained that when the Tibetans fled to India and Nepal after 1959, many young boys who lost their parents were sent to the monasteries and the few older monks who managed to escape simply could not control the hundreds of youngsters given into their charge.[15] In monasteries for girls and women, beatings appear to be much less common.

Ideally, monastery life should be a lifetime vocation, but there is a natural attrition rate. When they are young, children are given considerable leeway to adjust to the lifestyle and decide whether it suits them before taking even the novice precepts. Most wear robes, but some continue to wear lay clothes for some time. After they arrive at the monastery, children generally undergo a simple ritual known as *rabjung* ("renouncing" or "leaving the household life"). Children have many opportunities to leave, if they wish. If they decide they do not like living in the monastery, they may return home, let their hair grow, and revert to lay life. A certain stigma is attached to monastics who take precepts, live in the monastery for some time, and then abandon the renunciant life,[16] but little stigma attaches to children who drop out when they are young. Due to this natural process of attrition, the ones who stay are generally sincerely dedicated to the monastic pursuit. According to tradition, a person who wishes to leave should seek permission from the teacher or monastic community; it is considered bad form to simply disappear without any explanation. Since the monastery has provided all basic needs—food, shelter, education, training, and so on—for several years a person who leaves without permission is considered

15. The horrific living conditions of monks consigned to a refugee camp in Buxa, West Bengal, are described in David Patt, *A Strange Liberation: Tibetan Lives in Chinese Hands* (Ithaca, NY: Snow Lion Publications, 1992), 30–31.

16. The tradition of stigma against renouncing monastic life is evident in the language used, e.g., to "lose" being a monk or nun, or to "get ruined."

ungrateful. And because the person's teacher has gone to considerable effort to teach the acolyte, it is also considered quite disrespectful to leave without permission. Some monasteries may even impose a fine and require an apology in order for someone to be reinstated. For example, a twenty-three-year-old nun who ran away from a nunnery in Zangskar was required to formally apologize, prostrate in front of images of the Buddha, pay a fine of Rs. 2000, and provide a meal to the community before being allowed to return. A person who leaves the monastery because of romantic attraction usually does not return, whether or not the relationship works out, since it is assumed that the precept to refrain from sexual activity has been breached. Joining another monastery is not a simple matter. A person who leaves one monastery without permission is generally considered a high risk when applying to join another monastery; customarily, out of respect for the previous institution, monasteries do not accept runaways. When children are still small and have not yet taken precepts, however, the monastery and people in the community are quite understanding. Children are considered to be in a liminal state, so fewer restrictions and expectations are imposed upon them than on older monastics. This more lenient discipline allows children more time to decide whether they want to live as a monastic. It does not make sense to compel someone to do so against his or her will.

EDUCATION FOR THIS LIFE AND THE NEXT

For centuries, talented young men from Mongolia, Bhutan, Sikkim, and Himalayan border regions flocked to Tibet to study Buddhism. These opportunities were lost after the communist takeover, when Tibet's borders were effectively sealed. After H. H. Dalai Lama arrived in India in 1959, he set about reestablishing a wide variety of monasteries and cultural institutions in exile, thereby opening up new opportunities for young boys to study at monasteries in India. Whenever possible, families from Tibet and the Himalayan region send their sons to pursue a monastic education at one of several large monastic universities in south India. For example, Gomang College of Drepung Monastery, which has been reestablished near Mundgod (Karnataka State), has a long-standing connection with Buddhists in the Himalayan border areas. Over the last several decades a large number of boys from the Himalayan region—Tibet, Nepal, Kinnaur, Spiti, Zangskar, and Mon-Tawang—have enrolled in Buddhist studies programs at these monasteries and also at Buddhist institutes supported by the government of India, such as the Institute of Buddhist Studies in Leh and the Central Institute of Higher Tibetan Studies in Sarnath.[17]

17. The history and programs at these institutes, including the initial admission of girl students to the Central Institute of Higher Tibetan Studies in 1977, are described in Margaret Nowak, *Tibetan Refugees: Youth and the New Generation of Meaning* (New Bruswick, NJ: Rutgers University Press, 1984), 110–13.

In contemporary society, by contrast, universal secular education has become the norm. In the Himalayan region, too, there are more schools and the quality of education has steadily been improving. More local teachers have been trained and are returning to take up posts in village schools. These teachers are generally dedicated to helping improve educational standards in their homelands and are a great improvement over previous years, when teachers from outside the area were assigned to hardship areas to which they were poorly suited. The presence of energetic young local teachers is gradually contributing to a greater valuing of local languages, beliefs, and cultural practices. In the last twenty years, a trend toward gender equity in education is clearly visible, as more girls are attending school and completing higher grades. The improved quality and increased availability of education is having an impact on children and monastic life in the Himalayas.

There is evidence that a clash of cultures is occurring in monasterie today. Recent decades have brought major changes in the availability and quality of primary education in remote areas of the Himalayas. A major shift has also occurred in attitudes toward secular education for girls. Whereas parents previously regarded education as superfluous for girls, who were most often kept at home to work in the fields and care for younger siblings, today girls and boys are receiving primary education in almost equal numbers. Increasingly, parents encourage boys to do well in school, so that they can pursue higher education and compete for positions in the Indian government. Girls are less likely to be encouraged in this direction, since the chances of their obtaining government positions is far less likely, but parents increasingly recognize the benefits of schooling for girls, too. The rationale for sending children to school is at least partially economic; the earnings of educated children increase the family's income, enable them to be self-sufficient, and contribute to the economic health of the community. These new opportunities have resulted in observable tensions between secular and religious ideals. When one weighs educational alternatives, the choice is ultimately between traditional Buddhist knowledge, which offers spiritual and cultural benefits, and modern secular knowledge, which offers more worldly benefits. Although these alternatives may seem somewhat distant for children, the dichotomy of values intimately affects the younger generation, especially in border areas and cultures. As opportunities for girls to choose the monastic life open up, so do opportunities for them to pursue secular education. Whereas in earlier centuries a monastic career was prestigious and socially valued, as travel became easier in the latter half of the twentieth century, Himalayan peoples encountered new influences. Along with international trekkers came attractive new material goods as well as Western and Indian music, film, dance, and ideas that challenged traditional values and Buddhism's dominant position in cultural life.

In recent decades, Himalayan peoples' attitudes toward secular education have changed. Some parents are still ambivalent about the necessity of education for children in an agricultural society, especially since schools promote literacy in Hindi or Urdu rather than in local languages, but many are beginning to understand schooling as an important foundation for upward mobility and material prosperity. When possible, family members take children to urban centers, such as Leh, Shimla, Dharamsala, or Kathmandu, to provide them with a better education. As a result, the number of boys becoming monks has steeply declined in recent years.[18] Whereas parents previously sent at least one son to the monastery as a matter of course, today they routinely send boys to secular school. Instead of encouraging their sons to take up monastic life, they are likely to encourage them to aim for a position in government service or join the army—occupations that are far more lucrative. Until recently, the monastic vocation was regarded as both honorable and spiritually rewarding, but these days young men have many alternative life choices and may consider work as a trekking guide or driver to be more tangibly rewarding. As the number of monastic recruits dwindles, many older monks express concern that soon there will be too few monks to adequately perform the annual cycle of traditional rituals. Reportedly, some monks have begun refusing to perform *pūjās* in households unless the family agrees to send a son to the monastery.

THE GENDER DIFFERENTIAL

An old Tibetan saying goes: "When you need a master, make your son a monk, and when you need a servant, make your daughter a nun."[19] Another adage, "Nuns are neighbors' maids and monks are neighbors' leaders," similarly reveals the extent of gendered expectations in Himalayan religious life.[20] As these sayings attest, nuns traditionally existed on the peripheries of Buddhist monastic life and experienced considerable gender discrimination in religious education.[21] It is not difficult to imagine the impact such attitudes had on young boys and girls as they contemplated entering monastic life. Gendered patterns of expressing respect were instilled at a young age and reinforced in social interactions, supported by preconceptions about women's presumed inferiority. Even when girls were very intelligent, they were less likely than their brothers to get educational opportunities, either in monasteries or at school. The process of socialization included deprecating attitudes toward girls and women that were internalized and deeply affected the way in which women regarded their own capabilities. Affected by this worldview, women of previous generations generally were not very ambitious in matters of religion, in seeking higher teachings or aspiring to become teachers, but were instead content to

18. Christoph von Fürer-Haimendorf notes a decline in the number of novice monks and a concomitant decrease in the number of ritual specialists in Sherpa communities in northeastern Nepal since 1971, replenished somewhat by refugee lamas from Tibet. See his *Himalayan Traders* (New Delhi: Times Books International, 1988).

19. Recounted by Namgyal Lhamo Taklha in *Women of Tibet*, 9.

20. Namgyal Lhamo Taklha, *Women of Tibet*, 9

21. Karma Lekshe Tsomo, "Change in Consciousness: Women's Religious Identity in Himalayan Buddhist Cultures," in *Buddhist Women Across Cultures: Realizations* (Albany: State University of New York Press, 1999), 169–89.

practice quietly toward the goal of liberation. Until recently, the possibility of studying Buddhist philosophy seemed remote for women and opportunities for them to receive advanced teachings and empowerments were extremely limited. Even though opportunities for nuns to study Buddhism began to open up in the 1980s, the idea of a nun receiving higher ordination is still perceived as an unrealistic ideal for most. Unquestionably, girls' perceptions of their own potential change as they receive a monastic education and begin to realize that they have the capacity to learn, as long as they are willing to put in the effort. Still, their capacity to learn as much as they wish is constrained by perceptions of inadequacy, whether due to age, the lack of early childhood education, or simply the imagined handicaps of being female. Perceptions of inadequacy are instilled early on, even in very young girls, who grow up hearing the songs their mothers sing in the fields about wishing to be reborn as a male.

The conventional preconception that being a woman is a lower rebirth is deeply ingrained, fostered by language (the word for woman is *skye men*, literally "lower rebirth") and the belief that a female rebirth is the result of bad karma from past lives. Among nuns, this preconception of women's inferiority often leads nuns to denigrate themselves and to overcompensate by engaging in extreme practices. For example, nuns are famous for their practice of the *nyung ne* ritual that requires total fasting and silence on alternate days, combined with hundreds of full-length prostrations and contemplative practices beginning from early morning and continuing throughout the day. Nuns may complete the preliminary practices (*ngön dro*) multiple times in order to purify the nonvirtues they have accumulated over many lifetimes, evidenced by their status as a "lower rebirth" in this life, before embarking on retreats and higher tantric practices. Typically, nuns are extremely diligent in their Dharma practice and have completed more *ngon dros* than the average monk. Paradoxically, the biased attitudes toward women that are instilled in girls during childhood, such as the belief that a female rebirth is a misfortune and evidence of greater defilements, may inspire girls to become nuns and to exert extra effort in their practice, perhaps in an effort to compensate for their perceived inadequacies. Further, because of their marginal status, nuns may have more time to perform the preliminary practices and engage in higher tantric meditation practices than their male counterparts, who are busy maintaining their monasteries and attending to ritual responsibilities in the outside community.

Traditionally, whereas young boys would be encouraged to become monks, girls were rarely encouraged to become nuns, a reflection of culturally sanctioned gender discrimination. The respected Tibetan nun Yogini Gomchen recounts her family's opposition and her defiance:

> Since childhood, I wanted very much to become a nun, but my pleas did not get to the ears of my family members. It was either due to the religious influence in my present life or continuation from my past life that I always wanted to live a nun's life. It was our custom that young girls wear amber,

> coral, and turquoise necklaces and earrings, and have pieces of these stones strung through our hair, but I used to give mine away to my friends as I wanted to be a nun, and my mother used to be furious.... The older people in our region would talk about one's son marrying someone's daughter when the children were about eight or nine years of age...I used to pray that I would never have to get married.[22]

In some families with more than one daughter, the younger girl might be given the option of becoming a nun, if she wishes.

Girls may join a monastery because they see the defects of household life for women. Unless a woman becomes a nun, she has little choice but to marry and raise children, in addition to fieldwork and housekeeping duties. In some areas of the Himalayas, women are expected to do most of the work—both domestic and agricultural labor. A friend of mine, a former monk, once told me: "We have a custom in Spiti. Women do all the work," and his wife disparagingly confirmed the truth of his claim. The drudgery of hard labor is not the only reason girls become nuns, however. Many girls, even from a young age, feel a strong natural calling to practice the Dharma. Sometimes they are inspired by the example of a relative who lives a monastic life. For instance, a Zangskari nun named Sonam lived many years with her uncle, who was a monk at the local village monastery. She became so inspired by his practice and by reading the Buddhist teachings that she decided, against the wishes of her parents, to become a nun. Eventually, she ran away from home and traveled to Lahul, where she lived as a shepherd in a small monastery (*gon pa*) and performed her first *ngöndro* (an intensive set of preliminary practices) before gaining her parents' permission to become a nun.

Life in a nuns' monastery is definitely more difficult than life in a monks' monastery and therefore the life of a small girl in a monastery is very different from that of a small boy. Nuns get very little support from the lay community, whereas monks are well supported by donations of food, money, and labor.[23] Monasteries for monks often have large land holdings, a legacy of donations offered by local kings or landlords in adjacent areas. Villagers are expected to work these lands and contribute toward the upkeep of the monks and the monasteries. As a result, the needs of the monks are entirely met by the village community. In the past, monasteries for nuns were few or nonexistent; without the benefit of donors, nuns stayed in their family homes or in retreat. Throughout the Himalayan region, the economic disparities between monasteries for monks and those for nuns are clearly visible. Monks generally get support from their family members, but nuns generally do not. For young boys, the idea of going to a monastery and being liberally supported for life is

22. Namgyal Lhamo Taklha, *Women of Tibet*, 52.
23. Kim Gutschow, Being a Buddhist Nun: The Struggle for Enlightenment in the Himalayas. (Cambridge, MA: Harvard University Press, 2004).

an attractive option. By contrast, for young girls, the idea of "going forth into homelessness" with little or no encouragement from her family and little or no material support from the surrounding community is a rather dire prospect.

Currently, although monasteries for monks still benefit from land endowments and traditional patterns of lay support, social and economic changes in the region are beginning to reconfigure patterns of monastic support. Attitudes toward nuns are also changing, and their prospects are much better than before. In the last twenty years, throughout the Himalayan region, the status of nuns has improved and opportunities for women have expanded.[24] Although expectations persist that girls will grow up to marry and have children, some parents have now begun to recognize that their daughters might be happier as nuns, and it has become more common for parents to encourage their daughters' aspirations for monastic life. In Zangskar, for example, the number of nuns is increasing, while the number of monks is decreasing. In some areas, villagers more commonly invite nuns from the monasteries to perform basic rituals in their homes and in the village community. Although some rituals are still considered the exclusive purview of monks, there is an increasing recognition of nuns as skilled tantric practitioners with the merit and power to conduct ceremonies for the health and prosperity of their communities. When I first visited the village of Zangla in 2001, the villagers were still inviting monks to travel from Karsha Monastery to preside at funerals, but now many families invite nuns from nearby Changchub Chöling Monastery, even though a motorable road has been built. At the same time, many continue to call nuns, especially their relatives, to help them with domestic and agricultural chores—during harvest, for example—though they would never call monks to work in the fields. Since childhood, girls have been socialized to help their families and they may genuinely derive pleasure from doing so. Moreover, some nuns remain materially dependent on their families and therefore feel obligated to help in their households in return for material support. To refuse to help their families, even after they become nuns, could be viewed as arrogant and ungrateful behavior. For others, the connection to their natal household is much more psychological, ranging from affection to emotional dependency.

While monks struggle to get new recruits and may start to lose material support in an era of new economic priorities, nuns are learning to manage their new status as fields of merit for the villagers and as recipients of foreign donations. As the status of nuns improves, parents are likely to become more comfortable with the idea of their daughters becoming nuns; as more young women become nuns and gain access to the skills they need as religious specialists, nuns may begin to take more visible and important roles in the religious life of their communities, in a positive self-perpetuating cycle.

24. Karma Lekshe Tsomo, "Buddhist Nuns: New Roles and Possibilities," in *Exile as Challenge: The Tibetan Diaspora*, ed. Dagmar Bernstorff and Hubertus von Welck (Delhi: Orient Longman, 2003), 342–66.

Until recently, it was rare for girls to pursue higher education or travel far distances to become nuns and study the Dharma. Gradually, however, as opportunities for religious education for women open up, more and more religiously inspired women have begun to broaden their horizons. For example, after studying for a year at Changchub Chöling Monastery in Zangla, a young nun from Zangskar traveled to south India to further her studies at Jangchub Choeling Monastery in Mundgod, where she has become highly skilled in philosophical debate. In recent years, as perceptions of women's intellectual capabilities improved, Buddhist studies programs have gradually been established at monasteries in India and Nepal, and a large number of nuns from the Himalayan region have enrolled.[25] Some of these monasteries, in accordance with the wishes of H. H. Dalai Lama, welcome lay girls who wish to study Buddhism without necessarily becoming nuns, though few girls so far have taken advantage of the opportunity. Nuns and laywomen who meet the requirements may also enroll at the Institute of Buddhist Studies in Leh and the Central Institute of Higher Tibetan Studies in Sarnath. A large number of nuns who do not meet the requirements are now staying near the Institute in Sarnath and studying privately. One nun, from Bhutan Sonam Wangmo (Tenzin Dadon), is currently pursuing a Ph.D. in Gender and Religion at the University of Malaya. Positive changes in social attitudes toward nuns and increased educational opportunities for women in Buddhist studies have occurred in a remarkably short time. These changes have greatly improved self-perceptions among Himalayan laywomen and nuns and are very encouraging to young girls, inspiring some to act more independently in seeking religious and secular education.

One factor that may discourage a monastic vocation for girls is the glaring differences in the social status and material fortunes of nuns and monks. Despite Buddhist egalitarian principles, many monks, nuns, and laypeople in Tibetan and Himalayan societies believe that a male body is superior to a female body. There is no consensus on the matter, however. Some argue that, although a woman's body is not inherently inferior, it is preferable to be reborn as a man, because women have more sufferings and more work to do. Some believe that a woman must be reborn as a male before she can attain final awakening, while others believe that if a woman is a good practitioner, she can attain awakening in female form. In the sutrayana stream of Mahayana philosophy, a practitioner may pursue the bodhisattva path in either a male or a female body, but must achieve final awakening in a male body. In the *tantrayna* stream of Mahayana, a practitioner may achieve final awakening "in this very body, in this very life," clearly indicating that a woman can become a Buddha in a female body. The tantrayana stream of Mahayana, known as Vajrayana, is widespread in Tibetan cultural areas, and Buddhas such as Vajrayogini are the focus of visualization for male and female practitioners alike. Still, there are

25. Notable among these are Namdroling in Bylakuppe, Jangchub Chöling in Mundgod; Khachö Ghakhyil Ling in Kathmandu, and Dolma Ling, Dongyu Gatsal Ling, Gaden Chöling, and Jamyang Chöling in and near Dharamsala. A number of monasteries for women in Kinnaur, Ladakh, Spiti, and Zangskar also offer study programs.

shrine rooms in the monasteries that women cannot enter, particularly shrines housing the village protectors and tantric deities. Even though it is *au courant* to declare that boys and girls are equal, especially to outsiders and researchers, behavior discordant with this rhetoric reveals that gender prejudices persist at subtle and not-so-subtle levels. Young children still hear people make disparaging remarks about women and may hear women make prayers of aspiration to be reborn as a man. Even if they are not aware of the soteriological implications of gender, their monastic aspirations may be influenced by discriminatory social attitudes. Again, the disconnect between Buddhist compassion and gender bias is glaring and young girls are certainly not blind to it.

CHANGES, CHOICES, AND CHALLENGES

New opportunities are opening up for children who join monasteries in Himalayan societies, especially girls. Living conditions in the monasteries today are much improved, often better than at home. Young monks and nuns learn rituals, deportment, and Buddhist teachings both from senior monastics and from respected leading figures in the tradition, such as H. H. Dalai Lama and others, who visit their homelands to give teachings and conduct highly valued tantric empowerments and ceremonies. When these young monks and nuns travel outside their villages to Dharamsala, Bodhgaya, and other Buddhist sacred sites, they learn more about how to comport themselves, how to behave as a monk or nun, and what is expected of them as monastics. Monks who are talented or wish to study further are sent to the great monasteries of south India. Many young nuns, even as young as eleven, have also left their homelands to seek education in nunneries in Dharmasala, south India, or Nepal. Any discussion of monastic life in the Himalayas must take into consideration the historical, environmental, sociological, and economic circumstances of the region, especially the changes that are occurring so rapidly as to defy prediction.

The choice for young people these days is not only between the monastic pursuit and business success, but also between a poor local monastery and a well-endowed monastery in Kathmandu, Dharmasala, or Karnataka. Since the larger, financially successful monasteries are generally supported by foreign donors, admission may provide access to more in-depth Buddhist learning, advanced ritual skills, English classes, martial arts training, and even, eventually, foreign travel. The question is whether these places also support sincere Buddhist practice and a conducive environment for higher spiritual attainments. Monastics today must weigh the benefits of staying in Zangskar, despite the harsh living conditions, and fighting for better education there, or of leaving to join a well-endowed nunnery elsewhere where the educational infrastructure is already in place. Most are aware that well-traveled centers of Buddhist culture such as Dharamsala and Kathmandu are also full of distractions and temptations that may divert young monastics from the Dharma path to the attachments of the material world. Television, videos, music, the internet, and the lure of foreign travel can easily cause young monks and nuns to stray from sincere monastic practice and from the essence of the Dharma. As is illustrated in the film *The Cup*,[26] many young monks are more intrigued by soccer than by meditation. No one can deny that it is easier to surf the internet than to develop compassion and realize the selflessness of mind and phenomena. H. H. Dalai Lama now advises young monks to wait until they are a bit older before taking the novice precepts, to ensure that they are aware of the commitment they are making. He has also encouraged the introduction of secular subjects in addition to Buddhist studies, to prepare young monastics for life in the modern world. In the Tibetan Buddhist tradition, monastic ordination is viewed as a lifelong pursuit and the community cannot but feel disappointed when monks and nuns drop out. Still, it is always possible to return the precepts and revert to lay life, in which case children will have received a basic education and will be better prepared to make a living.

What will it take to maintain the monastic system and ensure its future development in the Himalayas, as well as ensure Buddhism's survival? Perhaps the most crucial element will be recruiting children to enter monastic life. Traditionally, young children gravitated to the monasteries, encouraged by their parents, relations, and social approval. What will attract more young people to monastic life in a time of dizzying distractions? Attracting them to the monasteries is not enough; it is essential to offer good teachers, training, encouragement, and a nurturing environment that are genuine reflections of Buddhist ideals. Young people everywhere are keenly attuned to hypocrisy, so the quality of training that children receive in the monasteries must accord with the liturgies they are asked to recite. Those who live a disciplined monastic life are motivated to keep traditions alive in order to provide an environment conducive to the study and practice of a cherished Buddhist heritage. They deserve appreciation for their contributions as models for future generations. Without monastics, there will be no one to perform the rituals that are necessary for prosperity and well-being, in both this life and the next.

Another change in the offing is an expansion of the monastic job description. H. H. Dalai Lama has publicly said that the time for monks and nuns to just sit and pray is over; monastics also need to train as teachers, doctors, lawyers, and social workers in order to address the needs of society. Extolling the work of Catholic nuns especially, he feels that monks and nuns should take active, visible roles in working for the social good. This advice seems both reasonable and timely. If monastics are well trained and educated, their celibate lifestyle frees them from many social and family obligations and allows them more time to benefit living beings. The younger generation is unlikely to feel satisfied by a life that is limited to simply reciting texts and performing

26. Khyentse Norbu, dir., *The Cup*, Festival Media, 2000.

rituals. Children need not only teachers who give teachings occasionally in public gatherings, but great teachers who stay at the monastery—teachers who not only teach texts, but are capable of guiding and mentoring a new generation with wisdom and compassion on a daily basis. With a variety of life paths available to them, those who choose monastic life today often have high expectations. They need teachers who are not only disciplinarians and ritual masters, but models of exemplary conduct and compassionate service to society. A disturbing aspect of globalization in the Himalayan region is the trend toward the commodification of Buddhism. The allure of Himalayan culture and its spiritual riches, combined with the material affluence of Western travelers, has the potential to exacerbate consumer impulses on all sides. Traditional values of humility and simplicity are often overlooked, while displays of power, splendor, and wealth create greater disparities between humble practitioners and popular icons. The foundation of monastic life—renunciation—becomes threatened by its very popularity. Although "leaving the household life" was rarely seen as a total break with one's natal family, the traditional definition of ordination as renunciation remains an ideal, even in the breach.

A final significant change afoot is redressing gender disparities in Himalayan monasteries. As long as male monastics are valued more highly and supported more handsomely than female monastics, boys and girls attracted to monastic life will be receiving mixed signals. In theory, they learn that men and women equally can become liberated and, through tantric visualization practices, even fully enlightened. In everyday life, however, they see that even though monks enjoy many privileges, many young men are drifting away from monastic life and toward the pleasures promised through worldly pursuits. At the same time, children cannot close their eyes to the fact that nuns, even when they are neglected or rejected by the lay community, continue to strive conscientiously in their daily religious devotions, preliminary practices, and intensive retreats. All things considered, the nuns' virtuous conduct is apt to improve perceptions of women's religious potential, in ways that are inspiring to a new generation of girls and, at the same time, encourage boys to keep up with them. If Buddhism is to continue to be the central focus of Himalayan cultural life, a revitalized system of education and training for children in the monasteries—girls and boys equally—is vital.

CHAPTER 17

The Westernization of Tulkus

ELIJAH ARY

One of Tibetan Buddhism's most distinctive characteristics is the recognition of young children as the reincarnations of highly realized Tibetan Buddhist masters of the past.[1] These reincarnates are given the title "Tulku," and they come to occupy a special and exalted place in the religious hierarchy as Tibetan Buddhism's spiritual elite. Great importance is placed on their discovery, recognition, and education. They are considered to embody the qualities of spiritual realization and therefore function as the spiritual, moral, and (later on) educational guides and role models for the communities, both monastic and lay, of which they are members.

Traditionally, only children from Tibetan cultural areas (Tibet, Mongolia, and Bhutan) were recognized as Tulkus.[2] Generally recognized at a young age, Tulkus are rapidly removed from their families and homes and sent to live and study in monasteries with the understanding that they will eventually take up the religious and administrative responsibilities of their predecessors' spiritual communities. In some cases, this momentous responsibility can come at a young age, as was the case with the present Dalai Lama, who fully assumed his religious and political functions at the age of fifteen.[3]

Following the abortive 1959 Tibetan uprising, the Chinese Cultural Revolution in the mid-1960s and early 1970s, and the subsequent crackdown on Tibetan religion and culture, a large number of Tibetans fled to India and Nepal. This mass exodus forced Tibetans to search for their reincarnated masters outside

1. The following discussion draws on both modern scholarship and personal accounts from within the Tulku tradition.

2. For example, the grandson of the Tümed Mongol ruler Altan Khan was recognized as the reincarnation of the third Dalai Lama c. 1602. He is now regarded as the only non-Tibetan to have been officially recognized as one of the Dalai Lamas.

3. Alexander Norman, "The Fourteenth Dalai Lama," in *The Dalai Lamas: A Visual History*, ed. Martin Brauen (Chicago: Serindia Publications, 2005), 164.

of Tibet. Children from Tibetan communities in both India and Nepal began to be recognized as Tulkus too. By the late-1960s a number of important Tibetan Buddhist masters had traveled to Europe and North America and begun teaching Western audiences. About a decade later, and for the first time in the institution's history, young Western boys were recognized as reincarnations.

This chapter looks briefly at the concept of reincarnation, at the history of the Tulku institution, and in particular at its development to include children who were born to Western parents (or at least one Western parent). It will explore how some Western Tulkus themselves see their roles within both the Tibetan Buddhist tradition and society in general. Particular attention will be paid to their education and their decision to not necessarily follow the path that tradition would dictate they take. Two important, and related, questions are: What are the implications of being recognized as the reincarnation of a revered Tibetan Buddhist master? And, how does this momentous event affect both the child (and the adult he[4] later becomes) and his parents?

One of the problems we are faced with when studying the Tulku institution is the fact that there is no clearly established, unequivocal theory or dogma to the Tulku phenomenon. The term "Tulku" itself carries with it the notion of an enlightened being, and the concept of recognized reincarnation is couched in the ideology of the benevolent bodhisattva come to save sentient beings from suffering in the world. But there is also the reality that some Tulkus do not quite live up to the expectations the tradition places on them. They are therefore criticized or their status is called into question. For the sake of simplicity, and in accordance with the Tibetan tradition, I take the term "Tulku" as a title given to those recognized as the reincarnations of Buddhist masters of the past. Whether or not these masters were bodhisattvas that reincarnated out of their immense compassion and desire to alleviate suffering of others, or even whether or not the reincarnations themselves live up to the tremendous expectations that are placed on them because of this ideology, are not the primary concern here. Furthermore, a Tulku's activity pans out during his lifetime, and it is only through his actions that he can be said truly to embody the bodhisattva ideal. Therefore, theoretically, it is only by the end of his life that such an assessment might be made.

THE CONCEPT

Various terms are used to describe those who reincarnate. The most prevalent is Tulku (*sprul sku*), which is in fact more of a title than an actual descriptive term. Technically, the term "tulku" is the Tibetan equivalent of the Sanskrit *nirmāṇakāya* (literally, "body of transformations"), which references the theory of the three bodies or aspects of enlightenment (*trikāya*): the "dharma body"

4. Since the majority of Tulkus are male, I will use the masculine pronoun when referring to them generally.

(*dharmakāya*), which is the impersonal and ineffable transcendent aspect of enlightenment; the "enjoyment body" (*sambhogakāya*), which is the glorified aspect seen in devotees' visions; and the "emanation body" (*nirmāṇakāya*), which refers to a Buddha's physical form.[5] *Tulku* is, in this regard, defined as the (physical) form in which a Buddha appears to ordinary beings.

There are three (or sometimes four) types of *nirmāṇakāya*. The first is the "Artist" or "Artisan" *nirmāṇakāya*, which is a bodily manifestation of an enlightened being in the specific form of an artisan or an artist.[6] In one Buddhist story, the Buddha manifests in the form of an immensely skilled musician in order to outplay and eventually liberate a talented but haughty Gandharvan musician named Supriya.[7] The second type of bodily manifestation of an enlightened being is called a "Born" *nirmāṇakāya* (*skye ba sprul sku*) and is a physical manifestation of enlightenment that appears through the ordinary process of birth for the sake of helping other sentient beings journey toward enlightenment. Finally, "Supreme" *nirmāṇakāya* (*mchog gi sprul sku*) are those physical manifestations of a Buddha endowed with all thirty-two major and eighty minor marks of an exalted being. An example of such a being would be the Buddha Shakyamuni himself, or any of the one thousand Buddhas that either are said to have passed through or are expected to appear in the world.

Defined in this way, a Tulku is supposed to be the earthly embodiment of enlightenment made manifest by means of the enlightened being's qualities of limitless compassion and wisdom. He or she can be perceived by everyday human beings; a physical, tangible, and interactive representation of an ideal that remains for most theoretical—an ideal that is difficult, if indeed possible, to attain. But are all Tulkus embodiments of enlightened beings and therefore Buddhas themselves? Many would argue that this is not the case. There are those who carry the title but do not necessarily fulfill the criteria for enlightenment. Nonetheless, the expectation is that all reincarnations should at least strive to embody the ideals of a *nirmāṇakāya* manifestation.

While *tulku* can be, and often is, used as a title, another term, *yangsi* (*yang srid*), which literally translates as "reexistence" or "rebecoming," is more typically used in describing whose reincarnation one might be (e.g., "X is the reincarnation (*yangsi*) of Y"). The term is perhaps closer to the English "rebirth" in that it implies a return to existence (Tib. *srid pa*, Skt. *bhava*). It is not used in quite the same way as "rebirth," however. While the concept of rebirth can apply to all sentient beings, human or animal, the term *yangsi* is usually used

5. Some traditions of *Vajrayāna* Buddhism have argued for a fourth aspect, the "essential body" (*svabhavavikāya*), which is sometimes described as the indistinctness of the three other aspects of a Buddha.

6. Some render this as "the Buddha as art." According to this definition, enlightenment may manifest itself in the form of a work of art (painting, sculpture, dance, or music) and is thus an inanimate form. See Jamgön Kongtrul Lodrö Thayé, *Enthronement: The Recognition of the Reincarnate Masters of Tibet and the Himalayas* (Ithaca, NY: Snow Lion, 1997), 23.

7. *Bodhisattvāvadānakalpalatā of Kṣemendra*, no. 80 ("Subhadrāvadāna"). *Sde dge bstan 'gyur*, Ke 1b1-Khe, 329a7 [Tōh. 4155].

only for reincarnated Buddhist masters. While *tulku*—the emanation or bodily aspect of enlightenment—is a concept that can be found throughout *Mahāyāna* Buddhism, the concept of *yangsi* reflects the uniquely Tibetan understanding that spiritually accomplished masters of yore return to this world specifically for the sake of benefitting other beings. In this sense, *yangsi* is better rendered as "reincarnation."

The confusion that can result from giving the title Tulku to beings that do not necessarily embody the ideals and standards expected of fully enlightened beings (*tulkus*), even though they are considered to have been highly realized masters in their previous lives, has prompted some to distinguish between *tulku* (the manifestation of enlightenment in physical form) and *yangsi* (the recognized reincarnation of a Buddhist master). Though there are indeed some who are both *yangsi* and *tulku*, all *yangsi* are not necessarily *tulkus*. Indeed, having the mere title Tulku does not in fact ensure one is a *tulku* (i.e., *nirmāṇakāya*). Recognized reincarnations that do not necessarily carry themselves in a way that is considered becoming of an enlightened being, or who are simply not very perseverant in their studies or interested in the duties of a Tulku, are seen as examples of this status.

There is yet another understanding of what a Tulku is, connected to the *Mahāyāna* Buddhist ideology of the *bodhisattva*: the perfectly altruistic and benevolent hero who strives for the enlightenment of all sentient beings above his or her own. A *bodhisattva* is considered capable of achieving full enlightenment at the end of his or her life, but instead takes the solemn vow to return and keep returning to cyclic existence so long as all sentient beings are not yet liberated from its throes, thereby delaying his or her own enlightenment. According to this view, a Tulku's birth in the world is the direct result of the *bodhisattva*'s vow to remain in and return to cyclic existence. Indeed, upon the *bodhisattva*'s death this vow keeps him or her from entering *nirvāna* and thereby leaving *saṃsāra* forever. Instead, he or she remains in cyclic existence, taking birth again in the world out of commitment to other sentient beings. This rebirth is a Tulku.[8]

According to this theory, however, all Tulkus would have to be de facto *bodhisattvas*. If this were indeed the case, why do not all Tulkus display the characteristic traits said to be associated with such exalted beings? Though possibly some, perhaps even many Tulkus are in fact *bodhisattvas*, there still remain those who would not seem to fit this particular definition. So what *is* a Tulku? How is it that reincarnations are given the title Tulku, even though they are not necessarily Buddhas or *bodhisattvas*?

The Tibetan *Tshigs mdzod chen mo* dictionary defines Tulku as "a title given to the reincarnations (*yang srid*) of high-ranking Buddhist masters."[9] This, of course, does not mean that they are in fact *nirmāṇakāya* manifestations. According to one explanation, the expression was originally merely a verbal

8. See Reginald Ray, "The Themes of a Tulku's Life," *Vajradhatu Sun* (August 1980), 7.
9. *Bod rgya tshig mdzod chen mo*, comp. Yi-Sun Zhang (Beijing: Mi rigs dpe skrun khang, 1993), s.v. "*sprul sku*."

sign of reverence given only to the highest of reincarnations. Over time, the expression became a title applied to all *yangsi*, even though these were not necessarily enlightened beings.[10]

According to Chögyam Trungpa, there are three types of Tulku. The first is a Tulku by name rather than by fact. This category consists of "ordinary people" who, though they are not really the direct reincarnations of the master they are supposed to be, are nonetheless placed by the tradition in the position of a Tulku in order that they "fulfill particular religious, social, and political functions."[11] Such a Tulku has no real connection to his alleged predecessor, but fulfils the needs of the tradition and may, depending on his actions, come to be seen as the legitimate heir to the master whose shoes he has been chosen to fill.

The second type of Tulku is the "Blessed Tulku." These are also not the direct reincarnations of their predecessors. Rather, they are the receptacles of a saint's or a great master's spiritual energy or character (and that of his entire lineage), which is transferred to a new individual (it is unclear when this happens), who might be the master's close acquaintance or disciple. Such individuals are supposed to be spiritually more advanced than most, and it is for this reason that they are chosen as successors. Such individuals must also undergo rigorous training and education so as to live up to the expectations tradition places upon them as the successors to a prominent saint or master.[12]

Finally, there is the "Direct Tulku," which corresponds to the earlier description of the benevolent and high-level *bodhisattva* who takes birth in the world repeatedly for the sake of saving other sentient beings. Such Tulkus constitute, according to Trungpa, the highest category, since they are the direct physical manifestations, the "actual, literal reincarnation[s] of a previous realized master."[13] Direct Tulkus may be divided into multiple incarnations so as to better carry out their enlightened activity (*phrin las*) in the world. Such is said to be the case with the great nineteenth-century Rimey (*ris med*) scholar Jamgön Kongtrul ('Jam mgon kong sprul—1813–1899), of whom there are supposed to be five incarnations, each corresponding to one of five aspects of his being (body, speech, mind, quality, and action). Of those Tulkus recognized as such, each has gone on to found his own reincarnation lineage.

Though I have never encountered a classification of Tulkus such as Trungpa's either in classical Tibetan literature or in the oral tradition, there would appear to be different types of reincarnations. Certain Tulkus are considered to be above the norm and to embody the true meaning of the term. The Dalai Lamas, the Panchen Lamas, the Karmapa hierarchs, and a select number of other reincarnation lineages are traditionally considered to be the highest types

10. Private discussion with Geshe Thupten Pelgye, Sera Monastery, India, January 2010.

11. Reginald Ray, *Secret of the Vajra World: The Tantric Buddhism of Tibet* (Boston: Shambhala, 2002), 375.

12. Ray, *Secret of the Vajra World*, 375–76.

13. See Ray, *Secret of the Vajra World*, 377.

of Tulkus and are regarded as embodiments of benevolent *bodhisattvas* who have come to help all sentient beings. And for such beings, the educational process is seen as a mere formality that has no real bearing on their spiritual understanding or realization, but instead provides them with the tools necessary for carrying out their activities in this world.

In some traditional contexts, there can be a clear means by which to rank Tulkus. In Sera Monastery, for example, a Tulku's status and place within the hierarchy of the assembly depend on what type of enthronement he was given. This will, in turn, depend somewhat, though not entirely, on the importance and popularity of the Tulku's predecessor. An influential and important predecessor, and a long lineage of predecessors too, will allow for the highest type of enthronement. A "lesser" Tulku (one whose predecessor was the first in the lineage or who was not very important or popular) may have a "low" or "middling" enthronement, depending on his finances. Indeed, a wealthy candidate can be given a higher enthronement, since this type of ceremony calls for a bigger celebration, thereby increasing his status within the monastery.

For most Tulkus, however, their status within Tibetan Buddhist hierarchy will depend largely on their actions in this life. To be sure, there are Tulkus who have an exalted status from the moment of their recognition owing to their predecessor's status. However, their activities in this life will still affect how they are thought of by the larger Tibetan tradition. Thus, as Reginald Ray has aptly put it:

> The stature of a tülku will undergo changes during his life, either ascending if he is a truly remarkable and selfless person, or perhaps declining if he has not been able to fulfill the expectations put upon him. Through this means, the reputation of a line of tülkus and its associated monasteries will usually undergo some shift in each generation. Sometimes a very modest line will, through the appearance of an extraordinary incarnation, suddenly become endowed with the greatest prestige. In Tibetan Buddhism, then, there is always the "official" status of a line of tülkus or a particular incarnation, but alongside this there is the unofficial, general consensus as to who are in fact the most accomplished masters.[14]

There is, therefore, an understanding that a Tulku's status, as well as that of his lineage, may change according to his activities and conduct in this life. This is an important point, as it intimates the fact, albeit implicitly understood, that lineage and status are not in fact static, but instead can be acquired, increased, or lost through the conduct of one being. It also implies that in order for a Tulku to maintain his or her status, or even be considered the legitimate heir to his or her alleged predecessor, he or she is expected to follow the course of education and training traditional for Tulkus, and must carry him or herself in

14. Ray, *Secret of the Vajra World*, 380.

a manner that is befitting of the memory of his previous life. But therein lies the rub: although Tulkus are expected to behave in a manner that tradition considers becoming of an enlightened or at least a spiritually elevated being, as incarnate *bodhisattvas* expected to work in countless ways for the benefit of others, they are also expected to know better than most what sentient beings really need and act in ways that are most conducive to their betterment, even if doing so means stepping outside of traditional boundaries and customs. An example of this is so-called "crazy" or "deviant wisdom" (*ye shes 'chol ba*)—when wisdom no longer conforms to the conventions of regular sentient beings—believed to have been manifested by Chögyam Trungpa (1939–1987), who was known for both his unconventional teaching methods and his unmonastic personal lifestyle.[15]

A LITTLE HISTORY

According to the late-nineteenth century British explorer Lawrence Austine Waddell, the Tulku system is a purely Tibetan invention dating to the fifteenth century and was initially "simply a scheme to secure stability for the succession to the headship of [a] sect against electioneering intrigues of crafty Lamas."[16] The origins of the tradition, which Waddell claims date back to the fifteenth century and have been "purposefully obscured so as to give the appearance of antiquity," most likely started out as a "simple reincarnation theory" but must not be confused with "the orthodox Buddhist theory of rebirth as the result of *karma*."[17] In Waddell's opinion, then, the Tulku concept—the recognition of one Tibetan as the reincarnation of and successor to an earlier Tibetan (or other) religious figure—is a purely Tibetan invention with little or no grounding in Indian Buddhism, and thereby has little or no value with regard to "orthodox Buddhism."

Waddell's assessment that the Tulku tradition is a Tibetan development would appear to be true. Indeed, although a number of cases have recently been documented in Sri Lanka of children claiming to recall their previous lives as monks, they are not necessarily awarded an exalted status within the Sri Lankan Buddhist community. To my knowledge, and in light of the lack of historical evidence to the contrary, no other Buddhist tradition or culture participates in the practice of enthroning young children as the reincarnations of their dead masters.[18]

15. See Fabrice Midal, *Chögyam Trungpa: His Life and Vision* (Boston: Shambhala, 2004).

16. L. A. Waddell, *Buddhism of Tibet or Lamaism, With Its Mystic Cults, Symbolism and Mythology and in Its Relation to Indian Buddhism* (London: W. H. Allen and Co., 1895), 229.

17. Waddell, *Buddhism of Tibet or Lamaism*, 229.

18. See E. Haraldsson and Gananath Obeyesekere, "Children Who Speak of Memories of a Previous Life as a Buddhist Monk: Three New Cases," in *Approaching the Dhamma: Buddhist Texts and Practices in South and Southeast Asia*, ed. Anne M. Blackburn and Jeffrey Samuels (Seattle: BPE Pariyatti Editions, 2003), 223–62.

Waddell's secondary claim, that the tradition has no orthodox Buddhist underpinnings (which, because of his lack of clarification, I take to refer to early Buddhist thought and practice), is not necessarily accurate, however. The theory of reincarnation, as Haraldsson and Obeyesekere have noted, is taken for granted in all Buddhist traditions, and there exists considerable literature on the theoretical aspects of reincarnation in ancient Pāli texts.[19] Furthermore and perhaps more important, Tibetans themselves typically understand the Tulku tradition to be based largely on early Buddhist theories of rebirth, though there are some slight differences.

Like his philosophical and spiritual predecessors, the Buddha maintained that birth and death recur in successive cycles for beings afflicted by ignorance about the true nature of the world. Contrary to his Indian predecessors, however, he denied the existence of an eternal and unalterable Self (*ātman*) grounding a world of transitory entities. Instead, he proclaimed the idea of "no-self" (*anātman*), namely, that everything that constitutes the empirical universe, including human beings, is the result of an uninterrupted, ever-fluctuating process of creation, decay, and destruction (birth, ageing, and extinction) according to the principle of Dependent Co-origination (*pratītyasamutpāda*): "If this exists, then that comes to be." Everything in the universe, and indeed the universe itself, is in flux. Everything perishes and is created anew in every instant; nothing remains the same from one moment to the next, from a single, tiny microbe to an entire galaxy.

But what, then, is person or personality, and what is it that reincarnates? Made up of five basic constitutive elements (*skandha*), themselves always in flux, a person is in fact a composite entity, the manifestation of a complex and continuous succession of psychosomatic moments propelled along a temporal continuum by the force of past actions (*karma*). As such, we are never the same from one moment to the next. We are constantly changing, being reborn, in some sense. We are therefore not the projection of a permanent self that transmigrates from one life to the next or even one body to another. In a way, a seemingly paradoxical and self-contradictory Buddhist teaching would be that there is nothing that transmigrates and yet there is rebirth.

The often-used analogy of a flame used to light candles may be helpful here. When a candle is lit with the fire from another candle, the second fire is the result of the first one. Although the second fire could not exist without the first having created it, in no way are the two identical, and in no way are they independent of one another. Similarly, in the continuum of consciousnesses, one instant informs and gives birth to the next through *karma* (moral choices and the actions consequent upon them). It is *karma* that coordinates the continuous flow of life-instances, becoming the life process itself. Each instant within the continuum has its own set of causal factors that come together to create it, and each one of these factors is itself the product of its

19. Haraldsson and Obeyesekere, "Children Who Speak of Memories of a Previous Life as a Buddhist Monk," 260.

own causal factors, and so on *ad infinitum*. In other words, we are not temporary physical projections of some universal Soul, as is the case according to most Hindu Advaita traditions, for example, but rather constant permutations of conditioned episodes in a continuum propelled by *karma*. Similar to rapid flashes that, when spaced close together, appear as a steady beam of light, we too appear to be constant and continuing entities. However, upon closer analysis, we are in fact transitory; coming into being and then dying out every instant. Everything around us is constantly changing, as are we, and birth and death thereby become nothing more than "dramatic interruptions or exceptional innovations in the ongoing life process."[20]

Technically, then, there is no single entity, let alone a conglomeration of entities, that passes across from one life form to the next. Yet somehow the continuity among phenomena carries forth. All of the constitutive elements of a person's life are considered to be present from the moment of conception, at least in a state of potentiality. Just like a sprout, whose growth is an effect of the seed meeting with particular conditions, potentially preexists in the seed itself and contains the sum of all the effects of its antecedent causal elements. The Tibetan understanding of reincarnation is in part based on this notion that we transmigrate from one life to the next, death being nothing more than a tangible interruption in a continuously recurring process. However, whereas regular beings are propelled along the continuum by the force of *karma*, the process is understood to be somewhat different for Tulkus.

A Tulku is in some ways very much like other beings, in making the seemingly interminable journey from life to life that characterizes cyclic existence. Yet at the same time the process remains theoretically different for Tulkus. Ordinary sentient beings are driven from one thing to the next throughout their lives primarily by their hopes and fears—mainly of satisfaction and well-being and of dissatisfaction and suffering, respectively. When they die, this process, which has been in operation "since beginning-less time," as the Tibetan expression goes, leads them to take rebirth instinctively. Confused, blind to the workings of their *karma*, and driven by their fears, passions, and emotions, they take rebirth in yet another state of confusion. Subjected to the workings of their karmic patterns and conditioning, they are literally thrown from one life to the next.

When a Tulku reincarnates, however, the process is seen instead as one of reincarnation from an enlightened point of view. A Tulku is said to be free from the karmic chains that bind one in *saṃsāra* and is considered to have thrown off the limitations of the ego. He or she does not, therefore, take rebirth out of confusion or propelled by his or her passion, aggression, or ignorance. Rather, the primary motive behind the process is understood to be the benefit of other sentient beings. Understanding the processes of rebirth and being free from the chains of karmic patterns, combined with a deep heartfelt sense of compassion for the very sentient beings that are thrown about from

20. J. Bruce Long. "Reincarnation," in *The Encyclopedia of Religion*, ed. Mircea Eliade (New York: Macmillan, 1986), 12: 267.

one life to the next like rag dolls in a dryer, he or she reincarnates voluntarily, taking on a particular physical manifestation.[21] This is conveyed in the very term "*tulku*," which, when broken down, carries a sense of intentionality to the process of manifesting. The Tibetan *sku* is the honorific form of "body." According to Reginald Ray:

> *Sku* in Tibetan is an honorific term for form or body. It means not an ordinary form, but rather a form of *truth* as opposed to a form of confusion. *Sku* is thus used to refer to something that is without neurosis, something that expresses things as they are, the dharma, clearly and directly.[22]

The term would therefore imply that the Tulku's physical form is not that of an ordinary being, but rather one in which are manifest wisdom and clarity as opposed to ignorance and confusion, and it is an embodiment of Truth as opposed to what is illusory and therefore flawed. I myself have never encountered such a meaning to the term *sku*, which is most often simply explained as "aspect" (as in the different aspects of enlightenment) or "body," both translating the Sanskrit term *kāya*.

The term *sprul pa* is a nominalized form of the transitive verb *sprul ba* (to manifest or produce) and therefore often translated as "manifestation." As opposed to the intransitive *'phrul ba*, which is better rendered as "to appear" or "manifest" unintentionally, as if by magic, *sprul ba* carries a clear sense of intentionality. The idea behind this is that a person who has freed him or herself from the fetters of karmic rebirth based on confusion and ignorance, faced with the suffering of sentient beings in the world, takes the decision to appear physically in the world so as to help alleviate suffering by whatever means necessary. Motivated thus by an altruistic sentiment, the person chooses a form (*sku*) that will be conducive to his or her task. For instance, if he or she chooses a physical form that is naturally unappealing, then the appearance may act as a barrier toward the goal of helping others. If, however, the chosen physical form is one that is appealing, then beings will naturally be attracted to the person and may even be more easily accepting of help.

A *bodhisattva*'s enlightened activities are not limited by worldly boundaries such as culture and race. Although a *bodhisattva* does incarnate in a specific place at a specific time and with a specific physical form chosen especially so as to be able to accomplish his or her goals of benefitting others, he or she is expected to work for the benefit of *all* sentient beings, not exclusively those within a particular cultural context or racial group. A Tulku's responsibility is toward everyone, not just a select few.

Another key to the development of the Tulku system is the notion that the Buddha Śākyamuni himself incarnated in this world repeatedly and intentionally for the benefit of other sentient beings, a tradition that, as Reginald

21. Ray, "The Themes of a Tulku's Life." 7.
22. Ray, "The Themes of a Tulku's Life," 7.

Ray has pointed out, is represented in the Pāli canon itself. According to such accounts, the Buddha often remembered and discussed persons, places, and even events from his past lives.[23] As will be discussed shortly, in the Tibetan Tulku tradition not only are reincarnates considered to take birth over and over for the sake of benefitting other beings trapped in cyclic existence, they too can sometimes remember key moments, places, and/or persons from their previous lives.[24] This notion that the reincarnation happens intentionally is an important one, since it gives the whole system its primary focus: the well-being of others.

Going back to Waddell's earlier comments, then, although the Tulku tradition is indeed an expression of Buddhism found almost exclusively in Tibet, it is nonetheless considered to be rooted in early Indian Buddhism. Therefore we cannot discount its important role in the history and development of Tibetan Buddhism, or even of Buddhism in general, particularly on the grounds that it is not an expression of "orthodox" Buddhism, if there even is such a thing.

Waddell's rather exaggerated dismissal of the whole Tulku system as little more than a cunning ruse to avoid political intrigue does raise the important issue of the origins and purposes of the recognition of Tulkus. Indeed, we must ask when did the Tulku tradition begin and why? What purposes might it have served, and what functions does it continue to serve? And what place and function do Western reincarnates have within this tradition?

Despite Waddell's certainty that the tradition dates back only to the fifteenth century, the origins of the Tulku tradition are in fact rather difficult to establish. Traditional Tibetan accounts maintain that the system in fact began with the second hierarch of the Karma branch of the Kagyu (*bKa' brgyud*) school of Tibetan Buddhism, Karma Pakṣī (1206–1283), who recognized himself as the reincarnation of the previous hierarch, Karmapa Dusum Khyenpa (Dus gsum mkhyen pa—1110–1193). Though Karma Pakṣī is the traditionally accepted starting point of the Tulku system, there appears to be evidence that an earlier figure, the Tantric master Chökyi Gyalpo (Chos kyi rgyal po—1069–1144), already considered himself to be the reincarnation of the great Kadampa (bKa' gdams pa) master Nagtso Lotsawa Tsultrim Gyalwa (Nag tsho lo tsā ba Tshul khrims rgyal ba—1011–1068), making him the earliest figure to be considered (or consider himself) a reincarnation.[25] Nonetheless, Karma Pakṣī's self-identification as the successor to the previous Karmapa hierarch would seem to be the earliest evidence of succession to religious and political power through reincarnation.

23. Ray, *The Secret of the Vajra World*, 363. See also P. D. Premasiri, "The Theravada Buddhist Doctrine of Survival After Death," in *Concepts of Transmigration: Perspectives on Reincarnation*, ed. S. J. Kaplan (New York: Edwin Mellen Press, 1996), 133–88.

24. The alleged recollection of past lives by children has been the subject of research by scholars such as Ian Stevenson, Antonia Mills, Jürgen Keil, Erlendur Haraldsson, and Gananath Obeyesekere.

25. Leonard van der Kuijp. "The Dalai Lamas and the Origins of Reincarnate Lamas," in *The Dalai Lamas: A Visual History*, ed. Martin Brauen (Chicago: Serindia Publications, 2005), 28–29.

Western scholars of Tibetan Studies have often held a similar, yet somewhat more moderate version of the views vehemently expressed by Waddell, namely that the tradition of recognizing the reincarnations of the heads of particular schools and lineages emerged out of the desire to keep the wealth and power accrued by the previous religious elite centralized within the lineages. Naming the child of a particular family as the Tulku and therefore heir of an influential and elevated religious figure allowed for that figure's followers and lineage to acquire the support (financial and/or political) of the family in question. It brought them into the fold, so to speak, strengthening alliances in some cases and creating them in others. Other succession practices, such as father to son or uncle to nephew, were not as effective in this respect. Thus, succession through reincarnation was a powerful tool for securing the fidelity and political allegiances of influential families. This viewpoint can be observed in the recognition of the grandson of the Tümed Mongol ruler Altan Khan (1507–1582) as the reincarnation of and therefore successor to the third Dalai Lama, circa 1602. Although this recognition could most likely not have taken place without the previous Dalai Lama's efforts to establish an alliance with the Mongol ruler, the ties between the Gelugpa tradition and the Mongol court were reinforced largely as a result of this recognition. The results of such an alliance were felt when the fifth Dalai Lama Ngawang Lobsang Gyatso (Ngag dbang blo bzang rgya mtsho—1617–1682) called upon Mongol forces to help support him in his attempt to claim Tibetan leadership in the mid-seventeenth century. Whatever the origins, the Tulku tradition has largely come to supplant others over the centuries since its inception as the preferred method of succession in all four major schools of Tibetan Buddhism.[26]

Despite the Tulku system's apparently purely politico-mercantile origins and function, Tibetan Buddhist tradition maintains that it above all serves a very important spiritual agenda that cannot be neglected. The traditional logic behind the phenomenon is putatively based on the ideals of altruism and compassion, as we have already discussed, rather than on political maneuvering or financial concerns. And according to some, the political and economic agendas were in fact grafted on to the tradition of recognizing reincarnations, not the other way around. Furthermore, such blatantly worldly concerns fail to take into account some important recent developments within the tradition, such as the recognition of so-called "lesser" incarnations and the recognition of reincarnations from European and North American backgrounds.[27]

26. For the Sakya (*Sa skya*) tradition, for example, succession was initially from father to son. Later on, with the scholar and celibate monk Sakya Paṇḍita (1182–1251), an uncleto-nephew scheme was implemented instead. In recent times the tradition has reverted to the father–son model of succession.

27. Some Tulkus are seen as being hierarchically superior to others. Often, the longer the lineage, the more important (and influential) the reincarnation. Furthermore, not all defunct masters will be searched for after their passing; this right is reserved for the more influential and renowned figures of Tibetan Buddhism. This does not mean that the masters not being searched for do not reincarnate. When they do, however, it can come as a surprise (albeit a welcome one) for the monastic communities from which they hailed.

DEVELOPMENTS IN THE INSTITUTION

With the increased spread of Tibetan Buddhism to Europe and North America in the late 1960s and early 1970s, the reincarnations of prominent (and sometimes less prominent) masters began to be recognized there too. Some of these Tulkus were either of Tibetan or mixed Tibetan and Western parentage, as is the case with the sons of the late Tibetan Buddhist teacher Chogyam Trungpa (1939–1987), or else were born to Tibetan and/or Mongolian parents who had settled in the United States, as is the case with Telo Tulku (Erdne Obadykow). In the late 1970s, however, a new development took place, and children born to Western parents also became recognized as the reincarnations of renowned Tibetan masters.

Initially Tibetans did not necessarily accept that these young Western boys were the reincarnations of their previous masters. Although some Tibetans were open to this new development in the tradition, many seemed to resist the idea that a Tibetan master would choose to be succeeded by a Westerner. They were wary that their recognition was perhaps due to the insistence of Western Buddhist practitioners who were overenthusiastic about their newfound beliefs. A number of Tibetans felt that the parents were trying to pass their children off as reincarnations in hopes of acquiring prestige. For most Western families whose sons were recognized as Tulkus, however, nothing could have been further from the truth.

The Tibetans' reaction to Western Tulkus underscores their perspective on reincarnation and the prestige of having a son recognized as a Tulku. To have a son recognized as a renowned master's reincarnation is an honor. It takes vast amounts of positive *karma* to "produce" a Tulku, and giving birth to such a being implies that one's own *karma* is particularly good and worthy of respect. Furthermore, there is the notion that an enlightened master chooses to reincarnate to particular parents, so that he, as a highly realized being, judged them to be morally worthy of his reembodiment. Also, giving birth to a Tulku can, in some circumstances, entail a heightened political status, as was the case with the parents of the Dalai Lamas, who automatically became members of the Tibetan government. Being a Tulku's parents can therefore carry with it great power and prestige. But with great power and prestige comes great responsibility, and this was an aspect that was sadly misunderstood by the parents of Western Tulkus.

By the mid-1980s, only a small handful of Western children had been officially recognized as Tulkus, but over the years, and with the increased exposure of Tibetan Buddhism to Western cultures (or vice-versa), their number has grown. Today Lama Osel, the Spanish reincarnation of the founder of the Foundation for the Preservation of the Mahayana Tradition, Lama Yeshe, is well-known to Western media despite his attempts to avoid the spotlight; he is a hot chat topic on internet Buddhist discussion forums, as are more disputed figures such as Steven Segal and Alyce Louise Zeoli (Jetsunma Ahkon Lhamo). Indeed, the recognition of these two latter figures by Penor Rinpoche has sparked some unease and debate within Tibetan Buddhist communities in India, Europe, and North America, as to whether or not they should be considered authentic Tulkus.[28] This argument raises important questions as to how and by whom Tulkus (Western or not) are, should, and can be recognized. By what processes are they discovered, and who has the authority to recognize them?

The recognition of a Tulku has, for the most part, remained an internal affair to each of the four schools of Tibetan Buddhism, though there is little if any divergence as to the methods by which a Tulku is recognized and confirmed. Masters from each school who feel they have found a reincarnation may request their own tradition's supreme hierarchs to confirm their suspicions.[29] Confirmation is not always given, and even in some cases where it is, such selections can sometimes lead to criticism or even dissention within the school (as in the case where different lineage masters recognize two different candidates as the successor to the sixteenth Karmapa hierarch).[30] In such cases, the request may be made that the Dalai Lama himself intercede in order to confirm one of the candidates above the other. In other cases, the candidate not chosen as the successor can also be recognized as a Tulku, though of another Tibetan Buddhist master.[31]

The recognition/confirmation process may differ with each candidate, but it is nonetheless possible to draw a few main trends. In cases where the deceased master was a highly revered and renowned religious figure, an official party will often be sent out in search of his reincarnation some time after his decease. Instructions are sometimes left behind by the teacher prior to his death as to where and when his followers should look, and inquire as discreetly as possible as to whether there are any children that show signs that are out of the ordinary. These children may then be individually met with, the names of the ones who display certain qualities (unusual generosity, compassion, or insight, or even a strong connection to religion or to a person in the search party), and a divination may be requested of an oracle.

In cases where no clear instructions have been given by the deceased master, other omens might be observed. Such was the case with the thirteenth Dalai

28. See "Statement by H. H. Penor Rinpoche Regarding the Recognition of Steven Seagal as a Reincarnation of the Treasure Revealer Chungdrag Dorje of Palyul Monastery" (http://palyul.org/docs/statement.html).

29. In some rare cases, a master from a different tradition may be called upon to recognize or confirm reincarnations. According to Jigdrel Dagchen Sakya Rinpoche (Jigs bral bdag chen sa skya Rin po che—b. 1929), he was asked at one time by the representatives of a Gelugpa monastery in eastern Tibet to locate and recognize the reincarnation of their defunct abbot. See Daniel Bärlocher, *Testimonies of Tibetan Tulkus: A Research Among Reincarnate Buddhist Masters in Exile* (Zürich: Tibet-Institut, 1982).

30. For a more detailed discussion of the "Karmapa controversy, *The Dance of 17 Lives* (London: Bloomsbury, 2004), and Lea Terhune, *Karmapa: The Politics of Reincarnation* (Boston: Wisdom Publications, 2004).

31. This is said to have been the case with the second candidate for the position of fifth Dalai Lama, who was later recognized as the reincarnation of the renowned scholar Panchen Sonam Dragpa (PaN chen bSod nams grags pa—1478–1554).

Lama, after whose passing certain signs were observed (the expired Lama's head is said to have turned toward the East after a few days, and an odd fungus developed on the northeastern pillar near his body) that were taken to signify that the next Dalai Lama would be reborn in eastern Tibet. Monks forming the initial search party are said to have also gone to Lake Lhamo Latso (*lha mo bla mtsho*), in which it is said one can see the future. According to the current Dalai Lama's own account, the Lama who had gone to look into the lake saw a monastery with roofs of jade and gold, a small house with a turquoise roof, and the letters *A*, *Ka*, and *Ma*.[32] All of these were taken as indications of where to find the defunct Dalai Lama's successor. But such signs are not reserved only for the highest reincarnations, and they are in fact looked for following the deaths of most masters.[33]

In some rare cases, masters may also leave details as to where to find their reincarnation in a letter or some other sort of instruction that is to be opened or revealed at a particular moment following the master's passing. This is said to have been the case with the sixteenth Karmapa hierarch, Rangjung Rigpay Dorje (Rang 'byung rig pa'i rdo rje—1924–1981), who allegedly left a letter providing key details concerning his future incarnation.[34] Tulkus do not necessarily leave behind indications as to their future rebirths. Sometimes, a potential candidate may be located even though no details have been left behind. In these cases, the candidate's identity is either confirmed or rejected by the head of a particular tradition and, especially in recent times, by the Dalai Lama himself.

A Tulku's confirmation as the legitimate successor to a particular master is sometimes dependant upon a "test" whereby the candidate is presented with various objects among which are those of his alleged predecessor. The candidate must recognize and "reclaim" the objects by picking them out from among other similar objects, providing, of course, that these are still readily available. Should the candidate pick up the wrong object, then his authenticity as the successor is called into question. The Current Dalai Lama is said to have chosen the wrong walking stick at first but then to have put it back and taken the right one. Upon reflection, the monks carrying out the testing realized that the first walking stick actually had originally belonged to the previous Dalai Lama but that he had given it away and favored the other. The fact that the young Dalai Lama chose this walking stick but then put it back

32. Dalai Lama Tenzin Gyatso. *My Land and My People: The Official Autobiography of His Holiness the Dalai Lama of Tibet* (New York: Grand Central Publishing, 1997), 8–10.

33. I was told a similar story about the founder of the Foundation for the Preservation of the Mahayana Tradition, Lama Yeshe (1935–1984), whose reincarnation was apparently found thanks in part to the appearance of signs in the form of unconventional cloud formations directly above his cremation site. I was told by Lama Yeshe's brother, Geshe Zopa, that these signs had in fact been key to locating his future reincarnation.

34. The authenticity of this letter is at the very heart of tensions between the two rival groups supporting different candidates as the seventeenth Karmapa. See Mick Brown, *The Dance of 17 Lives*.

is seen as his having remembered this and is therefore an even stronger confirmation of his identity, proving beyond any doubt that he was indeed the authentic reincarnation of the thirteenth Dalai Lama.[35] Because of the Tibetan migration to India following the events of 1959 and the loss of personal property that ensued, the aforementioned testing cannot always be carried out. In such cases, confirmation will depend largely on the word of authorities such as the Dalai Lama and the State oracle, or even the heads of the four schools of Tibetan Buddhism.

Other signs that may indicate a child's status as a reincarnation are those that are said to have occurred just prior to or at the time of the child's birth. Tibetan Buddhist biographies abound with accounts of miraculous events surrounding the birth of their respective heroes and, as Reginald Ray remarks, "virtually any Tibetan who has close contact with the tulku tradition typically has a wealth of memories and personal experiences of such things."[36] Miraculous dreams the parents had at the time of the child's conception are often reported, as are those that occur at the moment of birth. Such signs are not exclusive to the birth of Tulkus. Indeed, they surround the life stories of nearly all revered Tibetan Buddhist masters. But at the same time, many of these stories are tropes typically found in biographical rhetoric to support claims of their hero's grandeur. In this, they are similar to Tulkus in that these stories help authenticate them as members of the spiritual elite.[37]

Signs that a reincarnation is born into a family can also include the loss of riches and other such calamities, as was the case with the current Dalai Lama, whose family is said to have suffered the loss of nearly all of their livestock just prior to his birth. Loss, death, or even folly occurring in families after the rebirth of a major incarnation are sometimes explained through the notion that the birth of a Tulku is a most wonderful event, one that requires a large amount of previously accumulated good *karm*a. With the birth to the Tulku, that *karma* is used up all at once and the result is a sudden imbalance in the positive–negative *karma* ratio. Since much of one's good *karma* has been depleted, the *karma* accrued from past negative acts suddenly comes to fruition.[38]

35. Dalai Lama Tenzin Gyatso, *My Land and My People*, 10.

36. Ray, "The Themes of a Tulku's Life," 38.

37. Though he is not considered a Tulku per se, prior to the birth of the founder of the Gelugpa (*dge lugs pa*) school of Tibetan Buddhism, Tsongkhapa Lobsang Dragpa (Tsong kha pa Blo bzang grags pa—1357–1419), his parents are said to have had miraculous dreams in which divine beings appeared and conferred blessings upon them, even one in which Tsongkhapa personally chose his future mother in consultation with a goddess. See rTogs ldan 'Jam dpal rgya mtsho, *Rje btsun tsong kha pa'i rnam thar chen mo'i zur 'debs rnam thar legs bshad kun 'dus*, in *The Collected Works (gsun 'bum) of Rje Tsoṅ-Kha-Pa Blo-bzao-grags-p. Reproduced from an Example of the Old Bkra-śis-lhun-po Redaction from the Library of Klu-'khyil Monastery of Ladakh*, ed. Ngawang Gelek Demo (New Delhi: Ngawang Gelek Demo, 1979), 1: 144–66.

38. I have heard this mentioned often, but have yet to find a written source stating it clearly.

Specific comportment, attitudes, and behavioral traits can also be taken to lend authenticity to a candidate's status as a particular reincarnation. One often hears of young children later recognized as Tulkus being particularly friendly toward specific teachers or monks visiting them, as was the case with the current Dalai Lama, who is said to have wanted to sit on the lap of Keutsang Rinpoche, who led the search party for the fourteenth Dalai Lama.[39] This behavior is attributed to the Tulku's memory of the person in question and is seen as a clear sign of the reincarnation's authenticity.

In some cases, physical characteristics can also be considered signs of a Tulku's authenticity. For Tibetan Buddhists, one's physical appearance, particularly that of Tulkus, not only is the result of the combinations of genes and features found within one's family, but also is directly, and even primarily dependent upon the karmic results of one's past life and lives, and upon the decision to appear in a specific way. If a person is physically attractive, his or her appearance it is a result not only of biology, but primarily of his or her good *karma* (due to having practiced patience in a previous life, for example). For a Tulku, certain physical characteristics are considered to be directly linked to the actions, comportment, and physical appearance of his or her predecessor. This is not to say that a Tulku can be recognized solely on the fact that he is similar in appearance to a defunct master. However, physical markings such as a birthmark on a specific part of the body or resemblance to a predecessor can be considered signs of the authenticity of the reincarnation.[40] This most interesting notion that one can actually choose one's biological form, and even that one may influence one's appearance even prior to birth, contrasts rather sharply with the views espoused by modern life sciences that one's appearance depends primarily on particular gene combinations and the workings of dominant genes found within one's family.

Tibetans do not always seek out the reincarnations of their defunct religious figures; some are simply left to the annals of memory. This is not to say that they do not reincarnate at all—only that the search for their successors is not deemed of great importance, or else there is no one to carry out such a time-consuming and financially onerous task. Sometimes the master in question was not particularly well-known or influential, or did not have many disciples. A child may prove to be the reincarnation of a figure that was not in fact being searched for. The conjuncture of particular signs and events surrounding his birth, the connections his family had or has with particular masters, and his behavior and actions can all help signal that a child is not exactly ordinary. Parents who feel their child is indeed unusual will sometimes approach a local monk or a teacher who is particularly close to the family to signal the

39. Dalai Lama Tenzin Gyatso, *My Land and My People*, 8.

40. This was the case with the eleventh Lelung Jedrung Tulku, whom I met as a teenager in Drepung monastery in south India. He explained to me that the birthmark in the form of a small bluish dot on the sole of his foot is considered to be a sign confirming his status as an authentic reincarnation of the Jedrung lineage, as it is said that one of his predecessors had placed a drop of ink on the sole of that foot so that his reincarnation would be easily recognizable.

exceptionality of their child and ask who he might be. In such situations, the monks or teacher will address his school's authorities with the request that they decide just whose Tulku the child might be. In more rare cases, the child can also recollect names of teachers and friends, places, prayers, and rituals, and even events from his or her previous life, sometimes without being asked. With such Tulkus, the information gleaned from these recollections, which can come in the form of dreams, visions, or even ordinary experiences, is used to help determine who the child's predecessor was.

EXPERIENCING IT FIRST HAND

In 1980 I was recognized as a Western Tulku. Indeed, at age three, following an encounter with the ex-abbot of Drepung monastery and prominent scholar-teacher Khensur Pema Gyaltsen (mKhan zur Padma rgyal mtshan—d. c. 1985), I began telling my parents that I too had a teacher, that I had very special friends and a protector that was a horse with wings, and I proceeded to give them the teacher's name along with those of my "friends." When my parents, who were relatively new to Tibetan Buddhism, told Khensur Pema Gyaltsen of my "active imagination" and the stories I had told them, he responded that no ordinary child says such things and that he had known the people I had mentioned in Tibet, but most of them had already passed on. Khensur Pema Gyaltsen asked to see me again privately; I was brought before him and offered a ceremonial white scarf. He asked me to repeat the stories that I had told my parents, at which he seemed both surprised and overjoyed. He informed my parents that I was most likely a Tulku, but that he did not yet know of whom. He was to return to India shortly thereafter and look into whose reincarnation I might be.

I had given the name of my predecessor's teacher, Geshe Khornawa, so over the next four years Khensur Pema Gyaltsen compiled a list of names of the people who had studied with this figure, omitting those who were either still alive or else had already reincarnated. Since Geshe Khornawa had been a rather prominent teacher, however, the list remained rather long, and no clear conclusion concerning my identification could be arrived at. Khensur Pema Gyaltsen therefore consulted both the Nechung (gNas chung) Oracle and the Dalai Lama, requesting that divinations be done to decide for certain who my predecessor was.[41] Around 1979 my family received the news from both

41. The Nechung oracle, also known as Pehar (*Pe har*), occupies an important place within Tibetan Buddhist culture. Nechung is considered to be a type of worldly protector deity (a *rgyal po* spirit) attached to a particular place or person. These spirits are supposedly endowed with greater foresight—thanks to the deity's lack of a physical form—than human beings are capable of, and they are therefore often consulted on State matters. Following a long and precise ritual, the deity is believed to take possession of a particular person's body, at which time predictions might be made—though all do not necessarily come true—give advice, or answer specific questions asked of it. The State Oracle was traditionally consulted by the Tibetan government on various important matters of State, particularly because of Nechung's close connection to the Dalai Lamas.

Khensur Pema Gyaltsen and the Dalai Lama that I had been recognized as the reincarnation of Geshe Jatse (dGe bshes Bya rtse), a revered Gelugpa scholar and practitioner from Sera Monastery near Lhasa, who, I later learned, had passed away sometime in the mid-1950s.

At the time, my situation was still somewhat atypical. Though two other Tulkus born to Western parents had already been recognized in North America, both were the reincarnations of masters from the Kagyu (*bka' rgyud*) tradition.[42] I was the first Tulku born to Western parents to be officially recognized from within the Gelugpa tradition. Within a few months of my recognition by the Dalai Lama, my family received a letter from a group of monks at Sera Monastery in south India stating that since I had been recognized as the reincarnation of a member of their religious community, I should be "returned immediately" so as to resume my education as one of their spiritual elite. My parents and I decided that I was not quite old enough yet to go to India, and that I should continue school in Montreal. Personally, I did not feel ready to go. One evening, after a long discussion with my father as to what they should do, my mother came to my room to ask my opinion. "What do you want to do?" she asked. I looked up at her and very calmly said, "I will have to go one day. I cannot resist my *karma*. But I am not ready yet." I was eight years old. Our refusal to go to the monastery immediately provoked quite a bit of irritation on the part of the monks at Sera, and they showed it through a steady stream of progressively more adamant letters over the next few years insisting that I be returned to them as soon as possible.

The first reaction to this story is most often one of shock. Such tactics are seen as rather abrupt and even inconsiderate toward the Tulku's parents' feelings, and the Tulku is but a child. As my mother has said, "We were at once honored and quite shocked. My whole Western side rejected it. You don't just take a child and send him off to some foreign country, especially a country like India."[43] I find it interesting not only that my mother identifies a side to herself that is implicitly both Buddhist and therefore non-Westerner (as though the two were in some sense incompatible), but especially that there was a clear distinction in what is culturally acceptable for children. Though for Tibetan Buddhists it is an honor to remove a child from his or her family in order to send him or her off to a monastery far away, in modern Western culture this is just not so.[44]

Western parents' aversion to the idea of sending a child to live in a monastery far away would seem to be in part due to what we think the child's

42. I refer here to Ossian Maclise (Sangye Nyenpa) and Ananda Massoubre (Trinlay Tulku), both recognized in 1976 by the sixteenth Karmapa.

43. See Marcel Poulin. *Memories of a Previous Life* (documentary film, Montreal: Thuk Kar Productions, 1994).

44. This appears to be what was behind the reactions of the studio audience to an episode of The Oprah Winfrey Show in which Lama Osel's mother, when asked to explain her decision to send him to India too, was met with rather violent accusations that she could not be a good mother if she sent her young child so far away.

life there will be like. We imagine the child torn away from his or her family and all those who care for him or her, and placed in a strict, harsh context where he will just have to get over missing his parents. We visualize the child as being lonely, without help, in a hostile and dirty environment, fending for him or herself in a vast sea of strangers. But this is not necessarily the case. To be certain, family and parents are indeed missed, and there can be times when a child, particularly a Westerner, might feel secluded or different in the monastery. But he or she is far from such an imagined hostile and emotionally unfriendly environment. The relationship between a child and his parents, though perhaps impossible to substitute fully, is in fact reproduced in the teacher–disciple relationship that is forged from the moment a child enters the monastery and grows progressively from there on.

Needless to say, the exact nature of this relationship does depend on the teacher's own actions and understanding of his role vis-à-vis his new student. Generally speaking, a teacher comes to see himself as responsible for the child in every way. As one of my previous tutors from Sera Monastery recently told me, the relationship between a teacher and a young child is a very complex thing.

> I am responsible for this person's life and well-being. I have to be at once a parent, model, friend, and disciplinarian, sometimes all at the same time. And I have a responsibility towards the child's real parents too, for they trusted *me* with their son's education and upbringing. Having a pupil (*dge phrug*) can be a hindrance to merit-making (*dge 'khrug*), as it constantly challenges your patience and your capacity to do the right thing.[45]

This complex relationship is clearly seen in the interaction between teachers or even fellow monks and younger children in the monasteries. Teachers will often play with younger disciples, joke with or tease them on occasion, and at other times cuddle them like their own offspring or siblings. Disciplining when it is called for and comforting when parents or family members are missed is also part of the job. As such, a teacher's role is somewhat akin to that of the biological parents, though the biological connection is absent.[46] Interestingly, younger monks learn from this relationship and sometimes emulate it with the younger children too. Often older students within the same household will behave as older brothers and friends, even confidants for their younger housemates.

Another part of our own aversion toward the idea of sending a child away to live in a monastery seems to be a cultural understanding of what is acceptable for children. Though it may be true to some extent that the monks demanding my "return" to the monastery could and probably even should have employed other methods, and though the same methods, arguments, and tactics would

45. Conversation with Geshe Thupten Phelgye, Sera, January 2010.
46. In some cases, however, the child is indeed a member of the teacher's family.

most likely not be used nowadays (especially given the tensions they created back then), the incomprehension is in fact due to a cultural misunderstanding. It does in fact sometimes happen that a Tulku's parents refuse to send their child to the monastery. One such notable case is that of Dilgo Khyentse Rinpoche (1910–1991), whose father refused to send him as a child, despite his wishes to go there himself. Eventually, permission was granted, and Dilgo Khyentse Rinpoche composed a short but heart-wrenching poem thanking his parents for allowing him to fulfill his quest for enlightenment.[47] Another case is Kalu Rinpoche (1905–1989), one of the five incarnations of Jamgön Kongtrul Lodrö Thayé, whose father, himself a Tulku, refused to have his son recognized and enthroned in a monastery.[48]

But these figures are exceptions. For the most part, Tibetans see it as an honor and as part of their duty as the parents of a reincarnated master to send him or her to receive the education that will allow him or her to blossom into a full-fledged master. In many ways it is a privilege to have a Tulku in one's family. To prevent him from receiving the proper education and training is considered detrimental to one's own *karma*, not to mention that it hinders the Tulku's "enlightened activity" (*phrin las*) and the possibility of fulfilling his or her goal of helping all sentient beings. As Ngawang Zangpo points out in the introduction to his translation of Jamgön Kongtrul's work describing his master's enthronement:

> It is not an ethical dilemma most parents or societies have to face: if one is reasonably sure that a child is a reincarnation of a genius in a particular field, what does one do? (...) Does one wait for the child to reach maturity before allowing him or her to choose a career? If it could be proven to us that Shakespeare's (or Beethoven's, or Einstein's) reincarnation could be recognized, his or her talent nourished by a supportive environment, and that the results of such training consistently led to the greater happiness of the child and society-at-large, would we accept that system? Would we deny the world another Shakespeare, Beethoven, or Einstein? Would we prefer to leave the child in a "natural" setting—tending yaks and chickens on a farm, for example—for fear of controlling a child's life, or of stifling his or her own creativity and inclinations with our needs and ambitions? These are questions most Tibetan parents have answered by allowing the child to be enthroned in the position of his or her predecessor and to enter an education centered on religious training to the exclusion of all else.[49]

47. See Matthieu Ricard, *Journey to Enlightenment* (New York: Aperture Foundation, 1996).

48. Kalu Rinpoche was not assimilated into an institutional environment and did not have an official status as a Tulku until later on, but this position also allowed him the freedom from particular institutional and political responsibilities. He eventually went on to found his own monastic community and worked unrelentingly to establish Buddhist centers all over Europe and North America. See Jamgön Kongtrul Lodrö Thayé, *Enthronement*, 33–34.

49. Jamgön Kongtrul Lodrö Thayé, *Enthronement*, 27–28.

It is true that, to some extent, Tulkus are seen as valued and often vital assets to the monastic communities and subcommunities (i.e., regional houses) from which their predecessors hail. A Tulku is automatically affiliated with his predecessor's regional house, and his membership there is taken very seriously. A high-ranking, influential, and respected Tulku brings both prestige and financial support, among other things, to both his monastery and his regional house. To try to forcibly change a Tulku's affiliation to another house or institution can provoke rather strong reactions. I was recently told about a Tulku at Sera Monastery whose predecessor was affiliated with one regional house and whom another house tried to claim as their own. The affair caused quite a bit of animosity and accusations of attempted theft of the one regional house's Tulku, and it nearly prompted a physical confrontation between members of the two houses. As one monk somewhat jokingly put it, "We were preparing for war!" The standoff ended peacefully, but relations between the houses have since remained somewhat strained regarding the recognition of Tulkus.[50]

But perhaps more important and deeply embedded in this issue is the notion of to whom a child belongs. Is a child an independent entity, or does he belong to his parents? When the letters first came from the monastery in India, my parents were shocked. My father has said, "They wanted him to come there, as if he was theirs and not ours."[51] Are children property? Do they "belong" to us as other objects do? Can we do with them as we see fit? We tend to use possessive adjectives when referring to our offspring, but are children really owned by their parents?

The claim might be made that since the child's parents physically created the child, and then nourished and cared for him or her, sent him or her to school, and so forth, these actions make the child theirs. But when we factor in the concept of reincarnation, the perspective changes. Indeed, a child is no longer a finite entity whose existence begins at the time of birth (or conception, depending on the perspective) and ends with adulthood at eighteen or twenty-one years of age (when we are expected to "act our age"). He or she is now the *continuation* of a being with a past that now involves other people (and indeed other kinds of sentient beings) who did the same things that his or her current parents did for him or her in this life. It could even be argued that since, according to Buddhist thought, all beings have been our mother at some point in time, then theoretically we belong to everyone equally. In fact, Tulkus, as reincarnated beings, do indeed belong to more than one family. Not only are they their parents' children in this life, they are also members of the social, religious, and cultural communities of their predecessors. During my first trip to Tibet in 1999, I was able to visit my predecessors' home region, childhood monastery, and biological family. It was made very clear to me that

50. Conversation with Geshe Thupten Phelgye, Sera Monastery, India, January 2010.
51. Marcel Poulin, *Memories of a Previous Life*.

as the reincarnation of this figure I was also a member of all three. People from this particular region and monks from the local monastery all spoke to me as though I had grown up there, and members of my predecessor's family refer to themselves as my nephews, nieces, and cousins. On a recent trip back to Sera Monastery in India, my predecessor's niece's son, who has since become a monk there, referred to himself as my "family member" (*nang mi*). For him, I am not only a Tulku from the same regional house as him; I am the reincarnation of his maternal great-uncle.

Although Western reincarnations may nowadays be recognized at all ages (this was rare even in Tibet), in the early stages of the Tulku tradition's Western developments, this was done only with young boys. Many of these young, new Western Tulkus' parents, themselves often from Judeo-Christian backgrounds and only recently Buddhist, did not quite grasp the implications and responsibilities of such recognition. Whereas in the West, children are expected to remain with their parents and families, Western Tulkus are expected, just as are their Tibetan counterparts, to leave their families and homes in the West and "return" to their predecessors' monastic communities to undertake the rigorous training that had allowed the latter to achieve the heightened spiritual and hierarchical status they originally had. This training is considered essential in allowing Tulkus to become Tibetan Buddhist virtuosi in their own right.[52] As Penor Rinpoche has put it, "This training reawakens the Tulku's powers of insight and compassion and develops their skillful means for helping others. It is only after such training that a Tulku is ready to take on the role of a teacher." The Dalai Lama has said that Tulkus are like uncut diamonds. Without the proper attention, they are of little or no value. But once cut and shaped by the skilled hands of a master, they take on their full value. "Being recognized as a *tulku* is the beginning of the process, not the end of it."[53] But even in the monastic communities that recognize them, Tulkus are often implicitly expected to prove that they really are the reincarnations of their predecessors.

Being considered the continuation of a previous person, no less a Buddhist master, can be double-edged. Indeed, although it does give you a different understanding of family and kinship, it also can bring with it a heavy burden of expectations. In the monastery a Tulku is expected to perform better than other monks and is often criticized or chided for not doing so. One criterion by which a Tulku's authenticity can be judged is virtuosity at learning. The common assumption being that Tulkus are spiritually advanced, learned, and compassionate beings, there is an implicit assumption that they are also naturally endowed with the great wisdom that would come with such an exalted rank. But that knowledge is considered to be latent and must be coaxed to the surface through arduous training. Without the proper training, this latent wisdom

52. Only a handful of the Westerners recognized as tulkus have gone to study at monasteries, and many, if not all of them, have for one reason or another decided to leave earlier than traditionally expected.

53. Ringu Tulku, as cited by Mick Brown, *The Dance of 17 Lives*, 29–30.

remains dormant, and the Tulku cannot accomplish his or her goals of leading other sentient beings out of cyclic existence. When a Tulku manifests a particular talent for learning, he or she can be acknowledged as the true and authentic reincarnation of his or her successor. This is meant as a compliment and may be perceived by the Tulku as such. When the opposite is true (i.e. when the Tulku behaves poorly or shows little interest in study), however, then either nothing is said, or else blame is placed on his teachers, who in turn might discipline or criticize the child (or adult in some rare cases) for shaming them. In order to avoid such shame, some teachers continually critique the child's performances and conduct, as was the case for Chögyam Trungpa.[54]

In my own experience, I remember being scolded by my teacher for "misbehaving" during a prayer assembly. As the first and only Western Tulku in Sera Monastery in 1986, I was somewhat a novelty to the other Tulkus. My presence there attracted both their attention and their questions, which often came during prayer sessions. As a fourteen-year-old accustomed to playing, and hoping to make new friends in my new environment, I naturally responded. When I returned back to my household, my teacher strongly upbraided me for my lack of composure becoming of a Tulku, especially, I was told, one who should know better. Asked how I was supposed to know better, my teacher responded that as I was older than the others, I should act my age. When I drew his attention to the fact that I was at best of the same age as they, insinuating that I *had* been acting my age, he replied that since I was taller and of lighter skin, I stood out more and so had to behave. "Besides, he said, it is unbecoming of one who is supposed to be the reincarnation of someone as humble and wise as Geshe Jatse."

On multiple occasions, where I had performed particularly well in a debate, for example, I remember hearing other monks and teachers say, "He truly is Geshe Jatse's reincarnation, seeing how well he conducted that debate." On my first day as a monk at the monastery, teachers came to me and said, "Your predecessor Geshe Jatse was such a great and humble scholar. You too must study hard and not be pretentious!" And from the moment I was recognized, I was repeatedly told wondrous stories about his extremely humble demeanor and his great feats in both practice and debate.

All these actions (telling stories, encouraging emulation, and discouraging behavior deemed unbecoming of a master's reincarnation) help reinforce young Tulkus' identification with their predecessors. They are literally expected to behave just like these great masters of yore. But this also implies that as children, they are expected and continually encouraged to emulate and equal someone who is already a learned, "mature," and wise adult. As Ray puts it, a Tulku "typically received little sense of identity from his birth parents and formed his own sense of himself entirely from the *bodhisattva* ideal and model of his predecessor that were daily presented to him and from the culture of

54. Chögyam Trungpa, *Journey Without Goal* (Boston: Shambhala Publications, 1985), 97–99.

his monastic environment."[55] A Tulku is therefore encouraged to be less of a child and more of the adult he is said to have been. In the case of Western reincarnations, the child is in fact compared to and encouraged to identify with an adult of a completely different culture and historical setting—a rather complex task to accomplish. But expectations such as these are not entirely foreign to us. Western cultural trends also emphasize the values of children behaving like adults. We reward maturity and praise children who act "wise beyond their years" while we berate and criticize others for being "childish" or immature. But the degree to which this is done is different. In the West, we encourage children to behave *like* adults; in Tibetan culture, Tulkus are expected to almost *be* adults. In such circumstances, when can a child just be a child?

We must not forget, however, that within the Tibetan Buddhist context, young Tulkus are not seen merely as children. They are considered to have a potential, accumulated over the course of multiple lifetimes, to help and guide other sentient beings away from suffering and out of cyclic existence. Tulkus are considered to have already acquired to some extent the tools necessary for them to come to embody the Buddha's teachings and act as a role model and guide to others. But these tools remain latent, hidden under the surface, and must be coaxed out, developed, and honed through precise training. The propensity to teach and guide others would seem to come naturally to Tulkus. At times, it is almost as though we do this in spite of ourselves. And a Tulku who does not teach is often asked when he will begin to carry out his "mission" in this world. Without correct training, a Tulku might behave discordantly with the ideals he or she is supposed to uphold, misrepresent the teachings that are supposed to lead to true well-being, maybe even misguide other sentient beings away from the path to enlightenment. To the Tibetan community, the effects of an improperly trained Tulku are potentially disastrous to others and would be a disgrace to the Buddha's teachings.

EDUCATING THE ELITE

We can now better understand how important the recognition and confirmation of such beings is, and above all the importance of their education as guides and role models. It becomes easier, therefore, to understand how the religious groups that these spiritual elite are expected to lead and learn from might put pressure on their families so as to induce them to send their children to the monastery. Put in the right cultural and ideological context, then, the monastery's reaction with regard to my own recognition is not as surprising as it first may have appeared. This attitude, coupled with the fact that the people in question did not quite fathom the cultural differences that separated them from my parents in this regard, produced a difficult situation for all. My parents were in fact torn between sending me to receive the proper education

55. Ray, *Secret of the Vajra World*, 417.

that would allow me to flourish as a Tulku, and keeping me at home "where I belonged," according to Western culture. At the same time, they kept receiving letters pressuring them to "do the right thing" from a Tibetan Buddhist perspective and send me to the monastery. They were, in short, torn between what they saw as being good Buddhists and being good parents.

Exactly what constitutes a "proper education" may vary slightly from one Tibetan Buddhist tradition to the next. Each monastic (and some nonmonastic) setting will have its own course of study in which a Tulku is expected to excel. Generally speaking, however, a Tulku's education will focus primarily on instilling a sense of empathy and the Buddhist values of loving kindness and compassion for all sentient beings. After all, Tulkus are meant to be *bodhisattvas*, the very embodiments of compassion. They are educated accordingly, and the sense of responsibility toward others that comes with such values becomes a strong motivational force for his or her future activities. As Reginald Ray remarks:

> The kind of training that tülkus underwent, particularly beginning at such a young age, meant that their sense of identity was almost entirely shaped by their religious environment. From the moment they were recognized, they were told, 'You are a *bodhisattva*. The purpose of your life is to help others. There is no room for selfishness or unkindness here. Your predecessor was a realized master who helped countless suffering beings. You must aspire to emulate his greatness, and your training is for this purpose.'[56]

Ideally, the earlier a Tulku begins to receive training, the better. Indeed, as a young child a Tulku is a "past-oriented infant," to use Chögyam Trungpa's expression, whose mind is still relatively open and unimpeded by the notions of self, ego, duality, and other such elements of cyclic existence that come to taint our experience later in life. As the child grows older, his mind becomes more engrossed in its interaction with the outside world and the connection to past lives; the tools acquired during that time tend to wane, and with that the ease with which he can actualize his potential. This phenomenon is also said to be the reason why the recollections of Tulkus who remember their previous lives slow with time and eventually stop at a certain age.[57]

My own recollections ebbed at about age eight, though I have since had what some might call *déjà-vu*. One of these happened on my first visit to Sera Monastery in Lhasa in 1999, where my predecessor had lived most of his life. Upon my arrival there, I naturally found my way around the place and eventually made my way to my old regional house (*khang mtshan*), where I encountered an elderly monk prostrating himself before the altar. The sensation was in fact not one of *déjà-vu* (lit. "previously seen"), but rather one of *déjà-vécu* ("previously experienced"). With every step of the way I felt as though I had

56. Ray, *Secret of the Vajra World*, 417.
57. See Ray, "The Themes of a Tulku's Life," 40.

already been there, as though I were walking on familiar terrain, taking steps and feeling sensations that my feet already knew. As it turned out, the old monk had been a close disciple of Geshe Jatse. He had been charged with taking care of my predecessor's funerary remains after his passing circa 1956. When he realized who I was, he burst into tears and said, "I thought I would never see you again!"

THE WORK OF WESTERN TULKUS

I have discussed how the Tibetan Buddhist tradition considers a Tulku's role to be one of compassion and guidance toward other beings. As either embodiments of enlightenment and/or the manifestation of realized and benevolent beings returned to accomplish the greater good of all sentient beings, Tulkus have an important moral obligation toward others as both role models and incarnations of what is possible to achieve through properly following the Buddhist path. They also are expected to develop even further the "enlightened activities" undertaken by their predecessors. This task is considered to hold true for *all* reincarnations, regardless of time, place, or even social and cultural backgrounds. A Tulku therefore has specific goals to accomplish in this life. This idea is explained to Tulkus very early in their lives, possibly even embedded in us from the very outset. It produces a certain sense of urgency, necessity, and direction. I myself have felt this strong sense of direction from relatively early on in life, even though I am not always entirely certain by what means to achieve it.

Interestingly, it would appear that other Western Tulkus feel a similar sense of responsibility toward other beings. Some have decided to act on that in whatever way they deem necessary for achieving the well-being of others. Ananda Massoubre, for example, sees himself as having a degree of responsibility toward making the world a better place for others:

> *J'ai toujours pensé que ma responsabilité de tulkou, c'est de faire quelque chose pour participer à rendre le monde meilleur, en inspirant aux gens qui m'entourent le développement de la tendresse et de la compassion, si essentielles dans le bouddhisme. C'est ce à quoi j'aspire depuis toujours. Si je fais preuve de persévérance, peut-être que j'arriverai à certains résultats.*[58]

Osel Hita Torres, Lama Yeshe's reincarnation, has apparently decided that one way to work for the benefit of other sentient beings is through filmmaking, which, he says, can open the mind to new possibilities and can touch the hearts of millions of spectators.

58. http://www.psychologies.com/Culture/Philosophie-et-spiritualite/Pratiques-spirituelles/Articles-et-Dossiers/J-ai-ete-un-little-bouddha.

59. http://www.fpmt.org/teachers/osel/.

> I'm trying to find a different way for this future generation. One of the ways is through music, movies and audio-visual techniques. In a movie you can condense so many different stories. You can put in music, you can put in different situations and messages. Even just the sunset can be enough to give you peace to find a moment of meditation in yourself. There are so many different millions of possibilities in movies.[59]

A similar path appears to have been taken by Gesar Mukpo, one of the first Tulkus to be recognized in the West, and his teacher Dzongsar Khyentse Rinpoche, a Bhutanese Tulku who has directed multiple critically acclaimed films such as *The Cup* and *Travellers and Magicians*.

Some Tulkus, such as Dylan Henderson, who was also recognized by the sixteenth Karmapa, seem to have decided that a life of near-solitary practice with little teaching engagements is the best path to take this time around, and they find great pleasure and fulfillment in simple activities. Others, such as Ananda Massoubre, believe that a life of teaching, though not a personal ambition per se, is what very possibly lies in store for them. And in order to do this, they must receive the proper lineage teachings and transmissions that their predecessors held, so as to continue their work and live up to their identities as Tulku.

One might think that a Tulku's strong sense of responsibility toward other beings is merely the result of his or her education, with the constant reinforcement of his or her identification with the *bodhisattva* ideal. But not all recognized Western reincarnates actually go to receive a formal education in a monastery. In fact, very few of us have gone through or even begun a standard Tibetan Buddhist education. Ossian Maclise, Ananda, and I seem to have spent the most time in monastic settings receiving traditional Tibetan Buddhist training. This is not to say that others have not received such training at all. Many have tried to live in traditional Tibetan Buddhist settings. However, it is interesting to remark that even among the few who have gone to receive the training, most have decided to leave before what is considered the end. Indeed, many Western Tulkus seem to feel that although they have benefitted from their traditional education, their place still lies in the West, where they chose to be reborn, rather than in a monastery.

Some also feel that their place is in society, not cut off from it, and that they need to be free from the fetters of a conservative tradition in order to be able to truly walk their paths as Tulkus. Recently, there seems to be a new development whereby Tulkus, both Western and Tibetan, are rejecting the strict identification with their predecessors. This does not mean that they feel or believe they are not their reincarnations, only that they choose to walk the path differently from them. As Osel has put it, "Some people seem to expect that because this is Lama Yeshe's reincarnation, then he's going to be just like Lama Yeshe. But today is not like being in Tibet many years ago, or even when the hippies were in Nepal and India in the 1970s. The world has

60. http://www.fpmt.org/projects/loef/default.asp.

changed a bit, and so I'm trying to find a different way of communicating."[60] Similar sentiments have been expressed by other reincarnations.

The recognition of Western reincarnations is a complex and slippery issue. On one hand, Tulkus are naturally awarded a certain degree of respect from their immediate entourage and from the disciples and even families of their predecessors. When Gesar Mukpo was a child, his father's (adult) disciples often asked for his advice on important matters. Both Ananda and myself have had similar experiences. As reincarnated Buddhist masters, we are expected, even at a very young age, to have special knowledge and foresight that would not only allow us to comprehend the person's dilemma, but allow us to see matters clearly, even if the situation did not concern us directly. For children, this can be very a daunting responsibility, one that requires us to transcend our normal state as children and use skills (such as self-abstraction, the ability to imagine the outcome of a particular decision, and the capacity to take another's perspective) that are more typically used as adults. If we had been considered normal children, I doubt that we would have been asked our opinions with such high expectations. But we weren't; we were seen as Tulkus, new embodiments of old masters. As such, we were expected to have all the tools necessary to help these adults in distress.

On the other hand, many Tibetans seem to feel hesitant to accept Western Tulkus into the fold. This attitude would seem to underscore how strongly enmeshed with Tibetan culture the Tulku system really is. Tibetans themselves have a difficult time accepting the recognition of their spiritual elite among people from cultures that are not readily Buddhist. When I was a child, many Tibetans living in Montreal just would not accept my identity as a Western Tulku. For them, these two terms were antithetical. Even today I am still met with surprised faces and remarks when I explain to Tibetans (both laypersons and monks) that I am a Tulku.[61]

The promotion of Westerners among the ranks of a Buddhist spiritual elite that was created and largely dominated by Tibetans has raised some serious questions as to the validity and usefulness of such a system. Tulkus are meant to act as moral examples and spiritual guides to all beings affected by the suffering inherent to cyclic existence. Although Western Tulkus are expected to carry out these tasks, they are not necessarily regarded in quite the same manner as their culturally Tibetan counterparts. Western Tulkus often reject traditional expectations. Many do not join the spiritual communities their predecessors are said to have belonged to, while others leave those communities behind in search of a more active role in the Western world in which they were born.

Are these Tulkus merely fulfilling their destinies as models and guides for people living outside Tibetan cultural areas, or are they merely failed attempts

61. The situation has been made worse in recent years by an increasing number of Westerners proclaiming themselves reincarnations. Oddly, as a friend of mine pointed out, none of these self-styled Tulkus claim to be reincarnations of simple monks. Instead, they all claim to be reembodiments of major Buddhist figures of the past.

at the internationalization or rather Westernization of the Tulku phenomenon? How should the Tibetan Buddhist tradition, for which the Tulku system is so important, react? Oddly, in recent years many Tibetan Tulkus have also decided to leave their monastic lives, disrobe, and either establish centers or live "normal" lives elsewhere, often in Europe and North America. Does this development have anything to do with a trend set by Western Tulkus not remaining at their monasteries? Have Western Tulkus affected the Tulku tradition so that it has begun to follow the former's lead and adapt itself further to Western cultures and expectations? Or maybe it is merely that these times call for Tulkus to be active in more nontraditional spheres.

I am often asked during public talks whether I too will have a reincarnation. The question is an interesting one. It both betrays the inquirer's vision of the person before him, and invites reflection on whether or not Westerners will continue to have a place within the Tulku institution. Indeed, it proves that the person asking the question sees me first and foremost as a Westerner. It neglects the fact that this Western body is nothing more than a temporary physical form in which the consciousness continuum of my predecessor, Geshe Jatse, has chosen to incarnate. But what is also being asked is will I, a Westerner, have a Tulku? Will the reincarnation of a Westerner ever be recognized within the Tibetan Tulku tradition? Will a time come when children will be recognized as the reincarnations of influential Western practitioners and teachers as well?

The Dalai Lama has repeatedly said that he is not certain that the recognition of Tulkus in the West is a good thing. Most of them have chosen to leave the monasteries and therefore do not receive the full education they require. In an even stronger statement in an excerpt from Gesar Mukpo's autobiographical documentary "Tulku," Dzongsar Khyentse Rinpoche cautions that the Tulku system itself is potentially hazardous: "If Tibetans are not careful, this Tulku system is going to ruin Buddhism. And at the end of the day, Buddhism is more important than the Tulku system. Who *cares* about the Tulku system?"[62]

Perhaps the fact that Western Tulkus do not choose to follow the traditional path is just an adaptation of the traditional understanding of a Tulku's meaning and purpose in this life. Bardor Tulku, who has lived quite some time in the West, has said that a Tulku seems always to find the path that is most appropriate for him or her in this life. Perhaps our paths lie outside of the monastery, in the West. Perhaps by rebelling against a system that is perceived as trying to force us into a specific mold, we are actually fulfilling part of our calling as Tulkus by being trailblazers and guides for other sentient beings navigating unfamiliar terrain.

The Buddha is said to have advised his disciples to be lamps unto themselves; to trust in and follow their own hearts. Many Western Tulkus have done just that. We are navigating in uncharted waters and acting within the limits of our own understanding and intuition. Only time will tell whether or not the paths we have chosen are the right ones.

62. Gesar Mukpo, *Tulku* (documentary film, Canada: National Filmboard of Canada, 2009).

CHAPTER 18

"Give Me My Inheritance"

Western Buddhists Raising Buddhist Children

KRISTIN SCHEIBLE

Every parent understands tension. Every parent also knows experientially that while sometimes tension cannot be resolved, it can be transformed into productive tension. Just as tuning a string instrument requires proper tension, for the string and music will not be forthcoming if it is too loose or taut, so the tension felt by parents in balancing parenthood with personal lives and livelihood vibrates with creative potential.[1] Western Buddhist practice vibrates with a tension between the agency involved with the individualized, self-focused cultivation, and the demands on time and energy typifying family life in the West today. There

1. In a footnote to his translation of the *Ambalaṭṭhikārāhulovāda Sutta*, Thanissaro Bhikkhu explains that the term *samañña* (recluse) relates to the nature of tension and being tuned (and tuned in): "Throughout ancient cultures, the terminology of music was used to describe the moral quality of people and actions. Discordant intervals or poorly tuned musical instruments were metaphors for evil; harmonious intervals and well-tuned instruments, metaphors for good. In Pali, the term *sama*—"even"—described an instrument tuned on-pitch. There is a famous passage (in AN 6.55) where the Buddha reminds Sona Kolivisa—who had been overexerting himself in the practice—that a lute sounds appealing only if the strings are neither too taut nor too lax, but "evenly" tuned. This image would have special resonances with the Buddha's teaching on the middle way. It also adds meaning to the term *samanna*—monk or contemplative—which the texts frequently mention as being derived from *sama*. The word *samañña*—"evenness," the quality of being in tune—also means the quality of being a contemplative: the true contemplative is always in tune with what is proper and good. See "Ambalatthikarahulovada Sutta: Instructions to Rahula at Mango Stone" (MN 61), translated from the Pāli by Thanissaro Bhikkhu. *Access to Insight*, June 14, 2010, http://www.accesstoinsight.org/tipitaka/mn/mn.061.than.html.

is also tension between the desire to teach children in the ways of Buddhist thought and practice in order to disseminate the dharma, and the sense that it is one's child's right to encounter and choose to follow her own spiritual path in due time (just as many Western Buddhists discovered Buddhism for themselves). What models are there for first-generation Buddhists to consider when raising their own children? What are some of the sources Western Buddhists have skillfully tuned into for help in navigating the complexities and challenges of balancing their personal pursuits and perceived parenting responsibilities?

The historical Buddha asked of his adherents something quite radical, given the special place of family structure and obligation in his community and his time: abandon your station, your duty, your relationships, and reassemble with others who have renounced such ties as well. Structurally speaking, the Buddha called for an alternative community to the society of the day, a different clustering of people aimed toward a goal different from the householder's goal of getting by and perpetuating one's line. Since monastics relied on the broader community for material support, complete detachment from the householders was impossible. Inherent in the communal tradition of Buddhism that is the sangha, then, is the tension between renunciation and relationship. And yet far removed temporally and geographically from the first iteration of the sangha, Western Buddhists today feel the tension in palpable ways as family obligations and relationships impact their experience of the dharma.

Teaching, tradition, and lineage, the glue that binds the sangha, is not altogether different from the structures that bind family life. For that first generation of disciples, and for countless subsequent seekers, the Buddha became an iconic father figure: the paramount, the exemplar, the teacher. After his bodily demise, the dharma and sangha became the inheritance (or the dharma became the inheritance for the sangha, and the dharma and sangha together became the inheritance for all). For Buddhism, issues of inheritance bind the generations together; monastics and laypeople alike speak about their own teachers and lineages. The Buddha defined just what an inheritance might look like when his son Rāhula asked him for his own. Rather than give the expected property and rights that establish station in ordinary life, and that was the inheritance Rāhula's mother was angling for according to the commentary, the Buddha has his biological son brought into the sangha.[2]

If the dharma was the inheritance that the Buddha passed on to Rāhula and his sangha, and its delivery was initiated by Rāhula's lower ordination, does a contemporary Western lay practitioner have any claim to it? Many tensions are negotiated by the contemporary Western lay practitioner, especially if she claims the dharma inheritance and intends to pass it on in some fashion to her own children. There are historical tensions—that the Buddha lived then and this is now; issues pertaining to geography—East/West; the meaning of sangha—the monastic/layperson practical divide; and practical tensions felt by one raising a family—getting the lunches packed and kids to school/one's own meditative practice. Current parent/

2. For a discussion of this episode, see Kate Crosby's chapter in this volume.

practitioners negotiate these tensions for themselves, often with the support of communities of practice, while affirming their own claims to the inheritance. But just what is the inheritance that future generations of Western Buddhists will claim, and how has it been identified and prepared for further disbursement by current practitioners?

This question raises larger issues about what the dharma looks like and how it functions in the West today. At the time the Buddha would have disbursed the inheritance to Rāhula through his initial instruction, he focused on what was right at hand to communicate his dharma teaching. In the *Ambalaṭṭhikārāhulovāda Sutta* (*Majjhima Nikāya Sutta* no. 61), when Rāhula saw the Buddha approach, he prepared a seat for him and water for foot-washing, unwittingly participating in setting up a concrete metaphor for the Buddha to use. The Buddha didn't use all the water in the dipper for his feet; rather, he used a bit left in the dipper and the dipper itself to reflect on the worth, or lack thereof, of recluses who tell lies.[3] Parent/practitioners likewise focus on what is closer to home and what is concretely experienced: the common theme of raising children with some hope that they will move from mere exposure to the dharma through their parents' efforts to embracing the dharma on their own terms. How might one resolve the tension between one's individualized, self-focused, self-cultivation and the demands on time and energy that is family life? One resolution that is distinctive to Western Buddhist practice is recognizing that the seemingly polar pull of procreation and renunciation provides an opportunity to discern and sharpen one's own practice while defining just what the inheritance is.

A FUNDAMENTAL TENSION: PROCREATION AND RENUNCIATION

Parents feel an extraordinary sense of connection to their children; awe and responsibility comingle to tighten the bond. Reflecting on the Buddhist understanding of *karma*, however, complicates the relationship. The dependent child may have been one's parent, among many other relationships, in a past life.

Children themselves are iconically problematic in the Buddhist tradition. Visible reminders of the most basic cause-and-effect occurrence, they embody, implicate, and perpetuate *saṃsāra*. In the Buddha's own renunciation narrative, that he leaves his wife and newborn son serves to highlight the incredible sacrifice he makes to pursue his spiritual endeavors. He literally turns away from what binds him to *saṃsāra*, renouncing the relationships that act like glue to eventually create a highly governed community to support individualized practice. Ostensibly the most precious thing, his son, provides the rarest opportunity: the bodhisattva gives up his child not simply to follow some general

3. *Ambalaṭṭhikārāhulovāda Sutta*, PTS: M i 414; for further discussion of this episode, see Kate Crosby's chapter in this volume.

Buddha blueprint,[4] but because this particular event highlights the extreme to which he submitted himself in pursuit of dharma. A human birth is so dear, as Neil Gordon reflects: "Perhaps it has to do with the infinite improbability, in a classical Buddhist cosmology, of birth into this realm, and how infinitely precious human children therefore are. Nothing, after all, is as precious in our whole spectrum of experience as children."[5] How difficult it must have been to abandon his child, yet how critical for the renunciation to be complete.

The precious ideal, renunciation, comes at an obvious cost to the family. Later in the biography narrative, when Rāhula joined the sangha, Suddhodana was so distraught to lose his grandson as well as his son that he petitioned the Buddha to establish a rule that permission must be granted from one's family before one can be admitted to the sangha. Parents have always struggled with their children's decisions to lead paths aberrant to the perpetuation of the family line.

Even the origin story for the *patimokkha*, the explicit rules for the monks, derives from negotiating the tension between the societal and familial obligation for childrearing with personal renunciation. The story is a well-known one: the monk Sudinna, fairly recently ordained and pressured by his former family, "meets" with his former wife to fulfill his householder's obligation of procuring an heir.[6] He had been convinced by his mother that doing so was his duty, and the Buddha was not available to help him discern right practice; the result is a child. The bearing of children, the draw away from total renunciation, thus inspired the *patimokkha*![7]

The story that pervades Buddhist thought and practice, the Buddha's own biography, makes it abundantly clear that children are a problem. As Sasson explains, "The Buddha left home for a reason and this reason, be it the Four Sights, his meditation under the rose-apple tree, or his 'leper-like' wealth, is at the very heart of the Buddhist tradition."[8] The culminating event in this "reason," perhaps the penultimate nudge toward his leaving home, is parenthood—the most palpable bind to *saṃsāra*. In fatherhood, the bodhisattva experiences the realization firsthand of the shock of connection to another, a biological and social responsibility to that other. Leaving his home is a part of the same pattern of other significant goings: Queen Māyā left the palace to give birth to him, Queen Māyā dies (leaving him behind), and he leaves the palace to see the four sights, presaging his *parinibbāna*, his future departure from *saṃsāra*. With their model being the

4. John Strong, *The Buddha: A Short Biography* (Oxford: Oneworld Publications, 2001), esp. 10–14. Leaving his son is a required step in becoming a Buddha; for the Pāli list of thirty such requisite events, Strong cites *The Clarifier of Sweet Meaning*, trans. I. B. Horner (London: Pali Text Society, 1978), 429–30.

5. Neil Gordon, "Children and Dharma: An Introduction," in *Tricycle*, Spring 2002 (http://www.tricycle.com/feature/children-and-dharma-an-introduction).

6. For further discussion, see Kate Crosby's chapter herein.

7. *VinayaPitakam*, 5 vols., ed. H. Oldenberg (London: Pali Text Society, 1879–83), 3: 11–22.

8. See Vanessa R. Sasson's chapter in this volume.

Buddha, somewhat of an escape artist, why should parents feel so much emotion around leaving their children—temporarily—to intently practice meditation? And how do parents resolve the tension between the practical and symbolic goal of being present at this very moment, so central to the breathing practices and foci of meditation, and the goal of escape?

Beyond the samsaric bind that children represent symbolically, having children at all is an issue to consider mindfully. It is not that having children is inherently wrong; it is about the mindset of one embarking on the path of parenthood. Gross says, "Because physical reproduction and family life do not especially alleviate or even address these concerns and needs [that comprise *dukkha*], they are not the major focus of Buddhism. Indeed, from the Buddhist point of view, physical reproduction and family life, if pursued with a conventional mindset of attachment and desire, intensify rather than diminish suffering."[9] Attachments (love, responsibility) to children necessarily complicate a parent's ability to focus on the dharma. "Women who find in maternity the meaning they cannot find in their lives often fall into an extreme of attached parenting, living through their children."[10] When the children become "extensions of parents' egos," the relationship has a negative effect on both parent and child.

The biography of the Buddha provides one clear path: renunciation of the lay life, which is renunciation of the binds (physical, emotional, psychological) of parenthood. But for someone who is not aiming to follow the Buddha's own biography prescriptively or precisely, might there be some form of renunciation that is possible within lay life? Is renunciation a practical ideal, or even possible to adapt, for the Western lay Buddhist?

Renunciation is part of the parcel of dharma inheritance. Several dharma teachers recommend rethinking what renunciation means in practical terms, an expedient way for Western Buddhists to see the utility of renunciation within their lives. For example, Pema Chodron suggests a new definition:

> Renunciation does not have to be regarded as negative. I was taught that it has to do with letting go of holding back. What one is renouncing is closing down and shutting off from life. You could say that renunciation is the same thing as opening to the teachings of the present moment.... The whole journey of renunciation, or starting to say yes to life, is realizing first of all that you've come up against your edge, that everything in you is saying no, and then at that point, softening. This is yet another

9. Rita Gross, "Child and Family in Buddhism," in *Religious Dimensions of Child and Family Life: Reflections on the UN Convention on the Rights of the Child,* ed. Harold Coward and Philip Cook (Waterloo, ON: Wilfrid Waterloo, ON: University Press, 1996), 84.

10. Rita Gross, *Buddhism After Patriarchy* (Albany: SUNY Press, 1993), 236–37.

> opportunity to develop lovingkindness for yourself, which results in playfulness—learning to play like a raven in the wind.[11]

Practice can become an opportunity for renunciation, if only in temporary terms.[12] When the door shuts for a parent's undisturbed meditation, to some degree renunciation can occur. But what are the children of this generation's practitioners doing when that door is shut? Are Western Buddhists integrating what happens behind closed doors into their parenting, and if so, how?

For contemporary Buddhists there is a palpable, practical tension between the perceived ideal of the (even temporary) renunciant, let alone the monastic ideal of the celibate virtuoso, and the demands of lay life. This tension is even more pronounced for those who have discovered the relevance of Buddhism for themselves and those who had been brought up within a Buddhist home; renunciation may carry a different meaning for each. Rita Gross reflects:

> It is not so easy to maintain the open, aware, nonfixated state of mind of the small child in the shrine room, especially in a culture that encourages the exact opposite of those qualities. The clash between parenting and meditation practices comes because children can be extremely distracting and demanding, and because for biological reasons, people usually undertake childrearing while they are still relatively young and may not have a mature enough meditation practice to be able to carry mindfulness and awareness into such a difficult situation. Of course, children who grew up meditating would have a head start on their convert parents, and future generations of North American Buddhists may have an easier time with mindful parenting.[13]

The so-called "zeal of a convert," too, may inflate the assumption that the true, right path is one of celibacy, with the Buddha as exemplar. Refuge might include finding a refuge from the onslaught of daily family chaos. But for the convert or convinced Buddhist who does not immerse herself in the confining, protective social realm of the sangha but instead chooses to raise a family (or

11. Pema Chodron, "Like a Raven in the Wind," *Tricycle Magazine,*Fall 1991 (http://www.tricycle.com/dharma-talk/renunciation).

12. In a personal communication, Vanessa Sasson remarked that "according to the Bhagavadgita, renunciation has to do with abandoning the fruits of one's actions—it has little to do with abandoning particular lifestyles. It is a mental effort, not a physical one" (April 17, 2011). Rather than relegate the physical time, space, and energy needed for a full lifestyle of renunciation, parents may work instead toward cultivating the right mental environment for renunciation. Rather than having a quiet meditation space free of children, quiet space is created in the mind.

13. Rita Gross, "Buddhism and the Child in the United States," in *Children and Childhood in American Religion,* ed. Don Browning and Bonnie Miller McLemore (New Brunswick, NJ: Rutgers University Press, 2009), 177.

for one who has turned to the dharma after having children), there are many methods to choose from to help define and perpetuate the dharma inheritance. The closest at hand is reflection on one's own parenting experiences. A common theme arising in Western Buddhist writing on parenting is that children themselves are (typically inadvertent) dharma teachers or that parenting reveals or makes relevant the dharma.

REFLECTING ON CHILDREN RATHER THAN REFLECTIONS FOR CHILDREN: WHAT (AND HOW) CHILDREN CAN TEACH THE PARENT

For lay practitioners who have families, children often can be retooled into focusing points for dharmic instruction of the parent as well as, and sometimes instead of, the child. Parenting anecdotes dominate writing on "engaged Buddhism"—the experience of childhood through observation, vicarious experiences, and relationships leads to insight into the inner workings of the dharma. This genre of writing may explain more about the parents' paths, and of a certain kind of reflection on self-cultivation and one's own practice, than about the inheritance for their children. Much of what is being written for the popular audience (in books, magazines, and blogs) about Buddhist parenting tends to focus on the experience of the parent him- or herself, rather than the experience of the child. Anecdotes tend to either focus on making palpable some profound Buddhist teaching, such as one of the three marks of existence—impermanence (*anicca*) being the clear favorite for a topic that lends itself to ruminations on the fleeting nature of childhood[14]—or on practice. Focusing on what the experience of having a child in one's life might teach may affect the way the dharma is transmitted and inherited:

> My son never again awoke laughing—at least not loud enough to wake me—and soon that eight-month-old face was two years old, then three, and the fat cheeks had smoothed to show my wife's cheekbones, and the thin baby's hair had grown into the thick bangs I once had as a boy. And from that night and for a long time after, my experience of my children came to be infused with this pity of love. So much so, in fact, that

14. Typical of this genre: "My son was less than twenty-four hours old, and I knew he was going to die.... Veins no longer pricked, oxygen hood gone, lungs finally clear, he was healthy. Skye was coming home, yet I knew he would die. Some day.... Standing in the dawn, waiting for the doctor to say when we could take Skye home, I watched the mini-death and rebirths of his life marching past the nursery door: a first birthday, a tenth week of school, a third date with his future partner, a second year of work. And what of his death? His ninety-second day of kindergarten while climbing on the jungle gym? His ninety-second year while reaching to open the window?" Sarah Aceto, "On Parenting: As if I were your Mother," in Tricycle, Spring 2007, http://www.tricycle.com/-parenting/if-i-were-your-mother.

> I thought it was something very like depression. But as I became more versed in this emotion—and particularly as I watched it in my practice of meditation—I became more and more convinced that this pity was not pathological but existential; that there was within it a dharmic insight.... That was not a surprise. Nothing in my practice of meditation has been more powerfully illuminated than my experience of my children. And yet, I had found little that helped me understand what had happened to me, that night with my son. On retreats, in dharma talks, children were mentioned sometimes, but usually as part of the array of generously tolerated, somewhat tangential elements of the lay practitioner's life. But as I sat with the experience, I began to feel that the question posed by that night when my son was eight months old was not tangential to my practice but key—that it had, in fact, a very precise dharmic analogue. What was plaguing me was an insight into the irredeemable, nonnegotiable temporariness not of attachment—as I first thought—but of experience itself.[15]

Periodic absence of children can serve to put children into a prime position of reflection device. Lama John Makransky gained some perspective by entering a retreat where daily interaction with his family was curtailed. At the end of a silent retreat, a verbal exchange with his young son prompted reflection on Shantideva and how "the family is an intimate matrix for the exchange of self and other." In other words, the family is a practical tool, a focus for the work of meditation:

> Family can act as a charged arena within which all such ordinary thoughts and feelings, clinging and suffering can arise. And the family is an intimate matrix for the exchange of self and other, the heart of training.... The instant we perform Shantideva's exchange, infusing others around us with our sense of self, sensing them as the very focus of our "self"-concern, we find relief from our suffering, our self-obsession. The "mystery" is really something simple, accessible: it is the key to all our well-being, our deepest freedom.[16]

Far from rejecting or renouncing the intrusion of the family demands upon one's personal practice, he moves into a prescriptive mode and advocates the use of the family as a meditative object:

> It's good to first practice this exchange when alone for short periods: bring family members to mind, one by one. Allow your own sense of self,

15. Neil Gordon, "Children and Dharma: An Introduction" in *Tricycle* Spring 2002 (http://www.tricycle.com/feature/children-and-dharma-an-introduction).
16. John Makransky, "Family Practice" in *Tricycle*, Summer 2001, http://www.tricycle.com/-parenting/family-practice.

> your most intimate self-concern, to arise within each of them. A natural wish for their happiness as one's very "self" accompanies the shift. Radiate well-being and happiness to them from the heart. Secretly explore taking their suffering, worries, anxieties into yourself, and allow all this to dissolve completely into the empty ground of your being. Do this privately, secretly in daily practice. Feel its quiet power, the natural joy it elicits. Little by little let this secret exchange exercise itself in the bustle of family life. When you pick up your children from school, or when you do homework together, or play: exchange self for other. Take their subtle suffering, worries, anxieties into your empty nature and radiate your deepest well-being into them as if they were your very self. Allow the practice to naturally extend itself to neighbors, coworkers, all whom you pass on the highway, all who come to notice in the newspaper and evening news. Gradually, our practice senses them through the heart in just the way it has sensed our family: no difference. As we privately learn to do this practice with increasing rigor and continuity, family life itself transforms into training center, into multi-year "retreat": quietly, dharma communicates its own deep curriculum to us, our loved ones, and others.[17]

Sometimes the reflection on the child is used to explain or deepen one's appreciation for a dharma teaching, and sometimes parenting itself is valorized and seen as a parallel vehicle to other forms of practice for understanding. For example, in the introduction to her book *Buddhism for Mothers of Young Children: Becoming a Mindful Parent*, Sarah Napthali writes;

> ...motherhood opens your heart to a new way of being. So does practicing Buddhist teachings. We open ourselves to all kinds of experiences: to learning, to changing our perspective, to "not-knowing" and to letting go of what we cling to. A Buddhist practice encourages us to live in a state of receptivity: What are my experiences teaching me? Can I see that my children, in so many ways, are raising me?[18]

And sometimes parenting and Buddhism are not parallel paths, albeit mutually constitutive, to find a "new way of being" for the parent, a two-pronged pathway to uncover lessons for oneself; the paths are represented as completely conflated and challenges the self utterly. Karen Maezen Miller explains that the dharma/parenting tension assaults the parent, who barely has the energy to recognize or claim agency let alone wield it, the experience is so complete:

17. John Makransky, "Family Practice," *Tricycle*, Summer 2001 (http://www.tricycle.com/-parenting/family-practice).

18. Sarah Napthali, *Buddhism for Mothers of Young Children: Becoming a Mindful Parent* (NSW, Australia: 2007), xiv.

> We parents come to our Buddhism spontaneously and quite unintentionally. Almost none of us would even call it buddhadharma, but it is. From the get-go we are engaged, body and mind, in the most intense ego battle of all time. We are thrashed—indeed, we are slain—by the raw immediacy of our children and their insistent demands for care and attention. We are carried through this bloodbath by an encompassing and intimate love that is effortless and uncontrived. Repeatedly experiencing life's difficulties—often many times before dawn—we confront our egos as the source of our own suffering, and observe the impermanence of all phenomena. Then we make macaroni and cheese for the billionth time.... A day in the life of a mother is a short course in the complete, three-point teaching of the *Diamond Sutra*: realize no-self, realize no-other, and perform meritorious deeds. Parenthood is the most transformative experience that most of us mortals will undertake during our lifetimes, but the transformation does not occur without committed daily practice.[19]

The child–parent relationship is not always so violent and visceral a manifestation of *anicca*, *anatta*, and *dukkha*, however, nor so self-oriented. Upon reflection, the relationship provides a fundamental, experiential structure of reciprocal dependence and gratitude. Though experienced in individual ways to differing degrees, the relationship is universal—everyone has a mother, and regardless of how that relationship evolves through time, the very fact of birth and early nurturing provides an empirical model for the cultivation of compassion.

> The parent–child relationship, which does play a significant role in some Mahayana contemplations of compassion, deals with the experience from the child's point of view, of evaluating his mother as extremely compassionate because she took care of him in a fashion similar to his inspiration to care for all sentient beings as a bodhisattva. But that set of contemplations *does not* valorize parenting as a spiritual discipline from the parents' point of view.[20]

True enough, the mother–child relationship as a model for becoming a bodhisattva does stem from the child's point of view, but that is likely an adult child in a position to reflect critically on what the experience of being a child can teach. It does not valorize the child's experience, but the adult's understanding of what her childhood represents. The focus is not on the child.

19. Karen Maezen Miller, "Commentary: Looking Under the Bed," *Buddhadharma*, December 1, 2008 (http://archive.thebuddhadharma.com/issues/2008/winter/commentary.php).
20. Rita Gross, *Buddhism After Patriarchy* (Albany: SUNY Press, 1993), 276.

Family relationships may be the context, the matrix of compassion, the multiyear "retreat," the opportunity to practice, the inspiration or motivation for practice, or the reflection of *anicca*, *dukkha*, and the like. Children may provide their parents with multiple and multivalent enacted dharma lessons, or the opportunity to reflect dharma teachings through the prism of children's presence. But parenting is also a responsibility to care for another, not only to learn from their presence (even intrusion) in one's life. Neil Gordon hints at this multivalent and pressing nature of the dharma inheritance experienced by the parent:

> And then, there is the fact that the basis of our relationship with our children is our responsibility for them. That responsibility dictates that anything to do with children must be about *them* before it is about *us*. That responsibility, in dharmic terms, can be very complex, and confuses the possibility of their teaching us. And this, in turn, leads to the second prevalent attitude toward children in American Buddhism: that we practice in order to be better humans, and better parents, and so our children are the beneficiaries of our spiritual growth. This, too, is both true and inadequate. This, too, fails to reflect the fantastic complexity of practicing and parenting.[21]

IMPLICIT AND EXPLICIT INHERITANCE: HOW AND WHAT PARENTS TEACH THEIR CHILDREN

Just how much agency a parent can exert in shaping or determining the dharma inheritance for her child is debatable; there are too many variables in parenting to control disbursement. But a parent might actively try—by striving to be an exemplar for children or by explicitly teaching. Either way, the attributes of the exemplar or the content of the lesson depends upon the successful practice of the parent. Some Western Buddhist practitioners realize that need for authenticity leads them back to a focus on their own self-cultivation first and foremost:

> ...if I wanted to progress along the path—to begin to cut through habitual patterns, loosen the sense I had that I and the rest of my world were solid, have any ability to arouse bodhicitta—I was going to have to make practice my first priority, and Buddhism my life. The four reminders—the truth of precious human birth, impermanence, *karma*, and the futility of *samsara*—were going to have to become parts of my blood and bones through contemplative meditation. Not only that: it wasn't enough

21. Neil Gordon, "Children and Dharma: An Introduction," in *Tricycle*, Spring 2002 (http://www.tricycle.com/feature/children-and-dharma-an-introduction).

> for me to be a student of the dharma. I would have to set an example for my daughter by living the teachings in our life together. As far as I can tell, there is only one way to do this, to live a dharmic family life, to be a dharmic mom: daily practice.[22]

In much contemporary Western Buddhist writing, a common theme emerges: one must practice and work on oneself first and then allow practice to infuse daily life to represent the dharma to one's children as an exemplar. Mary Talbot explains that in working toward becoming the exemplar for their children, parents pay attention to their own "skills" that ought to be cultivated even if there were no audience. "We model generosity, we emphasize the importance of sticking with a task such as paying attention, or sitting in meditation, until it becomes a skill we're really good at—because that's when it's most pleasurable and meaningful and bears fruit. We are beefing up our own practice in the process, but the point here is that we are giving something really valuable to our children."[23] Perhaps it is a convenient truth that focus on one's own practice will generate good effects for one's children and that, by modeling good and right behaviors, parents teach by example.

Part of "mindful parenting" is staying tuned in—both to one's own needs and to those of the children. Unsurprisingly for a tradition that in all its diversity of practices and concerns centers around finding and treading the middle way, balance is advocated versus the extremes of self-focused work (where family concerns are eclipsed by personal needs) or child-focused ambition (the "Tiger Mother" approach).[24] External, societal challenges inform where the balance can be found. Jon Kabat-Zinn suggests:

> To do it [our work as parents], we need to nurture, protect, and guide our children and bring them along until they are ready to walk their own paths. We also have to be whole ourselves, each his or her own person, with a life of our own, so that when they look at us, they will be able to see our wholeness against the sky..... This is not always so easy. Mindful parenting is hard work. It means knowing ourselves inwardly, and working at the interface where our inner lives meet the lives of our children. It is particularly hard work in this era, when the culture is intruding more and more into our homes and into our children's lives in so many new ways.[25]

22. Trish Deitch Rohrer, "On Parenting: The Dharma of Motherhood," *Tricycle*, Winter 2001 (http://www.tricycle.com/columns/on-parenting-the-dharma-motherhood).

23. Mary Talbot, "Introduction: Teaching Your Children Buddhist Values," *Tricycle*, Fall 2008 (http://www.tricycle.com/special-section/introduction-teaching-your-children-buddhist-values).

24. For a somewhat tongue-in-cheek exaggeration of this stance, see Amy Chua, *Battle Hymn of the Tiger Mother* (New York: Penguin Press, 2011).

25. Jon Kabat-Zinn and MylaKabat-Zinn, *Everyday Blessings: The Inner Work of Mindful Parenting* (New York: Hyperion, 1997), 4.

"Mindful parenting" or "dharmic parenting" requires work from the parent beyond basic responsibility for one's children. It also moves beyond a passive modeling of right behaviors and attitudes into a more explicit, intentional terrain. As they navigate the various tensions that connect and threaten their own practice and parenting, parents regard children less as object lessons for personal growth and see their own responsibilities as greater than just exemplifying the dharma (to whatever degree this is possible). Neil Gordon asks, "What is dharmic parenting?" and what can mindfulness bring to parenting?

> Is mindfulness an R-rated activity, to be saved for when the kids are to bed or the babysitter is there? Over time, that thought has come to seem less and less adequate to me. Over time, in fact, to abandon my children to an education that is not informed by the dharma has come to strike me as unethical. Is it not possible that between the extremes of treating our children as the occasion for our own dharmic progression, and offering them only ourselves as models of mindfulness, that there is a middle path? This, I have come to think, is a challenge posed to the traditional Buddhist teaching by the particular circumstances of practice in the West.[26]

Finding the middle with this degree of reflection and mindfulness, naming the challenges with Buddhist terms, and evoking timeless dharma truths while muddling through the muck and mire might be what sets the Western Buddhist parent apart from the Western parent. This is a messy time and place to be raising well-adjusted kids, and messiness makes it harder for parents to be tuned in to their children's needs. While a Buddhist parent may process the challenges of parenting through Buddhist lenses, the challenges are not unique to the Buddhist parent, as is seen in this recent *New York Times* blog:

> Today's parents, critics tell us, are managing to mess up our kids in two contradictory yet somehow simultaneous ways. On one hand, we push them to grow up too fast, proud that they are reading before they are walking, pleased that they are taking college-level math in middle school. On the other hand, we keep them from really growing up at all, helicoptering in to solve all their problems well into young adulthood.... Is it possible that the answer lies, as most answers do, somewhere in the middle? Maybe if childhood was time to be, well, a child, the rest might sort itself into place?[27]

26. Neil Gordon, "Children and Dharma: An Introduction" in *Tricycle*, Spring 2002 (http://www.tricycle.com/feature/children-and-dharma-an-introduction).

27. Lisa Belkin, "Growing Up Too Fast?" *The New York Times*, May 4, 2009 (http://parenting.blogs.nytimes.com/2009/05/04/growing-up-too-fast).

But Western Buddhist parents aren't necessarily reassured that they are sufficient exemplars or that the dharma inheritance will be organically absorbed by their children. Many parents resolve (or surrender to) the tensions undergirding their own practice by tuning into teaching or explicitly imparting the dharma inheritance:

> When my older son turned seven, I began to wonder what kind of spiritual guidance I could offer him and his younger brother. At a minimum, I wanted them to learn enough about the practices and teachings of Buddhism so that as adults they could turn to these resources if they desired or needed to. I also thought it would be wonderful if they could feel at home in Buddhism so that no matter where they went in life, this home would always be available as a refuge. And finally, because the greatest wealth I know is the well-being, peace and compassion I have found through my Buddhist practice, I've often wondered how I can pass along these riches more broadly to the next generation as a kind of spiritual inheritance. Remembering that Rahula had entered his father's care when he was seven, I searched through the Pali discourses to learn what I could about how the Buddha taught his son.[28]

And just as when Rāhula asked his father for his inheritance, the Buddha had Sāriputta ordain him, so do parents in the West seeking instruction for their children turn to community. "First-generation Western Buddhists are struggling with questions of how to educate their children about Buddhism and how to raise Buddhist children in a non-Buddhist environment. This is not an issue that can be dealt with family by family."[29] The inheritance includes the community and the reciprocal duty to sustain it. Mary Talbot writes:

> In the *Rāhula Sutta*, the Buddha guides his son to cultivate friendships with wise adults who can help him make good choices—people in whom he can trust and confide. If we can position ourselves to be those friends to children—our own or other people's—we are providing a great service. The neurodevelopmentalist and pediatrician Mel Levine, who has written many books about child development in the U.S. today, believes we live in the first-ever historical period when children look more to their peers and the media for their social cues than to their elders. If we don't want Hannah Montana and Iron Man serving as our kids' only role models, we need to earn and maintain their respect.[30]

28. Gil Fronsdal, "The Buddha as Parent," *Inquiring Mind*, Spring 2008 (http://www.insightmeditationcenter.org/books-articles/articles/the-buddha-as-a-parent/).
29. Rita Gross, *Buddhism After Patriarchy*, 237.
30. Mary Talbot, "Introduction: Teaching Your Children Buddhist Values," *Tricycle*, Fall 2008.

Just as it is difficult for a parent to expect that modeling alone will effectively teach their children, so too a community resorts to explicit teaching to complement the more general supporting environment. How does the Buddhist community in the West foster a child's development?

Part of the inheritance received by Western Buddhists is structures proffered by other traditions, perhaps the non-Buddhist traditions in which one was raised. For example, Protestant Christianity has been well served by the Sunday School and youth group model, but this is a relatively recent development—the Sunday School model has been in operation only for the last couple of centuries. In dharma centers, frequently the teaching falls to a collective of parents. "Creating a Buddhist life for our kids means that we rejigger our approach to parenting, or we become big time volunteers, researching teaching methods, setting up programs, making paper Vesak lanterns and prayer flags with eight-year-olds, teaching meditation in schools."[31]

Several dharma centers offer child care concurrent with meditation for the adults, but they by no means follow a prescribed curriculum: some do this on a weekly basis, some monthly, some integrate children into the dharma teaching (for a set period of time, such as the first ten or fifteen minutes), some follow a curriculum (see the Dharma Rain Center or Zen Mountain Monastery websites, for examples), some keep the child care as open play, with no set curriculum.

The San Francisco Zen Center at Green Gulch Farm has successfully integrated children and the disbursement of the dharma inheritance, striving for a balance between exposing children to the teachings and community while preserving the space and practice so critical for adults. On the first Sunday of each month, children are included in the dharma teaching for the first ten to fifteen minutes. The Zen Center also offers a Coming of Age program for seventh and eighth graders that meets once a month during the school year, culminating in a ceremony celebrated by family members and friends.[32] They also celebrate an annual family day:

> On Saturday, October 16, a sunny, crisp fall day at Green Gulch Farm, families gathered to celebrate a Day of Gratitude together with leaders Furyu Nancy Schroeder and Nancy Petrin. Attending this annual event were about seventeen families and their children. With Fu and Nancy, the families had the opportunity to have Green Gulch Farm to themselves and to enjoy a full day together. There was zendo time, sitting silently, and moments during the day to stop at the sound of a mindfulness bell and give attention to the breath. Activities included harvesting chard and pumpkins for the families to take home and several boxes of chard for

31. Mary, "Introduction: Teaching Your Children Buddhist Values," *Tricycle*, Fall 2008.

32. http://www.sfzc.org/ggf/display.asp?catid=3,123&pageid=1651&mode=c (last accessed Feb. 26, 2011)

> the San Francisco Food Bank. Additionally, the day was wrapped in joy and play, with games, songs, and making prayer flags and mala bracelets as reminders of the shared experience. Two Green Gulch residents led the group in singing songs accompanied by guitar, which included Thich Nhat Hahn's "Breathing In, Breathing Out." During the closing tea in the zendo, each person had the opportunity to express what they most enjoyed during the day. One boy said, "Everything!"[33]

In spite of such community-centered efforts to support parents and periodic community-wide events, the hallmark of a place of Buddhist practice in the throes of practice is an absence of children in the midst.

Rita Gross explains that the lack of children in meditation halls may not be an accidental by-product of an adult-focused tradition but may instead be indicative of the work that has to happen before such an environment can be conducive to one's practice:

> People fare best in the meditation hall as adult individuals, which is why Buddhism is not especially oriented towards or focused on families and children, however important these concerns are to some Buddhists. Meditation halls, with their silence and aloneness, even in the midst of a crowd, are not especially "child friendly," as many Western Buddhists discover in their attempts to raise Buddhist children in Western societies ... The meditation hall is usually not interesting to people until they become adults, facing the sorrow and complexity of life as a human being in *samsara*, the infinite ocean of birth and death fuelled by *karma*, the inexorable law of cause and effect.[34]

Speaking to a nonspecialist audience concerned with the United Nations convention on the Rights of the Child, Rita Gross explains the crux of this conundrum:

> In its classic forms, whether doctrinally or institutionally, Buddhism does not especially focus on children or on the family. It is not a child-centered or a family-centered religion. This is because its deepest goals are not the worldly continuities so sought and valued by some religious orientations, but the transformation of conventional attitudes into enlightened mind. That is to say, seeing clearly that ceaseless impermanence is the deepest nature of reality brings freedom, tranquility, and compassion. This insight, experienced so deeply that it transforms one's very core, is far more valued than is maintaining cultural and familial or economic success.[35]

33. http://news.sfzc.org/content/view/920/52/.
34. Rita Gross, "Child and Family in Buddhism," 84.
35. Gross, "Child and Family in Buddhism," 82.

Thus, during an individually focused pursuit of enlightened mind, parents struggle to discern not only how best to guide their children to the dharma inheritance, but also whether to do so at all. Sumi Loundon considers the particular reticence of first-generation parents to directly teach or otherwise determine the religious education of their children:

> One unusual feature of the first generation of parents is that they are hands-off in teaching their own children about religion. Many of these parents say they remember, as children, being forced to attend church or the synagogue against their will. They came to dislike catechism, Sunday school, rituals, holidays, the authority of the clergy and the institution. As a result, many Buddhist parents decided they would not force their children to learn Buddhism for either of two reasons. One, they did not want their children to experience what they had from their own parents or, two, they secretly wanted their children to become Buddhist but knew that forcing them would make them rebel against it.[36]

The observation that one must find and nurture one's own experience of the dharma runs through both Western American Buddhist narratives and Asian American Buddhist expressions, as Sharon Suh discovered in her research among Korean Buddhist communities. Apparent parental ambivalence and the resulting lack of pressure on their children to be Buddhist are not unique components or "unusual features" specific to first-generation Buddhist parents, but are instead part of a technique, perhaps even expedient device, implemented effectively within Buddhist traditions. Suh discusses the "rhetoric of individuality" particular to Korean Buddhist communities in America, something that may develop within the parenting toolbox of second-generation Western Buddhists as well:

> Despite the hopes of many Buddhist parents that their own children would attend temple services, members of Sa Chal indicated that they believed that their children should choose their own religion. This choice for many Buddhists is, above all, the measure of what being a Buddhist is all about. Mrs. Jin, for example, a fifty-year-old mother of two, prides herself on having encouraged her sons to attend church so that when they decided for themselves what religion to practice, they would make an informed decision. "I even sent my kids to church. Why did I send them to church? I told them that they should try going to church and try to compare the merits of each faith. Since I have taken them to

36. Sumi Loundon, "Sunday School for Buddhists?: Nurturing Spirituality in Children," in *Nurturing Child and Adolescent Spirituality: Perspectives from the World's Religious Traditions*, ed. Karen Marie Yust (Lanham, MD: Rowman & Littlefield Publishers, 2006), 347.

temple with me since they were young, they were not influenced [by Christianity]. Rather than telling them not to go to church, I told them that they should try to understand the Christian faith in God so that later on, if they chose to believe in Buddhism, their beliefs would be deep and strong because they have chosen for themselves."[37]

And then there is the tension of timing: when is a good time to begin a more formal instruction, to move beyond the subtler work of exemplifying Buddhist practice? Is there such a thing as a Buddhist child? Or does one need sufficient life experience and reflective thought to identify oneself as Buddhist, to undertake refuge fueled by one's own conviction? As Sumi Loundon sought a younger generation's perspective on Buddhist thought and practice, she struggled to find more teen voices, noting that she "found that teens tended to be early in their self-identification."[38]

Does a Buddhist child need to self-identify as such? Can Buddhist practice be a family endeavor (with varying degrees of commitment and intentionality of the individuals) or is it inherently individual? A senior student at the Zen Mountain Monastery, Bethany Saltman reflects that while she has undertaken the Bodhisattva Vow, her five-year-old daughter has not. And yet the frustrations for a child of not getting what she wants—and then fixating on it—is a lesson that is played out daily, requiring at minimum some distraction or redirection by the parent if not more overt teaching.

Sometimes people ask, Can kids practice? I know there's a rule against answering a question with a question, but please allow me to ask three: Are they suffering? Do they want that suffering to stop? Can they drop their ideas about the way things are supposed to be and return to real life? Clearly the last question is the trickiest one, and that's where we and our perpetual bags of cashews [distractions] come in handy. The lucky thing is that we—adult or child practitioners—don't always need to see ourselves through our attachments or understand what is happening. For kids especially, they just need to be supported enough to actually feel the (inevitable) transformation of their experience, again and again and again. Without obsessive fixing. That's practice: a commitment to letting go of the agonizing self and easing into the luminous pool of things as they are. And it's a long haul, so lucky is the kid who starts young.[39]

37. Sharon Suh, "Asserting Buddhist Selves in a Christian Land: The Maintenance of Religious Identity Among Korean Buddhists in America," in *Religion and Spirituality in Korean America,* ed. David K. Yoo and Ruth H. Chung (Champaign: University of Illinois Press, 2008), 47.

38. Sumi Loundon, *Blue Jean Buddha: Voices of Young Buddhists* (Somerville, MA: Wisdom Publications, 2001), xvii.

39. Bethany Saltman, "Flowers Fall," *Chronogram,* March 2011, (http://www.chronogram.com/issue/2011/3/Whole+Living/Flowers-Fall-March-2011).

CONCLUSION

Looking at structures within Buddhist thought and practice for a useful paradigm to describe the transmission of dharma to children, Sandy Eastoak uses the metaphor of the lotus rising above the muck and mire of *saṃsāra*. The questions raised and compared to parts of the lotus—roots, stem, and flower—capture some of the temporally bounded understandings of truth that the Buddha touched upon in that first sermon to his seven-year-old son Rāhula when he advised examination of the skillfulness of past, present, and future bodily, verbal, and mental actions. The effective transmission of the dharma to children depends on reflection on the past and context, consideration of the present and methods, and attention to intention and the way to shape the future. Within a list of the "complex of dilemmas" that Eastoak defines as the root of practice, we find two interesting questions that underscore the therapeutic or self-focused stream of thought so prevalent in Western Buddhist reflection today. "How do we clean up our own *karma* so the pain we experienced as children is not passed on? How do we make parenting our vehicle for enlightenment?"[40] Both of these questions reflect more on the parent's experience than the child's; the child is in this case the tool or grounds for the parent's own use of the inheritance. The parent focus continues up the stem, perhaps drawing its sustenance not from a wider understanding of *saṃsāra* but from a particular experience of *saṃsāra* perceived through a Western parent's self-focus.

The stem, for Eastoak, is the "social context that honors parenting as a spiritual path." The stem raises other questions that are more immediate:

> Where do we find support for our efforts to solve our root dilemmas? How do we get recognition that the problems we are struggling with are not obstacles to spiritual practice, but *are* spiritual practice? How do Buddhist traditions guide us? How do we find or create guidance where the tradition is lacking? How do we dare suggest the tradition may be lacking? Where can we practice communally *with* our children? How can we establish children's programs and family practice days within our sanghas? How do parents and children function in the sangha? How does the sangha function in the passage of the generations?[41]

The bulk of these questions are very much rooted in parents' experience and perceived needs. If the only concern is on how parenting affects the parent, where are the children?

40. Sandy Eastoak, *Dharma Family Treasures: Sharing Buddhism with Children*, (Berkeley, CA: North Atlantic Books, 1994), xiv.
41. Eastoak, *Dharma Family Treasures*, xiv.

The stem leads to and supports the blossom, the imagined future flowering of one's parental efforts in the case of the child, or the next generation of the sangha in the case of the community. There is only so much agency a parent wields in directly influencing the flower, and only so much power one has in ensuring that the inheritance is passed on. And part of the hopes of parents is that the children will do even more with the inheritance, that the children will surpass the hopes of their parents and do so independently and authentically. "How can our children find their own way to the wisdom that beckons us? By what means will the mindfulness of their lives not be limited by the extent of our understanding, but grow and flourish beyond us?"[42] Parents may plant the seeds and cultivate the ground, but the children—as they grow (or not) into their own practice—determine the fruit.

We may fruitfully return to the iconic story of the Buddha's own son's inheritance to determine a model, of sorts, for transmission. There are obvious limits to its salience for and applicability to the modern family, of course. But thinking on the few vestiges of the father–son relationship between the Buddha and Rāhula that we find in the *suttas* may help Western Buddhists come to terms with what is otherwise ostensibly an untenable solution to the strains that family life puts on one's practice (and the converse). The basic structure—that the Buddha abandoned his fetter, his child, in favor of practice—threatens to overwhelm the subtleties of what is at work in the story.

Fu Schroeder picked up on one subtlety. Sarah Napthali, expert on Buddhist motherhood, concludes her book *Buddhism for Mothers: A Calm Approach to Caring for Yourself and Your Children*, with the following anecdote:

> As mothers, what can we make of that story of the Buddha leaving his family in the middle of the night? I asked Fu Schroeder. "Oh, but he wasn't the Buddha when he left his child. He was a young prince, in terrible pain," she answered. "If you're awake, you don't leave your child. Where would you go?"[43]

There is something else going on as well. The commentaries claim certain ages for the boy Rāhula during his lessons from the Buddha. Not to advocate a literal reading for a fixed chronology, narratively it does seem important which lesson comes first and when in the child's development. According to the commentary, in the *Ambalaṭṭhikārāhulovāda Sutta* (Instructions to Rāhula at the Mango Stone),[44] Rāhula was seven. Rāhula saw the Buddha approaching and set out water for washing the Buddha's feet. The lesson that is given is based on concrete observation—using the water dipper that the Buddha has at

42. Eastoak, *Dharma Family Treasures*, xiv.
43. Sarah Napthali, *Buddhism for Mothers: A Calm Approach to Caring for Yourself and Your Children* (New South Wales, Australia: Allen & Unwin, 2010), 218.
44. Pali Text Society, M i 414

hand—and illustrates the importance of staying tuned in to truth and observation for the practice of renunciation (Rāhula is a *samañña*).[45] It is a basic lesson on the harm done by lying; any parent of a seven-year-old knows just how salient a topic that is for that age.

And yet for many Western Buddhist parents, lying is an expedient mean employed in parenting on a regular—and dharmic—basis:

> So how do we raise children with the awareness that those few who actually do battle with injustice lose far more often than they win; that the vast majority of humanity lives and will probably always live in abject physical misery and political oppression; that anything like spiritual freedom may be hundreds of lifetimes away? Anyone who has ever walked their child to school in the morning knows the answer to this one, it's easy. What we do is, we lie. We conceal the basic truths of life from our children—the insatiability of desire, the radical truth of impermanence, the noble truths of the ubiquity of suffering. And while we lie we consistently teach them to rely on the very identity that later, if they are to be truly happy, they will struggle, for years and years—as we do—to dismantle: the self.[46]

Perhaps structurally speaking, Western Buddhists are on the cusp of adulthood themselves. Or perhaps, as Gross insinuated, the very nature of parenthood—the dependency, urgency, responsibility, and distraction—precludes the full immersion or renunciation needed for the full fruition of the dharma. Perhaps the inheritance becomes available in stages to adult practitioners, just as it is doled out by parents to their children in implicit and explicit ways over time.

It is only at age eighteen, according to the commentary, that Rāhula is deemed primed for meditation training. In the *Mahārāhulovāda Sutta* (The Greater Exhortation to Rāhula),[47] the Buddha said, "Rāhula, any form whatsoever that is past, future, or present; internal or external; blatant or subtle;

45. The lesson begins thus: "Then the Blessed One, having left a little bit of water in the water dipper, said to Ven. Rāhula, "Rāhula, do you see this little bit of left-over water remaining in the water dipper?" "Yes, sir." "That's how little of a contemplative [*samañña*, "tuned-in-one"] there is in anyone who feels no shame at telling a deliberate lie." Having tossed away the little bit of left-over water, the Blessed One said to Ven. Rāhula, "Rāhula, do you see how this little bit of left-over water is tossed away?" "Yes, sir." "Rāhula, whatever there is of a contemplative in anyone who feels no shame at telling a deliberate lie is tossed away just like that. . . ." See "Ambalatthika-rahulovadaSutta: Instructions to Rahula at Mango Stone" (MN 61), translated from the Pāli by Thanissaro Bhikkhu. *Access to Insight*, June 14, 2010 http://www.accesstoinsight.org/tipitaka/mn/mn.061.than.html.

46. Neil Gordon, "Children and Dharma: An Introduction" in *Tricycle*, Spring 2002 (http://www.tricycle.com/feature/children-and-dharma-an-introduction).

47. Pali Text Society, M i 420.

common or sublime; far or near: every form is to be seen as it actually is with right discernment as: 'This is not mine. This is not my self. This is not what I am.'"[48]

Notably, it is neither the Buddha as father or teacher, nor the son/student Rāhula who makes the next move to determine the appropriate lesson or the student's aptitude. It is another adult, an intercessor of sorts: "Ven. Sāriputta saw Ven. Rāhula sitting at the foot of a tree, his legs folded crosswise, his body held erect, and with mindfulness set to the fore. On seeing him, he said to him, 'Rāhula, develop the meditation of mindfulness of in-and-out breathing. The meditation of mindfulness of in-and-out breathing, when developed and pursued, is of great fruit, of great benefit.'" Rāhula works independently in seclusion, and, "[t]hen Ven. Rāhula, emerging from his seclusion in the late afternoon, went to the Blessed One and, having bowed down, sat to one side. As he was sitting there, he said to him, 'How, lord, is mindfulness of in-and-out breathing to be developed and pursued so as to be of great fruit, of great benefit?'" Rāhula, who is eighteen years old at this point, according to the commentary, asks for it. Another teacher has set him upon the path, but Rāhula determines its course.[49]

Considering the amount of material Western Buddhists have produced reflecting on their own practice and how it is hindered or augmented by family life—specifically child care—keeps the focus on the older generation. What is it that these children are inheriting, from whom, and how? A serious inquiry coming from a child's perspective, albeit a grown child, was raised by Sumi Loundon:

> Where, I wondered, are the young Buddhists of today who should be inheriting the dharma from the older Buddhists? Are they like me, do they share the same questions and interests? If they exist, what kind of sangha are they creating? What does it mean to be a Buddhist in America today and where will it take us tomorrow? What challenges do we face? Given how few young Buddhists I knew, I became a little concerned that there would not be anyone to inherit the dharma. Who would be *my* dharma teacher when I was fifty? Who would run the centers and temples?[50]

It is a challenge to survey the most current musings on lay practice and concerns, to weed through what is an extensive array of blogs, various journal articles, magazines, pop-media articles, and self-help manuals. The study of

48. "Maha-Rahulovada Sutta: The Greater Exhortation to Rahula" (MN 62), translated from the Pāli by Thanissaro Bhikkhu. *Access to Insight*, June 14, 2010 http://www.accesstoinsight.org/tipitaka/mn/mn.062.than.html.

49. "Maha-Rahulovada Sutta: The Greater Exhortation to Rahula" (MN 62).

50. Sumi Loundon, *Blue Jean Buddha: Voices of Young Buddhists*, vi.

Western Buddhism seems simultaneously established, entrenched even, and is still forming at a snail's pace. We might profitably look at one of the foremothers of this field for a sense of how far it has come, and how much work is left to do. In her now classic book *Buddhism after Patriarchy: A Feminist History, Analysis, and Reconstruction of Buddhism*, Rita Gross radically revisioned Buddhism for the West, supplying a new way into thought and practice. And yet in the concluding chapters she struggles to move into pointed, prescriptive language for laypeople regarding the tension between home life and practice. She lands on what she calls "the razor's edge" and recommends the tried and true Middle Way:

> While affirming the sacred potential of ordinary domestic householder concerns, one must also hold firmly to the Buddhist dissatisfaction with conventional attitudes and approaches to them.... That ongoing attitude of awareness will itself be the protection we need to keep us in balance and out of extreme behavior, whether the extreme behavior would take the form of a continual need to be in retreat from "worldly activities" or the temptation to lose and bury oneself in excessive involvement with career or family, by becoming a workaholic or by reproducing excessively.[51]

In other words, one should cultivate an "ongoing attitude of awareness" to mitigate the extremes inherent in parenting. With this attitude, there is no separate time or place that is most proper for mindfulness practice:

> The container for "true practice," whether it occurs in the meditation hall or the so-called "ordinary world," is the basic Buddhist mindfulness discipline, taught with many subtle variations. This is the training that allows one eventually to be able to maintain awareness, whether in one's own garden or the monastery garden.... True practice really is being here, aware, with "just this," whether "just this" is one's everyday occupation or one's seat in the meditation hall.[52]

Applying this to the conundrum of the dharma inheritance, an explicit time and place for explicitly teaching the dharma can be paired with modeling good practice (and hoping that a child may incline naturally as a result). An active community of support serves two purposes: a child is explicitly taught and a parent is given the room to work on his or her own practice knowing the children are cared for. The Buddha's sermon to his seven-year-old biological son can be just as effectively addressed to anyone in the position to inherit the

51. Gross, *Buddhism After Patriarchy*, 280.
52. Gross, *Buddhism After Patriarchy*, 278.

dharma. Rāhula may be a child, but what is a child within the Buddhist tradition? Might any practitioner, even a seasoned one, parent or not, be in this position?

Working as a constructive theologian, Rita Gross considers how childhood might be defined for Buddhists:

> It should come as no surprise then, that the state of childhood itself is not regarded as a special state. Children are neither especially endowed with innocence and goodness beyond what adults possess, nor are children in an unredeemed or depraved state of nature different in quality from that of adults who have been initiated or processed in some way. They are not waiting for some ritual, like baptism or circumcision to be performed upon them to transform them into human beings, members of a culture, beings capable of a state of grace. They are simply children—pre-adults going through the karmic process of moving from childhood, with its physical, mental, and spiritual conditions, into adulthood, at which point one is physically, mentally, and spiritually capable of practicing meditation to pursue enlightenment.[53]

The crux of the *Ambalaṭṭhikārāhulovāda Sutta* is that one should reflect on one's bodily, verbal, and mental actions before, during, and after the action., One should consider whether that action will lead to self-harm or harm done to others, whether it is an unskillful action that may lead to negative consequences (and if so, the intention to perform that action or the doing of the action should be prevented). After an action, too, one should submit to mindful contemplation of that action:

> Having done a [bodily, verbal, or mental] action, you should reflect on it: "This [bodily, verbal, or mental] action I have done—did it lead to self-affliction, to the affliction of others, or to both? Was it an unskillful [bodily, verbal, or mental] action, with painful consequences, painful results?" If, on reflection, you know that it led to self-affliction, to the affliction of others, or to both; it was an unskillful [bodily, verbal, or mental] action with painful consequences, painful results, then you should confess it, reveal it, lay it open to the Teacher or to a knowledgeable companion in the holy life. Having confessed it ...you should exercise restraint in the future. But if on reflection you know that it did not lead to affliction ...it was a skillful [bodily, verbal, or mental] action with pleasant consequences, pleasant results, then you should stay

53. Gross, "Child and Family in Buddhism," in *Religious Dimensions of Child and Family Life: Reflections on the UN Convention on the Rights of the Child,* ed. Harold Coward and Philip Cook (Waterloo, ON: Wilfrid Laurier University Press, 1996), 85.

mentally refreshed and joyful, training day and night in skillful mental qualities.[54]

Perhaps what we have considered here can be understood through the lens of a lesson delivered to a seven-year-old. Passing on the inheritance of the dharma is a bodily, verbal, and mental act. Parents and community members physically model the practice for children: this is done both in teaching right posture for meditation in the meditation hall and in the way lives are lived beyond it. Verbally, Buddhism is encapsulated and transmitted to the next generation through dharma teachings and manuals—there is a proliferation of children's books and books geared to teens and young adults, as Karen Derris's chapter in this volume amply demonstrates. And mentally, there is much consideration, only hinted at in this essay. The intention to transmit the tradition is there implicitly in the ways Western Buddhist parents are living their lives and explicitly in Sunday schools, retreats, and camps and how they represent themselves in print sources or on various web forums. But the reflexive piece—reflection not on one's own experience of "dharmic parenting" but instead on the experience of this generation's "children of the Buddha"—will have to come later.

54. "Ambalatthika-rahulovadaSutta: Instructions to Rahula at Mango Stone" (MN 61), translated from the Pāli by Thanissaro Bhikkhu. *Access to Insight*, June 14, 2010 http://www.accesstoinsight.org/tipitaka/mn/mn.061.than.html.

CHAPTER 19

Young Lord Maitreya

The Curious Case of Jiddu Krishnamurti

HILLARY RODRIGUES

Over the last two millennia, the notion of Maitreya, the teaching Buddha foretold to succeed Siddhārtha Gautama, has played a significant role in the religious imaginations of more than just Buddhists. Not only have various predictions been made about the circumstances of this Buddha's arrival and the nature of his persona and teachings, but there have been numerous persons who have declared themselves to be Maitreya or one of his incarnations.[1] Some have actually been regarded as Maitreya by certain religious communities. Notable among these contenders is the jolly rotund figure of Budai ("Hemp Sack"). According to folk tradition he was a Chinese Chan Buddhist monk named Qieci who lived during the Later Liang Dynasty (907–923 CE). Budai is often depicted as the "Laughing Buddha" in Chinese Buddhist temples. In fact, his image is so abundant in Chinatown stores throughout the world that many uninformed people mistakenly regard his image as that of the historical founder of Buddhism, Śākyamuni.[2] Another notable claimant, particularly because she was female, was the Chinese empress Wu Zetian (624705), who added the name Cishi (Maitreya) to her title five years after usurping the throne of the Tang Empire.[3] Belief in the empress's claim, however, was neither widespread nor enduring.

1. Between the fifth and early sixth centuries, in China alone, there were nine well-known messianic movements whose leaders sometimes claimed to be manifestations of Maitreya. See E. Zürcher, "'Beyond the Jade Gate': Buddhism in China, Vietnam, and Korea," in *The World of Buddhism*, ed. H. Bechert and R. Gombrich (London: Thames & Hudson, 1984), 202.

2. Taigen Daniel Leighton, *Faces of Compassion: Classic Bodhisattva Archetypes and Their Modern Expression* (Boston: Wisdom, 2003), 258.

3. Tansen Sen, *Buddhism, Diplomacy, and Trade* (Honolulu: University of Hawaii Press, 2003), 97. Also, a manuscript (S.6520) from the Dunhuang cave complex

This chapter focuses on one case of singular interest, that of the contemporary religious teacher or philosopher Jiddu Krishnamurti (1895–1986). In particular, it examines his childhood and early adulthood, a tumultuous period during which the young Krishnamurti was selected by the Theosophical Society as the physical vehicle for the next World-Teacher (*jagadguru*). Much has been written about Krishnamurti's life in the form of official biographies and reminiscences by people who were close to him.[4] Here I will highlight primarily the Buddhist features in his upbringing. According to the Theosophical Society's understanding of the spiritual evolution of humanity, a World-Teacher would emerge to spur the development of human consciousness. That teacher would be Lord Maitreya. Thus Krishnamurti was purposefully raised to become the physical vehicle for the consciousness of Lord Maitreya, the next teaching Buddha, a role that he initially accepted along the lines delineated by his Theosophist mentors. However, in a pivotal shift as a young adult, Krishnamurti disbanded his community of followers and trenchantly criticized all institutional forms of religion. In an enormous body of discourses that parallel the core of Buddhist teachings, but without Buddhism as it is conventionally configured, he spent the remainder of his life pointing to a transformative insight that he was convinced frees persons from the bondage of their conditioned thinking. Krishnamurti's curious case will be used here to explore a variety of issues, including transcultural notions of Buddhahood, institutional Buddhism(s), and organized spirituality. Particular focus will be on the issue of religious upbringing, and whether it is possible to be free from deeply conditioned childhood beliefs.

KRISHNAMURTI, THEOSOPHY, AND MAITREYA

Jiddu Krishnamurti was born in 1895 in Madanapalle, in the Indian state of Andhra Pradesh. He was the eighth child in a Telegu-speaking brahmin family. His mother died when he was ten, and in 1909 Krishnamurti's father, who had been a member of the Theosophical Society (TS) since 1882, found employment at the Society's headquarters at Adyar, a locality in Chennai (formerly Madras). The Jiddus moved to Adyar, and it was there that Krishnamurti was discovered by Charles Webster Leadbeater, one of the most influential leaders of the Society. Leadbeater claimed powers of clairvoyance and apparently discerned from Krishnamurti's aura that the boy (then fourteen) would be a

(along the Silk Road in China) claims that Empress Wu was the incarnation of Maitreya and should rule China (see Quang Ning, *Art, Religion, and Politics in Medieval China* [Honolulu: University of Hawaii Press], 112).

4. See, for instance, Pupul Jayakar, *Krishnamurti: A Biography* (Cambridge: Harper & Row, 1986), and Roland Vernon, *Star in the East: Krishnamurti, the Invention of a Messiah* (London: Constable, 2000). Jayakar knew Krishnamurti, whereas Vernon did not. Examples of reminiscences include Gabriele Blackburn's *The Light of Krishnamurti* (Ojai: Idylwild Books, 1996), and Donald Ingram Smith's *The Transparent Mind: A Journey with Krishnamurti* (Ojai: Edwin House, 1999).

suitable vehicle for Lord Maitreya, the next World-Teacher (*jagadguru*), a pivotal figure in the TS's envisioned scheme for the spiritual evolution of humanity. Leadbeater's assertion puzzled most onlookers, because Krishnamurti's undernourished physique, unkempt appearance, and vacant expression pointed to the contrary. Nevertheless, Krishnamurti, along with his younger brother Nityananda (b. 1898), were brought into tutelage by Theosophist mentors, including Annie Besant, then president of the TS, who eventually became the legal guardian of the two boys.[5]

Conceptions of Maitreya vary even among Buddhist groups. There is an early reference to him in the *Cakkavatisīhanāda-sutta* of the *Dīgha-nikāya*, part of the early core of canonical Buddhist scriptures, especially for the Theravāda tradition.[6] Several indicators suggest that the text has been tampered with and they may thus be insertions from a later period.[7] However, it is in the *Mahāvastu* (second century BCE to fourth century CE) that Maitreya first definitively emerges, heading a list of future Buddhas. As a proto-Mahāyāna text deriving from the Mahāsāṅghikas, the *Mahāvastu's* portrayal of Maitreya is surprisingly atypical of their notion of Buddhahood, which is characterized by supramundane (*lokottara*) attributes.[8] This suggests that the concept of a future Buddha likely predated the *Mahāvastu's* portrayal. Another early reference to Maitreya is found in the *Lalitavistara* (third century CE). There Maitreya is not specifically called a successor to Śākyamuni, but is entrusted with the task of instructing beings in the Tuṣita heaven after Śākyamuni's departure.[9]

When examining the thought of other religious groups of the period, such as the Jains, one realizes that notions about the periodic emergence of great spiritual figures (e.g., Tīrthaṅkaras) who presented the same doctrine in eons past and who will inevitably emerge in the future were not at all unusual, even when Śākyamuni was alive.[10] The theme of the future manifestation of a spiritual teacher may also have roots in ancient Middle Eastern teachings (e.g., Zoroastrianism), which were influential in northwest India at that time.[11] The portrayals of Maitreya vary in the

5. See Mary Lutyens, *Krishnamurti: The Years of Awakening* (New York: Farrar, Straus and Giroux, 1975), 40.

6. See the *Cakkavattisīhanāda-sutta* of the *Dīghanikāya* 26.25 in *The Dialogues of the Buddha*, trans. T. W. and C. A. F. Rhys-Davids (London: Oxford University Press, 1921), 3: 55–76.

7. Among these indicators is that Maitreya does not appear anywhere else in this literature, and that the style of the *sutta* is atypical. See Richard Gombrich, *Theravada Buddhism: A Social History from Ancient Benares to Modern Colombo* (New York: Routledge and Kegan Paul, 1988), 83–85.

8. See *Mahāvastu*, 1: 46, 67–69.

9. See *Lalitavistara*, 318.

10. See Padmanabh S. Jaini, "Stages in the Bodhisattva Career of the Tathāgata Maitreya," in *Maitreya, the Future Buddha*, ed. Alan Sponberg and Helen Hardacre (Cambridge: Cambridge University Press, 1988), 54–90.

11. Among these influences, A. L. Basham pointed to the doctrine of the Śaośyant (savior) in Zoroastrianism, who appears at the end-time to lead the forces of light in their conquest of the dark forces of evil. See A. L. Basham, *The Wonder That Was India* (New York: Grove Press, 1954), 274.

Buddhist literature that emerges after the *Mahāvastu*, but he progressively enters into both Mahāyāna and non-Mahāyāna texts and traditions, and despite variations in the particulars, develops a widely established persona as the next teaching Buddha, before the advent of the Christian era.[12]

Rhys-Davids points out that the Maitreya (Pali: Metteyya) legend mimics that of Siddhārtha Gautama in that he is reputed to have been a bodhisattva (an aspiring Buddha) for countless previous lives and currently resides in the Tuṣita Heaven. When it is time for his earthly manifestation, typically described as when the previous Buddha's teachings have essentially disappeared as an inevitable result of the distortions induced by human ignorance, Maitreya, like Siddhārtha, will take up birth as a prince, renounce his princely life, and ultimately attain buddhahood under a special kind of tree (a dragon flower), akin to Gautama's *bodhi* tree.[13] By the first few centuries of the Common Era, Maitreya's popularity had exploded and he often appeared in sculptures and paintings in Central Asia. He was frequently shown seated in the "European manner" (i.e., *pralambapadāsana*), or standing, as well as in some variant of the lotus posture, where one sits cross-legged with soles pointing upward (e.g., *ardha-padmāsana*).[14] He was "adopted by the Manicheans, who fused Mithras Invictus, Jesus Christ, and Ajita Maitreya into one composite savior figure."[15] Thus, while Maitreya himself may have emerged within Buddhism as a creative fusion influenced by similar ideas in other religious traditions (e.g., Zoroastrianism, Jainism, the Ājīvakas), his persona was also being adopted and melded into that of a savior-to-come by non-Buddhists, such as the Manicheans, more than 1,500 years ago. The Theosophical Society's adoption of Lord Maitreya into their scheme of humanity's spiritual evolution is thus hardly novel and has long-established precedents. Paralleling a figure such as Mani, who was configured as an amalgam of the expected saviors in various religious traditions, the Theosophical Society had chosen to designate their conceived savior-to-come, namely, the World-Teacher or *jagadguru*, as Lord Maitreya. This choice points to the robust influence of Buddhist symbols and doctrines within Theosophy. However, despite the many parallels with Buddhist conceptions, there are distinctive features in Theosophy and its notion of Maitreya to which we must first turn.

THE THEOSOPHICAL SOCIETY

The Theosophical Society was founded in New York City in 1875 by Madame Helena Petrovna Blavatsky, Colonel Henry Steel Olcott, and others. Blavatsky

12. Basham, *The Wonder That Was India*, 274.

13. T. W. Rhys Davids, "Anāgata Vaṃsa," in *Encyclopedia of Religion and Ethics*, Part I (Whitefish: Kessinger Publishing, 2003), 414.

14. See, for instance, Asha Das, *Maitreya Buddha in Literature, History and Art* (Kolkata: Punthi Pustak, 2003).

15. Richard H. Robinson, *The Buddhist Religion: A Historical Introduction* (Belmont, CA: Dickenson, 1970).

and Olcott eventually moved the Society's headquarters to Adyar, near Chennai, in the south Indian state of Tamil Nadu. Adopting the motto, "There is no religion higher than Truth," the TS defined itself as an institution composed of a nondiscriminatory universal fellowship dedicated to the comparative study of science, religion, and philosophy, and the investigation of humanity's latent powers and natural laws yet unknown.

The Theosophical vision of Ultimate Reality is an impersonal Absolute. This Absolute cognitively appears to manifest and then dissolve the creation, out of and back into itself periodically. However, this oscillation between manifestation with differentiation and dissolution back into the fundamental unity is an illusion generated through the mechanism of time. Nothing is actually created, although the differentiating manifestation appears to "evolve" or "emanate" in a process over huge phases of time. This cosmic evolution takes place in cyclic patterns, affecting all items within reality, including the consciousnesses of individual human beings who progress through many incarnations. The teleological outcome is that Ultimate Reality, concealed from itself through its manifestation, will eventually become conscious or self-aware. Toward that objective, humanity will evolve progressively into a Universal Brotherhood. This progress is facilitated by various beings, such as the Masters (Mahātmas), who possess more evolved states of consciousness than most human beings at this stage in the evolutionary cycle. Although they are at the lower end of the Occult Hierarchy, the Masters, who have reached the pinnacle of the development of human consciousness, assist in directing this development for those less evolved, through their energy and thoughts or even through the founding of a new religion. Individual beings are not coerced in their development, however; they must take responsibility for their own progress.[16]

It is difficult to ascertain just how many of the Theosophical Society's members know or accept these teachings, but it is certain that many do not. However, for those interested in entering more deeply into its esoteric teachings, Theosophy offers a path of five graded initiations by the Masters, purportedly leading to a condition of unbroken perception of the Unity that is the Absolute.[17] The Great White Brotherhood is composed of all initiates regardless of their initiatory levels.[18] The collective progress of humanity toward the

16. See Helena Blavatsky, *The Key to Theosophy, Being a Clear Exposition, in the Form of Question and Answer, of the Ethics, Science, and Philosophy for the Study of which the Theosophical Society Has Been Founded* (London: The Theosophical Publishing Company, 1889).

17. See Bruce F. Campbell, *Ancient Wisdom Revived: A History of the Theosophical Movement* (Berkeley: University of California Press, 1980), 31–74.

18. The term "Great White Brotherhood" is developed in C. W. Leadbeater's, *The Masters and the Path* (Wheaton, IL: Theosophical Publishing House, 1925). Earlier foundational notions of a secret organization of highly developed spiritual beings who oversee humanity's spiritual progress are found in Karl von Eckartshausen's "Council of Light" (see his *The Cloud Upon the Sanctuary*, trans. Mme. Isabel de Steige [San Diego: Book Tree, 2006]), and H. P. Blavatsky's concept of the "Masters of the Hidden Brotherhood" or the "Mahātmas." The British occultist Aleister Crowley

Universal Brotherhood is believed to be occurring through a sequential evolution of seven Root-Races. Humanity, situated at the level of the Fifth Root-Race was ripe for a change, and Madame Blavatsky predicted that the emergence of the Sixth Root-Race was imminent and would occur in Southern California. The hallmark of its consciousness would be a "spiritual intuition that illuminates the intellect."[19]

Another figure in Theosophy's Occult Hierarchy is the *mahāguru* (Great Teacher) or *jagadguru* (World-Teacher), a term conventionally used for the head of the monastic schools founded by Śaṅkarācārya, the renowned ninth-century proponent of nondualistic (*advaita*) Vedānta philosophy. However, the *jagadguru* in Theosophy is a different sort of figure. Theosophy's conception is similar to the typical Buddhist notion of a bodhisattva, particularly a highly advanced or celestial bodhisattva, who is very close to buddhahood or who already possesses the highest realization but chooses to refrain from final extinction out of compassion for sentient beings. The Theosophical Bodhisattva/World-Teacher functions especially during the evolutionary transition between two Root-Races.[20]

When World-Teachers (or even the lesser Masters) manifest, they do not typically do so through being born and undergoing physical development. Instead, a "disciple" whose body has been suitably prepared can serve as the physical vehicle for the consciousness of the World-Teacher who will possess that body permanently and through it teach the truth that will facilitate the evolutionary progress of human consciousness.[21] In Theosophical teachings, Lord Maitreya had previously descended into the body of the disciple Jesus of Nazareth, at about the age of twenty-nine, and remained there for the three or so years of the Christ's ministry.[22] According to Charles Leadbeater, Lord Maitreya is the "Great Head of the Department of Religious Education" in the divine Occult Hierarchy and after his appearances as Krishna, and the Christ, who formed a new religion, Maitreya's reappearance was imminent.[23] The Theosophists were entrusted with the task of raising and training the vehicle for the next World-Teacher. That boy was Krishnamurti, chosen at the age of fourteen and given the name Alcyone.[24]

linked his Hermetic Order of the Golden Dawn to the Great White Brotherhood, and conceptions of this community were developed later by the Theosophist Alice A. Bailey and occultist Dion Fortune.

19. Catherine Wessinger, *Annie Besant and Progressive Messianism* (Lewiston, NY: The Edwin Mellen Press, 1988), 211.

20. See René Guénon, *Theosophy: History of a Pseudo-Religion* (Hillsdale, NY: Sophia Perennis, 2003), 173.

21. An exception to this occurred when Lord Maitreya took birth as "Shri Krishna." See Guénon, quoting Leadbeater from the *Adyar Bulletin*, October 1913.

22. See Guénon, *Theosophy*, 177.

23. See Guénon, *Theosophy*, 179.

24. Alcyone in Greek mythology is the name of the daughter of Aeolus, the god of the winds, or one of the seven daughters of Atlas. It is also the name of the brightest star in the Pleiades star cluster in the Taurus constellation. The name may be rendered as meaning, "[She] who wards off evil."

BUDDHISM AND THEOSOPHY

Colonel Henry Steel Olcott's work in the revival of Buddhism in Ceylon is note worthy, and he is often credited with spearheading Buddhist studies among Westerners. Although they had privately declared themselves as Buddhists much earlier, Blavatsky and Olcott publicly took refuge in the Three Jewels and assumed the Five Precepts vow in Galle, Ceylon, in 1880. That act made them the first high-profiled Westerners (European-American) to become lay Buddhists.[25] Olcott founded the Buddhist Theosophical Society (BTS), which was eventually responsible for founding over 450 secondary and Sunday schools (205 at the time of his death in 1907) for the propagation of Buddhist knowledge. Mimicking the structures of his Christian heritage, Olcott is credited with being one of the key architects of what is sometimes called Protestant Buddhism. Besides the schools that were founded on Christian models, a key example of this Protestant approach to Buddhism was his composition in 1881 of the *Buddhist Catechism*. Published in both English and Sinhalese, it now exists in more than twenty languages, has gone through more than forty editions, and is still in use in schools throughout Sri Lanka. Although Olcott himself was not a monk, in 1884 high-ranking monks in Ceylon granted him the right to promote Buddhism by forming organizations and societies, to register persons from any country who wanted to declare themselves as Buddhists, and to administer to them the Five Precepts and Three Refuges. Essentially, this activity made Olcott the first Western Buddhist missionary to the West.[26] Olcott also helped to fund the Ceylonese representative, Anagarika Dharmapala, at the World Parliament of Religions in Chicago in 1893, thereby greatly enhancing the West's interest in Buddhism. Olcott's passionate involvement with Buddhism is an indicator of the stamp it left on the character of the early Theosophical Society, which he co-founded, and the enormously influential role the TS played in raising Buddhism's profile in south Asia and the West.

C. W. Leadbeater, who had been ordained as a priest of the Church of England, joined the Theosophical Society in 1883. He gave up his Church position, left for Adyar, and there, reputedly through contact with the Masters, enhanced his clairvoyant abilities. He journeyed with Henry Steel Olcott to Burma (Myanmar) and Ceylon (Sri Lanka) in 1884, and like Olcott and Blavatsky, he too publicly took the *pañcaśīla* (Five Precepts) vows upon his arrival in Colombo. Olcott wrote, "This was the first instance of a Christian clergy man having publicly declared himself a follower of the Lord Buddha, and the sensation caused by it may be easily imagined."[27] In Ceylon he worked as the first headmaster of the English Buddhist Academy, which he helped to

25. Stephen R. Prothero, *The White Buddhist: The Asian Odyssey of Henry Steel Olcott* (Bloomington: Indiana University Press, 1996), 96.

26. See Prothero, *The White Buddhist*, 111.

27. Henry S. Olcott, *Old Diary Leaves*, Part 3 (reprint, Whitefish: Kessinger Publishing, 2003), 196.

found.[28] Just as Olcott had written the *Buddhist Catechism*, Leadbeater had written *Sisya Bodhya* (*Elementary Catechism*), which was being circulated in their schools.[29] Despite their Christian backgrounds and the cultural proclivities these provided, Olcott and Leadbeater offer two telling examples of the strong Buddhist orientations of certain early Theosophists in Asia.

KRISHNAMURTI "JĀTAKAS"

Leadbeater returned to Adyar after spending seven years in England. There he had been involved in a scandal, accused of encouraging mutual masturbation among the teenage boys in his care. He resigned from the Society to save it from embarrassment but was supported by Annie Besant, who became president of the Society after Olcott's death in 1907. In 1909 Leadbeater was readmitted to the Theosophical Society and returned to Adyar. In the summer of that year, on the beach outside the TS's compound where the Adyar River joins the ocean of the Coromandel Coast of the Bay of Bengal, Leadbeater discovered Krishnamurti. He is reputed to have said that the boy possessed a wonderful aura, without a stitch of selfishness, and thus was a potential candidate as a vehicle for the World-Teacher, the Lord Maitreya. Krishnamurti's own recollection of his feelings before his first encounter with Leadbeater, in the latter's room, was fear. He writes that he had witnessed acts of cruelty by Europeans toward Indians and had a general bitterness toward Europeans, fueled by his imagination and the prevailing political and cultural attitudes of the time. However, Krishnamurti admits that his fears of Leadbeater were unfounded.[30]

Leadbeater utilized his psychic powers to investigate the past lives of the teenage boy, and in 1910 he began to publish his findings in *The Theosophist*, a Society periodical. They were eventually collectively published as *The Lives of Alcyone*, and like the Jātaka tales of Siddhārtha Gautama's previous lives, tell of forty-eight of Krishnamurti's consecutive previous lives ranging from 70,000 BCE to 694 CE.[31] The Masters, Adepts, and other members of the Occult Hierarchy appear in these tales, as well as prominent Theosophists and certain famous historical personages (e.g., Julius Caesar), often under the name of a star, a constellation, or a Greek hero. Thus Julius Caesar appears as Corona and Lao-Tzu as Lyra. Krishnamurti is Alcyone, Krishnamurti's younger brother, Nityānanda, is Mizar, and H. P. Blavatsky is Vajra. Alcyone's life spans ranged between 17

28. Mary Lutyens, *Krishnamurti: The Years of Awakening*, 13.
29. See Olcott, *Old Diary Leaves*, Part 3, 360, where he refers to the production of a new Sinhalese edition of 5,000 copies of his *Buddhist Catechism* and 2,000 of Leadbeater's *Sisya Bodhya*.
30. Mary Lutyens, *The Boy Krishna: The First Fourteen Years in the Life of J. Krishnamurti* (Brockwood Park, U.K.: The Krishnamurti Foundation Trust, 1995), 27–28.
31. See Annie Besant and C. W. Leadbeater, *The Lives of Alcyone*, Vols. I & II (Adyar, Madras: Theosophical Publishing House, 1924).

and 109 years, and there are often five hundred to a thousand years between each incarnation. In about a dozen incarnations Alcyone is female.

In the forty-seventh life, at the time of the Buddha, Alcyone (named Shivashankara in that life), who had often heard the Buddha preach and been deeply moved by his teachings, decided to become a follower. The Buddha accepted Alcyone's vow to commit himself to attaining buddhahood and predicted that it would be fulfilled. Alcyone then followed the Buddha in his wanderings throughout the north of India. Upon taking up his monastic robes, he assumed the name Maitribaladasa. The Buddha pointed out that this name was prophetic, for it means "the servant of the power of kindness" but could also be interpreted as "the servant of the power of Maitreya."

In the forty-eighth life, Alcyone (known then as Upasena but eventually as Dhammalankara when he took up the yellow robe) went on a pilgrimage, visiting many of the important Buddhist centers in north India. He did not know that he had done so in his previous incarnation, but occasionally he had strange visions remembering scenes from that past life. He eventually left his monastery in the plains and was invited to become abbot of a Buddhist monastery in the mountains of Nepal. After training the monks to manage their own affairs, he returned to his monastery in the lowlands. There he assumed responsibility for everything, ruled it wisely, but did so from behind the scenes, so that his old teacher maintained his nominal position.

I recount fragments of these lives in some detail to illustrate that from the earliest period of Krishnamurti's interaction with influential Theosophists such as Leadbeater, his life and even his recollections—imaginative though they might have been—were being shaped to wean him from his brahmin religious conditioning and orient him along the lines of a Theosophical worldview. Although this worldview was remarkably global in its sweep, culling from teachings from the Far East to the New World, Theosophy—particularly at the Adyar headquarters—through the influences of Olcott and Leadbeater, had robust strands of Buddhist symbolism and values embedded within it. For instance, in Alcyone's encounter (in his forty-seventh life) with Siddhārtha Gautama, we are reminded of the story of Sumedha's encounter with the Buddha Dīpaṅkara (the previous teaching Buddha, especially developed in Chinese Buddhist texts), Sumedha's commitment to attain buddhahood, Dīpaṅkara foretelling him that he would succeed, and Sumedha's subsequent rebirth as Siddhārtha who eventually became Śākyamuni Buddha. The young Krishnamurti was thus imbibing a generic array of moral values, including honesty and integrity, spiritual attitudes, such as that of renunciation, and metaphysical teachings, such as rebirth and the evolution/transformation of consciousness. In telling ways he was also learning many features of Buddhist Dharma, without its being labeled overtly or exclusively as Buddhism.[32]

32. After his break from Theosophy, Krishnamurti apparently expressed the wish that the *Lives of Alcyone* not be reprinted, because they conveyed information that he apparently did not want associated with his persona and teachings (see Foreword by Radha Burnier, President of the International Theosophical Society, in Joseph E. Ross, *Krishnamurti: The Taormina Seclusion, 1912* (Ojai: Edwin House, 2003), 9).

Moreover, in contrast to children who are selected as "recognized reincarnations" of deceased monks, a phenomenon particularly widespread in Tibetan Buddhism, Krishnamurti was not raised to believe that he was the incarnation of a recently deceased and known religious figure. His previous incarnation was perceived as occurring during the nineteenth year of the reign of King Harsha of Kanyakubja (i.e., 624 CE), and the one prior to that apparently took place at the time of Siddhārtha Gautama. Krishnamurti's case is all the more curious, because while we are not led to believe that Siddhārtha knew about his previous lives during his childhood—although the tradition asserts his capacity to remember past lives as he matured in his meditative practices—as a child, Krishnamurti was fed a steady diet of ideas about who he was and how he behaved in dozens of previous lifetimes.

BECOMING THE VEHICLE FOR LORD MAITREYA

Since the channeled past lives were deemed highly promising, Krishnamurti and his brother Nitya were brought more firmly under the care and tutelage of the Theosophists at Adyar. Krishnamurti's hair was cut, his teeth were straightened, and he was properly fed. He soon began to appear attractive, so much so that later on George Bernard Shaw is reputed to have remarked that Krishnamurti was "the most beautiful human being he ever saw."[33] The Theosophical tutelage may have been rather stern if not abusive. Krishnamurti talks about how if he and his brother said they wanted bicycles or liked porridge, they would get a bicycle but have to ride it every day on a rigorous schedule, or have to eat porridge daily, so much so that they stopped expressing their desires for anything.

Prior to his First Initiation into the Great White Brotherhood, for a period of five months Leadbeater took Krishnamurti daily (in "astral form") to visit Master Kuthumi (a.k.a. Koot Hoomi, or K.H.). Instructions received from there were transformed into a small book entitled *At the Feet of the Master*. Translated into twenty-seven languages and after some forty editions, it is still in print. Although the book is attributed to Alcyone, many doubt that authorship since Krishnamurti's grasp of English was still quite poor and the foreword claims that they are "the words of the master that taught me." Another book, *Education as Service,* attributed to the young Krishnamurti, is often credited to George Arundale, a Theosophist teacher. Some have seen suspicious parallels between the contents of *At the Feet of the Master* and the *Vivekacūḍāmaṇi,* attributed to Śaṅkara.[34]

33. Mary Lutyens, *Krishnamurti: The Years of Fulfilment* (London: John Murray, 1983), 28.

34. Personal communication with Dr. Radhika Herzberger, director of the Krishnamurti school at Rishi Valley, South India. In his post-Theosophical teachings, Krishnamurti would undoubtedly reject the premise of this book, which affirms the notion of serving a spiritual master and following a path to realization.

On January 10, 1910, Krishnamurti underwent his First Initiation, in the presence of Leadbeater and Annie Besant. He described his experience, during which he apparently met with Master Kuthumi and others, including the Buddha, and Lord Maitreya. Lord Maitreya asked him various questions to test his integrity, tested certain of his psychic capabilities (such as distinguishing between the astral body of a living and dead man), and asked for various commitments (e.g., forgetting himself completely for the good of the world), including that he keep secret certain instructions.[35]

Gossip of possible sexual misconduct had led Krishnamurti's father, Narianiah, to have grave concerns about Leadbeater's relationship with Krishnamurti.[36] He thus signed an agreement in which legal guardianship of Krishnamurti and Nitya was transferred to Annie Besant, who thereafter kept the boys close to her.[37] During the intervening years, Krishnamurti was officially selected as the vehicle for the manifestation of Lord Maitreya, and in 1911 he was placed at the head of the Order of the Rising Sun (later changed to the Order of the Star in the East), which would herald the arrival of the World-Teacher. Schisms and scandals followed. Rudolph Steiner left with most of the German lodges and formed the Anthroposophical Society.[38] According to Leadbeater's account, at a Theosophical Convention on December 28, 1911, members from all castes and religions, rich and poor, old and young, including Krishnamurti's brother Nitya, prostrated themselves in devotion at Krishnamurti's feet. A couple of days later a similar scene occurred—this time with Hubert van Hook (the other main contender for the role of Lord Maitreya's vehicle) also prostrating himself.[39] Krishnamurti's father, Narianiah, voiced his complaints, concerned that this deification of his son would make him and his family appear ridiculous. In early 1912 he threatened to launch a lawsuit against Annie Besant out of concerns about the direction that his son's life was taking, and he raised allegations of sexual misconduct by Leadbeater. He wanted a complete separation between the boys and Leadbeater but was persuaded to have Besant take the boys to England to be educated. However, while setting sail for England, Besant wrote to Narianiah requesting that he leave his residence at the TS Headquarters at Adyar, and Leadbeater eventually met with Krishnamurti in Taormina, Sicily. There was

35. Lutyens, *Krishnamurti: The Years of Awakening*, 29–39.

36. This included Leadbeater's teaching the children (through demonstration) to bathe naked in the European manner and to wash their genitals. Hubert van Hook swore to Besant that Leadbeater had sexually misused him, but Krishnamurti and Nitya held that nothing immoral had ever transpired between Leadbeater and themselves (see M. Lutyens, *Krishnamurti: The Years of Awakening*, 42).

37. Earlier, after Krishnamurti and Nitya had once been severely caned at school, Leadbeater had convinced Naraniah to move them into the care and tutelage of various Theosophists, including Annie Besant, and suggested that they might eventually continue their education in Europe (see Lutyens, *Krishnamurti: The Years of Awakening*, 25–26).

38. Lutyens, *Krishnamurti: The Years of Awakening*, 46.

39. See Lutyens, *Krishnamurti: The Years of Awakening*, 54–56.

an almost four-month period there during which Krishnamurti underwent his Second Initiation.[40]

Other initiations followed over the next decade and a half. The Fourth led to the status of Arahat and the Fifth (on August 13, 1925) to the status of Adept. Some of these initiations were done in the company of, and along with, Leadbeater, Besant, and others. One can only imagine how Krishnamurti experienced these astral encounters, what he saw, heard, and felt in the presence of disembodied beings such as the Master Kuthumi, as well as figures such as Śākyamuni Buddha, whose post-*parinirvāṇa* state in normative Buddhism does not seem to lend itself to such appearances.[41] Krishnamurti certainly accepted the reality of seeing these spiritual masters, at least in this early period. For instance, while in Taormina, another young Theosophist, George Arundale, had undergone his First Initiation, of which he remembered nothing. However, in a letter to George's aunt and foster mother, the wealthy Theosophist Francesca Arundale, Krishnamurti wrote that he had seen Master Morya and Master K.H. (Kuthumi) in the hall with George.[42]

Narianiah eventually filed a lawsuit against Besant. Besant maintained that, while Krishnamurti was technically a minor, he would soon turn eighteen and be legally free to return to his father if he so decided. Although Narianiah lost the case (the charge against Leadbeater was dismissed on account of insufficient evidence), as well as an appeal to the High Court of Madras (where the judge reprimanded Besant for breaching her promise to keep the boys away from Leadbeater), she eventually won a final appeal before the Privy Council of England. There Krishnamurti and Nitya testified on their own behalf, and since Krishnamurti was about to turn nineteen, the boys were free to choose with whom they stayed. The boys then spent about ten years being educated in Europe, exposed to the company and lifestyles of the aristocratic and wealthy.

During this period, beneath the allure of his aristocratic lifestyle, Krishnamurti's yearned for the Buddha's realization. He recalls being impressed by the story of the Buddha's awakening and teachings in *The Gospel According to the Buddha* by Paul Carus, and by Sir Edwin Arnold's *The Light of Asia*, a poetic telling of the Buddha's life. When reading *The Buddha's Way of Virtue* by W. D. C. Wagiswara and K. J. Saunders, he was so moved that he copied a passage for Lady Emily Lutyens, with whom he had developed a close and

40. An account of this period, drawing upon letters and journal entries by various participants during this period, is published in Joseph E. Ross, *Krishnamurti: The Taormina Seclusion, 1912* (Ojai: Edwin House., 2003).

41. Drawing upon the *trikāya* theory of the various Buddha bodies, some might suggest that such psychic encounters with the historical Buddha occur through his *sambhogakāya*, or enjoyment body, which appears to devotees in visions. See Elijah Ary's chapter in this volume for a discussion of this theory with respect to the Tulku phenomenon in Tibetan Buddhism.

42. Krishnamurti's letter was dated June 1, 1912. See Joseph E. Ross, *Krishnamurti: TheTaormina Seclusion*, 91.

loving filial relationship.[43] Lady Lutyens was the daughter of the First Earl of Lytton, once Viceroy of India, and her husband, Sir Edwin, was later appointed architect of New Delhi. Lady Lutyens' daughter, Mary, was a close companion of Krishnamurti, and in 1927 was even rumored to be engaged to him. Mary subsequently authored various superbly informative biographies. This is the passage cited by Krishnamurti: "All conquering and all knowing am I, detached, untainted, untrammelled, wholly freed by destruction of desire. Whom shall I call Teacher? Myself found the way."[44]

EMBODYING LORD MAITREYA?

One ought not to underestimate both the inspiration and the pressure induced by narratives of the Buddha's life upon the young Krishnamurti, absorbed not only from such readings, but from the certainly unusual experiences of his initiatory preparations and events. Stories of Siddhārtha's quest for realization have undoubtedly served as inspiration for countless Buddhists for over two millennia. While that makes the impetus for Krishnamurti's quest not particularly remarkable, he was under a unique configuration of pressures. He was not merely being inspired to be a good Buddhist, or even to pursue buddhahood along the lines of various traditional Buddhist paths in the Theravāda tradition or through the teachings of the Mahāyāna or Tibetan schools. He was expected to promulgate a radically new dispensation, one that would usher in a new phase in the spiritual evolution of humankind. He could not parrot any previously expressed teaching, for no matter how eloquently he did so, he would merely be proselytizing an existing tradition. He would simply be another Buddhist teaching Buddhism. Instead, Krishnamurti was expected to embody a state of consciousness that conveyed a teaching that was unique in its expression, if not in its essence.

Of course, many of Krishnamurti's mentors had hoped and expected that the new religious dispensation he would deliver would align itself with the vision formulated by Theosophy. This hope initially appeared to hold promise, as the young Krishnamurti began writing editorials for the *Herald of the Star*, a quarterly magazine. At gatherings of the Order of the Star in the East, a subset of the TS with branches in some forty countries, he was speaking with growing confidence.[45] The order's name was eventually changed to the Order of the Star, and earlier in that same year, 1927, Annie Besant publicly proclaimed that the World-Teacher had indeed arrived.[46]

43. Lady Emily documents her maternal relationship with Krishnamurti in *Candles in the Sun* (London: Rupert Hart-Davis, 1957).
44. Lutyens, *Krishnamurti: The Years of Awakening*, 120.
45. Lutyens, *Krishnamurti: The Years of Awakening*, 232n.
46. Lutyens, *Krishnamurti: The Years of Awakening*, 241.

Some years earlier, in 1922, Krishnamurti and his brother Nityananda had retreated to Ojai, California, where the climate was thought to be good for Nitya's tuberculosis. In August of that year, Krishnamurti had a life-transforming three-day experience, the culmination of some weeks of regular meditation. He described the event this way: "During that period of less than three weeks, I concentrated to keep in mind the image of the Lord Maitreya throughout the entire day, and I found no difficulty in doing this. I found that I was getting calmer and more serene. My whole outlook on life was changed."[47] An acute pain in the nape of his neck made him almost unconscious but led to a "most extraordinary experience" of unity. He wrote: "I was in everything, or rather everything was in me, inanimate and animate, the mountain, the worm, and all breathing things. All day long I remained in this happy condition."[48] The next day he sat cross-legged in meditation under a pepper tree by the house to deal with the debilitating physical and psychological after-effects. Nitya, reporting on his memory of those events, heard Krishnamurti chanting a mantra that was sung every night in the Shrine Room at Adyar. He said:"[A]s Krishna [Krishnamurti], under the young pepper tree, finished his song of adoration, I thought of the Tathagata under the Bo tree, and again I felt pervading the peaceful valley a wave of that splendor, as if again He [i.e., the Great Lord, Maitreya] had sent a blessing upon Krishna." Nitya's comments reveal the prevailing view of Krishnamurti held by the members of his closest circles, namely, to regard Krishnamurti as an embodiment of divinity. His actions were thus often interpreted in terms of the religious figures with whom he was supposed to identify—in particular, the Buddha.

DISEMBODYING LORD MAITREYA?

Krishnamurti himself described the ensuing events this way:

> When I had sat thus for some time, I felt myself going out of my body, I saw myself sitting down with the delicate tender leaves of the tree over me.... Then I could feel the vibrations of the Lord Buddha; I beheld Lord Maitreya and Master K. H. I was so happy, calm and at peace.... There was such profound calmness both in the air and within myself, the calmness of the bottom of a deep unfathomable lake. Like the lake I felt my physical body, with its mind and emotions, could be ruffled on the surface but nothing, nay nothing, could disturb the calmness of my soul. The Presence of the mighty Beings was with me for some time and then They were gone. I was supremely happy, for I had seen. Nothing could ever be the same. I have drunk at the clear and pure water at the source of the fountain of life and my thirst was appeased. Never

47. Lutyens, *Krishnamurti: The Years of Awakening*, 158.
48. Lutyens, *Krishnamurti: The Years of Awakening*, 158.

> more could I be thirsty, never more could I be in utter darkness. I have seen the Light. I have touched compassion which heals all sorrow and suffering.[49]

One cannot ascertain with any certainty the exact nature of this experience, when all we have are the words used to describe it to others. However, from Krishnamurti's telling of it, it was marked by a deep sense of peacefulness at the core of his being. His image of an unfathomably deep lake suggests a realization of an undifferentiated and ineffable reality—akin to ideas of Buddhist realization—seamlessly conjoined with his bodily, emotional, and mental processes. He seems to regard these body-mind processes as far less significant (like ripples on the lake's surface) than an unfathomable reality. The various masters, such as K.H. (i.e., Kuthumi), the Buddha, and Lord Maitreya, that seemingly manifest to Krishnamurti in this vision appear to belong to this latter body-mind category, for they initially appear but then are gone. Krishnamurti describes Lord Maitreya merely as one of the beings that manifested to his consciousness ("they were with me for some time"), but one who also then vanishes. He gives no indication in this account that Lord Maitreya's consciousness had taken possession of his body as a vehicle. However, Krishnamurti's descriptive language of this experience does point to what he appears to regard as an irreversible fulfilment, satiation, enlightenment, and a salvific attainment of interconnectedness.

Krishnamurti continued his role at the head of the Order of the Star in the East, but simultaneously experienced a painful physical ailment which he called "the process," characterized by headaches, bodily sensitivity, visions of light, and the hearing of voices. Both Besant and Leadbeater were baffled by the condition, which lasted for about a year and recurred occasionally over the course of Krishnamurti's life.

On November 13, 1925, Krishnamurti's brother, Nitya, succumbed to his tuberculosis. The full reach of Nitya's death on Krishnamurti is difficult to ascertain, but although Krishnamurti had initially embraced his role, apparently ceding to the growing presence of Lord Maitreya within him, he thereafter began to distance himself from other teachings and tenets of Theosophy. Thus in April 1927 Annie Besant had declared in a statement to the Associated Press of America: "The Divine Spirit has descended once more on a man, Krishnamurti, one who in his life is literally perfect, as those who know him can testify.... The World-Teacher is here."[50] Her sense of confidence that the consciousness of Lord Maitreya had fully occupied his physical vehicle was evident. But this idea contrasted with the message being delivered by Krishnamurti himself. In August 1927 Krishnamurti explained his understanding of the Masters and other such beings in the Theosophical hierarchy, and what he meant by "the Beloved," a term that he had begun to use, this way:

49. Lutyens, *Krishnamurti: The Years of Awakening*, 159.
50. Lutyens, *Krishnamurti: The Years of Awakening*, 241.

> When I was a small boy I used to see Sri Krishna, with the flute, as he is pictured by the Hindus, because my mother was a devotee of Sri Krishna.... When I grew older and met with Bishop Leadbeater and the T. S., I began to see the Master K. H.—again in the form that was put before me, the reality from their point of view—and hence the Master K. H. was to me the end. Later on, as I grew, I began to see the Lord Maitreya. That was two years ago, and I saw him constantly in the form put before me.... Now lately, it has been the Buddha whom I have been seeing, and it has been my delight and my glory to be with Him. I have been asked what I mean by "the Beloved." To me it is all—it is Sri Krishna, it is the Master K. H., it is the Lord Maitreya, it is the Buddha, and yet it is beyond all these forms.... If I say, and I will say, that I am one with the Beloved, it is because I feel it and know it.... In your own hearts, in your own experience, you will find the Truth, and that is the only thing of value... My purpose is not to create discussions on authority, on the manifestations in the personality of Krishnamurti, but to give the waters that shall wash away your sorrows, your petty tyrannies, your limitations, so that you will be free.[51]

It is clear that Krishnamurti continued to experience mental images of the deities and divine teachers of his upbringing (e.g., Krishna, Master K. H., Lord Maitreya, and the Buddha). One might also reasonably interpret that he underwent some sort of psychological disassociation from reality and accepted his role as the embodiment of Lord Maitreya. However, a compelling interpretation of his comments is that his new apprehension of reality (i.e,. the Beloved) at the time of this statement penetrated beyond these divine entities which he seems to regard as images or mind-constructed forms ("the Beloved...is beyond all these forms"). Following this line of interpretation, he actually does not appear to be interested in reinforcing his identification as the vehicle for Lord Maitreya, nor as being Lord Maitreya himself ("My purpose is not to create discussions on...the manifestations in the personality of Krishnamurti"). From that perspective, being "one with the Beloved" points to a merging into, not the possession of one's body by the consciousness of a different being, and "the Beloved" appears to be a totality, a "Truth" that transcends the particularity of Lord Maitreya's consciousness. For a few years that follow, Krishnamurti continued to use the personal pronoun "I" when speaking about himself, but in later years he would avoid personal pronouns when referring to himself in public discourses. Objective analysis cannot lead to definitive conclusions about the actual nature of Krishnamurti's self-understanding and subjective experience, although he did spend the remainder of his life trying to convey his realization to his audiences. He certainly appears to believe that he had experienced something that transformed his understanding of the world and himself, a "Truth" or "realization" that could overcome human conflict ("your sorrows, your petty tyrannies").

51. Lutyens, *Krishnamurti: The Years of Awakening*, 250.

Krishnamurti's subsequent condemnation of disciples, ritualism, and stages of spiritual evolutionary progress, values so crucial to Theosophy, is evident in the following early passage, and these teachings began to take their toll on the structures of the Theosophical Society.

> I say again that I have no disciples.... The only manner of attaining Truth is to become disciples of the Truth itself without a mediator.... There is no understanding in the worship of personalities.... I still maintain that all ceremonies are unnecessary for spiritual growth.... I say that liberation can be attained at any stage of evolution by a man who understands, and that to worship stages as you do is not essential. I am not going to be brought into a cage for your worship.[52]

The effect of such comments on the Theosophical Society was marked, as disenchanted members began to disown him. Annie Besant initially attempted to reconcile his teachings with Theosophy, for instance, by shutting down the Esoteric Section of the Society, but this step proved unsuccessful and damaged her credibility in the organization. Even Leadbeater confided to others that the Coming of Lord Maitreya had gone astray.

In August 1929, at the age of thirty-four, in Ommen, Switzerland, Krishnamurti delivered perhaps his most memorable early speech at Castle Eerde, which together with 5,000 acres had been donated to him by Baron Philip van Pallandt. In the course of that speech, presented to some 3,000 members of the Order of the Star, he disbanded that organization, saying:

> I maintain that Truth is a pathless land, and you cannot approach it by any path whatsoever, by any religion, by any sect. That is my point of view, and I adhere to it unconditionally. Truth, being limitless, unconditioned, unapproachable by any path whatsoever, cannot be organized; nor should any organization be formed to lead or coerce people along any particular path.... I desire those who seek to understand me, to be free, not to follow me, not to make out of me a cage which will become a religion, a sect.... I have now decided to disband the Order, as I happen to be its Head. You can form other organizations and expect someone else. With that I am not concerned, nor with creating new cages, new decorations for those cages. My only concern is to set men absolutely, unconditionally free.[53]

In 1930 Krishnamurti resigned from the Theosophical Society and spent most of the remainder of his life traveling the world, giving discourses and discussing the truth he believed he had discovered. He spoke more than 150 times

52. Lutyens, *Krishnamurti: The Years of Awakening*, 262.
53. Lutyens, *Krishnamurti: The Years of Awakening*, 272–275.

per year, on average, to crowds ranging from 50 to 8,000.[54] In 1980 he met with Radha Burnier, then president of the Theosophical Society, and reconciled the rift that seemingly existed between him and the Society. Most of his teachings are preserved in the form of audio and video recordings of his discourses, from which a variety of books have been published. In 1953 *Education and the Significance of Life* was published; it presented his philosophy on teaching and learning. His concerns with proper education led him to form schools in India, the United States, and England. Krishnamurti died of pancreatic cancer on February 17, 1986, in Ojai, California. There, where the Krishnamurti Foundation of America (KFA) is headquartered, is an archive collection that contains about "5,000 pages of letter and handwritten manuscripts, an estimated 120,000 pages of typed manuscripts, roughly 7,000 photographs, 2,500 audio programs, 550 video tapes and 20 films," dating from the early 1900s to the year of his death.[55] In 1995 His Holiness the fourteenth Dalai Lama spoke at the ceremonies held to inaugurate Krishnamurti's birth centenary. Lobsang Tenzin, the fifth Samdhong Rimpoche, former Kalon Tripa (Prime Minister) of the state of Tibet in exile and former principal of the Central Institute of Higher Tibetan Studies at Sarnath, is a member of the Board of Trustees of the Krishnamurti Foundation of India, further suggestive of the strong affinities between Krishnamurti's teachings and those of Buddhism.

KRISHNAMURTI'S TEACHINGS AND BUDDHISM

A close analysis of Krishnamurti's teachings reveals compelling parallels with those of Buddhism. While a detailed analysis of these is not possible here, I have explored some of the similarities elsewhere.[56] For instance, just as the Buddha's point of departure was human suffering (*duḥkha*), as articulated in the first of the Four Noble Truths, so too Krishnamurti frequently begins his discourses with the predicament of conflict in the world. External social conflict, Krishnamurti teaches, is a reflection of one's inner psychological turmoil. Like the Buddha, Krishnamurti points to the ephemeral and illusory nature of the "I" or the "me," conceptual thoughts that serve as a hub for a constellation of psychological phenomena that produce the sense of self, and thus reinforce and sustain the roots of suffering. There are striking parallels with Buddhism's *anātman* doctrine and its teachings on dependent arising (*pratītya-samutpāda*). The profound psychological transformation to which Krishnamurti points, which is essentially a deep insight into the

54. Information provided by the Krishnamurti Foundation of America (KFA).

55. Letter to Albion W. Patterson, former Trustee of the Krishnamurti Foundation of America (KFA), dated December 20, 1993.

56. See Hillary Rodrigues, *Krishnamurti's Insight: An Examination of His Teachings on the Nature of Mind and Religion* (Varanasi: Pilgrims, 2001), and "Movement in Emptiness: Assessing Jiddu Krishnamurti's Life and His Teachings on Religion," *Religious Studies and Theology* 15 nos. 2–3 (1997), 45–60.

mechanisms through which conceptual thought constructs and sustains inadequate representations of the self and reality, is akin to the Buddha's nirvanic realization.

Notable points where Krishnamurti differs from classical Buddhism as it has developed include his rejection of a formally constituted religious community, monastic or lay, and his rejection of the authority of religious teachers and systems. So, unlike the Buddhist Saṅgha, which has a system of monks and nuns, laymen and laywomen, and monastic regulations (*pratimokṣa*), Krishnamurti teaches that all such communities based on designations and regulations are impediments to attaining the pivotal, transformative insight. Krishnamurti would reject various notions of levels of attainment found in the Theravāda (e.g., stream-winner to *arhat*), and Mahāyāna (e.g., bodhisattva *bhūmis*) traditions, and would certainly also reject the value of high ritual and initiatory progress, as found in the Vajrayāna and other Tantric forms of Buddhism, in the attainment of insight. Krishnamurti's teachings essentially have an either/or quality about them: either one has attained radical psychological transformation or one has not. He entertains no substantial notion of grades or levels of advancement, for these notions of progress are embedded in the illusion of time. In this regard, his teachings parallel those found in those Zen Buddhist traditions where instantaneous enlightenment is the paramount goal; they differ in their rejection of the formal techniques found in Zen and its rigid master–disciple hierarchy. Although he offers no "method" for the attainment of pivotal insight, Krishnamurti does point to the value of simple awareness in which one chooses no particular focal point. In this choiceless awareness, consciousness moves freely and thus has parallels to Buddhist mindfulness (*smṛti*), but without any associated preferred or prescribed techniques of sitting, breathing, walking, and so on.

And yet, despite these connections, Krishnamurti's post-Theosophical teachings, for which he is most widely known, rarely make reference to the Lord Maitreya, the Buddha, Buddhism, or Dharma. In fact, the renowned Buddhist monk and scholar Walpola Rahula appeared frustrated during conversations with Krishnamurti, who ignored or sidestepped the frequent comparisons that the venerable Rahula suggested exist between Krishnamurti's teachings and those of the Buddha and Buddhism.[57] In all his discourses, Krishnamurti was insistent on dismissing any attempts to compare his teachings to other systems. He felt that pointing out similarities and differences among philosophical or religious schools of thought, their terms and categories, historical developments, and other such intellectual activities, were merely academic. They were of little or no value in the awakening of true "intelligence," his term for the wisdom associated with the attainment

57. See J. Krishnamurti and Walpola Rahula, *Discussion on Truth* (England, audiotape discussion, 1979) and *Discussion on Death* (England, audiotape discussion, 1979).

of pivotal transformation through total insight. His public discourses and discussions were rarely if ever directed at anything other than pointing to the urgency of change in the very moment that the discourse or discussion was underway.

LIBERATION FROM CHILDHOOD CONDITIONING?

During his childhood, Krishnamurti was deeply conditioned to become nothing less than a vessel and a mouthpiece for a programmatic dispensation. This dispensation, which was constructed by his Theosophist mentors, was intended to be delivered to the world. The Theosophical Society, at the time of Krishnamurti's impending embodiment of "Lord Maitreya," had an estimated worldwide membership of 45,000 (its largest ever), many of whom were wealthy and influential in their countries. Krishnamurti's message would constitute a "new teaching" that would be appropriate to usher humankind into its next level of spiritual consciousness along the scheme envisioned by Theosophy. It is evident that Krishnamurti initially took up this role for himself and functioned along the lines for which he had been programmed.

However, after his resignation from the TS, Krishnamurti spent several years of his early adulthood in Ojai, California, in quiet reflection and contemplation. There, he began to detach from the memories of his intense Theosophist psychological conditioning. As he struggled for a language with which best to express his teachings, he began to refer to himself less frequently with the pronoun "I" and quite frequently in the third person, often referring to himself simply as "the speaker," or as "K." When speaking of his experiences with the Theosophists, he would speak of "the boy" as if that were another person. He actually claimed to have very few memories of those preawakening years, teaching that personal memories are generally unnecessary since such remembering contributes to constructions of the illusory self and taints the experience of the present moment.

According to his biographer, Mary Lutyens, Krishnamurti reflects the most on his childhood—although it is still very little. In *Krishnamurti's Journal*, published in 1982, the book consists of writings he produced during six weeks in 1973 as a result of her encouragement. Throughout that text, he refers to himself in the third person. In one excerpt Krishnamurti states:

> He only discovered recently that there was not a single thought during these long walks.... Ever since he was a boy it had been like that, no thought entered his mind. He was watching and listening and nothing else.[58]

58. Lutyens, *Krishnamurti: The Years of Fulfilment*, 196.

In another entry, he wrote:

> There was never a wall between him and another. What they did to him, what they said to him never seemed to wound him, nor flattery to touch him.... He was not withdrawn, aloof, but like the waters of a river. He had so few thoughts; no thoughts at all when he was alone.[59]

This excerpt suggests that Krishnamurti assesses himself as being relatively untouched by the conditioning efforts of his Theosophical mentors. He quietly watched, observed, and evidently "did" as he was asked to do, until he was able to "do" differently. He did not regard the effects of his Theosophical upbringing as damaging to his psyche. For instance, he states:

> He has never been hurt though many things happened to him, flattery and insult, threat and security. It is not that he was insensitive, unaware; he had no image of himself, no conclusion, no ideology. Image is resistance and when that is not, there is vulnerability but no hurt.[60]

On his discovery by the Theosophists, he wrote:

> He was standing by himself on the low bank of the river.... He was standing with no one around, alone, unattached and far away. He was about fourteen or less. They had found his brother and himself quite recently and all the fuss and sudden importance given to him was around him. He was the centre of respect and devotion and in the years to come would be the head of organizations and great properties. All that and the dissolution of them still lay ahead. Standing there alone, lost and strangely aloof, was his first and lasting remembrance of days and events.[61]

Krishnamurti describes how he was once approached by his former teacher who was needlessly respectful after hearing his talks and surprised that this Krishnamurti was the same student he once taught. The teacher admitted how he would cane Krishnamurti almost daily (for not studying and not remembering anything he was told), and put him out on the school veranda, where he would remain until someone came to take him home. Krishnamurti remarked:

> All those years passed without leaving scars, memories, on his mind; his friendships, his affections, even those years with those who had ill-treated him—somehow none of these events, friendly or brutal, have left marks on him.[62]

59. Lutyens, *Krishnamurti: The Years of Fulfilment*, 197.
60. Lutyens, *Krishnamurti: The Years of Fulfilment*, 197.
61. Lutyens, *Krishnamurti: The Years of Fulfilment*, 197.

He also recounts how these are memories provided to him by others about his childhood, both before and during his Theosophical years. He tells how one frustrated author sneeringly suggested that he was pretending and simply "putting on airs" by claiming that his experiences left no enduring trace of memory.[63]

It is evident that Krishnamurti was strongly affected by the physical and psychological manipulation that he underwent as a child, both prior to and during his Theosophical years. A crucial part of his legacy is his formation of schools based on his educational philosophy. While it is beyond the scope of this paper to elaborate extensively upon these teachings, Krishnamurti's efforts to influence the upbringing of children is worth noting. He felt that the hope for humanity's future lay in the transformation of individuals, but that persons—particularly adults—are so heavily conditioned that they are disenfranchised from their true natures and fragmented by their conceptual attachments from the wholeness of reality. Education, he taught, must allow children to grow into unique, creative expressions of Life (an early synonym he used for the ineffable mystery of existence), without the authoritarian processes typically used by educators to shape them to suit prevailing social and cultural agendas. Self-awareness, through sensitive observation of one's inner and outer world, is a key value in Krishnamurti's philosophy of education.

Did Krishnamurti actually free himself from the Theosophical agenda of serving as the physical vehicle for the consciousness of Lord Maitreya, a conditioning for which he was evidently thoroughly programmed? While he almost certainly felt that he had, it remains an open question. Certainly, besides the immediate effect of his formal break from the TS, Krishnamurti's subsequent teachings also had significant negative long-term repercussions on the Society,[64] so it is highly unlikely that his entire post-Theosophy life was merely a conscious playing out of the role for which he had been conditioned as a child. His self-proclaimed, pivotal insight certainly appears to have empowered him to free himself from the psychologically manipulative environment and hands of his Theosophical mentors. However, it is reasonable to wonder whether he was free from the enduring effects of his conditioning at their hands. It is also reasonable to wonder if his amnesia about his childhood experiences was a coping mechanism for dealing with the powerful psychological pressures he endured during his childhood.[65] While one might reasonably suggest that a loss of identification with a personal self is

62. Lutyens, *Krishnamurti: The Years of Fulfilment*, 197.

63. Lutyens, *Krishnamurti: The Years of Fulfilment*, 198.

64. At its peak in the 1920s, when expecting Krishnamurti to be the World-Teacher, the membership of the TS was estimated at about 45,000. In 1980 the Adyar Society had about 35,000 members (see B. F. Campbell, *Ancient Wisdom Revived*, 176.)

65. There are innumerable psychological studies that point to amnesia (psychogenic, dissociative) as a means of coping with abuse (physical, sexual, etc.) during childhood and with post-traumatic stress (e.g., during warfare, natural disasters, etc.).

generally conceded as the outcome of a nirvanic insight within the parameters of classical Buddhist teachings (e.g., the Buddha frequently refers to himself as "the Tathāgata" rather than by personal pronouns), one is also led to wonder whether Krishnamurti's use of the third person ("the boy" or "K") when speaking about himself in public was the result of a dissociative psychological mechanism.

Krishnamurti's post-Theosophy struggles to handle his private relationships (sexual, inimical), without tainting his public persona (seemingly celibate, free from conflict), which might thwart his sense of mission are touched upon in various books, most notably in the autobiography by Radha Rajagopal Sloss, whose mother, Rosalind, had a long, extramarital relationship with Krishnamurti.[66] It is tempting to suggest that Krishnamurti was merely so conditioned by his childhood upbringing that he was compelled to carry out the mission for which he was programmed. His absence of memory about his childhood (even prior to his Theosophical conditioning) could suggest a tacit acceptance that the boy Krishnamurti had disappeared and was now replaced with the consciousness of Lord Maitreya. There is possibly more than a kernel of truth in that suggestion, but there are crucial caveats that cannot be ignored.

The most significant of these is the argument that he may have undergone a genuine nirvanic awakening, if not attaining *nirvāṇa* itself.[67] Objectively it is impossible to ascertain whether such a realization is at all possible, and if so whether or not he attained it. However, those who resonate with Krishnamurti's teachings (and with traditional Buddhism as well), would certainly argue that his attainment of a genuine nirvanic insight is a significant possibility that is worth entertaining. Nevertheless, both those who tacitly revere and those who scorn Krishnamurti tend to marginalize such an experience.[68] Among those of a devotional turn, many regard it as a unique kind of realization, or extremely rare, thus making Krishnamurti very special and almost worthy of veneration. In fact, among those who have followed Krishnamurti's teachings extensively, it is difficult to have anyone acknowledge either his or her own attainment of the radical transformation to which Krishnamurti points, or for them to accept that anyone else has attained it.[69] It would be as if in the entirety of the

66. Radha Rajagopal Sloss, *Lives in the Shadow with J. Krishnamurti* (London: Bloomsbury Publishing 1991).

67. One should note that some people deny the actuality of such a nirvanic realization for anyone. They suggest that all such claims are either erroneous or forms of delusion and that a master's acknowledgement of such attainments by students within traditions such as Zen merely indicate that the student has mastered an appropriate knowledge base of behaviors and linguistic responses to appear awakened and thus keep the tradition alive.

68. Incidentally, the word "experience" is eschewed by certain teachers and disciples, who feel that a "self" is needed to have an experience, and thus realization is not an experience, but an event.

69. A pervasive notion that plays into this silence is that "no one" attains insight, because upon realization, the "I" is recognized as merely a thought construction. An assertion that one has transformed is viewed with suspicion and seen as an indicator that one is deluded.

Buddha's career, none of his close disciples attained *nirvāṇa* or were acknowledged as having done so by their fellows in the fourfold assembly. Ironically, several others, often from beyond—or pushed beyond—Krishnamurti's close circles, do claim such an attainment and acknowledge his influence on their realizations.[70]

Of Krishnamurti's critics—and there are many, especially among adherents of established religious traditions, including Buddhism—many regard his purported "attainment" as a psychological aberration. His personality is a crucial concern for both factions. The "devotees" are hurt by any evidence of Krishnamurti's seeming moral failings, while his critics rejoice in these validations of his all-too-human character. But the possibility of a nirvanic awakening has been a cornerstone teaching of Buddhism and Hinduism (where, despite noteworthy metaphysical distinctions, it is known as *mokṣa*) for at least two and a half millennia, and in the mystical wings of most of the world's religious traditions. It is at the heart of the teachings of perennial philosophy and received one of its best earliest examinations as simply a human experiential possibility in William James's *The Varieties of Religious Experience: A Study in Human Nature*. In other words, there is a long and widespread history of testimonies that a nirvanic insight is desirable and, although rare, potentially available to anyone sincerely intent on attaining it. As a relatively rare subjective experience, it is a problematic category for those attempting to conduct detached objective and scientific study of a nirvanic insight. For those who have not attained such deep insight, its reality is reasonably subject to doubt, and even for those who claim they have, there is general consensus that it cannot be adequately described, thus making objective academic appraisals, comparisons, and categorizations challenging.[71] On the basis of his study, James characterized the full-blown mystical experience as ineffable, yet possessed of a noetic quality of such potency that its certainty cannot be denied by the experiencer. Quite important, it is held in the highest regard by all who have experienced it, despite the scepticism and doubt of others.

If one follows the argument that Krishnamurti actually had a profound, life-transforming insight which was akin to the ultimate realization pointed to in spiritual liberation philosophies such as Buddhism, then Krishnamurti's awakening evidently freed him from parroting the Theosophical dispensation. However, it left him struggling to articulate in his own words the truth that

70. Vimala Thakar is one example of someone with this discordant relationship. See P. Jayakar, *Krishnamurti: A Biography*, 204–6.

71. Steven T. Katz, for instance, questions the contention that all deep mystical experiences lead to the same realization. He feels that the goal is mediated by a person's upbringing, and thus the realization is shaped by that conditioning. Ultimately, it is expressed in the terminology of the person's conditioning. See his *Mysticism and Philosophical Analysis* (Oxford: Oxford University Press, 1978). Perennialists may agree with aspects of his argument but generally situate his understanding in the category of clear, rational thinking on the subject, that is not informed by the actual experience.

he believed he had discovered. While there was a certain intrinsic alignment between the message of Theosophy and that of his own realization, there were significant differences, and it is these that led to the eventual rift with the Society. An example of such alignment is that Krishnamurti, who had been conditioned to be a tireless teacher of the Theosophical dispensation, became instead a tireless teacher of the truth he believed he had realized. Nevertheless, it is reasonable to suggest that, even if freed by his insight, his childhood conditioning played itself out in many other instances (e.g., the languages he spoke, his food, and other esthetic preferences), other than in those areas where conditioned actions and responses apparently ran counter to his realization (e.g., accepting that he was the embodiment of Lord Maitreya, articulating a teaching that promoted the Theosophical Society, the Theosophical system of graded initiations, acknowledging its worldview of disembodied masters (including the World-Teacher, the Mahātmas, etc.), and its notions of the spiritual evolution of humanity).[72]

Put differently, features of Krishnamurti's post-Theosophical life aligned itself in certain respects with the dispositions to which he was conditioned as the physical vehicle for "Lord Maitreya," but veered away from those dispositions in certain crucial areas, particularly within the teachings that he delivered. In the West, for instance, he often sat in a simple straight-backed chair, evoking the classic depictions of Maitreya's *pralambapadāsana*, whereas in Asia he often sat cross-legged in a lotus posture or variant. His life paralleled the narrative of the historical Buddha's in various ways, and it is not clear how much of this parallel, or the emphasis of details in its portrayal, was consciously constructed by his Theosophist mentors.[73]Just as Queen Māyā died shortly after Siddhārtha Gautama's birth, Krishnamurti's mother died when he was young (ten years old), and he too was raised by "foster mothers" such as Annie Besant and Lady Emily Lutyens, figures akin to Queen Prajāpatī in the Buddha's legendary story.

72. The Krishnamurti Foundations, which are entrusted with the preservation and distribution of his teachings, are conflicted about where to draw the line when publishing his "Complete Works." Krishnamurti apparently instructed the Trustees of the Foundations that he did not want anything prior to 1933 associated with "his teachings." These include works such as *At the Feet of the Master*, *Education as Service*, his writings in the *Herald of the Star*, and other such pieces. Of course, for historians and other scholars, as well as for Theosophists, the pre-1933 writings (as well as works not *by* him but *about* him from that period—such as the *Lives of Alcyone*, letters by those around him, etc.) reveal much about the full compass of his life. I serve on the Advisory Council of the Complete Works project and am thus aware of some of these discussions.

73. Although the connections are more tacit, Nitya's comparison between Krishnamurti's experience under the pepper tree in Ojai and the Tathāgata under the Bo tree is an explicit example of such links. Comparisons continued even after Krishnamurti left the Theosophical Society. For instance, after hearing one of Krishnamurti's discourses in Switzerland, Aldous Huxley wrote, "among the most impressive things I ever heard. It was like listening to a discourse of the Buddha—such power, such intrinsic authority, such an uncompromising refusal to allow the *homme moyen sensuel* any escapes or surrogates, any *gurus* or saviours, *führers*, churches." Cited in Lutyens, *Krishnamurti: The Years of Fulfilment*, 114.

Leadbeater's perception of the young Krishnamurti's aura is reminiscent of the sage Asita's discerning signs that predicted the future potential of the young Siddhārtha. While in Europe, Krishnamurti lived an aristocratic lifestyle—like prince Siddhārtha—raised and cared for by wealthy members of British and American society. He was even given Castle Eerde in Switzerland with 5,000 acres, by Baron Philip van Pallandt, one of his many wealthy lay benefactors, akin to Anāthapiṇḍika in the Buddha narrative. The effects of the death of Krishnamurti's brother, Nityānanda, has resonances with the third of the Four Noble Sights that Siddhārtha encountered, which spurred him on his quest for realization. And Krishnamurti's renunciation of the Theosophical Society and the support of its membership, his surrogate family (Besant, Leadbeater, etc.), and his leadership of the Order of the Star parallels Siddhārtha's great renunciation of his kingship in his quest for truth. Or perhaps one might suggest that when Krishnamurti took up the mantle of "Lord Maitreya," he renounced his worldly, aristocratic life, and that his departure from the Theosophical Society was akin to Siddhārtha's departure from his religious teachers, Ārāḍa Kālāma and Udraka Rāmaputra, as well as his five ascetic companions and whatever system of practice they followed. The Buddha, too, renounced the traditional religious organizations and paths of his day. Although he was, broadly speaking, a *śramaṇa*, a mendicant seeker, at the time of his attainment Siddhārtha did not belong to any form or school of "Buddhism" of his culture and historical period.

The tension between the householder and ascetic's life in the spiritual quest is frequently depicted as requiring a renunciation of the material world. The spiritual path then may involve joining a religious community, such as the Buddhist Saṅgha or some church. Krishnamurti was groomed to be the head of a potentially enormously influential religious organization, with substantial political clout in an India struggling for independence from British rule. Most would-be founders of new religious movements would have found Krishnamurti's status at the outset of his religious mission to be highly enviable. He had a widespread cadre of educated, politically and socially influential, and financially well-endowed disciples ready to implement his teachings, provided he remained within the confines of the Theosophical mandate. Much greater than Castle Eerde and other material interests, it was this infrastructure provided by the Theosophical Society and the willing obedience of the members of the Order of the Star, Krishnamurti's cadre of disciples, that was the particularly remarkable renunciation. In this respect Krishnamurti's story differs from that of the historical Buddha, who apparently spent years building up a large following of disciples whom he would then instruct with the mission of spreading his teachings.

Krishnamurti's abdication of his role is almost as if a young boy, recognized as a reincarnated Tibetan Buddhist lama, who held sway over a large number of monasteries and monks dispersed worldwide, were to suddenly declare that the entire system of incarnate lamas, stages of attainment on the bodhisattva path, and so on were actually hindrances to the attainment of *nirvāṇa*. It would be as if such a lama were to call an assembly of all the monks under his jurisdiction and there publicly doff his robes, criticize the rituals, initiations, and other structural forms of the Vajrayāna tradition. Moreover, it would be as if such a monk were then to continue to teach "dharma" with a different vocabulary, without ever calling it Buddhist Dharma, and without paying homage to notions of the guru, or the Saṅgha, and critique the canonical literature and the Vajrayāna path in general. Perhaps this is why there is more than a tacit respect for Krishnamurti among some circles of "recognized as reincarnated" Tibetan lamas who have been thrust into roles of great status and influence, even though his teachings do earn the ire of most adherents of organized religious traditions. Elijah Ary's chapter in this volume deals extensively with the processes and procedures entailed in finding and acknowledging a recognized reincarnate lama, or Tulku.[74] He details the pressures placed on the (generally male) child and his family once the recognition is officially sanctioned, for the child is no longer seen as belonging to his parents, but rather to his monastic community or, more broadly, the world. Krishnamurti renounced not only his aristocratic and materialistic life, he renounced leadership of organized religion as well. And he did not abdicate these in order to enter into a life without the pressures and responsibilities that go with such leadership. Instead, for the remainder of his lifetime he continued tirelessly to teach by pointing to the truth he believed he had discovered.

CURIOUSER AND CURIOUSER

But did Krishnamurti utterly break free from his childhood conditioning or is such freedom impossible to achieve? About nine days before his death, in a physically debilitated state, weak-voiced, but with clear intent, he recorded a statement that puzzled members of his Foundations and gives reason to raise this question by way of conclusion. I quote the statement completely (as presented by his biographer, Mary Lutyens) for the sake of clarity. He said, in faltering words:

> I was telling them this morning—for seventy years that super energy—no—that immense energy, immense intelligence, has been using this body. I don't think people realise what tremendous energy and intelligence went through this body—there's [sic.] twelve cylinder engine. And for seventy years—was a pretty long time—and now the body can't stand any more. Nobody, unless the body has been prepared, very carefully, protected and so on—nobody can understand what went through this body. Nobody. Don't anybody pretend.

74. Ary expands on the various interpretations about the nature of Tulkus, their status regarding Buddhahood, and the ways in which they manifest and are "recognized. Some modern Tulkus have begun to reject or resist monastic life."

> Nobody. I repeat this: nobody amongst us or the public know what went on. I know they don't. And now after seventy years it has come to an end. Not that intelligence and energy—it's somewhat here, every day, and especially at night. And after seventy years the body can't stand it—can't stand anymore. It can't. The Indians have a lot of damned superstitions about this—that you will and the body goes—all that kind of nonsense. You won't find another body like this, or that supreme intelligence operating in a body for many hundred years. You won't see it again. When he goes, it goes. There is no consciousness left behind of *that* consciousness, of *that* state. They'll all pretend or try to imagine they can get in touch with that. Perhaps they will somewhat if they live the teachings. But nobody has done it. Nobody. And so that's that.[75]

One must exercise caution in interpreting these words, given the circumstances under which they were spoken, with Krishnamurti's body engaged in a losing battle with pancreatic cancer. However, his expression of an immense intelligence using his body smacks of a sort of bodily possession by some other consciousness, a process that took its toll on the physical vehicle that gave it embodiment. The immense energy and intelligence to which he refers almost comes across as an entity of some sort. His comments also suggest that Krishnamurti understood himself to possess a unique status, derived from the special circumstances of his childhood. Essentially, he voices (at the time of this recording) that his body had been specially groomed for such an embodiment and protected thereafter, making no one else capable of understanding what his body actually experienced. That supreme intelligence was now releasing hold of his body, manifesting periodically through the day and night. All this could certainly be interpreted as being in alignment with his childhood conditioning through the Theosophical agenda which had him understand himself as the physical vehicle for the consciousness of Lord Maitreya. "Who was doing the talking?" one must wonder: the shell, the supreme intelligence, or both?

Furthermore, he states that with the demise of his body, that supreme intelligence would not take hold of a body again ("any body," we might interpret that he intended) for several hundred years. How he would be capable of making such a bold assertion about the future behavior of that supreme intelligence is certainly puzzling, for it seems to run contrary to the majority of his teachings in the previous seventy years where he promoted the possibility of awakening that intelligence for anyone who was passionately disposed toward it. Was he speaking as "that consciousness" with whom he believed he had identified, the bodily vehicle that he believed it possessed, or both? The latter interpretation of the intent of his words is a possibility because he

75. Mary Lutyens, *Krishnamurti: The Open Door* (New York: Farrar Straus Giroux, 1988), 148–49.

further suggests that "that consciousness"—the conflation of his body with the supreme intelligence he believed was operating in his body—would depart forever. This notion does appear to be consistent with his teachings which point to a unique and ever-creative unfolding of reality and everything within it. He might well have been suggesting that the particular manifestation of the being that was Krishnamurti would depart forever. However, that does not seem to point to anything distinctive or unique about him, which contrasts with the tone of the statement and the seeming rationale behind his providing it. But while the idea that a person is a unique manifestation who departs upon death never to return is common in Western metaphysical systems, the notion of repeated reincarnations is endemic in Eastern worldviews. Krishnamurti seemed to be implying that he was not going to be reborn.

From the statement, Krishnamurti definitely seems concerned that after his death many people would pretend that they had somehow connected with "that consciousness." Just what he meant by "get in touch" is also unclear. Perhaps it was partly a reference to a range of issues tied to notions of spiritual authority and the construction of religious traditions against which he was consistently outspoken. It is not uncommon for disciples to claim that their master had officially passed the mantle of authority to them. This claim often leads to the formation of religious traditions built upon the notion of authorized spiritual transmission. The concept of authoritative lineage is enormously important in Eastern religious traditions, and Krishnamurti was adamantly against endorsing the creation of any kind of religious tradition or sanctioned transmissions. When he emphatically says that "nobody has done it," he could have been circumventing the capacity for individuals to claim that they had tapped into the same consciousness as he had. This would include the sort of contact that individuals might claim as transmission holders, or the claims of individuals who were "channeling" Krishnamurti's consciousness or engaging with it in some other psychic manner. Most emphatically, through this statement Krishnamurti undercut attempts by anyone to assert that they are his reincarnation. It effectively undermines the notion of his being labeled a bodhisattva, because the general thrust of his comments seems to suggest "nonreturn" rather than future repeated reincarnations. While such concerns about one's post-death persona may appear unusual to most persons raised in Western religious milieus, we must remember that Krishnamurti was raised by a community that regularly took him to meet ("in astral form") with a wide array of disembodied masters. Krishnamurti was evidently emphatic about not having his persona manipulated after his death to suit the agendas of others. Here too we may recognize an effort by Krishnamurti to undermine any attempt by others to influence any child into believing he or she is a recognized incarnation of Krishnamurti, and thereby forcing that child into satisfying those persons' needs and desires.

Krishnamurti's curious recorded statement appears to have been an elaboration upon a question posed to him earlier that morning. It asked, "When Krishnaji dies what *really* happens to that extraordinary focus of understanding and energy that is K?" Mary Zimbalist, his close companion, scribbled his immediate response, which was, "It is gone. But if someone goes wholly into the teachings perhaps they might touch that; but one cannot *try* to touch it." On more than one occasion, Krishnamurti spoke about how "trying" was a means of avoiding "doing," because it bought into the erroneous notion that transformative realization was a slow process, involving stages of development and spanning time.

However much one may puzzle about the curious life of Krishnamurti, about which there are innumerable questions without unambiguous answers, it is clear that despite any unusual personal notions he may have harbored about himself, during almost the entirety of his public life, he—perhaps unsuccessfully—pointed people away from their ongoing fascination with his persona. One could also reasonably argue that he did not point people toward an undue fascination with the corpus of his teachings. Rather, he encouraged them to embrace a mode of existence entailing a sensitive awareness that he believed would immediately free them from their thought-constructed ailments and allow them to touch the immensity or the "vast emptiness" that was his truth, which he maintained was the Truth, to which they would otherwise be oblivious.

BIBLIOGRAPHY

Abé Ryūichi and Peter Haskel, trans. *Great Fool: Zen Master Ryōkan*. Honolulu: University of Hawaii Press, 1996.

Aceto, Sarah. "On Parenting: As if I were your Mother." *Tricycle*, Spring 2007 (http://www.tricycle.com/-parenting/if-i-were-your-mother).

Acharya, Diwakar, trans. *The Little Clay Cart by Shūdraka*. New York: New York University Press, 2009.

Adams, Gillian. "The First Children's Literature? The Case for Sumer." *Children's Literature* 14 (1986), 1–30.

Adams, Vincanne, Renqing Dongzhu, and Phuoc V. Le. "Translating Science: The Arura Medical Group at the Frontiers of Medical Research." Pp. 111–36 in *Studies of Medical Pluralism in Tibetan History and Society (Proceedings of the 11th Seminar of Iats, Bonn 2006)*. Edited by Sienna Craig, Mingji Cuomu, Frances Garrett, and Mona Schrempf. Halle: International Institute for Tibetan and Buddhist Studies GmbH, 2011.

Agostini, Giulio. "Partial *Upāsakas*." Pp. 1–34 in *Buddhist Studies*. Edited by Richard Gombrich and Christina Scherrer-Schaub. Delhi: Motilal Banarsidass, 2008.

Akamatsu Toshihide and Philip Yampolsky. "Muromachi Zen and the Gozan System." Pp. 313–29 in *Japan in the Muromachi Age*. Edited by John Whitney Hall and Toyoda Takeshi. Berkeley: University of California Press, 1977.

Allen, Michael. "Girls' Pre-Puberty Rites Amongst the Newars of the Kathmandu Valley." Pp. 179–210 in *Women in India and Nepal*. Edited by Michael Allen and S. N. Mukherjee. Canberra: Australian National University Press, 1982.

Amino Yoshihiko. *Muen, kugai, raku*. Tokyo: Heibonsha, 1978.

An, Yang-Gyu. *The Buddha's Last Days. Buddhaghosa's Commentary on the Mahāparinibbāna Sutta*. Oxford: The Pali Text Society, 2003.

Anālayo. "Theories on the Foundation of the Nuns' Order: A Critical Evaluation." *Journal of the Centre for Buddhist Studies, Sri Lanka* 6 (2008), 105–42.

Anālayo. "Vinaya." Pp. 647–50 in *Encyclopaedia of Buddhism*. Edited by W. G. Weeraratne, vol. 8, no. 3. Sri Lanka; Department of Buddhist Affairs, 2009.

App, Urs. *Facets of the Life and Teaching of Chan Master Yunmen Wenyan* (864–949). Ph.D. Diss., Temple University, 1989.

App, Urs, trans. *Master Yunmen: From the Record of the Chan Master "Gate of the Clouds."* New York: Kodansha America, 1994.

Ariès, Philippe. *Centuries of Childhood: A Social History of Family Life*. Translated by Robert Baldick. New York: Alfred A. Knopf, 1970.

Ariès, Phillippe. *L'enfant et la vie familial sous l'Ancien Régime*. Paris: Éditions du Seuil, 1973.

Āśa Kāji, Paṇḍit Vaidya (a.k.a. Gaṇeś Rāj Vajrācārya). *Daśakarma vidhi*. Autograph, 345, complete. Large exercise book, black ink. In 2010 in the possession of Saddharma Vajrācārya, son of the author. NS 1087 [1966/1967 CE].

Asha Kaji, Pandit Vaidya (Ganesh Raj Vajracharya). *The Daśakarma Vidhi: Fundamental Knowledge on Traditional Customs of Ten Rites of Passage Amongst the Buddhist Newars*. Translated by N. B. Bajracharya. Edited, Annotated, and Typeset by Michael Allen. Kathmandu: Mandala Book Point, 2010.

Ashiwa, Yoshiko, and David L. Wank, eds. *Making Religion, Making the State: The Politics of Religion in Modern China*. Stanford, CA: Stanford University Press, 2009.

Ashvaghosha, *Handsome Nanda*. Translated by Linda Covill. Clay Sanskrit Library. New York: New York University Press, 2007.

Ashvaghosha. *Life of the Buddha*. Translated by P. Olivelle. Clay Sanskrit Library. New York: New York University Press, 2008.

Atkinson, Jane Monig, and Shelly Errington, eds. *Power and Difference: Gender in Island Southeast Asia*. Stanford, CA: Stanford University Press, 1990.

Aziz, B. N. *Tibetan Frontier Families: Reflections on Three Generations from D'ing-Ri*. Durham, NC: Carolina Academic Press, 1978.

Baker, Simon. *Child Labour and Child Prostitution in Thailand: Changing Realities*. Bangkok: White Lotus, 2007.

Bailey, Greg, and Ian Mabbett. *The Sociology of Early Buddhism*. Cambridge: Cambridge University Press, 2003.

Bal, Mieke. *Narratology: Introduction to the Theory of Narrative*. Toronto: University of Toronto Press, 1997.

Balbir, Nalini. "La question de l'ordination des enfants en milieu jaina." Pp. 153–85 in *Les Ages de la vie dans le Monde Indien*. Edited by Christine Chojnacki. Paris: Boccard, 2001.

Bāldev Juju. "Ihi Saṃskārayā Abhiprāya." Pp 32–33 in *Svakvaḥgu Ihi Munejyā. Smarikā, edited by Javāharabhāi Prajāpati, Gaṇgārāma Prajāpati, and Śyāma Prajāpati*. Yem̆? (Kathmandu): Dharmacakra taḥnanī khalaḥ, NS 1118 [1997 CE].

Banerjee, Anukul Chandra. *Sarvāstivādan Literature*. Calcutta: Calcutta Oriental Press, 1957.

Banerjee, Anukul Chandra. *Two Buddhist Vinaya Texts in Sanskrit*. Calcutta: World Press Private Limited, 1977.

Bansat-Boudon, Lyne, ed. *Théâtre de l'Inde ancienne*. Paris: Gallimard, 2006.

Bareau, André. *The Buddhist Schools of the Small Vehicle*. Translated by Sara Boin-Webb. Honolulu: University of Hawaii Press [forthcoming].

Bareau, André. "La jeunesse du Buddha dans les Sūtrapiṭaka et les Vinayapiṭaka anciens." *Bulletin de l'école Française d'Extrême Orient* 61 (1974), 199–274.

Bareau, André. *Les sectes bouddhiques du petit véhicule*. Paris: L'École Française d'Extrême-Orient, 1955.

Bärlocher, Daniel. *Testimonies of Tibetan Tulkus: A Research among Reincarnate Buddhist Masters in Exile*. Zürich: Tibet-Institut, 1982.

Bartholomeusz, Tessa. *Women Under the Bo Tree: Buddhist Nuns in Sri Lanka*. New York: Cambridge University Press, 1994.

Basham, A. L. *The Wonder That Was India*. New York: Grove Press, 1954.

Batchelor, Stephen. *Confessions of a Buddhist Atheist*. New York: Spiegel and Grau Trade, 2011.

Bays, G., trans. *The Lalitavistara Sutra: The Voice of the Buddha, The Beauty of Compassion*. 2 vols. Berkeley, CA: Dharma Publishing, 1983.

Bazin-Foucher, E. "Une représentation de Pañcika et Hārītī à Sāñchi." *Journal asiatique* (1933), 348–49.

Bcod pa klu rgyal and 'Brug mo byams. *Byis pa'i rab byed*, Blo 'byed klog deb dpe tshogs. Lan kru'u: Kan su'u mi rigs dpe skrun khang, 2010.

Beal, Samuel, trans. *Si-Yu-Ki, Buddhist Records of the Western World: Translation from the Chinese of Hiuen Tsiang (AD. 629–645)*. 2 vols. New Delhi: Asian Educational Services, 2003.

Behnke Kinney, Anne, ed. *Chinese Views of Childhood*. Honolulu: University of Hawaii Press, 1995.

Behnke Kinney, Anne. "The Theme of the Precocious Child in Early Chinese Literature." *T'oung Pao* 81 (1995), 1–24.

Belkin, Lisa. "Growing Up Too Fast?" *The New York Times*, May 4, 2009 (http://parenting.blogs.nytimes.com/2009/05/04/growing-up-too-fast).

Bennett, Lynn. *Dangerous Wives and Sacred Sisters: Social and Symbolic Roles of High-Caste Women in Nepal*. New York: Columbia University Press, 1983.

Besant, Annie, and C. W. Leadbeater. *The Lives of Alcyone*, 2 vols. Adyar, Madras: Theosophical Publishing House, 1924.

Blackburn, Anne. *Buddhist Learning and Textual Practice in Eighteenth-Century Lankan Culture*. Princeton, NJ: Princeton University Press, 2000.

Blackburn, Gabriele. *The Light of Krishnamurti*. Ojai: Idylwild Books, 1996.

Blavatsky, Helena. *The Key to Theosophy, Being a Clear Exposition, in the Form of Question and Answer, of the Ethics, Science, and Philosophy for the Study of Which the Theosophical Society Has Been Founded*. London: The Theosophical Publishing Company, 1889.

Bloch, Jules. *Les inscriptions d'Asoka*. Paris: Société d'Édition "Les Belles Lettres," 1950.

Blum, Susan D. "Margins and Centers: A Decade of Publishing on China's Ethnic Minorities." *The Journal of Asian Studies* 61 no. 4 (2002), 1287–310.

Bodhi, Bhikkhu. *The Connected Discourses of the Buddha. A New Translation of the Saṃyutta Nikāya*. 2 vols. Boston: Wisdom Publications, 2000.

Bodhisattvāvadānakalpalatā of Kṣemendra, no. 80 ("Subhadrāvadāna"). *Sde dge bstan 'gyur*, Ke 1b1-Khe, 329a7 [Tōh. 4155].

Boisvert, Mathieu. "A Socio-cultural Analysis of the Burmese *Shin pyu* Ceremony." *Journal of Beliefs and Values* 21 no. 2 (2000), 203–11.

Bokenkamp, Stephen R. "Scripture of the Inner Explanations of the Three Heavens." Pp. 186–29 in *Early Daoist Scriptures*. Edited and translated by Steven Bokenkamp. Berkeley: University of California Press, 1997.

Borchert, Thomas. *Educating Monks: Buddhism, Politics and Freedom of Religion on China's Southwest Border*. Ph.D. Diss., University of Chicago, 2006.

Borchert, Thomas. "Worry for the Dai Nation: Sipsongpanna, Chinese Modernity and the Problem of Buddhist Modernism." *The Journal of Asian Studies* 67 no. 1 (2008), 107–42.

Bouchard, David. *Buddha in the Garden*. Vancouver: Raincoast Books, 2001.

Boucher, Daniel. *Bodhisattvas of the Forest and the Formation of the Mahāyāna*. Honolulu: University of Hawaii Press, 2008.

Brang ti dpal ldan rgyal mtshan. "Sa skya sman grong ba'i man ngag thun mong ma yin pa dngul bre ma bzhugs so." In *Man ngag gser bre ma dang dngul bre ma zhes bya ba bzhugs so*. Pe cin: Mi rigs dpe skrun khang, 2004.

Brookshaw, Sharon. "The Material Culture of Children and Childhood." *Journal of Material Culture* 14 no. 3 (2009), 365–83.

Brown, Mick. *The Dance of 17 Lives*. London: Bloomsbury, 2004.

Brown, Richard C. "Educating the Warrior: A Tibetan Buddhist Approach to Spiritual Growth." Pp. 157–73 in *Nurturing Child and Adolescent Spirituality: Perspectives from the World's Religious Traditions*. Edited by K. M. Yust et al. Lanham: Rowman & Littlefield, 2006.

'Brug mo skyid, Charles Kevin Stuart, Alexadru Anton-Luca, and Steve Frediani. "Stag Rig Tibetan Village: Hair Changing and Marriage." *Asian Highlands Perspectives* 6 (2010), 151–217.

Buddhaghosācariya. *Papancasūdanī Majjhimanikāyaṭṭhakathā*. Edited by I. B. Horner. 3 vols. Oxford: Pali Text Society, 1977.

Buddhist Text Translation Society. *The Giant Turtle*. Burlingame: Dharma Realm Buddhist Association, 2000.

Bunge, Marcia J., ed. *The Child in Christian Thought*. Grand Rapids, MI: Eerdmans, 2001.

Bunge, Marcia J., ed. *The Child in the Bible*. Grand Rapids, MI: Eerdmans 2008.

Bunge, Marcia J., and Don S. Browning, eds. *Children and Childhood in World Religions*: Primary Sources and Texts. New Brunswick, NJ: Rutgers, 2009.

Bunge, Marcia J.. and Don S. Browning, "Introduction." Pp. 1–14 in *Children and Childhood in World Religions: Primary Sources and Texts*. Edited by Don S. Browning and Marcia J. Bunge. New Brunswick, NJ: Rutgers, 2009.

Bunnag, Jane. *Buddhist Monk, Buddhist Layman: A Study of Urban Monastic Organization in Central Thailand*. Cambridge: Cambridge University Press, 1973.

Burnouf, Eugène. *Introduction à l'histoire du Buddhisme indien*. Paris: Imprimerie royale, 1844.

Bunyavong, Khongdeuane. *Thao Hung Thao Cheuang*. Vientiane: Toyota Foundation, 2000.

Byis Pa'i Shes Bya'i Mdzod Chung. Translated by Bkra shis sgrol ma. Si khron mi rigs dpe skrun khang, 2000.

Cabezón, José Ignacio, ed. *Tibetan Ritual*. New York: Oxford University Press, 2009.

Cambrosio, Alberto, Allan Young, and Margaret Lock. "Introduction." Pp. 1–16 in Living *and Working with the New Medical Technologies: Intersections of Inquiry*. Edited by Margaret Lock, Alan Young, and Alberto Cambrosio. Cambridge: Cambridge University Press, 2000.

Campbell, Bruce F. *Ancient Wisdom Revived: A History of the Theosophical Movement*. Berkeley: University of California Press, 1980.

Carlson, Gyokuko, and Domyo Burk. "The ABC's of Enlightenment." *Tricycle: The Buddhist Review* (Fall 2008), 78–79, 117–18.

Carrithers, Michael. *The Buddha*. Oxford: Oxford University Press, 1983.

Celli, Nicoletta. "The Birth of the Buddha and Related Episodes as Represented in Chinese Art." Pp. 305–20 and 437–51 in *The Birth of the Buddha: Proceedings of the Seminar Held in Lumbini, Nepal, October 2004*. Edited by Cristoff Cueppers, Max Deeg, and Hubert Durt. Lumbini International Research Institute, 2010.

Chab 'gag rdo rje tshe ring, ed. *Yul Srol*. Lan kru'u: Kan su'u mi rigs dpe skrun khang, 2006.

Chaiyotha, Danai. *Buddhism for Young Children*. 6 vols. Bangkok: Mahamakut Buddhist University Press, 2519 [1976].

Chakrabarti, D. K. "Buddhist Sites Across South Asia as Influenced by Political and Economic Forces." *World Arachaeology* 27 no. 2 (1995), 185–202.

Chalmers, Robert, ed., *The Majjhima-Nikāya*. Vols. 2 and 3. London: Henry Frowde, 1898.

Chandra, Lokesh. "The Khotanese Mural of Hārītī at Dandan-Uiliq." Pp. 243–49 in *Purābhāratī. Studies in Early Historical Archaeology and Buddhism*. Vol. 2. Delhi: Sharada Publishing House, 2006.

Changhub, Gyalwa, and Namkhai Nyingpo. *Lady of the Lotus Born: The Life and Enlightenment of Yeshe Tsogyal*. Translated by Padmakara Translation Group. Boston: Shambhala, 2002.

Ch'en, Kenneth. *The Chinese Transformation of Buddhism*. Princeton, NJ: Princeton University Press, 1973.

Ch'en, Kenneth. "Filial Piety in Chinese Buddhism." *Harvard Journal of Asiatic Studies* 28 (1968), 81–97.

Chen, Yuhneu. "Mingdai Funu Xinfo De Shehui Jinzhi Yu Zizhu KongJian." *Chengda Lishi Xuebao* 29 (2005), 121–64.

Cheng, Wei-yi. *Buddhist Nuns in Taiwan and Sri Lanka: A Critique of the Feminist Perspective*. London & New York: Routledge, 2007.

Childs, Geoff. *Tibetan Diary: From Birth to Death and Beyond in a Himalayan Valley of Nepal*. Berkeley: University of California Press, 2004.

Childs, Geoff, M. C. Goldstein, Ben Jiao, and Cynthia Beall. "Tibetan Fertility Transitions in China and South Asia." *Population and Development Review* 31 no. 2 (2005), 337–49.

Childs, Margaret H. "Chigo Monogatari: Love Stories or Buddhist Sermons?" *Monumenta Nipponica* 35 no. 2 (1980), 127–51.

Ching, Heng, trans. *Sutra of the Past Vows of Earth Store Bodhisattva*. Revised by Heng Ch'ih, polished by Heng K'uan, certified by Master Hsuan Hua. New York, Buddhist Text Translation Society, The Institute of Advanced Studies of World Religions, 1974.

Chögyam Trungpa. *Journey Without Goal*. Boston: Shambhala, 1985.

Chos kyi 'byung gnas. Bka' 'gyur (sde dge par phud). 103 vols. TBRC W22084. Delhi: delhi karmapae chodhey gyalwae sungrab partun khang, 1976.

Chou, Chuing Prudence, and Ho Ai-Hsin. "Schooling in Taiwan." Pp. 344–77 in *Going to School in East Asia*. Edited by Gerard A. Postiglion and Jason Tan. Greenwood eBooks. 2007. <http://ebooks.greenwood.com/reader.jsp?x=GR3633&p=344&bc=EGR3633> (12 May 2009).

Chua, Amy. *Battle Hymn of the Tiger Mother*. New York: Penguin, 2011.

Clarke, Shayne. "The Existence of the Supposedly Non-existent *Śikṣādattā-śrāmaṇerī*: A New Perspective on *Pārājika* Penance." *Bukkyo Kenkyu* 29 (2000), 149–76.

Clarke, Shayne. "Family Matters in Indian Monastic Buddhism." Ph.D. Diss., UCLA, 2006.

Clarke, Shayne. "*Vinaya Mātṛkā*—Mother of the Monastic Codes, or Just Another Set of Lists? A Response to Frauwallner's Handling of the Mahāsāṃghika *Vinaya*." *Indo-Iranian Journal* 47 (2004), 77–120.

Clart, Philip. "Confucius and the Mediums: Is There a 'Popular Confucianism.'" *T'oung Pao* 89 (2003), 1–38.

Clart, Philip, and Charles B. Jones. *Religion in Modern Taiwan: Tradition and Innovation in a Changing Society*. Honolulu: University of Hawaii Press, 2003.

Cleary, Thomas. *The Flower Ornament Scripture: A Translation of the Avatamsaka Sutra*. 3 vols. Boulder, CO: Shambhala, 1984–87.

Coatsworth, Elizabeth. *The Cat Who Went to Heaven*. New York: Aladdin Paperbacks, 2008.

Coberly, Margaret. "Crisis as Opportunity: Nuns and Cultural Change in the Spiti Valley." Pp. 193–204 in *Buddhist Women and Social Justice: Ideals, Challenges, and Achievements*. Edited by Karma Lekshe Tsomo. Albany, NY: State University of New York Press, 2004.

Cohen, Ada. "Introduction: Childhood between Past and Present." Pp. 1–22 in *Constructions of Childhood in Ancient Greece and Italy*. Edited by Ada Cohen and Jeremy B. Rutter. Princeton. NJ: The American School of Classical Studies at Athens, 2007.

Cohen, Richard S. "Nāga, Yakṣiṇī, Buddha: Local Deities and Local Buddhism at Ajaṇṭa." *History of Religion* 37 (1998), 360–400.

Cole, Alan. *Mothers and Sons in Chinese Buddhism*. Stanford, CA: Stanford University Press, 1998.

Collcutt, Martin. *Five Mountains: The Rinzai Zen Monastic Institution in Medieval Japan*. Cambridge, MA: Harvard University Asia Center, 1981.

Collcutt, Martin. "Zen and the *Gozan*." Pp. 583–652 in *The Cambridge History of Japan: Medieval Japan*. Edited by Kōzō Yamamura and John Whitney Hall. Cambridge: Cambridge University Press, 1990.

Collins, Steven. and Justin McDaniel. "Buddhist 'Nuns' (*mae chi*) and the Teaching of Pali in Contemporary Thailand." *Modern Asian Studies* 44 no. 6(2010), 1373–408. Coningham, Robin. "The Archaeology of Buddhism." Pp. 61–95 in *Archaeology and World Religion*. Edited by Timothy Insoll. London: Routledge, 2001.

Conover, Sarah. *Kindness: A Treasury of Buddhist Wisdom for Children and Parents*. Spokane: Eastern Washington University Press, 2001.

Couture, André. "Kṛṣṇa's Initiation at Sāndīpani's Hermitage." *Numen* 49 no. 1 (2002), 37–57.

Cowell, E .B. et al., ed. *The Jātaka or Stories of the Buddha's Former Births*. 6 vols. Cambridge: Cambridge University Press, 1895.

Cowell, E. B. and R. A. Neil, eds. *The Divyāvadāna: A Collection of Early Buddhist Legends*. Cambridge: Cambridge University Press, 1886.

Crosby, Kate. "'Only If You Let Go of That Tree:' Ordination without Parental Consent in Theravāda *Vinaya*." *Buddhist Studies Review* 22 (2005), 155–73.

Crosby, Kate. "Gendered Symbols in Theravada Buddhism: Missed Positives in the Representation of the Female." *Hsuan Chuang Journal of Buddhist Studies* 9 (March 2008), 31–47.

Crosby, Kate. "*Uddis* and *Ācikh*: Buddhaghosa on the Inclusion of the *Sikkhāpada* in the *Pabbajjā* Ceremony." *Journal of Indian Philosophy* 28 no. 5–6 (2000), 461–77.

Crosby, Kate, Andrew Skilton, and Amal Gunasena. "The Sutta on Understanding Death in the Transmission of *borān* Meditation from Siam to the Kandyan Court." *Journal of Indian Philosophy* 40, no. 2 (2012), 177–98

Cuevas, Bryan J. "The 'Calf's Nipple' (*Be'u Bum*) of Ju Mipham (*'Ju Mi Pham*): A Handbook of Tibetan Ritual Magic." Pp. 165–86 in *Tibetan Ritual*. Edited by José Ignacio Cabezón. Oxford and New York: Oxford University Press, 2010.

Cunningham, Hugh. *Children and Childhood in Western Society Since 1500*. London: Longman, 1995.

Cunningham, Hugh. *The Children of the Poor: Representations of Childhood Since the Seventeenth Century*. Oxford: Blackwell, 1991.

Dalai Lama. *Ethics for the New Millennium*. New York: Riverhead, 1999.

Dalai Lama Tenzin Gyatso. *Freedom in Exile: Autobiography of His Holiness the Dalai Lama of Tibet*. New York: HarperOne, 1991.

Dalai Lama Tenzin Gyatso. *My Land and My People: The Official Autobiography of His Holiness the Dalai Lama of Tibet*. New York: Grand Central, 1997.

Dalai Lama Tenzin Gyatso. *Ngos kyi yul dang ngos kyi mi dmangs*. Dharamsala: Bod gzhungs shes rig par khang, n.d.

Das, Asha. *Maitreya Buddha in Literature, History and Art*. Kolkata: Punthi Pustak, 2003.

Davison, Gary Marvin, and Barbara E. Reed. *Culture and Customs of Taiwan*. Westport and London: Greenwood Press, 1998.

de Bernon, Olivier. *Le manual des maîtres de kammaṭṭhan: étude et presentation de rituals de meditation dans la tradition du bouddhisme khmer,* PhD thesis, 2 volumes. Paris: Institut National des Langues et Civilisations Orientales, 2000.

Deitch Rohrer, Trish. "On Parenting: The Dharma of Motherhood." *Tricycle,* Winter 2001 (http://www.tricycle.com/columns/on-parenting-the-dharma-motherhood).

De La Vallee Poussin, Louis. "Documents d'Abhidharma, part 2." *Mélanges Chinois et Bouddhiques* 1 (1932), 65–125.

Demi. *Buddha*. New York: Henry Holt and Company, 1996.

Deqing, Hanshan. "The Spiritual Autobiography of Te-ch'ing." Pp. 67–92 in *The Unfolding of Neo-Confucianism*. Edited by W. T. de Bary. New York: Columbia University Press, 1975.

Derrett, J. Duncan. *A Textbook for Novices: Jayarakṣita's "Perspicuous Commentary on the Compendium of Conduct by Śrīghana."* Torina: Indologica Taurinensia, 1983.

de Silva, C. R. "Categories, Identity and Difference: Buddhist Monks (*Bhikkhus*) and Peace in Lanka." *Lines* (2003), 1–18.

De'u dmar bstan 'dzin phun tshogs. "Byis pa'i rna pra brtag pa gsal snang sha yi me long g.ta' bral." Pp. 431–44 in *De'u dmar gso rig gces btus*. Pe cin: Mi rigs dpe skrun khang, 2007.

de Woskin, Kenneth. "Famous Chinese Childhoods." Pp. 57–78 in *Chinese Views of Childhood*. Edited by Anne Behnke Kinney. Honolulu: University of Hawaii Press, 1995.

Dickson, J. F. "The Upasampadā-Kammavācā Being the Buddhist Manual of the Form and Manner of Ordering of Priests and Deacons." *Journal of the Royal Asiatic Society of Great Britain and Ireland* 7 (1874), 1–16.

Doobninin, Peter. "Tough Loving Kindness." *Tricycle: The Buddhist Review* (Fall 2008), 74–77.

Dōwa kenkyūkai, ed. *Ijin to eiyū: kyōkun dōwa*.Vol. 2. Osaka: Sekibunkan Shōten, 1925.

Dri me 'od zer, ed. *Byis pa gso ba*, Dus rabs 21 pa'i bod lugs gso rig dngos tshan slob gso'i 'char 'god slob deb. Pe cin: Mi rigs dpe skrun khang, 2004.

Dudbridge, Glen. *The Legend of Miao-shan*. London: Ithaca Press for the Board of the Faculty of Oriental Studies, Oxford University, 1978.

Dudbridge, Glen. *The Legend of Miaoshan*. Revised Edition. Oxford: Oxford University Press, 2004.

Durt, Hubert. "La 'visite aux laboureurs' et la "méditation sous l'arbre *jambu*' dans les biographies sanskrites et chinoises du Buddha." Pp. 95–120 in *Indological and Buddhist Studies: Volume in Honour of Professor J. W. de Jong on his Sixtieth Birthday*. Edited by L. A. Hercus et al. Delhi: Indian Books Centre, 1982.

Durt, Hubert. "Two Interpretations of Human-Flesh Offering: Misdeed or Supreme Sacrifice." *Kokusai Bukkyōgaku daigaku kenkyū kiyō* (1999), 57–83.

Dutt, Nalanaksha. *Gilgit Manuscripts*. Delhi: Sri Satguru Publications, 1939, 1984.

Dutt, Sukumar. *Buddhist Monks and Monasteries of India*. London: Allen and Unwin, 1962.

Dutt, Sukumar. *Early Buddhist Monachism 600 B.C.–100 B.C.* London: Kegan Paul, Trench, Trubner & Co., 1924.

Eastoak, Sandy. *Dharma Family Treasures: Sharing Buddhism with Children*. Berkeley, CA: North Atlantic Books, 1994.

Eberhardt, Nancy. *Imagining the Course of Life: Self-Transformation in a Shan Buddhist Community*. Honolulu: University of Hawaii Press, 2006.

Eco, Umberto. *Six Walks in the Fictional Woods*. Cambridge: Harvard University Press, 1994.

Eichenbaum Karetzky, Patricia. "The Recently Discovered Chin Dynasty Murals Illustrating the Life of the Buddha at Yen-shang-ssu, Shansi." *Artibus Asiae* 42 no. 4 (1980), 245–60.

Emmerick, R. E. trans. *Sutra of Golden Light*. Oxford: The Pali Text Society, 1970.

Ericson, Joan E. "Introduction." Pages vii–xv in *A Rainbow in the Desert: An Anthology of Early Twentieth-Century Japanese Children's Literature*. Translated by Yukie Ohta. Armonk, NY: M.E. Sharpe, 2001.

Evans, Grant. "Transformation of Jing Hong, Xishuangbanna, PRC." Pp. 162–82 in *Where China Meets Southeast Asia*. Edited by Grant Evans, Christopher Hutton, and Kuah Khun Eng. Singapore: Institute of Southeast Asian Studies, 2000.

Falco Howard, Angela. *Summit of Treasures: Buddhist Cave Art of Dazu, China*. Boston: Weatherhill, 2001.

Falk, Monica Lindberg. "Thammacarini Witthaya: The First Buddhist School for Girls in Thailand." Pp. 61–71 in *Innovative Buddhist Women: Swimming Against the Stream*. Edited by Karma Lekshe Tsomo. Richmond, Surrey: Curzon Press, 2000.

Falk, Monica Lindberg. *Making Fields of Merit: Buddhist Female Ascetics and Gendered Orders in Thailand*. Copenhagen/Washington: NIAS Press/University of Washington Press, 2007.

Falk, Monica Lindberg. "Gender and Religious Legitimacy in Thailand." Pp. 95–120 in *Gender Politics in Asia: Women Manoeuvring within Dominant Gender Orders*. Edited by Wil Burghoorn, Kazuki Iwanaga, Cecilia Milwertz, and Qi Wang. Copenhagen: NIAS Press, 2008.

Faure, Bernard. *The Red Thread: Buddhist Approaches to Sexuality*. Princeton, NJ: Princeton University Press, 1998.

Fausboll, V., ed. *The Jātaka Together with Its Commentary: Being Tales of the Anterior Births of Gotama Buddha, For the First Time Edited in the Original Pāli*. 3 vols. Oxford: The Pali Text Society, 1990.

Feer, M. L. "Le Karma-śataka." *Journal Asiatique* 17 (1901), 53–100.

Fongkaew, Warunee. "Gender Socialization and Female Sexuality in Northern Thailand." Pp. 147–64 in *Coming of Age in South and Southeast Asia: Youth, Courtship and Sexuality*. Edited by Lenore Manderson and Pranee Liamputtong. Richmond: Curzon Press, 2002.

Fontein, Jan. *The Pilgrimage of Sudhana: A Study of Gaṇḍavyūha Illustrations in China, Japan and Java*. The Hague: Mouton, 1967.

Foucault, Michel. *Mental Illness and Psychology*. Translated by Alan Sheridan. Berkeley: University of California Press, 1987.

Foucher, Alfred. *La vie du Bouddha d'après les textes et les monuments de l'Inde*. Paris: Payot, 1949.

Frauwallner, Erich. *The Earliest Vinaya and the Beginnings of Buddhist Literature*. Rome: Instituto Italiano per il Medio ed Estremo Oriente, 1956.

French, Rebecca Redwood. *The Golden Yoke: The Legal Cosmology of Buddhist Tibet*. Ithaca, NY: Cornell University Press, 1995.

Fronsdal, Gil. "The Buddha as Parent." *Inquiring Mind,* Spring 2008 (http://www.insight-meditationcenter.org/books-articles/articles/the-buddha-as-a-parent).

Gade, Anna M. *Perfection Makes Practice: Learning, Emotion, and the Recited Qur'an in Indonesia*. Honolulu: University of Hawaii Press, 2004.

García Márquez, Gabriel. *Love in the Time of Cholera*. Translated by E. Grossman. New York: Penguin, 1989.

Garrett, Frances. "Buddhism and the Historicizing of Medicine in Thirteenth Century Tibet." *Asian Medicine: Tradition and Modernity* 2 no. 2 (2007), 204–24.

Garrett, Frances. *Religion, Medicine and the Human Embryo in Tibet*. Critical Studies in Buddhism. New York: Routledge, 2008.

Garrett, Frances. "Shaping the Illness of Hunger: A Culinary Aesthetics of Food and Healing in Tibet." *Asian Medicine: Tradition and Modernity* 6 (1): 33–54. Garrett, Frances, Andrew Erlich, Nick Field, Barbara Hazelton, and Matt King. "Narratives of Hospitality and Feeding in Tibetan Ritual." *Journal of the American Academy of Religion* (forthcoming).

Gellner, David N. "Hinduism, Tribalism and the Position of Women. The Problem of Newar Identity." *Man* (NS) 26 (1991), 105–25.

Gellner, David N. "Initiation as a Site of Cultural Conflict." Pp. 167–81 in *Hindu and Buddhist Initiations in India and Nepal*. Edited by Astrid Zotter and Christof Zotter. Wiesbaden: Harrassowitz, 2010.

Gellner, David N. *Monk, Householder and Tantric Priest: Newar Buddhism and Its Hierarchy of Ritual*. Cambridge: Cambridge University Press, 1992.

Gellner, David N. "Ritualized Devotion, Altruism, and Meditation: The Offering of the Guru Maṇḍala in Newar Buddhism." *Indo-Iranian Journal* 34 (1991), 161–97.

Gellner, David, and Declan Quigley, eds. *Contested Hierarchies: A Collaborative Ethnography of Caste among the Newars of the Kathmandu Valley, Nepal*. Oxford: Oxford University Press, 1995.

Gerke, Barbara. "The Authorship of the Tibetan Medical Treatise 'Cha Lag Bco Brgyad' (Twelfth Century AD) and a Description of Its Historical Background." *Traditional South Asian Medicine* 6 (2001), 27–50.

Gethin, Rupert. *The Foundations of Buddhism*. Oxford: Oxford University Press, 1998.

Giersch, C. Patterson. *Asian Borderlands: The Transformation of Qing China's Yunnan Frontier*. Cambridge, MA: Harvard University Press, 2005.

Gladney, Dru. *Muslim Chinese: Ethnic Nationalism in the People's Republic*. Cambridge, MA: Harvard University Press/Council on East Asian Studies, 1991.

Gnoli, Raniero. *The Gilgit Manuscript of the Sanghabhedavastu, Being the 17th and Last Section of the Vinaya of the Mūlasarvāstivādin*. Roma: Instituto Italiano per il Medio ed Estremo Oriente, 1977.

Golden, Mark. *Children and Childhood in Classical Athens*. Baltimore: The Johns Hopkins University Press, 1990.

Goldstein, M. C. "Fraternal Polyandry and Fertility in a High Himalayan Valley in Northwest Nepal." *Human Ecology* 4 (1976), 223–33.

Goldstein, M. C. "New Perspectives on Tibetan Fertility and Population Decline." *American Ethnologist* 8 (1981), 721–38.

Goldstein, Melvyn. "The Revival of Monastic Life in Drepung Monastery." Pp. 15–52 in *Buddhism in Contemporary Tibet*. Edited by Melvyn Goldstein and Matthew Kapstein. Berkeley: University of California Press, 1998.

Goldstein, M. C. "Stratification, Polyandry, and Family Structure in Central Tibet." *Southwestern Journal of Anthropology* 27 (1971), 64–74.

Gombrich, Richard. "Temporary Ordination in Sri Lanka." *Journal of the International Association of Buddhist Studies* 7 no. 2 (1984), 41–65.

Gombrich, Richard. *Theravada Buddhism: A Social History from Ancient Benares to Modern Colombo*. London: Routledge, 1988.

Gonda, J. "Ancient Indian Kingship from the Religious Point of View." *Numen* 3 no. 1 (1956), 36–71.

Gonda, J. "Ancient Indian Kingship from the Religious Point of View (continued)." *Numen* 3 no. 2 (1956), 122–55.

Gonda, J. "Ancient Indian Kingship from the Religious Point of View (conclusion)." *Numen* 4 no. 2 (1957), 127–64.

Gonda, J. *Change and Continuity in Indian Religion*. London: Mouton, 1965.

Gordon, Neil. "Children and Dharma: An Introduction." *Tricycle*, Spring 2002 (http://www.tricycle.com/feature/children-and-dharma-an-introduction).

Granoff, Phyllis. "Fathers and Sons: Some Remarks on the Ordination of Children in the Medieval Śvetāmbara Monastic Community." *Asiatische Studien* 60 no. 3 (2006), 607–33.

Greenway, Christine, and Todd Lewis. "The Use of Visual Media in the Study of Religious Belief and Practice." Pp. 223–71 in *Selected Readings in the Anthropology of Religion: Theoretical and Methodological Essays*. Edited by Stephen Glazier and Charles A. Flowerday. Westport, CT: Praeger, 2003.

Greenwold, Stephen M. "Buddhist Brahmins." *Archives Européennes de Sociologie* 15 (1974), 483–503.

Grimshaw, Anna. *Servants of the Buddha: Winter in a Himalayan Convent*. Cleveland: The Pilgrim Press, 1992.

Gross, Rita. *Buddhism After Patriarchy*. Albany: SUNY Press, 1993.

Gross, Rita. "Buddhism and the Child in the United States." Pp. 165–79 in *Children and Childhood in American Religion*. Edited by Don Browning and Bonnie Miller McLemore. New Brunswick, NJ: Rutgers University Press, 2009.

Gross, Rita M. "Buddhism and Children in North America." Pp. 165–79 in *Children and Childhood in American Religions*. Edited by Don S. Browning and Bonnie J. Miller-McLemore. New Brunswick, NJ: Rutgers University Press, 2009.

Gross, Rita. "Child and Family in Buddhism." Pp. 79–98 in *Religious Dimensions of Child and Family Life: Reflections on the UN Convention on the Rights of the Child*. Edited by Harold Coward and Philip Cook. Waterloo: Wilfrid Laurier University Press, 1996.

Gross, Rita M. "Scarce Discourse: Exploring Gender, Sexuality, and Spirituality in Buddhism." Pp. 411–22 in *Nurturing Child and Adolescent Spirituality: Perspectives from the World's Religious Traditions*. Edited by K. M. Y et al. Lanham, Ont.: Rowman & Littlefield, 2006.

Gross, Rita M. *Soaring and Settling: Buddhist Perspectives on Contemporary Social and Religious Issues*. New York: Continuum, 1998.

Guangming, Yin. *Dunhuang shiku quanji: Baoenjing huajuan*. Hong Kong: The Commercial Press, 2000.

Guénon, René. *Theosophy: History of a Pseudo-Religion*. Hillsdale, NY: Sophia Perennis, 2003.

Gunaratne, Ruwanthi Herat. "From Layman to Monk in Two Weeks." *Sunday Times*. February 3, 2002, Plus.

Gutschow, Kim. *Being a Buddhist Nun: The Struggle for Enlightenment in the Himalayas*. Cambridge, MA: Harvard University Press, 2004.

G.yu thog gsar ma yon tan mgon po. "Sri'u gso ba med thabs med pa." Pp. 495–98 in *Cha lag bco brgyad ces bya ba bzhugs so*. Pe cin: Mi rigs dpe skrun khang, 2004.

G.yu thog gsar ma yon tan mgon po. "Sri'u gso ba med thabs med pa bzhugs." Pp. 338–40 in *Yuthok's Treatise on Tibetan Medicine*, edited by Lokesh Chandra. New Delhi: International Academy of Indian Culture, 1968.

G.yu thog gsar ma yon tan mgon po. "Sri'u gso ba med thabs med pa bzhugs so." Pp. 13–14 in *Sngags bcos be'u bum phyogs bsgrigs*. Pe cin: Mi rigs dpe skrun khang, 2006.

G.yu thog gsar ma yon tan mgon po. "Sri'u gso ba med thabs med pa bzhugs so." Pp. 701–4 in *Cha lag bco brgyad*. Edited by Blo bzang and Bkra shis rdo rje. Lan kru'u: Kan su'u mi rigs dpe skrun khang, 1999.

G.yu thog gsar ma yon tan mgon po, et al. "Sri'u gso ba med thabs med pa." Pp. 161–67 in *Las sna tshogs pa'i sngags bcos be'u bum*. Pe cin: Mi rigs dpe skrun khang, 2008.

Hansen, Anne. *How to Behave: Buddhism and Modernity in Colonial Cambodia, 1860–1930*. Honolulu: University of Hawaii Press, 2007.

Hansen, Mette Halskov. *Lessons in Being Chinese: Minority Education and Ethnic Identity in Southwest China*. Seattle: University of Washington Press, 1999.

Hansen, Mette Halskov. "Ethnic Minority Girls on Chinese School Benches: Gender Perspectives on Minority Education." Pp. 403–29 in *Education, Culture and Identity in Twentieth-Century China*. Edited by Glen Peterson, Ruth Hayhoe, and Yongling Lu. Ann Arbor: University of Michigan Press, 2001.

Haraldsson, Erlendur, and Gananath Obeyesekere. "Children Who Speak of Memories of a Previous Life as a Buddhist Monk: Three New Cases." Pp. 223–62 in *Approaching the Dhamma: Buddhist Texts and Practices in South and Southeast Asia*. Edited by Anne M. Blackburn and Jeffrey Samuels. Seattle: BPE Pariyatti Editions, 2003.

Hare, E. M. *The Book of the Gradual Sayings*, London: Luzac and Company for the Pali Text Society, 1961.

Harris, Nancy, Patricia Crawford, Yeshe Yangzom, Lobsang Pinzo, Palden Gyaltsen, and Mark Hudes. "Nutritional and Health Status of Tibetan Children Living at High Altitudes." *New England Journal of Medicine* 344 no. 5 (2004), 341–47.

Harrison, Paul. "Sanskrit Fragments of a Lokottaravādin Tradition." Pp. 211–34 in *Indological and Buddhist Studies: Volume in Honour of Professor J. W. de Jong on His Sixtieth Birthday*. Edited by L. A. Hercus et al. Delhi: Indian Books Centre, 1982.

Hayashi Yukio. *Practical Buddhism among the Thai-Lao: Religion in the Making of a Region*. Kyoto: Kyoto University Press, 2003.

Heller, Natasha. "The Chan Master as Illusionist: Zhongfeng Mingben's Huanzhu Jiaxun." *Harvard Journal of Asiatic Studies* 69 no. 2 (2009), 271–308.

Hill, Ann Maxwell. *Merchants and Migrants: Ethnicity and Trade among Yunnanese Chinese in Southeast Asia*. New Haven, CT: Yale University Press/Center for Southeast Asian Studies, 1998.

Hiltebeitel, Alf. "Aśvaghoṣa's Buddhacarita: The First Known Close and Critical Readings of the Brahmanical Sanskrit Epics." *Journal of Indian Philosophy* 34 no. 3 (2006), 229–86.

Hiraoka Satoshi. *Setsuwa no kōkogaku: Indo Bukkyō setsuwa ni himerareta shisō*. Tokyo: Daizō Shuppan, 2002.

Hodgson, Brian H. *Essays on the Languages, Literature, and Religion of Nepal and Tibet*. New Delhi: Manjushri, 1972 (1874).

Holland, Patricia. *Picturing Childhood: The Myth of the Child in Popular Imagery*. London: I. B. Tauris, 2004.

Hood, Ralph, Jr., Bernard Spilka, Bruce Hunsberger, and Richard Gorsuch. *The Psychology of Religion: An Empirical Approach*. New York & London: The Guilford Press, 1996.

Horner, I. B., trans. *The Book of the Discipline*. 6 vols. London: The Pali Text Society, 1938–1966.

Horner, I. B., trans. *Chronicle of Buddhas, Minor Anthologies III*. London: The Pali Text Society, 1975.

Horner, I. B., trans. *The Clarifier of Sweet Meaning*. London: Pali Text Society, 1978.

Horner, I. B., trans. *The Collection of the Middle Length Sayings*. 3 vols. London: Luzac & Company, 1957.

Horner, I. B., trans. *Milinda's Questions*. 2 vols. Oxford: Pali Text Society, 1996.

Horner, I. B. trans. *Women Under Primitive Buddhism: Laywomen and Almswomen*. Delhi: Motilal Banarsidass, 1930, 1989.

Horner I. B., and Padmanabh S. Jaini. *Apocryphal Birth-Stories (Paññāsa-Jātaka)*. Vol. 1. London: Pali Text Society, 1985.

Hsieh Shih-chung. "On the Dynamics of Tai/Dailue Ethnicity: An Ethnohistorical Analysis." Pp. 301–38 in *Cultural Encounters on China's Ehnic Frontier*. Edited by Stevan Harrell. Seattle: University of Washington Press, 1995.

Hsiung, Ping-chen. *A Tender Voyage: Children and Childhood in Late Imperial China*. Stanford, CA: Stanford University Press, 2005.

Hsü, Sung-peng. *A Buddhist Leader in Ming China: The Life and Thought of Han-Shan Te-Ch'ing*. University Park: Pennsylvania State University Press, 1979.

Htun, Hmat Win, Sao. *The Initiation of Novicehood and the Ordination of Monkhood in the Burmese Buddhist Culture*. Rangoon: Department of Religious Affairs, 1986.

Huang, Hui, annotator. *Lunheng jiaoshi*. Taipei: Taiwan shangwu yinshuguan, 1964.

Huber, Toni. *The Holy Land Reborn: Pilgrimage and the Tibetan Reinvention of Buddhist India*. Chicago: The University of Chicago Press, 2008.

Hum chen and Nyi zla, eds. *Sngags bcos be'u bum phyogs bsgrigs*, Sngags Mang Dpe Tshogs. Pe cin: Mi rigs dpe skrun khang, 2006.

Humphries, Jeff. *Reading Emptiness*. Albany: SUNY Press, 1999.

Hur, Nam-lin. *Death and Social Order in Tokugawa Japan: Buddhism, Anti-Christianity, and the Danka System*. Cambridge, MA: Harvard University Asia Center, 2007.

Huxley, Andrew. "The *Vinaya*: Legal System or Performance-Enhancing Drug?" Pp. 141–63 in *The Buddhist Forum*. Vol. 4. Edited by T. Skorupski. SOAS, London 1996.

Idema, Wilt L. *Personal Salvation and Filial Piety: Two Precious Scroll Narratives of Guanyin and Her Acolytes*. Honolulu: University of Hawaii Press, 2008.

Iwaya Sazanami, ed. *Kaitei shūchin nihon otogibanashi*. Tokyo: Hakubunkan, 1911.

Jackson, Peter. A. "Withering Centre, Flourishing Margins: Buddhism's Changing Political Roles." Pp. 75–93 in *Political Change in Thailand: Democracy and Participation*. Edited by Kevin Hewison. London: Routledge, 1997.

Jackson, Roger R. "A Tantric Echo in Sinhalese Theravada? Pirit Ritual, the Book of Paritta and the Jinapanjaraya." *Journal of the Rare Buddhist Texts Research Project* 18 (1994), 121–40.

Jacobs, Janet. "Deconversion from Religious Movements: An Analysis of Charismatic Bonding and Spiritual Commitment." *Journal for the Scientific Study of Religion*. 26 no. 3 (1987), 294–308.

James, William. *The Varieties of Religious Experience*. New York: Longmans, Green, 1916.

Jamgön Kongtrul Lodrö Thayé. *Enthronement: The Recognition of the Reincarnate Masters of Tibet and the Himalayas*. Ithaca, NY: Snow Lion Publications, 1997.

Jang, Li-ju. *The 921 Earthquake: A Study of the Effects of Taiwanese Cultural Factors on Resilience*. Ph.D. Diss., University of Denver, 2005.

Jayakar, Pupul. *Krishnamurti: A Biography*. Cambridge: Harper & Row, 1986.

Jayarakṣita. *Sphuṭārtha Śrīghanācarasaṃgrahaṭīkā*. Edited by Sanghasena. Patna: K. P. Jayaswal Research Institute, 1968.

Jayawickrama, N. A., trans. *The Sheaf of Garlands of the Epochs of the Conqueror*. London: The Pali Text Society, 1978.

Jayawickrama, N. A., trans. *The Story of Gotama Buddha (Jātaka-nidāna)*. Oxford: Pali Text Society, 1990.

Jinananda, B. ed. *Upasampadājñaptiḥ*, Tibetan Sanskrit Works Series, Volume VI. Patna: Kashi Prasad Jayaswal Research Insitute, 1961.

Johnson, Charles. *Dreamer: A Novel*. New York: Scribner, 1999.

Johnson, Charles. *Middle Passage*. New York: Scribner, 1998.

Johnson, Charles. *Oxherding Tale: A Novel*. New York: Scribner, 2005.

Johnson, Charles. *Soul Catcher and Other Stories*. New York: Mariner Books, 2001.

Johnson, Charles. *Turning the Wheel: Essays on Buddhism and Writing*. New York: Scribner, 2003.

Johnston, E. H., trans. *Aśvaghoṣa's Buddhacarita or Acts of the Buddha*. New Delhi: Motilal Banarsidass, 1995.

Johnston Laing, Ellen. "Chin 'Tartar' Dynasty (1115–1234) Material Culture."*Artibus Asiae* 49 no. 1/2 (1988–1989), 73–126.

Jones, B. Charles, *Buddhism in Taiwan: Religion and the State: 1660–1990*. Honolulu: University of Hawaii Press, 1999.

Jones, J. J., trans. *The Mahāvastu*. 3 vols. London, The Pali Text Society, 1987.

Jory, Patrick. "Thai and Western Scholarship in the Age of Colonialism: King Chulalongkorn Redefines the Jatakas." *Journal of Asian Studies* 61 no. 3 (2002), 892–96 and 911–1.

Joshi, L. M. *Discerning the Buddha: A Study of Buddhism and of the Brahmanical Hindu Attitude to It*. Delhi: Munshiram Manoharlal, 1983.

Kabat-Zinn, Jon, and Myla Kabat-Zinn. *Everyday Blessings: The Inner Work of Mindful Parenting*. New York: Hyperion, 1997.

Kabilsingh, Chatsumarn. *Thai Women in Buddhism*. Berkely ,CA: Parallax Press, 1991.

Kaelber, W. O. "The 'Dramatic' Element in Brahmanic Initiation: Symbols of Death, Danger, and Difficult Passage." *History of Religions* 18 no. 1 (1978), 54–76.

Kaelber, Walter O. "Tapas, Birth, and Spiritual Rebirth in the Veda." *History of Religions* 15 no. 4 (1976), 343–86.

Kakar, Sudhir. *The Inner World: A Psycho-analytic Study of Childhood and Society in India*. 2nd edition. Delhi: Oxford University Press, 1990.

Kamala Tiyavanich. *Forest Recollections: Wandering Monks in Twentieth-Century Thailand*. Honolulu: University of Hawaii Press, 1997.

Kamala Tiyavanich. *Sons of the Buddha: The Early Lives of Three Extraordinary Thai Masters*. Boston: Wisdom Publications, 2007.

Kane, Pandurang Vaman. *History of the Dharmaśāstra*. Poona: Bhandarkar Oriental Research Institute, 1974.

Karatani Kōjin. *Origins of Modern Japanese Literature*. Translation edited by Brett de Bary. Durham, NC: Duke University Press, 1993.

Karma chags med. "Byis pa'i gdon chen bco lnga'i mdos bzhugs so." Pp. 363–69 in *Gto 'bum*. Thimphu: Kunsang Topgay, 1978.

Karma rang byung kun khyab [Ka lu rin po che]. "Sri'u gso ba'i gdams pa bzhugs so." Pp. 843–45 in *Dpal ldan shangs pa'i chos skor rnam lnga'i rgya gzhung*. Sonada (TBRC ID W23922).

Katz, Steven T. *Mysticism and Philosophical Analysis*. Oxford: Oxford University Press, 1978.

Keene, Donald. "The Portrait of Ikkyū." *Archives of Asian Art* 20 (1966/1967), 54–65.

Keyes, Charles F. "Ambiguous Gender: Male Initiation in a Northern Thai Buddhist Society." Pp. 66–96 in *Gender and Religion: On the Complexity of Symbols*. Edited by Caroline Walker Bynum, Stevan Harrell, and Paula Richman. Boston: Beacon Press, 1986.

Keyes, Charles F. "Mother and Mistress but Never a Monk: Buddhist Notions of Female Gender in Rural Thailand." *American Ethnologist* 11 no. 2 (1984), 223–41.

Keyes, Charles F. ed. *Reshaping Local Worlds: Formal Education and Cultural Change in Rural Southeast Asia*. New Haven, CT: Yale Centre for International and Area Studies, 1991.

Keyes, Charles. "Who Are the Lue Revisited? Ethnic Identity in Laos, Thailand and China." Working Paper, Center for International Studies. Cambridge, MA: MIT, 1992.

Khan, Noor Inayat. *Twenty Jātaka Tales*. Rochester, VT: Inner Traditions International, 1983.

Khoroche, Peter, trans. *Once the Buddha was a Monkey*. Chicago: Chicago University Press, 1989.

Kirsch, Thomas A. "Buddhism, Sex-Roles, and the Thai Economy." Pp. 13–32 in *Women of Southeast Asia*.Edited by Penny Van Esterik. Southeast Asia Monograph Series. Dekalb: Northern Illinois University, 1996.

Klautau, Orion. "Against the Ghosts of Recent Past: Meiji Scholarship and the Discourse on Edo-Period Buddhist Decadence." *Japanese Journal of Religious Studies* 35 no. 2 (2008), 263–303.

Kloppenborg, Ria. "The Earliest Buddhist Ritual of Ordination." Pp. 158–68 in *Selected Studies on Ritual in the Indian Religions: Essays to D. J. Hoens*. Edited by Ria Kloppenborg. Leiden: Brill, 1983.

Knapp, Keith Nathaniel. *Selfless Offspring: Filial Children and Social Order in Medieval China*. Honolulu: University of Hawaii Press, 1995.

Knodel, John. "The Closing of the Gender Gap in Schooling: The Case of Thailand." *Comparative Education* 33 no. 1 (1997), 61–86.

Kong Rithdee. "Taking the Middle Path: Animated Thai Buddha Epic Proves Far from Timeless." *The Bangkok Post*, December 14, 2007.

Krishnamurti, J. *Discussion on Death*. England: Audiotape discussion, 1979.

Krishnamurti, J., and Walpola Rahula. *Discussion on Truth*. England: Audiotape discussion, 1979.

Kujira Tōichirō. *Kinkakuji ni hisokamuro: tonchi tantei no Ikkyū-san*. Tokyo: Shōdensha, 2002.

Kyan, Winston. *The Body and the Family: Filial Piety and Buddhist Art in Late Medieval China*. Ph.D. Diss., University of Chicago, 2006.

Lafleur, William R. *Liquid Life: Abortion and Buddhism in Japan*. Princeton, NJ: Princeton University Press, 1992.

Lamotte, Etienne. *History of Indian Buddhism from the Origins to the Saka Era*. Translated by Sara Webb-Bonn. Louvain-la-Neuve: Universite Catholique de Louvain Institut Orientaliste, 1988.

Landaw, Jonathan. *Prince Siddhartha: The Story of Buddha*. Boston: Wisdom, 2003.

Las sna tshogs pa'i sngags bcos be'u bum. Bod kyi gso ba rig pa'i gna' dpe phyogs bsgrigs dpe tshogs. Pe cin: Mi rigs dpe skrun khang, 2008.

Lave, Jean, and Etienne Wenger. *Situated Learning: Legitimate Peripheral Participation*. Cambridge: Cambridge University Press, 1991.

Leadbeater, C. W. *The Masters and the Path*. Wheaton, IL: Theosophical Publishing House, 1925.

Lee, Jeanne. *I Once Was a Monkey*. New York: Farrar, Straus and Giroux, 1999.

Leighton, Taigen Dan, and Shohaku Okumura, trans. *Dogen's Extensive Record: A Translation of the Eihei Koroku*. Cambridge: Wisdom Publications 2010.

Levering, Miriam. *Chan Enlightenment for Laymen: Ta-hui Tsung-kao and the New Religious Culture of the Sung*. Ph.D, Diss., Harvard University, 1978.

Levering, Miriam. "Stories of Enlightened Women in Ch'an and the Chinese Buddhist Female Bodhisattva/Goddess Tradition." Pp. 137–76 in *Women and Goddess Traditions*. Edited by Karen King. Minneapolis: Fortress, 1997.

Levine, Nancy. "Differential Childcare in Three Tibetan Communities: Beyond Son Preference." *Population and Development Review* 13 (1988), 281–304.

Lewis, Todd T. "Buddhist Merchants in Kathmandu: The Asan Tol Market and *Urāy* Social Organization." Pp. 38–79 in *Contested Hierarchies: A Collaborative Ethnography of Caste among the Newars of the Kathmandu Valley, Nepal*. Edited by David Gellner and Declan Quigley. Oxford: Oxford University Press, 1995.

Lewis, Todd T. "Childhood and Newar Tradition: Chittadhar Hridaya's *Jhī Macā*." *Asian Folklore Studies* 48 no. 2 (1989), 195–210.

Lewis, Todd T. "Growing Up Newar Buddhist: Chittadhar Hridaya's *Jhī Macā* and Its Context." Pp. 301–18 in *Selves in Time and Place: Identities, Experience, and History in Nepal*. Edited by Debra Skinner, A. Pach, and D. Holland. Lanham: Rowman and Littlefield, 1998.

Lewis, Todd T. "The *Nepāl Jana Jīvan Kriyā Paddhati:* A Modern Newar Guide for Vajrayāna Life-Cycle Rites."*Indo-Iranian Journal* 37 (1994), 1–46.

Lewis, Todd T. "Patterns of Religious Belief in a Buddhist Merchant Community, Nepal." *Asian Folklore Studies* 55 no. 2 (1996), 237–70.

Lewis, Todd T. *Popular Buddhist Texts from Nepal: Narratives and Rituals of Newar Buddhism*. Albany: State University of New York Press, 2000.

Lewis, Todd T. *Sugata Saurabha: A Poem on the Life of the Buddha by Chittadhar Hridaya of Nepal*. [with Subarna Man Tuladhar]. New York: Oxford University Press, 2009.

Lewis, Todd T. *The Tulādhars of Kathmandu: A Study of Buddhist Tradition in a Newar Merchant Community*. Ph.D. Diss., Columbia University, 1984.

Lhun grub rdo rje. "Bod lugs gso rig las byis pa'i bde srung skor bshad pa." *Krung go'i bod kyi gso rig* 3 no. 2 (2009), 26–35.

Libu Lakhi, Charles Kevin Stuart, and Gerald Roche. "Calling Back the Lost Namuyi Tibetan Soul." *Asian Highlands Perspectives* 1 (2009), 65–115.

Lienhard, Siegfried. "Nepal: The Survival of Indian Buddhism in a Himalayan Kingdom." Pp. 108–14 in *The World of Buddhism*. Edited by Richard Gombrich and Heinz Bechert. New York: Facts on File, 1984.

Link, Arthur E. "Biography of Shih Tao-an." *T'oung Pao* 46 no. 1/2 (1958), 1–48.

Locke, John. *Karunamaya*. Kathmandu: Sahayogi Press, 1980.

Long, J. Bruce. "Reincarnation." Pp. 265–69 in *The Encyclopedia of Religion*. Vol. 12. Edited by Mircea Eliade. New York: Macmillan, 1986.

Lopez, Donald S., Jr., ed. *A Modern Buddhist Bible: Essential Readings from East to West*. Boston: Beacon Press, 2002.

Loundon, Sumi. "Sunday School for Buddhists?: Nurturing Spirituality in Children." Pp. 338–51 in *Nurturing Child and Adolescent Spirituality: Perspectives from the World's Religious Traditions*. Edited by Karen Marie Yust. Lanham: Rowman & Littlefield Publishers, 2006.

Loundon, Sumi, ed. *Blue Jean Buddha: Voices of Young Buddhists*. Somerville, MA: Wisdom Publications, 2001.

Lowdin, Per. *Food, Ritual and Society: A Study of Social Structure and Food Symbolism among the Newars*. Kathmandu: Mandala Point Books, 1998.

Lu, Z. A., trans. *A Pictoral Biography of Śākyamuni Buddha*. Taiwan: The Corporate Body of the Buddha Educational Foundation, 1997.

Lutyens, Lady Emily. *Candles in the Sun*. London: Rupert Hart Davis, 1957.

Lutyens, Mary. *Krishnamurti: The Years of Awakening*. New York: Farrar Straus and Giroux, 1975.

Lutyens, Mary. *Krishnamurti: The Years of Fulfilment*. London: John Murray, 1983.

Lutyens, Mary. *Krishnamurti: The Open Door*. New York: Farrar Straus and Giroux, 1988.

Lutyens, Mary. *The Boy Krishna: The First Fourteen Years in the Life of J. Krishnamurti*. Brockwood Park: The Krishnamurti Foundation Trust, 1995.

Mackerras, Colin. *China's Ethnic Minorities and Globalization*. London: Routledge/Curzon, 2003.

MacLean, Kerry Lee. *Peaceful Piggy Meditation*. Morton Grove, IL: Albert Whitman & Company, 2003.

Madsen, Richard. *Democracy's Religious Renaissance and Political Development in Taiwan*. Berkeley: University of California Press, 2007.

Madsen, Richard. "Secularism, Religious Renaissance and Social Conflict in Asia." *Religion and Culture Web Forum*, University of Chicago Divinity School, September 2008 (divinity.uchicago.edu/martycenter/publications/webforum/092008/index.shtml; accessed August 2009).

Maheshwari, Madhurika K. *From Ogress to Goddess. Hārītī A Buddhist Deity*. Mumbai: IIRNS Publications, 2009.

Maiden, Anne Hubbell, and Edie Farwell. *The Tibetan Art of Parenting: From before Conception through Early Childhoos*. Boston: Wisdom Publications, 1997.

Mair, Victor. "The Linguistic and Textual Antecedents of the Sutra on the Wise and Foolish." *Sino-Platonic Papers* 38 (1993), 3–18.

Malalasekera, G. P. *Dictionary of Pali Proper Names*. 3 vols. London: Indian Text Series, 1937–1938.

Malalgoda, K. *Buddhism in Sinhalese Society 1750–1900*. Berkeley: University of California Press, 1976.

Manos, Helen. *Samsara Dog*. San Diego, CA: Kane Miller, 2007.

Mapel, Tim. "The Adjustment Process of Ex-Buddhist Monks to Life After the Monastery." *Journal of Religion and Health* 46 no.1 (2007), 19–34.

Makransky, John. "Family Practice." *Tricycle*, Summer 2001 (http://www.tricycle.com/-parenting/family-practice.

Marsden, Carolyn. *The Buddha's Diamonds*. Cambridge: Canlewick Press, 2008.

Martin, Rafe. *The Monkey Bridge*. New York: Alfred A. Knopf, 1997.

Mass, Jeffrey P. *The Origins of Japan's Medieval World: Courtiers, Clerics, Warriors, and Peasants in the Fourteenth Century*. Stanford, CA: Stanford University Press, 2002.

Mather, Richard B. "Filial Sons and Spoiled Brats: A Glimpse of Medieval Chinese Children in *Shishuo xinyu*." Pp. 111–20 in *Chinese Views of Childhood*. Edited by Anne Behnke Kinney. Honolulu: University of Hawaii Press, 1995.

Mazard, Eisel "Be Warned: Thai Film: "The Life of Buddha," March 1, 2008. http://www.prachatai.com/english/node/461

McCarthy, Susan. *Communist Multiculturalism*. Seattle: University of Washington Press, 2009.

McDaniel, Justin Thomas. *Gathering Leaves and Lifting Words: Histories of Buddhist Monastic Education in Laos and Thailand*. Seattle: University of Washington Press, 2008.

McDaniel, Justin. *Invoking the Source: Nissaya Manuscripts, Pedagogy and Sermon-Making in Northern Thailand and Laos*, Ph.D. Dissertation. Cambridge: Harvard University, 2003.

McDaniel, Justin. "Liturgies and Cacophonies in Thai Buddhism," *Aséanie* 18 (2007), 119–50.

McGinnis, Mark W. *Buddhist Animal Wisdom Stories*. Boston: Weatherhill, 2004.

McGuire, Meredith B. *Religion: The Social Contest*. Belmont, CA: Wadsworth, 1997.

McRae, J. R. "Ordination." Pp. 614–18 in *Encyclopedia of Buddhism*. Edited by Robert E. Buswell. New York: MacMillan Reference, 2004.

Mendelson, E. Michael. *Sangha and State in Burma: A Study of Monastic Sectarianism and Leadership*. Edited by John P. Ferguson. Ithaca, NY: Cornell University Press, 1975.

Michaels, Axel. *Hinduism: Past and Present*. Translated by B. Harshav. Princeton, NJ: Princeton University Press, 2004.

Midal, Fabrice. *Chögyam Trungpa: His Life and Vision*. Boston: Shambhala, 2004.

Mikame Tatsuji and the Zen Bunka Kenkyūjo, eds. *Ikkyū banashi shūsei*. Kyoto: Zen Bunka Kenkyūjō, 1993.

Miller, Karen Maezen. "Commentary: Looking Under the Bed." *Buddhadharma* (December 1, 2008), (http://archive.thebuddhadharma.com/issues/2008/winter/commentary.php)

Mi pham. "Las sna tshogs pa'i sngags kyi be'u bum dgos 'dod kun 'byung gter gyi bum pa bzang po bzhugs so." Pp. 233–414 in *Las sna tshogs pa'i sngags bcos be'u bum*. Pe cin: Mi rigs dpe skrun khang, 2008.

Mi pham 'jam dbyangs rnam par rgyal ba. *Las sna tshogs kyi be'u bum bzhugs so*. Zhang kang then ma dpe skrun khung zi, 1999.

Mitra, R. L., trans. *The Lalita Vistara: Memoirs of the Early Life of Sakya Sinha (chs. 1–15)*. Delhi: Sri Satguru Publications, 1998.

Miyao Shigeo. *Ikkyū-san*. Tokyo: Dai Nihon Yūbenkai Kōdansha, 1938.

Mlecko, Joel D. "The Guru in Hindu Tradition." *Numen* 29 no. 1 (1981), 33–61.

Moreno, Manuel. "Pañcāmirtam: God's Washings as Food." Pp. 147–78 in *TheEternal Food: Gastronomic Ideas and Experiences of Hindus and Buddhists*. Edited by R. S. Khare. Delhi: Sri Satguru Publications, 1993.

Morris, Richard, ed. *The Aṅguttara-Nikāya*. 6 vols. London: The Pali Text Society, 1976–1981.

Mounier, Alain, and Phasina Tangchuang, eds. *Education and Knowledge in Thailand: The Quality Controversy*. Chiang Mai: Silkworm Books, 2010.

Mrozik, Susanne. *Virtuous Bodies: The Physical Dimensions of Morality in Buddhist Ethics*. New York: Oxford University Press, 2007.

Murray, Julia K. "The Evolution of Buddhist Narrative Illustration in China after 850." Pp. 125–50 in *The Latter Days of the Law: Images of Chinese Buddhism 850–1850*. Edited by Marsha Weidner. Honolulu: University of Hawaii Press, 1994.

Murray, Julia K. "The Temple of Confucius and Pictorial Biographies of the Sage." *The Journal of Asian Studies* 55 no. 2 (1996), 269–300.

Murray, Julia K. "What Is 'Chinese Narrative Illustration'?" *The Art Bulletin* 80 no. 4 (1998), 602–15.

Muth, Jon J. *Stone Soup*. New York: Scholastic Press, 2003.

Muth, Jon J. *The Three Questions*. New York: Scholastic Press, 2002.

Muth, Jon J. *Zen Ghosts*. New York: Scholastic Press, 2010.

Muth, Jon J. *Zen Shorts*. New York: Scholastic Press, 2005.

Muth, Jon J. *Zen Ties*. New York: Scholastic Press, 2008.

Nakagawa Yoshiharu, 2006. "The Child as Compassionate Bodhisattva and as Human Sufferer/Spiritual Seeker: Intertwined Buddhist Images." Pp. 33–42 in *Nurturing Child and Adolescent Spirituality: Perspectives from the World's Religious Traditions*. Edited by Karen Marie Yust, et al. Boulder, CO: Rowman & Littlefield, 2006.

Nakamura, H. *Gotama Buddha*. Los Angeles: Buddhist Books International, 1977.

Ñāṇamoli Bhikkhu. *The Minors Readings, The First Book of the Minor Collection*. Oxford: The Pali Text Society, 1997.

Ñāṇamoli Bhikkhu and Bhikkhu Bodhi. *The Middle Length Discourses of the Buddha. A Translation of the Majjhima Nikāya*. Boston: Wisdom Publications, 2001.

Napthali, Sarah. *Buddhism for Mothers: A Calm Approach to Caring for Yourself and Your Children*. NSW, Australia: Allen & Unwin, 2010.

Napthali, Sarah. *Buddhism for Mothers of Young Children: Becoming a Mindful Parent*. NSW, Australia, 2007.

Natchā, Laohasirinadh. *Sipsongpannā: Raat Carit* [Sipsongpanna: a Traditional State]. Bangkok: The Thailand Research Fund/Foundation for the Promotion of Social Sciences and Humanities Textbook Project, 1995.

Nebesky-Wojkowitz, Rene De. *Oracles and Demons of Tibet: The Cult and Iconography of the Tibetan Protective Deities*. The Hague: Mouton, 1956.

Negi, J. S. *Bod skad dang legs sbyar gyi tshig mdzod chen mo*. 16 vols. Sarnath: Central Institute of Higher Tibetan Studies, 2004.

Ning, Quang. *Art, Religion, and Politics in Medieval China*. Honolulu: University of Hawaii Press.

Niwano Nikkyo. *A Guide to the Three-fold Lotus Sutra*. Tokyo: Kosei Publishing Company, 1981.

Nobuyuki Yamagiwa. "Vinaya Manuscripts: State of the Field." *Indica et Tibetica* (2007), 607–16.

Nolot, Edith. *Règles de Discipline des Nonnes Bouddhistes*. Paris: College de France, 1991.

Norberg-Hodge, Helena, and Hazel Russell. "Birth and Child-Rearing in Zangskar." Pp. 519–32 in *Himalayan Buddhist Villages: Environment, Resources, Society and Religious Life in Zangskar, Ladakh*. Edited by John Crook and Henry Osmaston: University of Bristol, 2001.

Norbu, Khyentse, dir. *The Cup*, Festival Media, 2000.

Norman, Alexander. "The Fourteenth Dalai Lama." Pp. 162–71 in *The Dalai Lamas: A Visual History*. Edited by Martin Brauen. Chicago: Serindia, 2005.

Norman, H. C., ed. *The Commentary on the Dhammapada*. 5 vols. London: Henry Frowde, 1906.

Norman, K. R., trans. *The Group of Discourses (Sutta-nipāta)*. Vol. 2. Oxford: The Pali Text Society, 1992.

Norman, K. R., trans. *The Elders' Verses I: The Theragāthā*. 2nd edition. Lancaster: The Pali Text Society, 2007.

Nowak, Margaret. *Tibetan Refugees: Youth and the New Generation of Meaning*. New Brunswick, NJ: Rutgers University Press, 1984.

Oakley, Ann. "Women and Children First and Last: Parallels and Differences between Children's and Women's Studies." Pp. 13–32 in *Children's Childhoods: Observed and Experienced*. Edited by Berry Mayall. London: The Falmer Press, 1994.

Obeyesekere, Gananath. "Child Monks: Good or Bad?" *The Sunday Times*, July 8, 2001, Plus Section.

Obeyesekere, Gananath. "The Death of the Buddha: A Restorative Interpretation." Pp. 17–45 in *Approaching the Dhamma: Buddhist Texts and Practices in South and Southeast Asia*. Edited by Anne M. Blackburn and Jeffrey Samuels. Seattle, WA: BPS Pariyatti Editions, 2003.

Obeyesekere, Gananath. *Medusa's Hair: An Essay on Personal Symbols and Religious Experience*. Chicago: Chicago University Press, 1981.

Obeyesekere, Ranjini. *Jewel of the Doctrine*. Albany, NY: SUNY, 1991.

Oguibenine, Boris. "From a Vedic Ritual to the Buddhist Practice of Initiation into the Doctrine." Pp. 107–23 in *Buddhist Studies Ancient and Modern*. Edited by Philip Denwood and Alexander Piatigorsky. London: Curzon, 1983.

Ohnuma, Reiko. "The Gift of the Body and the Gift of Dharma." *History of Religions* 37 no. 4 (1998), 323–59.

Ohnuma, Reiko. *Head, Eyes, Flesh, and Blood: Giving Away the Body in Indian Buddhist Literature*. New York: Columbia University Press, 2006.

Ohnuma, Reiko "Mother-Love and Mother Grief: South Asian Buddhist Variations on a Theme." *Journal of Feminist Studies in Religion* 23 no.1 (2007), 95–116.

Olcott, Henry S. *Old Diary Leaves*, Part 3. Reprint: Whitefish: Kessinger, 2003.

Oldenberg, Hermann, ed. *The Vinaya Piṭakam: One of the Principal Buddhist Holy Scriptures in the Pāli Language*. 5 vols. London: Williams and Norgate, 1879.

Oldenberg, Hermann. *Vinaya Texts, Volumes 1, 2, 3*. Forgotten Books, 1881, 2007.

Olivelle, Patrick. *The Aśrāma System: The History and Hermeneutics of a Religious Institution*. New York: Oxford University Press, 1993.

Olivelle, Patrick. "Amṛtā: Women and Indian Technologies of Immortality." *Journal of Indian Philosophy* 25 no. 5 (1997), 427–49.

Olivelle, Patrick. "Introduction." Pp. xix–lvii in *Life of the Buddha* by Ashvaghosha. Translated by Patrick Olivelle. Clay Sanskrit Library. New York: New York University Press, 2008.

Olivelle, Patrick. *Collected Essays I: Language, Texts, and Society. Explorations in Ancient Indian Culture and Religion*. Firenze: Firenze University Press, 2005.

Olivelle, Patrick. *Manu's Code of Law: A Critical Edition and Translation of the Mānava-Dharmaśāstra*. New York: Oxford University Press, 2005.

Ortner, Sherry. *High Religion: A Cultural and Political History of Sherpa Buddhism*. Delhi: Motilal Banarsidass, 1989.

Ōtsubo Sōjirō, *Ikkyū-san*. Tokyo: Nihonbunka Shuppan, 1949.

Paknam, No Na. *Wat Pathumwanaram*. Bangkok: Muang Boran, 2539 [1996].

Palanee, Dhitiwatana. "Buddhism and Thai Education." *The South East Asian Review* 7 no. 1–2 (1982), 75–86.

Palden Gyatso. The *Autobiography of a Tibetan Monk*. New York: Grove Press, 1998.

Pandey, Rajbali. *Hindu Samskaras: Socio-Religious Study of the Hindu Sacraments*. 2nd ed. Delhi: Motilal Banarsidass, 1969, 1994

Panglung, Jampa Losang. *Die Erzählstoffe des Mūlasarvāstivādavinaya analysiert auf Grund der tibetischen Übersetzung*. Studia Philologica Buddhica Monograph Series III. Tokyo: The Reiyukai Library, 1981.

Pannapadipo, Phra Peter. *Little Angels*. Bangkok, Thailand: Post Books, 2001.

Parkes, Graham. "The Role of Rock in the Japanese Dry Garden Landscape Garden." Pp. 85–146 in François Berthier's *Reading Zen in the Rocks: The Japanese Dry Landscape Garden*. Chicago: University of Chicago Press, 2000.

Pāsādika, Bhikkhu. "Rahula." P. 711 in *Encyclopedia of Buddhism*. Edited by Robert Buswell. New York and London: Macmillan, 2003.

Patt, David. *A Strange Liberation: Tibetan Lives in Chinese Hands*. Ithaca, NY: Snow Lion Publications, 1992.

Pei-yi, Wu. *The Confucian's Progress: Autobiographical Writings in Traditional China*. Princeton, NJ: Princeton University Press, 1992.

Pema Chodron. "Like a Raven in the Wind." *Tricycle Magazine*. Fall 1991 (http://www.tricycle.com/dharma-talk/renunciation).

Penor Rinpoche. "Statement by H. H. Penor Rinpoche Regarding the Recognition of Steven Seagal as a Reincarnation of the Treasure Revealer Chungdrag Dorje of Palyul Monastery" (http://palyul.org/docs/statement.html).

Peri, Nöel. "Hārītī, la Mère-de-démons." *Bulletin de l'École française d'Extrême-Orient* 17 (1917), 1–102.

Phongpaichit, Pasuk. *Rural Women in Thailand: From Peasant Girls to Bangkok Masseuses*. Geneva: International Labour Office, 1980.

Phrabat Somdet Phra Chao Yu Hua Phummiphol Adunyadet, *Phra Mahachanok chabab kartun*. Bangkok: Amarin, 2542 [1999].

Pidaev, Shakirjan, Tukhtash Annaev, et Gérard Fussman. *Monuments bouddhiques de Termez*. 2 vols. Paris: Collège de France, 2011.

Pissin, Annika. *Elites and Their Children: A Study in the Historical Anthropology of Medieval China*, 500–1000 AD. Ph.D. diss., University of Leiden, 2009.

Pittman, Don A. *Toward A Modern Chinese Buddhism: Taixu's Reforms*. Honolulu: University of Hawaii Press, 2001.

Postman, Neil. *The Disappearance of Childhood*. New York: Vintage, 1994.

Poulin, Marcel. *Memories of a Previous Life*. Documentary film. Montreal: Thuk Kar Productions, 1994.

Powers, John. *A Bull of a Man: Images of Masculinity, Sex, and the Body in Indian Buddhism*. Cambridge, MA: Harvard University Press, 2009.

Prebish, Charles S. *Buddhist Monastic Discipline: The Sanskrit Prātimokṣa Sūtras of the Mahāsāṃghikas and Mūlasarvāstivīns*. University Park: The Pennsylvania State University Press, 1975.

Prebish, Charles S. "Review: Theories Concerning the Skandhaka: An Appraisal." *Journal of Asian Studies* 32 no.4 (1973), 669–78.

Prebish, Charles S. *A Survey of Vinaya Literature*. Taipei: Jin Luen Publishing House, 1994.

Premasiri, P. D. "The Theravada Buddhist Doctrine of Survival After Death." Pp. 133–88 in *Concepts of Transmigration: Perspectives on Reincarnation*. Edited by S. J. Kaplan. New York: Edwin Mellen Press, 1996.

Prothero, Stephen R. *The White Buddhist: The Asian Odyssey of Henry Steel Olcott*. Bloomington: Indiana University Press, 1996.

Quagliotti, Anna Maria. "An Inscribed Image of Hārītī in the Chandigarh Government Museum and Art Gallery." *Silk Road Art and Archaeology* 6 (1999/2000), 51–60.

Rabten, Geshe. *The Life and Teachings of a Tibetan Monk*. Mount Pelerin, Switzerland: Edition Rabten, 2000.

Rahula, Bhikkhu Telwatte. *A Critical Study of the Mahāvastu*. Delhi: Motilal Banarsidass, 1978.

Rajapatirana, Tissa. "Suvarṇavarṇāvadāna." Translated and Edited together with Its Tibetan Translation and the Lakṣacaityasamutpatti. Ph.D. Diss., Australian National University, 1974.

Ram-Prasad, C. "Promise, Power, and Play: Conceptions of Childhood and Forms of the Divine." *International Journal of Hindu Studies* 6 no. 2 (2002), 147–73.

Rappaport, Roy A. *Ritual and Religion in the Making of Humanity*. Cambridge University Press, 1999.

Ray, Reginald A. *Buddhist Saints in India: A Study in Buddhist Values and Orientations*. New York and Oxford: Oxford University Press, 1994.

Ray, Reginald. "The First Tulku." *Vajradhatu Sun* (October-November 1980), 29 and 36.

Ray, Reginald A. "Nāgārjuna's Longevity." Pp. 129–59 in *Sacred Biography in the Buddhist Traditions of South and Southeast Asia*. Edited by Juliane Schober. Honolulu: University of Hawaii Press, 1997.

Ray, Reginald. *Secret of the Vajra World: The Tantric Buddhism of Tibet*. Boston: Shambhala, 2002.

Ray, Reginald. "The Themes of a Tulku's Life." *Vajradhatu Sun* (August 1980), 7 and 38–40.

Reeves, Gene, trans. *The Lotus Sutra: A Contemporary Translation of a Buddhist Classic*. Cambridge, MA: Wisdom, 2008.

Reinders, Eric. "Blessed Are the Meat Eaters: Christian Antivegetarianism and the Missionary Encounter with Chinese Buddhism." *Positions* 12 no. 2 (2004), 509–37.

Reynolds, Craig. *The Buddhist Monkhood in Nineteenth Century Thailand*. Ph.D. Diss., Cornell University, 1972.

Rhi, Juhyung. "The Birth of the Buddha in Korean Buddhism: Infant Buddha Images and the Ritual Bathing." Pp. 321–44 and 452–58 in *The Birth of the Buddha: Proceedings of the Seminar Held in Lumbini, Nepal, October 2004*. Edited by Cristoff Cueppers, Max Deeg, and Hubert Durt. Lumbini International Research Institute, 2010.

Rhys-Davids, T. W. "Anāgata Vaṃsa." P. 414 in *Encyclopedia of Religion and Ethics*, Vol. I. Edited by James Hastings. Edinburgh: T. and T. Clark, 1908. Reprint: Whitefish: Kessinger Publishing, 2003.

Rhys-Davids, T. W. *Buddhism, Its History and Literature*. New Delhi: Asian Educational Services, 2000.

Rhys Davids, T. W., and J. E. Carpenter, eds. *Dīghanikāya*. 3 vols. London: Pali Text Society, 1890–1911.

Rhys Davids, T. W., and C. A. F. Rhys Davids, trans. *The Dialogues of the Buddha*. 3 vols. London: Oxford University Press, 1921.

Rhys Davids, T. W., and Hermann Oldenberg, trans. *Vinaya Texts, Part I*. Sacred Books of the East Series, vol. 13. Oxford: Oxford University Press, 1881. Rprt. Delhi: Motilal Banarsidass, 1968.

Rhys Davids, T. W., and William Stede. *Pali-English Dictionary*. London: The Pali Text Society, 1972.

Ricard, Matthieu. *Journey to Enlightenment*. New York: Aperture Foundation, 1996.

Riccardi, Theodore, Jr., "Buddhism in Ancient and Early Medieval Nepal." Pp. 265–81 in *Studies in the History of Buddhism*. Edited by A. K. Narain. New Delhi: B. R. Publishing, 1980.

Richards, Paul. "Dressed to Kill: Clothing as Technology of the Body in the Civil War in Sierra Leone." *Journal of Material Culture* 14 nos. 4 (2009), 495–512.

Ridgely Bales, Susan. *When I Was a Child: Children's Interpretations of First Communion*. Chapel Hill: University of North Carolina Press, 2005.

Robinson, Richard H. *The Buddhist Religion: A Historical Introduction*. Belmont, CA: Dickenson, 1970.

Rodrigues, Hillary. "An Instance of Dependent Origination: Are Krishnamurti's Teachings Buddhadharma?" *Pacific World*, Third Series 9 (Fall 2007), 85–102.

Rodrigues, Hillary. *Krishnamurti's Insight: An Examination of His Teachings on the Nature of Mind and Religion*.Varanasi: Pilgrims, 2001.

Rodrigues, Hillary. "Movement in Emptiness: Assessing Jiddu Krishnamurti's Life and His Teachings on Religion." *Religious Studies and Theology* 15 nos. 2–3 (1997), 45–60.

Rongxi, Li, trans. *Buddhist Monastic Traditions of Southern Asia. A Record of the Inner Law Sent Home from the South Seas by Śramaṇa Yijing*. Berkeley, CA: Numata Center for Buddhist Translation and Research, 2000.

Ross, Joseph E. *Krishnamurti: The Taormina Seclusion, 1912*. Ojai: Edwin House, 2003.

Roth, Gustav. *Bhikṣuṇī-Vinaya: Manual of Discipline for Buddhist Nuns*. Patna: K. P. Jayaswal Research Institute, 1970.

Roy, Sita Ram. *Suvarṇavarṇāvadāna. Decipherment and Historical Study of a Palm-Leaf Sanskrit Manuscript: An Unknown Mahāyāna (avadāna) Text from Tibet*. Patna: K. P. Jayaswal Research Institute, 1971.

rTogs ldan 'Jam dpal rgya mtsho. *Rje btsun tsong kha pa'i rnam thar chen mo'i zur 'debs rnam thar legs bshad kun 'dus*. Pp. 144–66 in *The Collected Works (gsun 'bum) of Rje Tsoṅ-Kha-Pa Blo-bzao-grags-pa. Reproduced from an Example of the Old Bkra-śis-lhun-po Redaction from the Library of Klu-'khyil Monastery of Ladakh*. Vol. 1. Edited by Ngawang Gelek Demo. New Delhi: Ngawang Gelek Demo, 1979.

Ryōshū Michibata. "Chūgoku Bukkyō to shokuninniku no mondai." Pp. 391–404 in *Jikaku Daishi kenkyū*. Edited by Fukui Kōjun. Tōkyō: The Association for the Tendai Sect for Buddhist Studies, 1964.

Ryugen Tanemura, ed. *Kriyāsaṃgraha of Kuladatta*. Chapter VII. Tokyo: The Sankibo Press, 1997.

Saddhatissa, Hammalawa. *Before He Was Buddha: The Life of Siddhartha*. Berkeley, CA: Seastone, 1998.

Saltman, Bethany "Flowers Fall," *Chronogram*, March 2011 (http://www.chronogram.com/issue/2011/3/Whole+Living/Flowers-Fall-March-2011).

Samuel, Geoffrey. *Civilized Shamans: Buddhism in Tibetan Societies*. Washington, DC: Smithsonian Institution Press, 1993.

Samuels, Jeffrey. *Attracting the Heart: Social Relations and the Aesthetics of Emotion in Sri Lankan Monastic Culture*. Honolulu: University of Hawaii Press, 2010.

Samuels, Jeffrey. "Buddhism and Caste in India and Sri Lanka." *Religion Compass* 1 no. 1 (2007), 120–30.

Samuels, Jeffrey. "Establishing the Basis of the Sasana: Social Service and Ritual Performance in Contemporary Sri Lankan Monastic Training." Pp. 105–24 in *Approaching the Dhamma: Buddhist Texts and Practices in South and Southeast Asia*. Edited by Anne Blackburn and Jeffrey Samuels. Seattle: BPS Pariyatti Editions, 2003.

Samuels, Jeffrey. "Texts Memorized, Texts Performed: A Reconsideration of the Role of *Paritta* in Sri Lankan Monastic Education." *Journal of the International Association of Buddhist Studies* 28 no. 2 (2005), 339–67.

Samuels, Jeffrey. "Toward an Action-Oriented Pedagogy: Buddhist Texts and Monastic Education in Contemporary Sri Lanka." *Journal of the American Academy of Religion* 72 no. 4 (2004), 955–71.

Samuels, Jeffrey. "When Words Are Not Enough: Eliciting Children's Experiences of Buddhist Monastic Life Through Photographs." Pp. 197–224 in *Visual Research Methods: Image Society, and Representation*. Edited by Gregory C. Stanczak. Thousand Oaks, CA: Sage Publications, 2007.

Sanford, James. *Zen-Man Ikkyū*. Chico, CA: Scholar's Press, 1981.
Sangs rgyas rgya mtsho. *Gso rig sman gyi khog 'bugs*. Dharamsala: Tibetan Medical and Astro Institute, 1994.
Sankrityayana, Rahul, ed. *Vinayasūtra of Bhadanta Gunaprabha*. Bombay: Bharatiya Vidya Bhavan, 1981.
Śāntideva, *Śikṣāsamuccaya*. Edited by P. L. Vaidya. Dharbhanga: Mithila Institute, 1961.
Sasson, Vanessa R. *The Birth of Moses and the Buddha: A Paradigm for the Comparative Study of Religions*. Sheffield: Sheffield Phoenix Press, 2007.
Sasson, Vanessa R. "Māya's Disappearing Act: Motherhood in Early Buddhist Literature" in *Family in Buddhism: Buddhist Vows and Family Ties*. Edited by Liz Wilson (forthcoming).
Sasson, Vanessa R. "A Womb with a View: The Buddha's Final Fetal Experience." Pp. 55–72 in *Imagining the Fetus: The Unborn in Myth, Religion, and Culture*. Edited by Vanessa R. Sasson and Jane Marie Law. New York: Oxford University Press, 2009.
Sawada, Janine Anderson. *Confucian Values and Popular Zen: Sekimon Shingaku in Eighteenth-Century Japan*. Honolulu: University of Hawaii Press, 1993.
Scharfe, Hartmut. *Education in Ancient India*. Leiden: Brill, 2002.
Schein, Louisa. *Minority Rules: The Miao and the Feminine in China's Cultural Politics*. Durham, NC: Duke University Press, 2000.
Schlütter, Morten. *How Zen Became Zen: The Dispute Over Enlightenment and the Formation of Chan Buddhism in Song-Dynasty China*. Honolulu: University of Hawaii Press, 2008.
Schopen, Gregory. *Bones, Stones, and Buddhist Monks: Collected Papers on the Archaeology, Epigraphy, and Texts of Monastic Buddhism in India*. Honolulu: University of Hawaii Press, 1997.
Schopen, Gregory. *Buddhist Monks and Business Matters: Still More Papers on Monastic Buddhism in India*. Honolulu: University of Hawaii Press, 2004.
Schopen, Gregory. "Counting the Buddha and the Local Spirits in A Monastic Ritual of Inclusion for the Rain Retreat." *Journal of Indian Philosophy* 30 no. 4 (2002), 359–88.
Schopen, Gregory. *Figments and Fragments of Mahāyāna Buddhism in India. More Collected Papers*. Honolulu: University of Hawaii Press, 2005.
Schopen, Gregory. "On Buddhist Monks and Dreadful Deities: Some Monastic Devices for Updating the Dharma." Pp. 169–73 in *Gedenkschrift J. W. de Jong*. Edited by H. W. Bodewitz and Minoru Hara. Tokyo: The International Institute for Buddhist Studies, 2004.
Schopen, Gregory. "Taking the Bodhisattva into Town: More Texts on the Image of 'the Bodhisattva' and Image Processions in the Mūlasarvāstivāda-vinaya." *East and West* 55 (2005), 299–311.
Schopen, Gregory. "The Urban Buddhist Nun and a Protective Rite for Children in Early North India." Pp. 359–80 in *Pāsādikadānaṃ. Festschrift für Bhikkhu Pāsādika*, hrsg., Martin Straube et al. Marburg: Indica et Tibetica Verlag, 2009.
Schuler, S. R. *The Other Side of Polyandry*. Boulder, CO: Westview Press, 1987.
Seeger, Martin. "'Against the Stream': The Thai Female Buddhist Saint Mae Chi Kaew Sianglam (1901–1991)." *South East Asia Research* 18 no. 3 (2010), 555–95.
Sen, Tansen. *Buddhism, Diplomacy, and Trade*. Honolulu: University of Hawaii Press, 2003.
Seneviratne, H. L. *The Work of Kings: The New Buddhism in Sri Lanka*. Chicago: University of Chicago Press, 1999.
Sethakul, Ratanaporn. "Tai Lue of Sipongpanna and Müang Nan in the Nineteenth-Century." Pp. 319–29 in *Civility and Savagery: Social Identity in Tai States*. Edited by Andrew Turton. Richmond: Surry: Curzon, 2000.

Sénart, Emile. *Le Mahāvastu: Texte Sanskrit publié pour la première fois et accompagné*. Tokyo: Meicho-Fukyu-kai, 1977.

Sharf, Robert H. "Buddhist Modernism and the Rhetoric of Meditative Experience." *Numen* 42 (1995), 238–83.

Sharma, G. R. "Excavations at Kauśāmbī, 1949–1955." *Annual Bibliography of Indian Archaeology* 16 (1958), xxxvi–xlv.

Shengbao, Xie. *Dunhuang fojing gushi*. Lanzhou: Gansu shaonian ertong chubanshe, 1992.

Shirakabe Yukio, Shirakabe Takehiro, Takeshi Kishimoto, Takayanagi Susumu, and Kikui Tomoko. "Expressions of Faces in Sculptures and Paintings as Seen from an Anatomical Viewpoint." *Aesthetic Plastic Surgery* 5 (1981), 329–42.

Shufen, Liu. "Art, Ritual and Society: Buddhist Practice in Rural China during the Northern Dynasties." *Asia Major* 8 part 1 (1995), 19–46.

Silber, Ilana Friedrich. "Dissent through Holiness: The Case of the Radical Renouncer in Theravada Buddhist Countries." *Numen* 28 no. 2 (1981), 164–93.

Silber, Ilana Friedrich. *Virtuosity, Charisma, and Social Order: A Comparative Sociological Study of Monasticism in Theravada Buddhism and Medieval Catholicism*. Cambridge: Cambridge University Press, 1995.

Silk, Jonathan A. "Child Abandonment and Homes for Unwed Mothers in Ancient India: Buddhist Sources." *Journal of the American Oriental Society* 127 no. 3 (2007), 297–314.

Silk, Jonathan. *Managing Monks: Administrators and Administrative Roles in Indian Buddhist Monasticism*. New York: Oxford University Press, 2008.

Silver, Gail. *Anh's Anger*. Berkeley, CA: Plum Blossom Books, 2009.

Sister Susan. *Each Breath a Smile*. Berkeley, CA: Plum Blossom Books, 2001.

Skidmore, Monique. "The Future of Burma: Children Are Like Jewels." Pp. 249–70 in *Burma at the Turn of the 20th Century*. Edited by M. Skidmore. Honolulu: University of Hawaii Press, 2005.

Skorupski, Tadeusz, and Crystyn Cech. "Major Tibetan Life Cycle Events—Birth and Marriage Ceremonies." *Kailash* 11 no. 1–2 (1984), 5–32.

Sloss, Radha Rajagopal. *Lives in the Shadow with J. Krishnamurti*. Indiana: Bloomsbury, 1991.

Slote, Walter H., and George A. De Vos. *Confucianism and the Family*. Albany: State University of New York Press, 1998.

Slusser, Mary S. *Nepal Mandala*. Princeton, NJ: Princeton University Press, 1982.

Smith, Brian K. "Ritual, Knowledge, and Being: Initiation and Veda Study in Ancient India." *Numen* 33 no. 1 (1986), 65–89.

Smith, Donald Ingram. *The Transparent Mind: A Journey with Krishnamurti*. Ojai: Edwin House, 1999.

Smith, Douglas C. "Foundations of Modern Chinese Education and the Taiwan Experience." Pp. 1–61 in *The Confucian Continuum: Educational Modernization in Taiwan*. Edited by Douglas C. Smith. New York: Praeger, 1991.

Smith, Helmer, ed. *Khuddakapātha*. London: Pali Text Society, 1915.

Snellgrove, David. "Buddhism in Nepal." Pp. 362–80 in *Indo-Tibetan Buddhism: Indian Buddhists and Their Tibetan Successors*. Vol. 2. Boston: Shambhala, 1987.

Sony Music Corporation. "R.O.D. (Read or Die)." Accessed June 8, 2010. http://www.sony-music.co.jp/Animation/ROD/archive/media/ovaindex.html.

Soper, Alexander Coburn. "Literary Evidence for Early Buddhist Art in China." *Artibus Asiae Supplementum* 19 (1959), iii–296.

Speyer, J. S. *Avadānaśataka: A Century of Edifying Tales Belonging to the Hīnāyāna* (The Hague: Mouton & Co., 1958.

Spiro, Melford E. *Buddhism and Society: A Great Tradition and Its Burmese Vicissitudes*. 2nd ed. 1970. Repr. Berkeley: University of California Press, 1982.

Sponberg, Alan, and Helen Hardacre, eds. *Maitreya, The Future Buddha*. Cambridge: Cambridge University Press, 1988.

"*sprul sku*," *Bod rgya tshig mdzod chen mo*. Comp. Yi-Sun Zhang. Beijing: Mi rigs dpe skrun khang, 1993.

Srivastava, K. M. "Archaeological Excavations at Piprāhwā and Ganwaria and the Identification of Kapilavastu." *Journal of the International Association of Buddhist Studies* 30 no. 1 (1980), 103–10.

Stark, Rodney, and William Sims Bainbridge. "Networks of Faith: Interpersonal Bonds and Recruitment to Cults and Sects." Pp. 307–24 in *The Future of Religion: Secularization, Revival and Cult Formation*. Edited by Rodney Stark and William Sims Bainbridge. Berkeley: University of California Press, 1985.

Strong, John S. *The Buddha: A Short Biography*. Oxford: Oneworld, 2001.

Strong, John S. *The Experience of Buddhism: Sources and Interpretation.*: 3rd ed.. Belmont, CA: Thomson Wadsworth, 2008.

Strong, John S. "A Family Quest: The Buddha, Yaśodhara, and Rāhula in the *Mūlasarvāstivāda Vinaya*." Pp. 113–28 in *Sacred Biography in the Buddhist Traditions of South and Southeast Asia*. Edited by Juliane Schober. Honolulu: University of Hawaii Press, 1997.

Strong, John S. *The Legend and Cult of Upagupta: Sanskrit Buddhism in North India and Southeast Asia* (Princeton, NJ: Princeton University Press), 1992.

Strong, John S. *The Legend of King Aśoka: A Study and Translation of the Aśokāvadāna*. Delhi: Motilal Banarsidass, 1983.

Struve, Lynn A. *Deqing's Dreams: Markers in a Reinterpretation of His Autobiography*. Unpublished draft of March 2011.

Suh, Sharon. "Asserting Buddhist Selves in a Christian Land: The Maintenance of Religious Identity Among Korean Buddhists in America." Pp. 40–59 in *Religion and Spirituality in Korean America*. Edited by David K. Yoo and Ruth H. Chung. Champaign: University of Illinois Press, 2008.

Sukanya Hantrakul. "Prostitution in Thailand." Pp. 115–36 in *Development and Displacement: Women in Southeast Asia*. Edited by Glen Chandler, Norma Sullivan, and Jan Branson. Monash Papers on Southeast Asia, No. 18. Clayton, Australia: Centre of Southeast Asian Studies, Monash University, 1988.

Swearer, Donald K. "Bimba's Lament." Pp. 541–52 in *Buddhism in Practice*. Edited by Donald S. Lopez, Jr. Princeton, NJ: Princeton University Press, 1995.

Swearer, Donald K. *The Buddhist World of Southeast Asia*. Albany: State University of New York Press, 1995.

Taddei, Maurizio. "The Dīpaṃkara-jātaka and Siddhārtha's Meeting with Rāhula: How Are They Linked to the Flaming Buddha?" *Annali rivista del dipartimento di studi Asiatici e del dipartimento di studi e ricerche su Africa e paesi Arabi* 52, fasc.1 (1992), 103–7.

Taklha, Namgyal Lhamo. *Women of Tibet*. Dehra Dun: Songtsen Library, 2005.

Talbot, Mary. "Introduction: Teaching Your Children Buddhist Values." *Tricycle*, Fall 2008 (http://www.tricycle.com/special-section/introduction-teaching-your-children-buddhist-values).

Tambiah, Stanley J. *World Conqueror and World Renouncer: A Study of Buddhism and Polity in Thailand against a Historical Background*. Cambridge: Cambridge University Press, 1976.

Tanemura, Ryugen. *Kuladatta's Kriyāsaṃgrahapañjikā: A Critical Edition and Annotated Translation of Selected Sections*. Groningen: Egbert Forsten, 2004.

Tan Leshan. *Theravada Buddhism and Village Economy*. Ph.D. Diss., Cornell University, 1995.

Tantiwiramanond, Darumee, and Sashi Ranjan Pandey, "The Status and Role of Thai Women in the Pre-Modern Period: A Historical and Cultural Perspective." *Sojourn* 2 no. 1 (1987), 125–49.

Tatar, Maria. *Enchanted Hunters: The Power of Stories in Childhood*. New York: W. W. Norton & Company, 2009.

Tatelman, Joel. *The Trials of Yaśhodharā: A Critical Edition, Annotated Translation and Study of the Bhdrakapāvadāna II-V.* 2 vols. Ph.D. Diss., Oxford University, 1996.

Tatelman, Joel. "The Trials of Yaśodharā: The Legend of the Buddha's Wife in the *Bhadrakalpāvadāna* (from the Sanskrit)." *Buddhist Literature* 1 (1999), 176–261.

Tawada Yoko. "Is Europe Western?" *Kyoto Journal* 61 (2005). Accessed April 23, 2011. http://www.kyotojournal.org/kjselections/Tawada_Europe.html.

Teiser, Stephen F. *The Ghost Festival in Medieval China*. Princeton, NJ: Princeton University Press, 1988.

Teramura Teruo. *Ikkyū-san*. Tokyo: Akane Shobo, 1976.

Terhune, Lea. *Karmapa: The Politics of Reincarnation*. Boston: Wisdom Publications, 2004.

Thanissaro Bhikkhu (Geoff DeGraff). *The Buddhist Monastic Code Volume 1: The Patimokkha Training Rules*. Valley Center, CA: Metta Forest Monastery, 1994.

Thanissaro Bhikkhu, trans. "Maha-Rahulovada Sutta: The Greater Exhortation to Rahula (MN 62). *Access to Insight* (http://www.accesstoinsight.org/tipitaka/mn/mn.062.than.html).

Thich Nhat Hanh. *The Coconut Monk*. Berkeley, CA: Plum Blossom Books, 2009.

Thich Nhat Hanh. *The Hermit and the Well*. Berkeley, CA: Plum Blossom Books, 2003.

Thich Nhat Hanh. *A Pebble for Your Pocket*. Berkeley. CA: Plum Blossom Books, 2010.

Thich Nhat Hanh. *Under the Rose Apple Tree*. Berkeley,CA: Parallax Press, 2002.

Thomas, E. J. *The Life of Buddha as Legend and History*. Delhi: Motilal Banarsidass, 1997.

Thupten Sangay (trans. Gavin Kilty). "Tibetan Traditions of Childbirth and Childcare." *Tibetan Medicine* 7 (1984), 3–24.

The Tibetan Tripitaka. Taipei Edition. Edited by A. W. Barber. Taipei: SMC Publishing, 1991.

Toei Animation. "Ikkyu-san." (English) Accessed April 23, 2011. http://corp.toei-anim.co.jp/english/film/ikkyusan.php.

Toei Animation. "Ikkyu-san." (Japanese) Accessed April 23, 2011, http://www.toei-anim.co.jp/lineup/tv/ikkyu.

Toffin, Gérard. "Études sur les Newars de la Vallée Kathmandou: *Guthi*, Funérailles et Castes," *L'Ethnographie* 2 (1975), 206–25.

Toshiichi Endo. *Buddha in Theravada Buddhism: A Study of the Concept of Buddha in the Pali Commentaries*. 2nd ed. Dehiwala: Buddhist Cultural Centre, 2002.

Treckner, V., ed. *The Majjhima-Nikāya*. 4 vols. London: The Pali Text Society, 1971–1991.

Treckner, V., ed. *The Milindapañho: Being Dialogues Between King Milinda and the Buddhist Sage Nāgasena*. London: The Pali Text Society, 1986.

Tsering Bum. *A Northeastern Tibetan Childhood*. Xining City: Plateau Publications, 2007.

Tsomo, Karma Lekshe. "Buddhist Nuns: New Roles and Possibilities," Pp. 342–66 in *Exile as Challenge: The Tibetan Diaspora*. Edited by Dagmar Bernstorff and Hubertus von Welck. Delhi: Orient Longman, 2003.

Tsomo, Karma Lekshe. "Change in Consciousness: Women's Religious Identity in Himalayan Buddhist Cultures." Pp. 169–89 in *Buddhist Women across Cultures: Realizations*. Edited by Karma Lekshe Tsomo. Albany: State University of New York Press, 1999.

Turton, Andrew, ed. *Civility and Savagery: Social Identity in Tai States*. Surrey: Curzon, 1999.

Tweed, Thomas A. "Nightstand Buddhists and Other Creatures: Adherents, Sympathizers and the Study of Religion." Pp. 71–90 in *American Buddhism: Methods and Findings in Recent Scholarship*. Edited by Duncan Ryuken Williams and Christopher Queen. Richmond, Surrey: Curzon Press, 1999.

Vaidya, P. L., ed. *Lalitavistara*. Buddhist Sanskrit Texts, no. 1. Darbhanga: Mithila Institute, 1958.

Vajrācārya, Badri Ratna. *Daśakarma pratiṣṭhā, chāhāyeke vidhi va balimālā*. Yeṁ? [Kathmandu]: Candramāna Mālākāra, Surendramāna Mālākāra, Pradipamāna Mālākāra, Prakāśamāna Mālakāra: Mālākāra Prinṭiṅa presa, VS 2045 [1988 CE].

Vajrācārya, Cundā. "Ihi. " Pages 1–7 in *Svakvaḥgu Ihi Munejyā*. Edited by Javāharabhāi Prajāpati, Gaṅgārāma Prajāpati, and Śyāma Prajāpati. Yeṁ? (Kathmandu): Dharmacakra taḥnanī khalaḥ, NS 1118 [1997 CE].

Vajrācārya, Nareś Mān. "Daśakarma." Paper presented at the IVth Conference on the Buddhist Heritage of Nepal Mandala, Kathmandu, Sept. 7–10, 2005.

Vajrācārya, Ratna Kāji. *Yem Deyā Bauddha Pūjā Kriyāyā Halaṃjvalam*. Kathmandu: Saṅkata Printing Press, 1981

Vālmīki. *Rāmāyana, Book One: Boyhood*. Translated by R. P. Goldman. Clay Sanskrit Library. New York: New York University Press, 2005.

van der Kuijp, Leonard. "The Dalai Lamas and the Origins of Reincarnate Lamas." Pp. 14–31 in *The Dalai Lamas: A Visual History*. Edited by Martin Brauen. Chicago: Serindia Publications, 2005.

van de Wetering, Janwillem. *Little Owl: An Eightfold Buddhist Admonition*. Boston: Houghton Mifflin Company, 1978.

van Esterik, Penny, ed. *Women of Southeast Asia*. Southeast Asia Monograph Series. Dekalb: Northern Illinois University, 1996.

Vargas-O'Bryan, Ivette. "Disease, the Demons and the Buddhas: A Study of Tibetan Conceptions of Disease and Religious Practice." Pp. 81–99 in *Health and Religious Rituals in South Asia: Disease, Possession and Healing*. Edited by Fabrizio Ferrarri. London: Routledge, 2011.

Vargas-O'Bryan, Ivette. "Legitimising Demon Diseases in Tibetan Medicine: The Conjoining of Religion, Medicine, and Ecology." Pp. 379–404 in *Studies of Medical Pluralism in Tibetan History and Society: Proceedings of the Eleventh Seminar of the International Association for Tibetan Studies, Konigswinter, 2006*. Edited by Sienna Craig, Mingji Cuomu, Frances Garrett, and Mona Schrempf. Halle: IITBS GmbH International Institute for Tibetan and Buddhist Studies, 2011.

Vergati, Anne. *Gods, Men and Territory: Society and Culture in the Kathmandu Valley*. New Delhi: Manohar, 1995.

Vernon, Roland. *Star in the East: Krishnamurti, the Invention of a Messiah*. London: Constable, 2000.

von Eckartshausen, Karl. *The Cloud Upon the Sanctuary*. Translated by Mme. Isabel de Steige. San Diego: Book Tree, 2006.

von Fürer-Haimendorf, Christoph. *Himalayan Traders*. New Delhi: Times Books International, 1988.

von Hinüber, Oskar. *Beiträge zur Erklärung der Senavarma-Inschrift*. Stuttgart: Franz Steiner Verlag, 2002.

von Hinüber, Oskar. "Buddhist Law According to the Theravāda-Vinaya: A Survey of Theory and Practice." *Journal of the International Association of Buddhist Studies* 18 no.1 (1995), 7–45.

von Hinüber, Oskar. "The Foundation of the Bhikkunīsaṃgha: A Contribution to the Earliest History of Buddhism." *Annual Report of the International Research Institute for Advanced Buddhology* 11 (2008), 3–29.

von Hinüber, Oskar. *Selected Papers on Pāli Studies*. Oxford: The Pali Text Society, 1994.

von Rospatt, Alexander. "The Consecration Ceremony in the *Kriyāsaṃgraha* and Newar Buddhism." Pp. 197–260 in *Hindu and Buddhist Initiations in India and Nepal*. Edited by Astrid Zotter and Christof Zotter. Wiesbaden: Harrassowitz, 2010.

von Rospatt, Alexander. "The Transformation of the Monastic Ordination *(pravrajyā)* into a Rite of Passage in Newar Buddhism." Pp. 199–234 in *Words and Deeds: Hindu and Buddhist Rituals in South Asia*. Edited by Jörg Gengnagel, Ute Hüsken, and Srilata Raman. Wiesbaden: Harrassowitz Verlag, 2005.

Vongtalam, Bosaenggam et al. *Vannakhati Lao*. Vientiane: Kaxuang Seuksa, 1987.

Wada Tokutarō. *Rekishi sōdan: shūshin gadan.*Vol. 9. Tokyo: Shun'yōdō, 1898.

Waddell, L. A. *Buddhism of Tibet or Lamaism, with Its Mystic Cults, Symbolism and Mythology and in Its Relation to Indian Buddhism*. London: W. H. Allen and Co., 1895.

Walters, Jonathan S. "Communal Karma and Karmic Community in Theravada Buddhist History." Pp. 9–39 in *Constituting Communities: Theravada Buddhism and the Religious Cultures of South and Southeast Asia*. Edited by John Clifford Holt et al. Albany: SUNY, 2003.

Walters, Jonathan S. "Gotamī's Story." Pp. 113–38 in *Buddhism in Practice*. Edited by Donald S. Lopez, Jr. Princeton, NJ: Princeton University Press, 1995.

Watson, Burton, trans. *The Lotus Sutra*. New York: Columbia University Press, 1993.

Wayman, Alex. "Buddhism." *Historia Religionum* 2 (1971), 372–464.

Weber, Max. *The Religion of India: The Sociology of Hinduism and Buddhism*. Glencoe, IL: The Free Press, 1958.

Weeraratne, Amarasiri. "Vinaya—Rules and the Sangha." *The Island*, August 19, 2003. Features.

Weidner, Marsha. "Imperial Engagements with Buddhist Art and Architecture," Pp, 117–44 in *Cultural Intersections in Later Chinese Buddhism*. Edited by Marsha Weidner. Honolulu: University of Hawaii Press, 2001.

Welch, Holmes. *The Practice of Chinese Buddhism: 1900–1950*. Cambridge, MA: Harvard University Press, 1967.

Wells, K. E. *Thai Buddhism: Its Rites and Activities*. New York: AMS Press, 1960.

Wessinger, Catherine. *Annie Besant and Progressive Messianism*. Lewiston, NY: The Edwin Mellen Press, 1988.

Whalen-Bridge, John, and Gary Storhoff, eds. *The Emergence of Buddhist American Literature*. Albany: SUNY Press, 2009.

Wheeler, Kate Lila. "How a Buddhist Decides Whether or Not to Have Children." Pp. 405–24 in *Women's Buddhism, Buddhism's Women: Tradition, Revision, Renewal*. Edited by Ellison Banks Findley. Boston: Wisdom, 2000.

White, Rosalyn. *The Rabbit in the Moon: A Jātaka Tale*. Oakland: Dharma Publishing, 1989.

Wickremegamage, Candra. "Tavakalika Paevidda Ratata Yahapatak [Temporary Ordination Is Better for the Country]." *Lankadipa*, December 27, 1999.

Wijayaratna, M. *Buddhist Monastic Life: According to the Texts of the Theravada Tradition*. Translated by Claude Grangier and Steven Collins. Cambridge: Cambridge University Press, 1990.

Wiley, Andrea S. "A Role for Biology in the Cultural Ecology of Ladakh." *Human Ecology* 25 no. 2 (1997), 273–95.

Williams, Duncan Ryūken. *The Other Side of Zen: A Social History of Sōtō Zen Buddhism in Tokugawa Japan*. Princeton, NJ: Princeton University Press, 2005.

Wilson, Liz. *Charming Cadavers: Horrific Figurations of the Feminine in Indian Buddhist Hagiographic Literature*. Chicago: University of Chicago Press, 1996.

Witzel, Michael. "How to Enter the Vedic Mind? Strategies in Translating a Brāhmaṇa Text." Pp. 163–76 in *Translating, Translations, Translators from India to the West*. Vol.

1. Edited by Enrica Garzilli. Harvard Oriental Series, Opera Minora. Cambridge, MA: Harvard Oriental Series, 1996.

Wogihara Unrai, ed., *Bodhisattvabhūmi*. Tokyo: Sankibo, 1971.

Woodward, F. L., trans. *The Book of the Gradual Sayings (Aṅguttara-Nikāya) or More-Numbered Suttas*. Vols. 1 and 2. Oxford: The Pali Text Society, 1932.

Woodward, F. L., trans. *The Minor Anthologies of the Pali Canon, Part II*. Oxford: The Pali Text Society, 1996.

Wyatt, David K. "The Buddhist Monkhood as an Avenue of Social Mobility in Traditional Thai Buddhism." *Sinlapakon* 10 no. 1 (1966), 41–52.

Wyatt, David K. *Studies in Thai History: Collected Articles*. Chiang Mai: Silkworm Books, 1994.

Yoneo Ishii. *Sangha, State and Society: Thai Buddhism in History*. Honolulu: University of Hawai'i Press/Center for Southeast Asian Studies Kyoto University, 1986.

Xiaoshami Zhanjie, "Woshilongshupusazhuanshi." *Liberty Times*, April 1, 2009 (http://www.libertytimes.com.tw/2009/new/apr/1/today–life13.htm).

Xiushen, Sun. "Dunhuang Mogaoku di 296 ku Xusheti gushi di yanjiu." *Dunhuang yanjiu* (1992), 1–10.

Xueyong, Mu comp. *Jiange Jueyuan si Mingdai fozhuan bihua*. Beijing: Wenwu chubanshe, 1993.

Yang, Fenggang. "The Red, Black and Grey Markets of Religion in China." *The Sociological Quarterly* 47 (2006), 93–122.

Yang, Lien-sheng. *Studies in Chinese Institutional History*. Cambridge, MA: Harvard University Press, 1961.

Yangzom, Yeshe, Yunden Droma, Osamu Kunji, Mingna Shan, Lobsong Pingzo, and Pa Song. "The Dietary Habits of Non-Asthmatic Schoolchildren in Lhasa, Tibet." *Journal of Asthma* 44 no. 4 (2007), 317–24.

Yangzong, P. Nafstad, C. Madsen, and E. Bjertness. "Childhood Asthma under the North Face of Mount Everest." *Journal of Asthma* 43 no. 5 (2006), 393–98.

Yeh, Fan et al. *Hou Han shu*. Beijing: Zhonghua shuzhu, 1965.

Yongning, Li. *Dunhuang shiku quanji: bensheng gushi huajuan*. Hong Kong: Commercial Press, 2000.

Yoshiharu Nakagawa. "The Child as Compassionate Bodhisattva and as Human Sufferer/Spiritual Seeker: Intertwined Buddhist Images." Pp. 33–42 in *Nurturing Child and Adolescent Spirituality: Perspectives from the World's Religious Traditions*. Edited by K. M. Yust et al. Lanham: Rowman & Littlefield, 2006.

Yü, Chün-fang. "Chan Education in the Sung: Ideals and Procedures." Pp. 57–104 in *Neo-Confucian Education: The Formative Stage*. Edited by Wm. Theodore de Bary and John W. Chaffee. Berkeley and Los Angeles: University of California Press, 1989.

Yü, Chün-fang. "Chung-feng Ming-pen and Ch'an Buddhism in the Yüan." Pp. 419–77 in *Yuan Thought: Chinese Thought and Religion under the Mongols*. Edited by Hok-lam Chan and William Theodore de Bary. New York: Columbia University Press, 1982.

Yü, Chün-fang. *Kuan-yin: The Chinese Transformation of Avalokiteśvara*. New York: Columbia University Press, 2001.

Yü, Chün-fang. "P'u-t'o Shan: Pilgrimage and the Creation of the Chinese Potalaka." Pp. 190–245 in *Pilgrims and Sacred Sites in China*. Edited by Susan Naquin and Chün-fangYü. Berkeley: University of California Press, 1992.

Zhang, Rujia, and Yuhai Zhang. "Zhongguo Chuantong Renlunguan Jiqi Xiandai Qishi." *Journal of University of Science and Technology Beijing* 23 no.4 (2007), 157–61.

Zhao Shilin and Wu Jinghua. *Daizu Wenhua Zhi* (A Cultural History of the Dai Nationality). Kunming: Yunnan Minzu Chubanshe, 1997.
Zhonglin, Qiu. "Buxiao zhi xiao," *Xinshixue* 6 (1995), 1–48.
Zürcher, E. "'Beyond the Jade Gate': Buddhism in China, Vietnam, and Korea." Pp. 193–211 in *The World of Buddhism*. Edited by H. Bechert and R. Gombrich. London: Thames and Hudson, 1984.
Zurcher, E. *The Buddhist Conquest of China*. Leiden: E.J. Brill, 1931; 1959.

INDEX

abbot, 13, 145, 255, 256, 259, 265, 281, 415, 461
- Ikkyū as, 328–330

adoption, 27, 274, 361, 456
adventure story, 291, 294, 296, 301, 302, 304
ailment
- *See* disease

Anagarika Dharmapala, 459
Ānanda, 106, 112, 162, 164, 176
- nephews of, 9, 50, 52, 53, 56, 60, 72, 73, 231

Anāthapiṇḍada / Anāthapiṇḍika, 39, 40, 478
ancestors, 91, 109, 126, 157, 158, 364–368, 370, 379
animals, 114, 115, 117, 149, 188, 189, 191, 193, 214
- caring for, 377, 379, 382, 384, 385
- as characters in children's books, 217, 219, 221
- children as wild, 346
- children playing with, 381
- domestic, 27
- eating, 51
- hunting, 174
- *jātaka*, 211–213
- plowed and overturned, 83, 99, 223
- rebirth as, 400
- stray, 54
- wild, 154

Aniruddha, 22–24, 32, 67–69
anti-family, 3, 4
Apadāna, 101–103, 105, 119
Asceticism
- Buddha and, 65, 108, 302, 478
- as Buddhist priority, 3, 8, 9, 13, 43, 245, 295, 302, 356
- female, 73, 266, 269, 271
- following-after-, 59, 64, 66, 67
- Jainism and, 57
- Yaśodharā and, 98

Asha Kaji, Pandit Vaidya (Ganesh Raj Vajracarya), 360–363, 365–370
Asita, 84, 132, 153, 478
Avadānaśataka, 22, 24, 32, 38, 63, 67, 68, 370
Avalokiteśvara
- acolyte of, 146, 152
- devotion to, 351
- invoking power of, 140
- Princess Miaoshan as, 157, 158
- statue or icon of, 353, 357
- temple dedicated to, 350
- *See also* Guanyin

Baldev Juju, 360, 363–370
bedtime story Buddhists, 208, 219, 225
Besant, Annie, 455, 458, 460, 463, 464, 467, 469, 477, 478
birth
- and age calculation, 231
- Buddha's, 11, 78, 81, 84–86, 127, 129, 132–139, 142, 145, 156, 214, 302, 363, 431, 477
- ceremony, 22
- Chen Lian's, 153
- Confucius', 135
- Dalai Lama's, 413
- Hou Chi's, 130, 131
- Ikkyū's, 332
- Maitreya's, 456, 458
- ontological, 92, 93
- order, 375, 377
- Rāhula's, 64, 66, 97–99, 104–106
- ritual, 65, 71, 185
- Sudhana's, 146–148